精选汉英计算机词典

（含汉语通用词汇）

顾问 朱三元　　审阅 白英彩
编者 高建华 黄人杰 邱国华

上海科学技术文献出版社

图书在版编目(CIP)数据

精选汉英计算机词典／ 高建华,黄人杰,邱国华编.—上海:上海科学技术文献出版社,2002.1
ISBN 7-5439-1927-3

Ⅰ.精… Ⅱ.①高…②黄…③邱… Ⅲ.计算机技术—词典-英、汉 Ⅳ.TP3-61

中国版本图书馆 CIP 数据核字(2001)第 092627 号

责任编辑:袁仲江

精选汉英计算机词典
（含汉语通用词汇）

....

高建华 黄人杰 邱国华 编

....

*

上海科学技术文献出版社出版发行
（上海市武康路2号 邮政编码 200031）
全国新华书店 经销
上海长鹰印刷厂印刷
2002 年 1 月第 1 版 *2002 年 1 月第 1 次印刷
开本 787× 1092 1/60 印张 10.5 字数 822 000
印数:1－5 100
ISBN 7-5439-1927-3/Z・995
定价:24.00 元

前　言

《精选英汉计算机词典》在全国畅销并评为九八年第十一批科技类全国优秀畅销书后，许多读者要求出版精选的汉英计算机词典，以便于计算机专业的汉英翻译和对外交流，或网上发表英语文字信息及电子邮件等。

目前，汉英计算机类词典已渐有出版，但是，既便于携带而又兼收汉语通用词汇的工具书尚缺，《精选汉英计算机词典》的出版，希望能满足广大科技人员和涉及计算机的读者的这一愿望。

本词典收入汉语通用词汇逾1万个，收入计算机软硬件、办公自动化、通信、多媒体、互联网、电子商务等方面的专业词超过2.8万，内容基本上包涵了所有常用的通用词和专业词。

本词典按照汉字的拼音排序，属于每一单字词目的通用词紧接在单字的译义后，然后再分列专业词条以及英语词组的缩写。

本词典在编纂中能得到上海计算机软件中心顾问朱三元研究员、上海交通大学白英彩教授的热情指导和审阅，中国科学院陈国治编审也提出了许多宝贵建议，在此表示衷心的感谢。

编者

使用说明

本词典以放大的单个汉字起首,属于每一单字的汉语通用词汇紧接在单字的释义后,汉语专业词汇则再分行顶格列出。汉语单字和词汇均按其拼音排序。

单个汉字有多种读音时,将列在各个拼音下,并在每处用"另见"提示其它的各个拼音。

本词典篇眉标示该页的四声拼音及单个汉字,篇眉过长时四声合并,对应汉字间用逗号分隔。

本词典其它标点符号的用法如下:
1) 2)... 表示单汉字不同释义间的分隔
① ②... 表示不同释义间的分隔
, 表示同义汉语词或同一词义英译间的并列
　　如:荒谬,荒唐 absurd, preposterous
; 表示差异较大英译间的分隔
– 汉语连字符
– 英语连字符
　　如:二-十进制码 binany-coded decimal
/ 表示可前后择一的英语单词
　　如:转移操作 jump/transfer operration
( ) 1)表示对前面内容的说明
　　如:会章(协会章程) the constitution of ...
2)表示对后面内容的说明
　　如:眠(睡眠) sleep
3)表示汉语词汇中"可有可无"的部分
　　如:单稳(态)的 monostable
4)表示英语单词中"可有可无"的部分
　　如:非彩色 achromatic color(s)
[ ] 表示汉语词汇中"可以替代"的部分
　　如:标准检查[评估]程序 benchmark
{ } 表示前面英语词组的"英语缩写"
　　如:风险投资 venture capital {VC}
【 】 表示汉语拼音
〈 〉 表示词性、语种、学科等的不同
　　如:〈名〉〈动〉、〈法语〉、〈电子〉等
◇ 表示汉语字或词的扩词用例
// 表示该汉语扩词的其它用例
　　如:"表"词条的 2)(测量器具)一项中有
　　◇电表 ...// 水表 ...// 钟表 ...

A a

【ā】

阿 阿拉伯 Arabian, Arabic, Arab 阿拉伯数字 Arabic numerals, Arabic figure(s), Arabic cipher

阿尔法测试 alpha test

阿奇(工具) Archie

【ái】

癌 cancer

挨 (遭受)suffer, endure

【ǎi】

矮 1)(身材短)short 2)(高度小,级别,地位低)low 矮子 a short person, dwarf

【ài】

爱 love, like, be fond of 爱好 ① love, like, be fond of, be keen on ② interest, hobby 爱好者 amateur, enthusiast, fan, lover (of art, sports, etc.) 爱护 cherish, take good care of

碍 (妨碍)hinder, obstruct

【ān】

安 安定 stable 安放 lay, set, place, put in a certain place 安静 quiet, peaceful 安排 arrange, fix up, plan 安全 safety, security 安全操作 safe operation 安全措施 safety measures, safety precautions 安稳 safe and steady 安置 arrange for, find a suitable place for 安装 fix, install, set up, mount

安全策略 security policy

安全的 safe

安全的超文本传输协议 secure hypertext transport protocol {SHTIP}

安全电子交易 secure electronic transaction {SET}

安全服务 security services

安全工作域 secure working area

安全过滤器 security filter

安全环 safety ring

安全接口层 secure layer {SL}

安全节点 security node

安全码 safety code

安全描述体 security descriptor

安全特性 security feature

安全停机 safe shutdown

安全外壳软件包 secure shell package {SSP}

安全[保密]通信 secure communication

安全[保密]通信业务 secure traffic

安全网 guard net, safe net

安全系数 coefficient/ factor of safety, safety factor, security coefficient

安全系统 security/safe system
安全[保密]线路 secure line
安全协议 secure protocol
安全卸出 security dump
安全性 security, safety, secure, fail-safe, safeness
安全性维护 security maintenance
安全余量 safety margin
安全帐户管理程序 security accounts manager {SAM}
安全注意键 secure attention key {SAK}
安全转储 security dump
安全状态 security status
安装程序 installation program, installer
安装的用户程序 installed user program {IUP}
安装服务程序 installer
安装进程 installation process
安装卷宗 mount a volume
安装软盘 installation diskette
安装手稿 installation script
安装性能说明 installation performance specification {IPS}
安装验证过程 installation verification procedure {IVP}
安装预置文件 installation profile

鞍 saddle

【àn】

岸 bank, coast, shore ◇ 海岸 coast, seashore

按 1)(用手指压)press, push down 2)(用手压住不动) keep a tight grip on 按理 in the ordinary course of events, normally 按期, 按时 on time, on schedule 按语 note, comment 按照 according to, in accordance with, in the light of, on the basis of
按比例扩大 scale up
按比例缩小 scale down, scaling-down
按表检验法 check list method
按词序排列 word by word
按地址调用 call by location
按地址访问 address reference
按动(鼠标器) click
按二减 decrement by two
按关键字选择路由 routing by key
按"或"查找 disjunction search, disjunctive search
按基线排齐 base alignment
按键 key, key stroke, touch
按键标定序 keyed sequence
按键电话设备 key telephone equipment
按键法 touch method
按键访问 keyed access
按键开关 key switch
按键顺序存取法 keyed sequential access method {KSAM}
按键误码率 error rate of keying
按键选择路径 routing by key
按结构等价 structural equivalence
按客户要求设计 custom design
按块分配 block allocation
按类通信协议 bracket protocol
按零转移指令 branch on zero instruction
按描述符调用 call by descriptor
按名传送 pass by name
按名赋值 assignment by name
按名字等价 name equivalence
按模数N校验 module-KRN check
按内容查找 contextual search
按内容存取 content access

按内容访问存储器 content-addressable/addressed memory {**CAM**}
按钮 button, knob, push, push-button, touch
按钮赋值 button assignment
按钮复位 push-button reset
按钮开关 press button
按钮开关阵列 push-button array
按钮式拨号 key pulse, tone dialing
按钮型设备 button device
按实例查询 query by example {**QBE**}
按位编码 encoding by bit
按位表示法 positional representation
按位处理 serial-by-bit
按位的补码 digital complement
按位对准器 site by site aligner
按位记数(数) positional number
按位进位 step-by-step carry
按位开关 bit switch
按位运算 digitwise operation
按行发送 line transmission
按性能分类 property sort
按需拨号选路 dial on demand routing {**DDR**}
按序 in-sequence
按序编址 sequential addressing
按序存取 sequential access
按序调度系统 sequential scheduling system
按序排队 sequential queue
按页发送 page transmission
按页寻址 paged addressing
按"与"检索 conjunctive search
按帧编码 framing code
按值调用 call by value
按指针转移 branch on indicator
按字节寻址 byte addressing
按字节寻址计算机 byte address machine
按字母分类 alphabetic sorting
按组编码 encoding by group

案 案件(law) case, legal case

暗 dark, dim, dull 暗淡 dim, faint, dull 暗含着 imply 暗号 secret sign(al), secret code, cipher 暗示 hint, suggest, clue
暗电流 dark current

【āng】

肮 肮脏 dirty, filthy

【áng】

昂 昂贵 expensive, costly

【àng】

盎 盎司 ounce (略作 oz.)

【āo】

凹 concave, sunken, dented 凹凸不平 full of bumps and holes, uneven

【ào】

奥 奥秘 profound mystery 奥妙 profound and subtle

懊 懊悔 feel remorse, regret, repent

B b

【bā】

八 eight 八方 all directions 八月 August
八二进制编码 octal-coded binary code
八进制编码 octal code
八进制地址 octal address
八进制记数法 octal notation
八进制加法 octal addition
八进制码 octonary code
八进制数 octal number, octal numeral
八进制译码器 octal decoder
八位寄存器 eight bit register
八位加法器 eight bit adder

巴 bar (unit of pressure) ◇ 毫巴 millibar // 微巴 microbar
巴科斯范式 Backus normal form {BNF}, normal form Backus

【bá】

拔 1)(拉出,抽出)pull out, pull up 2)(挑选)choose, pick, select ◇选拔 select
拔除 pull out, remove

跋 (书等后的短文)postscript

【bǎ】

把 1)(握住)grasp, hold 2)(看守)guard, watch 3)(车把)handle 把手 ①(指领导)grip, handle, knob ②(指握持器)lug 把握 ①(抓住)grasp, hold ◇把握时机 seize the opportunity ②(可靠性)confidence, assurance, certainty

钯 palladium (Pd)

靶 target 靶心 bull's-eye, centre of a target

【bà】

坝 dam, dike

罢 1)(停止)cease, stop 2)(免去)dismiss 罢工(go on) strike 罢免 recall, be removed from (a post) 罢免权 right of recall

【bái】

白 1)(弄清楚)clear 2)(徒然)in vain, for nothing 3)(无代价)free of charge, gratis 4)(空白)blank 白热 white heat, incandescence 白色 white 白天 daytime
白板 whiteboard
白体活字 light face (=lf)
白箱测试 white box testing
白页 white page
白噪声 white noise

【bǎi】

百 hundred 百倍 a hundred-fold, hundred times 百分 per cent, percent ◇百分之三 3 per cent, 3% 百分比 percentage 百货 general merchandise 百货商店 department store
百万次浮点运算 megaflops
百万二进制位 megabit
百万分之一 micro
百万条指令每秒 million instructions per second {MIPS}
百万位(兆位) megabit

摆 1)(安放)put, place, arrange 2)〈机械〉pendulum
摆动 swing, sway 摆脱 cast off, shake off
摆动扫描头 oscillating scan head
摆动转移托架 swinging delivery tray
摆杆式缓冲机构 swing bar buffer mechanism

【bài】

败 1)(失败)be defeated, lose, fail 2)(打败)defeat, beat

【bān】

扳 pull, turn
扳倒 pull down

班 1)(班组)class, team 2)(班次)shift, duty ◇三班倒 work in three shifts 3)〈量〉(交ààrip班次)末班车 last bus, train, etc. (of the day) 班级 classes and grades in school

斑 斑点 spot, stain, dot, speckle

颁 颁布 promulgate, issue, publish 颁发 ①(发布)issue, promulgate ②(授与)award

搬 (移位)take away, move, remove 搬用 apply indiscriminately, copy mechanically 搬运 carry, transport

【bǎn】

板 board, plank, plate, slab
板式 on-board

版 edition ◇修订版 revised edition ∥ 原版 original edition ∥ 再版 second edition
版本 edition, release, version
版本管理 version control, version management
版本修正 version revision
版本注释 release note
版面调整 copy fitting
版权 copyright
版税 royalty
版图编辑程序 layout editor

【bàn】

办 1)(处理)do, handle, manage, tackle 2)(创办、经营)set up, run 办法 way, means, measure 办公 handle official business, work (usu. in an office) 办公室 office 办理 handle, conduct, transact 办事 handle affairs, work 办事处 office, agency
办公打字机 office typewriter
办公活动 office activity
办公(用)计算机 office computer
办公流程 office procedure

办公软件 officeware
办公室(间)网络 intraoffice network
办公室自动化 office automation {**OA**}
办公通信系统 office communication system
办公信息系统 office information system {**OIS**}
办公用套装软件 office suites
办公用显示终端 office display terminal
办公桌附件 desk accessory {**DA**}
办公自动化 office automation {**OA**}, bureautique

半 1)(一半) half, semi- ◇半小时 half an hour // 增加一半 increase by 150% 2)(在…中间) in the middle, halfway 3)(部分) partly, about half 半…半… partly ... partly ◇半真半假 partly true, partly false 半工半读 part work, part study 半公开 semi-overt, more or less open 半径 radius 半路 halfway, midway, on the way 半天 half of the day 半途而废 give up halfway 半夜 midnight 半月刊 bi-weekly, semimonthly, fortnightly
半编译的程序 semicompiler
半导体 semiconductor
半导体材料 semiconductor material
半导体存储器 semiconductor memory
半导体光电子器件 semiconductor photoelectronic device
半导体激光器 semiconductor laser
半导体集成电路 semiconductor integrated circuit
半导体开关元件 thyristor
半导体盘存储设备 semiconductor disk device
半导体物理学 semiconductor physics
半动画 partial animation
半读电流 read half-current
半读脉冲 partial read pulse, read half-pulse
半范数 seminorm
半负定矩阵 negative semidefinite matrix
半固定长度记录 semifixed length record
半机器翻译 half-machine translation
半加 false add, half-add
半加器 half-adder, one-digit adder, two-input adder
半减器 half-subtracter, one-digit subtracter, two-input subtracter
半进位 half-carry
半进位标志 half-carry flag
半群 semigroup
半群同态 semigroup homomorphism
半弱密钥 semiweak key
半色调 half-tone
半色调处理机 half tone processor
半色调单元 half-tone cell
半色调图 half-tone image
半色调原件 half-tone original
半色调字体 half-tone font
半双工 half-duplex {**HD, HDX**}
半双工传输 half-duplex transmission
半双工电路 half-duplex circuit
半双向 either-way, half-duplex {**HD, HDX**}
半双向操作 either-way opera-

半线性的 semilinear
半写脉冲 write half-pulse
半信关 half-gateway
半序集 half-ordered set, partially ordered set
半序空间 partially ordered space
半序任务 partially ordered task
半选电流 half-current
半选脉冲 half-select pulse
半英寸磁带机 half-inch tape drive
半永久数据 semipermanent data
半周期 semi-period
半自动报文交换 semiautomatic message switching
半字 half-word
半字二进制数 half-word binary
半字符 half-half
半字节 half-byte, nib (=nibble), nybble
半字节串 nibble serial
半字空格 en space
半字压缩 half-byte packing
半字组 half block

伴 (同伴) companion, partner 伴随 accompany, follow 伴同 accompany
伴随方程 adjoint equation
伴随记录 incident record
伴随矩阵 adjoint matrix
伴随空间 adjoint space
伴随式矩阵 syndrome matrix
伴随网络 adjoint network

拌 mix

绊 (cause to) stumble, trip

【bāng】

邦 nation, state, country
邦交 relations between two countries, diplomatic relations

帮 (集团) gang, band, clique 帮忙 help, give/lend a hand, do a favor 帮手 helper, assistant 帮助 help, assist
帮助命令 help command
帮助屏幕 help screen

【bǎng】

绑 bind, tie
绑定 binding

榜 1)(张贴的名单) a list of names posted up ◇光荣榜 honor roll 2)(文告) announcement, notice 榜样 example, model

【bàng】

傍 傍晚 toward evening, at dusk, at nightfall

磅 1)(质量单位) pound 2)(磅秤) scales 3)(称重量) weigh

镑 (货币单位) pound (£)

棒 stick, club, rod, bar

【bāo】

包 1)(裹起来) wrap 2)(包好的东西) bundle, package, pack, packet, parcel 包办 take care of everything concerning a job 包产 make a production contract, take full responsibility for output quotas 包袋 bag, sack 包袱 ①(包布) cloth-wrappers

②(布包) a bundle wrapped in cloth ③(负担) load, weight, burden 包干 be responsible for a task until it is completed 包工 contract for a job 包裹 ① wrap up, bind up ② bundle, package, parcel 包含 contain, include 包括 include, consist of, comprise, incorporate 包罗万象 all-embracing, all-inclusive 包围 surround, encircle 包扎 wrap up, bind up, pack 包装 pack, package 包租 hire, charter

包报头 packet head
包标题 packet head
包布局 packet layout
包长度 packet length
包成帧 packet framing
包处理 packet processing
包处理模块 packet handling module
包传输程序 packet transfer procedure
包传送 packet transport
包错误检测 packet error detection
包的最长寿命 maximum packet lifetime {MPL}
包地址识别 packet address recognition
包分割 packet fragmentation
包含操作 include function
包含的 comprehensive
包含关系 inclusion relation, relation of inclusion
包含集 include set
包缓冲池 packet pool
包缓冲器 packet buffer
包过滤 packet filtering
包格式 packet format
包格式 packet packtize
包级逻辑接口 packet level logical interface
包交换 packer/ packet switching
包交换实验网络 experimental packet switching service {EPSS}
包交换网 packet switching network
包交换协议 packet switching protocol
包交换终端 packet terminal
包交换总线 packet switched bus
包交替 packet interleaving
包接口 packet interface
包控制 packet control
包(程序)库 package library
包络 envelope
包络延时畸变 envelope delay distortion
包络原理 envelope principle
包媒体 package media
包模 packet module
包容对象 container object
包容法 containment method
包设计 packet layout
包式[分组式]终端 packet mode terminal
包首部 packet header
包信息 package information
包信息位 packet bit
包延迟 packet delay
包中继器 packet repeater
包重传输 packet retransmission
包装域 packed field

剥 另见【bō】
shell, peel, skin

褒 praise, honor, commend
褒义 commendatory 褒义词 commendatory term

【báo】

雹 hail

薄 另见【bó】
1)（与"厚"相对）thin 2)（淡）weak, light 3)（不肥沃）infertile, poor
薄膜 film, pellicle, thin film
薄膜磁盘 film disk, thin film disk
薄膜磁头 film head, thin film head
薄膜磁阻磁头 thin film magnetoresistive head
薄膜存储器 film memory/storage, thin film memory/storage
薄膜打字机带 film ribbon
薄膜电路 thin film circuit
薄膜集成电路 film integrated circuit, thin film IC
薄膜键盘 membrane keyboard
薄膜晶体管(显示屏) thin film transistor {TFT}
薄膜微电子器件 thin film microelectronics
薄片 slice, wafer
薄片开关 diaphragm switch

【bǎo】

宝 1)（珍贵物）treasure 2)（珍贵的）precious, treasured
宝贵 valuable, precious
宝石 precious stone, gem, jewel
宝藏 precious (mineral) deposits

保 （担保）stand guarantor for sb 保安 ensure public security, ensure safety 保安措施 security measures 保安人员 security personnel 保持 keep, maintain, preserve, hold 保藏 keep in store, preserve 保存 preserve, conserve, keep 保管 take care of 保护,保卫 protect, defend 保健 health protection, health care 保健事业 public health work 保留 ①（保持不变）continue to have, retain ②（暂不处理）hold back, keep back, reserve 保密 maintain secrecy, keep sth secret 保暖 keep warm 保全 save from damage, preserve 保守 ①（使不失去）guard, keep ②（守旧的）conservative ◇保守派 conservatives 保税区 bonded area 保卫 defend, safeguard 保卫部门 public security bodies 保温 heat preservation 保温瓶 vacuum flask, vacuum bottle, thermos (bottle) 保险 ①（保险业务）insurance ②（可靠）safe ③（保证）be sure, be bound to 保险法 insurance law 保险范围 insurance coverage 保险金额 insurance amount, insured amount, sum insured 保险箱 safe, strong-box 保险费 (insurance) premium 保修 free repair within the period of guarantee 保养 maintain, keep in good repair ◇机器保养 maintenance of machinery, upkeep of machinery 保障 ensure, guarantee, safeguard 保证 pledge, guarantee, assure, ensure 保证金 earnest money, cash deposit, bail 保证人 guarantor, bail 保证书 written pledge, letter of guarantee 保质保量 guarantee both

quality and quantity
保持按钮 hold button
保持电压 keeper voltage
保持队列 hold queue
保持符号 hold mark
保持能力 hold facility
保持请求 hold request
保持时间 retention time, hold time, holding time
保持信息表 hold list
保持要求 hold request
保持页面队列 hold page queue
保持应答 hold acknowledge
保持状态 freeze mode
保存点 save point
保存期限 storage life
保存区表 save area table {SAVT}
保存区目录 save area table {SAVT}
保存图像 save image
保存文件 save file
保存系统 saved system
保存现场 spot saving
保存序列 saving sequence
保存值 save value
保管费用 inventory carrying cost, storage cost
保护 lock-out, protect, protection, safeguard
保护标志 protect tab
保护槽 protect notch
保护层 protective coating/covering
保护程序 defender
保护带 guard band
保护单元 protected location
保护的 guarding
保护的会话 protected conversation
保护范围 protection domain
保护方式 guard/ protected mode
保护符 protection character

保护管理器 protection manager
保护环 guard/protection ring
保护机制 protection mechanism
保护级 protected level
保护间隔 guard band
保护键 protected/ protection key
保护交换 protection switch
保护码 protected/ protection code
保护膜 resist film
保护目标 protected object
保护器 defender
保护区 field- protected, protected field
保护冗余 protective redundancy
保护设计 protection design
保护数据 protected data
保护数位 guard digit
保护态 protected mode
保护特性 protection feature
保护体系结构 protection architecture
保护通道 protection channel
保护涂层 protective coating
保护网 guard net
保护位 guard bit/ digit/ position
保护系统 protection system
保护信号 guard signal
保护装置 guard
保护字段 protected field
保护字节 guard byte
保留操作数 reserved operand
保留存储器 reserve storage
保留段 retained segment
保留符号 stet
保留进位加法器 carry-save adder
保留卷 reserved volume
保留名 reserved name

bào 刨抱暴爆曝 bēi 杯背悲卑

message telephone network
报文交换[处理]过程 message switching procedure
报文交换数据服务 message switching data service {MSDS}
报文交换系统 message switching system
报文交换中心 message switching center
报文截取处理 message intercept processing
报文结构 message structure
报文[消息,信文,信息]结束符 end of message {EOM}
报文开始 start of message {SOM}
报文控制程序 message control program {MCP}
报文链路 message link
报文路由选择 message routing
报文模型 message model
报文起始字符 start-of-text character {STX}
报文日志功能 message journaling function
报文冗余度 message redundancy
报文输出描述符 message output descriptor {MOD}
报文输入描述符 message input descriptor {MID}
报文数据组 message data set
报文速率 message rate
报文探询 message polling
报文头 heading, message head, message header, report heading
报文头部缓冲 header buffer
报文文本 message text
报文应用编程接口 message application programming interface {MAPI}
报文优先级 message priority

报文源 message source
报文再同步程序 message resynchronization
报文转接[接收]器 message sink
报文字段 message field
报文组装 depacketize

刨 另见【páo】
plane sth down, (knife) plane, shave

抱 hold or carry in the arms, embrace 抱负 aspiration, ambition 抱歉 be sorry, feel apologetic, regret 抱怨 complain

暴 sudden and violent 暴跌 steep fall (in price), slump 暴力 violence, force 暴露 expose, reveal 暴雨 rainstorm 暴涨 rise suddenly and sharply

爆 explode, burst 爆发 erupt, burst out, break out 爆炸 explode, burst, blow, blast 爆炸性 explosive
爆炸命令 explosion command
爆炸性文件 exploded file

曝 曝光 exposure

【bēi】

杯 cup ◇玻璃杯 glass

背 另见【bèi】
carry on the back

悲 sad, sorrowful 悲观 pessimistic

卑 1)(低下)low 2)(低劣)inferior, humble 卑劣 base,

mean, despicable

【běi】

北 north

【bèi】

贝

贝尔实验室 Bell laboratory

备 1)(具备)be equipped with, have 2)(防备)provide against, prepare against, take precautions against 备案 put on record, put on file, enter in the records 备查 for (future) reference 备忘录 memo, memorandum 备用 reserve, spare, alternate 备有 prepare, get ready 备注 remarks
备读[可读]卡片 ready-read card
备份 backup, spare
备份版本 backup version
备份[替代,替换]磁道 alternate track
备份[后备]存储器 backup storage
备份[复制]记录 duplicated record
备份拷贝 backup copy
备份频度 backup frequency
备份冗余 standby redundancy
备份软盘 backup diskette
备份扇区 alternate sector, alternative sector
备份设备 alternate device
备份文件 backup file
备份系统 standby system
备份项目 backup item
备份应用 standby application
备份域控制器 backup domain controller
备份周期 backup cycle
备件 appendage, spare part, spares
备用部件 spare unit
备用程序 back-up program
备用处理机 spare processor
备用磁道 spare track
备用磁头 spare head
备用带 spare tape
备用代码 alternate code
备用的 spare
备用电源 standby power supply {SPS}
备用功能键 alternate function key
备用机 spare machine
备用集 trim set
备用寄存器 standby register
备用键 alternate key, spare key
备用库 alternate library
备用块 standby block
备用零部件 spare part
备用路线 alternate route (=alt-route)
备用密钥 alternate key
备用文件 back file
备用[后备,后援]系统 backup system
备用显示器 standby display
备用线 spare wire
备用线路 off-premises line, standby line
备用信道 reserve channel
备用站 reservation station
备用值 backed-up value
备用装置 standby unit
备用总线 auxiliary bus-bar

背 另见[bēi]
1)(脊背)the back of the body
2)(瞒)hide sth from, do sth behind sb's back 3)(违背) act contrary to, violate, break 背包 knapsack, rucksack 背后 behind, at the

back 背景 background, back drop 背离 deviate from, depart from 背面 the back of an object 背面 the back, the reverse side, back face 背诵 recite from memory, lean by heart 背着 with the back towards

背景颜色索引 background color index
背面电极 backplate
背面馈送 face-down feed

倍 1) times, -fold ◇五倍 five times, fivefold 2) (加倍) double

倍长寄存器 double register
倍加器 doubler
倍率 multiplying power
倍密度 double density
倍密度编码 double-density encoding
倍密度软盘 double-density diskette
倍频制 frequency doubling {FD}
倍数 factor
倍数发生器 multiple generator
倍增电极 dynode
倍增器 multiplicator

焙 bake over a slow fire

钡 barium (Ba)

被 被动 passive 被迫 be compelled, be forced 被子 quilt

被保护单元 protected location
被采用权限 adopted authority
被操作数位 operated digit
被测部件 unit under test {UUT}
被测系统 system under test {SUT}
被乘数存储器 icand/multiplicand register
被除数 dividend
被调程序 called program
被调度的操作 scheduled operation
被调分程序 invoked block
被调入位置 called station
被动安全 passive security
被动传感器 passive sensor
被动打开 passive open
被动方式 passive mode
被动模拟 passive simulation
被加队排队 passive queue
被动站 passive station
被呼叫的终端 terminal called
被呼叫方 called party
被呼叫站 called station
被呼叫子地址 called sub-address
被激励网络 energized network
被检测数据载体 data carrier detected {DCD}
被减数 minuend
被叫用户 dialed line
被截站 intercepted station
被截终端 intercepted terminal
被截[截听]资源 intercepted resource
被控过程 controlled process
被控位移 controlled slip
被隶属任务 attached task
被零除的俘获 divide by zero trap
被零除的自陷 divide by zero trap
被驱动的 driven
被扫描符号 scanned symbol
被扫描文档 scanned document
被扫描字符 scanned character
被锁卷 locked volume
被锁名 locked name
被锁文件 locked file

被锁页面 locked page
被锁资源 locked resource
被选单元 selected cell
被选择的地址 selected address
被占终端 occupied terminal
被作用集 affected set

【bēn】

奔 奔驰 run quickly
奔腾微处理器 (Pentium) microprocessor
奔腾芯片 Pentium chip

【běn】

本 1)(根本)foundation, basis, origin 2)(现今的)this, current, present 3)(簿本) book, notebook 本国 one's own country 本国语 native language, mother tongue 本行 one's line, one's own profession 本来 ①(原有的) original ②(原先)originally, at first ③(理所当然) it goes without saying, of course 本领 skill, ability, capability 本能 instinct 本钱 capital, principal 本人 I, me, myself, oneself, in person 本身 itself, in itself 本性 natural instinct, natural character, nature 本义 original meaning, literal sense 本意 original idea, real intention 本质 essence, nature, entity 本着 in line with, in the light of
本地安全性 local security
本地标题 local title
本地传输包 local packet
本地传送方式 local mode
本地到远地链路 local-local link
本地到远地链路 local-remote link
本地的 local
本地登记机构 local registration authority {LRA}
本地地址 local address
本地对话标识(符) local session identification {LSID}
本地多重访问 local multiple access
本地服务区 local service area
本地共享资源 local shared resources {LSR}
本地呼叫 local call
本地[内部]环境 home environment
本地计算机 local computer
本地交换中心 local exchange center
本地节点 local node
本地控制器 local controller
本地设备 local device
本地事务 local transaction
本地通道 local channel
本地网络 local area network {LAN}
本地系统 local system
本地线路 local line
本地信道 local channel
本地信息 local information
本地虚拟协议 local virtual protocol
本地循环 local loop
本地站 local station
本地中心局 local central office
本地终端[设备,机] local terminal
本地[本机,局部]资源 local resource
本存储器 local memory
本机的 local, native
本机电池 local battery
本机调用 native call
本机附件[连接] native attachment
本机信号处理器 native signal

processor {NSP}
本机映像 native image
本体 body
本体语言 body language
本性非负矩阵 essentially non-negative matrix
本性上确界 essential supremum
本性正矩阵 essentially positive matrix
本原多项式 primitive polynomial
本原空间 primitive coordinates/space
本原流程表 prime flow table
本原问题 primitive problem
本原演绎 primitive deduction
本原有向图 primitive digraph
本原字符集 native character set
本原字体 primitive font
本征半导体 intrinsic semiconductor
本征根 latent root
本征函数 eigenfunction
本征图像 intrinsic image
本征向量 eigenvector, latent/proper vector
本征值问题 eigenvalue problem
本征字体 intrinsic font

苯 benzene, benzol(e)

【bèn】

笨 1)(智力差) stupid, dull, foolish 2)(不灵巧) clumsy, awkward 笨重 heavy, cumbersome 笨拙 clumsy, awkward, stupid

【bēng】

崩 崩溃 collapse, crumble, fall apart 崩裂 burst apart, break apart, crack

绷 stretch tight, draw tight

【bèng】

泵 pump

【bī】

逼 逼近 close in on, approach, draw near 逼迫 force, compel 逼真 lifelike, true to life

【bí】

鼻 nose

【bǐ】

比 比方 analogy, instance 比分 score 比价 price relations, rate of exchange 比较 ①(对比) compare, contrast ②〈副〉fairly, comparatively, relatively, quite, rather 比例 proportion, scale 比率 ratio, proportion 比拟 compare, draw a parallel, match 比如 for example, for instance, such as 比赛 match, competition 比试 have a competition 比喻 metaphor, analogy, figure of speech 比重 proportion, specific gravity
比较表达式 comparison expression
比较操作符 comparison operator
比较电路 comparator
比较法 relative method
比较函数 comparison function
比较器 comparator
比较数 comparand
比较运算符 comparison operator
比较指令 compare instruction, comparison order

比较装置 comparing unit
比较字符串 compare string
比较字寄存器 comparand register
比例(尺) scale
比例乘法器 scale multiplier
比例乘数 rate multiplier
比例法 ratio/scaling method
比例仿真 scale simulation
比例模型 scale model
比例失调 miss ratio
比例误差 ratio error
比例因子 scale coefficient, scale/scaling factor
比例字符 proportional character
比例字体 proportional font
比率 rate, ratio
比率检验法 ratio test
比赛树 game tree
比特 bit (=bigit, binary digit)
比特/样本 bit per sample {BPS}
比特矩阵 bit matrix
比特数据流 bit stream
比特/秒 bits per second (=bits/second) {bit/s}
比特差错率 bit error rate
比值控制 ratio control

彼 1)(那个)that, those, the other, another 2)(对方)the other party 彼此 each other, one another

笔 pen ◇钢笔 fountain pen // 铅笔 pencil // 圆珠笔 ball-point pen 笔记 ① take down (in writing) ② notes 笔名 pen name, pseudonym 笔试 written examination/test 笔误 a slip of the pen 笔译 written translation 笔者 the author, the writer 笔直 perfectly straight, bolt upright
笔触输入 pen touch input
笔层次 stroke level
笔画抽取 stroke extraction
笔画发生器 stroke generator
笔画分析 stroke analysis
笔画符号发生器 stroke character generator
笔画集合 stroke set
笔画宽度 stroke width
笔画面积 stroke area
笔画模式 stroke pattern
笔画(输入)设备 stroke device
笔画书写器 stroke writer
笔画数据 stroke data
笔画显示 stroke display
笔迹 script
笔迹学 graphology
笔记录器 pen register
笔式绘图机[绘图仪] pen plotter
笔式系统 pen system
笔输入[笔式]计算机 pen computer

【bì】

币 money, currency ◇外币 foreign currency // 银币 silver coin // 硬币 coin 币值 currency value

必 必定 be bound to, be sure to; certainly, necessarily, surely 必然 inevitable, certain 必修 essential, indispensable 必须 must, have to 必需[必要] essential, indispensable, necessary 必需品 necessities, necessaries ◇生活必需品 daily necessaries
必读文件 required reading file
必然区域 sure region

毕 finish, accomplish, conclude 毕竟 after all, all in all 毕生 all one's life, lifetime 毕业 graduate, finish school 毕业典礼 graduation (ceremony), commencement 毕业论文 graduation thesis/dissertation 毕业设计 graduation project 毕业生 graduate 毕业证书 diploma, graduation certificate

闭 shut, close 闭幕 ① the curtain falls, lower the curtain ② close, conclude 闭幕词 closing address, closing speech 闭幕式 closing ceremony 闭塞 ① (堵塞) stop up, close up ② (交通不便) hard to get to, inaccessible ③ (消息不灵通) uninformed, ill-informed
闭包 closure
闭包代数 closure algebra
闭包公理 closure axiom
闭包关系 closure relation
闭包假设 closure assumption
闭包条件 closure condition
闭包运算 closure operation
闭博弈 closed game
闭操作 closed operation
闭调用 closed call
闭对策 closed game
闭对应 closed correspondence
闭合定理 closure theorem
闭合环路 closed loop
闭合拓扑 closed topology
闭合循环 closed cycle
闭合阵列 closed array
闭环 closed loop
闭环传递函数 closed loop transfer function
闭环控制回路 close loop control circuit
闭环控制系统 close loop control system
闭环频率响应 closed loop frequency response
闭环适配器 closed loop adapter
闭环增益 closed loop gain
闭环转接器 closed loop adapter
闭迹 closed trail
闭集 closed set/aggregate
闭路 closed path, closed-open
闭路传真系统 intrafax
闭路电视 closed-circuit television {CCTV}
闭算子 closed operator
闭锁 latching, latch-up
闭态 closed state
闭凸包 closed convex hull
闭凸集 closed convex set
闭途径 closed walk
闭文件 closed file
闭型(例行)程序 closed routine
闭型法 closed method
闭映射 closed mapping
闭语言 closed language
闭运算 closed operation
闭子句 closed clause
闭总线 closed bus

铋 bismuth (Bi)

弊 1) (蒙骗) fraud, abuse ◇作弊 cheat 2) (毛病) disadvantage 弊病 malady, evil, malpractice 弊端 malpractice, abuse, corrupt practice

蔽 cover, shelter

壁 wall

避 (防止) prevent, keep away, repel 避开 avoid, evade, keep away from 避免

avoid, refrain from, avert
避免错误[故障] fault avoidance
避免死锁 deadlock avoidance

臂 arm

【biān】

边 1)（某一边）side 2)（界线）limit, bound 边界 border, frontier, boundary 边框 frame, rim 边缘 ① edge, fringe, verge, rim, periphery ② margin(al), borderline
边读边写 write-while-read-reading
边割集 edge cut set
边界 bound, boundary, frontier, verge
边界处理 boundary treatment
边界错误 boundary error
边界点 boundary point
边界对准[调整] boundary alignment
边界估算 boundary estimation
边界函数[功能] boundary function
边界集 frontier set
边界节点 border/boundary node
边界路由器 border router
边界面 boundary face
边界区域 border region
边界曲线 boundary curve
边界设备 edge device
边界填充 boundary fill
边界网关协议 border gateway protocol {BGP}
边界网络节点 boundary network node {BNN}
边界像素 boundary pixel
边界[界限]元法 boundary element method
边距 edge spacing
边图 edge graph
边线 border
边缘标度 margin scale
边缘标题 side head
边缘发射二极管 edge emitting diode
边缘检测 edge detection
边缘检验 bias test, marginal test
边缘接插件 edge connector
边缘量化 edge quantization
边缘拟合 edge fitting
边缘识别 edge recognition
边缘试验 marginal test
边缘缩进 margin indent
边缘填充 edge filling
边缘校验 bias check, high-low bias test, margin check, marginal checking

编 （排列）organize, group, arrange 编导 ① write and direct (a play, film, etc.) ② playwright-director 编号 number 编辑 ①（指工作）edit, compile ②（指人员）editor, compiler 编辑部 editorial department 编排 arrange, lay out 编选 select and edit, compile 编译 translate and edit, translate and compile 编造 ①（组织资料）compile, draw up, work out ②（捏造）fabricate, invent, make up ③（想象）create out of the imagination 编造预算 draw up a budget 编者 editor, compiler 编者按 editor's note, editorial note 编织 weave, plait 编制 compilation, composition 编著 compile, write
编程[程序设计] programming
编程环境 programmed/

programming environment
编程检验 programmed check
编程逻辑 programmed logic
编程序模块 programming module
编程[程序设计]语言 programming language
编档单位 filing unit
编档段 filing section
编档规则 filing rule
编档准则 filing criteria
编辑操作 editing operation
编辑程序缓冲器 editor buffer
编辑程序命令 editor command
编辑程序软件 editor software
编辑程序设计 editor programming
编辑处理中心 editorial processing centre {EPC}
编辑窗口 edit window
编辑的 editorial
编辑动画制作 edit animation
编辑对话 editing session
编辑方式 edit/editing mode
编辑符号 edit/editing symbol
编辑复本 edited copy
编辑工具语言 author tool language
编辑功能 edit/editional function
编辑缓冲区 edit buffer
编辑汇编 edit assemble
编辑记录 reference record
编辑检查 edit check
编辑键 editing key
编辑决策表 edit decision list {EDL}
编辑控制 edit/editing control
编辑控制符 edit control character
编辑控制器 edit controller
编辑类型 editing type
编辑模式操作符 edit pattern operator

编辑能力 editing capacity
编辑器 editor
编辑区 editing area
编辑筛选程序 edit filter
编辑显示器 edit display
编辑项目 edit item
编辑掩膜 edit mask
编辑语句 edit/editing statement
编辑语言 author language
编辑转储 edit dump
编辑状态 editing mode
编码 code, coded, coding, encode, encoding
编码表示法 coded representation
编码的十进制 coded decimal
编码地址 coded address
编码点 coded/encoded point
编码调试 coding debug
编码方案 coding/encoding scheme
编码风格 coding style
编码符号 code symbol, coded identification
编码格式 code/coded format, coding form, encoded format
编码规则 code rule, coding rule/scheme
编码机 code machine
编码集 coded set
编码控制 encoded control
编码理论 coding theory
编码率 code rate
编码脉冲 coded pulse
编码器 code device, coder, encoder
编码区 code area
编码树 code tree
编码数 coded number
编码条 encoding strip
编码图 code pattern
编码图灵机 encoded Turing machine

编码图像 coded/ encoded image
编码图形 coded graphic
编码网络 coding network
编码消息 coded message
编码效率 code/ coding efficiency
编码信号 code/coded signal
编码信息 coded message/word
编码形式 coded/coding form
编码行 coding line
编码序列 coded sequence
编码译码器 codec, coder-decoder {**CODEC**}
编码元素 code element
编码制图学 coded graphics
编码装置 code device
编码字符 code/ coded character
编码字符串 coded string
编码字符集[组] coded character set
编目 catalog (=catalogue), cataloging, categorization, listing
编目表 list table
编目光标 list cursor
编目理论 inventory theory
编目目录 catalog directory
编目数据集 cataloged data set
编目文件结构 list file structure
编目系统 cataloging system
编排板 patch panel
编排符号 editing symbol
编入 indit
编校 redact, redaction
编译 compilation, compile, intercompilation
编译表 compile list
编译程序 compile routine, compiler (program)
编译程序编写系统 compiler writing system
编译程序调入 compiler call
编译程序调试 compiler debugging
编译程序辅助工具 compiler aids
编译程序构造 compiler construction
编译程序基准程序 compiler benchmark
编译程序接口 compiler interface
编译程序结构 compiler structure
编译程序结合 compiler binding
编译程序开关 compiler switch
编译错误 compile error
编译代价 compiler cost
编译单位 compilation unit
编译功能 compilation facility/function
编译级 compiler level
编译阶段 compilation phase
编译代码 compiler directive
编译命令 compiler directive
编译模块 collector
编译期间 compile duration
编译器 compiler
编译器装帧 compiler binding
编译算法 compile/ compiler algorithm
编译完成日期 date-compiled
编译语言 compiler language
编译运行 compilation run
编译知识 compiled knowledge
编译周期 compiling duration
编址 addressing
编址存储器 addressed memory
编址矩阵 addressing matrix
编址[寻址]空间 addressing space
编址容量 addressing capacity
编址[寻址]系统 addressing system
编组记录 group record

鞭 whip, lash 鞭策 spur on, urge on

【biǎn】

扁 flat 扁圆 oblate 扁平电缆 flat cable

贬 贬低 belittle, depreciate, play down 贬义 derogatory sense 贬义词 derogatory term 贬值 ① devalue, devaluate, deflate ② depreciate

【biàn】

变 1)(改变)change, become different 2)(使改变)transform, change, alter 变成 change into, turn into, become 变动 change, alteration 变革 transform, change 变更 change, alter, modify 变化 change, vary 变换 transform, alternate, vary 变迁 change, vicissitude 变形 be out of shape, become deformed; deformation, distortion 变异 variation, mutation 变质 go bad, deteriorate

变更方式 alter mode
变更符号 change sign
变更级 change level
变更记录 change record
变更开关 alternation switch
变更位 change bit
变更文件 change file, file change
变更指示符 change bar
变化的 variable, variant
变化点 change point
变换编码 transform coding
变换窗口 mapping window
变换地址 map(ping) address
变换点 change point
变换定义语言 transformation definition language {TDL}
变换分析 transform analysis
变换功能 transformation function
变换故障 mapping fault
变换规则 transformation rule
变换码 conversion code
变换器 changer, converser, transducer, transformer
变换中心 transform center
变换装置 mapping device
变换状态 transition state
变换字段 mapping field
变量 variable, variable quantity
变量标识符 variable identifier
变量表 argument table
变量表达式 variable expression
变量结合 variable binding
变量空间 variable space
变量名 variable name
变量说明 variable declaration
变量替换 variable substitution
变量引用 variable reference
变量状态字 variable state word
变量字段标记 variable field mark
变频器 frequency converter
变速控制 variable speed control
变态 mutation
变态程序 mutator
变体 variant
变体部分 variant part
变体记录 variant record
变体字符 variant character
变形镜装置 deformable mirror device {DMD}
变址 index, indexed address, indexing, map, modify
变址编加 indexed addressing
变址表 index/mapping table
变址部分 index part
变址操作 indexing operation

变址磁道 index track
变址磁盘 index disk
变址存储器 index memory/storage
变址存取方法 indexed access method {IAM}
变址访问 indexed access(ing)
变址级 index level
变址寄存器 B- box, B- line, B-register, B-store, loop box
变址记录 index record
变址加法器 index adder
变址数据名 indexed data name
变址数据项 index data item
变址位 index bit
变址寻址 indexed addressing
变址值 index value
变址字 index word

便 另见【pián】

1)（方便）convenient, handy 2)（非正式的）informal, plain, ordinary 便利 convenient, easy 便条 (informal) note 便携的 portable 便于 easy to, convenient for
便携(式)计算机 pocket computer
便携(式)计算器 pocket calculator
便携式 luggable, ultra-light
便携式程序编译器 portable compiler
便携式打印机 portable typewriter
便携式观察器 hand viewer
便携式计算机 luggable/portable/transportable/ultralight computer
便携式数据捕获器 portable data capture device
便携式数据终端 portable data terminal
便携式台式计算机 handy-type computer

遍 1)（普遍）all over, everywhere 2)〈量〉a time, once through 3)〈计算机〉pass
遍布 be found every- where, spread all over 遍及 extend all over, spread all over
遍历 traversal, traverse
遍历(性)的 ergodic
遍历性 ergodicity
遍历状态 ergodic state
遍历状态表 traversal state list

辨 辨别 differentiate, distinguish, discriminate, identify 辨别方向 take one's bearings 辨认 identify, recognize 辨析 differentiate and analyse
辨别测试 distinguishing test
辨别能力 resolving ability
辨别序列 distinguishing sequence

辩 argue, dispute, debate 辩驳 dispute, refute 辩护 speak in defense of, defend 辩解 provide an explanation, try to defend oneself 辩论 argue, debate 辩证 ① dialectical ② investigate

【biāo】

标 标本 specimen, sample 标兵 example, model 标点 ① punctuation ② punctuate 标明 put a mark, label 标签 tag, label 标题 title, topic, heading, headline, caption 标志 indicate, mark, sign, symbolize
标尺 scale
标尺行 ruler line
标点符号 punctuation

mark/symbol
标点位 punctuation bit
标点字符 punctuation character
标度 density scale, off-scale reading, scale
标号 label, tab
标号编码 label coding
标号变量 label variable
标号变址方式 label index mode
标号标识符 label identifier
标号表 label list/table
标号地址表 label address table
标号格式记录 label format record
标号跟踪 label trace
标号集 label set
标号记录 label record
标号检验 label check
标号描述符 label descriptor
标号前缀 label prefix
标号区 label area
标号区段 labeled field
标号实体 label incarnation
标号属性 label attribute
标号网络 labeled network
标号下标 label subscript
标号原型 label prototype
标号直方图 label histogram
标号终结符 label terminator
标号柱面 label cylinder
标号追踪 label trace
标号字段 label(led) field
标号组 label group, label set
标记 badge, blip, flag, guide line, label, labeling, mark(er), mark(ing), sentinel, sign, tab, tag, ticking, token
标记[令牌]环 token ring
标记窗 index window
标记存储槽 tag slot
标记读出 mark reading, mark-sense, mark-sensing
标记检测 mark detection
标记卡片 mark/token card
标记卡阅读器 labelling reader
标记块 mark block
标记逻辑功能 flag logic function
标记脉冲 mark impulse
标记命令 tab command
标记排序 tag sort
标记偏置 marking bias
标记识别 marker sense
标记算法 labelling algorithm
标记终结符 flag line
标记终结符 marked termination
标记(域) signature
标记域 tag field
标记阅读器 badge reader
标记终结符 marked terminal
标记状态 flag state
标记字段 flag/tag field
标记字节 flag byte
标记[令牌]总线 token bus
标量 scalar, scalar quantity
标量变量 scalar variable
标量表达式 scalar expression
标量常数 scalar constant
标量乘法 scalar multiplication
标量处理机体系结构 scalar processor architecture {SPARC}
标量赋值 scalar assignment
标量功能部件 scalar functional unit
标量函数 scalar function
标量计算机 scalar computer
标量属性 scalar attribute
标量数据类型 scalar data type
标量排序 tag sorting
标签文件 label file
标识 identification, identify, identifying, token
标识部分 identification division
标识点 identification point
标识符 identifier {ID}, tag
标识符长度 identifier length

标识符计数 identifier count
标识符令牌 identity token
标识符名 identifier name
标识号 identification number
标识卡片阅读器 identification card reader
标识空段 identify dummy section
标识控制段 identify control section
标识码 identification code, identifying code
标识区 tag slot
标识图 markgraph
标识(符)字 identifier word
标识字段 identification field
标题表 header sheet/table
标题开始符 start-of-heading character {SOH}
标题文件 header file
标题项 header entry
标题行 header/ heading line, headline
标题页 title page
标题帧 heading frame
标题字 banner/header word
标头开始 start of header {SOH}
标尾 mark end
标线 guide line
标记磁道错误 mark track error
标志符 denoter, designator
标志符号 tag mark
标志寄存器 flag register
标志检测 mark detection
标志位 flag/zone bit, Q-character
标志行 flag line
标准 standard, criterion (复数 criteria), canon, norm, etalon, reference level
标准包协议 standard packet protocol
标准报文格式 standard message format {SMF}
标准操作符 standard operator
标准测试 normative testing, standard test
标准产品手册 data book
标准程序 standard program, general routine
标准打字 standard writer
标准单元 standard block, standard cell
标准[常规]地址 normal address
标准电池 standard cell
标准调色板 standard palette
标准[普通]二进制 ordinary binary
标准二进制码 standard binary code
标准方式 standard mode
标准方位 normal orientation
标准工具箱 standard tool kit
标准归约 standard reduction
标准过程 standard procedure
标准函数 standard function
标准化 normalize, standardization, standardize
标准环境 standard environment
标准基 canonical base
标准积 standard product
标准记数法 standard notation
标准检查[评估]程序 benchmark
标准件 modular unit
标准交互设计系统 standard interactive design system
标准接口 standard interface
标准接口总线 standard interface bus
标准卷标号 standard volume label
标准控制字段 normal control field
标准库 standard order
标准块 standard block
标准框[样板] template, templet

标准类型	standard type
标准模式	standard mode
标准偏差	standard deviation
标准屏幕	standard screen
标准设备	conventional equipment
标准时间	allowance, standard time
标准数据格式	standard data format
标准数据交换	standard data interchange {SDI}
标准通用标记语言	standard generalized markup language {SGML}
标准图像交换格式	standard interchange format {SIF}
标准图像文件	standard image file {SIF}
标准谓词	standard predicate
标准误差	standard error
标准形式	normalized form
标准页面描述语言	standard page description language {SPDL}
标准语言	standard language
标准字符	standard character

【biǎo】

表 1) (外表) surface, external, outside 2) (测量器具) meter, gauge ◇ 电表 electric meter // 水表 water meter // 钟表 watch **表达** express, show, voice, convey **表格** table, list, form **表决** decide by vote, vote **表决权** right to vote **表面** appearance **表面化** become apparent, come to the surface **表面上** superficially **表明** make known, make clear, state clearly **表示** show, express, indicate, demonstrate **表现** ① expression, manifestation ② show, display, manifest **表扬** praise, commend **表彰** commend, honor

表编址	table addressing
表变换	table transform
表标记	list notation
表参数	list parameter
表层结构	surface structure
表层模型	surface-level model
表层知识	surface knowledge
表处理程序	list processor {LISP}
表存储	list storage
表存储残片	table fragmentation
表达式	expression
表达式分析	expression parsing
表达式精度	expression precision
表达式区段	expression field
表达式语句	expression statement
表达树	expression tree
表大小	table size
表访问	table access
表分段	table segmenting
表分隔符	list separator
表封锁	table-lock-up
表格层次	table hierarchy
表格处理	form processing
表格打印机	form printer
表格调度法	list schedule
表格顶部	top of form {TOF}
表格矩阵	table matrix
表格数据结构	list data structure
表格显示	tabular display
表格语言	table language
表格指示符	table indicator
表函数	table function
表检索	table search
表结构	list structure, table

structure
表结束 end of list {EOL}
表决机 voter
表决元件 voting element
表空间 table space
表块 table block
表面安装技术 surface mount technology {SMT}
表面安装器件 surface mount device {SMD}
表面安装组件 surface mount component {SMC}
表面模型 surface model
表面势垒 surface barrier
表面纹理 surface texture
表面显影 surface development
表模式 list pattern
表目 entry, list cell
表目块 entry block
表目录 table directory
表排序 list sorting
表情符号 emotions
表区 list area
表(格)驱动程序 table-driven program
表驱动的 list-drived, table-drived
表驱动技术 table-driven technique
表实用程序 list utility
表式路由选择 directory routing
表式输入 list-directed input
表式说明 table description
表示层 presentation layer
表示法 notation, representation
表示分类 presentation class
表示服务层 presentation services layer
表示格式 presentation format
表示规范 presentation specification
表示[演示]空间 presentation space

表示媒体 presentation medium
表数据结构 list data structure
表索引 table index
表头 head of list, list head, table header
表文件 table file
表显示 table display
表项目 table entry
表寻址 table addressing
表引用字符 table reference character {TRC}
表语言 list language
表域 list area
表元 list cell
表元素 table element
表征 characterization
表组 map group

裱 mount, paste up

【bié】

别 1)(离别) leave, part 2)(另外) other, another 3)(类别) distinction ◇性别 sex (distinction) 4)(差别) difference, distinction 5)(区别) differentiate, distinguish 别称 another name, alternative name 别处 else where, another place
别名 alias
别名分析 alias analysis
别名联合 alias association
别名描述体 alias description entry
别名名字 alias name
别名网络地址 alias network address
别名文件 alias file

【bīn】

宾 guest ◇贵宾 distinguished guest

滨 bank, shore ◇海滨 sea-shore

濒 濒临 be close to, border on 濒于 on the verge of

【bīng】

冰 ice 冰冻 freeze, ice

兵 soldier, fighter

【bǐng】

丙 third

柄 handle, arm, holder

饼 (round flat) cake 饼干 biscuit, cracker
饼形图 pie chart

屏 另见【píng】
1)(抑止)hold 2)(除去)reject, get rid of, abandon 屏除 remove, get rid of 屏弃 discard, abandon, reject

秉 1)(拿着)grasp, hold 2)(掌握)control 秉公 justly, impartially 秉性 nature, disposition

【bìng】

并 1)(合并)combine, merge, incorporate 2)(同时)simultaneously, side by side 3)〈连〉and, moreover
并存 exist side by side, coexist 并进 keep abreast of, advance together 并举 develop simultaneously 并立 exist side by side, exist simultaneously 并列 stand side by side, be juxtaposed 并且 ①(同时)and, also, as well, in addition ②(进一步)besides, moreover, furthermore 并入 merge into, incorporate in 并重 lay equal stress on, pay equal attention to
并串行变换 parallel serial conversion
并发 concurrency
并发(的) concurrent
并发程序设计 concurrent programming
并发程序验证 prove of concurrent program
并发处理机 concurrent processor
并发关系 concurrency relation
并发进程 concurrent process
并发控制机制 concurrent control mechanism
并发位 syndrome
并发协议 concurrent protocol
并集 join, union, union set
并集函数 union function
并接 cascade
并联 parallel, shunt, shunting
并联的 parallel
并联电路 parallel circuit, shunt circuit
并联呼叫 paracall
并联结 union join
并联[并行]连接 parallel connection
并联入口 parallel entry
并联文档 relevant document
并联系统 parallel system
并联字符 parallel character
并联总线 parallel bus
并列显示器 side by side display
并列子句 coordinate clause
并模式 union pattern
并行 parallel
并行插入 parallel insertion

并行查找 parallel search
并行程序 parallel program
并行处理 parallel processing, multiprocessing
并行处理机 parallel processor
并行传输 parallel transmission
并行存储器 parallel storage/memory
并行存取 parallel access, simultaneous access
并行的 collateral
并行调度 parallel scheduling
并行动作 collateral action
并行读出 parallel reading
并行端口 parallel port
并行方式 parallel mode/manner
并行访问 parallel access
并行工程 parallel engineering
并行计算机 parallel computer
并行计算模型 parallel computational model
并行检测 parallel detection
并行检索 parallel search
并行接口 parallel interface
并行累加器 parallel accumulator
并行联结 parallel join
并行链接 parallel link
并行流 parallel flow
并行模拟 parallel simulation
并行任务 parallel task
并行入口 parallel entry
并行设备 parallel device
并行式 parallel mode
并行输入 parallel in
并行输入输出 parallel input/output {**PIO**}
并行数据 parallel data
并行数据库 parallel database
并行[平行]算法 parallel algorithm
并行体系结构 parallel architecture
并行通道 parallel channel
并行通话 parallel sessions
并行推理 parallel inference
并行外部[外围]操作 concurrent peripheral operation {**CPO**}
并行系统 parallel system
并行性 parallelism
并行执行 parallel execution
并行转换 parallel conversion
并置 concatenation, catenation, juxtaposition, side by side
并置符号 concatenation character
并置键 concatenated key
并置数据集 concatenation data set
并置算符 concatenation operator
并置索引 concatenated index
并置字段 concatenated field

病 1)(疾病)illness, sickness, disease 2)(生病)be ill, be taken ill 3)(缺陷)fault, defect 病人 patient 病态 sick
病毒 virus
病毒变种 virus mutation
病毒标志 virus marker
病毒程序 virus program
病毒繁殖 virus breeding
病毒防范 virus defence
病毒分类 virus taxis/classification
病毒分析 virus analysis
病毒复制 virus replication
病毒隔离 virus isolation
病毒蔓延 virus spread
病毒免疫 virus immunity
病毒剖析 dissection of virus
病毒侵袭 virus attack
病毒渗透 virus infiltration
病毒特征 viral signature
病毒疫苗 viruses vaccine

病毒预防 virus precaution
病毒载体 virus carrier
病态耦合 ill coupling

【bō】

拨 (用手拨动) stir, poke, turn ◇拨钟 set a clock 拨款 ①〈动〉appropriate funds, allocate funds ②〈名〉appropriation 拨正 set right, correct ◇拨正航向 correct the course
拨出 dial-out
拨号 dial, dialing, dial-up
拨号代码 dial-code
拨号电路 dialed circuit
拨号调制解调器 dial modem
拨号范围 dialing area
拨号服务 dial-up service
拨号后时延 post dialing delay
拨号呼叫[访问] dial-up
拨号话音网 dial-up voice network
拨号机 dial set
拨号键 dial key
拨号交换机 dial exchange
拨号局 dial office
拨号卡 dial number card
拨号目录 dialing directory
拨号识别服务 dialed number identification sevrice {DNIS}
拨号数位 dial digit
拨号数字显示 dialed number display
拨号网络 dial-up networking
拨号线 dial-up line, dialed line
拨号音 dial tone
拨号账号 dial up account
拨号指示灯 dial pilot lamp
拨号终端 dial-up terminal, dial-up
拨回 dial back
拨动开关 thumb wheel switch
拨入 dial in

波 wave 波动 undulate, fluctuate, rise and fall 波及 spread to, involve, affect 波浪 wave
波长 wavelength
波长测量计 wavemeter
波带 wave band
波动作用 wave action
波段 band
波分复用 wavelength division multiplexing {WDM}
波分析 wave analysis
波峰焊 wave-soldering
波及效果 spread effect
波特 baud
波特率 baud rate
波形 waveform
波形处理机 wave processor
波形存储器 wave form memory
波形发生器 waveform generator
波形监控器 waveform monitor
波形数字化 waveform digitization
波形数字滤波器 wave digital filter

玻 玻璃(杯) glass ◇防弹玻璃 bullet-resisting glass ∥ 钢化玻璃 tempered glass ∥ 光学玻璃 optical glass ∥ 磨沙玻璃 frosted glass

剥 另见【bāo】
剥夺 deprive, expropriate, strip 播放 broadcast 剥落 peel off

播 播送 broadcast, transmit

【bó】

泊 另见【pō】
be at anchor, moor, berth

铂 platinum (Pt)

驳 驳斥 refute, denouce 驳船 barge, lighter

脖 脖子 neck

博 1)(丰富)rich, abundant, plentiful 2)(取得)win, gain 博览 read extensively 博览会 fair 博物馆 museum 博士 doctor
博多码 Baudot code
博弈 game, game playing, gaming
博弈程序 game program
博弈论 game theory
博弈模拟 gaming simulation
博弈图 game graph

搏 搏动 beat rhythmically, pulse 搏斗 wrestle, fight, struggle

薄 另见【báo】
slight, thin, meager, small 薄利 small profits 薄利多销 small profits but quick turnover 薄弱 weak

箔 foil, tinsel, leaf ◇金箔 gold foil

【bǒ】

跛 lame 跛子 lame person, cripple

【bǔ】

补 1)(修补)mend, patch, repair 2)(填补)fill, supply, make up for 补充 ① replenish, supplement, complement ② additional, complementary, supplementary 补充规定 additional regulations 补充说明 additional remarks 补给 supply, provision 补救 remedy 补救措施 remedial measure 补考 make-up examination 补偿 compensation 补贴 subsidy, allowance 补遗 addendum, supplement 补助 subsidy, allowance 补助金 grant-in-aid, subsidy 补足 bring up to full strength, make up a deficiency, fill (a vacancy, gap, etc.)

补偿(值) offset
补偿参数 offset parameter
补偿调整 compensation adjustment
补偿法 penalty method
补偿放大器 compensated amplifier
补偿函数 penalty function
补偿技术 compensation technique
补偿器 compensator, equalizer
补偿事务 compensating transaction
补偿数据 offset data
补偿算法 back-off algorithm
补偿误差 compensating error
补偿系统 back-off system
补偿线路 equalize circuit
补充的文件属性 additive file attribute
补充[追加]记录 additional record
补充项 additional item, addition item

补集 complementary set, supplementary set
补码表示 complement(ed) representation
补码地址 complement address
补码二进制 complementary binary
补码规则 complement rule
补码基 complement base
补码形式 complement form
补码指令 complement instruction
补数记数法 complementary notation
补算码 make-up code
补算时间 make-up time
补图 complement of a graph, complement

捕 捕获 capture 捕捉 catch, seize, arrest
捕获半径 capture radius
捕获带 capture zone
捕获地址 trap address
捕获键 capture key
捕获区域 capture region
捕获时间 capture time
捕获向量 trap vector
捕捉范围 catching range
捕捉效应 capture effect
捕捉语句 catch statement

哺 哺养 feed, rear 哺育 feed, nurse, nurture

【bù】

不 （否定）not, no 不必 need not, not have to 不必要 unnecessary, dispensable 不便 inconvenient 不…不… ①（表示否定）◇~清~楚 not clear ②（表示"既不…又不…"）◇~大~小 neither too big nor too small, just right 不测 accident, mishap, contingency 不错 ①（正确）correct, right ②（好）not bad, pretty good 不大 ①（不经常）not often, seldom, rarely, hardly, scarcely ②（程度不深）not very, not quite 不但 not only 不当 unsuitable, improper, inappropriate 不道德 immoral 不得 ①（不能够）cannot, not to ②（不可以）should not, must not, be not supposed to, not be allowed 不得不 have no choice but to, have to, cannot but 不定 indefinite 不断 unceasing, uninterrupted, continuous 不法 lawless, illegal, unlawful 不符 not agree with, not conform to 不敢 dare not, not dare 不够 not enough, insufficient, short of, lack 不辜负 be worthy of, live up to 不顾 disregard, ignore, in spite of 不关心 be indifferent to, not concern oneself with 不管 no matter, regardless of 不过 ①〈副〉（只，仅）only, just, merely, nothing but, no more than ②〈连〉（语意转折）but, nevertheless, however, only 不仅 not only 不禁 can't help, can't refrain from 不久 soon, before long 不可避免 be inevitable 不可分割 indivisible, inseparable 不可估量 inestimable, incalculable, beyond measure 不可调和 irreconcilable, incompatible 不合法 illegal 不利 ① unfavorable, disadvantageous, harmful ② unsuccessful 不料 unexpectedly, to one's surprise 不留余地 leave no room, make no allowance (for) 不论 no matter, irrespective of, regardless of 不免 unavoidable 不明 not clear, unknown, fail to understand 不能 not have to, cannot but 不怕 be not afraid of, not fear 不配 be unworthy of, be not qualified to 不如 ① (比不上) not equal to ② (还是) had better, would rather 不失时机 lose no time 不时 ① frequently ② at any time 不通 ① (阻隔) be obstructed, be blocked up ② (文理错误) not make sense, be illogical, be ungrammatical 不外 not beyond the scope of, nothing more than 不惜 ① not stint, not spare ② not hesitate (to do sth) 不行 ① (不可以) will not do, be not allowed ② (不中用) be no good, not work ③ (不好) not good, poor 不幸 ① (灾祸) misfortune ② (不希望的) unfortunately 不朽 immortal, not second to, as good as 不言而喻 it goes without saying, it is self-evident 不一 vary, differ ◇长短不一 differ in length 不遗余力 spare no pains, spare no efforts, do one's utmost 不再 no longer, not any more 不折不扣 to the full, one hundred percent 不止 ① (超出范围) more than, not limited to ② (不停止) incessantly, without end 不至于 cannot go so far as to, not to such an extent as to 不准 not allow, forbid, prohibit ◇不准人内！ No admittance // 不准吸烟！ No smoking! 不足 ① not enough, insufficient, inadequate ② (不满某个数目) less than

不安全的 unreliable, unsafe
不安全文件 unsafe file
不变标量 invariant scalar
不变量 invariant
不变式计算 invariant computation
不变数 numerical invariant
不变系统 invariant system
不变信息 fixed information
不变性 invariance, immutable
不变性定理 invariance theorem
不变性论题 invariance thesis
不变因子 invariant factor
不变运算 invariant operation
不变整数 invariant integer
不常变记录 master record
不常变数据 master data
不常变文件 master file
不等 inequality, not equal to {NE}
不等长编码 nonequal length code
不定长记录 nonfixed-length record, undefined-length record
不定点 nonpoint
不定积分 indefinite integral
不定矩阵 indefinite matrix
不定型 indefinite form
不[确]定性 uncertainty, nondeterminacy
不定性原理 uncertainty principle
不对称曲线 skew curve
不对称人字形 asymmetric

chevron
不对称设备 asymmetric devices
不对称失真 asymmetric distortion
不符合 mismatch
不工作单元 dead zone unit
不工作区 dead band, dead space, dead zone
不规则 irregularity, fortuitous
不规则的文本 unjustified text
不规则格式 scramble pattern
不规则函数 scramble function
不规则节点 irregular node
不规则偏差 irregular variation
不规则失真 fortuitous distortion
不规则跳动 random jump
不规则问题 irregular problem
不规则系统 scramble system
不归零 non-return-to-zero {NRZ}
不归零"1"制记录 non-return-to-zero on one recording {NRZ1}
不活动 deactivation, inaction
不活动窗口 inactive window
不活动的 inactive
不活动记录 inactive record
不活动节点 inactive node
不活动页 inactive page
不活动站 inactive station
不活跃端口 disabled port
不活跃状态 disabled state
不间断电源 uninterrupted power supply {UPS}
不可比性 incomparability, incommensurability
不可变换[交换]的 inconvertible
不可擦除[删去]的 non-erasable
不可擦(除)存储器 nonerasable storage
不可擦媒体 nonerasable medium
不可分操作 indivisible operation
不可分图 nonseparable graph
不可分页动态区 nonpageable dynamic area
不可分页分区 nonpageable partition
不可分页区 nonpageable region
不可改正的错误 nonrecoverable error
不可更改指令 unmodified instruction
不可更换磁盘 nonremovable disk
不可恢复(的)错误 fatal error, irrecoverable error, nonrecoverable error
不可恢复的事务处理 nonrecoverable transaction
不可恢复数据 nonrecoverable data
不可见的 invisible, unviewable
不可见性 nonvisibility
不可交换存储器 nonswappable storage
不可解节点 unsolvable node
不可靠的 unreliable
不可控变量 uncontrolled variable
不可能事件 impossible event
不可逆状态 irreversible state
不可排序(的) unordered
不可判定的 undecidable
不可屏蔽中断 NI interrupt, nonmaskable interrupt {NMI}
不可省略回车 required carrier return {RCR}
不可校正的错误 uncorrectable error
不可约的 irreducible
不可约多项式 irreducible polynomial
不可约矩阵 irreducible matrix

不可约马尔可夫链 irreducible Markov chain
不可约图 irreducible graph
不可约映像 irreducible image
不可约元 irreducible element
不可中断模块 disabled module
不可中断页故障 disabled page fault
不连通图 disconnected graph
不连续 discontinuous
不连续保存段 discontinuous save segment {DCSS}
不连续的 discrete
不连续函数 discontinuous function
不灵活 dumb
不灵活的 inflexible
不能读的 unreadable
不能接受的 unacceptable
不匹配 mismatch
不平衡性 unbalance
不确定程序 nondeterministic program
不确定模型 ambiguous model
不确定算法 nondeterministic algorithm
不确定推理 uncertain reasoning
不确定系统 uncertain system
不确定性故障 indeterminate fault
不确定性决策 uncertain decision
不确定性有限自动机 nondeterministic finite automaton
不确定知识 uncertain knowledge
不确定状态 indeterminate state
不确定自动机 nondeterministic automaton
不确切概念 inexact concept
不确切函数 inexact function
不确认 non-acknowledge
不停顿 nonstop

不同接口 distinct interface
不透明的 opaque
不透明屏蔽 opaque mask
不透明屏幕 opaque screen
不透明区 opaque area
不透明映射 opacity map
不完全模型 incomplete model
不完全识别 partial recognition
不完全有限自动机 incomplete finite automat(a)
不稳定的 unstable, labile, crank
不稳定调节 undamped control
不稳定平衡 unstable equilibrium
不稳定条件 instability condition
不相干的 incoherent
不相干光 incoherent light
不相关 irrelevance, uncorrelated
不相关变量 uncorrelated variable
不相关函数 uncorrelated function
不相交和 disjoint sum
不相交集(合) disjoint set
不相交事件 disjoint event
不相接的回路 disjoint circuit
不相容动作 incompatible action
不相容事件 incompatible event
不相容性 inconsistency
不相容原理 exclusion principle
不一致的 inconsistent
不一致性 discordance, inconsistency
不一致知识 inconsistent knowledge
不正确长度 incorrect length

布 cloth, fabric **布告** notice, bulletin, proclamation **布告栏** notice board, bulle-

tin board 布局 overall arrangement, lay-out, distribution 布置 ①（陈设）fix up, arrange, decorate ②（安排）arrange, make arrangements for, give instructions about
布尔 Boolean (=boolean)
布尔变量[变数] Boolean variable
布尔标志 Boolean denotation
布尔标志符 Boolean marker
布尔表达式 Boolean expression
布尔差分 Boolean difference
布尔常数 Boolean constant
布尔超正方体 Boolean hypercube
布尔乘法 Boolean multiplication
布尔初等量 Boolean primary
布尔代数 algebra Boolean, Boolean algebra
布尔代数符 boolean operator
布尔法 Boolean method
布尔方程 Boolean equation
布尔符号 Boolean (symbol)
布尔函数 Boolean function
布尔合取 Boolean conjunction
布尔环 Boolean ring
布尔加 Boolean add
布尔检索 Boolean search
布尔矩阵 Boolean matrix
布尔类型 Boolean type
布尔连接 Boolean conjunction/connective
布尔量 Boolean quantity
布尔逻辑 Boolean logic
布尔模式 Boolean pattern
布尔求反 Boolean complementation
布尔数组 Boolean array
布尔搜索 boolean search
布尔算符 Boolean operator
布尔条件 Boolean condition
布尔系数 Boolean coefficient
布尔项 Boolean term
布尔演算 Boolean calculus
布尔因子 Boolean factor
布尔域 Boolean field
布尔运算 Boolean calculation/operation
布尔运算符 Boolean operator
布尔值 Boolean (=boolean), Boolean value
布局规划 allocation plan
布线 routing, wire layout, wiring
布线背面 wired back
布线[发送]程序 router
布线电容 wiring capacitance
布线逻辑 hardwired logic, wired logic
布线通道 routing channel
布线图 wiring diagram
布线图案 wiring pattern
布线问题 wiring problem

步

步 step, pace 步步 step by step, at every step 步调 pace, step 步伐 step, pace 步骤 step, measure, move
步长 step, step-length, step-size, step-width
步进电(动)机 stepper motor
步进机构 proportional spacing mechanism
步进技术 stepping technique
步进计数器 step counter
步进记录 step record
步进(式)开关 step-by-step switch
步进开关 stepper, stepper switch
步进控制 step-by-step control
步进逻辑 step logic
步进时间 stepping time
步进式乘法器 step multiplier
步进式寄存器 stepping register

步进伺服电机 step-servo motor
步进系统 step-by-step system
步进项目 advance item
步控制 step control
步命令 step command
步式重新启动 step restart

钚 plutonium (Pu)

部 1)(单位) unit, department 2)(政府的部) ministry
部分 part, section
部件 parts, components, assembly
部门 department, branch, division
部位 position, place, location, placement
部长 minister, head of a department
部分定序 partial ordering
部分和 partial sum, subtotal
部分进位 partial carry
部分名称 division name
部头 division header
部件表目 component entry
部件[单元,设备]地址 unit address
部件地址 component address
部件符号 symbolic unit
部件故障影响分析 component failure impact analysis {CFIA}
部件接口 unit interface
部件结构 unit architecture
部件控制 unit control
部件入口 component entry
部件异常 unit exception
部件诊断 unit diagnostics
部名 division name
部首 division header, radical

簿 book

C c

【cā】

擦 1)(摩擦)rub 2)(涂抹) spread sth on ◇给机器擦油 oil a machine 擦净 wipe 擦去 abrade, erase 擦拭 clean, cleanse

擦除 erase, erasing, letter out, scratch, wipe
擦除磁头 erase head
擦除动作 erasing move
擦除符 erase character
擦除命令 erase command
擦除模板 wipe pattern
擦除器 eraser
擦时删除 erase-on-scratch
擦写替换 erase/writer alternate {EWA}

【cāi】

猜 guess 猜测 guess, speculate, conjecture 猜想 suppose, guess, assume
猜测 guess, conjecture
猜测法 conjecture method

【cái】

才 (有才能的人)capable person, talent 才干 ability, competence 才能 ability, talent, gift 才智 ability and wisdom

材 (木料)timber 材料 ① material ② makings, stuff

材料工程 material engineering
材料管理 material control
材料计划 material planning
材料需求计划 material requirements planning {MRP}

财 wealth, money 财宝 money and valuables 财产 property, assets, fortune 财富 wealth, riches, fortune 财务 financial affairs
财务报表 financial statement
财务管理 financial management
财务计划 financial planning
财政分析 financial analysis
财政管理 financial administrative control {FAC}

裁 cut (paper, cloth, etc.) into parts 裁剪 cut out; clipping
裁剪[限幅,显示]边界 clip boundary
裁剪表 clip list
裁剪路径 clip path
裁剪路线 clipping path
裁剪平面 clipping plane
裁剪区域 clipping region
裁剪数据 trimming data
裁决点 decision point
裁切[剪切]标记 crop marks

【cǎi】

采 1)(摘)pick 2)(开采)

mine, extract 采集 gather, collect 采纳 accept, adopt 采取 adopt, select 采用 adopt, use, employ
采集时间 acquisition time
采集装置 pick device
采样 sample, sampling
采样保持 sample (and) hold
采样定理 sampling theorem, sampling theory
采样方式 sample mode
采样间隔 sample interval
采样率 sampling rate
采样频率 sampling frequency
采样(周)期 sampling period
采样数据 sample/sampled data

彩
彩色 color, chromatic color, technicolor, multicolor
彩色板 see-through plate
彩色编码 color coding
彩色变换 color transformation
彩色(对照)表 color map
彩色表 color scheme, color table
彩色查找表 color look-up table {CLUT}
彩色打印机 color printer
彩色调节器 color corrector
彩色调色板 color palette
彩色分域法 color-range method
彩色过滤器 color filter
彩色号 color index
彩色活动图像压缩规范 motion picture experts group {MPEG}
彩色监视器 color monitor
彩色解调器 chroma demodulator
彩色滤光阵列 color filter array
彩色扫描器 color scanner
彩色数据 color data
彩色缩微胶片 color microfilm

彩色图像 color image
彩色图像恢复 color image restoration
彩色图形包 color graphic package
彩色图形适配器 color graphic adapter {CGA}
彩色显示 color display
彩色显像管 color kinescope
彩色消失 color disappearing
彩色校正 color correction
彩色形成器 color plexer
彩色循环 color cycling
彩色元素 color cell
彩色增强 color enhancement
彩图 color graph

踩
step on, trample ◇
踩油门 step on the gas (accelerator)

【cài】

菜
1) (蔬菜) vegetable, greens 2) (泛指副食) food
菜单 menu, bill of fare 菜肴 dish, course
菜单安全保护 menu security
菜单参数 menu parameter
菜单操作 menu operation
菜单程序 menu program, menu routine
菜单窗口 menu window
菜单界面 menu interface
菜单卡 menu card
菜单栏 menu bar
菜单命令 menu command
菜单内容 menu text
菜单驱动软件 menu-driven software
菜单数据 menu data
菜单提示 menu prompt
菜单条 menu bar
菜单外壳 menu shell
菜单文本 menu text

菜单文件 menu file
菜单系统 menu system
菜单项 menu item
菜单选择 menu selection, selecting menu
菜单(选择区)域 menu area
菜单正本 menu script

【cān】

参 另见【cēn】
(加入)join, enter, take part in 参观 visit, look around 参考 ① consult, refer to ② reference 参加 join, attend, take part in 参加者 participant, have a hand in 参与 participate in, have a hand in 参阅 ① consult ② read sth for reference 参照 consult, refer to
参变元件 parametron
参考 reference
参考[基准]变量 reference variable
参考标记 reference mark
参考波 reference wave
参考层 reference level
参考带 reference tape
参考地址 reference address
参考电路 reference circuit
参考电平 reference level
参考电源 reference (power) supply
参考调用 reference call
参考记录 reference record
参考卷 reference volume
参考类 reference class
参考码 reference code
参考时间 reference time
参考手册 guide book, reference manual
参考索引 reference key
参考向量 reference vector
参考信号 reference signal
参考音量 reference volume
参考帧 frame of reference
参考资料手册 data book
参数 parameter
参数包 parameter pack
参数变换 parameter variation
参数传送 parameter passing
参数分界符 parameter delimiter
参数分析 parametric analysis
参数规划 parametric programming
参数过程 procedure as parameter
参数化 parameterization, parameterize
参数化模块库 library of parameterized module {LPM}
参数记录 reference record
参数界限 parameter bound
参数描述符 parameter descriptor
参数偏移 parameter shift
参数相关 parameter correlation
参数选择菜单 parameter selection menu
参数用户 parametric user
参数字 parameter word

餐 1)(吃饭)eat 2)(饭食)food, meal ◇快餐 snack ‖ 西餐 Western food ‖ 中餐 Chinese food 餐厅 ①(饭厅,食堂)dining room, dining hall ②(餐馆)restaurant

【cán】

残 (剩余)remnant, remaining 残存 remnant, remaining, surviving 残废 crippled, disabled 残酷 cruel, brutal, ruthless 残缺 incomplete, deficient
残留数据问题 residue problem

cán 惭 cǎn 惨 càn 灿 cāng 仓舱 cáng 藏 cāo 操

残留误差 offset, residual error
残片 fragment
残数 residue
残数定理 residue theorem
残数校验 residue check

惭
惭愧 be ashamed

【cǎn】
惨 惨败 crushing defeat, disastrous defeat 惨祸 horrible disaster, frightful calamity 惨剧 tragedy, calamity 惨重 heavy, grievous, disastrous

【càn】
灿 灿烂 magnificent, splendid

【cāng】
仓 storehouse, warehouse 仓储 warehousing 仓促 hurriedly, hastily
仓库 warehouse, repository
仓库费用 warehouse cost

舱 1) cabin, compartment ◇货舱 hold // 客舱 (passenger) cabin 2)〈宇航〉module ◇指令舱 command module

【cáng】
藏 1)(隐藏) hide, conceal 2)(储藏) store, stock

【cāo】
操 操练 drill, practice 操心 worry about, trouble about, take pains 操纵 control, steer, manipulate 操作 operation, manipulation, working
操纵杆 control stick, joy-stick (=joystick), operating lever
操纵[控制]杆接口 joystick interface
操纵杆式(光标)指示器 joystick pointer
操纵盒 joybox
操纵机构 motivator
操纵力 operating force
操作表 operation table
操作表达式 operation expression, operational expression
操作(码)部分 operation part
操作程序 operating program, operational program
操作次数/秒 operations per second
操作单位 operating unit
操作的 active, functional, operated, operative
操作地址寄存器 operational address register
操作对象格式 operand format
操作分析 operation analysis
操作符 operator, operational character, control character {CTRL}, actor, instruction character
操作符表 operator table
操作[运算]符号 operation/operator symbol
操作符栈 operator stack
操作功能 operating function
操作管理程序 operation supervisor
操作管理员 operation manager
操作规程 working instruction
操作环境 operating/operational environment
操作缓冲区 operation buffer
操作键 operational key
操作开关 function switch
操作空格 operation blank
操作空间 operating space
操作控制板 operation control panel

操作控制开关 operation control switch
操作控制台 operator's console, utility control console
操作控制语句 operation control statement
操作控制语言 operation control language {OCL}
操作例行程序 function routine
操作流程图 operation(al) flowchart
操作流水线 operation pipeline
操作码 action/ command/ function/ order code, operation(al) code (=op code)
操作码表 operation code table
操作码部分 operator part
操作码方式 operating code mode {OPCMOD}
操作码寄存器 operating code register (= op register), operation code register
操作码字段 operating code field (=op code field), operator field
操作面板 guidance panel
操作命令 operating/ operation/ oprand command
操作模式 operator schema
操作期间 operational period
操作起动装置 operational trigger
操作权利 operational rights
操作软盘 operating/ operational diskette
操作时间 operating/ operation time
操作事故 operation exception
操作手 manipulator
操作手册[指南] operation manual
操作[运算]属性 operational attribute

操作数 operand
操作数标识 operand identification
操作数表 operand table
操作数部分 operand part
操作数存取 operand access
操作数地址 operand address
操作数段 operand field
操作数队列 operand queue
操作数对 operand pair
操作数寄存器 operand register
操作数接口 operand interface
操作数进入 operand entry
操作[运算]数据 operational data
操作数据安全 operational data security
操作数据表 function data table {FDT}
操作数类型 operand type
操作数取出指令 operand fetch instruction
操作数说明符 operand specifier
操作数位 operand bit
操作数误差[错误] operand error
操作数寻址操作 operand addressing operation
操作数延迟(时间) operand delay
操作数页面 operand page
操作数有效地址 effective operand address
操作数值 operand value
操作数指定 operand designation
操作数字长 operand wordlength
操作说明 operation declaration
操作说明书 operating manual/ specification
操作台 (control) console, operating console, operation

board
操作台缓冲器 console buffer
操作台[操作员]指示灯 operator indicator
操作特权 operating privilege
操作特性 operating characteristic
操作条件 operating/operational condition
操作图 operation chart
操作位 done bit, function digit
操作文档编制 operations documentation
操作系统 operating system {OS}, executive system {EXEC system}, operation system
操作系统安全性 operating system security
操作系统分时 operating system time-sharing
操作系统管理程序 operating system supervisor
操作系统核心 operating system kernel
操作系统模块 operating system module
操作系统内核 operating system nucleus
操作系统配置 operating system configuration
操作系统生成 operating system generation
操作系统特性 operating system characteristic
操作系统体系结构 operating system architecture
操作系统文件 operating system file
操作系统优化 operating system optimization
操作系统族 operating system family

操作显示面板 operating/displaying panel
操作延误时间 operating delay
操作译码器 operation decoder
操作异常 operation exception
操作语义模型 operational semantic model
操作语义学 operational semantics
操作员 operator
操作员存取码 operator's access code
操作员错误 operator error
操作员调度问题 operator scheduling problem
操作员服务程序 operator services
操作员干预 operator intervention
操作员监督 operator oversight
操作员监视 operator monitor
操作员接口控制块 operator interface control block {OPICB}
操作员开工文件 operator profile
操作员控制板 operator control panel
操作员控制单元 operator control element {OPCE}
操作员控制命令 operator control command {OCC}
操作员控制台 operator console, operator's station
操作员控制台程序 operator console facility {OCF}
操作员控制台面板 operator control panel
操作员控制语言 operator control language {OCL}
操作员逻辑分页 operator logic(al) paging
操作员命令 operator command
操作员确认记录 operator au-

thorization record {OAR}
操作员识别 operator identification
操作员特权 operator privilege
操作员特许记录 operator authorization record {OAR}
操作员通信管理程序 operator communication manager {OPCOM}
操作员信息 operator message
操作员引导码 operator guidance code
操作员站 operator station
操作员站任务 operator station task {OST}
操作员中断 operator interrupt
操作栈 active/operator stack
操作栈寄存器 operation stack register
操作指令 operating instruction, operational order
操作周期 operation/operational cycle
操作状态 operating state/status, operation state
操作字 operational word (=opword)
操作字段 operation field

糙 rough, coarse

【cáo】

槽 groove, slot, channel, chute, trough
槽沟 chamfer
槽口 slot, notch
槽名 slot name

【cǎo】

草 grass, straw 草案 draft, ground plan 草草 carelessly, hastily 、草稿 rough draft, rough copy 草签 initial ◇ 草签合同 sign a contract // 草签文本 initiated text // 草签协定 initial an agreement
草率 careless, perfunctory, sloppy
草案拷贝 draft copy
草稿打印机 draft-quality printer
草稿带 scratch tape
草稿文件 scratch file
草稿字体方式 draft mode
草稿字体印刷质量 draft quality
草体 script
草图 layout, rough, rough draft, rough sketch, schematic drawing, sketch map/pad, sketch(ing)
草图模板 sketch template
草图模式 draft mode
草图设计 layout design

【cè】

册 1)(簿册) volume, book 2)〈量词〉copy

厕 厕所 lavatory, toilet, W.C., restroom, washroom

侧 1)(旁边) side 2)(向旁边歪斜) incline, lean 侧面 side, aspect, flank 侧重 lay particular emphasis on
侧板 side plate
侧壁 side wall
侧电路 side circuit
侧放 side lay
侧流 side flow
侧面图 profile
侧视图 side view

测 survey, measure 测定 determine 测量 survey, measure, gauge 测算 measure, calculate

测度 measure
测度空间 measure space
测度论 measure theory
测绘仪 coordinate machine
测量点 measuring point
测量范畴 measurement category
测量范围 measurement range
测量技术 measurement technique
测量脉冲 metering pulse
测量器件 sensing device
测量误差 measurement error, error of measurement
测量系统 measurement system
测试 checkout, test, testing
测试板 test card
测试报告 test report
测试编码器 test encoder
测试表 test table
测试步 test step
测试程序 test program, testing program
测试初始化 test initialization
测试点 test point
测试范围 test range, test specification
测试方法学 test methodology
测试覆盖率 test coverage
测试工具 test tool
测试管理程序 test supervisor program
测试规格 test specification
测试环境 test environment
测试阶段 test phase
测试空间 test space
测试控制 test(ing) control {TC}
测试库 test library
测试理论 theory of testing
测试码生成程序 test generator
测试模拟器 test simulator
测试模型 test model
测试器 tester

测试请求 request for test {RFT}
测试请求信息[报文] test request message {TRM}
测试任务 test task
测试日志 test log
测试软件 testing software
测试设备 test equipment/facility, instrumentation
测试时间 test time, testing time
测试事件 test event
测试[检查,试验]数据 test data
测试数据生成 test data generation
测试说明 test specification
测试条件 test condition
测试文件 test file
测试向量 test vector
测试信号 pilot signal
测试指示器 test indicator
测试自动化 test automation

策 plan, scheme, strategy 策划 plan, plot, scheme, engineer 策划者 sponsor, plotter, schemer 策略 tactics, strategy
策略计划 strategic planning

【cēn】
参 另见[cān]
参差 irregular, uneven; staggering, diversity, jagging 参差不齐 uneven, not uniform
参差文本 ragged text

【céng】
层 1)〈量词〉layer, tier, stratum 2)〈楼层〉story, floor
层次 hierarchy, level, gradation
层次[分层] layer module

层次编码 hierarchical coding
层次查询语言 hierarchical query language
层次法 stratification
层次分割 hierarchical cut
层次分解 hierarchical decomposition
层次分析法 analytic hierarchy process {AHP}
层次划分 hierarchical division
层次化存储管理系统 hierarchical storage management system
层次接口 layer interface
层次结构 hierarchical structure
层次控制 hierarchical control
层次类别 layer class
层次[分层]路径 hierarchical path
层次模型 hierarchical model
层次片段 hierarchy segment
层次嵌套 hierarchy nesting
层次设计法 hierarchical design method
层次式菜单 hierarchical menu
层次数据结构 hierarchical data structure
层次[分层]数据库 hierarchical database
层次数据模型 hierarchical data model
层次顺序 hierarchical sequence, hierarchical sequential {HS}
层次图 hierarchical/ hierarchy chart, hierarchical graph
层次协议 layer protocol
层次型命名机制 hierarchy naming
层次直接 hierarchical direct {HD}
层次直接存取法 hierarchical direct access method {HDAM}

层次字体 level font
层管理 layer management
层号 level number
层流 laminar flow
层内通信 intralayer communication
层状结构 sandwich

【chā】

叉

叉积 cross product

差 另见【chà】【chāi】

〈数学〉difference 差错 mistake 差额 difference, balance 差距 ① gap, disparity ② 〈机械〉difference 差异 difference, divergence, discrepancy, inequality
差错 error {ERR}
差错程序 error routine
差错处理器 error handler
差错[错误]恢复 error recovery
差错检测 error detection
差错纠正 error correction
差错控制命令 error control command
差错率 error rate
差错潜伏期 error latency
差错数据分析 error data analysis {EDA}
差错文件 error file
差错校验 error checking and correction {ECC}
差动放大器 differential amplifier
差动线圈 hybrid coil
差动装置 compensator, differential gear
差分 difference
差分表 difference table
差分表示式 difference expression
差分方程 difference equation

差分机 difference engine
差分结构 difference structure
差分算子 difference operator
差分系数 difference coefficient
差分校正 difference correction
差分序列 difference sequence
差分压缩 differential compression
差分移相键控 differential phase-shift keying {DPSK}
差模时延 differential mode delay {DMD}
差拍 beat
差频 beat frequency

插 stick in, insert, interpose, thrust 插话 interpose (a remark, etc.), chip in 插手 ①(参加)take part, lead a hand ②(参与)have a hand in, poke one's nose into, meddle in
插板式计算机 card-board computer
插槽 slot
插件 field replaceable unit {FRU}, package card, plug-in board/card/package
插件(板) package board
插件板 plug-in card/sheet, (add-on) board
插件边框 card frame
插件编程 board programming
插件插头座 card connector
插件导轨 board guide, card guide
插件底盘 card chassis
插件电源 card power supply
插件盒[架] card cage
插件机框 card frame cage
插件级模件 card level module
插件模件 card module
插件片 plug-in sheet
插件总线 card bus
插脚 connector pin
插脚兼容(的) pin-compatable
插接 pin contact
插接板 control panel, pinboard, plugboard
插接瓣 lobe
插接瓣旁路 lobe bypass
插接[转接]矩阵 relay matrix
插接线 plug wire
插孔 jack, plug jack, socket, hub
插孔板 jack panel
插孔布局 hub layout
插入 insert, patch, interpolate, break-in, in-lay
插入板 add-in card
插入表示法 infix notation
插入程序 plugged program
插入点 insertion point
插入方式 insert mode
插入键 Ins key (=Insert key)
插入类型 insertion class
插入模式 insert mode
插入排序[分类] insertion sort
插入式存储器 plug-in type memory
插入式电路板 plug-in circuit card
插入式接口插件 plug-in interface card
插入算符 infix operator
插入形式 infix form
插入字符 insertion character
插入组装 in-line assembly
插头 jackplug, male connector, plug contact, spigot
插针 connector pin, pin
插针间距 contact spacing
插针阵列 pin grid array {PGA}
插值 interpolation
插值多项式 interpolation polynomial
插值公式 interpolation formula
插座 plug socket, hub,

socket, jack

【chá】

茶 tea

查 1)(检查)check, examine 2)(调查)look into, investigate 3)(察看)look up, consult　查获 hunt down and seize, track down　查勘 survey, exploration　查明 find out, ascertain　查阅 look up, consult　查找 search, look up, seek
查表 look-up, table look-up {TLU}
查表法 look-up table
查错模块 debugging module
查核 check up
查看功能 look facility
查全因子 recall factor
查索指南 access guide
查线系统 seek wire system
查询 polling, query, enquiry (=inquiry){ENQ}
查询表 polling list
查询策略 query strategy
查询层次 query hierarchy
查询对话 inquiry session
查询方式 inquiry mode
查询访问 queried access
查询工具 query facility
查询会话 inquiry session
查询间隔 polling interval
查询路径 query path
查询事例 query instance
查询事务 inquiry transaction
查询台 requester station
查询网络 requester network
查询握手认证协议 challenge handshake authentication protocol {CHAP}
查询系统 polling system
查询线 information trunk
查询优化 query optimization
查询语言 inquiry language
查询周期 polling cycle
查询[轮询]字符 polling character
查询作业 inquiry job
查寻报告 hunt report
查寻方式 hunt mode
查寻阶段 hunt phase
查寻组 hunt group
查页表 page table look-up
查找操作 search operation
查找长度 search length
查找程序 finder, search program, looker
查找方向 search direction
查找关键字 search key
查找过程 search procedure
查找键 search key, key for searching, seek key
查找路径算法 search path algorithm
查找码 search key
查找能力 search capability
查找区 seek area
查找区域 region of search, seek area
查找时间 search time
查找树 search tree
查找语句 search statement
查找周期 search cycle

搽 put (powder, ointment, etc.) on the skin

察 examine, look into, scrutinize　察觉 be conscious of, become aware of, perceive　察看 watch, look carefully at, observe

碴 broken pieces, fragments

【chà】

差 另见 【chā】【chāi】
1) (不相同) differ from, fall short of 2) (错误) wrong, mistake 3) (缺少) wanting, short of, missing 4) (不好) bad, inferior ◇质量差 poor quality **差不多** ① (相差有限) almost, nearly, without much difference ② (过得去) just about enough **差很多** (不同) very different, entirely different

【chāi】

拆　**拆除** demolish, dismantle, remove **拆穿** expose, unmask **拆开** tear open, take apart **拆毁** demolish, pull down **拆开** take apart, open, separate; disconnection, unsealing, uncoupling **拆散** break up **拆卸** pull down, take-down, dismantle,
拆卸键 eject key
拆卸控制 eject control

差 另见 【chā】【chà】
1) (派遣) send on an errand, dispatch ◇因公出差 be away on official business **差事** errand, job

【chái】

柴　柴油 diesel oil

【chān】

搀　**搀扶** support sb with one's hand **搀和、搀杂** mix, mingle **搀假** adulterate

掺　mix

【chán】

缠　twine, wind, wrap

【chǎn】

产　1) (生育) give birth to, breed 2) (生产) produce, yield 3) (物产) product, produce **产地** place of production, producing area **产量** output, yield **产品** product **产权** property right **产生** ① (使出现) produce, engender, bring about, generate, yield ② (出现) emerge, come into being **产业** ① estate, property ② industrial **产值** output value
产品概览 product summary
产品规格说明 product specification
产品开发 product development
产品目录[样本] catalog (=catalogue)
产品确认测试 product validation
产品认证 product certification
产品说明 product description
产品研制 product development
产生规则 generation rule
产生集 productive set
产生器 creator
产生式 production
产生式表示 production representation
产生式规则 production rule
产生式规则的右部 right hand side {RHS}
产生式语言 production language
产生式左部 left hand side {LHS}
产生树 generation tree
产生(式)系统 production system

chǎn 铲闸 chàn 颤 chāng 昌猖 cháng 长尝常

铲 （清除）lift or move with a shovel 铲子 shovel, spade

闸 explain 阐明 illuminate, expound, clarify 阐述 expound, set forth, represent

【chàn】

颤 quiver, tremble, vibrate 颤动 vibrate, quiver

【chāng】

昌 昌盛 prosperous

猖 猖獗 be rampant, run wild

【cháng】

长 另见【zhǎng】
1)（距离大）long 2)（时间久）of long duration 长处 good qualities, strong points 长度 length 长久 for a long time, permanently 长期 over a long period of time; long-term, long-period(ic), long-time 长期贷款 long-term loan 长寿 long life, longevity 长远 long-term, long-range
长报文 long message
长串 long string
长度 size, length
长度检验 length check
长度说明 length specification
长浮点数 long floating point
长格式 long format/form
长途电话 toll, long distance call
长途电话呼叫 toll call
长途电话交换局 toll office
长途电话局间干线 intertoll trunk
长途电话中心 toll center
长途电话中心局 toll point {TP}
长途电缆 toll cable
长途电码 trunk code
长途电信业务提供商 interexchange carrier {IXC}
长途话务员拨号 operator distance dialing {ODD}
长途局间中继线 intertoll trunk
长途线 long-distance terminal
长途直接拨号电话 direct distance dialing {DDD}
长途中继线 trunk junction
长文件 long file
长整型常数 long constant
长指令格式 long instruction format
长字 long word
长字界 long word boundary
长字运算 long word operation

尝 1)（辨味）taste, try the flavor of 2)（感受）experience 尝试 attempt, try 尝试法 trial-and-error method

常 1)（平常）ordinary, common, normal 2)（经常）constant, invariable 常常 frequently, often, usually 常规 convention, routine, normal procedure 常见 common 常年 ① throughout the year ② year in year out 常识 ① general knowledge ② common sense 常态 normality; proper, normal 常用 in common use 常驻 residence; permanent
常规闭合 normally closed {NC}
常规程序设计 conventional programming
常规磁头 conventional head

常规存储器 base memory, conventional memory
常规的 convention, conventional, custom
常规内存 conventional memory
常规事务 regular transaction
常规文件 ordinary file
常量 constant
常数 constant, invariable
常数标记 constant mark
常数标志符 constant identifier
常数表达式 constant expression
常数部件 coefficient unit
常数存储库 constant pool
常数存储区 constant area
常数地址 constant address
常数块 constant block
常数区 constant area
常数区域 constant section
常数说明部分 constant declaration section
常数维数 constant dimension
常数字 constant word
常数字段 constant field, control store literal
常态网络 proper network
常用对数 common logarithm
常用卡片 active card
常值故障率 constant failure rate {CFR}
常驻[驻留]程序 resident program
常驻程序 core program
常驻程序段 resident segment
常驻管理程序 resident executive, resident supervisor
常驻核心程序 resident nucleus
常驻区 resident area
常驻任务 resident task
常驻系统 resident system
常驻系统(程序) system residence {SYSRES}

常驻系统卷 system residence volume
常驻执行程序 resident executive
常驻主存(储器)程序 core resident routine
常驻生存的 core-resident
常驻装入模块 resident load module {RLM}
常驻字型 resident font

偿 repay, compensate for
偿还 repay, pay back

【chǎng】
厂 factory, mill, plant, works 厂房 factory building, workshop 厂商 ① firm, factory ② factory owner 厂长 factory director
厂方软件 manufacturer software

场 1)(农场)farm 2)〈物理〉field ◇磁场 magnetic field // 电场 electric field 场地 ground, field, yard, place ◇会场 meeting-place 场合 stage, spot, scene, occasion 场所 place, arena
场控晶体管 field transistor
场论 field theory
场密度 field density
场频 field frequency
场强 field strength
场效应晶体管 field effect transistor {FET}

敞 1)(无遮拦)spacious, open 2)(张开)open, uncovered 敞开 ①(大开)open wide ②(尽量)unlimited, unrestricted

【chàng】

畅 1)（无阻碍）smooth, unimpeded 2)（尽情）free, uninhibited 畅谈 speak glowingly of 畅通 unblocked, open and smooth 畅销 be in great demand, sell well

倡 initiate, advocate ◇首倡 initiate, take the lead 倡导 initiate, propose 倡议 propose, sponsor

唱 sing

【chāo】

抄 抄写,抄录 copy, transcribe
抄送 carbon copy {CC}

钞 ◇现钞 cash 钞票 bank note, paper money, bill

超 超常 super-, extra- 超出 transcend, go beyond, overrun, exceed 超额 excess; surpass 超过 exceed, surpass, overtake 超级 super- 超越 surmount, transcend, surpass, overpass 超支 overspend
超边 hyperedge
超标量 superscalar
超标量计算机 superscalar computer
超长控制 jabber control
超长指令字 very long instruction word {VLIW}
超出（额定）范围 over range
超大规模集成 very large-scale integration {VLSI}, grand scale integration {GSI}
超大规模集成(电路) ultra-large-scale integration {ULSI}
超大规模集成电路 very large-scale integrated circuit {VLSI}, super-large-scale integration {SLSI}, miracle chip
超大规模计算机 super-way computer
超大内存 very large memory {VLM}
超大(型)数据库 very large database {VLDB}
超导 superconductivity
超导存储器 superconducting memory, superconductor memory
超导单元 superconducting cell
超导隧道效应 superconductive tunnel effect
超导体 superconductor
超导性 superconductivity
超高频 ultra-high frequency {UHF}, super-high frequency {SHF}
超高速计算机 ultra-fast computer, very-high speed computer
超过 excel, override
超级电脑 super computer
超级访问软件 hyperaccess
超级计算 supercomputing
超级[巨型]计算机 ultracomputer
超级计算机 supercomputer
超级加密 superencipherment
超级流水技术 superpipeline
超级图像图形阵列 super-video-graphics array {SVGA}
超级网络 ultranet
超级微型计算机 super-micro-computer
超级文本系统 hypertext system
超级纹理 hypertexture

超级系统 supersystem
超级性能 superperformance
超级[特权]用户 superuser
超级用户授权 superuser authority
超级组 supergroup
超卡 hypercard
超块 superblock
超类 superclass
超立方体仿真程序 hypercube emulator
超立方体数据库 hypercube database
超立方网(络) hypercube network
超链接 hyperlink
超流水线超标量计算机 superpipelined superscalar computer
超路由 superroute
超码 supercode, superkey
超媒体[媒质] hypermedia
超媒体通信 hyper media communication
超媒体应用 hypermedia application
超前 advance, look ahead
超前进位生成器 look ahead carry generator
超前控制 advanced control
超软件 supersoft
超声 ultrasound
超声波传感器 ultrasonic sensor
超声测量 ultrasonic measurement
超时 time over, time-out, timing out
超时传输 jabber
超时传输控制 jabber control
超时错误 time-out error
超时断开 disconnect time-out
超时恢复 time-out recovery
超时检查 time-out check
超时检验 time-over check
超时控制 time-out control
超视图 superview
超收敛性 superconvergence
超数据系统 hyper data system
超图 supergraph
超图编辑程序 supergraphic editor
超图数据结构 hypergraphic based data structure
超网络媒质 supernetwork media
超微结构 ultrastructure
超(级)文本 hypertext
超文本标记语言 hypertext markup language {HTML}
超文本传输协议 hyper text transmit protocol {HTTP}
超文本技术 hypertext technology
超文本链 hypertext link
超纹理结构 hypertexture
超稀疏 supersparsity
超线性 superlinear
超小型 subminiature
超小型磁盘 superminiature disk
超小型化 microminiaturization
超小型(计算)机 super minicomputer
超行距走纸 paper slew, paper throw
超越保护 overreach protection
超载 overload
超帧 superframe
超字 superword

【cháo】

巢 nest

朝 另见【zhāo】
朝代 dynasty 朝向 orientation

潮
(社会潮流)(social) upsurge, current 潮流 ① tide, tidal current ② trend 潮湿 moist, damp 潮汐 tide

嘲
嘲笑 ridicule, laugh at

【chē】
车 1)(车辆)vehicle, car, carriage 2)(机器)machine ◇停车 stop the machine // 试车 trial run, test run 3)(用车床切削)lathe, turn 车间 workshop, shop 车库 garage, shed, barn 车厢 carriage 车站 station, bus stop

【chě】
扯 1)(拉)pull 2)(撕)tear 扯裂 tear, divulsion 扯碎 discerp, devil

【chè】
彻 thorough, penetrating 彻底 thorough, thoroughgoing 彻底检查 overhaul, examine throughout 彻头彻尾 out and out

掣
pull, tug

撤
(除去)remove, take away 撤换 dismiss and replace, recall, replace 撤退 withdraw, evacuate 撤销 cancel, revoke 撤职 dismiss sb from his post, remove sb from office
撤销授权 drop authority
撤消 scratch, undo, withdrawal
撤消语句 cancel statement
撤消原语 destroy primitive

【chén】
尘 dust, dirt 尘土 dust

辰 1)(日,月,星)celestial bodies ◇星辰 stars 2)(时光,日子)time, day, occasion ◇诞辰 birthday

沉 sink, settle, submerge 沉淀 sedimentate, precipitate, deposit, settle 沉没 submerged, sunk, immersed 沉陷 sink, cave in, depress 沉渣 sediment, dregs 沉重 heavy 沉着 cool-headed, calm

陈 1)(铺开)lay out, put on display 2)(旧的)old, stale 陈规 outmoded conventions 陈货 old stock, shopworn goods 陈旧 outmoded, obsolete, out-of-date, old-fashioned 陈列 display, set out, exhibit 陈列馆 exhibition hall 陈设 display, set out; furnishings 陈述 state, declare, statement

晨 morning

橙 另见【chéng】
橙子 orange

【chèn】
衬 衬里 lining, liner 衬托 line, place sth underneath

称 另见【chēng】
fit, match, suit 称心 find sth satisfactory, be content with; to one's liking 称职 fill a post with credit, be competent

趁 趁机 take advantage of the occasion, seize the chance 趁早 as early as possible, (do sth) before it is too late

【chēng】

称 另见【chèn】
1) (叫做) call 2) (名称) name 3) (测重) weigh 4) (说) say, state 称号 title, name, designation 称呼 ① call, address ② form of address 称赞 praise, commend

撑 1) (抵住) prop up, support 2) (支持) maintain, keep up 3) (张开) open, unfurl

【chéng】

成 …成 one tenth ◇增产一成 a 10% increase in output 成本 cost, self-cost 成分 composition, constituent 成份 part, composition, component, ingredient 成功 accomplish, succeed 成果 achievement, result, fruit 成绩 result, achievement, success 成见 prejudice 成交 strike a bargain, conclude a transaction 成就 achievement, accomplishment, attainment, success 成立 ① found, establish, set up ② be tenable, hold water 成名 become famous, well-known 成年 grow up, come of age 成年人 adult, grown-up 成批 group by group; batch, mass 成品 end product 成群 grouping, bunching 成人 ① 〈动〉grow up, become full-grown ② 〈名〉adult, grown-up 成色 ① (含纯金银量) the percentage of gold or silver in a coin, etc. ② (质量) quality 成熟 ripe, mature 成套 gang, complete set, packaged, unitized 成为 become, turn into 成效 effect, result 成语 phrase, idiom 成长 grow up, grow to maturity
成本分析 cost analysis
成本估算 cost estimate, cost estimation
成本会计 cost accounting
成本价格 cost price
成本结构 cost structure
成本系数 cost coefficient
成本向量 cost vector
成本效率 cost effectiveness {CE}
成本资料报表 cost information reporting {CIR}
成对比较 paired comparison
成块记录 blocked record
成块文件 blocked file
成批表 batch table
成批查询 batch query
成批初启 batch initiation
成批处理 batch process, batch processing
成批打印 type batch
成批调度程序 batch sceduler
成批对话 batch session
成批加工 batch processing
成批控制 batch control
成批[批量]请求 batch request
成批[批量]设备 batch device
成批数据处理 batch data processing
成批数据交换 batch data exchange {BDE}
成批系统 batch system
成批询问 batch query
成批用户 batch user

chéng 呈承诚城乘

成批远程通信 batched telecommunication
成批运行 batch execution, batch run
成批作业 batch job, batched job
成套备用工具 outfit
成套程序 suite of programs
成套处理器插件板 kit processor card
成套汇编程序 kit assembler
成套计算机 complete machine
成套软件工具 software kit
成套实用程序 kit utility
成套芯片 chip set
成像技术 imaging
成像设备 imaging device
成像系统 imaging system
成形字符 formed character
成员 member, membership, tenancy
成员表 membership table
成员服务器 member server
成员号 member number
成员记录 member record
成员类型 member type
成员名 member name
成员指示字[指针] member pointer
成员状态 member condition
成组 blocking, ganging
成组编码记录 group coded record(ing) {GCR}
成组标识 group identification
成组出现 group occurrence
成组传送 block transfer
成组存取 block access, burst access
成组打印 group printing
成组的 packed
成组[组合]技术 group technology {GT}
成组记录 group record, blocked record, grouped record
成组检查 group check
成组进位 group carry
成组控制 ganged control
成组输出 group out
成组显示 group display
成组协同工作方式 team operation

呈 呈报 submit a report, report a matter 呈递 submit, present 呈现 assume (form, color, etc.), appear, emerge

承 (托) bear, hold, carry 承办 undertake (with) 承包 contract (with), contract (to do a job), bear, assume 承蒙 be indebted (to sb for a kindness), be granted a favor 承认 admit, acknowledge 承受 bear, support, endure

诚 sincere, honest 诚恳 sincere 诚实 honest 诚意 good faith, sincerity 诚挚 sincere, cordial

城 city, town 城墙 city wall, wall ◇长城 the Great Wall
城域网 metropolitan area network {MAN}

乘 1)(搭乘) ride, take, go by 2)(利用) take advantage of, avail oneself of 乘便 when it is convenient, at one's convenience 乘机 seize the opportunity
乘除指令 multiply-divide instruction
乘法 multiplication, multiply

乘法器 multiplier
乘法算符 multiplication operator
乘积 (arithmetic) product
乘积发生器 product generator
乘积寄存器 product register
乘积空间 product space
乘积区 product area
乘积选择器 product selector
乘积字 product word
乘数 multiplicator, multiplier (=ier), multiplier factor
乘数寄存器 multiplier register
乘数商数寄存器 multiplier-quotient register {MQR, MQ register}
乘数因子 multiplier factor

盛 另见【shèng】
1) (装) fill, ladle 2) (容纳) hold, contain

程 rule, regulation ◇规程 rules // 章程 rules, constitution 程度 ① (知识或能力水平) level ② (达到的状况) extent, degree 程式 form, pattern, formula 程序 ① order, procedure, sequence ② program, routine 程序设计 programming
程控硬件 program control hardware
(计算机)程序 program(me), procedure, routing process
程序包 package program, program package, routine package, software package
程序包生成程序 package generator
程序包体 package body
程序包文件 package file
程序保护 program(med) protection
程序编译 program compilation/compiling
程序编制器 programmer
程序变更登录 programming change log
程序变量 program variable
程序标识 program identification {program ID}
程序表 program list, program table
程序表达式 program expression
程序步长 program step
程序部分 program part
程序参数 program parameter
程序操作员 program operator
程序测试 program testing
程序产品 program product
程序初始化 program initialization
程序处理机 program processor
程序窗口 program window
程序存取(代)码 program access code
程序错误 program error
程序错误[出错]中断 program error interrupt
程序错误转储 program error dump
程序代数 program algebra
程序单位 program unit
程序单元 program element, program unit
程序的安全性 program security
程序的再设计 programming redesign
程序调入[装入] program loading
程序调试 program debug
程序动态装入 dynamic program loading
程序段 program segment, segment, program section

{PSECT}
程序段表 program segment table
程序断点 program breakpoint
程序对象[目标] program object
程序翻译 program translation
程序仿真器 program emulator
程序分析 program analysis
程序分析员 analyst-programmer, programmer analyst
程序分页功能 program paging function
程序复杂性 program complexity
程序复执 program retry
程序格式 program format
程序跟踪 program trace
程序功能键 program function key
程序共享 program sharing
程序固有停机指令 program halt
程序规范 program specification
程序划分 program partitioning
程序环 program ring
程序环境 program environment
程序级 program level
程序监视器 program monitor
程序兼容(性) program compatibility
程序检验 program/ routine test, programmed check
程序接口 program interface, routine interface
程序结构 program structure/organization, structure program
程序结构块 program structure block
程序结构流程图 program structure flow chart

程序结束标志 program end flag
程序卷回 program roll-back
程序开发 program development
程序开发工具 program development tool
程序开发时间 program development time
程序开发系统 program development system
程序可靠性 program reliability
程序控制 program(med) control
程序控制表 program control table
程序控制部件 program controlling element
程序控制的逻辑 programmed logic
程序控制的学习 programmed learning
程序控制计算机 program controlled computer
程序控制卡 program card
程序控制流 program control flow
程序控制器 program controller, programmator, programming controller
程序控制台 program board
程序控制通道 programmed channel
程序控制系统 process/program control system
程序控制语句 program control statement
程序控制指令 program control instruction
程序控制中断 progra-controlled interruption
程序控制转移 program control transfer
程序库 program library, libra-

ry, routine library, facilities library, program package
程序库例行程序 library routine
程序库目录 library directory
程序块 procedural/ program block, brick, module
程序块地址 block address
程序块访问 block access
程序块级存取 block level access
程序块首部 block head(er)
程序块装入 block loading
程序框图 flow diagram, flowchart, flowsheet, program flowchart/chart
程序链 program chain
程序列表 program listing
程序灵活性 program flexibility
程序流程图 program flow diagram, program flowchart
程序逻辑 logic of program, program logic
程序逻辑流图 program logic flowchart
程序逻辑阵列 program logic array
程序逻辑指令 routine logical instruction
程序描述符 program descriptor
程序名 program/routine name
程序模块化 program modularity
程序模拟器 program simulator
程序模式 program scheme
程序模型 programs model
程序评价 program evaluation
程序破坏 program crash
程序请求 program request
程序区 program area, program region
程序驱动 program-driven
程序取出 program fetch
程序权限[审定] program authority
程序日期 program date

程序设备 program device
程序设计 program design/ composition, programming
程序设计标准 programming standards
程序设计成本 programming cost
程序设计范例 programming paradigm
程序设计方法 programming method/approach
程序设计风格 programming style
程序设计工具 programming tool/aid
程序设计规格说明 programming specification
程序设计过程 programming procedure
程序设计环境 programming environment
程序设计技术 programming techniques, programmatics
程序设计检验 programming check
程序设计接口 programmatic interface
程序设计控制板 programming control panel
程序设计框图 programming flowchart
程序设计理论 programming theory
程序设计灵活性 programming flexibility
程序设计流程框图 programming flow diagram
程序设计逻辑 programming logic
程序设计模块 programming module
程序设计模型 programming model
程序设计起始地址 program

origin
程序设计师 programmer
程序设计实现 programming implementation
程序设计透明性 programming transparency
程序设计效应 programming effect
程序设计性能 programming performance
程序设计学 programmatics
程序设计语义学 programming semantics
程序设计支持环境 programming support environment
程序设计质量 programming quality
程序生成 program generation
程序时钟标记 program clock reference {PCR}
程序数据 program data
程序说明 program description
程序算法 programmed algorithm
程序体 program body
程序体系结构 program architecture
程序停机 program(med)/ coded stop, programmed halt
程序头 program header
程序图表 process sheet, sequence chart
程序维护 program maintenance, maintenance of program
程序文本 program text
程序文档 program documentation
程序文法 program syntax
程序文件 program file
程序系统测试 program system testing
程序校验 program checkout/ test/ testing, programmed/ routine check
程序校验中断 program check interruption
程序行 program line
程序验证 program verification
程序移植 program portable
程序异常 program exception
程序异常中断 program check interrupt {PCI}
程序引用 program reference
程序映像 program image
程序优化 program optimization
程序优先级 program priority
程序语句 program/ routine statement
程序语言 program language
程序员 programmer
程序员检查 programmer check
程序员控制板 programmer control panel
程序员逻辑单元 programmer logical unit
程序再设计 reprogramming
程序正确性 program correctness
程序证明 program certification/ proof/ proving
程序支持库 program support library
程序执行 program execution
程序指令 program(med) instruction
程序中断 program interrupt
程序中断条件 program interrupt condition
程序中断信号 program interrupt signal
程序中断转移 program interrupt transfer
程序终端 program terminal
程序终止 program determination
程序重叠 program overlay

chéng 惩澄橙 chèng 秤 chī 吃 chí 池弛驰迟持匙 chǐ 尺

程序重定位 program relocation
程序重构技术 program restructuring technique
程序注释 program comment
程序转储 programmed dump
程序转换 program conversion, programming transformation
程序装入 program load
程序状态 program status, progstate

惩 punish, penalize 惩办 punish; punishment 惩罚 punish, penalize

澄 澄清 clear, transparent; clear up, clarify

橙 另见【chén】
橙色 orange color 橙子 orange

【chèng】

秤 balance, steelyard, (weighing) scale ◇电子秤 electronic scale ‖ 杆秤 steelyard, lever scales ‖ 台秤 platform balance, platform scale ‖ 弹簧秤 spring balance

【chī】

吃 eat, take, have one's meals 吃饭 eat, have a meal 吃惊 be startled, be shocked 吃苦 bear hardships 吃亏 suffer losses 吃力 entail strenuous effort

【chí】

池 pool, pond
池队列 pool queue

弛 relax, slacken, ease

驰 驰名 well-known, famous, renowned

迟 1)(慢)slow, tardy 2)(晚)late 迟到 be late, come late, arrive late 迟钝 slow (in thought or action), dull-witted 迟缓 slow, tardy, sluggish 迟误 delay, procrastinate 迟延 delay, retard 迟疑 hesitate 迟早 sooner or later 迟滞 slow-moving, sluggish; retarding, lagging

持 1)(拿着)hold, grasp 2)(支持)support, maintain 3)(主管)manage, run ◇主持 take charge of, manage 持久 endurance, permanence; lasting, persistent 持平 unbiased, fair 持续 continue, sustain; endurance, persistence; durative 持有 hold
持续故障 sustained fault
持续会话 persistent session
持续时间 duration, duration-time
持续振荡 persistent oscillation
持续状态 persistent state

匙 spoon

【chǐ】

尺 (量具)rule, ruler ◇丁字尺 square ‖ 折尺 folding rule
尺寸 measurement, dimensions, size ◇加工尺寸 finish size ‖ 名义尺寸 nominal size
尺寸变化 scale change
尺寸度量 dimensioning
尺寸选择 size select

齿 tooth 齿轮 gear wheel, gear
齿距 pitch

耻 shame, disgrace

【chì】

斥 1)(责备)scold, denounce 2)(使离开)repel, exclude

赤 (红色)red 赤膊 bare 赤字 deficit

炽 炽热 red-hot, blazing; candescence, red heat

翅 wing

【chōng】

冲 另见【chòng】
冲淡 dilution 冲动 impulse, actuation 冲击 impact, impulse, shock 冲破 break through, smash ◇冲破障碍 charge, rush, dash, thrust 冲散 break up, scatter, disperse 冲刷 erode, scour, wash out, wash away 冲洗 rinse, flush, wash ◇冲胶卷 develop a roll of film 冲撞 clash, collide

冲突 collision, conflict, contention, interfere, warfare
冲突分解 conflict resolver
冲突分析 conflict analysis
冲突环 conflict ring
冲突集 conflict set
冲突检测 collision detection {CD}
冲突模型 conflict model
冲突图 conflict graph
冲突信号 collision signal
冲突状态 contention state

充 (装满)fill, charge 充当 serve as, act as, play the part of 充分 sufficient, full, ample 充公 confiscate 充满 full of, brimming with, permeated with 充任 fill the post of, hold the position of 充实 substantial, rich; substantiate, enrich 充填 fill up, pack 充裕 abundant, ample, plentiful 充足 adequate, sufficient, sufficiency, abundant, ample
充电 charging
充电装置 charge unit
充分条件 sufficient condition, sufficiency

【chóng】

虫 insect, worm 虫子 insect, worm

重 另见【zhòng】
(再)again, once more 重叠 one on top of another, overlap, superpose, superimpose 重复 repeat, duplicate, reiterate 重合 coincide, reclose 重建 rebuild, reconstruct, reestablish 重申 reaffirm, reiterate, restate 重提 bring up again 重温 review 重现 reappear, reproduce 重新 again, anew, afresh
重安排 reschedule
重版 added edition
重编 reassemble
重编程序 reprogramming
重标页码 repaginate
重拨 redial
重传输 retransmit
重调度 reschedule
重叠操作 overlapped operation, overlap

重叠查找 overlapping seek
重叠处理 overlap processing
重叠定义 overlay defining
重叠段 overlay segment
重叠方式 overlap mode
重叠访问 overlapped access
重叠控制程序 overlay controller
重叠路径 overlay path
重叠区 overlay region
重叠树(图) overlay tree
重叠通路 overlay path
重叠因子 overlap factor
重叠执行 overlapped execution
重叠字段 overlapping field
重定格式 reformat, reformatting
重定位 dynamic relocation
重定向 redirect
重读 reread, rereading
重发 retransmission, retry
重赋值 reassignment
重复编址 repeat to address {RA}
重复操作 repetitive operation {REPOP, REP/OP}
重复打印 repeat print
重复地址 repeat to address {RA}
重复分组 duplicate packet
重复符号 replicator
重复构造 repetitive construct
重复呼叫 recall
重复击键 repeat key stroke
重复计数 repeat count
重复记录 duplicate record
重复加 repetitive addition
重复键 repeat key
重复码 duplication code
重复数据 repeating data
重复说明 repeat specification
重复因数[因子] duplication factor
重复运算 repetitive operation {REPOP, REP/OP}
重复占位 overlaying
重复指令 repetition instruction, repetitive instruction
重复字符 repeat character {RPT}
重构 rebuild, reconfiguration, reconstitution, reconstruct, reconstruction, restructure
重构程序 reorganizer, restructuring program
重构系统 reconfiguration system
重合[双重,重复]校验 duplication check
重画 redrawing, repaint
重建索引 reindex
重命名 rename
重排 rearrangement, shifting
重入 reentrance, re(-)entry
重入点 reentry point, rescue point, restart point
重写 overwrite, overwriting, regenerate, rewrite
重写操作 rewrite operation
重写错误[误差] overwriting error
重写方式 overwrite mode
重写规则 rewriting rule
重写误差 overwrite error
重写语句 rewrite/rewriting statement
重新安装 reinstallation, full install
重新编号 renumbering
重新编译 recompile
重新定标 rescale
重新定义 redefine
重新分配 deallocate, deallocation
重新分页 repaginate, repagination
重新构建 reconstruction
重新开始 resume

重新连接 reconnect
重新排序 rearrange, restart sorting
重新配位表 relocation dictionary {**RLD**}
重新配置 reconfiguration, reconfigure
重新启动 reboot, restart {**RST**}, bring up
重新启动程序 restart routine
重新启动调用 restart call
重新启动键 restart key
重新同步 resync, resynchronization
重新选择路由 rerouting
重新引导 reboot
重新运行点 rerun point, rescue point, roll-back point
重新装入 resume load
重新组成 reconstitution
重新组织 reorganization, reorganize
重印 overprinting, reprint
重影 ghost image
重用 reuse
重置 reset
重置按钮 reset button
重置信息数据集 reset information data set {**RIDS**}
重装 reassemble
重装入 reload
重做 redo

崇 崇高 lofty, high, esteemed 崇敬 esteem, respect, revere

【chòng】
冲 另见【chōng】〈机械〉punch

【chōu】
抽 1) (取出) take out (from in between), take a part from a whole 2) (吸取) obtain by drawing, pumping, etc. 抽查 random inspection, selective examination 抽打 lash, whip 抽调 transfer (personnel or material) 抽动 twitch, jerk 抽空 ① manage to find time ② underpressure, exhaustion, evacuation 抽象 abstract 抽样 sampling, spot test, exampling 抽象(概念)abstraction
抽出 extract, extraction, drawer, eject
抽出键 eject key
抽点打印 snapshot, snapshot dump
抽点拷贝 snapshot copy
抽点转储 snapshot dump
抽签法 lottery
抽签问题 ballot problem
抽取 extract, extracting
抽取命令 extraction instruction
抽取[析取、选取]指令 extract instruction
抽象操作 abstract operation
抽象测试套 abstract test suite {**AST**}
抽象层次 abstraction level
抽象代码 abstract code
抽象代数 abstract algebra
抽象单体 abstract individual
抽象单形 abstract simplex
抽象动词 abstract verb
抽象范数 abstract norm
抽象方法 abstract method
抽象符号 abstract symbol
抽象工具 abstraction tool
抽象化语法表示1 abstract syntax notation one {**ASN.1**}
抽象机 abstract machine
抽象集 abstract set
抽象计算机 abstract computer
抽象结构 abstract structure

抽象空间 abstract space
抽象控制 abstract control
抽象类 abstract class
抽象名词 abstract noun
抽象模块 abstract module
抽象模型 abstract model
抽象术语 abstract term
抽象数据 abstract data
抽象数据结构 abstract data structure
抽象数据类型 abstract data type {ADT}
抽象算法 abstract algorithm
抽象文件 abstract file
抽象系统 abstract system
抽象语法 abstract syntax, abstract syntactic
抽象语法表示法 abstract syntax notation {ASN}
抽象语言理论 abstract language theory
抽象语言族 abstract family of languages {AFL}
抽象自动机 abstract automaton
抽象自动机理论 abstract automaton theory
抽象字母 abstract alphabet
抽样程序 sample program
抽样单位 sampling unit
抽样点 sample point
抽样调查 sample survey
抽样定理 sampling theorem
抽样范围 sampling range
抽样方案 sampling plan
抽样方法 sampling method
抽样函数 sampling function
抽样间隔 sampling interval
抽样检查 sampling inspection
抽样检验 sample survey
抽样率 sample rate
抽样脉冲 sampling pulse
抽样模拟数据 sampled analog data
抽样生成算法 sample span algorithm
抽样时间 sample time
抽样输入 sample input
抽样数据 sample data, sampled data
抽样误差 sampling error
抽样性质 sampling property
抽样正态分布 sampling normal distribution
抽样周期 sampling period

【chóu】

仇 仇恨 hatred, enmity, hostility

绸 silk fabric, silk

愁 worry, be anxious

畴 1)〈种类〉kind, division ◇范畴 category 2)〈物理〉domain

筹 筹办 make preparations, make arrangements 筹备 prepare, arrange 筹建 prepart to construct or establish 筹资 raise money or funds

稠 (浓) thick 稠密 dense, crowded
稠密集 dense set
稠密矩阵 dense matrix
稠密索引 dense index
稠密子图 dense subgraph

酬 酬报 reward, repay, recompense 酬金 monetary reward, remuneration 酬劳 recompense, reward

踌 踌躇 hesitate

【chǒu】

丑 1)(难看)ugly, ill-looking 2)(厌恶)disgraceful, shameful 丑恶 ugly, repulsive, hideous 丑事 scandal

【chòu】

臭 另见【xiù】
1)(难闻)smelly, foul, stinking 2)(讨厌)disgusting, disgraceful
臭虫 bug

【chū】

出 1)(出去)go out, come out 2)(超出)exceed, go beyond 3)(拿出)issue, put up, give, offer 4)(生产)produce, turn out 5)(发生)arise, happen, take place, occur 出版 publish 出差 be away on official business, be on a business trip 出产 produce, manufacture, output 出发 ① set out, start off ② start from, proceed from 出发点 starting point, point of departure 出格 go beyond the limit 出国 go abroad, leave one's native land 出价 bid 出口 exit, outlet, vent; export 出路 way out, outlet 出卖 ①(卖)offer for sale, sell ②(背叛)sell out, betray 出毛病 be go out of order, go wrong, break down 出门 ①(外出)go out ②(离家)leave home, be away from home 出名 famous, well-known 出品 ① produce, manufacture, make ② product 出色 outstanding, remarkable, splendid 出示 show, produce, present 出事 meet with a mishap, have an accident 出售 offer for sale, sell 出席 attend, be present 出现 appear, arise, emerge, turn up 出众 outstanding, prominent, distinctive 出租 hire, let, lease
出租汽车 taxi, cab
出版软件 publishing soft
出版系统 publishing system
出版语言 publication language
出错 mistake, malfunction, syndrome
出错报告 error report
出错程序 error routine
出错处理 error handling
出错登记 error log
出错返回 error return
出错范围 fault domain
出错记录 error record
出错列表 error listing
出错率 error rate/ratio
出错数据 error data
出错文件 error file
出错信号 error signal
出错[错误]信息 error message
出错指示符 error indicator
出度 out-degree, outgoing degree
出口标号 exit label
出口表 exit list {**EXLST**}
出口程序 exit procedure/program/routine
出口处理程序 exit handler
出口点 exit point
出口和进口 export/import
出口条件 exit condition
出口位置 exit position
出口语句 exit statement
出口指令 exit instruction
出纳终端 teller terminal
出入口 gangway, port
出文件 outfile
出纸 paper delivery, paper out

初 (开始) just beginning, for the first time 初步 preliminary, initial, the first time 初级 elementary, primary, preliminary, rudimentary 初期 preliminary stage, first stage 初始 at the beginning of, in the early part of; initial

初步的 elemental
初步设计 preliminary design
初等变换 elementary transformation
初等的 primary
初等函数 elementary function
初等矩阵 elementary matrix
初等数论 elementary number theory
初等算术 elementary arithmetic
初等图 primary graph
初等项 elementary item, elemental term, primary
初稿 draft
初级 primary
初级操作员 junior operator
初级程序员 junior programmer
初级输入与输出 primary input/output
初级用户 naive user
初级语言 low level language
初期错误 initial error
初期的 infant
初启 init
初始 initiation
初始(的) initial
初始变元 original argument
初始表 initial table, initial/starting tableau
初始部分 initial portion
初始程序 initial program/routine, initiator program
初始程序装入 initial program load {IPL}
初始窗口 home window
初始的 original
初始地址段 origin address field {OAF}
初始点 initial point
初始定义 initial definition, original definition
初始段 initial segment
初始方式 initial mode
初始符号 initial symbol
初始复位 initial reset
初始负载 initial load
初始光标 original cursor
初始过程 initial procedure
初始函数 initial function
初始化 initialization, initialize
初始化程序 initializer
初始化向量 initialization vector {IV}
初始化指令 initialization directive
初始间隔 initial gap, initial interval
初始进程名 initial process name
初始控制字 initial control word {ICW}
初始链接值 initial chaining value {ICV}
初始逻辑单元 initiating logic unit {ILU}
初始模型 initial model
初始目录 home directory
初始配置 initial configuration
初始请求 initial request
初始入口点 primary entry point
初始属性 initial attribute
初始数据 primary data, source data
初始条件 initial condition
初始文档 original document
初始信息 initial information
初始行 initial line, initial row
初始值 starting value

初始装入 initial load, initial loading
初始状态 initial/original state
初项 initial term
初值 initial/starting value
初值化语句 initiate statement

【chú】

除 1)(去掉)get rid of, exclude, eliminate, remove 2)(不计)except, except for 3)(此外)besides, in addition to 4)〈数学〉divide **除非** only if, only when, unless **除外** except, not counting
除法 division
除法程序 division routine
除法器 divider
除法时间 divide time
除法溢出 divide overflow
除法语句 divide statement
除法子程序 division subroutine
除零自陷 divided by zero trap

橱 cabinet, closet ◇书橱 bookcase

【chǔ】

处 另见(chù)
(相处)get along (with sb) **处理品** goods sold at reduced prices **处罚** punish, sentence, penalize **处于** be in a certain condition 处置 ① handle, deal with, manage, dispose of ② punish
处理 processing, treatment, handle, handling, manipulation, massaging
处理表 processing list
处理部件 processing element/unit
处理程序 handler, processor
处理程序调度 processor scheduling
处理单元 processing unit
处理方法 processing method
处理方式 process mode, processing mode
处理功能 processing function
处理机 processor, handling machine, manipulator, processing element
处理机表 processor table
处理机部件 processor element
处理机操作 processor operation
处理机插板 processor board
处理机对 processor pair
处理机共享 processor sharing
处理机管理 processor management
处理机互连 processor interconnection
处理机间通信 interprocessor communication
处理机间中断 interprocessor interrupt
处理机接口 processor interface
处理机节点 processor node
处理机结构 processor architecture/structure
处理机连线 processor link
处理机模块 processor module
处理机配置 processor configuration
处理机性能 processor performance
处理机状态位 processor state bit
处理机状态字 processor state word
处理机组织 processor organization
处理级 processing level
处理链 processing chain
处理能力 processing capacity
处理器分配 processor alloca-

处理速度 processing speed
处理项目 process entry
处理中断 processing interrupt
处理装置 processing unit
处理资源 processing resource

储 store up, keep in reserve, have in reserve 储备 ①(储存备用)store for future use, lay in, lay up ②(储藏品)reserve, store ◇黄金储备 gold reserve // 外汇储备 foreign exchange reserve 储藏 store, preserve 储存 memory, store, storage
储墨槽 ink duck

【chù】

处 另见【chǔ】
1)(地方)place 2)(机关,部门)department, office ◇人事处 personnel department, personnel section // 售票处 booking office // 问讯处 inquiry office 处处 everywhere, in all respects

畜 domestic animal, livestock

触 touch, contact, strike, hit 触犯 offend, violate, go against
触板 touch plate
触板开关 touch panel switch
触笔 stylus
触发电路 trigger, trigger circuit
触发电平 level triggered, trigger level
触发器 binary pair, flip-flop, toggle, toggle circuit / switch, trigger
触键 touch key
触摸(输入)板 touch pad
触摸传感器 touch sensor
触摸屏(幕) touch screen
触摸区域 touch area

矗 矗立 stand, erect, tower over sth

【chuān】

川 1)(河流)river 2)(平原)plain

氚 tritium

穿 (通过)pass through, cross, go through 穿透 pierce through, penetrate 穿着 wear, put on, be dressed in
穿卡机 punch
穿孔 punch, perforate, perforation
穿孔板 plugboard
穿孔带 perforated tape, pertorated tape
穿孔卡 punch card
穿透深度 penetration depth
穿透性 penetrability
穿线 thread
穿芯电容 feedthrough capacitor

【chuán】

传 另见【zhuàn】
传 spread, propagate 传达 pass on (information, etc.), transmit, relay, communicate 传达室 reception office, janitor's room 传导 transmit, conduct 传递 pass, pass on, transmit, deliver, transfer 传授 pass on (knowledge, skill, etc.), teach, impart 传统 tradition, convention 传统产业 con-

ventional industries 传真 fax, facsimile, electrofax
传播D立方 propagation D-cube
传播[传输]时间 propagation time
传播损耗 propagation loss
传播延迟 propagation delay
传递 convey, deliver, passing, posting, transmission {XMT}
传递闭包 transitive closure
传递关系 transitive relationship
传递归约 transitive reduction
传递函数 transfer function
传递依赖 transitive dependency
传动的 driven
传感器 sensing device, sensing element, sensing unit, sensitive pick-up, transducer, sensor
传感器(芯)片 sensor chip
传感数据 sense data
传感头 sensing head
传感线路 sensor line
传感元件 sensor element
传染 contagion, infection
传染方式 infection way
传声线 audio line
传输 entrainment, transfer, transmission {XMT}, transmit {TRAN}, transmittal, transput
传输标题 transmission header {TH}
传输参数 transmission parameter
传输层 transport layer
传输层安全协议 transport layer security {TLS}
传输差错控制 transmission error control
传输代码 transmission code
传输等待时间 timeout
传输地址 transport address
传输电平 transmission level
传输端口 transmit port
传输[传送]方式 transmittal mode, transmission mode
传输格式 transformat
传输极限 transmission limit
传输检验 transfer check
传输接口 transmission interface
传输结束 end of transmission {EOT}
传输介质 transmission medium
传输控制 transmission control {TC}
传输控制协议 transmission control protocol {TCP}
传输控制字符 transmission control character
传输(数据)块 transmission block
传输连接 transport connection, liaison
传输链路 transmission link
传输流量控制 transmit flow control
传输路径 transmission path
传输率 transfer rate, transmissibility, transmission rate
传输码 transmission code
传输脉冲 transmission pulses
传输媒体 transmission medium
传输目标 transmission objectives
传输驱动程序接口 transport driver interface {TDI}
传输设备 transmission equipment
传输时间 delivery time, transfer time
传输时延 propagation delay
传输数据 transmit data
传输数据组 transmit data set, transmission data set

传输速度 transmission speed, transfer speed, transfer rate
传输损耗 transmission loss
传输通路 transmission path
传输网络 transport(ation)/transmission/transit network
传输系数 transmission coefficient
传输线 transmission line
传输线控制块 line control block {LCB}
传输协议 transport protocol
传输信息包 transmission packet
传输性能 transmission performance
传输延迟 transfer/ transit/ transmission/ transport delay, wait before transmission {WABT}
传输业务 transport service
传输优先级 transmission priority
传输站 transfer/ transport station {TS}
传输帧 transmission frame
传输中断 transmission interruption
传输装置 transport unit
传输阻抗 line impedance
传送 carry, delivery, pass, propagate, propagation, transfer, transmission {XMT}, transmit {TRAN}, transmittal, transport
传送操作 transfer operation
传送地址 transfer address
传送电路 transfer circuit
传送方式 load/move mode
传送机构 delivery mechanism
传送记录纸 transfer sheet
传送检验 transfer check
传送键 transfer key
传送控制 transfer control, transmission control {TC}, transport control
传送类型 transmission type
传送门 pass gate
传送名 pass name
传送[输送]平台 delivery platform
传送请求 transfer request
传送数据集 transmit data set
传送数据组 passed data set
传送托盘 delivery tray
传送校验 transfer check
传送语法 transfer syntax
传送[输送]语句 move statement
传送[输送]圆筒 delivery cylinder
传送站 transfer station
传送[传输]终止符 end of transmission {EOT}
传送走带机构 transport deck
传统的 classical, traditional
传统的决策支持系统 traditional decision support system {TDSS}
传统方法 classical way
传统系统 legacy system
传真报纸 telenewspaper
传真传输 facsimile transmission
传真打印机 facsimile printer
传真电报 facsimile telegraph, electrograph, phototelegraphy, telautograph
传真(报文)分组 facsimile packet
传真服务 facsimile service
传真复制 facsimile copy
传真广播 facsimile broadcasting
传真机 facsimile machine
传真计算机 fax computer
传真记录器 facsimile recorder
传真(感光)记录纸 facsimile

paper
传真接口 facsimile interface
传真接收机 facsimile receiver
传真卡 fax board
传真扫描器 facsimile scanner
传真摄像机 facsimile camera
传真适配器 fax adapter
传真收发机 facsimile transceiver
传真通信 facsimile communication {FAX}
传真通信业务 fax service
传真同步 facsimile synchronizing
传真图解 teleprinter diagram
传真系统 facsimile {FAX, fax}
传真信函 facsimile mail
传真信号 facsimile signal
传真印件 telecopy
传真照相术 telephotography

船 boat, ship ◇驳船 barge, lighter // 油船 oil tanker 船厂 shipyard 船货 cargo 船只 shipping, vessels ◇船只失事 shipwreck

【chuàn】

串 1)(连贯)string together 2)〈量词〉string, bunch, cluster ◇一串钥匙 a bunch of keys
串编辑程序 string editor
串变量 string variable
串标志 string denotation
串表 string list
串表达式 string expression
串并转换器 deserializer, serial to parallel converter, staticizer
串部件 string unit
串参数 string parameter
串操作 string manipulation
串操作符 string operator
串操作数 string operand
串常数 string constant
串处理 string handling
串处理系统 string process system {SPS}
串断点 string break
串分类 string sort(ing)
串符号 string symbol
串赋值 string assignment
串归约 string reduction
串函数 string function
串话 crosstalk {XTALK}
串级 cascade connection/stage, tandem
串级表 cascade table
串级控制 cascade/tandem control
串接表 cascade list
串接表目 cascade entry
串开关 string switch
串框架 string frame
串联补偿 cascade compensation
串联的 serial
串联电路 serial/series circuit
串联过程 cascade process
串联门 series gate, series gating
串联桥 cascaded bridges
串联系统 series system
串联线圈 series coil
串联校正 cascade compensation
串列顺序 cascade sequence
串描述符 string descriptor
串模式 string pattern
串扰 crossfire, interference
串属性 string attribute
串文法 string grammar
串文件 string file
串行半加器 serial half-adder
串行半减器 serial half-subtracter
串行编号 serial numbering
串行操作 serial operation

串行处理 serial processing
串行传输 serial transmission
串行传送 serial transfer
串行存取 serial access
串行存取存储器 serial access memory {SAM}
串行打印机 serial printer
串行调度 serial scheduling
串行方式 serial mode
串行访问 serial access
串行分类 serial sort
串行分量 serial component
串行分析 serial analysis
串行格式 serial format
串行化 serialization, serialize
串行环 serial loop
串行[行波]计数器 ripple counter
串行计算机 serial computer, consecutive sequence computer, sequential computer, series machine
串行加法器 serial adder
串行接口 serial interface
串行进位 cascaded carry, serial carry
串行可重用资源 serially reusable resource {SRR}
串行口 serial port
串行流 serial flow
串行逻辑 serial logic
串行排序 serial sort
串行设备 serial device
串行输出 serial output
串行输入 serial entry, serial input
串行输入输出 serial I/O {SIO}
串行输送 serial feeding
串行鼠标(器) serial mouse
串行数据 serial data
串行体系结构 series architecture
串行通信 serial communication
串行网络 serial network
串行线因特网协议 serial line internet protocol {SLIP}
串行移位 serial shift
串行运算 serial arithmetic
串行终端(设备) serial terminal
串语句 string statement
串运算符 string operator

【chuāng】

窗 window 窗户 window, casement
窗口 aperture, window
窗口边缘 window edge
窗口编号 window number
窗口标识 window ID
窗口部件类 widget class
窗口裁剪 window clipping
窗口操作 window operation
窗口成分 window component
窗口程序 window program
窗口大小 window size
窗口管理器 window manager
窗口环境 windows/windowing environment
窗口缓冲器 window buffer
窗口类 window class
窗口列 window column
窗口流 window stream
窗口流程 window flow
窗口目标 window object
窗口屏幕 window screen
窗口软件 window software
窗口软件设计工具 widget
窗口题标 windows title
窗口图 window diagram
窗口图像移动 window zoom
窗口文件 window file
窗口系统 window system
窗口箱 window box
窗口信号 window signal
窗口[终端]装置 agent set
窗口坐标(系) window coordinates

【chuáng】

床 bed ◇车床 lathe

【chuǎng】

闯 (直冲) rush in, charge, dash 闯祸 get into trouble, cause a disaster 闯破 break through, temper oneself 闯入 burst into, intrude

【chuàng】

创 start, achieve, initiate, establish, create ◇创纪录 establish a new record, set a record 创办 establish, originate 创建 found, establish 创立 found, originate 创新 originality, innovation 创造 create 创造性 creativity
创建原语 create primitive
创建者 creator
创造能力 genius
创作 authoring
创作的 creative
创作工具 authoring tools
创作软件 authoring software

【chuī】

吹 吹风 ①(被风吹) be in a draught, catch a chill ②(透露消息) give sb a briefing in advance ③(送风,充气) blow, aerate 吹气 blow, puff 吹奏 play (wind instruments)

炊 cook a meal

【chuí】

垂 hang down, droop, sag 垂直 perpendicular, vertical
垂直处理 vertical processing
垂直分段 vertical fragmentation
垂直分支 vertical branch
垂直格式 vertical format
垂直划分 vertical division
垂直回扫 vertical retrace
垂直(磁)记录 vertical recording
垂直间距 vertical spacing
垂直卷动 vertical scrolling
垂直奇偶校验 vertical parity check
垂直冗余校验 vertical redundancy check {VRC}
垂直微码 vertical microcode {VMC}
垂直微指令 vertical microinstruction
垂直位置 vertical position
垂直校验 vertical check

捶 beat, thump

锤 锤打 hammer into shape 锤子 hammer, beater 锤状物 weight ◇秤锤 steelyard weight

槌 mallet

【chūn】

春 spring 春假 spring vacation, spring holidays 春节 the Spring Festival

【chún】

纯 pure, unmixed, fine 纯粹 virgin, pure, entire, undiluted 纯洁 ①(清白) pure, clean and honest ②(使纯洁) purify
纯量 scalar, scalar quantity
纯量积 scalar product
纯量矩阵 scalar matrix
纯整数规划 pure integer programming

chún 唇醇 chuō 戳 chuò 辍绰 cī 疵 cí 词瓷辞磁

唇 lip

醇 alcohol, spirit

【chuō】

戳 jab, poke, thrust 戳穿 ①(刺穿) pierce through, puncture ②(揭穿)lay bare, expose 戳记 stamp, seal, counter mark

【chuò】

辍 stop, cease 辍工 stop work

绰
绰号 alias

【cī】

疵 疵点 flaw, fault, defect, blemish, weak spot

【cí】

词 (讲话)speech, statement ◇开幕词 opening speech 词典 dictionary 词根 root 词汇 vocabulary, glossary, lexicon 词条 entry 词头 prefix 词尾 suffix 词语 word, term ◇同义词 synonym 词缀 affix
词典的 lexical, lexicographic
词典顺序 lexicographic order
词法包 lexical closure
词法标记 lexical token
词法程序 lexical routine
词法单位 lexical unit
词法多义性 lexical ambiguity
词法分析 lexical analysis, morphology parsing
词法符号 lexical symbol
词法功能 lexical function
词法基础 lexical base
词汇表 vocabulary, entry, glossary
词汇节点 lexical node
词汇矩阵 lexical matrix
词类范畴 lexical category
词频索引 word frequency index
词组 word combination, word group, phrase

瓷 porcelain, china

辞 辞别 bid farewell, say good-bye, take one's leave 辞典 dictionary 辞退 dismiss, discharge 辞职 resign

磁 magnetism 磁铁 magnet
磁表面存储器 magnetic surface memory/storage
磁场 magnetic field
磁存储单元 magnetic cell
磁带 mag(netic) tape, storage tape, tape
磁带标号 magnetic tape label
磁带标记 tape mark
磁带标识 tape identification
磁带标准接口 magnetic tape formatter
磁带操作系统 tape operating system {**TOS**}
磁带存储器 tape storage
磁带存取 magnetic tape access
磁带读出方向 tape travel
磁带分类 tape sorting
磁带格式 magnetic tape format
磁带盒 cartridge, tape cartridge
磁带机接口 tape reader interface
磁带记录密度 tape recording density
磁带加载 magnetic tape loading
磁带检测 magnetic tape testing

磁带检索 tape search
磁带结束 end-of-tape {EOT}
磁带卷 tape reel, tape volume, reel
磁带卷标号 reel label
磁带开始 beginning-of-tape {BOT}
磁带控制器 magnetic tape controller
磁带库 tape library/pool
磁带馈送 tape feed
磁带录像机 video magnetic tape recorder, videotape recorder {VTR}
磁带录音机 tape machine/recorder
磁带密度 magnetic tape density
磁带奇偶校验 (magnetic) tape parity
磁带驱动器 magnetic tape driver
磁带入口 tape entry
磁带设备 tape unit
磁带设备数据块 tape device data block {TDB}
磁带适配器 magnetic tape adapter, magnetic type adapter
磁带条 tape strip
磁带头 tape head, leader
磁带尾 magnetic tape trailer, tape trailer
磁带文件 magnetic tape file, tape file
磁带系统 mag(netic) tape system
磁带箱 tape bin
磁带信息块 tape block
磁带装置 magnetic tape unit
磁带走带机构 magnetic tape deck
磁单元 magnetic cell
磁道 magnetic track, track
磁道标号 track label

磁道标记 track mark
磁道错误 track error
磁道单元 track element, track spot
磁道格式 track format
磁道置换 track replacement
磁道挂起 track hold
磁道恢复 track recovery
磁道畸变 track distortion
磁道间距 track pitch, track spacing
磁道宽 track width
磁道密度 track density
磁道选择器 track selector
磁道/英寸 tracks per inch {TPI}
磁道柱面 cylinder
磁鼓 drum, magnetic drum
磁光存储器 magneto-optical memory
磁光记录 magneto-optical recording
磁光盘 magneto-optic(al) disk {MO}
磁光软盘 floptical
磁光显示器 magneto-optic display
磁光效应 magneto-optical effect
磁光学 magneto-optics
磁(性)记录 magnetic recording
磁记录方式 magnetic recording mode
磁记录媒体[介质] magnetic recording medium
磁记录文件 magnetic record file
磁记录字符 magnetic character
磁卡文件 magnetic card file
磁卡系统 magnetic card system
磁卡阅读机 strip-card reader
磁卡装置 magnetic card device
磁盘 disk (=disc), magnetic cartridge, magnetic disk

磁盘部件[装置] disk unit
磁盘操作系统 disk(-based) operating system {**DOS**}
磁盘尺寸 disk size
磁盘磁头 disk head
磁盘存储 disk storage
磁盘存储设备 disk storage device
磁盘存取 disk access, disk accessing
磁盘存取臂 disk arm
磁盘存取方法 disk access method
磁盘存取时间 disk access time
磁盘单元 disk cell, diskette unit
磁盘道 disk track
磁盘地址 disk address
磁盘调度策略 disk scheduling policy
磁盘队列 disk queue
磁盘队列控制块 disk queue control block {**DQCB**}
磁盘访问时间 disk access time
磁盘分配表 disk allocation table {**DAT**}
磁盘分区 disk partition
磁盘封装 disk enclosure
磁盘复制 disk copy, disk duplexing
磁盘管理程序 disk manager
磁盘盒[座] disk cartridge
磁盘机 disk drive/unit, magnetic disk unit
磁盘机电源 disk unit supply
磁盘机系统 disk drive system
磁盘记录格式 disk record(ing) format
磁盘接口 disk interface, disk interfacing
磁盘镜像技术 disk mirroring
磁盘卷(宗) disk volume
磁盘拷贝 disk copy
磁盘控制器 (magnetic) disk controller
磁盘库文件 disk library
磁盘类型 disk type
磁盘区 disk partition
磁盘驱动器 disk driver, disk drive unit, (magnetic) disk drive
磁盘冗余阵列 redundant array of independent disk {**RAID**}
磁盘杀手病毒 disk killer virus
磁盘扇区 disk sector
磁盘设备 disk device
磁盘适配器 magnetic disk adapter
磁盘双工 disk duplexing
磁盘图符 disk icon
磁盘文件 (magnetic) disk file
磁盘文件管理程序 disk file manager
磁盘文件结构 disk file organization
磁盘文件控制器 disk file controller
磁盘文件索引 disk file index
磁盘文件系统 disk file system
磁盘文件寻址 disk file addressing
磁盘文件引用 disk file reference
磁盘文件组织 disk file organization
磁盘系统 disk system
磁盘写保护 disk write protect
磁盘写入器 diskette writer
磁盘信息块 disk information block
磁盘阵列 disk array
磁盘组 disk cartridge, disk volume, magnetic disk pack
磁泡 magnetic bubble, domain tip
磁泡存储器 bubble memory, magnetic bubble memory, magnetic bubble storage

磁片 magnetic sheet
磁数据记录纸 magnetic sheet
磁条 magnetic stripe
磁条记录 magnetic strip record
磁条卡 magnetic stripe card
磁条文件 magnetic strip file
磁条系统 magnetic stripe system
磁条阅读机 magnetic stripe reader
磁通 flux
磁头 magnetic head, head, record head
磁头臂 access arm, head (support) arm
磁头标志 head marker
磁头槽 head slot
磁头磁盘组合件 head disk assembly {HDA}
磁头存取窗 head access window
磁头定位 head positioning
磁头读写口 head slot
磁头缝隙 head gap
磁头号 head number
磁头合一 head unification
磁头碰撞 head crash
磁头启停区 head landing zone
磁头切换 head switching
磁头驱动器 head driver, head actuator
磁头卸载 head unloading
磁头组 head stack, yoke
磁透明水印 watermark magnetics
磁线 magnetic wire
磁芯 magnetic core
磁性薄膜 magnetic film, magnetic thin film
磁性存储器 magnetic memory
磁性墨水 magnetic ink
磁性涂层 magnetic coating
磁性氧化物 magnetic oxide
磁学 magnetism

磁延迟线 magnetic delay line
磁元件 magnetic cell
磁滞 hysteresis
磁滞回线 magnetic hysteresis loop
磁(片)组 disk pack

雌 female

【cǐ】

此 this 此地 this place, here 此后 after this, hereafter, henceforth 此刻 now, this moment, at present 此时 this moment, right now 此外 besides, in addition, moreover

【cì】

次 1)(次序)order, sequence ◇车次 train number // 依次 in due order, in succession, one by one 2)〈量词〉◇一次 once // 两次 twice // 三次 three times 3)(第二)second, next 4)(质次)second-rate 次级(的)secondary, sublevel, ungraded
次品 substandard product, defective goods, minus material; ungraded 次数 number of times, frequency 次序 order, sequence 次要 secondary, auxiliary, minor
次对话端 secondary half-session
次功能 secondary function
关键字 secondary key
次级存储器 second-level storage
次级调制解调器 secondary modem
次级回路 secondary loop
次级控制器 secondary control-

次级目录 second-level directory
次级请求 secondary request
次记录键 alternate record key
次节点 minor node
次(级)逻辑单元 secondary logical unit {SLU}
次入口点 secondary entry point
次设备 secondary device
次索引 secondary index
次要的 minor
次要决策 minor decision
次要控制 minor control
次应用块 secondary application block {SAB}
次站 secondary station

刺 thorn, splinter (扎刺) sting, stab, prick 刺伤 stab and wound 刺激 stimulation

赐 grant, favor 赐复 kindly favor us with reply 赐予 grant, bestow

【cōng】

匆 匆忙 hastily, in a hurry, in haste

聪 聪明 intelligent, bright, clever

【cóng】

从 1)(跟随)follow ◇顺从, 听从 comply with, obey 2)(表示起于)from 从不 never 从此 from this time on, from now on, from then on 从而 thus, thereby 从简 conform to the principle of simplicity 从来 always, at all times, all along 从略 be omitted 从前 before, formerly, in the past 从容 ①(镇静) calm, unhurried, leisurely ②(宽裕)plentiful, sufficient, enough 从事 go in for, be engaged in 从属 subordinate, dependent, secondary, slave, auxiliary 从属地位 subordinate status 从头 from the beginning, anew, once again 从中 out of, from among, therefrom
从(属)触发器 slave flip-flop
从动部分 secondary part
从方式 slave mode
从(属)计算机 slave computer
从略数据 ignore data
从属部件[设备] slave
从属处理机 slave processor
从属存储器 slave memory, slave store
从属的 slave, tributary
从属方式 slave mode
从属分析 dependent analysis
从属工作站 dependent workstation
从属故障 misjudgement failure
从属关系 subordinate relation
从属任务 subordinate task
从属系统 slave system
从属应用 slave application
从属站 slave station, tributary station
从属装置 slave unit
从态 slave state
从系统 slave system
从站 secondary station, slave station, passive station

【còu】

凑 gather together, pool, collect 凑巧 luckily, fortunately, by chance

【cū】

粗 (声音粗) gruff, husky 粗大 wide (in diameter), thick 粗放型 extensive form 粗略 rough, sketchy 粗浅 superficial, shallow, simple 粗率 rough and careless, ill-considered 粗细 thickness 粗心 careless, thoughtless 粗糙 coarse, crude, rough
粗黑体 extrabold (=xbld)
粗体(字) body face, boldface {bf}
粗像素 thick primitive

【cù】

促 1) (短促) short, hurried, urgent 2) (推动) urge, promote ◇催促 urge, hurry 促成 help to bring about, facilitate 促动 actuate, motivate 促进 promote, advance, accelerate 促使 impel, urge, spur

猝 猝然 suddenly, abruptly, unexpectedly

醋 vinegar

簇 1) form a cluster, pile up 2)〈量词〉cluster, bunch 3)〈数学〉manifold 簇新 brand new
簇表目 cluster entry
簇代理 cluster agent
簇功能 cluster function
簇计算 cluster computing
簇目录表 cluster entry

【cuàn】

窜 1) (乱跑) run about, flee, scurry 2) (改动) change 窜改 alter, tamper with, adulterate

【cuī】

催 (加快变化) hasten, expedite, speed up 催促 urge, hurry up, spur on, press

摧 break, destroy, crush 摧残 wreck, destroy, ruin 摧毁 destroy, smash

【cuì】

脆 1) (易碎) fragile, brittle, frangible 2) (味脆) crisp 3) (声音清脆) clear, ringing, clear and sharp 脆弱 fragile, frail, weak

翠 fresh green 翠绿 emerald green, jade green

【cūn】

村 village

【cún】

存 1) (存在) exist, live, survive, be 2) (保存) store, keep 3) (聚集) accumulate, collect 4) (储蓄) deposit 5) (寄存) leave with, check 6) (保留) reserve, retain 7) (结存) remain on balance, be in stock 8) (怀有) cherish, harbor 存放 ① deposit ② leave with, leave in sb's care 存折 deposit book, bankbook
存储 storage, memory, inventory, store, storing
存储板 memory board
存储保护 storage protection, memory protection, memory guard, store protection

存储(器)变换 memory mapping

存储标志 storage mark

存储表 storage list

存储部件 storage device

存储残片[碎片] fragmentation

存储操作 memory operation, store operation

存储层次 memory hierarchy

存储程序计算机 stored program computer

存储程序控制 stored program control {SPC}

存储程序逻辑 stored program logic

存储池 storage pool

存储冲突 memory contention

存储带宽 memory bandwidth

存储单元 memory cell, storage cell, store cell, memory location, cell, location, storage location

存储地址寄存器 memory address register {MAR}, storage address register, store address register

存储地址驱动器 memory address driver

存储段 store section

存储方式寄存器 bank mode register

存储访问故障 memory access fault

存储分块表 memory block table {MBT}

存储分配 memory/ storage allocation

存储分配策略 storage allocation policy

存储管理 memory/ store management, storage administration

存储管理部件[单元] memory management unit {MMU}

存储管理系统 storage management system {SMS}

存储缓冲器[区] memory buffer

存储矩阵 memory/storage matrix

存储(器)开关 storage switch

存储空间 dedicated space, memory/storage space

存储控制器 storage control unit, store controller

存储块 block of memory, storage/store block

存储类 storage class {SC}

存储(器)空间 memory space

存储密度 memory/ storage/ packing density

存储(器)模块 storage module

存储模式 storage pattern

存储奇偶校验 memory parity

存储保护 storage protection

存储编址 memory addressing

存储器测试 storage testing

存储器冲突 memory conflict

存储器存取保护 memory access protection

存储器存取[访问]冲突 memory access conflict

存储器存取方式 memory access mode

存储器地址线 memory address line

存储器地址指针 memory address pointer

存储器访问保护 memory access protection

存储器访问控制部件 storage access control unit

存储器分配算法 storage allocation algorithm

存储器工作空间 memory workspace

存储器交叉存取 memory across access, storage interleaving

存储器奇偶性 memory parity
存储器数据总线 memory data bus
存储器写周期 memory write cycle
存储器易失性 storage volatility
存储器溢出 storage overflow
存储器诊断(程序) memory diagnostic
存储器重新配置 storage reconfiguration
存储(信息)转储 storage dump
存储器字长 memory word length
存储器总线 memory bus
存储区 memory area, storage area, storage region, area in storage, zone
存储区标识符 location identifier
存储区定界符 location delimiter
存储区域 storage region
存储区域网络 storage area network {SAN}
存储(器)容量 memory/storage/store capacity
存储上溢 overflow
存储设备 storage device/facility
存储设备控制器 storage device controller
存储数据 storage data, stored data
存储数据寄存器 memory data register {MDR}
存储碎片 storage fragmentation
存储体 memory module, memory stack, storage volume, bank, memory bank
存储体冲突 bank conflict
存储条 sliver

存储图 storage map
存储图像 memory/storage image
存储位 bank bit, storage bit
存储位置 storage site
存储系统 inventory/memory system
存储性能 memory property
存储映射[映像] storage mapping, storage image, memory map
存储映像函数 storage mapping function
存储优先权[级] memory priority
存储元件 memory/storage element, storage cell
存储指令 store instruction
存储周期 memory/storage cycle
存储转储 storage dump
存储转发 forward and store, store and forward
存储装置 storage apparatus, storing device
存储资源共享 memory resource sharing
存储字 memory/storage word, stored word
存储字段 memo field
存储字符 store character
存档 archive, archiving, grandfather
存档转储 archive dump
存取 (一般对硬件),访问(对非硬件) access
存取臂 access arm
存取表 access list
存取部件 access unit
存取层 level of access
存取点 access point
存取法 access method
存取法服务 access method services {AMS}

存取方式 access mode
存取卷 access volume
存取孔 access hole
存取控制 access control
存取控制表 access control list
存取控制键 access control key
存取控制机制 access control mechanism
存取控制寄存器 access control registor
存取控制矩阵 access control matrix
存取控制块 access control block {ACB}
存取控制类别 access control category
存取控制码 access control code
存取控制锁 access control lock
存取控制字段 access control field
存取[访问]能力 access capability
存取权 access authority/right
存取授权 access authorization
存取速率 access rate
存取特权 access privilege
存取位 access bit
存取位数 access width
存取限制 access restriction
存取线(路) access line
存取协议 access protocol
存取优先级 access priority
存取周期 (store) access cycle {AC}

【cùn】

寸 寸步 a tiny step, a single step

【cuō】

搓 1) (捻) twist, twine 2) (摩擦) rub, scrub, rub with the hands

磋 磋商 consult, exchange views

【cuò】

挫 挫败 frustrate, foil, defeat, thwart 挫折 setback, reverse

措 1) (安排,处置) arrange, manage, handle 2) (筹划) make plans ◇筹措款项 raise funds 措施 measure

锉 file ◇方锉 square file // 木锉 (wood) rasp

错 1) (参差) interlocked and jagged, intricate, complex 2) (不正确) wrong, mistaken 3) (过错) fault, demerit, error 错开 stagger 错综复杂 intricate, complex, very complicated
错读 dirty read
错位 out of position, skewing, transposition
错误 error {ERR}, bug, fault, fallacy, mistake
错误标记 bug patch, error flag/mark
错误表 error list
错误捕捉 error trapping
错误出口 error exit
错误处理程序 error handler
错误调用 error call
错误计数器 error counter
错误记录 error logging, error record
错误记录程序 error logger
错误监测 bug monitor, error detecting program, error detecting routine
错误检测码 error detecting code, error detection code

错误检测器 error detector
错误检验和纠正 error checking and correction {ECC}
错误卷分析 error volume analysis {EVA}
错误控制符 error control character
错误控制码 error control code
错误控制设备 error control equipment
错误类别 error category
错误类型 error pattern, error type
错误模式 bug pattern, error pattern
错误模型 error model
错误日志 error log
错误日志表 error log table
错误日志管理程序 error log manager {ELM}
错误式样 error pattern
错误数据 misdata
错误校验码 error checking code
错误校正码 error correcting code {ECC}
错误[误差]校正系统 error correcting system
错误延迟时间 error latency
错误诊断 error diagnostic
错误中断请求向量 error interrupt request vector {EIRV}
错误状态码 error status code
错误状态字 error status word
错误自陷 error trapping

D d

【dā】

搭 搭配 arrange in pairs or groups, mate, match

答 另见【dá】
答应 ① (应答) answer, reply, respond ② (许诺) promise, comply with ③ (同意) agree, consent

【dá】

打 另见【dǎ】
〈量词〉dozen ◇半打 half a dozen

达 1) (通达) extend 2) (表达) express, communicate 达成 reach (agreement) 达到 reach, attain, amount to, achieve 达意 express one's idea, convey one's ideas
达林顿放大器 Darlington amplifier

答 另见【dá】
1) (回答) answer, reply, respond 2) (还报) return (a visit, etc.), reciprocate 答案 answer, solution, key 答辩 reply, defence 答词 thank-you speech, answering speech, reply 答卷 ① answer sheet ② answered test paper 答谢 express appreciation, acknowledge (a favor) 答复 reply {REP, RPLY}, answer
答话终端 audio terminal

【dǎ】

打 另见【dá】
1) (敲打) strike, hit, knock 2) (攻打) fight, attack 3) (锻造) make, forge 4) (搅拌) mix, stir, beat 5) (凿) open, dig 打败 ① (战胜) defeat, beat ② (失败) suffer a defeat, be defeated 打包 bale, pack, tie up 打草稿 prepare a draft 打断 ① (折) break ② (使中断) interrupt, cut short 打发 ① (派出去) send, dispatch ② (使离开) dismiss, send away ③ (消磨) while away (one's time), kill time 打翻 overturn, strike down 打官司 go to court, go to law, engage in a lawsuit 打夯 ramming, tamping 打击 hit, strike, attack, impact, knock 打搅 disturb, trouble 打开 ① (揭开) open, unfold ② (开电视机等) turn on, switch on ③ (攻开) break through ④ (展开) open up, spread ◇打开僵局 break the impasse, find a solution to a problem 打乱

throw into confusion, upset **打破** break, smash **打气** ①(充气) inflate, pump up, aerate ②(鼓励) boost the morale, cheer (up) **打拳** box, practice boxing **打扰** disturb, trouble **打散** break up, scatter **打算** ①(考虑) intend, plan, consider ②(想法) idea, opinion **打碎** break-in, breaking-down, pounding; smash, shatter, destroy **打听** ask about, inquire about **打通** open up ◇打通电话 get through (on the telephone) **打退** beat back, beat off, repulse **打折扣** sell at a discount, give a discount, rebate **打中** hit the mark, hit the target, hit **打转** spin, rotate, revolve **打字** typewrite, type **打字带** typewriter ribbon **打字机** typewriter **打字员** typist

打点式 dot type
打断键 break key
打击键 key stroke
打开文件 file opening, open file
打入 type in, typing-in
打印 print, printing
打印板 type plate
打印表征 print attribute
打印部件 type carrier, type element
打印操作员 print operator
打印错误 misprint, type error
打印(色)带 print band
打印点 print point
打印服务器 print server
打印杆 print bar, type bar
打印格式符 layout character
打印鼓 print drum, type drum
打印机 print unit, printer, writing machine
打印机挂起 printer hang
打印机芯 printer engine
打印机警告 printer alert
打印机控制语言 printer control language {PCL}
打印机驱动程序(器) printer driver
打印机占用 printer busy
打印机字体 printer font, monospace font
打印记录号[数] print record number
打印假脱机 print spooler
打印架 printing frame
打印键 printing/type key
打印禁止 print inhibit
打印控制符 control character {CTRL}, print control character
打印宽度 print span
打印密度 character pitch
打印速度 print speed, printing speed, typing speed
打印体 type-script
打印头 print head, typing head
打印图表 print plot
打印位置 imprint position
打印文件 print file, printer file
打印线 print line, typing line
打印样式 type style
打印页 type face
打印预览 print preview
打印针 print wire
打印字符尺寸 type size
打字机 typewriter, writer
打字拉杆 type rod
打字员 typist

【 dà 】
大 1)(范围)big, large, great 2)(程度)heavy (rain, etc.), strong (wind, etc.), loud 3)

(规模)general, main, major 4)(年龄)age, old 大半 ①(过半数)more than half, greater part, most ②(很可能)very likely, most probably 大部分 greater part 大大地 greatly, enormously 大胆 bold, daring, audacious 大地 the earth, mother earth, the world 大典 grand ceremony 大都市 a large city, a metropolis 大多 for the most part, mostly 大多数 great majority, vast majority 大风 (fresh) gale, strong wind 大幅度 by a wide margin, by a big margin, substantially 大概 ①(大致内容)general idea, broad outline ②(大约)general, rough, approximate ③(可能)probably, most likely, presumably 大纲 outline 大哥大 cellular telephone, mobile telephone 大规模 large-scale, extensive, massive, mass 大号子 large size 大会 ①(社团会议)plenary session, general assembly, conference ◇联合国大会 the General Assembly of the United Nations ②(群众会议)mass meeting, rally 大家 ①(专家)great master, authority ②(大伙)all, everybody 大局 overall situation, general situation, whole situation 大考 end-of-term examination, final exam 大礼堂 hall, auditorium 大力 energetically, vigorously 大量 a large number, mass, (great) quantity, bulk, multitude 大楼 multi-storied building 大陆 continent, mainland 大陆架 continental shelf 大略 ①(大致情况)general idea, broad outline ②(大约)generally, roughly, approximately; about 大门 entrance door, front door, gate 大批 large quantities, large numbers, large amounts, multitude 大气压 atmospheric pressure 大权 power over major issues, authority 大厦 large building, mansion 大师 (great) master 大使 ambassador 大事 great event, major important matter, major issue 大事记 chronicle of events 大体 roughly, more or less, on the whole, by and large, for the most part 大厅 hall 大写 capitalization 大型 large-scale, large-size(d) 大学 university, college 大学生 university student, college student 大意 ①(主要意思)general idea, main points ②(疏忽)careless, negligent, absent-minded 大雨 heavy rain 大约 ①(约略)approximately, about ②(可能)probably 大致 roughly, approximately, more or less 大众 masses, people, general public 大众化 popular; popularize 大自然 nature 大宗 a large amount, a large quantity

大规模并行处理机[系统] massively parallel processor {MPP}

大规模并行计算机 massively parallel computer {MPC}

大规模集成电路 large-scale in-

tegration {LSI}
大量数据 mass data
大量转储 massive dump
大模式 large model
大容量传输协议 bulk transfer protocol {BTP}
大容量存储记录 mass storage record
大容量存储卷 mass storage volume
大容量存储媒体 mass media
大容量[海量]存储器 mass storage
大容量存储器 bulk store, large capacity memory, bulk storage
大容量存储系统 mass storage system {MSS}, high capacity storage system {HCSS}
大容量光存储器 mass optical memory
大容量数字设备 high capacity digital device
大项 maxterm
大小 dimension, magnitude, size
大写体 upper case
大写字母 caps, capital letter
大型机 mainframe, large computer, mainframe computer
大型计算机 large scale computer, large computer, maxicomputer
大型芯片 jumbo chip
大样本 large sample
大于或等于 greater than {GT} or equal to {GE}
大众传播媒体(指广播、电视等) mass media

【dài】

代 1)(历史年代)historical period ◇古代 ancient times 2)(世代)generation 代办所 agency 代表 deputy, delegate, representative 代表大会 congress, representative assembly, representative conference 代表团 delegation, mission, deputation 代号 code name, code number, symbol 代价 price, cost 代理 ①(代人负责)act on behalf of, acting 代理厂长 acting manager of a factory ②(代表别人工作)act as an agent, act as a procurator 代理人 agent, deputy, proxy, procurator 代数 algebra 代替 replace, supersede, substitute for, take the place of, be in place of 代用 substitute, transpose 代用品 substitute, ersatz
代理 proxy, agent
代理服务器 proxy server
代理进程 agent process
代理主机 proxy
代码 code, coded representation
代码表 code page
代码单位 code element
代码点 code point
代码行 code line
代码号 code number {CODEN}
代码间距 code distance
代码检查[检验] code check/inspection
代码键 code key
代码禁止 code inhibit
代码审查[计] code audit
代码审计[检查]程序 code auditor
代码识别系统 code recognition system
代码编码系统 coding system
代码相关系统 code sensitive

system, coded dependent system

代码再生[重写] code rewriting

代码转换 code conversion, code convert

代码字 code word, coded word

代数闭包 algebraic closure

代数变换 algebraic manipulation/transformation

代数表达式 algebraic expression

代数等价 algebraically equivalent

代数符号 algebraic sign, sign digit

代数复型 algebraic complex

代数构形 algebraic configuration

代数规划 algebraic program

代数简化 algebraic simplification

代数解析 algebraic analysis

代数式 algebraic expression

代数同构 algebra isomorphism

代数拓扑学 algebraic topology

代数系统 algebra system, algebraic system

代数元 algebraic element

带 1)(带子)belt, ribbon, band 2)(地带)zone, area, belt 3)(携带)take, bring, carry 4)(含有)bear, have 5)(附带)having sth attached 带领 lead, guide 带头 take the lead, be the first, take the initiative, set an example

带操作系统 tape operating system {TOS}

带(磁带) band, bar, ribbon, tape, tape spool, zone

带点的十进制表示 dotted decimal notation

带点地址 dot address

带电操作 power operation

带符号字段 signed field

带缓冲的键盘 buffered keyboard

带缓冲的键盘式打印机 buffered keyboard printer

带缓冲的行式打印机 buffered line printer

带基数 based number

带宽 bandwidth {BW}, tape width

带宽保留协议 bandwidth reservation protocol

带宽范围 bandwidth range

带宽管理 bandwidth management

带宽控制 bandwidth control

带式打印机 band printer, belt printer, strip printer, tape printer

带通 bandpass

带通滤波器 band pass filter {BPF}

带状[扁平]电缆 ribbon

带状电缆 flat (flexible) cable, ribbon cable, ribbon type cable, tape cable

带状物 ribbon

带状线 strip line

贷 1)(借入)borrow 2)(借出)lend 贷款 provide a loan, extend credit to, make an advance to, loan, credit

贷方 credit {CR, CRD}, creditor

待 1)(对待)treat, deal with 2)(招待)entertain 3)(等待,留待)wait for, await 待遇 ①treatment ②(报酬)pay, wages, salary

待发 clear to send {CTS}, due

out

待命中断 arm, armed interrupt

待命状态 armed state

待用 standby application

待用状态 dormant/ inactive state

怠 idle, slack, lazy 怠工 slow down, go slow

袋 bag, sack, pocket

戴 put on, wear, have on

【dān】

担 另见【dàn】
carry with a shoulder pole 担保 assure, guarantee, secure 担保人 guarantor, guarantee 担当 take on, undertake, assume 担风险 take risks, face the risk 担负 bear, shoulder, take on, be charged with 担任 hold the post of, act as 担心 worry, feel anxious 担忧 worry, be anxious

单 1)(一个)one, single 2)(奇数)odd 3)(仅只)only, alone 4)(清单)bill, list ◇ 菜单 menu ∥ 提货单 bill of lading 单纯 ① (简单)simple, pure, plain ② (单一)alone, purely, merely 单词 word 单调 monotonous, dull 单独 alone, by oneself, on one's own; single, independent, individual 单方面 one-sided, unilateral 单个 single, solitary, odd, solo 单价 unit price 单据 receipt, voucher, invoice, bill 单位 unit, unity 单向 one-way, unidirectional, unilateral, monodirectional

单板 on-board

单板(计算)机 on-board computer

单板计算机 board computer, single board computer {SBC}

单板计算机控制器 single board computer controller

单板微型(计算)机 single-board microcomputer, monoboard microcomputer, one board microcomputer

单版本 single version {1V}

单倍字长运算 single-length arithmetic

单倍(字长)精度 single precision

单标记 single token

单步(执行) single step

单步操作 one-shot operation, one- step operation, single shot operation, single- step operation

单步处理 single-step process

单步调试 single step debugging, single-step debug

单步法 one-step method, single step, single-step process

单步方式 single shot/ step mode

单步陷阱 single step trap

单触发电路 one-shot circuit

单处理器 monoprocessor, single processor, uniprocessor

单穿孔 single column punch

单串行处理机 single serial processor

单纯域 simple domain

单错校正双错检测码 single error correcting/ double error detecting code {SEC/ DEC code}

单地址 one-address, single address, unique address
单地址报文 single address message
单调 monotone, monotony
单调的 monotonic, quiet
单调递减 monotone decreasing
单调递增 monotone increasing
单调分析 monotonic analysis
单调关联系统 coherent system
单调函数 monotonic function
单调逻辑 monotonic logic
单调收敛 monotone convergence
单调推理 monotonic reasoning
单调性 monotonicity
单端 single end
单端放大器 monoamplifier
单个任务 individual task
单工 oneway
单工(的) simplex
单工传输 simplex transmission
单工电路 simplex circuit {SPX circuit}
单工方式 simplex mode
单工/双工终端 simplex/duplex terminal
单工通信 simplex communication
单工线路 simplex circuit {SPX circuit}, simplex line, single circuit
单工信道 simplex channel
单功能流水线 unifunctional pipeline
单环 lone loop
单回路 individual loop, lone loop
单会话(期) single session
单击[鼠标] click
单机系统 stand-alone system, single-machine system, one-of-a-kind system
单极传输 unipolar transmission
单极(性)的 unipolar
单极(型)晶体管 unipolar transistor
单级 single stage, single level
单级互连网络 single stage interconnection network
单计算机 stand-alone computer
单计算机系统 single-computer system, unicomputer system
单间隔 monospacing, monospacing, single space
单间隔字符 monospaced characters
单间隔字体 monospace font
单晶 single crystal
单(倍)精度 single precision
单精度运算 single precision arithmetic
单精度整数 single precision integer
单块 inblock
单块存储器 monolithic storage
单块芯片 monolithic chip
单连通的 simply connected
单链表 simply linked list
单列直插式存储器模块 single in-line memory module {SIMM}
单列直插式组件 single in-line package {SIP}
单路(通信) simplex
单路操作 one-way only operation
单路推理 one-line inference
单脉冲 single pulse
单门 simple gate
单密度 single density
单密度磁盘 single-density disk
单密度(记录)格式 single density format
单密度记录 single density recording
单密度软盘 single density

单面倍密度软盘 single-sided double-density diskette
单面磁盘 single-sided disk
单面软盘 single-sided diskette
单命令 single command
单模 single mode
单模光纤 monomode/single-mode optical fiber
单目运算 unary operation
单目运算符 unary operator
单片 monochip
单片处理机 monolithic processor, single chip processor
单片存储器 monolithic memory/storage, on-chip memory
单片的 monolithic
单片方式 single chip mode
单片高速缓冲存储器 on-chip cache
单片工艺 monolithic technology
单片混合微电路 monobrids
单片(计算)机 computer on a chip, computer on-slice
单片集成电路 monolithic integrated circuit
单片技术 monolithic technology
单片寄存器结构 chip register architecture
单片结构 single chip architecture
单片微处理机 chip microprocessor
单色 monochrome, solid shade
单色激光打印机 monochrolaser printer
单色(图形)适配器 monochrome graphics adapter, monographics adapter
单色显示(器) monochrome display
单色显示适配器 monochrome display adapter {MDA}
单色性 monochromatic
单输出系统 single output system
单输入单输出系统 single-input single-output system {SISO system}
单体磁头 monolithic head
单通道 single channel
单通道单载波 single carrier per channel {SCPC}
单同态 monomorphism
单位[单元]分隔符 unit separator {US}
单位[时间]间隔 unit interval
单位间隔 unit gap, unit space
单位间距[距离]码 unit distance code
单位矩阵 identity/unit/unitary/unity matrix
单位立方 unit cube
单位码 unitary code
单位元素 unit element
单位面积 elemental area, unit area
单位模块 unital module
单位退格符 unit backspace character {UBS}
单位向量 unit vector, unity vector
单位元素 unit element, unity
单谓词演算 unary predicate calculus
单稳(态)的 monostable
单稳态触发器 monostable flip-flop/trigger
单稳态多谐振荡器 monostable multivibrator, single shot multivibrator, start-stop multivibrator
单线程方式 single threading
单线程应用程序 single-thread

application program
单线函数 single line function
单线数字用户线 single line digital subscriber line {SDSL}
单相 single phase
单相感应电机 single phase induction motor
单项 single entry, single item
单项算符 unary operator
单项系统 uniterm system
单项消解 unit resolution
单向 one way
单向传导 unilateral conductivity
单向传输 one-way transmission, unidirectional transmission
单向传送 one-way transmission
单向连通图 unilaterally connected graph
单向链接表 single linked list
单向流 uniflow
单向密码 one-way cipher
单向搜索 unidirectional search
单向通道 forward channel, one-way only channel
单向通信 one-way/ simplex communication
单向元件 unidirectional element
单向中继线 one-way trunk
单向总线 unidirectional bus
单芯 single core
单循环 individual loop, single loop
单页 cut form
单页馈送 single sheet feeding
单一 unity
单一表目 single entry
单一程序启动程序 single program initiator {SPI}
单一进位 single carry
单一目的 single goal
单一网络管理协议 Single Network Management Protocol {SNMP}
单一总线 unibus
单元 cell, unit, element, location, primitive
单元变量 element variable, unit variable
单元表 cell list
单元表征(属性) cell attribute
单元分离符 unit separator character {US}
单元机组 monoblock
单元级 cell level
单元计算机 transputer
单元记录设备 unit record device
单元(程序)库 cell library
单元名 cell name, uniterm
单元区 cellular zone
单元体 cell cube
单元阵列 cell array, cellular array
单值公式 monadic formula
单值函数 monodrome/ monotropic/ uniform function, single-valued function
单指令单数据流 single-instruction single-data stream {SISD}
单指令多数据流 single-instruction multiple-data stream {SIMD}
单指数光纤 step-index fiber
单中断请求 single interrupt request
单字 unique word
单字长寄存器 single-length register
单字长运算 single precision arithmetic
单字节校正 single byte correction {SBC}
单字节字符集 single-byte character set {SBCS}

单总线操作 single-bus operation

耽 耽搁 ① (停留) stop over, stay ② (拖延) delay, hold up

【dǎn】
胆 (内胆) a bladder-like inner container 胆量 courage, guts, bravery

【dàn】
旦 day, daybreak ◇元旦 New Year's Day

但 (只,仅) only, merely 但是 but, yet, still, nevertheless

担 另见【dàn】
〈量词〉tan, picul (= 50 kilograms) 担子 load, burden

淡 1) (稀薄) thin, light 2) (颜色浅) light, pale 3) (冷淡) indifferent 淡季 slack season, dull/off season 淡出 fade-out, fading out 淡入 fade in, fading in

弹 另见【tán】
(枪弹) bullet, bomb ◇导弹 guided missile 弹子 ball, pellet

诞 诞辰 birthday 诞生 be born, come into being, emerge

氮 nitrogen [N]

【dāng】
当 另见【dàng】

1) (相称) equal 2) (应当) ought to, should, must 3) (正在…) just at a certain time or place 4) (充当) work as, serve as, be 5) (承官) bear, accept, deserve 6) (掌管) direct, manage, be in charge of 当班 be on duty by turn 当场 on the spot, then and there 当初 originally, at the beginning 当代 the present age, the contemporary era 当地 at the place in question, in the locality; local 当即 at once, right away 当今 now, at present, nowadays 当局 the authorities 当面 in sb's presence, to sb's face 当年 in those years, in those days 当前 at present, current 当然 ① (合情合理) without doubt, certainly, of course, to be sure ② (应这样) as it should be, only natural 当时 then, at that time 当天 the same day, the very day 当心 take care, be careful, look out 当选 be elected 当中 ① (正中) in the middle, in the center ② (中间) among(st) 当众 in public, in the open, publicly 当做 treat as, regard as, look upon as

当前版本 current release
当前窗口 active window, current window
当前磁道号 current track number
当前打印位置 current print position
当前代码段 current code segment
当前单元 active cell

当前地址 current address
当前堆 current heap
当前工作目录 current working directory
当前记录 current record
当前块号 current block number
当前目录 current directory
当前设备 current device
当前位置 current location, current position
当前文件 current file
当前行 current line
当前行指示字 current line pointer {CLP}
当前[活动,现时]用户 active user
当前指针 current pointer
当前值 current value, present value, currency
当前指令 present instruction
当前状态 current state

挡 【dǎng】
1)(挡住)keep off, block, shelter 2)(遮蔽)block, get in way of 3)汽车排挡)gear

党 1)(政党)political party, party 2)(集团)clique, faction, gang 党员 party member

【dàng】
当 另见【dāng】
1)(适当)proper, right 2)(相当)match, equal to 3)(认为)think 当时 that very day/ month/ year, right away, at once, immediately 当真 ①（信以为真）take seriously, accept sth as true ②(果然)really true; really 当作 treat as, regard as, take for

档 档案 files, archives, record
档案柜 file cabinet
档案文件 archive file

【dāo】
刀 knife, sword

氘 〈化学〉deuterium, diplogen

【dǎo】
导 1)(引导)lead, guide 2)(传导)transmit, conduct 3)(开导)instruct, teach, give guidance to 导出 derive, develop, induce 导弹 guided missile 导论 introduction 导入 import, input 导师 tutor, teacher 导体 conductor 导向 lead, pilot 导致 lead to, bring about, result in, give rise to

导出范数 induced norm
导出句型 derived sentential form
导出数据 deductive data, derived data
导杆 guard bar
导航系统 navigation aid, navigation system
导航者 netscape navigator
导孔 carrier hole, feed through, guide hole
导孔穿孔 feed punch
导孔间距 feed pitch
导轮 guide roller
导数 derivation, derivative
导体间距 conductor spacing
导线延迟 line delay
导引 prologue (=prolog), steering
导引程序 steering routine

导引树 homing tree
导引图 derivation graph
导引向量 steering vector
导引指令 steering order
导纸板 paper deflector
导纸机构 paper guide

岛 island, islet

捣 pound with a pestle, etc.; beat 捣毁 smash up, demolish, 捣碎 pound to pieces, triturate, mash 捣碎机 stamp mill, gravity mill

倒 另见〔dào〕
(失败) collapse, fail 倒闭 close down, go bankrupt, go out of business 倒换 ① (替换) rotate, take turns ② (换掉) rearrange sequence, rearrange order, replace 倒买倒卖 speculative buying and selling, illegal dealings 倒塌 collapse, fall down 倒下 fall, topple

【dào】

到 1)(往)go to, leave for 2)(止)until, up to 到岸价格 cost, insurance and freight (C.I.F.) 到处 at all places, everywhere 到达 arrive, reach, get to 到底 ①(到尽头)to the end, to the finish ②(最后)at last, in the end, finally ③(究竟)ever, indeed 到目前为止 so far, by now, up to now 到期 become due, expire, terminate

倒 另见〔dǎo〕
1)(颠倒) upside down, inverted, reverse 2)(反向移动) move backward, turn upside down 3)(倾倒) pour, tip 倒车 back a car 倒流 flow backwards 倒退 go backwards, fall back 倒转 reverse, inverse, converse; flyback
倒带 tape rewind
倒带时间 rewind time
倒排表 inverted list
倒排索引 reverse/ inverted index
倒相(器)门 inverter gate
倒置 inversion, invert
倒置器 inversor
倒置树 inverted tree
倒置网络 inverse network
倒转方式 inversion mode
倒装法 flip chip

悼 悼念 mourn, grieve over

盗 steal, rob; thief, robber, bandit 盗用 embezzle usurp ◇盗用名义 usurp the name of
盗版软件 bootleg
盗版软件者 bootleger

道 1)(道路) road, way, path 2)(水道) channel, course 道德 morality, ethics 道理 ①(原理) principle, truth ②(理由) reason, sense, justification 道歉 apologize, make an apology 道谢 express one's thanks, thank
道号 track number
道间串扰 crosstalk {XTALK}, intertrack crosstalk
道间距 track pitch
道宽 track width
道密度 track density

道密度单位 tracks per inch {TPI}

【dé】

得 get, obtain, gain 得不偿失 the loss outweighs the gain, the game is not worth the candle 得出 reach (a conclusion), obtain (a result) 得到 get, obtain, gain, receive 得分 score, point 得奖 win a prize, be awarded a prize 得失 gain and loss, success and failure 得益 benefit, profit 得意 proud of oneself, pleased with oneself, complacent

锝 technetium (Tc)

德 virtue, morals, moral character 德国 Germany 德国人 German 德语 German (language)

【dēng】

灯 lamp, lantern, light 灯光 the light of a lamp, lamplight, lighting 灯泡 bulb

登 (刊登)publish, record 登记 register, check in, enter one's name, login 登陆 land, disembark, go ashore 登上 ascend, mount 登载 publish
登记(通信)表 polling list
登记器 logger
登录 logon, log-in
登录安全性 logon security
登录策略 account policy
登录对话(期) login session
登录方式 log-on mode
登录号 accession number, postings
登录机构 registration authority
登录脚本 logon script
登录进程 logon process
登录领域 login domain, logon domain
登录名(称) login name
登录目录 login directory
登录请求 log-on request
登录时间 logged on time, logon hours
登录手稿 logon script
登录原语 login script

【děng】

等 (相等)equal 等次 place in a series, grade 等待 wait, await 等等 and so on, and so forth, etc. 等候 wait, await, expect 等级 class, grade, rank 等价 of equal value, equal in value; equivalence, parity 等同 equate, be equal, identify 等外品 substandard product, reject 等于 equal to, equivalent to
等差级数 arithmetic progression, arithmetic series
等长(度编)码 equal length code
等待表 wait list, waiting list/table
等待时间 latency, think time, latency time, time waiting, wait(ing) time
等待系统 standby system, waiting system
等待应答 wait acknowledge
等待状态 idle
等级 class, gradation, grade, rank, tier
等级分类 hierarchical classification

等级服务 quality of service {QOS}
等价(的) equivalent
等价变换 equivalence/ equivalent transformation
等价关系 equivalence/ equivalent relation
等价群 equivalence group
等价[等效]系统 equivalent system
等角速 constant angular velocity {CAV}
等距的 isometric
等距视图 isometric view
等离子打印机 plasma printer
等时服务 isochronous service
等势 equipotence, equipotent
等势面 equipotential surface
等同关系 identity relation
等同说明 identity declaration
等同性 identity property
等同字符 equate character
等位面 equipotential surface
等效 equivalence
等效电路 equivalent circuit
等效(符号)串 equivalent string
等压线 isobar
等值命题 biconditional/ equivalence proposition
等值线 isoline

【dèng】
凳 凳子 stool

【dī】
低 1)〈形〉low 2)〈动〉let droop, hang down 低估 underestimate, belittle, underrate 低级 elementary, lower, rudimentary, low-grade 低廉 cheap, low-priced 低等(的) inferior, low-grade 低声 in a low voice 低温 ① low temperature ② microtherm
低部字节 low order byte
低层报文 low-level message
低层树 lower height tree
低差异编码 low disparity code {LDC}
低成本码 low cost code
低存储区 low memory
低地址保护 low address protection
低点 low point
低电平[电压] low level
低电平逻辑 low level logic
低端内存 low memory
低级网络 low level network
低级语言 low level language, lower level language
低能[哑]终端 dumb
低频(率) low frequency
低速 low speed, slow speed
低速存储器 slow memory
低速度 low speed
低通 low pass
低通滤波器 low pass filter
低位 low order
低位字符 low order character
低位字节 lower order byte
低温电子学 cryoelectronics
低温管 cryotron
低温器件 cryogenic device
低温学 cryogenics
低温元件 cryogenic element
低效运行方式 fallback mode
低音 bass sound
低优先级 low priority
低字 lower word
低字节 low byte

堤 dike, embankment, dam
堤岸 embankment 堤坝 dikes and dams

提 另见【tí】
提防 take precautions against,

be on guard against

滴 〈量词〉drop ◇一滴水 a drop of water 滴落 drip

镝 dysprosium (Dy)

【dí】

的 的确 indeed, really

敌 (力量相等) match, equal 敌对 hostile 敌人 enemy, foe 敌手 match, opponent, adversary

涤 wash, cleanse

笛 笛卡儿乘积 Cartesian product 笛卡儿坐标 Cartesian coordinate

【dǐ】

抵 抵触 conflict, contradict 抵抗 resist, stand up to, counteract 抵赖 deny 抵消 offset, cancel out, counteract 抵押 mortgage 抵制 resist, boycott

底 1)(末尾)end ◇年底 the end of a year 2)(衬底) ground, background, foundation 底部 bottom, base 底稿 draft, manuscript 底片 negative, photographic plate 底下 ① under, below, beneath ② next, later
底板 back panel, backplane, bay, board, chassis, pallet, panel, platter
底板互连(总线) backplane interconnect
底板接口 backplane interface
底板总线 backplane bus
底边 bottom margin
底部阴影 bottom shadow
底面 bottom-layer
底片[负片] negative, negative matrix
底片底纸 marigold
底片胶卷 master film
底片图案 negative pattern
底区 base area
底色 base color
底色墨水 background ink
底数 basic number

【dì】

弟 younger brother

地 1)(陆地) land, soil 2)(田地) fields 地产 landed estate, real estate 地带 region, zone 地道 tunnel 地点 place, site 地段 a section of an area 地方 ①(行政区)locality ②(当地的) local ③(某一地区) place, space 地基 ground (work), foundation 地面 ground, floor, land, earth 地壳 the earth's crust 地球 the earth 地区 area, district, region, local 地图 map 地位 position, status, standing, place 地下 underground, subterranean, subsurface 地下铁道 underground (railway), tube, subway 地域 region, district 地震 (earth)quake, seism
地方局 regional center {RC}
地理编码 geocoding
地理管理信息系统 geographic management information system {GMIS}
地理数据库 geographical

database
地理网络 geonetwork
地理信息系统 geographical information system {GIS}, geometric information system
地球站 earth station
地区的 local
地区交换中心 local exchange center
地区码 area code
地区[国家]语言支持 national language support {NLS}
地区中心 regional center {RC}, sectional center
地址 address {ADDR, ADR}, location
地址变换[映射,修正] address mapping, address modification
地址变换表 address mapping table
地址标号 address label
地址标记 address mask
地址表 address list/table, map
地址簿 address book
地址部分 address component, address port(ion)
地址单元 address location, address unit
地址对齐 address aliasing
地址翻译信关 address translation gateway {ATG}
地址访问类型 address access type
地址分隔符 address separator
地址分配 address assignment
地址格式 address format
地址交错 address interleaving
地址结束(符) end of address {EOA}
地址解析协议 address resolution protocol {ARP}
地址类 address class
地址流 address stream

地址屏蔽 address mask
地址区 address area
地址识别协议 address resolution protocol {ARP}
地址线 address line
地址选通 address strobe
地址掩码 address mask
地址译码器 address decoder
地址引用 address reference
地址映射 address mapping table {AMT}
地址转换 address translation
地址(递)增量 address increment
地址[目的]域 destination field
地址转换机构 address translator

帝 1)(上帝) God 2)(皇帝) emperor

递 1)(传送) hand over, pass, give 2)(顺次) successively, in the proper order 递加 progressive increase; increase successively, increase by degrees 递减 decrease progressively, decrease successively, decrease by degrees 递交 hand over, present, submit 递送 send, deliver 递增 increase progressively, increase by degrees
递归 recursion, recurrence
递归表 recursive list
递归表处理 recursive list processing
递归并行性 recursive parallelism
递归长度 recursion length
递归程序 recursion/ recursive routine
递归调用 recursive call/invocation
递归定义 recursive definition

递归对策 recursive game
递归方式 recursive fashion
递归分析 recursive analysis
递归规则 recursive rule
递归过程 recursion procedure
递归函数 recursive function
递归结构 recursive structure
递归算法 recursive algorithm
递归算子 recursive operator
递归文法 recursive grammar
递减 decrement, descending
递降因子 degradation factor
递阶控制 control hierarchy, hierarchical control
递升 ascending
递升排序 ascending sort
递增 increment

第 第一 first, primary, foremost 第一产业 primary industry 第一流 first-rate, first-class, top-notch
第二代计算机 second generation computer
第二范式 second normal form {2NF}
第三范式 third normal form {3NF}
第四代语言 fourth generation language {4GL}
第四范式 fourth normal form {4NF}
第五代计算机 fifth-generation computer
第五范式 fifth normal form {5NF}
第一范式 first normal form {1NF}
第一引导 first boot

缔 缔结 conclude, establish 缔造 found, create 缔造者 founder

碲 tellurium (Te)

【diān】

颠 top, summit 颠簸 jolt, bump, toss; turbulence, roughness 颠倒 inverse, reverse, overturn, upset

巅 mountain peak

【diǎn】

点 1)（小点）spot, dot 2)（液滴）drop 3)（小数点）decimal point, point 4)（地点或起点）place, point ◇沸点 boiling point 5)（钟点）o'clock 点滴 a bit, spot, droplet 点火 ① (把火点着) burn, light a fire, light-up, kindle ② 〈机械〉(起动) ignition, firing 点名册 roll book, roll 点燃 light, kindle, ignite, inflame 点数 check the number, count 点子 ① spot, dot ② key, point, idea
点大小 dot size
点一点连接 point to point connection
点一点协议 point to point protocol {PPP}
点对 dot pair, dotted pair
点对点隧道协议 point to point tunneling protocol {PPTP}
点对多点连接 point to multipoint connection {PMP}
点割集 vertex cut set
点积 scalar product
点距 dot pitch
点命令 dot command
点模式 dot pattern
点式穿孔机 spot punch
点(阵)式打印机 dot printer

点式显示 point-mode display
点速度 dot speed
点提示符 dot prompt
点图 point diagram, dot chart, point chart
点位图 bit mapped image
点文件 dot file
点阵 dot matrix, wire matrix
点阵打印机 dot matrix printer
点阵格式 dot matrix format
点阵网络 lattice network
点阵显示 dot matrix display
点阵字符发生器 dot matrix character generator

典 law, standard 典范 model, example 典礼 ceremony, celebration 典型 typical case, typical example, model, type, representative
典型抽样 representative sampling
典型控制 classical control
典型试验 type test
典型问题 typical problem

碘 iodine (I)

【diàn】

电 electricity 电报 telegram, cable 电冰箱 refrigerator, freezer 电池 cell, battery 电灯 electric lamp, electric light 电动机 motor 电风扇 electric fan 电费 charges for electricity 电话 telephone, phone ◇长途电话 trunk call, long distance call // 公用电话 public telephone, pay telephone // 市内电话 local call 电话簿 telephone directory, telephone book 电话分机 extension (telephone) 电话号码 telephone number 电话机 telephone (set) 电话接线员 telephone operator, switchboard operator 电话局 telephone office, telephone station 电话总机 central exchange 电力 electric power, power 电脑 computer, electronic brain 电钮 push button 电器 electrical equipment 电视 television (TV), radiovision 电视播送 telecast, televise 电视电话 video telephone, videophone 电视台 television station 电台 ① transmitter, receiver, transceiver ② broad-casting station, radio station 电梯 (electric) elevator, (electric) lift 电线 wire 电压 voltage 电影 film, movie ◇宽银幕电影 wide-screen film // 立体电影 stereoscopic film // 电影院 cinema, movie (house) 电子 electron
电报传真机 telewriter
电报电路 telegraph circuit
电波测量 electrical wave measurement
电传 radio teletype {RTTY}
电传打印机 teleprinter {TTY}
电传打字机[设备] teletype {TTY}
电传机接口 teleprinter interface
电传文本 teletext
电磁波 electromagnetic wave
电磁场 electromagnetic field
电磁辐射 electromagnetic radiation
电磁干扰 electromagnetic interference {EMI}
电磁环境 electromagnetic environment

电磁兼容性 electromagnetic compatibility {EMC}
电动会计机 electric accounting machine {EAM}
电动势 electromotive force {EMF}
电感 inductance
电感器 inductor
电光器件 electro-optic
电光神经元计算机 electro-optic neural computer
电光效应 electro-optic effect
电荷 charge
电荷耦合器件 charge-coupled device {CCD}
电话拨号控制 dial-up control
电话传真 telefacsimile
电话代码 telephone code
电话购物 telemarketing
电话会议 telecon
电话机 teleset
电话教学 telelecture
电话网络 telephone network
电话学 telephony
电话银行 telephone bank, call bank
电机 electric machine
电可编程序只读存储器 electrically programmable ROM {EPROM}
电可擦除只读存储器 electrically erasable ROM {EEROM}
电可改写只读存储器 electrically alterable ROM {EAROM}
电缆 cable, harness
电缆测试 cable test
电缆电视 cable television {CATV}
电缆调制解调器 cable modem
电缆干扰 cable noise
电缆接头 cable joint
电缆连接器 cable connector
电缆匹配器 cable matcher
电缆套管 cable jacket
电缆网 cable network
电缆用具套 cable harness jacket
电缆终端网络 cable termination network
电力电缆 power cable
电力线 power line
电流 current
电流开关 current switch
电流开关逻辑电路 current mode logic {CML}
电流密度 current density
电流探头 current probe
电流源 current source
电流重合法 coincident-current selection
电路 circuit
电路板 board, circuit board
电路保护 circuit protection
电路参数 circuit parameter
电路测试器 circuit tester
电路插件板 circuit card
电路设计 circuit design
电路图 electrical schematic
电脑病毒 virus
电脑犯罪 computer crime
电脑黑客 hacker
电脑恐惧症 cyberphobia
电平 level
电平补偿器 level compensator
电平相关扫描设计(法) level-sensitive scan design {LSSD}
电气工程 electric engineering
电气与电子工程师学会 Institute of Electronic and Electrical Engineering {IEEE}
电桥 bridge
电容 capacity, capacitance
电势 (electric) potential
电视点播 video on demand {VOD}

电视[传真,可视]电话 videophone
电视电缆 television cable
电视会议 video conference, videoconferencing
电视书刊 teletext
电视图像 video
电视网 television network
电视[视频]文本 videotex
电视许可证 television license
电视影院 telecine
电视邮件 video mail
电视[电子]游戏 video game
电网继电器 network relay
电位 (electric) potential
电位差 potential difference
电位图 potential diagram
电文 text
电信 telecommunication, telecom
电信购物 teleshopping
电信会议 teleconference
电信线路 telecommunication line
电信营销 telemarketing
电压电平 voltage level
电压馈送 voltage feed
电压跳跃 voltage jump
电源 power supply, power source, power
电源保护系统 power supply protection system
电源测试 power supply test
电源电缆 power cord
电源管理 power management
电源切断 power dump
电源适配器 power adapter
电源系统 power (supply) system
电源线 power line
电子百科全书 electronic encyclopedia
电子报纸 electronic newspaper(s), telenewspaper
电子笔 electronic pen/stylus
电子表格软件包 electronic spreadsheet package
电子布告栏 bulletin board system {BBS}
电子测量 electron measurement
电子产品 electronic product
电子秤 electronic scales
电子出版系统 electronic publishing (system) {EPS}
电子电路 electronic circuit
电子白板 electronic whiteboard
电子服务提供 electronic service delivery
电子工程 electronic engineering
电子工业联合会 Electronics Industry Association {EIA}
电子工业协会 Electronic Industries Association {EIA}
电子购物 electronic shopping
电子管 electron tube, electronic tube
电子函件[邮件] electronic mail(ling) {E-mail}
电子黑板 electronic blackboard
电子会议系统 electronic conference system
电子汇款 electronic funds transfer {EFT}
电子货币 electronic money, cybercash, digital cash, electronic cash
电子计算机 electronic computer
电子计算器 electronic calculator
电子交换系统 electronic switching system {ESS}
电子开关 electronic switch
电子开关系统 electronic switching system {ESS}
电子器件 electron device, electronic device
电子枪 electron gun

电子收款机 electronic cash register {ECR}
电子书 dynabook
电子书刊 electronic journal
电子书写 electronic writing
电子束 electron beam (=E beam)
电子数据处理 electronic data processing {EDP}
电子数据交换 electronic data exchange, electronic data interchange {EDI}
电子数据系统 electronic data system {EDS}
电子数字积分计算机 electronic numerical integrator and calculator {ENIAC}
电子探测 electron detection
电子通报 electronic bulletin board
电子图书 electronic book
电子图书馆 electronic library
电子文本 hypertext
电子文档 electronic document
电子现金 electronic cash
电子信息系统 electronic message system
电子学 electronics
电子音乐 electronic music
电子银行 electronic bank
电子邮箱 electronic mailbox
电子邮政 electronic post
电子语音识别 electronic speech recognition
电子杂志 electronic journal
电子支付 electronic payment
电子支票 electronic check
电子转换系统 electronic switching system {ESS}
电子转帐 electronic transfer account
电子资金转账 electronic funds transfer {EFT}
电子自动交换机 electronic automatic exchange {EAX}
电子字典 electronic dictionary
电阻-电阻耦合晶体管逻辑(电路) resistor-transistor logic {RTL}

店 shop, store 店员 shop assistant, salesman or saleswoman 店主 shop-keeper, storekeeper

垫 pad, cushion, mat

奠 奠定 establish, settle 奠基 lay a foundation

【diāo】

雕 雕刻 carve, engrave, cut 雕塑 sculpture 雕像 statue

【diào】

吊 (悬挂)hang, suspend 吊车 crane 吊物 lift up or let down with a rope, etc. 吊销 revoke, withdraw

调 另见【tiáo】
1)(乐调)key 2)(声调)tone, tune 调拨 allocate and transfer (goods or funds), allot 调查 investigate, inquire into, look into, survey 调查报告 findings report 调查人 investigator, inquirer 调查提纲 outline for investigation, questionnaire 调动 transfer, shift, move 调度 dispatch (trains, buses etc.), manage, control, schedule ◇生产调度 production management 调度员 dispatcher, controller 调换 exchange, change, swap 调配 allocate, deploy 调用 transfer (a per-

son), reallocate (goods) 调子 ①(曲调)tune, melody ②(论调)tone (of speech)
调查研究 investigation
调度表 dispatch list, dispatching list
调度策略 dispatch strategy, scheduling strategy
调度程序 scheduler program, scheduler, dispatcher
调度程序工作区 scheduler work area {SWA}
调度队列 scheduling queue
调度规则 scheduling discipline/rule
调度开销 scheduling overhead
调度控制表 dispatcher control table {DCT}
调度器 dispatcher
调度器排队 dispatcher queue
调度任务 scheduler task
调度算法 dispatch(ing) algorithm, scheduling algorithm
调度网络 dispatch network
调度问题 scheduling problem
调度优先级 dispatching/scheduling priority
调度员 dispatcher
调度[发送]中心 dispatching center
调度周期 dispatching cycle
调度资源 scheduling resource
调度作业 schedule job
调分页区 paging area
调入 call in
调入地址 call address
调入[调用]语句 call statement
调入指令 call instruction
调页装置 paging device
调页组 clustering
调用变元 calling argument
调用程序 call program, caller, calling program
调用级 call level
调用块 invoking block
调用[呼叫]请求 call request {CRQ}
调用入口 call entry
调用序列 call sequence, calling sequence

掉 1)(落)fall, drop, shed, come off 2)(遗失)lose, be missing
掉电 power down, power failure, power-fail, ac dump

【diē】

跌 fail, drop 跌价 go down in price; fall, drop in price
跌落 fall, drop

【dié】

迭 迭次 repeatedly, again and again
迭代 iterate, iteration
迭代布局算法 iterative placement algorithm
迭代步 iterative step
迭代操作 iterative operation
迭代插值法 iterated interpolation method
迭代程序 iterative program, iterator, iterative routine
迭代对策 iterated game
迭代法 iterative method, method of iteration, process of iteration
迭代过程 iterative process
迭代计算 iterative computation
迭代器 iterator
迭代算法 iteration algorithm
迭代图 iteration diagram
迭代循环 iteration loop
迭代因子 iteration factor
迭代语句 iterative statement
迭代阵列 iterative array

迭代指令 iterative instruction

叠 1)(重叠)pile up, repeat 2)(折叠)fold 叠加 overlap, overlay, superpose, superimpose 叠式 superimpose, superpose
叠加器 superimposer
叠加原理 principle of superposition, superposition principle
叠式图表 stacked graph
叠式组件 stacked wafer module

【dīng】

丁 (第四)fourth 丁等 the fourth grade, grade D 丁字 T-shaped 丁字尺 T-square

钉 nail, tack

酊 (酊剂)tincture

【dǐng】

顶 顶点 apex, zenith 顶端 peak, top, head, crown 顶峰 peak, summit, pinnacle 顶替 take the place of, substitute, replace 顶住 push up, prop up 顶撞 retort, talk back
顶部 top, upper curtate
顶层文档 top document
顶端菜单 top menu
顶端节点 top node
顶行 top row

【dìng】

订 1)(制订)conclude, draw up, agree on 2)(预定)subscribe to, book, order 订单 order for goods, order form
订费 subscription (rate) 订购、订货 order (goods), place an order for goods, book, subcribe 订户 subscriber 订立 conclude, make ◇订立合同 conclude a contract 订阅 subscribe to
订单号 order number
订货合同 purchase contract
订正 revision

定 1)(稳定)calm, stable 2)(决定)decide, fix, set ◇定方针 decide on a policy 3)(已确定的)fixed, settled, established 4)(预定)subscribe to, book (seats, tickets, etc.), order 定额 quota, norm, quantum, ration ◇生产定额 production quota 定稿 finalize (a manuscript, test, etc.); final version or text 定货 order goods, place an order for goods 定货单 order form 定价 fix a price 定金 deposit 定局 foregone conclusion, inevitable outcome 定论 final conclusion 定名 name, denominate 定期 ①(定下日期)fix a date ②(有一定期限的)regular, at regular intervals, periodical 定期付款 payment on terms 定期交货 delivery on term 定期存款 fixed deposit, time deposit **定期刊物** periodical (publication) 定向 directional 定性 ① determine the nature ② determine the chemical composition of a substance 定义 definition
定标 calibrate, scale, scaling, calibration
定标操作 scale operation
定标电路 scaling circuit

定步 pacing
定步参数 pacing parameter
定步窗口 pacing window
定步响应 pacing response
定长 fixed-length
定长变量 fixed-length variable
定长操作 fixed-length operation
定长串 fixed-length string
定长符号 fixed-length symbol
定长记录 fixed length record, fixed-size record
定长块 fixed-length block
定长数据 fixed-length data
定长行 fixed-length string
定点 fixed decimal, fixed-point
定点表示法 fixed-point representation
定点部分 fixed-point part
定点常数 fixed-point constant
定点格式 fixed-point format
定点计算 fixed-point calculation
定点计算机 fixed-point computer
定点数 fixed-point number, fixed-point numeral
定点小数 fractional fixed point
定点溢出 fixed overflow
定点运算 fixed-point calculation/operation
定界 delimit
定界标识符 delimited identifier
定界符 delimiter, delimiting character
定界符表 delimiter table
定界符行 delimiter line
定界记号 delimiter token
定界语句 delimiter statement
定界元素 delimiter element
定界字符 delimiting character
定理 axiom, theorem
定理证明 theorem proving
定量 quantify

定量分析方法 quantitative analysis method
定律 law, rule
定时 clocking, timing
定时程序 timer routine, timing routine
定时错误 timing error
定时电路 time circuit, timing circuit, timer circuit
定时发生器 timing generator
定时[控时]开关 time switch
定时脉冲 timing pulse, time control pulse, commutator pulse
定时门 time gate
定时时钟 time clock, timing clock
定时图 timing diagram
定时信号 clocked signal, timing signals
定时已过 timing out
定时中断 timer interruption
定位板 positioning board
定位操作 positioning operation
定位方式 locate mode, location mode
定位符号 position mark
定位码 alignment code, position code
定位器 detent, localizer, locator, mouse, positioning device
定位系统 positioning system
定位装置 locator device, positioner
定相 phasing
定向器 direction finder {DF}
定向搜索 beam search
定性分析 qualitative analysis
定义变量 defined variable
定义标量 defining scalar
定义表 define table, definition table
定义部分 definitional part

dìng 锭 diū 丢 铥 dōng 东冬氡 dǒng 董懂 dòng 动

定义部件 definition component
定义常数 define constant
定义点 define point, definition point
定义范围 defining range
定义方法 define method
定义数组 defined array
定义语句 define statement, definition statement
定义域 domain
定义状态 definition status
定义字 defined word
定义字节 define byte
定制 customize
定制菜单 custom menu
定制插件 custom card
定制程序 custom program
定制工具 customized tool
定制模式 customized pattern
定制软件 customized software
定制系统 custom system

锭 ingot; 〈纺织〉spindle

【diū】
丢 (扔)throw, cast, toss 丢失 lose, mislay
丢"1" drop-out
"丢失"符 throw-away character
丢失信息 drop-out

铥 thulium (Tm)

【dōng】
东 east 东方 ①(东)east ②(指亚洲)the East, the Orient 东南 southeast 东南亚 Southeast Asia 东欧 Eastern Europe 东西 thing, goods

冬 winter

氡 radon (Rn), niton (Nt)

【dǒng】
董 董事 director, trustee 董事会 ①(企业的)board of directors ②(学校等的)board of trustees 董事长 chairman of the board

懂 understand, know

【dòng】
动 1)(运动)move 2)(行动)act 3)(改动)change 4)(触动)touch, arouse, stir up 动工 begin construction, start working 动机 motive, intention 动力 ① motive power, power ② motive force, impetus 动手 start work, get to work 动态 dynamic state, dynamic motion, trend 动物 animal 动向 trend, tendency 动议 motion 动用 put to use, employ, draw on 动作 movement, motion, action
动笔 pen-on
动臂机构 actuator
动画 animate, animation, picture animation
动画片 cartoon
动画影片方式 comic-strip oriented mode
动画制作成套设备 animation kit
动画制作软件 animation software
动画制作语言 animation language
动态安装库 dynamic load libraries {DLL}
动态保护 dynamic protection
动态变量 dynamic variable
动态程序结构 dynamic program structure

动态程序再定位 dynamic program relocation
动态处理 dynamic handling
动态存储分配 dynamic memory allocation, dynamic storage allocation
动态存储管理 dynamic memory management
动态MOS存储器 dynamic MOS memory
动态存储器 dynamic storage
动态存储器接口 dynamic memory interface {DMI}
动态存储器刷新 dynamic memory refresh
动态存取 dynamic access
动态打印管理 dynamic print management
动态登录 dynamic log
动态地址变换[转换] dynamic address translation {DAT}
动态地址再定位 dynamic address relocation
动态调度 dynamic dispatching, dynamic scheduling
动态调试程序 dynamic debugging routine
动态多功能流水线 dynamic multifunctional pipeline
动态范围 dynamic range
动态访问 dynamic access
动态分配 dynamic assignment, runtime allocation
动态分区 dynamic partition
动态分析 dynamic analysis
动态规划 dynamic programming {DP}
动态控制 dynamic control
动态连接 dynamic connection, dynamic link(ing)
动态连接库 dynamic link library {DLL}
动态链接 dynamic link
动态模型 dynamic model {DYNAMO}
动态设备配置 dynamic device reconfiguration {DDR}
动态设计方法 dynamic design approach
动态树 dynamical tree
动态数据 dynamic data
动态数据交换 dynamic data exchange {DDE}
动态数据模式 dynamic data schema
动态数学模型 dynamic mathematical models
动态刷新 dynamic refresh
动态瞬时页池管理 dynamic transient pool management {DTPM}
动态瞬时页池区 dynamic transient pool area {DTPA}
动态搜索算法 dynamic search algorithm
动态算法 dynamic algorithm
动态特性 dynamic behavio(u)r, dynamic characteristic
动态图像 dynamic image
动态网络收集 dynamic network collection {DNC}
动态网页 active server page {ASP}
动态响应 dynamic response
动态选路 dynamic routing
动态循环 dynamic loop
动态页池块 dynamic pool block {DPB}
动态映射 dynamic mapping
动态再定位 dynamic relocation
动态阵列 dynamic array
动态重复 dynamic replication
动态主机配置协议 dynamic host configuration protocol {DHCP}
动态资源分配 dynamic resource allocation
动态资源管理 dynamic re-

dòng 冻洞 dǒu 抖陡 dòu 斗逗 dū 都督 dú 毒独

source management
动态自适应寻径 dynamic adaption routing
动态总线分配 dynamic bus allocation
动态组 dynamic set
动态组合块 dynamic pool block {DPB}
动作表 action list, action schedule, action table
动作[触发]脉冲 action pulse
动作条 action bar
动作语句 action statement, imperative statement
动作周期 action cycle

冻 freeze 冻结 freeze, congeal
冻结窗口 window freeze
冻结帧 freeze-frame
冻结状态 freeze mode

洞 hole, cavity 洞察 see clearly, have an insight into

【dǒu】

抖 抖动 shake, vibrate, tremble, dither, jitter
抖动矩阵 dither matrix

陡 steep, sharp
陡度 steepness
陡前沿脉冲 steep pulse

【dòu】

斗 (对打)fight 斗争 struggle against, fight, combat

逗 逗号 comma "," 逗留 stay, stop
逗号符号 comma symbol

【dū】

都 1)(首都)capital 2)(大城市)big city, metropolis

督 督促 supervise and urge

【dú】

毒 (有毒的)poisonous, noxious, toxic 毒品 narcotic drugs, narcotics 毒物 poison, toxin ◇服毒 take poison 毒性 toxicity, poisonousness

独 only, single 独创 original (unique) creation 独家代理 sole agency 独力 by one's own efforts, on one's own 独立 stand-alone, independent, self-supporting 独特 unique, distinctive, unusual 独占 have sth all to oneself, monopolize 独资企业 enterprises with exclusive investment, enterprises solely owned by sb 独自 alone, by oneself
独立操作 independent operation
独立程序 stand-alone program
独立的 free-standing, independent
独立进程 independent process
独立例程 independent routine
独立软件供应商 independent software vendor {ISV}
独立式 self contained type
独立事件 independent event
独立数据项 independent data item
独立文件 unique file
独立项 independent entry, noncontiguous item
独立信号单元 alone signal unit {ASU}
独立性 independence

独立性检查 independent check
独立性检验 independence test
独立元 independent entry

读 read, read aloud **读书** ①(看书)read, study ②(上学)attend school **读物** reading matter, reading material
读者 reader
读 read {R}
读保护的 read-protected
读被提交 read committed
读标记 mark-sense, read flag
读操作 read operation
读程序 reader
读出 sensing, sense, reading, read out, playback
读出磁头 magnetic read head
读出电路 sense circuit
读出放大器 read amplifier, sense amplifier
读出码 sense code
读出脉冲 read pulse
读出器 reader unit, sensor
读出时间 read time, read-out time
读出数据 sense data
读出速度 reading speed, reading rate, reading velocity
读出头 read head
读出位 sense bit
读出误差 read-out error
读出线 sense line, sensor line
读出响应 sense response
读出信号 sense signal
读出装置 read-out device
读出字节 sense byte
读出总线 read bus
读窗口 reading window
读错误 read error
读访问类型 read access type
读后写 write after read
读恢复 read recovery
读脉冲 read pulse

读请求 read request
读驱动器 read driver
读取 fetch, read {R}
读取部件 fetch unit
读取策略 fetch policy
读取程序 fetch program
读取过程 fetch process
读取权 read rights
读入读出 read-in/read-out
读入原语 read primitive
读入装置 reader
读数据选通 read data strobe {RDS}
读通路 read path
读位 read bit
读校验 read verify
读写 read/write {R/W, RW, read-write}
读写保护 read/write protection
读写操作 read/write operation
读写磁头 magnetic read/write head, read/write head, write/read head
读写存储器 read/write memory {RWM}
读写存取方式 read/write access mode
读写等待时间 read/write waiting time
读写访问方式 read/write access mode
读写兼用磁头 (magnetic) read/write compatible head
读写器 reader-writer
读写头 read/write head
读写校验 R/W check
读信号 read signal
读指针 read pointer
读周期 read cycle time

【dǔ】

堵 堵塞 stop up, block up, plug, close, lock ◇交通堵塞 traffic jam

【dù】

杜 prevent 杜绝 stop, put an end to 杜撰 fabricate, make up

妒 妒忌 be jealous of, be envious of, envy

度 1)(程度) degree, extent 2)(千瓦小时) kilowatt-hour (kwh) 3)(限度) limit 度过 spend, pass

渡 1)(通过) cross (a river, a lake, etc.) 2)(运载过河) ferry (people, goods, etc.) across 渡过 tide over, pull through 渡越 transit

镀 plate, coat, overlay, clad

【duān】

端 1)(开头) beginning 2)(平举) hold sth level with both hands, carry 端部 end, head, tip, extremity, terminal 端正 ① (不歪斜) upright, regular ② (正派) proper, correct ③ (使端正) rectify
端到端 end to end
端到端服务 end to end services
端到端信令 end to end signaling
端到端选路 end to end routing
端点 terminal, endpoint, terminal endpoint, terminal point, terminal vertex, termination point
端端加密 end-to-end encryption
端接线 terminated line
端节点 end node, tip node
端局 end office {EO}
端口 port
端口到端口协议 port-to-port protocol
端口地址 port address
端口共享部件 port sharing unit {PSU}
端口号 port number
端口控制器 port controller
端口宽度 port width
端口令 port number
端口识别器 port identifier
端口数 port number
端口选择 port select
端口组 port group

【duǎn】

短 1)(不长) short, brief 2)(缺少) lack, owe 短处 shortcoming, failing, fault, weakness 短期 short-term 短途 short distance 短小 short and small, short, small 短暂 of short duration; transient, brief, temporal, transitional
短报文 short message
短程 short-haul
短程调度 short-term schedule
短串 short string
短格式 short form, short format
短类型 short type
短路 short circuit, short circuiting
短缩寻址 abbreviated addressing
短消息 small message
短循环 small-size loop
短语 phrase
短指令 short instruction
短指令格式 short instruction format

短周期 short cycle
短转移 short jump
短字 short word

【duàn】

段 〈量词〉section, segment, part 段落 ①(文章的一段) paragraph ②(阶段)phase, stage
(区)段保护 segment protection
段编号 segment number
段编码 segment encode
段编址 segment addressing
段标 segment mark
段标号 segment labeling
段标记 segment mark
段标题 section header
段表 segment table {SGT, ST}
段表表目 segment table entry {STE}
段表长度寄存器 segment table length register {STLR}
段表基址寄存器 segment table base register {STBR}
段表起始地址 segment table origin {STO}
段表入口 segment table entry {STE}
段长度 segment size (length)
段存储器 segment memory
段单元 segment unit
段范围 segment limit
段方式 segment mode, segmented mode
段共享 segment sharing
段管理程序 segment manager
段号 segment number, fragment number {FR-NB}, section number
段级 segment level
段类型 segment type
段名 section/ segment/ paragraph name
段前缀 segment prefix

段式 segmentation
段式程序 program segmentation
段式存储系统 segmented memory system
段式调度 segmentation scheduling
段式管理 segment management
段式系统 segmentation system
段式硬件 segmentation hardware
段头 section header, paragraph head, paragraph header
段映像表 segment map table {SMT}

断 (决断)judge, decide ◇ 当机立断 make a prompt decision 断定 conclude, form a judgment 断断续续 off and on, intermittently 断绝 break off, cut off, sever 断开 break, snap, cut off 断裂 break, fracture, rupture, disrupt, crack 断然 absolutely, flatly, categorically 断言 say with certainty, assert
断点 breakpoint
断点程序 breakpoint program
断点地址 breakpoint address
断点俘获 breakpoint trap
断点寄存器 breakpoint register
断点监视 breakpoint watch
断点开关 breakpoint switch
断点指令 breakpoint instruction
断电 power cut, power down
断电保护 power-off protection
断电后重新启动 dump and restart
断开 cut-off, set-off, switch-off, turn-off, disconnect(ion), release connection

断开方式 break mode, disconnect mode {DM}
断开[释放]节点 release node
断面 section
断面图 cross section, cross sectional view
断线 break, open wire
断言表 assertion list
断言逻辑 assertion logic

【duàn】

锻 forge 锻炼 ①(体育锻炼)take exercise, have physical training ②(磨炼)temper

【duī】

堆 〈量词〉pile, heap, crowd
堆成物 heap, pile, stack
堆积 pile up, heap up, stack
堆叠 heap
堆叠分类 heap sort
堆叠符号 heap symbol
堆栈 stack
堆栈表 stack list
堆栈操作 stack operation
堆栈操作指令 stack operation instruction
堆栈存储器 stack storage
堆栈单元 stack cell
堆栈的底部 bottom of stack
堆栈的指针 pointer to stack
堆栈结构 stack architecture
堆栈控制逻辑 stack control logic
堆栈区 stack area
堆栈上托 stack pop-up
堆栈算法 stack algorithm
堆栈下推 stack push-down
堆栈指示符 stack indicator
堆栈自动机 stack automata, stack automaton {SA}
堆阵 heap

【duì】

队 队伍 team, group 队员 team member 队长 captain, group leader, team leader
队列 queue
队列表 queue list
队列管理 queue management
队列请求 queue request
队列深度 queue depth
队列元(素) queue element {QE}

对 1)〈量词〉(双)pair, couple 2)(朝着)be directed at 3)(对面的)opposite 4)(核对)compare, check, identify 5)(调整)set, adjust 6)(正确)right, correct 对比 contrast, balance 对不起 pardon me, I beg your pardon 对答 answer, reply 对待 treat, approach, handle, cope with 对得起 not let sb down, treat sb fairly, be worthy of 对等 reciprocity, equity, balance 对调 exchange, swap 对方 the other side, the other party, the opposite side 对付 deal with, cope with, tackle 对抗 ①(对立)confrontation ②(抵抗)oppose, counteract 对立 oppose, set sth against; contradictory 对立面 opposite, antithesis 对面 ①(对过)opposite ②(正前方)right in front ③(面对面)face to face 对内 internal, domestic; at home 对手 ①opponent, adversary ②match, equal 对外 external, foreign; abroad 对外关系 external relations, foreign relations 对外经济贸易部 Ministry of Foreign Economics and Trade 对外开放 opening to the outside

world 对外贸易 foreign trade
对象 target, object 对消 offset, cancel each other out; eliminate 对应 corresponding, homologous 对于 toward 对照 contrast, compare 对折 50% discount, half price
对比度 contrast ratio, contrast
对比度操纵 contrast manipulation
对比度控制 contrast control
对比灵敏度 contrast sensitivity
对比图 area chart
对策 game, gaming
对策仿真 gaming simulation
对策论 game theory
对策模拟 game simulation, gaming simulation
对策树 game tree
对称 balanced, homology, symmetry
对称比赛 symmetric game
对称闭包 symmetric closure
对称变换 symmetric transformation
对称表 symmetric list, symmetrical list
对称部分 symmetric part
对称差分 symmetric difference
对称处理机 symmetric processor
对称多处理机 symmetric multiprocessor
对称多项式 symmetrical polynomial
对称关系 symmetric relation
对称合并 balanced merge
对称加密 symmetric cryptography
对称矩阵 symmetric matrix
对称联结 symmetric junction
对称链表 symmetric linked list
对称群 symmetric group
对称态 symmetrical state
对称图 symmetric graph
对称线性规划 symmetric linear programming
对等(通信) peer to peer
对等(层)实体 peer entities
对等网络 per-to-per network
对分查找 binary chop
对分查找树 binary search tree
对分法 bisection method, method of bisection
对分搜索 binary search
对合 involution
对合矩阵 involuntory matrix
对话 conversation, dialog (=dialogue), session, talk
对话层 dialog layer
对话窗口 dialog window
对话端 session end
对话方式 interactive mode
对话[会话]控制 session control {SC}
对话控制记录 conversation control record {CCR}, conversational control record
对话框 dialog box
对话命令 session command
对话日期 session date
对话式程序设计系统 conversational programming system {CPS}
对话式图解 interactive graphics {IG}
对话式终端 talking terminal
对话系统 interactive system
对讲电话装置 intercommunication
对角矩阵 diagonal matrix
对角线 diagonal
对角元素 diagonal element
对阶 match exponents, matching of exponents
对抗 confrontation
对抗策略 counterplot

对抗措施 countermove
对抗对策 countermeasure
对抗计划 counter-planning
对抗记号 confrontation token
对抗能力 counterforce
对抗手段 countermove
对抗性 antagonicity
对抗性对策 antagonism game
对立 contradictory
对立事件 contrary event
对偶 dual
对偶变量 dual variable
对偶操作 dual operation
对偶超图 dual hypergraph
对偶定理 dual(ity) theorem
对偶图 dual graph
对偶网络 dual mesh, dual network
对偶系统 dual system
对偶性 duality, duality property
对偶原理 duality principle, principle of duality
对齐 align, alignment, justified
对齐规则 alignment rule
对数 log (=logarithm)
对数变换 logarithmic transformation
对数表 logarithmic table
对数螺线 logistic spiral
对数分析 logit analysis
对数函数 logarithmic function
对数曲线 log curve, logistic curve
对数正态分布 logarithmic normal distribution, log-normal distribution
对象标识 object identity
对象表 object list
对象表示 object representation
对象窗口 object window
对象定义 object definition
对象动作 object-action
对象分解 object decomposition
对象分配 object distribution
对象服务 object service
对象管理程序[管理器] object manager
对象管理集团[管理组] object management group {OMG}
对象管理体系结构 object management architecture {OMA}
对象管理组 object management group {OMG}
对象句柄 object handle
对象空间 object space
对象(分)类 object class
对象类型 object type
对象历史模型 object history model
对象链接与嵌入 object linking and embedding {OLE}
对象领域 object domain
对象模块 object module
对象模型 object model
对象目录对象 object directory object
对象内容系统结构 object content architecture {OCA}
对象请求代理 object request broker {ORB}
对象属性 object attribute
对象数据管理器 object data manager {ODM}
对象数据库 object database
对象数据模型 object data model {ODM}
对象数据语言 object data language {ODL}
对象协议模型 object protocol model
对象用户 object user
对象语言 object language
对象再用[复用] object reuse
对映信令 antipodal signaling
对照表 reference listing
对照法 contrast

duì 兑 dūn 吨敦 dùn 钝顿遁 duō 多

对准 alignment, align
对准标记 alignment/ registration marks
对准标线 alignment target
对准网络 alignment network

【duì】

兑 exchange, convert 兑现 cash (a cheque, etc.) 兑换 exchange, convert

【dūn】

吨 ton (t.) 吨位 tonnage, shipping ton

敦 敦促 urge, press 敦请 earnestly invite, earnestly request

【dùn】

钝 (不锋利) blunt, dull, obtuse, pointless

顿 1)(停顿) pause 2)(安顿) arrange, settle 3)(跺脚) stamp 顿时 immediately, at once

遁 escape, flee, fly

【duō】

多 1)(数量大) many, much, more 2)(较多) more than the original figure 3)(过分的) excessive, too much 多半 ① (大半) the great part, most ② (大概) probably, most likely 多边 multilateral 多变 changeable, changeful, varied 多次 many times, time and again, repeatedly, on many occasions 多方 in many ways, in every way 多方面 many-sided; in many ways 多久 how long 多亏 thanks to 多面手 a many-sided person, a versatile person 多少 ①(数量大小) number, amount ②(或多或少) somewhat, more or less, to some extent ③(问数量) how many, how much 多数 majority, most 多疑 suspicious 多余 unnecessary, surplus, redundant 多种多样 varied, manifold
多版本 multiversion {MV}
多报文方式 multiple message mode
多倍长 multiple length
多倍字长精度 multiple precision
多变量 multivariate
多变量分析 multivariate analysis
多变性 polytrope
多遍程序 multiple pass program
多遍打印 multiple-pass printing
多遍翻译 multipass translation
多遍排序 multipass sort
多标量 multiscalar
多表 multilist
多表处理器 multilist processor
多表组织[结构] multilist organization
多播地址识别服务器 multicast address resolution server {Mars}
多播主干 multicast backBONE {MBONE}
多步法 multistage method, multistep method
多步分类 polynomial sort
多步公式 multistep formula
多步公式 polyphase merging
多步控制 multistep control
多步任务 multistep task

多操作 multioperation
多层 multilayer, polylaminate
多层布线 multilayer metallization
多层结构 multilayer structure
多层芯片 superlattice
多层印制板 multilayer board, multilayer printed circuit board
多重处理系统 multiprocessing system {MPS}
多重符合 multiple coincidence
多重积分 multiple integral
多重模块访问 multiple module access
多重目标函数 multiple objectives
多重目录表 multiple directory
多重判定(决策) multiple decision
多重嵌套 multinest
多重请求 multiple request
多重任务 multitask
多重索引 cumulative index
多重图 multigraph, multiple graph, polygraph
多重文本 multiple context
多重文件界面 multiple document interface {MDI}
多重线索 multiple thread
多重相关 multiple correlation
多重响应 multiple response
多重校验 multiple check
多重效果 multiple effect
多重协调 multiple coordination
多重中断请求 multiple request
多重中断系统 multiple interrupt system
多处访问 multiaccess
多处理机[器] multiprocessor, polyprocessor
多处理机网 polyprocessor reticulum {PPR}
多处理机系统 multiprocessing system {MPS}, multiprocessor system
多窗口 multiwindow
多次编译程序 multipass compiler
多存取控制器 multiaccess controller {MAC}
多单元 polycell
多单元消息 multiunit message {MUM}
多道 multiple tracks
多道程序 multiprogram
多道程序分时系统 multiprogrammed time-sharing system
多道程序设计 multiple programming, multiprogramming, multirunning
多道程序(设计)系统 multiprogramming system {MPS}
多道处理 multiprocessing
多道磁头 multitrack head
多道功能 multitrack function
多道作业 multijob
多地址 multiaddress, multiple address
多地址报文 multiple address message
多地址空间 multiple address space
多地址指令 multiaddress instruction, multiple address instruction
多点 multidrop
多点传播服务 multicast server
多点传输 multicast communication
多点传送 multileaving
多点广播地址 multicast address
多点接口 multipoint interface
多点结构 multipoint configuration
多点链路 multipoint link

多点拓扑 multidrop topology
多点网络 multidrop network
多端的 multitailed
多端点连接 multiendpoint connection
多端[多级]开关 multipole switch
多端口存储器 multiport memory
多端口共享 multiple port sharing {MPS}
多端连接 multitail connection
多端网络 multiterminal network
多端用户 multiple end-user
多对多关系 many-many relationship
多对多通信 many-to-many communication
多对一 several-for-one, many-one, many-to-one
多对一联系 many to one relationship
多方法 multimethod
多方式通信 multiway communications
多分区支持 multiple partition support {MPS}
多格式方式 forms mode
多格式设计 forms design
多格式输入 forms input
多格式重叠 forms overlay
多工 multiplex {MUX}, multiplexing
多功能(插件)板 multifunction board
多功能流水线 multifunctional pipeline
多功能阅读机 multifunction reader
多故障 multiple faults
多关联处理机 multiassociative processor {MAP}
多光谱扫描器 multispectral scanner {MSS}
多环 polycyclic
多回路控制系统 multiloop control system
多基地主机 multihomed host
多机系统 multiple system
多机种数据库 heterogeneous database
多机种网络 heterogeneous network
多级 multiple level, multiple order, multistage
多级编址 multilevel addressing
多级层次体系 multilevel hierarchy system
多级存储系统 hierarchical/multilevel memory system
多级地址 multilevel address
多级法 multistage method
多级互连网络 multistage interconnection network
多级决策 multidecision
多级控制 control hierarchy, multilevel control
多级链路 multilink
多级索引 multilevel index
多级网络 multistage network
多级寻址 multilevel system
多计算机通信 multicomputer communication
多继承性 multiple inheritance {MI}
多价 polyvalent
多价数 polyvalent number
多阶 n-order
多阶段 multistage, many stages, multiphase
多节点 multinode
多卷分类 multireel sorting
多卷文件 multivolume file
多客户系统 multiclient system
多控制台支持 multiple console support {MCS}
多链表 multilinked list

多链路点对点协议 multilink point to point protocol {MLPPP}
多链路接口驱动器 multiple link interface driver
多路 multipath, multiplexing, multipling
多路操作 multipled operation, multiplexed operation
多路传输 multiplex {MUX}, multiplexing
多路传送 multiplexer {MUX}
多路传送方式 multiplex mode
多路存取 multiaccess
多路存取控制器 multiaccess controller {MAC}
多路复用 multiplexed
多路复用操作 multiplex operation
多路复用方式 multiplex mode
多路复用接口 multiplex interface
多路复用链路 multiplex link
多路复用设备 multiplexed device
多路径 multiple path
多路开关 multiplexer {MUX}
多路入口 multientry
多路信道 multiplex {MUX}
多路由选择 multiple routing
多路终端 multiplex terminal
多媒体 multimedia
多媒体编辑工具 multimedia editing tool
多媒体标题 multimedia title
多媒体窗口 multimedia window
多媒体方法 multimedia scheme
多媒体工具包 multimedia toolset
多媒体环境 multimedia environment
多媒体计算(技术) multimedia computing
多媒体计算机 multimedia computer
多媒体教学(教材) multimedia tutorial
多媒体卡 multimedia card
多媒体课件 multimedia courseware
多媒体路由器 multimedia router
多媒体平台 multimedia platform
多媒体软件 multimedia software
多媒体视频 multimedia video
多媒体视频处理器 multimedia video processor {MVP}
多媒体数据库 multimedia database
多媒体数据模型 multimedia data model
多媒体通信 multimedia communication/traffic
多媒体文档 multimedia document
多媒体系统 multimedia system
多媒体信息 multimedia information
多媒体演示系统 multimedia presentation system
多媒体应用程序接口 multimedia application programming interface {MAPI}
多媒体用户界面 multimedia user interface
多媒体资料 multimedia document
多模板 multitemplate
多模光纤 multimode (optical) fiber
多目标 multiple objective
多目标规划 multi-objective programming
多表链 multilist chain
多片电路 multichip circuit
多频(率)接收机 multifrequency

receiver {MFR}
多平台 multiplatform
多区操作 multiregion operation {MRO}
多任务操作系统 multiple task operating system
多任务处理 multitasking
多色图形阵列 multi-color graphics array {MCGA}
多扇区 multisector
多视端口 multiview port
多视区 multiple viewports
多数据库系统 multidatabase system {MDBS}
多数逻辑 majority logic
多数元件 majority element
多数原则 majority principle
多态性 polymorphism
多条图 multiple bar chart
多通道 multichannel
多微处理器 multi-microprocessor
多维 many-dimensions
多维存取存储器 multidimensional access memory
多维数据库 dimension database
多维数组 multidimensional array
多维下标 multidimensional subscript
多维最优控制 multidimensional optimal control
多位谓词 n-place predicate
多系统 multisystem
多系统环境 multisystem environment
多纤维光缆 multifiber cable
多线程操作系统 multithreaded operating system
多线程技术 multithreading
多线索结构 multithread architecture
多相 multiphase, polyphase
多相分类 polyphase sort

多项式 polynomial, multinomial
多项式定理 multinomial theorem
多项式空间 polynomial space
多项式系数 multinomial coefficient
多协议标签交换 multiprotocol label switching {MPLS}
多谐振荡器 astable multivibrator, freerunning multivibrator, multivibrator
多信息文本格式 rich text format {RTF}
多形代码 polymorphic code
多形系统 polymorphic system
多虚拟存储器 multiple virtual storage {MVS}
多义性 ambiguity, multiple meaning, polysemy
多用户 multi-user
多用户虚拟数字线路 multiple virtual line {MVL}
多用户许可证 multiuser license
多用途 multiple use, multipurpose, multi-use
多用途因特网函件扩展 multipurpose internet mail extension {MIME}
多余信号 superfluous signal
多余信息 redundant information, superfluous message
多语言系统 multi-language system
多元分布 multivariate distribution
多元分析 multivariate analysis
多元关系 n-tuple relation
多元样本 multivariate sample
多原件打印 multiple original print {MOP}
多运算 multioperation
多站 multistation
多站点访问单元 multistation access unit {MAU}

多站结构 multistation configuration
多值 multiple value
多值函数 multivalued function
多值逻辑 many-valued logic, multiple value logic, multiple-valued logic {MVL}, multivalue logic
多值依赖 multivalued dependence
多指令单数据流 multiple instruction-single data stream
多指令多数据流 multiple instruction-multiple data stream {MIMD}
多终端编址 multiterminal addressing
多终端存取 multiple terminal access {MTA}
多准则 multiple criteria
多准则决策 multiple criteria decision making {MCDM}
多字 multiword
多字节 multibyte
多字节指令 multiple byte instruction
多字指令 multiple word instruction, multiword instruction
多总线 multibus {MULTIBUS}
多总线结构 multiple bus architecture
多总线系统 multiple bus system
多作业调度 multijob scheduling

【duó】

夺 1)（强取）take by force, seize, grab 2)（争取）contend for, compete for, strive for **夺得** take by force, seize **夺回** recapture, retake, seize back

【duǒ】

躲 躲避 avoid, dodge 躲藏 hide (oneself)

【duò】

剁 chop, cut

垛 pile, stack

舵 rudder, helm

堕 fall, sink 堕入 sink into, lapse into, land oneself in

惰 lazy, indolent
惰性计算 lazy evaluation

E e

【é】

锇 osmium (Os)

额 (规定的数目) a specified number or amount ◇超额 above quota ‖ 贸易额 volume of trade 额定 specified (number or amount), rated, normal, nominal 额头 forehead 额外 supplementary, extra, additional

额定速度 nominal speed, rated speed

额定值 nominal value, rating

额外开销 overhead

【è】

扼 clutch, grip 扼杀 strangle, smother 扼要 to the point

恶 另见【wù】
bad, evil 恶毒 vicious, malicious 恶化 worsen, deteriorate, penalize, take a turn for the worse 恶劣 wicked, disgusting 恶性 malignant, pernicious, vicious

恶病毒 malicious viruses

恶逻辑 malicious logic

饿 hungry

遏 遏止 check, hold back 遏制 keep within limits, be under control, inhibit

【ēn】

恩 kindness, favor, grace

【ér】

而 but, yet, while 而且 ①(平列) and ②(用在"不仅"后) but also

儿 (小孩) child 儿女 sons and daughters, children 儿童 children 儿子 son

【ěr】

耳 (耳朵) ear; lug, bump, handle; aural, auditive, auditory

耳机 earphone, headphone, phone

铒 erbium (Er)

【èr】

二 two, binary, dyad 二倍 double, diploid 二倍体 dual, duplex, diploid 二重性 duality, duplexity, duplicity 二次 secondary, quadratic, quadric 二等 second-class, second-rate 二元 binary; dual, bidimensional, bibasic 二月 February

二倍行距 double leaded

二叉查找树 binary search tree
二叉节点 binary node
二叉树 binary tree
二叉树查找[检索] binary tree search
二叉树的遍历 binary tree traversal
二叉树排序 binary tree sort
二叉有向树 binary directed tree
二次插值法 quadratic interpolation
二次分配 secondary allocation
二的补码记数法 two's complement number notation
二地址 double-address, two-address
二地址结构 two-address architecture
二分法 binary method
二极管 diode
二级编码 two-level encoding
二级存储器 secondary memory, secondary storage, second-level storage
二级目录 second-level directory
二阶谓词演算 second-order predicate calculus
二进制 binary, binary normal, binary number system, binary ordinary, binary system
二进制"0" binary zero
二进制"1" binary one
二进制编码的十进制 binary-coded decimal {BCD}
二进制变量 binary variable
二进制表示(法) binary representation
二进制布尔代数 binary Boolean algebra
二进制常数 binary constant
二进制串 binary string
二进制代码 binary code
二进制单元 binary cell, binary element
二进制反码 complement of one's, one's complement
插体 field replaceable unit {FRU}, package card, pluggable unit, plug-in board, plug-in card, plug-in package
二进制方式 binary mode
二进制符号 binary character
二进制浮点数 binary-floating-point data
二进制格式 binary format
二进制基数 binary radix
二进制计数 binary counting
二进制记数法 binary notation
二进制加法器 binary adder
二进制链 binary chain
二进制流 binary stream
二进制码元 binary element
二进制模式 binary pattern
二进制属性 binary attribute
二进制数 binary number, binary numeral
二进制数组 binary array
二进制条件[状态] binary condition
二进制同步通信 binary synchronous communication {BISYNC, BSC}
二进制同步通信适配器 binary synchronous communication adapter {BSCA}
二进制位 binary bit, bigit (=bit)
二进制文件 binary file
二进制运算 binary operation
二进制运算符 binary operator
二进制阵列 binary array
二进制整数 binary integer
二进制转储 binary dump
二进制转换 binary conversion
二进制字 binary word

二进制字符 binary-coded character
二进制字母表 binary alphabet
二目关系 binary relation
二目运算符 binary operator
二人博弈 two-person game
二冗余码 two-redundant code
二-十进制码 binary-coded decimal {BCD}, binary-coded decimal code {BCD code}
二输入端加法器 two-input adder
二态[二值]变量 binary-state variable
二态的 binary
二态元件 binary component
二维 two-dimension
二维表 two-dimensional table
二维[二元]分布 bivariate distribution
二维码 two-dimension code
二维数组 dyadic array, two-dimensional array
二位字节 doublet, two-bit byte
二五混合进制码 biquinary code
二相环 two-phase loop
二项式 binomial
二项式定理 binomial theorem
二项式队列 binomial queue
二项式分布 binomial distribution
二义访问 ambiguous reference
二义性 ambiguity
二义性句子 ambiguous sentence
二义性文法 ambiguous grammar
二义性消除 disambiguating
二义性引用 ambiguous reference
二义性语言 ambiguous language
二元变量 binary variable
二元查询 binary query
二元公式 dyadic formula
二元关系 binary relation
二元化 dualization
二元矩阵 binary matrix
二元连接 binary connection
二元数组 dyadic array
二元算子 dyadic operator
二元图 binary pattern
二元向量 binary vector
二元性 duality
二元有向树 binary directed tree
二元域 two element field
二元运算 dyadic operation
二元字符[符号]集 binary character set
二值 two-value
二值变量 two-valued variable
二值逻辑 two-valued logic
二值模式 binary pattern
二值图像 binary image, binary picture
二值图像传输 binary-image transfer
二重插值 double interpolation
二重差分 double difference
二重积分 double integral
二重系统 dual system
二重性 ambiguity, duality

F f

【fā】
发 另见【fà】

发表 publish, issue 发布 issue, release 发出 issue, send out, give out 发达 developed, flourishing 发电 generate electricity 发动 start, launch ◇发动机器 start a machine 发放 provide, grant, extend 发给 issue, distribute, grant 发挥 ①(表能力)bring into play, give play to ②(详尽论述)develop (an idea, a theme, etc.) 发货 send out goods, deliver goods 发货单 dispatch list 发奖 award prizes 发奖仪式 prize-giving ceremony 发觉 find, detect, discover 发刊词 foreword to a periodical 发明 invent 发票 bill, receipt 发起 initiate, sponsor 发起人 initiator, sponsor 发射 ①launch, project, discharge, shoot, fire ②〈物理〉transmit, emit 发生 happen, occur, take place, generate 发售 sell, put on sale 发现 find, discover 发信 post a letter 发信人 addresser 发行 issue, publish, distribute, put on sale 发言 ①〈动〉speak, make a speech ②〈名〉speech

发言权 right to speak 发言人 spokesman 发扬 develop, carry on 发音 pronunciation 发源 rise, originate 发展 develop, expand, grow, evolve
发动机 engine
发光 glow, luminescence
发光的 luminous
发光二极管 light-emitting diode {LED}
发光体 illuminant
发话端 first speaker
发话人地址 talker address
发话人回声 talker echo
发件箱 outbox
发散 divergence, evaporation
发散级数 divergent series
发散矩阵 divergent matrix
发散理论 divergence theory
发散序列 divergent sequence
发射基地 firing base
发射极 emitter
发射器脉冲 emitter pulse
发声 intonation
发声模型 sonification model
发生器 generator
发送 dispatch, dispatching, forwarding, send, sending, transmission {XMT}, transmit {TRAN}, transmittal
发送窗口 send window
发送符 transmit symbol
发送缓存器 transmit buffer
发送就绪 ready for sending

【fā】

发送开始[起始]码 transmitter start code {TSC}
发送流控制 transmit flow control
发送器 sender, source, transmitter, transponder
发送时间 send time
发送时钟 transmitter clock
发送数据 transmitter data
发送信号 sending signal
发送信息 transmitted information, transmitter data
发送状态 send state
发送准备 transmitter ready
发信号 signalling

【fá】

乏 1)(缺少)lack 2)(疲乏)tired, weary 乏(尔)var (unit of reactive power)

罚 punish, penalize

阀 valve

【fǎ】

法 (方法)method, way 法案 proposed law, bill 法定 legal, statutory; official 法定代理人 legal representative 法定人数 quorum 法官 judge, justice 法规 laws and regulations, statutes 法国 France 法国人 the French, Frenchman 法郎 franc 法律 law 法人 legal person, juridical person 法庭 court, tribunal 法语 French (language) 法院 court (of justice), law court 法则 rule, law 法制 legal system, legal institutions
法定单位 legal unit

【fà】

发 另见【fa】
hair ◇理发 haircut

珐 (珐琅)enamel

【fān】

帆 sail

翻 1)(推翻)reverse 2)(使成倍增长)multiply 翻版、翻印 reprint, reproduce, republish 翻滚 roll, tumble, toss 翻新 renovate, refresh 翻修 rebuild, overhaul, reconstruct 翻译 ①〈动〉translate, interpret ②〈名〉translator, interpreter 翻越 cross, get over 翻转 turn over, tip, tilt, tumble; turnover, roll-over, retroflection
翻译表 interpret table
翻译程序 translating program, translation program, translator, version
翻译程序适配器 translator adapter
翻译程序书写系统 translator writing system {TWS}
翻译程序语言 translator language
翻译方法 translation approach
翻译(程序)命令 translator command
翻译时间 translate duration, translating time
翻译算法 translation algorithm
翻译文法 translation grammar
翻译语言 translation language

【fán】

凡 (平凡)commonplace, ordinary 凡是 every, any, all

钒 vanadium (V)

烦 1)(厌烦)be tired of, be sick of, be fed up with 2)(烦劳)trouble 烦恼 be worried, be irritated 烦琐 loaded down with trivial details

繁 繁多 various, a great number of 繁华 flourishing, busy 繁忙 busy, bustling 繁荣 ①〈形〉flourishing, prosperous, booming ②〈动〉make sth prosper 繁重 heavy, strenuous, arduous 繁体字 the complex form of Chinese character, unsimplified Chinese character

【fǎn】

反 1)(翻,转)turn over 2)(背向)in an opposite direction, in reverse 3)(相反的,反向的)converse, inversive 反驳 retort, rebut, refute 反常 unusual, abnormal, strange, anomalous 反对 oppose, be against, fight (against) 反而 on the contrary, instead 反复 repeatedly, again and again, over and over again; repeat, iterate, reiterate 反感 be disgusted with, feel sick of 反抗 revolt, resist 反面 ①(与正面相反)reverse side, opposite side, the other side ②(消极面)opposite, negative side 反义词 antonym 反应 response, reaction; respond, react 反映 ①(报告上级)report ②(反射)reflect, mirror; inversion 反正 anyway, anyhow, in any case 反之 conversely, in the contrary, otherwise 反作用 counteraction, reaction, retroaction, opposition
反编译 decompiling
反编译(程序) decompiler
反编译系统 anti-compiler
反弹 bounce
反调制器 demodulator
反迭代 inverse iteration
反读 backward read, read backward/ reverse, reverse read
反对称的 antisymmetric(al), skew-symmetric
反对称矩阵 antisymmetric/ skew-symmetric matrix
反对称律 antisymmetric law
反对称性 antisymmetry, skew-symmetry
反对数 antilogarithm
反复字符 repeat character {RPT}
反函数 inverse function
反号 opposite sign
反汇编 disassemble, disassembling, disassembly
反汇编程序 disassembler, reverse assembler
反馈 feedback
反馈编码 feedback encoding
反馈变量 feedback variable
反馈部件[环节] feedback element
反馈电路 feedback circuit
反馈调整 feedback adjustment
反馈函数 feedback function
反馈回路 feedback loop
反馈检索 feedback searching
反馈控制 feedback control, reaction control
反馈桥接故障 feedback bridging fault

反馈搜索 feedback search
反馈系数 feedback coefficient
反馈系统 feedback system
反馈信息 feedback information
反馈增益 feedback gain
反馈指数 feedback index
反馈装置 feedback device
反链 anti chain
反码 anticode, one's/ (b−1)'s complement
反命题 inverse proposition
反偏压 reverse bias
反三角函数 inverse trigonometric
反射 mirror, mirroring, reflection
反射原理 reflection principle
反数 inverse number
反顺序 reverse order
反同构 anti-isomorphism
反相 antiphase
反相(位) opposite phase
反相处理 reversal processing
反相放大器 see-saw amplifier, sign-reversing amplifier
反相缓冲器 inverter/ inverting buffer
反相门 inverse gate, invert gate, inverting gate
反相器 inverter
反相输出 inverted output
反相输入 inverted input
反相显示 reverse video
反向 backward, reversal
反向处理 backward processing
反向地址识别协议 reserve address resolution protocol {**RARP**}
反向读出 backward reading, read backward
反向访问 inverted access
反向恢复 back recovery, backward recovery
反向计数 counting in reverse

反向计数器 reverse counter
反向结构 inverted structure
反向纠错 backward error correction {**BEC**}
反向链接 back(ward) chaining, backward link
反向搜索 backward/ reverse search
反向索引 reverse indexing
反向通道 reverse channel
反向推理 backward chained reasoning, backward reasoning
反向学习 backward learning
反向引用 backward reference
反向中断 reverse break, reverse interrupt {**RVI**}
反向中断字符 reverse-interrupt character {**RVI**}
反斜杠符号 backslash
反序 antitone, inverted sequence
反序映射 antitone mapping
反依赖 antidependence
反应 echo, reaction, response
反应方式 reactive mode
反应关系 response relation
反应式 reactive mode
反正切 arctan
反转 flux reversal, inversion, invert

返 return 返工 do a task again (because of poor quality)
返回 backspace {**BS**}, backspacing, loopback, regression, return {**RET**}
返回次序 back order
返回地址 return address
返回点 reentry point, return point
返回符号 carriage return character {**CR**}, return character

返回键 return key, backspace key
返回连接 return link
返回路径 return path
返回码 return code
返回信号 backward signal
返回信息[消息] return message
返回语句 return statement
返回栈 return stack
返回值 returned value, exit value, return value
返回指令 bridging order, link order, return instruction
返回指针 return pointer
返回状态 return state
返回字符 return character

【fàn】

犯 犯法 break/violate a law 犯规 break the rules 犯人 prisoner, convict 犯罪 commit a crime

泛 (广泛) extensive, general, nonspecific 泛滥 flood 泛指 make a general reference
泛代数(学) universal algebra
泛关系 universal relation
泛函 functional
泛函方程 functional equation
泛函分析 functional analysis

范 ◇典范 example // 示范 demonstrate 范例 example, model, paradigm
范畴 category, domain
范畴的 categorical
范畴分析 categorical analysis
范畴关系 categorical relation
范畴文法 categorical grammar
范例机 paradigm machine
范式 normal/canonical form
范式项 normal term

范数 norm
范数空间 norm space
范围 range, area, bound, circumscription, extent, limit, reach, region, scale, sphere, zone
范围变量 range variable, bound variable
范围查询 range query
范围调整 range adjustment
范围检查 range check
范围结束(符) end of extent {EOE}
范围索引 range index

饭 饭菜 meal, repast 饭店 ①(旅馆)hotel ②(饭馆)restaurant 饭厅 dining hall

贩 贩卖 peddle, sell

【fāng】

方 1)(正方) square 2)(立方) cube 3)(乘方) power 4)(响度单位) phon 方便 convenient 方才 just now 方格 check 方面 respect, aspect, side, field 方位 position, direction 方形 square 方向 direction, course, bearing, orientation 方言 dialect 方针 policy, guiding principle
方案 scheme, version, conception, layout
方案[概念]分析 conceptual analysis
方案阶段 conceptual phase, conceptual level
方案视图 conceptual view
方波 square wave
方差 variance
方差分析 analysis of variance, variance analysis
方差检验 variance test

方差律 variance law
方程 equation
方程语句 equation statement
方程组 equation set, system of equations
方法 method, approach, fashion, manner, philosophy, methodology, resource, technique, tool, way
方法分析 method analysis
方法库 method base
方法论 methodology
方法描述符 method descriptor
方法名称 method name
方法学 methodology
方块 square
方块图 block chart, skeleton diagram
方括号 bracket, square bracket
方式 mode, fashion, form, manner, philosophy, way
方式标识符 mode identifier
方式说明符 mode specifier
方式位 mode bit
方式字段 mode field
方位角 bearing angle, bearing, azimuth angle
方位向量 position vector
方向键 direction key, arrow key
方向控制 direction control
方向图 directivity pattern
方向性天线 directive antenna
方向性系数 directivity factor
方向耦合器 directional coupler
方阵 matrix (=matrices), square matrix

钫 francium (Fr)

【fáng】

防 防爆 explosion-proof, flame-proof, antiknock 防备 guard against, take precautions against 防尘 dust protection; dirt-proof, dust-laying 防范 be on guard, keep a look out 防护 guard, protect, shelter, prevent; proof, shielding, protection 防火 fireproof, flame-proof, incombustible 防漏 antidrip, antidrop; leakproof 防霉 fungus-proof, anti-mildew 防湿 moisture-proof, waterproof, non-hygroscopic 防守 defend, guard 防水 waterproof, watertight, water-repellent, water-resistant 防污 antifouling 防线 line of defense 防锈 rust-prevention; antirusting, non-rust(ing), rust-proof 防雨 rainproof, raintight 防止 prevent, avoid 防治 provention and cure
防病毒程序 antivirus program
防错程序设计 defensive programming
防光晕 anti-halation
防护频带 guard band
防护装置 protector
防护装置[罩,栏] safeguard
防火墙 fire wall, firewall
防空导弹 guided air defence rocket
防空系统 air defence system
防卫数据网 defense data network {DDN}

妨 妨碍 hinder, hamper 妨害 impair, harm

房 (房子) house 房间 room 房屋 house, building 房租 rent (for a house)

【fǎng】

仿 (类似) resemble, be like **仿佛** seem; as if **仿效** imitate, copy **仿照** imitate, follow **仿制品** imitation, replica, copy

仿射环 affine ring
仿射集 affine set
仿射空间 affine space
仿射密码 affine cipher
仿射映射 affine mapping
仿射坐标 affine coordinate
仿生(物)芯片 biochip
仿效 emulate, imitate, modelling
仿效程序 emulation program {EP}
仿形变量 profile variable
仿形终端 profile terminal
仿形装置 profile device
仿样函数 spline function
仿真 emulation, emulate, simulate, simulation
仿真测试 emulation testing, simulation testing
仿真程序 emulation program {EP}, emulate routine, emulator program, simulation program, simulator
仿真程序/虚拟系统 emulation program/ virtual system {EP/VS}
仿真的 artificial
仿真法 simulation method
仿真方法学 simulation methodology
仿真方式 emulator mode, emulation mode
仿真技术 emulative technique, technique of simulation
仿真计算机 emulation computer, simulating computer, simulation computer
仿真结构 simulation architecture
仿真理论 simulation theory
仿真命令 emulation command
仿真器 emulator, simulator
仿真软件技术 simulation software technology
仿真时间 simulation time
仿真实验 simulation examination
仿真数据 simulation data
仿真算法 simulation algorithm
仿真系统 emulator system
仿真向量 artificial vector
仿真硬件 simulation hardware
仿真语声 artificial voice
仿真语言 emulational language, simulation language {SIMULA}
仿真终端 emulation terminal
仿真[模拟]总线 emulation bus

访

访 访求 seek, search for **访问** visit, call on; access, inquiry, reference

访管指令 supervisor call instruction {SVC}
访管中断 supervisor call interruption {SVC interruption}, supervisor interrupt
访问策略 access strategy, access policy
访问程序 access program, access routine, fetcher
访问冲突 access conflict
访问存储器 access memory
访问对象 access object
访问法 access method, method of access
访问方法 access(ing) method
访问方式 access mode
访问符 enquiry character {ENQ}
访问环境 access environment
访问级别 accession level

访问记录 access record
访问键 access key
访问控制 access control
访问控制表 access control list
访问控制块 access control block {ACB}
访问控制码 access control code
访问控制器 access controller
访问控制项 access control entry {ACE}
访问控制域 access control field
访问控制字 access control word
访问口令 access password
访问类 access category
访问类型 access type
访问令牌 access token
访问路径 access path
访问码 access code
访问模式 access patterns
访问周期 access period
访问权 access right
访问权限 access authority
访问时间 access time
访问属性 access attribute
访问速度 access speed
访问算法 access algorithm
访问位 access bit, reference bit
访问许可 access permission
访问周期 access cycle

纺 spin

【fàng】

放 put, place 放长 lengthen 放出 give out, let out, emit, eject, bleed, expel 放大 enlarge, magnify, amplify 放过 let off, let skip 放假 have a holiday or vacation, have a day off 放宽 relax restrictions 放宽期限 extend a time limit 放宽条件 soften the terms 放弃 abandon, give up 放射 radiate 放松 relax, slacken, loosen 放下 lay down, put down 放心 set one's mind at rest, be at ease 放行 let sb pass 放置 lay up, lay aside
放大 amplify, amplification, enlargement, magnify, zoom
放大倍数 magnification, gain
放大矩阵 amplification matrix
放大器 amplifier
放大系数 amplification coefficient
放大选择 zoom out option
放大因数 multiplier factor
放射器 emanator
放射性分析 activation analysis
放像器 enlarger
放音 playback

【fēi】

飞 (飞翔) fly, flit 飞船 airship 飞机 aircraft, aeroplane, plane 飞机场 airport, airdrome 飞行 flying, flight, aviation 飞跃 leap
飞(母拖)(单位前缀) femto- (=10^{-15})
飞机订票系统 airline reservation system
飞行计算机 flight computer
飞行模拟器 flight simulator
飞行速度 flying speed

非 negation, not, no 非常 extraordinary, unusual, special 非法 unlawful, illegal, illicit 非凡 outstanding, extraordinary, uncommon
非卖品 (articles) not for sale
非正式 unofficial, informal
非洲 Africa
"非" NOT, negation, Boolean complement, Boolean com-

plementation, negate
非保护系统文件 unprotected system file
非保护域 unprotected field
非饱和记录 nonsaturation recording
非本地网络 nonnative network
非本域资源 otherdomain resource
非本征的 extrinsic, extrinsical
非本征增益 extrinsic gain
非编号回答 unnumbered acknowledge {UA}, unnumbered response
非编码信息 noncoded information {NCI}
非变体部分 non-variant part
非变换方式 nonmapping mode
非标准标号 nonstandard label
非拨号中继 nondial trunks
非彩色 achromatic color(s)
"非"操作 NOT operation
非操作方式 nonoperational mode
非操作[空操作]码 no-operation code
非存储设备 nonstorage device
非打印代码 non-print code
非打印字符 nonprint character
非单调逻辑 non-monotonic logic
非单调推理 nonmonotonic reasoning
非导体 nonconductor
非等价 nonequivalence
非递归规则 nonrecursive rule
非定界符 non-delimiter
非定向的 astatic
非对称多处理 asymmetrical multiprocessing
非对称多重处理系统 asymmetric multiprocessing system {ASP}
非对称关系 asymmetric/non-symmetric relation
非对称数字用户线 asymmetric digital subscriber line {ADSL}
非对称系统 asymmetric system
非对变量性 unsymmetry
非法变量名 illegal variable name
非法操作 illegal operation
非法存储器访问 illegal memory access
非法存取 illegal access
非法代码 false code, forbidden code, illegal code, improper code, nonexistence code, nonexistent code, unallowable code, unused code
非法翻印 pirate, piracy
非法防护方式 illegal guard mode
非法函数名 illegal function name
非法码 unallowable code
非法命令 illegal command, improper command, unused command
非法请求 illegal request
非法引用 no-valid reference
非法指令 disable instruction, illegal instruction
非法状态 illegal state
非法[禁用]字符 improper character
非分组方式终端 non-packet mode terminal {NPT}
非封锁 nonblocking, unblock
非冯·诺依曼(计算)机 non von Neumann machine
非负象限 nonnegative quadrant
非格式化磁带 unformatted tape
非格式化方式 unformatted mode
非格式化请求 unformatted re-

非格式化图像 unformatted image
非关联文档 nonrelevant document
非管(理状)态 nonsupervisor mode
非规范关系 unnormalized relation
非规格化数 unnormalized number
非规则点 irregular point
非过程化 deproceduring
非合取 nonconjunction
非活动时间 inactive time
非活跃段 inactive segment
非基本变量 nonbased variable
非记录面 non-recording surface
非加权码 non-weighted code, no-weighted code
非兼析取 exclusive disjunction
非接受状态 nonaccepting state
非结构文件 unstructured file
非禁止[非屏蔽]中断 noninhibit interrupt {NI}
非均匀分布 non-uniform distrubution
非均匀取样 nonuniform sampling
非均匀系统 nonhomogeneous system
非可编程终端 nonprogrammable terminal {NPT}
非空输入栏 nonblank input column
非空格 unblank
非空集合 nonempty set
非空类 non-null class
非空序列 nonempty sequence
非控解 nondominated solution
非控制系统 noncontrol system
非连通图 unconnected graph
非零位 nonzero digit

非零向量 non-vanishing vector
非零整常数 nonzero integer constant
非逻辑的 illogical
非忙等待 nonbusy waiting
非"忙"中断 not busy interrupt
非忙状态 nonbusy condition
"非"门 NOT gate, negation gate, negator, NOT element
非平衡树 unbalanced tree
非屏蔽中断 nonmaskable interrupt {NMI}
非破坏性读出 nondestructive read {NDR}
非奇异性 nonsingularity
非齐次 inhomogeneous
非齐次方程组 inhomogeneous system of equations
非确定的分析 nondeterministic parsing
非确定图灵机 nondeterministic Turing machine {NDTM, NTM}
非确定性 nondeterminism
非确定性系统 nondeterministic system
非任务 nontask
非软件的 nonsoftware
非实时处理 nonreal-time processing
非实时仿真 nonreal time simulation
非数据输入 nondata input
非数据应用 nonumeric application
非数值[数字]文字 nonnumeric literal
非数值[数字]项 nonnumeric item
非数值应用 nonnumeric application
非数字操作 nonnumeric operation
非数字字符 nonnumeric char-

非顺序计算机 nonsequential computer
非伺服机器人 nonservo robot
非算术移位 nonarithmetic shift
非随机存取[访问] nonrandom access
非锁定 nonlocking
非锁定转义符 nonlocking shift character
非特权程序 non-privileged program
非特权方式 non-privileged mode
非特权状态 unprivileged state
非条件转移 unconditional jump
非通用语言 special language
非同步的 nonsynchronous
非透明方式 nontransparent mode
非透明属性 nontransparent attribute
非图形数据 non-graphical data
非物理设备 non-physical device
非线性 nonlinearity
非线性方程 nonlinear equation
非线性放大器 nonlinear amplifier
非线性估计 nonlinear estimation
非线性规划 nonlinear planning/programming
非线性回归 nonlinear regression
非线性集成电路 nonlinear integrated circuit
非线性流水线 nonlinear pipeline
非线性耦合 nonlinear coupling
非线性平滑[光顺] nonlinear smoothing
非线性失真 nonlinear distortion
非线性时变模型 nonlinear time-varying model
非线性数据结构 nonlinear data structure
非线性网络 nonlinear network
非线性系统 nonlinear system
非线性优化 nonlinear optimization
非线性预测 nonlinear prediction
非线性运算 nonlinear operation
非线性最优控制 nonlinear optimal control
非相关干扰 noncoherent jamming
非向量中断 non-vectored interrupt {NVI}
非形式语法树 informal syntax tree
非形式证明 informal proof
非循环网络 acyclic network
非循环序集 acyclic set
非循环有向图 acyclic directed graph (= acyclic digraph)
非叶节点 non-leaf node
非一致的 incomparable, inconsistent
非一致性 nonuniformity
非映射窗口 unmapped window
非映射系统 unmapped system
非用词表 stop list
非优先中断 nonpriority interrupt
非预定维修 unscheduled maintenance {UM}
非阈值逻辑电路 non-threshold logic circuit {NTL}
非正常 improper
非正常停机 disorderly closedown
非正规的 denormal
非正规集 nonregular set
非正式文件 informal documentation

非正式信息 chat message
非正态性 abnormality, non-normality
非执行 non-execution
非致命错误 nonfatal error
非智能终端 nonintelligent terminal
非终(结符)节点 nonterminal node
非终结符 nonterminal
非终结符顶点 nonterminal vertex
非终结符号表 nonterminal vocabulary
非重复次序 non-repetitive sequence
非周期 acyclic, aperiodic
非周期链 aperiodic chain
非周期网络 acyclic network
非周期性 aperiodicity
非专用的 nondedicated
非转换存储器 untranslated storage
非自反的 non-reflexive
非自反关系 irreflexive relation
非最终状态 nonfinal state

扉
扉页 title page

【féi】
肥 (肉肥) fat 肥沃 fertile, rich

【fěi】
斐
斐波纳契数 Fibonacci number

【fèi】
肺 lung

废 1) (无用) waste, useless, unwanted 2) (残废) disabled, maimed 废除 abolish, annul, do away with 废话 nonsense, rubbish 废品 ① waste product, reject ② scrape, waste 废物 waste material, trash
废除功能 undo function
废进废出 garbage-in garbage-out {GIGO}

沸 boil 沸水 boiling water

费 1) (花费) cost, spend, expend 2) (浪费) wasteful, consuming too much, expending sth too quickly 费解 hard to understand, obscure 费力 need great effort, be strenuous 费时 take time 费事, 费心 give or take a lot of trouble 费用 / fee, dues, expense, charge
费用 charge, cost, expenditure, expense, outlay, toll
费用分析 cost analysis
费用计算 cost account
费用结构 cost structure
费用模型 cost model
费用曲线 cost curve
费用向量 cost vector
费用效益 cost effectiveness {CE}
费用种类 cost category

镄 fermium (Fm)

【fēn】
分 另见【fèn】
1) (分开) divide, separate, part, share, segregate 2) (分配) distribute, assign, allot 3) (表示分数) fraction 4) (中国货币单位) fen 5) (时间与角度单位) minute 6) (记分) point, mark 分辨 distinguish, differentiate, recognize; resolution 分别 ① (离

别)part, leave each other ② (各自)respectively, separately **分布** distribute, allocate, spread; partitioned, extended **分担** share responsibility for **分发** distribute, hand out, issue, assort **分割** divide, division, part(ition), excise, excision, dissect, segment, split **分隔** separate, divide, compart **分工** divide the work, division of labour **分号** semi-colon **分级** grade, classify, assort, fractionate, cascade; sectional, stepped, hierarchic(al) **分解** resolve, decompose, dissolve, disintegrate, dissociate; breakdown **分类** class(ify), category, categorization, grade, rank, sort(ing), systematic **分离** separate, dissociate, detach, split, isolate; discrete **分裂** ①（分开）split, divide, break up, disintegrate ②〈生物〉〈物理〉fission, division ◇核分裂 nuclear fission **分母** denominator **分批** in batches, in turn **分期** by stages **分期付款** instalment plan **分歧** difference, divergence ◇消除分歧 iron out difference **分散** break up, scatter, dispersion **分数** ① fraction ② mark, score, grade **分析** analyze, dissect; analytic(al) **分享** share (joy, rights, etc.) partake of **分支** branch **分子** ①〈数学〉numerator ②〈化学〉molecule **分组** divide into groups, grouping

分贝 decibel (=dB, db)
分辨率 definition, resolution, resolution factor, resolution ratio
分辨能力 resolving ability
分辨误差 resolution error
分别编译 separate compilation
分布 distribute, distribution, layout
分布表 distribution list, distribution table
分布参数 distributed parameter
分布程序 distribution program
分布处理系统 distributed processing system {DPS}
分布[分散]的 dispersal
分布的 distributed
分布队列 distribution queue
分布方法 location mode
分布计算(机)环境 distributed computing environment {DCE}
分布(式)控制 distributed control
分布逻辑 distributed logic
分布逻辑存储器 distributed logic memory
分布律 distribution law
分布密度 distribution density
分布模型 distributed model
分布排序 distribution sorting
分布区 distribution zone
分布式办公支持系统 distributed office support system {DISOSS}
分布式并行控制 distributed concurrency control
分布式操作系统 distributed operating system
分布式查找 distributed search
分布式程序设计 distributed programming
分布式处理系统 distributed processing system {DPS}
分布式登录安全性 distributed logon security

分布式队列双总线 distributed queue dual bus {DQDB}
分布式对象构件模型 distributed component object model {DCOM}
分布式对象管理系统 distributed object management system {DOMS}
分布式对象系统 distributed object system
分布式访问系统 distributed access system
分布式功能终端 distributed function terminal {DFT}
分布式关系数据库体系结构 distributed relational database architecture {DRDA}
分布式管理环境 distributed management environment {DME}
分布式环境 distributed environment
分布式计算 distributed computing
分布式计算环境 distributed computing environment {DCE}
分布式计算机控制系统 distributed computer control system {DCCS}
分布式计算机网络 decentralized computer network, distributed computer network {DCN}
分布式计算机系统 distributed computer system {DCS}
分布式结构 distributed frame
分布式决策支持系统 distributed decision support system {DDSS}
分布式媒体访问控制 distributed media access control
分布式容错计算系统 distributed fault-tolerant computing system
分布式事务处理 distributed transaction process(ing)
分布式搜索引擎 distributed search engine
分布式数据 distributed data
分布式数据测试系统 distributed data test system {DDTS}
分布式数据处理 distributed data processing {DDP}
分布式数据管理 distributed data management {DDM}
分布式数据交换 distributed data switching
分布式数据库管理系统 distributed database management system {DDBMS}
分布式数据库机 distributed database machine
分布式算法 distributed algorithm
分布式随机访问机器 distributed random access machine {DRAM}
分布式索引存取方法 distributed indexed access method {DXAM}
分布式通信结构 distributed communication architecture {DCA}
分布式网络系统 distributed network system {DNS}
分布式文件系统 distributed file system
分布式系统 distributed system
分布式系统对象模型 distributed system object model {DSOM}
分布式选路 distributed routing
分布式询问处理 distributed query processing
分布式阵列处理机 distributed array processor {DAP}
分布式知识 distributed know-

分布式知识库系统 distributed knowledge base system {DKBS}
分布式智能系统 distributed intelligence system {DIS}
分布式自适应路由选择 distributed adaptive routing
分布式组织 distributed organization
分布(式)刷新 distributed refresh
分布文档 distribution document
分布系统结构 distributed system architecture {DSA}
分布项目 distribution entry
分步 substep
分步解决 divide and conquer
分步区域 step region
分层 gradation, grade, layering, layers, level, quantization, stratification, stratify
分层层次 hierarchy of layer
分层的 hierarchical
分层接口 layered interface
分层结构 layered structure, sandwich structure
分层决策 hierarchical decision making
分层路由选择 hierarchical routing
分层模型 hierarchical model
分层取样 stratified sampling
分层数 hierarchy number
分层算法 hierarchical algorithm
分层图 hierarchical diagram
分层拓扑 hierarchical topology
分层[分级]网络 hierarchical network
分层文件 hierarchical file
分层(结构)系统 hierarchical system
分层协议 layered protocol
分层语言 stratified language
分叉 bifurcation, fork
分叉级 fork level
分叉进程 fork process
分程序 block, split routine
分程序号 block number
分程序标识符 block identifier
分程序表 block list
分程序层次 hierarchy of blocks
分程序出口 block exit
分程序体 block body
分段 partition, burst, sectioning, sectoring, staging, segment(ation), grading, graduation
分段表示法 fragment notation
分段播放项目 segment play item
分段参数 segmentation parameter
分段插值 piecewise interpolation
分段差错 segment fault
分段程序 segmentation routine, segmented program
分段处理 period processing
分段存储 fragment, fragmentation
分段地址空间 segmented address space
分段法 segmentation
分段覆盖 segment(ation) overlay
分段格式 zoned format
分段回归 piecewise regression
分段汇编程序 sectional assembly
分段寄存器表 segmentation register table {SRT}
分段码 fragment code
分段区 segment field
分段搜索 sectioning search
分段算法 segmentation algorithm
分段文件 segmental file

分段寻址(系统)结构 segmented addressing architecture
分段译码器 segment decoder
分段运行 partition running
分段重叠 segmentation overlay
分割成芯片 chipping
分割窗口 split window
分割[切除]定理 excision theorem
分割定理 partition theorem
分割法 division method
分割范式 partitional normal form {PNF}
分割键标 split key
分隔符 delimiter, separator
分隔符记录 separator record
分隔控制字符 separating control character
分隔区域 separated region
分隔页 separator page
分隔语句 delimiter statement
分隔字符 break/ separator character
分级操作系统 hierarchical operating system
分级存储器 hierarchical memory
分级存取时间 hierarchy access time
分级管理 hierarchical management
分级规划 hierarchical planning
分级监视程序 hierarchical monitor
分级结构 hierarchical structure
分级控制 hierarchical control, step control
分级控制表 level control table {LCT}
分级模拟 hierarchical simulation
分级顺序的 hierarchical sequential {HS}
分级文件结构 hierarchical file structure
分级文件系统 hierarchical file system
分级系统 hierarchical system
分级智能 hierarchical intelligence
分交换数据网络 packet switching data network {PSDN}
分解查询 decomposition query
分解法则 resolution principle
分解描述 decomposition description
分解器 resolver
分解器程序 resolver routine
分解行 scanning line
分解原理 resolution principle
分界网络节点 boundary network node {BNN}
分块 blocking, constructing, deblock, partition, partitioning
分块编译 blocked compiling
分块查找 block search
分块的 blocked
分块[分区]方式 partitioned mode
分块规划 partition programming
分块过程 blocking process
分块矩阵 matrix in block form
分块逻辑 partitioned logic
分块系数 blocking factor
分块因子 block factor
分块作业 blocked job
分缆 drop cable
分类表合并 sorted list merging
分类参数 sort parameter, sorting parameter
分类层次 class hierarchy
分类插入法 insert method
分类程序 sort(ing) program/ routine
分类程序段 sorting phase

分类程序设计 categorical programming
分类传送 sort pass
分类代码 category code
分类法 class method, classification
分类符 classifier
分类符号 class symbol
分类关键词[字] sort key, sorting key
分类归并[合并] clustering, sort merge
分类号 category number, class number
分类间隔[区间] class interval
分类模式 category pattern
分类目录 systematic bibliography
分类器 categorizer, classifier, sorter
分类扫描 sort pass
分类数据 categorical data, category data
分类算法 sort(ing) algorithm
分类索引 classified index
分类条件 class condition
分类图像 classification image
分类网 sorting net
分类文件 sort file
分类系统 classification system
分类向量 class vector
分类协议 bracket protocol
分类信息 category message
分类选择 sort selection
分类学 taxonomy
分类应用 sort application
分类语句 sort statement
分类语言 classification language, specification language
分类阵列 sort array
分类子句 class clause
分离符[器] separator
分离集 disjoint set
分离技术 splitting technique
分离节点 separate node
分离理论 separation theorem
分离时钟 separated clock
分离式键盘 detached/ split keyboard
分离系统 separating system, split system
分离原理 separation principle
分离装置 segregating unit, stripper
分离总线 separate bus
分立电路 discrete circuit
分立元件 discrete component
分量电视信号 component video
分裂法 splitting method/ technique, tearing method
分裂技术 splitting technique
分流电路 shunt circuit
分目录 subdirectory
分派 detach, dispatch
分派过程 allocation process
分派进程 detached process
分派问题 assignment problem
分配 allocate, allocation, assignation, deal, despatch, distribute, distribution, imputation
分配表 assign table, distribution list
分配表目 distribution entry
分配部件 allocation units
分配程序 allocator, assignor
分配放大器 distribution amplifier
分配分类 distribution sort
分配符 allocator
分配节点 allocate node
分配控制板 distribution panel
分配列表 distribution list
分配任务 allocating task
分配式磁带卷 distribution tape reel {DTR}
分配图文件 map file

分配网络 distribution network
分配位图[表] allocation bit map
分配文件 allocate file
分配问题 allocation/ assignment problem
分配语句 allocate statement
分批 batching
分批法 batch process
分批流 batch stream
分批事务文件 batch transaction file
分片 slicing
分片存取法 partitioned access method {PAM}
分频器 frequency divider, counterdown
分区 partition, sectoring, space-sharing
分区(制) zoning
分区标识符 partition identifier
分区存取(方)法 partitioned access method {PAM}
分区断点 regional breakpoint
分区法 partition allocation method
分区访问 regional addressing
分区格式 zoned format
分区检索 area search
分区控制表 partition control table {PCT}
分区控制描述符 partition control descriptor {PCD}
分区说明表 partition specification table {PST}
分区图 area chart
分区网络 partition network
分区文件 partitioned file
分区中心 regional center {RC}
分散表 scatter table
分散处理 decentralized processing
分散存储 scatter storage
分散读入 scatter read

分散格式 scatter format
分散控制 decentralized control
分散网络 decentralized network
分散式控制系统 distrbuted control system {DCS}
分散系统 decentralized system
分散原则 decentralization principle
分时 time share, time-shared
分时(技) time-sharing {T/S}
分时操作系统 time-sharing operating system
分时程序设计 time-shared programming
分时处理 time-sharing processing
分时调度规则 time sharing scheduling rule
分时对话 time-shared conversation
分时方式 time-sharing format, time-sharing mode
分时分配 time-sharing allocation
分时记帐 time-sharing accounting
分时控制 time-shared control
分时控制任务 time-sharing control task {TSC}
分时控制系统 time-sharing control system
分时轮询 time-sharing polling
分时软件 time-sharing software
分时时钟 time-sharing clock
分时网络 time-share/ shared sharing network
分时系统 time-shared/ sharing system {TSS}
分时制 time-sharing system {TSS}
分时中断 time-sharing interrupt
分时终端 time-sharing terminal

分时总线　time-shared bus
分式规划　fractional program
分数步长法　fractional steps method
分数部分　fractional part
分数迭代　fractional iteration
分数规划　fractional programming
分析程序　analysis program, analytic program, analyzer, parser
分析法　analysis method, analytic method
分析方式　analysis mode
分析过程　parsing process
分析机　analyzer
分析控制　analytic control
分析模型　analytic model, analytic modelling
分析树　parse tree
分析算法　parsing algorithm
分析拓扑学　analytic topology
分析员　analyst
分形　fractal
分形笔　fractal pen
分形理论　fractal theory
分形模型　fractal model
分形内插　fractal interpolation
分形曲线　fractal curve
分形图案　fractal pattern
分形维数　fractal dimension
分页　page, page break
分页(法)　paging
分页[调页]策略　page fetch policy
分页[调页]管理程序　paging supervisor
分页区　paging area
分页设备　paging device
分帧　framing
分帧位　framing bit, framing bits
分帧线　frame line
分支程序　branching program
分支带　branch strip
分支点　branch/ branching/ winding point
分支动作　descendant action
分支节点　branch node
分支结构　branch construct
分支连接　branch linkage {BAL}
分支请求　branch demand
分支算法　branching algorithm
分支网络　branch network
分支系统　branch system
分支[转移]指令　branch, branch instruction
分支指令　branch order
分组　burst, grouping, packet
分组编码　block coding, block encoding
分组抽样　group sampling
分组传送协议　packet transfer protocol {PTP}
分组单元数据流　packetized elementary stream {PES}
分组调度程序　packet scheduler
分组格式　packet format
分组记录　group record
分组交换　packet switch
分组交换节点　packet switch node {PSN}
分组交换数据　packet switched data
分组交换网络　packet switch network
分组密码　block cipher
分组驱动程序　packet driver
分组冗余技术　group redundant technique {GRT}
分组突发传输方式　packet burst mode
分组误差　grouping error
分组[群体]限额　group allowance
分组寻址　packet addressing
分组因子　grouping factor

【fēn】

芬 sweet smell, fragrance

吩 吩咐 tell, instruct

纷 1)(杂乱)confused, disorderly 2)(多)numerous 纷繁 numerous and complicated

酚 phenol

【fén】

焚 burn

【fěn】

粉 powder, flour 粉碎 smash, shatter, crush, pulverize 粉末 powder

【fèn】

分 另见 fēn
1)(成分)component 2)(职分)what is within one's right or duty 分量 weight 分内 one's job, one's duty 分外 ① particularly, especially ② not one's job, not one's duty

奋 奋斗 struggle, fight, strive 奋发 rouse oneself, exert oneself

份 share, portion ◇股份 stock, share

【fēng】

丰 丰产 high yield, bumper crop 丰富 ①〈形〉rich, abundant, plentiful ②〈动〉enrich 丰硕 plentiful and substantial, rich

风 wind 风暴 windstorm, storm 风格 style 风俗 custom 风险 risk, hazard, venture 风景画式的 landscape 风景画页面 landscape page 风扇 fan 风险分析 risk analysis 风险估计 risk assessment 风险[危险]管理 risk management 风险函数 risk function 风险投资 venture capital {VC}

疯 mad, insane, crazy

封 (信封)envelope 封闭 ①(关住)seal, enclose, encapsulate ②(查封)seal off, close 封面 cover, front cover 封锁 blockade, block, seal of, latch
封闭(式体系)结构 closed architecture
封闭数组 closed array
封闭特性 closed property, closure property
封闭系统 closed system
封闭线 closure line
封闭用户组[群] closed user group {CUG}
封锁进程 blocked process
封锁卷 locked volume
封锁卷/开锁功能 lock/ unlock facility
封锁域 locked field
封锁状态 blocked state
封套 wrapping
封装 encapsulation, pack, package, packaging
封装程序 canned program
封装工艺 packaged technology
封装级 package level
封装技术 packaging technique
封装晶体管 packaged transistor
封装密度 packaging density,

feng 峰锋蜂,冯逢缝,奉缝 fǒu 否 fu 夫肤敷,伏扶

packing factor
封装密封 package sealing
封装式软件 packaged software
封装体 package body
封装型 encapsulated type

峰 peak, summit
峰位漂移 peak shift
峰值 crest value, peak value
峰值保持 peak holding
峰值点 peak point
峰值电流 peak current
峰值电位 spike potential
峰值负载 peak load
峰值检测 peak detection
峰值识别 peak recognition
峰值限制 peak limiting

锋 锋利 sharp, keen

蜂 蜂鸣 buzz, singing 蜂音 buzz, hum(ming)
蜂鸣器 buzzer
蜂窝数据链路控制 cellular data link control {CDLC}
蜂窝数据通信系统 cellular data communication system
蜂窝数字分组数据 cellular digital packet date {CDPD}

【féng】

冯
冯·诺依曼(计算)机 von Neumann machine

逢 meet, come across
逢"1"变化不归零制 non-return-to-zero change-on-one {NRZI}

缝 另见【fèng】
stich, sew

【fèng】

奉 奉命 act on orders 奉行 pursue (a policy, etc.)

缝 另见【féng】
(结合缝) seam ◇无缝钢管 seamless steel tube 缝隙 crack, crevice

【fǒu】

否 否决 vote down, veto, turn down 否认 deny, repudiate 否则 otherwise, if not, or else
否定 deny, negate, negation, negative acknowledgement {NAK}
否定回答 negative acknowledge, negative acknowledge character {NAK}, negative response
否则 else
否则符号 else symbol
否则规则 else rule

【fū】

夫 夫妇,夫妻 husband and wife 夫人 lady, madam, Mrs. (Mistress)

肤 skin 肤浅 superficial, shallow

敷 apply (powder, ointment, etc.) 敷设 lay, install 敷衍 perfunctory, inattentive

【fú】

伏 bend over, lean over, stoop
伏特 volt {V}

扶 support with the hand
扶植 foster, prop up
扶助 help, assist, support

服 1)（衣服）clothes, dress 2)（信服）be convinced, obey 服从 obey, comply with, submit to 服务 give service to, serve 服务性行业 service trade, service industries 服务员 attendant, waiter 服用 take (medicine) 服装 dress, clothing, costume

服务报文 service message
服务表 agent list
服务菜单 service menu
服务查询 service-seeking
服务程序 server, service facility/program, servicer
服务等级 grade of service {GOS}
服务点 service point {SP}
服务方式 service mode
服务访问点 service access point {SAP}
服务公告协议 service advertising protocol {SAP}
服务(等)级 class of service {COS}
服务器 server, server machine
服务器报文块 server message block {SMB}
服务器捕捉 server grabbing
服务器集群 server clustering
服务器进程 server process
服务器镜像 server mirroring
服务器名 server name
服务器网络 server network
服务器站点 server side
服务请求 service request
服务区 service area
服务设施 service facility
服务授权 service authority
服务数据块 service data unit {SDU}
服务消息 service message
服务原语 service primitive
服务质量 quality of service {QoS}
服务中心 service center
服务周期 service cycle
服役[活动, 有效]时间 active time

俘 俘获 capture, trap, entrap
俘获字 trap word

浮 float 浮动 ①（漂浮）float, drift, levitate; floating, non-locating, relocatable ②（不稳定）unsteady, insecure
浮点 floating-point
浮点表示(法) floating-point representation
浮点常数 float constant, floating-point constant
浮点程序 floating-point program
浮点除法 floating-point division
浮点处理器 floating-point processor
浮点二进制 floating-point binary
浮点格式 floating-point format
浮点功能部件 floating-point feature
浮点基数 floating-point base, floating-point radix
浮点计算 floating-point calculation/computation
浮点记数法 floating-point notation
浮点阶 floating-point exponent
浮点精度 floating-point precision
浮点数 floating number/numeral, floating-point number/numeral
浮点数据 floating data

浮点算术符号 floating arithmetic sign
浮点特性 floating-point feature
浮点尾数 floating-point coefficient
浮点溢出 floating-point overflow
浮点运算 floating-point operation {FLOP}
浮点指令组 floating-point instruction group
浮点转换 floating-point transformation
浮雕字符 embossed character
浮动磁头 float head, floating head, flying head
浮动地址表 relocation dictionary {RLD}
浮动符号 floating sign
浮动缓冲区 floating buffer
浮动库 relocatable library
浮动零点 floating zero
浮动区 floating area
浮动通道 floating channel
浮动头 air supported head, float(ing) head
浮动位 floating bit
浮动性 relocatability
浮动因子 float factor
浮动主机 floating master
浮动字典 relocation dictionary {RLD}

符

符号 symbol, mark, sign, notation ◇标点符号 punctuation mark　符合 accord with, agree with, conform to; coincidence, agreement, correspondence, compliance; valid, congruent
符号保持 mark hold
符号笔画 character stroke
符号编辑 symbolic editing
符号编码 symbolic coding, symbolic programming
符号变换 symbol manipulation
符号变量 symbolic variable
符号标号 symbolic label
符号标记 sign digit, sign flag
符号表 symbol table, tableaux, tag list
符号表达式 symbolic expression
符号表控制 symbol(ic) table control
符号表示 symbolic representation
符号表示法 symbolic notation
符号表指针 symbolic table pointer
符号布局 symbolic layout
符号参数 symbolic parameter
符号操作码 symbolic operation code
符号操作数 symbolic operand
符号测试 sign test
符号差 signature
符号差分析 signature analysis
符号常量 symbolic constant
符号程序 symbolic program
符号触发器 sign flip-flop
符号处理[操作] symbol manipulating/ manipulation/ processing, symbolic manipulation/processing
符号处理语言 symbol manipulation/processing language
符号传播 sign propagation
符号传输 character transfer
符号串 symbol string
符号地址 symbolic address
符号调试 symbolic debugging
符号定义 symbol definition
符号(字)段 sign field
符号发生器 symbol generator
符号分析 symbolic analysis
符号功能 mark function
符号汇编语言 symbolic assem-

bly language
符号绘图 symbol plotting
符号机器 symbolic machine
符号集 set of symbol, symbol set, vocabulary
符号计算 symbolic computing
符号检定 sign test
符号控制表 symbol control table
符号控制符 sign control symbol
符号栏 symbolic field
符号列 symbol rank
符号逻辑 logistics, symbol(ic) logic
符号码 character code
符号密度 character density
符号名 symbolic name
符号模式 sign pattern
符号模型 sign model, symbol(ic) model
符号数字 symbolic number
符号替换 symbol substitution
符号条件 sign condition
符号图 stick diagram
符号推理 symbol(ic) inference, symbol(ic) reasoning
符号位 sign bit, sign digit, sign position, symbol bit
符号文件 symbolic file
符号演算 symbolic calculus
符号引用 symbolic reference
符号语言 symbol(ic) language
符号域 sign field
符号原子 symbolic atom
符号运动 stick motion
符号运算 symbolic operation
符号指令 symbolic instruction
符号指针 symbolic pointer
符号转换程序 symbolic conversion program {SCP}
符号转换器 signal converter
符号状态 sign condition
符号字符 sign character
符号字体[字型] symbol font
符号组 character set, field {FLD}
符合电路 coincidence circuit
符合归并 match-merge
符合门 coincidence gate, identity gate
符合条件 match condition
符合停机 match stop
符合字 matching word

氟 fluorine (F), fluor

幅 width, size 幅度 range, scope, extent, amplitude
幅度 amplitude
幅度分割 amplitude segmentation
幅度畸变 amplitude distortion
幅度量子化控制 amplitude quantize control
幅度调制 amplitude modulation {AM}

辐 spoke 辐射 radiation
辐射干扰 radiate radiated interferense
辐射能 radiant energy
辐射区 radiation field

福 good fortune, happiness, luck 福利 material benefits, well-being, welfare

弗
弗林分类法 Flynn classification schema

【fǔ】

抚 (安慰)comfort, console
抚养 foster, bring up, take care of

斧 斧子 axe

俯

俯 bow, lower 俯瞰 look down on, overlook

辅

辅 assist, supplement 辅导 give guidance in study or training, coach 辅助 ①(从旁帮助) assist ②(非主要的) supplementary, auxiliary, subsidiary, aided, assistant
辅导程序 tutorial program
辅导规则 tutorial rule
辅段 secondary segment
辅键码 secondary key
辅索引 secondary index
辅向量 secondary vector
辅站 extension station
辅助变量 auxiliary variable
辅助操作 nonproductive operation
辅助操作[工作,运算] auxiliary operation
辅助(例行)程序 auxiliary routine
辅助程序 bootstrapping
辅助处理机 attached processor {AP}
辅助磁道 cue track
辅助存储池 auxiliary storage pool {ASP}
辅助存储器 auxiliary memory/ storage/ store, second(ary) memory, secondary storage, supplementary storage
辅助存储器管理程序 auxiliary storage manager {ASM}
辅助地址向量表 secondary address vector table {SAVT}
辅助调页设备 secondary paging device
辅助段 secondary segment
辅助功能 auxiliary/ secondary function
辅助关键字 secondary key
辅助缓冲器 auxiliary buffer
辅助寄存器 auxiliary register
辅助寄存器组 secondary register set
辅助记号 mnemonic mark
辅助接口 satellite interface
辅助卡 daughtercard
辅助控制台 auxiliary console, secondary console
辅助路由 auxiliary route
辅助设备 accessories, ancillary equipment, auxiliary, secondary device
辅助索引 alternate/ secondary index
辅助条件 subsidiary condition
辅助通道 secondary channel
辅助位 overhead bit, service bit
辅助文件 auxiliary file, secondary file
辅助系统 secondary system
辅助信号 cue signal
辅助站 tributary station
辅助终端 accessory terminal
辅助子程序 subsidiary subprogram
辅助字符 special character
辅助总线 satellite bus line, secondary bus

腐

腐烂 decomposed, putrid
腐蚀 ① corrode, etch ② corrupt, corrode

【fù】

父

父 father, parent
父节点 father node
父链接 father link
父母链 parent's chain
父目录 parent directory
父文件 father file
父域 father field
父字段 father field

付

1) 〈支付〉pay 2) 〈交付〉hand over to, turn over to **付现** pay in cash **付诸实施** bring into effect

负

1) 〈亏欠〉owe 2) 〈失败〉lose 3) 〈〈数学〉小于零的〉minus, negative 4) 〈电气〉negative **负担** ①〈动〉bear (a burden), shoulder ②〈名〉burden, load **负责** ①〈担负责任〉be responsible for, be in charge of ②〈认真〉conscientious **负债** be in debt, incur debts, owe a debt

负半定矩阵 negative semidefinite matrix
负标志 minus flag
负的(负数) negative, subzero
负定(的) negative definite
负定函数 negative definite function
负定矩阵 negative definite matrix
负反馈 degenerative feedback, negative feedback
负号 minus flag
负号的 subtractive
负区位[负区,负数区] minus zone
负荷 load
负荷[负载]分布图 load chart
负荷[负载]控制 load control
负荷[负载]容量 load capacity
负基数 negative base number
负畸变[失真] negative distortion
负极 cathode
负角 negative angle
负进位 negative carry
负矩阵 negative matrix
负馈系统 negative feeding system
负逻辑 negative(-true) logic
负平衡 negative balance
负全息图 negative hologram
负熵 negentropy
负数 negative, subzero
负压磁头浮动块 negative pressure slider {**NPS**}
负载 charge, load
负载调整 load regulation
负载额量 capacity
负载均衡组 load balancing group {**LBG**}
负载类型 load type
负载率 operating factor
负载匹配 load matching
负载平衡 load balance/ balancing
负载问题[故障] loading problem
负载系数 load factor
负载线路 loaded line
负载线圈 loading coil
负载映像图 load image
负载运行 underrun
负载阻抗 load impedance
负值 negative value

妇

woman, married woman, wife

附

附带(顺便) in passing **附加** ①〈额外加上〉add, attach, append ②〈附带的〉additional, attached, extra, subsidiary, supplementary, auxiliary **附加费** extracharge, surcharge **附加条款** additional article **附近** ①〈靠近〉nearby, neighboring ②〈接近〉close to, in vicinity of **附录** appendix, addendum **附设** have as an attached institution **附属** subsidiary, auxiliary, attached, accessory, appendant **附属机构** subsid-

iary body 附上 attach, attachment 附言 appendix, postscript (P.S.) 附注 remark, excursus, note 附着 adhere to, stick to, cohere, attach
附加板 add-in card
附加报文 extra message
附加表 add list
附加拨号 additional dialing
附加程序 appendage, extracode
附加存储器 add-on memory, annex memory/storage
附加打印指令 extra print order
附加代码 extracode
附加单元 extra cell
附加的 extra, additional, additive
附加地址 extra address
附加[备用,终端]电池 end cells
附加电路 applique, building-out circuit
附加电平 extra level
附加符号 additional character
附加缓冲区 extra buffer
附加基板 attachment base
附加级 extra level
附加[相邻]寄存器 adjunct register
附加记录 incident record
附加检验 additional test
附加控制板 attachment base
附加款目 added entry
附加码 extracode
附加门 extra gate
附加时间 additional period
附加条件 auxiliary/subsidiary condition
附加位 additional bit, overhead bit
附加文件 append file
附加消息 extra message
附加信息 extraneous information
附加印刷 overprinting
附加约束 additional constraint
附加指令 extra instruction
附加状态 additional state
附加字节 extra byte
附件 accessories, accessory, add-in, appendage, equipment, attachment
附加处理机 attached processor {AP}
附加电路 accessory channel
附属通道 accessory channel
附属信息 satellite information
附随软件 bundled software
附托硬件 piggyback hardware

复 1) (重复) compound, complex 2) (回答) answer, reply 3) (恢复) recover, resume 4) (再,又) again 5) (双重) binary 复本 duplicate copy 复查 recheck, reexamine; reinspection 复发 relapse, recur 复核 check 复核 compound, complex, composite 复习 review, revise 复写 copy, duplicate 复信 write a letter in reply 复印 duplicate, copy 复原 return, reset, unset, renew, restore, restitution, reinstatement, recuperation, rehabilitation 复杂 complicated, complex 复制 duplicate, replicate, copy, reproduce
复变量[变数] complex variable
复常数 complex constant
复打 strike-on
复合编码 composite coding
复合表达式 compound expression
复合乘 complex product
复合串 compound string
复合窗口 composite window

复合磁带 composite tape
复合电缆 composite cable
复合[组合]电路 composite circuit
复合电平 composite level
复合电视广播信号 composite video broadcast signal {CVBS}
复合调制 complex modulation
复合动作 composite move
复合对象 complex object(s), compound object, composite object
复合反馈系统 composite feedback system {CFS}
复合关系 composite relation
复合函数 compound function
复合节点 composite node
复合卡 composite card
复合控制 combination control
复合名字 stowed name
复合命题 combination of sentence, composite statement, compound proposition
复合设备 complex equipment
复合视频信号 composite video
复合特性 composite attribute
复合体 solid object
复合条件 complex/compound condition
复合条形图 composite bar chart
复合文本块 composed-text block
复合系统 composite system {CS}
复合显示(器) composite display
复合项 compound term
复合语句 component statement, composite statement
复合值 stowed value
复合指令 compound instruction
复合终点节点 composite end node {CEN}
复数 complex number, plural number
复数乘法 complex multiplication
复数符号 complex symbol
复数据 complex data
复数类型 complex type
复数属性 complex attribute
复数数据 complex (numeric) data
复数型 complex number type
复数型常数 complex constant
复位 clear, homing, reset, unset
复位程序 reset routine
复位冲突 reset collision
复位[重置,清除]方式 reset mode
复位机构 cancelling release mechanical system
复位键 anti-clash key, reset button, reset key
复位禁止 reset inhibit
复位开关 reset switch
复位控制逻辑 reset control logic
复位脉冲 reset pulse
复位门 reset gate
复位线 reset line
复位信号 reset signal {RES}
复位周期 reset cycle
复现性 reproducibility
复写操作 copy operation
复写规则 copy rule
复写器 polygraph
复写[碳精,炭质]色带 carbon ribbon
复写语句 copy statement
复写纸 carbon paper, copy paper
复印机 copier, copying machine, duplicator, platen

复印件 hard copy, carbon copy {CC}
复印术 reprography
复印语句 copy statement
复印纸 copy paper
复印纸传送机构 conveyer delivery mechanism
复印周期 copy cycle
复原程序 reposition routine
复原卷 recovery volume
复原指令 release command
复杂度 complexity, order of complexity
复杂对象 complex object(s)
复杂性 complexity
复杂性层次 complexity hierarchy
复杂性度量 complexity measure
复杂性类 complexity class
复杂指令集计算(机) complex instruction(s) set computing {CISC}
复杂网络管理 sophisticated network management
复值函数 complex function
复制(品) replication
复制操作 copy operation
复制程序 reproducer
复制错误报文 duplicate error message
复制的程序 version
复制定标 reproduction scale
复制副本 reproduction replica
复制记录 copy write
复制检查 copy check
复制键 duplicate key
复制件 copy cell, hard copy
复制卷 copy volume, duplicate volume
复制目录 directory replication
复制品 clone, copy
复制品尺寸 copy size
复制区 duplicate field
复制术 reprography
复制图 copy pattern
复制位 copy bit
复制写入文件 copy write file
复制修订 copy revision
复制原版 duplicate original
复制纸 transfer sheet
复制装置 duplicating unit

赴 go to, attend, take part in

副 1)(居第二位的)deputy, assistant, vice 副部长 vice-minister 副教授 associate professor 副经理 assistant manager 副秘书长 deputy secretary 2)(辅助的)auxiliary, secondary, subsidiary, supplementary 3)〈量词〉pair, set 副本 duplicate (copy), transcript, (backup) copy, second sheet 副手 assistant 副业 sideline, side occupation 副作用 ① side effect, by-effect ② secondary action
副本 copy, back(up) copy, carbon copy {CC}
副本保护 copy protect
副本保护带 copy guard tape
副本卷 copy volume
副本文件 save file
副插件 subboard
副处理机 subprocessor
副环 inner loop
副键盘 companion keyboard

赋 bestow on, endow with
赋有 possess (naturally), be gifted (with)
赋名规则 naming rule
赋值 assign, assignment,

bind, evaluation
赋值表达式 assignment expression
赋值地址 assigned address
赋值符号 assignment symbol
赋值过程 valuation process
赋值兼容 assignment compatible
赋值设备 valuator, valuator device
赋值算符 assignment operator
赋值语句 assignment statement
赋值运算 assignment operation
赋值转换 assignment conversion
赋值转移 assigned branch
赋值子句 value clause

富 rich, wealthy, abundant 富强 prosperous and strong 富饶 richly endowed, fertile, abundant 富余 have more than needed, have enough to spare 富裕 prosperous, well-to-do, well-off

腹 belly, abdomen, stomach

覆 覆盖 cover, overlay, overlap
覆盖层 blanket
覆盖[重叠]程序 overlay program
覆盖程序段 overlay segment
覆盖管理程序 overlay supervisor
覆盖[重叠]结构 overlay structure
覆盖率 coverage, coverage ratio
覆盖模块 overlay module
覆盖模式 replace mode
覆盖平面 overlay planes
覆盖区(域) overlay area, overlay region
覆盖时间 cover time
覆盖树 overlay tree
覆盖数 covering number
覆盖图 covering graph
覆盖网络 overlay network
覆盖文件 overlay file

傅
傅里叶变换 Fourier transform
傅里叶分析 Fourier analysis
傅里叶积分 Fourier integral

G g

【gā】
伽 gal (Gal, unit of acceleration)

【gá】
钆 gadolinium (Gd)

【gǎi】
该 1)（应当）ought to, should 2)（用于公文）this, that, the side, the above mentioned

【gǎi】
改 （修改）alter, revise
改编 ①（改写作品）adapt, rearrange, revise ②（重新组织）reorganize, redesignate
改变 change, transform 改动 change, after, modify 改革 reform 改换 change over to, change 改建 reconstruct, rebuild 改善 improve, refine, reform, innovate 改造 transform, reform, remold, remake 改正 correct, amend, rectify, put right 改装 reequip, refit, remodel, repack 改组 reorganize, reshuffle
改变 alter, change, modify, stepping, varying
改变长度字符串 varying length string
改变符号 change sign
改变位 change bit
改变文件 file change
改变优先级 change priority
改变装置 modifier
改错 error correcting
改进 reforming, retrofit, upgrade
改进的改进调频制 modified- modified frequency modulation {M²FM}
改进首次适合规则 refined-first-fit rule {RFF}
改进系统 modified system
改进型 second generation
改进型调频制 modified frequency modulation {MFM}
改名 rename
改写方式 typeover mode
改型 version up
改正 correction
改正错误(纠错) error correcting
改正带 amendment tape
改正记录 amendment record
改正码 amendment code
改正文件 amendment file
改址 redirection
改组目录 shifting

【gài】
钙 calcium (Ca); calcic

盖 1)（盖子）lid, cover 2)（覆盖）cover 盖房 build 盖

章 affix a seal, stamp a seal
盖写 overwrite

概
概况 general situation, survey 概括 summarize, generalize 概括地 briefly, in broad outline 概略 outline, summary, skeleton; schematic 概论 outline, introduction, topic 概念 concept, conception, notion, idea 概要 essentials, outline, general remark, general view
概率 probability
概率(方)法 probabilistic method
概率仿真 probabilistic simulation
概率分布 probability distribution
概率分析 probability analysis
概率估计 probability estimate
概率规划 probabilistic programming
概率函数 probability function
概率机 probabilistic machine
概率极限 probability limit
概率检验 probabilistic testing
概率空间 probability space
概率论 probability theory
概率逻辑 probabilistic logic
概率密度 probability density
概率模型 probabilistic/probability model
概率算法 probabilistic algorithm
概率图灵机 probabilistic Turing machine {PTM}
概率推理 probabilistic reasoning
概率微分 probability differential
概率[随机]系统 probabilistic system
概率相关 probability correlation
概率向量 probability vector
概率预测 probabilistic forecasting
概率预算 probabilistic budgeting
概率支配 probabilistic dominance
概貌 profile
概念层 conceptual level
概念层次体系 concept hierarchy
概念范畴 concept field
概念方法 conceptual schema
概念分类 concept classification
概念构造 concept formation
概念化框架 conceptual framework
概念机 concept machine
概念节点 concept node
概念模式[模型,框图] conceptual model, conceptual schema
概念群集 concept clustering
概念数据库 conceptual database
概念协调 concept coordination
概念形成 concept formation, concept making
概念依赖 conceptual dependency
概要报表 summary report
概要设计 summary design

【gān】
干 另见【gàn】
(干燥)dry, waterless 干净 ①(清洁)clean, neat and tidy ②(完全)completely, totally 干扰 disturb, jam, interfere, confuse 干涉 interfere, intervene 干预 intervene, meddle 干燥 dry, arid
干扰测试 disturbed test
干印法 xerography

gān 甘杆竿 gǎn 杆赶敢感 gàn 干 gāng 刚

干油墨 dry ink

甘 (甜)sweet, pleasant 甘心,甘愿 willingly, readily

杆 另见【gǎn】
1) pole, staff, post, mast ◇电线杆 pole 2)〈量词〉pole (unit of length)

竿 1) pole, rod 2)〈量词〉rod (unit of length)

杆 另见【gǎn】

pole, rod, bar, link, lever, arm
杆式[棒式]存储器 rod memory
杆式打字[打印]机 bar typewriter

【gǎn】

赶 赶快 at once, quickly 赶忙 hurry, hasten, make haste 赶任务 rush through one's work 赶上 ①(追上)overtake, catch up with, keep pace with ②(及时)be in time for

敢 dare, make bold 敢说敢为 dare speak and act 敢于 dare to, be bold in

感 (觉得)feel, sense 感到 feel, sense 感动 move, touch 感官 sense organ, sensory organ 感激 feel grateful, be thankful, feel indebted 感觉 ① sense perception, sensation, feeling ② feel, perceive, become aware of 感情 emotion, feeling, sentiment 感受 ①(受到)be affected by ②(体会) experience, feel 感想 impressions, reflections, thoughts 感谢 thank, be grateful 感谢信 letter of thanks, thank-you note 感兴趣 be interested in
感光层 photographic layer
感光绘图机 photo plotter
感应 induct, induction, influence
感应马达 induction motor
感应式读写磁头 inductive read/write head
感应线圈 induction coil
感知 perception
感知段 sensitive segment
感知功能 perceptive function
感知机[器] perceptron
感知原语 perceptual primitive
感知字段 sensitive field

【gàn】

干 另见【gān】
1)(主体)trunk, main part 2)(做)do, work 干劲 drive, vigor, enthusiasm
干线 main line, trunk line
干线电缆 trunk cable
干线放大器 trunk amplifier
干线耦合器 trunk coupling unit

【gāng】

刚 firm, strong 刚才 just now, a moment ago 刚刚 only a short while ago, just 刚好 ①(正合适)just, exactly ②(正巧)happen to, it so happened that
刚-挠多层印制板 flex-rigid multilayer printed board
刚使用过的 least recently used {LRU}
刚性方程组 stiff systems

刚性稳定 stiff stability
刚性系统 stiff system

纲 1)(总纲)key link, guiding principle 2)(大纲)outline, program 3)〈生物〉class 纲领 program, guiding principle 纲要 outline, sketch; essentials, compend(ium), key

钢 steel ◇炼钢 steelmaking 钢笔 pen, fountain pen 钢材 steel products, steels, rolled steel 钢琴 piano 钢铁 iron and steel

缸 vat, jar; cylinder

【gǎng】

岗 (山岗)hillock, mound 岗哨 sentry, guard 岗位 post, position

港 港口(sea)port, harbor

【gàng】

杠 (thick)stick; bar 杠杆开关 lever key

【gāo】

高 1)(高度)tall, high 2)(等级高)of a high level or degree 高产 high yield, high production 高超 superb, excellent 高潮 ① high tide ② upsurge, climax, high tide 高大 tall and big, lofty 高度 ① altitude, height ② a high degree of; highly 高峰 peak, summit, height 高级 ① (级别高)senior, high-ranking, high-level, high, higher order, top grade ② (质量高)high-grade, high-quality, advanced 高技术 high tech, high technology 高精尖 high, refined and peak; high level, perfected and most advanced 高明 brilliant, wise 高尚 noble, lofty 高深 advanced, profound 高速 high speed 高温 high temperature 高兴 ① (愉快)glad, happy, cheerful ② (喜欢)be willing to, be happy to 高压 ① high pressure ② high tension, high voltage 高涨 rise, boom, run high
高保真度 high fidelity
高保真图像 high fidelity image
高部位 high-order bit
高层次 up leveling
高层集 upgrade set
高层网络协议 high level network protocol
高层信息 high-level message
高冲击强度[冲力] high impact
高存储器 high memory
高档 high-end
高档语言 high-order language {HOL}
高电平 high level
高电位[电压] high potential
高度对称图 highly symmetric graph
高度[深度]平衡树 height balanced tree
高度相关 high correlation
高端存储器 high memory
高端内存区 high memory area {HMA}
高反差 high-contrast
高分辨率 high resolution (= hi-res)
高峰时间 rush hours
高负载 high capacity

高功能终端 high function terminal {HFT}
高级办公室系统 advanced office system {AOS}
高级编程接口 high-level programming interface {HLPI}
高级编译程序 high-level compiler
高级查询 advanced query
高级程序设计 advanced programming
高级程序员 senior programmer
高级电视 advanced television {ATV}
高级调度 high-level scheduling
高级对等互连网 advance peer-to-peer internetworking {APPI}
高级对等连网 advanced peer-to-peer networking {APPN}
高级对等通信 advance peer-to-peer communications {APPC}
高级格式 high level format
高级功能打印 advanced function printing {AFP}
高级绘图软件 high-level graphics software
高级教程 advanced course
高级控制系统 advanced control system {ACS}
高级目标 high level goal
高级软件技术 higher-order software technology {HOS}
高级声音编码 advanced audio coding {AAC}
高级声音编码工具 advanced audio coding tool
高级数据库系统 advanced database system
高级数据链路控制 high-level data link control {HDLC}
高级数据链路控制规程(协议) high level data link control {HDLC}
高级数据通信控制进程 advanced data communications control procedure {ADCCP}
高级文本管理系统 advanced text management system {ATMS}
高级系统分析员 senior system analyst
高级系统设计员 senior system designer
高级协议 high-level protocol
高级信息技术 advanced information technology
高级语言 higher language, higher-order language, high-level language {HLL}
高级语言机 high-level language machine
高级原语 high-level primitive
高技术工业 high technology industry
高技术区 high technic area
高阶函数 higher-order function
高阶逻辑 higher-order logic
高阶目的 higher-order goal
高阶微分 higher differential
高阶位 higher-order position
高阶谓词 higher-order predicate
高阶[高位]字节 high-order byte
高抗扰逻辑 high-noise immunity logic {HNIL, HiNIL}
高宽比 aspect ratio
高密度磁盘 high-density disk
高密度集成存储器 superintegrated storage
高密度数字存储器 high-density digital storage
高密度双极性编码 high-density bipolar {HDB}
高内存区 high memory area {HMA}
高能 high energy
高能磁带 high-energy tape

高能的 energetic
高频 high frequency
高频总线 high-frequency bus
高强度 high tension
高清晰度(数字)电视 high-definition television {HDTV}
高韧度[性] high tenacity
高容量 high capacity
高数位 high-order digit, high-order position, top digit
高速处理技术 high-speed processing technology
高速串行接口 high speed serial interface {HSSI}
高速存储器 high-speed memory, cache memory
高速存储器系统 cache system
高速存储区 scratchpad area {SPA}
高速打印机 high-speed printer {HSP}
高速电路交换数据 high speed circuit switching data {HSCSD}
高速度 high speed
高速仿真 high-speed simulation
高速环 high-speed loop
高速缓冲器[区] high-speed buffer
高速缓冲存储器 cache (buffer) memory, cache storage
高速缓冲存储器命中 cache storage hit
高速缓存参数 cache parameter
高速缓存冲突 cache conflict
高速缓存存取 cache access
高速缓存单元 cache unit
高速缓存访问失败 cache miss
高速缓存管理程序 cache manager
高速缓存接口 cache interface
高速缓存进入 cache entry
高速缓存控制程序 cache controller
高速缓存控制字 cache control word
高速缓存命中 cache hit
高速缓存模拟程序 cache simulator
高速缓存目录 cache directory
高速缓存器的相关性 cache coherency
高速缓存驱动程序 cache driver
高速缓存网络 cache network
高速缓存一致性 cache coherence
高速缓存置换 cache replace
高速缓存周期 cache cycle
高速控制器 high-speed controller
高速通路 speedway
高速阅读器 high-speed reader {HSR}
高通 highpass
高通滤波器 highpass filter
高维阵列 higher array
高位[高序,高阶] high order
高位地址 high address
高位端 high-order end
高位列 high-order column
高位数(位) left-hand digit, high-order digit
高位值 high-value
高位字符 high-order character
高位字节 high byte
高性能并行接口 high performance parallel interface {HPPI}
高性能存储器 high-performance memory
高性能计算 high performance computing
高性能文件系统 high performance file system {HPFS}
高真空 high vacuum
高质通信线路 conditioned line
高阻(状)态 high-impedance state

膏 1)(油膏)fat, grease, oil 2)(糊状物)paste, cream, ointment

【gǎo】

搞 (做)do, carry on, be engaged in

镐 pick, pickaxe

稿 稿件 manuscript, contribution 稿子 draft, sketch

【gào】

告 tell, inform 告别 leave, bid farewell to 告成 accomplish, complete 告急 ①(情况紧急)be in an emergency ②(请求援救)report an emergency, ask for immediate help 告警 report an emergency, give an alarm 告示 official notice, bulletin, announcement 告诉 tell, let know 告知 inform, notify 告终 come to an end, end up

告警分类 alarm category

告警指示信号 alarm indication signal {AIS}

锆 zirconium (Zr)

【gē】

戈 (瑞)gray (Gy, unit of absorbed dose)

哥 (elder) brother

胳 胳臂 arm

搁 搁置 shelve, lay aside

割 cut 割除 cut off, cut out, excise 割断 sever, cut off 割裂 cut apart, separate, isolate

割点 cut vertex, cut-point

割集 cutset

割集方程 cutset equation

割集矩阵 cutset matrix

歌 (唱歌)sing 歌曲 song

【gé】

革 1)(皮革)leather, hide 2)(改变)change, transform 3)(开除)remove from office, expel 革除 abolish, get rid of 革命 revolution 革新 innovation

格 squares formed by crossed lines, check 格调 style 格局 pattern, setup, structure 格式 form, pattern, format, style, layout 格外 especially, unusually

格点 lattice point

格式背景 form overlay

格式编им formatting

格式变换 format transformation, reformatting

格式标识 format identification {FID}

格式标识符号 formatter symbol

格式标志 format denotation

格式标识符 format designator

格式标准 format standard

格式表 form sheet, format list

格式参数 format parameter

格式常量 layout constant

格式成员 format member

格式程序 formatted program

格式串 format string

格式存储 format storage

格式错误 format error

格式打印程序 reformatter

格式定义 form definition {FORMDEF}, format definition
格式翻译 format translate
格式符(号) format/ layout character, format symbol
格式管理 form management
格式化 format, formatting
格式化程序 formatted program, formatter
格式化磁带 formatted tape
格式化磁道 format track
格式化方式[状态] formatting mode
格式化软盘 formatted diskette
格式化图像 formatted image
格式化信文[报文] formatted message
格式集 format set
格式(化)记录 formatted record
格式检验 format check
格式控制表 form control table {FCT}
格式控制符 format effector (character) {FE}
格式控制字符 effector
格式馈给[进纸] form feed {FF}
格式类型 format type
格式描述 format description
格式明细符 format effector {FE}
格式识别 format identification {FID}, format recognition
格式数据 formatted data, layout data
格式图像 format-pattern
格式文本 format text
格式文件 format(ted) file
格式项 format item
格式选择 format selection
格式语句 FORMAT statement
格式指令 format order
格式转换 format conversion/ translate

格网 mesh
格网间隔 mesh spacing
格网区域 mesh region
格栅 grid
格栅图表 grid chart
格子填充 slot-filling

隔 (间隔)at a distance from, after or at an interval of 隔壁 next door 隔绝 isolate, exclude 隔开 separate, stand or lie between, partition, divide, space 隔离 isolate, segregate, buffer
隔离层 spacer
隔离的 isolated
隔离放大器 buffer amplifier
隔离码 barrier code
隔离器 isolator
隔离位置 isolated location
隔行 interleave
隔行驱动 nonstaging drive
隔行扫描 interlacing, interleave, staged scanning

镉 cadmium (Cd)

【gè】
个 个别 ①（单个）individual, specific ②（极少数）very few, one or two, exceptional 个人 individual (person) 个人财产 personal property 个体 individual 个体经济 individual economy 个体户 individual entrepreneur 个性 individual character, individuality, personality
个别控制 individual control
个人标识符 personal identifier
个人计算机 personal computer {PC}
个人识别号码 private identifi-

cation number {PIN}
个人识别码 personal identification number {PIN}
个人识别数据 personal identification data {PID}
个人通信业务 personal communication services {PCS}
个人网站服务程序 personal web server
个人泄密 personal disclosure
个体变量[变项] individual variable

各 each, every, all 各半 half and half, fifty-fifty 各别 distinct, different 各个 ①（每个）each, every, various ②（分别）one by one, separately 各行各业 the various walks of life, all trades and professions 各级 all or different levels 各式各样 various, of all kinds 各种 diversified, various, different 各自 each, respectively, individually
各向异性 anisotropy

铬 chromiun (Cr), chrome

【gěi】
给 另见【jǐ】
1)（交给）give, grant, hand 2)（为）for 3)（让）let, allow 4)（被）by
给定装置 setter

【gēn】
根 1)（植物的根）root 2)〈数学〉(方程的解)root, (记数根) radix ◇立方根 cube root 3) 〈化学〉(带电的基)radical ◇ 酸根 acid radical 根本 ①（最重要的）basic, fundamental ②（用于否定）at all ③（彻底）radically, thoroughly 根除 thoroughly do away with, eradicate 根据 ①（依据）on the basis of, according to, in the light of, in line with ②〈名〉basis, grounds, foundation 根源 source, origin, root
根窗口 root window
根记录 base node, root record
根节点 root node
根路径 root path
根算符 root operator

跟 （脚跟）heel 跟随 follow 跟踪 follow the tracks of, trace, track, tail
跟随复制指令 follow copy {FC}
跟随[随动]控制 follow-up control
跟随控制 self-aligning control
跟踪包 trace packet
跟踪表 trace table
跟踪[检测,追踪]程序 trace routine
跟踪[示踪,追踪]程序 trace program
跟踪程序模块 tracer module
跟踪分析程序 tracking analyzer
跟踪工具 trace tool
跟踪记录 audit log
跟踪进程 trace d(a)emon
跟踪[追踪]例行程序 tracing routine
跟踪能力 trackability
跟踪器 tracker
跟踪日志 trace log
跟踪文件 follow-up file
跟踪文件,追踪文件 trace file
跟踪装置 follower, tracking apparatus

【gēng】

更 另见【gèng】

更动,更改 change, alter
更换,更替 change, replace, supersede, transpose; renewal
更正 correction, amendment, rectification
更换位 change bit
更名 rename
更替例程 alternate routine
更替路径 alternate path
更新 update, refresh, retrofit, replacement, renew(al)
更新安装 update install
更新标记 update mark
更新操作 update operation
更新分析 replacement analysis
更新过程 innovation process, renewal process
更新理论 renewal theory
更新请求 refresh request
更新权 update authority, update rights
更新速度 refresh rate
更新文件 update file
更新状态 update mode

【gěng】

梗 stalk, stem 梗概 broad outline, main idea, gist, generality, skeleton, synoptic

【gèng】

更 另见【gēng】
1)(更加) more, still more, even more 2)(再,又) further, furthermore

【gōng】

工 工厂 factory, mill, plant, works 工场 workshop 工程 engineering, project 工程师 engineer 工地 site 工段 work section, department 工具书 reference book 工龄 length of service, standing, seniority 工人 worker, workman, laborer 工序 working procedure, process 工业 industry 工资 wages, pay 工作 work, labor 工作日 work-day 工作者 worker 工作证 employee's card, ID card
工厂布局 plant layout
工程抽样[试样] engineering sample
工程费用 engineering cost
工程更改 engineering change {EC}
工程计划 engineering effort
工程控制论 engineering cybernetics
工程设计 engineering design
工程数据 engineering data
工程数据库系统 engineering database system {EDBS}
工程数学 engineering mathematics
工程说明书 engineering specification
工程图 schedule graph
工件 work piece
工具 tool, implement(ation), instrument
工具板 tool palette
工具包 toolkit
工具角色 instrument case
工具类 widget typewidget
工具设计 tool design, facility design
工具箱 toolbox, toolkit, instrument case
工具组 tool set
工序图 schedule graph
工业安全 industrial security
工业标准体系结构 industry

standard architecture {ISA}
工业产品 industrial product
工业工程 industrial engineering {IE}
工业管理 industrial management
工业控制机 industrial control unit {ICU}
工业控制组件 industrial control module
工业生产报文规范 manufacturing message specification {MMS}
工业通信协会 industrial communication association {ICA}
工业微型计算机 industrial microcomputer
工业应用程序 industry application program {IAP}
工艺过程 process
工艺模型 process modeling
工艺设计 process planning
工资报表 payroll journal
工资单 payroll
工资计算 payroll accounting
工作 role, run, working
工作测定 work measurement
工作程序 production routine, working routine
工作抽样 work sampling
工作磁带 work tape
工作存储节 working storage section
工作[暂时]存储器 working storage {WS}
工作存储区 working area
工作带 working tape
工作单元 work unit, working cell, work package
工作单元表 temporary table
工作单元块 temporary block
工作队列 work queue
工作对话 work session
工作范围 operating range, working range
工作方式 working mode
工作分解结构 work breakdown structure {WBS}
工作分配图 work distribution chart
工作负荷 work load
工作负载 live load, operating load
工作过程 working process
工作集 working set
工作卷 work volume
工作空间 working space, workspace
工作框 operation box, process box
工作流程 workflow
工作流分析 workflow analysis
工作流计算 workflow computing
工作流软件 workflow software
工作流语言 workflow language {WFL}
工作码 working code
工作目录 working directory
工作盘 scratch diskette
工作区 working area, work area, working space, workspace
工作区单元 workspace location
工作区结构 workspace architecture/structure
工作区控制 working set control
工作区指示字 workspace pointer
工作日报 daily activity report {DAR}
工作软盘 working diskette
工作设备 working equipment
工作设计 work design
工作时间 active session, on time, operating time
工作时间片 work slice

工作数据文件 working data file
工作台 desktop, operating board, work table
工作条件 operational condition
工作位置[状态] operating position
工作文档 work document
工作文件 work file, working paper
工作系数 operating factor
工作因子 work factor
工作语言 work language
工作原理 operational principle
工作栈 work stack
工作站 work station, working station, active station
工作站地址 workstation address
工作站服务 workstation service
工作站过程 work station process
工作站领域 workstation domain
工作周期 work cycle, work period
工作[活动,有效]状态 active state
工作组 workgroup

弓 bow, arch

公 1)(共同的) common, general 2)(雄性的) male (animal) 公安 public security 公报 communique, bulletin 公布 promulgate, announce, publish 公尺 meter 公道 ①(正义) justice ②(公平) fair, just, reasonable, impartial 公分 centimeter 公告 announcement 公共 public, common 公共财产 public property 公共汽车 bus 公关 public relations 公家 public, state-owned, collective 公斤 kilogram 公开 ①〈形〉open, public ②〈动〉make public, make known to the public 公里 kilometer 公立 established and maintained by the government, public 公立学校 public school 公路 highway, road 公民 citizen 公平 fair, just, impartial, equitable 公顷 hectare 公认 generally acknowledged, (universally) accepted 公式 formula 公事,公务 public affairs, official business 公司 company, corporation 公用 for public use, public, communal 公有 publicly-owned, public 公元 the Christian era 公园 park 公正 just, fair, impartial, fair-minded 公职 public office, public employment 公众 the public

公告牌系统 bulletin board system {BBS}
公共表达式 common expression
公共操作 public operation
公共操作服务 common operations service {COS}
公共存储器区 common storage area
公共代码 common code
公共电话交换网 general switched telephone network {GSTN}
公共动作 common action
公共队列 public queue
公共对象模型 common object model {COM}
公共对象请求代理体系结构 common object request broker architecture {CORBA}
公共管理信息协议 common

management information protocol {CMIP}
公共键 common key, public key
公共交换数据网 public switched data network {PSDN}
公共决策 public decision making
公共开放软件环境 common open software environment {COSE}
公共控制单元 common control unit
公共库 public library
公共领域软件 public domain software {PDS}
公共密匙 public key
公共密匙基础 public key infrastructure {PKI}
公共密钥加密 public key encryption
公共目录 public directory
公共耦合 common coupling
公共权限 public authority
公共数据网 public data network {PDN}
公共说明 common declaration
公共通路 highway
公共网 public network
公共网关接口 common gateway interface {CGI}
公共[公用]通信适配器 common communication adapter {CCA}
公共信息 public information
公共应用服务元素 common application service element {CASE}
公共用户访问 common user access {CUA}
公共语言 common language
公共中间格式 common intermediate format {CIF}
公共注记 public note
公共总线 common bus
公开策略 open policy
公开密钥 clear cryptographic key, public key
公开数据 public data
公开信道 overt channel
公理 axiom
公理格式 axiom schema
公理探索 axiomatic approach
公理系统 axiom system
公认程序 authorized program
公式处理 formula manipulation
公式处理编译程序 formula manipulation compiler {FORMAC}
公式化 formulate, formulation
公式控制 formula manipulation
公式模型 formula model
公式识别 formula recognition
公式语言 formula language
公司开发的图像文件存储格式 graphics interchange format {GIF}
公因子 common factor
公用部件 global facility
公用程序 common program, utility
公用程序库 public library
公用存储器端口 common memory port
公用的 common
公用地址空间段 common address space section {CASS}
公用电话交换网 public switched telephone network {PSTN}
公用电话网络 public telephone network
公用段 common section/ segment, public segment
公用队列 common queue,

public queue
公用功能 utility function
公用缓冲区 common buffer
公用汇编程序 common assembler
公用(软)件 shareware
公用交换 public exchange
公用交换电话网 public switched telephone network {PSTN}
公用交换网络 public switched network {PSN}
公用卷 public volume
公用空间 public space
公用控制器 common control
公用控制区 common control section
公用库 common library
公用块 common block
公用例程 utility routine
公用区 common area/ field, global area
公用软件 common software
公用数据 common data
公用数据网(络) public data network {PDN}
公用索引 common index
公用天线电视 community antenna television {CATV}
公用网络 common network
公用文件区域服务 public domain service
公用线 multiparty line
公用信号量 global semaphore
公用掩码 common mask
公用页 common page
公用语言 common language
公用域 common field, public domain {PD}
公用源 common source
公用资源 common resource
公用字段 common field
公钥加密 public key encryption
公钥密码学 public key cryptography

公正性 fairness
公正准则 fairness doctrine
公制 international system of units {SI}

功 1)(成绩) merits, achievement, result 2)〈物理〉work 功绩 merits and achievements, contribution 功课 schoolwork, homework 功劳 contribution, meritorious service, credit 功能 function, facility 功效 efficacy, effect 功用 function, use, duty
功率 power
功率比 power rate
功率操作 power operation
功率电平 power level
功率放大器 power amplifier
功率函数 power function
功率级 power level
功率晶体管 power transistor
功率控制 power control
功率频谱 power spectrum
功率系数 power factor
功率增益 power gain
功能按钮 function button
功能标记 functional label
功能标识符 function identifier
功能表示法 function representation
功能并行性 functional parallelism
功能部分 function part
功能部件 function unit, functional unit
功能部件冲突 functional unit collision
功能测试 functional test
功能层 functional layer
功能程序 function program, functionality
功能单元 functional unit
功能定义 functional definition

gōng 攻

功能分类 functional classification
功能分配 allocation of function, function allocation
功能分析 functional analysis
功能符 function character
功能管理数据 function management data {FMD}
功能划分 functional division, functional partitioning
功能恢复例行程序 functional recovery routine {FRR}
功能级 function level
功能检查 function check
功能键 function key
功能键盘 function keyboard
功能键区 function key area
功能键小键盘 function pad
功能接口 functional interface
功能结构 functional configuration
功能开关 functional switch
功能控制块 function control block {FCB}
功能控制序列 function control sequence {FCS}
功能块 function block, module, functional block
功能流程图 function flowchart
功能逻辑 function logic
功能码 function code
功能名 function name
功能模块 functional module
功能模拟 functional simulation
功能模式 functioning pattern
功能模型 functional model
功能配置 functional configuration
功能软盘 function diskette
功能(部件)设计 functional design
功能设计 function design
功能设计图 function diagram
功能失效 disabler
功能识别符 function identifier
功能授权使用凭证 function authority credentials {FAC}
功能说明 function specification
功能特性 functional performance
功能特许证 function authority credentials {FAC}
功能完备性 functional completeness
功能位 function digit
功能系统分析 functional analysis system technique {FAST}
功能型指令 functional instruction
功能性应用 functional application
功能需求 functional requirement
功能选择表 option list
功能依赖 functional dependency
功能异常 malfunction
功能元 functional primitive
功能元件 functor, function element, functional element
功能阵列 function array
功能转变 functional shift
功能状态块 function status block
功能子程序 function subprogram
功能子系统 functional subsystem {FSS}
功能子系统接口 functional subsystem interface {FSI}
功能子系统应用 functional subsystem application {FSA}
功能字 function word
功能字符 function(al) character
功能组织 function organization

攻
攻读 study assiduously, study diligently 攻关 tackle

gōng 供恭 gǒng 巩汞拱 gòng 共

key problems 攻克 capture, take

供 另见【gòng】

(提供) for (the use or convenience of) ◇仅供参考 for reference only 供不应求 supply falls short of demand 供给 supply, feed, provide, furnish 供销 supply and marketing 供应 supply, delivery, provide
供带盘 feed reel, supply reel
供电部分 power pack
供电线路 power supply circuit
供给标准 pay standard
供给中心 backbone
供货水平 service level
供应者 provider
供纸板 feedboard
供纸检测器 sheet detector
供纸控制器 feed control
供纸量 paper delivery
供纸器 feeder, sheet feeder

恭
恭候 await respectfully 恭敬 respectful, with great respect 恭喜 congratulations

巩
巩固 ①〈动〉consolidate, strengthen ②〈形〉consolidated, strong, solid, stable

汞
mercury (Hg), quicksilver, hydrargyrum

拱
arch, bow

【gòng】
共
common; share 共存 coexist, survive together 共计 amount to, add up to, total 共事 work together 共同 ①(共有)common ②(一起)together, jointly 共享 enjoy together, share 共性 general character, generality
共存[共用]程序 symbiont
共存控制 symbiont control
共存模式 coexistence model
共存系统 symbiotic system
共存性 coexistence
共电路 cocircuit
共调度 coscheduling
共轭 conjugate
共轭函数 conjugate function
共轭弦 conjugate chord
共轭像 conjugate image
共模[共态]操作 common mode operation
共生进程 symbiont
共生系统 symbiotic system
共式[共模]抽样 common mode sampling
共属性段 sibling segment
共态协调 costate coordination
共态抑制比 common mode rejection ratio {CMRR}
共体 covolume
共同体描述表 community profile
共同作用 synergism
共享变量 shared variable
共享策略 sharing policy
共享程序 shared routine, sharer
共享磁道 shared track
共享磁盘 sharing disk
共享存储器 shared memory/storage
共享打印机 printer sharing
共享地址 shared address
共享端口 shared port
共享段 shared segment
共享访问通路 shared access path
共享分类 shared class

gòng 贡供 gōu 勾沟钩 gòu 构

共享分区 shared partition
共享环境 shared environment
共享计算 share count
共享假脱机 shared spooling
共享(软)件 shareware
共享结构 shared structure
共享控制器 shared control unit
共享控制网关 shared control gateway
共享库 share(d) base {SB}
共享逻辑 shared logic
共享名 sharename
共享目录 shared directory
共享批处理[作业]区 shared batch area {SBA}
共享请求 share request
共享任务组 shared task set
共享入口 shared port
共享数据集 shared data set
共享数据库 shared database
共享(型)锁 shared lock
共享网络 sharing network
共享文件 share file, shared file
共享文件夹 shared folder
共享系统 shared/ sharing system
共享虚拟存储器 shared virtual area {SVA}, shared virtual memory
共享页表 shared page table
共享页面 shared page
共享者 sharer
共享资源 shared resource, sharing resource
共享总线 shared bus
共用成批程序区域 shared batch area {SBA}
共用磁盘 shared disk
共用存取转换设备 common access switching equipment {CASE}
共用调制解调器 modem sharing unit {MSU}
共用控制器 shared control unit
共用例程 shared routine
共用路径 shared path
共用目录 directory shared
共用[共享]设备 shared device
共用视图 community view
共用通路 shared path
共用外围设备 shared peripheral
共用网络 community network
共用文件 shared file
共用系统 sharing system
共用虚拟区 shared virtual area {SVA}
共用页面表 shared page table
共用总线 shared bus
共域 codomain
共驻主存的 coresident

贡 tribute 贡献 contribute, dedicate, devote

供 另见【gōng】
供认 confess 供职 hold office

【 gōu 】

勾 勾画 draw the outline of, delineate, sketch 勾销 cancel, write off, strike out

沟 ditch, drain, channel; groove 沟通 link up

钩 hook, crook
钩链 hook chain

【 gòu 】

构 构成 constitute, construct, compose, form, make up; built-up 构想 idea, conception, concept 构造 structure, construction
构成文法 constituent grammar
构成[结构]帧 configuration frame
构架 truss

构件 structure
构件对象模型 component object model {COM}
构件赋值 structure assignment
构件属性 structure attribute
构思模型 mental model
构图 compose
构像 constellation
构形 topography
构造性证明 constructive proof
构造子集 subsetting

垢 dirt, filth ◇ 尘垢 dust and dirt // 油垢 grease stain

购 purchase, buy 购买 purchase, buy 购买力 purchasing power 购销 purchase and sale, buying and selling
购买系统 purchase system
购物系统 shopping system

够 enough, sufficient, adequate 够格 be qualified, be up to the standard

【gū】

估 估价 appraise (prices of goods) 估计 estimate, appraise, reckon 估量 appraise, estimate, assess, evaluate 估算 estimate, provisional estimate, rough estimate; appraise, reckon
估计方差 estimate variance
估计费用 cost estimate
估算单元 evaluation unit
估算技术 estimation technique
估算理论 estimation theory

孤 (孤单) solitary, isolated, alone 孤立 isolate
孤立点 acnode, isolated point, isolated vertex
孤立顶点 isolated vertex
孤立节点 isolated node
孤立解 isolated solution
孤立网络 isolated network
孤立字 isolated word
孤行 orphan, widow line

箍 hoop, band, buckle, collar

【gǔ】

古 ancient 古代 ancient times 古典 classical 古董 antique, curio 古老 ancient, age-old
古典方法 classical approach
古典控制 classical control

谷 (山谷) valley, gorge 谷物 cereal, grain

股 1)(大腿) thigh 2)(组织单位) section (of an organization) ◇ 财务股 accounting section 3)(绳子的一股) strand 股本 capital stock 股东 shareholder, stockholder 股份 share, stock 股份有限公司 limited company (Ltd.) 股票 share, stock 股息 dividend

骨 骨架 skeleton, framework ◇ 钢骨水泥 reinforced concrete 骨干 backbone, mainstay 骨头 bone
骨架 skeletal, skeleton
骨架数据 skeleton data
骨图 skeleton view
骨架系统 shell system, skeletal system

钴 cobalt (Co)

鼓 (乐器)drum 鼓动 agitate, arouse 鼓励 encourage, urge 鼓掌 clap one's hands, applaud

鼓式打印机 barrel printer, drum printer

鼓式绘图机 drum plotter

鼓式扫描 drum scanning

鼓式印刷 barrel printing

鼓形扫描 drum scanning

毂 hub, nave

【gù】

固 1)〈形〉solid, firm 2)〈动〉strengthen 固定 ①〈形〉fixed, regular ②〈动〉fix, regularize 固然 ① no doubt, it is true ② of course, admittedly 固体 solid body, solid 固有 intrinsic, inherent, innate

固定保持 fixed retention

固定比特率 constant bit rate {CBR}

固定变量 fixed variable

固定标记 mark hold

固定标识 constant mark

固定长度 fixed-length

固定长度编码 fixed-length code {FLC}

固定程序 fixed program, program fix

固定磁盘 fixed disk, nonremovable disk

固定磁头 fixed head

固定存储器 fixed memory, fixed storage, nonerasable storage

固定读写头 fixed head

固定方式 fixed mode

固定分区 fixed partition

固定格式 canned format, fixed form(at), F-format

固定功能 fixed function

固定"0"故障 stuck-at-zero fault

固定"1"故障 stuck-at-one fault

固定故障 permanent fault

固定级 fix level

固定间隔 fixed spacing

固定键 dead key

固定空格 fixed space, fixed spacing

固定空间 fixed space

固定控制区 fixed control area

固定块 fixed block

固定块长度 fixed block length

固定块传输 fixed block transmission

固定块格式 fixed block format

固定块结构 fixed-block-architecture {FBA}

固定宽度字体 monospace font

固定框 fixed box

固定路由选择 fixed routine

固定名 fixed name

固定模式 fixed mode

固定区域 fixed area {FX}, fixed field

固定软件 canned software

固定设备 fixed resource

固定十进制 fixed decimal

固定顺序 permanent order

固定网络 fixed network

固定文件属性 fixed file attributes

固定形式 fixed-form

固定行号 fixed line number

固定性错误 solid error

固定性故障 constant fault

固定页面 fixed page

固定溢出 fixed overflow

固定优先级 fixed priority

固定域 fixed field

固定周期 fixed cycle

固定字 fixed word

固定字长 fixed word-length

固定字段 fixed field, fixed

filed
固定字宽体 monospace font
固件 firmware
固件程序 firmware program/routine
固件工程 firmware engineering
固件结构 firmware structure
固件驱动(的) firmware-driven
固件设备 firmware device
固态逻辑技术 solid logic technology {SLT}
固态元件 solid state component
固体成像 solid image
固体电路 solid state circuit
固有存储器 inherent-memory device
固有错误 inherited error
固有名字 proper name
固有[自然]频率 natural frequency
固有区 proper area
固有值 intrinsic value
固有字型 intrinsic font

故 1) (事故) incident, happening 2) (缘故) reason, cause 3) (从前的) former, old **故意** intentionally, willfully, deliberately, on purpose
故事病毒 story virus
故障 failure, fault, bug, casualty, down, malfunction, accident, mischief
故障保护 error protection
故障报警 error warning, malfunction alarm
故障标识 failure identification
故障表 error/fault list, fault dictionary, syndrome table
故障表征 fault signature
故障部件[部分] trouble block, trouble unit
故障测试 fault testing, syndrome test
故障测试生成 fault test generation
故障插入 fault insertion
故障查找器 fault finder
故障场所 trouble spot
故障串 syndrome serial
故障单位 failure unit
故障单元 trouble unit
故障登记 failure logging
故障等效 fault equivalence
故障点 point of failure, trouble spot
故障定位测试(法) fault location test {FLT}
故障定位程序 fault locator
故障分布 failure distribution
故障分类 failure category, fault grading
故障分析 failure analysis, fault analysis
故障覆盖 fault-coverage
故障隔离 fault isolation
故障跟踪 fault trace
故障管理 fault management
故障恢复 fault recovery, recovery from the failures
故障恢复例行程序 damage assessment routine {DAR}
故障记录 failure logging
故障检测 failure testing, fault detect(ion)
故障矩阵 fault matrix
故障块 trouble block
故障类别 fault category
故障模拟 fault simulation
故障模式分析 failure mode analysis {FMA}
故障模型 bug model, failure/fault model
故障屏蔽 fault masking
故障缺陷 fault defect
故障软化 soft-fail

故障撒播 bug seeding
故障树 fault tree
故障树分析 failure tree analysis {FTA}, fault tree analysis {FTA}
故障数据 accidental data, failure data
故障探测 fault detection
故障条件 fault condition
故障停机 disorderly closedown, down
故障位 fault bit, syndrome bit
故障位置指示器 fault location indicator {FLI}
故障现象 symptom
故障线路 faulty line
故障影响分析 failure effect analysis {FEA}
故障[失效]预测 failure prediction
故障原因 failure cause
故障诊断 failure/ fault diagnosis, fault diagnostics
故障指示器 fault indicator
故障致命性分析 failure criticality analysis {FCA}
故障中断 trouble interrupt
故障字 syndrome word
故障字典 fault dictionary

雇 hire, employ 雇员 employee 雇主 employer

顾 (回头看) turn round and look at, retrospect 顾及 attend to, take into consideration 顾客 customer, client 顾虑 misgiving, worry 顾问 adviser, consultant

【guā】

瓜 melon, gourd

刮 scrape, shave

【guǎ】

寡 few, scant 寡头 oligarch ◇金融寡头 financial oligarchy

【guà】

挂 1)(悬挂) hang, put up 2)(钩住) hitch, get caught 3)(打电话) call up, put sb through to 挂号 register (at a hospital, etc.) 挂号处 registration office 挂号信 registered letter 挂名 titular, nominal, only in name 挂起 hang, hung, suspend
挂钩 hooking
挂号通信 poll
挂机 on-hook
挂起 suspend
挂起(状态) suspension
挂起原语 suspended primitive
挂起终端 held/hung terminal

【guǎi】

拐 拐角 corner, turning 拐弯 turn a corner, turn
拐点 inflection point, knee
拐角点 corner point

【guài】

怪 1)(奇怪) strange, odd, queer, bewildering 2)(责怪) blame 怪不得 no wonder

【guān】

关 1)(合拢) shut, close 2)(禁闭) lock up, shut in 3)(切断电源) turn off 4)(倒闭) close down 5)(海关) custom(s)house 6)(重要转折点) barrier, critical juncture ◇技术难关 technical barriers 7)(关系) concern, involve

◇有关方面 the parties concerned/involved 关闭 ①(合拢) close, shut ②(歇业) close down, shut down ③(切断电源) turn off 关键 key, hinge 关联 be related, be connected, be correlated with, associate, relevant to 关系 ①(相互关系) relation, relationship ②(有影响) bearing, impact, significance ③(关联) concern, affect, have a bearing on, have to do with 关于 about, on, with regard to, concerning 关注 follow with interest, pay close attention to, show solicitude for

关闭符号 close symbol
关闭节点 closed node
关闭框 close box
关闭设备 closing device
关闭文件 close file, closing file
关闭语句 close statement
关闭状态 inactive state
关断 turn-off
关机 closedown, cut-off, shutdown
关键操作 key operation
关键词 keyword
关键词表 antistop list, go-list, keyword table
关键对象 key object
关键范围 key range
关键活动 critical activities
关键技术 key technology
关键路径法 critical path method {CPM}
关键码 key, keyword
关键码表 key table
关键码数据库 key database
关键码条件 key condition
关键码位置 key position
关键码文件 keyed file
关键码压缩 key compression
关键码值 key value
关键码字段 key field
关键器件 key device
关键区域 key area
关键事件 key event
关键属性 keyed attribute
关键(码)树 key tree
关键帧 key frames, keyframe
关键指令 key instruction
关键状态 key state
关键字 key, key word
关键字变量 key argument
关节点 articulation point
关节集 articulation set
关联变量 correlation variable
关联变址 context indexing
关联表 association list
关联处理 associative processing
关联词 associated word, correlative
关联矩阵 incidence matrix, interconnection matrix
关联数据 associated data
关联算子 associate operator
关联图 associated/ association diagram
关联向量 interconnection vector
关联因子 association factor
关系标识符 relation identifier {RID}
关系操作符 relational operator
关系查询 relational query
关系代数 relational algebra
关系方法 relational approach
关系矩阵 matrix of relation
关系类型 relation type
关系理论 relational theory
关系逻辑 relational logic
关系模式 relation schema/ scheme, relational schema
关系模型 relation model, relational model

关系匹配 relational matching
关系(表达)式 relational expression
关系树 relational tree
关系数据库 relational database
关系数据库管理系统 relational database management system {RDBMS}, relational DBMS
关系数据库模式 relation(al) database schema
关系数据库语言 relational database language
关系数据理论 relational data theory
关系数据模型 relational data model
关系数据语言 relational data language
关系图 graph of relation
关系演算 relation(al) calculus
关系语言 language of relations
关系约束 relation constraint
关系运算符 relation(al) operator

观 1) (观看) look at, watch, observe, view 2) (景观) sight, view 观察 observe, watch, survey 观测 observe, collimate 观点 outlook, point of view, viewpoint, standpoint 观光 go sightseeing, visit, tour 观摩 watch and learn from each other 观念 sense, idea, concept 观众 spectator, viewer, audience
观察点 observation point, point of view {POV}, viewpoint
观察映像 view mapping
观点推理 reasoning by view
观念处理机 idea processor
观念简图 idea sketch
观念数据库 idea database

官 government official, officer 官方 ①〈名〉the authorities ②〈形〉governmental, official 官方消息 news from government source, official sources 官司 lawsuit 官员 official

【guǎn】

管 1) (管子) tube, pipe 2) (过问) bother about 管道 pipeline, conduit 管道工 pipelayer 管道工程 plumbing 管理 manage, run, be in charge of, administrate, supervise 管辖 have jurisdiction over, administer 管辖权 jurisdiction 管制 control ◇交通管制 traffic control
管道名 pipename
管道系统 piping system
管脚 pins
管脚插孔 pin jack
管理 administer, administration
管理报表[报告] managerial report
管理操作系统 management operating system {MOS}, supervisor operation system
管理操作员 administrative operator
管理策略 administrative strategy
管理[监督, 监控]程序 monitor program
管理程序 management program, control procedure, manager, hypervisor, master routine, monitor, supervisor, supervisor program
管理程序调用命令 supervisor

call instruction {SVC}
管理程序仿真 supervisory program simulation
管理程序中断 supervisor interrupt
管理磁盘 hyperdisk
管理存取 supervisor access
管理的 supervisory
管理的作用 managerial role
管理对策 management game
管理对象 management object
管理方式 supervisory mode
管理分析 management analysis
管理服务 supervisor(y) service
管理工程 administrative engineering
管理工具 management tool
管理环境 management environment
管理计算机 supervisory computer
管理决策 administrative decisionmaking, management decision
管理科学 administrative/management science {MS}
管理控制 management control, supervisory control
管理控制级 management control level
管理控制台 supervisor console, supervisory console
管理框架 administrative framework
管理类别 management class
管理例程 supervisory routine
管理模型 administrative model
管理能力 supervisory capability
管理器 supervisor
管理人 guardian
管理(程序)软件 supervisor software
管理授权 supervisor authority
管理通道 supervisory channel
管理文件 management file
管理系统 management system
管理信息服务 management information service {MIS}
管理信息库 management information base {MIB}
管理信息系统 management information system {MIS}
管理域 administrative domain
管理员 administrator, controller
管理者 manager
管理(执行)指令 executive instruction
管理指令 execute instruction, supervisory instruction
管理终端系统 administrative terminal system {ATS}
管理状态 supervisor state
管路网 piping system
管态 supervisor state, supervisor mode

馆 1)(宾馆) accommodation for guests, guest house, hotel 2)(大使馆) embassy, consulate 3)(商店) shop ◇茶馆 teahouse ◇饭馆 restaurant 4)(公共场所) a place for cultural activities ◇图书馆 library // 文化馆 cultural center

【guàn】
贯 贯彻 carry out, implement, put into effect 贯穿、贯串 run through, penetrate, pierce; breakthrough 贯通 ①(透彻了解) have a thorough knowledge of, be well versed in ②(接通) link up, thread together
贯穿布线 feed throughs

guǎn

冠 冠军 champion 冠军赛 championships

惯 惯例 convention, usual practice
惯例 custom, tradition
惯性制导系统 inertial guidance system

盥 盥洗室 washroom 盥洗用具 toilet articles

灌 irrigate, pour 灌注 pour into, bottle, impregnate

罐 jar, jug, pot, tin, can, tank

【guāng】

光 1)(用完)used up 2)(只,仅)solely, only, merely 光彩 luster, splendor, radiance
光亮 bright(ness), luminous, shiny 光临 presence of (honored guests) ◇敬请光临 Your presence is cordially requested. 光明 ①〈名〉light ②〈形〉bright, promising 光滑 smooth, glossy, polished 光荣 honor, glory, credit
光线 light, ray
光暗真值逻辑 dark true logic {DTL}
光斑 optical pattern
光倍增器 photomultiplier {PMT}
光笔 light pen, selector pen, light gun, light stylus, pen light, control pen
光笔触击 light pen strike
光笔跟踪 light pen tracking
光笔检测 light pen detection, light pen strike, light pen hit
光笔控制 pen control
光笔系统 light pen system
光笔选通 light pen strobe
光笔中断 light pen attention, light-pen interrupt
光笔装置 light pen unit
光标 cursor
光标操作 cursor operation
光标窗口 cursor window
光标存储器 cursor memory
光标打印机 cursor printer
光标代码 cursor code
光标发生器 cursor generator
光标开关 cursor switch
光标识别 optical character recognition {OCR}, optical mark recognition {OMR}
光标位置 cursor position
光标线 cursor line
光标移动 cursor remove
光标右移 cursor right
光标指针 cursor stylus
光标左移 cursor left
光程 optical distance
光处理机 optical processor
光传感器 optosensor
光窗口 optical window
光磁存储器 photomagnetic memory
光磁的 optomagnetic
光磁软盘 floptical
光(学)存储器 optical memory
光存储器 light memory, optical storage
光导材料 light guide
光导管 light conduit
光导体 photoconductor {PC, pc}
光导纤维 optical fiber
光点尺寸 spot size
光点扫描 spot scan
光电池 photoelectric cell, photovoltaic cell, photocell
光电导体 phoroconductor, photoconductor {PC, pc}

光电二极管 photodiode
光电管 eye, phototube
光电检测 photoelectric detection
光电晶体管 phototransistor
光电矩阵 photocell matrix
光电开关 photoswitch
光电耦合器 photocoupler
光电排版 photocomposition
光电器件 photoelectric device
光电摄像管 iconoscope
光电设备 optoelectronic device
光电输入 optoelectronic input
光电输入机[阅读器] photoreader
光电校验 photocell light check
光电效应 photoelectric effect
光电阴极 photocathode
光电阅读器 photoelectric reader
光电转换系统 photo-translating system
光电子 opto-electronic
光电子技术 optoelectron technique
光电子器件 optoelectronic device
光电子学 optoelectronics, photoelectronics
光电阻 photoresister
光(读写)头 optical head, optical read/write head
光放大器 optical amplifier
光(盘)轨 optical track
光互连 optic connection
光绘机 photo plotter
光机鼠标器 optomechanical mouse
光计算机 optical/photo computer
光记录 optical recording
光检测 optical detection
光检测器 photodetector
光接收器 optical receiver
光绝缘体 photo-isolator
光刻 photoetching, photolithography
光刻工艺 photoetching technology
光刻蚀 photoetch
光控制 optical control
光控制设备 light guide
光缆 optical cable, optical fiber cable, fiber-optic cable
光缆网络 fiber cable network
光链路 optical link
光亮真值逻辑 bright true logic {BTL}
光流 optical flow
光路 optical path
光逻辑元件 optical logic element
光敏 light-sensitive
光敏电池 photoconductive cell
光敏二极管 photosensitive diode
光敏元件 optical sensor, photosensor
光模拟计算机 optical analog computer
光模式识别 optical pattern recognition {OPR}
光耦合器 optical coupler, photocoupler
光盘 compact disk {CD}, optical disk, video disk
光盘驱动器 optical disk drive
光盘头 optical head
光盘系统 video disk system
光盘只读存储器 compact disk-read-only memory {CD-ROM}
光偏转器 optical deflector
光频 optical frequency
光谱段 spectrum segment
光谱分析器 spectrum analyzer
光谱路径 spectrum routing
光谱区域 spectral domain

光谱色彩 spectral color
光谱学 spectroscopy
光器件 optical device
光驱(动) optical drive
光圈盘 aperture disk
光全息存储器 optic holography memory
光扫描 optical scanning, photoscanning
光扫描器 optical scanning device {OSD}
光神经计算机 optic neural computer, optical neurocomputer
光输入机 optical reader
光鼠标器 optical mouse
光束存储器 beam store
光束定位器 beam positioner
光束控制 beam control
光束扫描 optical beam scanning
光束位移 pattern displacement
光数据总线 optical data bus
光塑胶片 photoplastic film {PPF}
光条带 light bar
光通信 optical communication, optical channel
光通信技术 optical communication
光纤 optical fiber
光纤包层 fiber clading
光纤波导 optical fiber waveguide
光纤电缆 fiber-optic cable, fiberoptic cable
光纤分布(式)数据接口 fiber distributed data interface {FDDI}
光纤缓冲 fiber buffer
光纤连接器 fiber connector
光纤束 fiber bundle
光纤数据链路 fiber data link
光纤通信 fiber optics communication {FOC}, optical fiber communication
光纤涂层 fiber coading
光纤网络 fiber optic network
光纤网络单元 optical network unit {ONU}
光纤维 fiber optic(s)
光纤信道 optical fiber channel, fiber channel
光纤以太网 fiber ethernet
光显示终端 optical display terminal
光学标记识别 optical mark recognition {OMR}
光学标记阅读器 optical mark reader {OMR}
光学处理 opticals, photo-process
光学传递函数 optical transfer function {OTF}
光学传感器 optic sensor, optical sensor
光学存储器 photo-optic memory
光学读写头 optical read/write head
光学分解[分辨]率 optical resolution
光学符号读出 optical character recognition {OCR}
光学工程 optical engineering
光学机构 optical facilities
光学检测器 optical detector
光学模式调节器 optical mode conditioner {OMC}
光学模式识别 optical pattern recognition {OPR}
光学[光敏]器件 opto-device
光学扫描 optical scanning
光学识别 optical recognition
光学识别字体 optical font
光学鼠标器 optical mouse
光学数据识别 optical data recognition {ODR}
光学数字式数据盘 optical

digital data disk {ODDD}
光学特性 optical characteristics
光学图像 optical image
光学图形 optical pattern
光学信息 optical information
光学元件 optical element, opto-element
光学阅读器 optical reader
光学字符 optical character
光学字符识别 optical character recognition {OCR}
光掩膜 photomask
光源 lamphouse
光阅读机 optical reader
光栅 grating, optical grating, raster
光栅常数 grating constant
光栅绘图仪 raster plotter
光栅间距 grating space
光栅宽度 raster width
光栅扫描 raster scan
光栅失真 raster distortion
光栅数据 raster data
光栅图示(法)技术 raster graphics
光栅图像 raster image
光栅图形显示器 raster plotter
光栅显示设备 raster display device
光栅字体 raster font
光中继器 optical repeater
光轴 optical axis
光子 photon
光字符识别 optical character recognition {OCR}
光字符阅读机 optical mark reader {OMR}

【guǎng】

广 wide, vast, extensive
广播 broadcast, announce
广大 ①(宽阔)vast, wide, extensive ②(巨大)large-scale, wide-spread ③(众多)numerous 广泛 extensive, wide-ranging, widespread 广告 advertisement 广阔 vast, broad 广义 broad sense
广播传输 broadcast transfer
广播地址 broadcast address, all-stations address
广播风暴 broadcast storm
广播和未知服务器 broadcast and unknown server {BUS}
广播会议 broadcast conference
广播频段 broadcast band
广播通道 broadcast channel
广播通信 broadcast communication, broadcasting
广播拓扑 broadcast topology
广播卫星 broadcast satellite
广义方差 generalized variance
广义方程 generalized equation
广义管理模型 generalized management model {GMM}
广义链表 generalized list
广义模型 generalized model
广义网论 general net theory
广义相关 generalized correlation
广义样条 generalized splines
广义指令 generalized instruction
广域网 wide-area network {WAN}
广域信息服务器[系统] wide area information server {WAIS}

【guī】

归 (返回)go back to, return
归根结底 in the final analysis
归功于 give the credit to, owe the success to 归还 give back to, return sth to, revert 归结 sum up, come to a conclusion 归纳 induce, conclude, sum up 归于 ①

(属于) belong to, be attributed to ② (趋向于) tend to, result in, end in
归并 merge, merging
归并程序 merge program
归并分类 merge sorting
归并[合并]排序 ordering by merging
归并排序[分类] merge sort
归并排算法 conflation algorithm
归并网络 merge network
归档 archive, archiving
归档处理[过程] archiving process
归类 categorization, subsumption
归零制 return-to-zero {RZ}, return-to-zero method
归纳 extrapolation, summary
归纳断言 inductive assertion
归纳法 induction, inductive approach/ method, method of induction/resultant
归纳命题 inductive proposition
归纳算法 induction algorithm
归纳学习 inductive learning
归属代理 home agent
归约 reduce, reduction, reductive
归约定理 deduction theorem
归约关系 reduction relation
归约规则 reduction rule
归约文法 reduced grammar

规 1)(圆规) compasses, dividers 2)〈机械〉gauge ◇ 线规 wire gauge 规定 stipulate, provide 规范 norm, model, standard, specification 规格 specifications, standards, norms 规律 law, regular pattern 规模 scale, scope, dimensions, size 规划 plan, program 规则 rule, regulation, discipline 规章 rules, regulations
规程 discipline, procedure, protocol
规范次序 canonical order
规范化 normalization, normalize
规范化条件 normalization condition
规范化形式 normalized form
规范文件 authority file, authorization file
规范[标准,典型]形式 canonical form
规格化 normalization, standardization
规格化浮点 normalized floating point
规格化数 normalized number
规格化形式 normal form, normalized form
规划决策 programmed decision-making
规则库 rule base {RB}
规则库系统 rule-based system
规则[正规]命令 regular command
规则数据库 rule database
规则子句 rule clause
规则组 rule group

硅 silicon (Si)
硅编译 silicon compilation
硅(片)编译程序 silicon compiler
硅(片)编译器 silicon compiler
硅二极管 silicon diode
硅岛 silicon island
硅谷 Silicon Gulch, Silicon Valley
硅(片)汇编程序 silicon assembler
硅胶 silicon gel
硅晶体 silicon crystal

硅晶体管 silicon transistor
硅片 silicon chip, silicon die
硅圆片 silicon wafer

【guǐ】

鬼 ghost, spirit 鬼怪 ghosts, monsters, devils

轨 rail, track 轨道 ① track ② course, path ③ orbit, trajectory
轨迹 locus, pathway, track

诡 deceitful, tricky, cunning 诡辩 sophistry, fallacy
诡计 cunning scheme, trick

【guì】

柜 cupboard, cabinet 柜台 counter, bar

贵 expensive, costly, dear 贵宾 honored guest, distinguished guest 贵重 valuable, precious

【gǔn】

辊 roller, roll, expansion cylinder

滚 roll 滚动 roll, scroll, trundle
滚动方框 scroll box
滚动屏幕 roll screen
滚动条 scroll bar
滚筒 drum, roller
滚筒绘图仪 drum plotter

【gùn】

棍 rod, stick

【guō】

锅 pot, pan, boiler 锅炉 boiler

【guó】

国 country, state, nation
国宾 state guest 国产 made in one's own country, made in China 国防 national defence 国会 parliament, (美) Congress 国籍 nationality 国家 nation 国际 international 国际组织 international organization 国库 national treasury, exchequer 国立 state-maintained, state-run 国民经济 national economy 国内直拨 domestic direct dial (DDD) 国旗 national flag 国庆 National Day 国事 national affairs 国事访问 state visit 国外 external, oversea, abroad 国王 king 国有化 nationalize 国有化 nationalization 国债 national debt
国标区位码 national standard region-position code
国防数据网 defense data network {DDN}
国际标准 international standard {IS}
国际标准期刊编号 International Standard Serial Number, ISSN
国际标准书号 International Standard Book Number {ISBN}
国际代码标志符 international code designator {ICD}
国际标准(化)组织 International Standards Organization {ISO}
国际单位制 international system of units {SI}
国际互联网 internet
国际互联网服务供应商 internet service provider {ISP}

国际计算中心 International Computation Center {ICC}
国家标准符号 national characters
国家电视制式委员会 National Television System Committee {NTSC}
国家科学基金会 national science foundation {NSF}
国家科学基金网 national science foundation network {NSFNET}
国家数据编码 data country code {DCC}
国家无线电高级数据通信服务 advanced national radio data service {ARDIS}

【guǒ】

果 1)(果实)fruit 2)(后果)result, consequence 果断 resolute, decisive 果然 really, as expected, sure enough 果真 if indeed, if really

裹 bind, wrap

【guò】

过 1)(通过)cross, pass 2)(穿过)across, past, through, over 3)(度过)spend (time), pass (time) 4)(超过)exceed, go beyond 过程 process, procedure, routine, course 过错 fault, mistake 过度,过分 undue, over, excessive(ly) 过关 ①(通过关口)pass a barrier ②(通过检验)pass a test, reach a standard 过后 afterwards, later 过户 transfer ownership 过境 pass through the territory of a country, be in transit 过量 excessive, over-dose, surfeit 过滤 filter, filtrate 过去 in the past, formerly, previously 过时 out-of-date, outmoded, out of fashion, overdue
过程 procedure, process
过程表 process list
过程表目 process entry
过程部 procedure division
过程层次 procedure level
过程抽象 procedural abstraction
过程出口 procedure exit
过程段 procedure section/segment
过程队列 process queue
过程划分 procedure division
过程级 procedure level
过程节 procedure section
过程节点 process node
过程控制台 process console
过程描述符 procedure/process descriptor
过程首部 procedure head
过程说明 procedure declaration
过程[进程]异常 process exception
过程引用 procedure invocation/reference
过程预置 procedure initialization
过程指针 procedure pointer
过零检测器 zero-crossing detector
过滤模型 filtering model
过滤器 filter
过期文件 scratch file
过载 overload, override
过载保护 breakaway action, overload protection
过载能力 overload rating
过载失真 blasting

H h

【hā】

哈 哈夫曼压缩代码 compact Huffman code
哈密顿图 Hamiltonian graph

铪 hafnium (Hf)

【hái】

孩 child

还 另见【huán】
1)(仍旧)still, yet 2)(更加)even, more 3)(另外)also, too, as well, in addition 还好 ① (不坏)not bad ② (幸运)fortunately 还是 still, nevertheless, all the same

【hǎi】

海 sea, big lake 海拔 height above sea level, elevation 海滨 seashore, seaside 海港 seaport, harbor 海关 customhouse, customs 海军 navy 海事 maritime affairs 海外 overseas, abroad 海湾 bay, gulf 海峡 strait, channel 海洋 sea, ocean 海员 seaman, sailor 海运 sea transportation, ocean shipping
海量存储控制器 mass storage control {MSC}
海量存储器 mass storage device
海量存储系统 mass storage system {MSS}
海量存储装置 mass storage facility {MSF}
海量数据 mass data

【hài】

害 1)〈名〉evil, harm, calamity 2)〈形〉harmful, destructive, injurious 3)〈动〉do harm to, impair, cause trouble to 害处 harm 害怕 be afraid, be scared

氦 helium (He)

【hán】

含 1)(口含) keep in the mouth 2)(包含) contain 含糊 ambiguous, vague 含量 content 含义 meaning, implication 含有 contain, have

函 letter
函件爆发器 mail exploder
函件交换机 mail exchanger
函件网关 mail gateway
函数变换 function mapping, functional transformation
函数变量 function variable
函数表 function table
函数程序 function program

hán 焓涵寒 hǎn 罕喊 hàn 汉汗旱焊 hāng 夯

函数调用 function call, function reference
函数定义 function definition
函数段 function segment
函数发生 function generation
函数返回值 function return value
函数关系 functional relation
函数首部 function head
函数说明 function declaration
函数体 function body
函数引用 function reference
函数应用 function application
函数值 function value
函询 mail survey

焓
〈物理〉enthalpy, total heat, heat content

涵
涵义 connotation

寒
cold 寒带 frigid zone 寒假 winter vacation 寒冷 cold, frigid

【hǎn】
罕
罕见 seldom seen, rare 罕有 rare, unusual, exceptional

喊
1)（大声叫）shout, cry out, yell 2)（叫人）call

【hàn】
汉
（男子）man 汉语 Chinese (language) 汉字 Chinese character
汉卡 Hanzi card
汉明距离[间距] Hamming distance
汉明码 Hamming code
汉明权 Hamming weight
汉明校验 Hamming check
汉语 Chinese
汉语语音识别 Chinese speech recognition
汉语语音输入 Chinese speech input
汉字(指字符) Chinese character
汉字编码方案 Hanzi coding scheme
汉字打印[印刷]机 Chinese printer, Hanzi printer
汉字打印机 Chinese character printer
汉字键盘 Hanzi keyboard
汉字库 Chinese character library
汉字(机)内码 Hanzi internal code
汉字生成器 Hanzi generator
汉字识别 Hanzi recognition
汉字使用频度 Hanzi frequency count
汉字输出 Hanzi output
汉字输入 Hanzi input
汉字输入设备 Chinese input device
汉字外形 character outline
汉字信息处理系统 Chinese information processing system {CHIPS}
汉字终端 Hanzi terminal
汉字字(形)库 Hanzi font library

汗
sweat, perspiration

旱
dry spell, drought 旱灾 drought

焊
weld, solder ◇气焊 gas welding

【hāng】
夯
ram, tamp, pound

【háng】

行 另见【xíng】
line, row, string（商行）business firm ◇银行 bank **行话** jargon **行家** expert, specialist **行列** line, row, string **行情** quotations (on the market), prices **行业** trade, profession, industry
行编号 line number
行编辑 line editing
行编辑程序 line editor, line-editor program
行标尺 line ruler
行标号 line label
行波传送进位 ripple-through carry
行波[脉动]加器 ripple adder
行波进位法 ripple carry method
行长度 string length
行超松弛 line overrelaxation
行尺 line ruler
行处理语言 string manipulation language
行次序 row order
行地址 line address, row address
行地址选通 row address strobe {RAS}
行迭代 row iteration
行方式 line mode
行方向 inline direction
行访问 row access
行号 line number
行间隔 line spacing
行间距 line pitch, line space
行间空白 interline space
行结束 end of line
行距 line space/ pacing, (row) pitch
行控制块 line control block {LCB}
行宽 line measure, line width
行馈送字符 line feed character {LF}
行栏地址 row column address
行列式 determinant
行密度 row density
行末对齐 line-end adjustment
行频 horizontal scanning frequency
行扫描 line scanning, row scanning
行失真 line distortion
行式打印机 line printer {LP}
行式设备 line device
行首缩进 indent, indentation
行数 linage, line number
行选 row selection
行译码 row decoding
行状态 row state

航 navigate (by water or air) ◇民航 civil aviation **航班** scheduled flight, flight number **航道** channel, lane, course **航空** aviation **航天** spaceflight, aerospace; astronautic(al), cosmonautic **航天飞机** space shuttle **航线** air or shipping line, route; airway, course line, flightpath **航向** course (of a ship or plane), heading **航行** ① navigate by water, sail ② navigate by air, fly **航运** shipping

【háo】

毫 （千分之一）milli- **毫不** not in the least, not at all **毫米** millimeter (mm)

豪 **豪华** luxurious

【hǎo】

好 另见【hào】
1)（优良）good, fine, nice
2)（友好）friendly, kind
3)（健康）be in good health
好处 ①（益处）good, benefit, advantage ②（利益）gain, profit
好话 ① a good word, word of praise ② fine words
好看 ①（美观）good-looking, nice ②（吸引人）interesting
好评 favorable comment, high opinion
好事 good deed, good turn
好像 seem, be like
好转 take a turn for the better, take a favorable turn, improve

【hào】

好 另见【hǎo】
1)（喜爱）like, love, be fond of
2)（易于）be liable to

号 1)（商号）business house ◇分号 branch (of a firm, etc.)
2)（标号）mark, sign, signal
3)（等级）size
4)（日期）date
号称 ① be known as ② claim to be
号码 number
号召 call, appeal
号码表 directory
号码构成 number building
号码组 number group

浩
浩大 very great, huge, vast
浩荡 vast and mighty

耗
耗费 consume, exhaust, use up
耗尽方式 depletion mode

【hé】

合 （结合）join, combine
合并 merging, union, fold(ing), incorporation, consolidation
合成 ① compose, compound ②〈化学〉synthetize, synthesize
合法 legal, lawful, legitimate, rightful
合格 qualified, up to standard, competent
合股 pool capital, form a partnership
合伙 form a partnership
合伙经营 run a business in partnership
合计 be equal to, add up to, amount to
合金 alloy
合理 rational, reasonable, justified
合理化 rationalize
合理化建议 rationalization proposal
合理性 justification, rationality, reasonableness
合力 ①（一起出力）join forces, pool efforts ②〈物理〉resultant of forces, resultant (force)
合拢 close, shut
合适 suitable, appropriate, proper
合算 paying, worthwhile
合同 contract
合资 joint venture
合资企业 joint venture
合作 cooperate, collaborate, work together

合并比较	merge match
合并次序	merge order
合并定理	union theorem
合并节点	merge node
合并模式	merging patterns
合并排序[分类]	merge sorting
合并算法	union algorithm
合并通道[旁路]	merge pass
合并文件	merge file
合并语句	merge statement
合成地址	generated address, synthetic address
合成关系	composite relation, synthetic relationship
合成图像	composite

synthevision
合成向量 composite vector
合成映像 composite mapping
合成语言 synthetic language
合法程序 legal program
合法地址 legal address
合法句子 legal sentence
合法模式 legal pattern
合法状态 legal state
合格检查 validation test {VT}
合计 summarizing, figure out
合理(的) reasonable, legitimation
合取 conjunction
合取范式 conjunctive normal form
合取式 conjunct
合式公式 well-formed formula {WFF, wff}
合一 unification, unity
合一部件 unification unit
合用 serve
合用线 shared line, party line
合作式处理 cooperative processing

和 1) (平和) gentle, mild, kind 2) 〈连〉and, with 3) 〈数学〉sum 和解 become reconciled 和平 peace, mild 和谐 harmonious
和的积 product-of-sum
和检验 sum check
和数 sum
和数读出 sum readout
和数脉冲 sum pulse
和数校验 sum check, summation check
和数子句 sum clause

何 何必 there is no need, why 何等 what, how 何况 much less, let alone 何谓 what is a meant by, what is the meaning of 何以 how, why

河 river 河岸 river bank 河道 river course 河流 river 河堤 dike

荷 另见【hè】
荷兰 the Netherlands, the Holland

核 1) (果核) pit, stone 2) (核状物) nucleus 3) (查对) examine, check 核定 check and ratify, appraise and decide 核实 verify, check 核算 business accounting 核算单位 accounting unit 核心 nucleus, core, kernel 核武器 nuclear weapon 核准 examine and approve
核对 matching, verification, verify
核对检验 verify check
核对总和 check sum {CKS}
核心程序 core program, engine, nucleus
核心初始化程序 nucleus initialization program {NIP}
核心窗口部件 core widget
核心对象 kernel object
核心目标 kernel object
核心软件 kernel software
核心网关 core gateway

盒 盒子 box, case, casket
盒带 tape cartridge
盒带存储器 cartridge store
盒式磁带 cassette (magnetic) tape, tape cassette
盒式磁带机 cassette (unit), cartridge
盒式磁盘 cartridge disk, disk cartridge

hè 贺荷赫褐 hēi 黑 hen 痕,很狠,恨 heng 亨,恒

盒式存储器 memory cartridge
盒式记录装置 cassette recorder
盒式录相机 video cassette recorder {VCR}
盒式录像带 video cassette/cartridge, cassette videotape
盒式录音机 cassette recorder
盒装缩微胶片 microfilm jacket

【hè】

贺 congratulate 贺词 speech of congratulation, greetings 贺电 congratulatory telegram 贺礼 gift (as a token of congratulation) 贺年 extend New Year greeting, pay a New Year call 贺年片 New Year card 贺信 congratulatory letter, letter of congratulation

荷 另见【hé】
1)（杠，背）carry on one's shoulder or back 2)（负担）burden, responsibility 荷载 load 荷重 loading; weight

赫 （显赫）conspicuous, grand
赫(兹) hertz {Hz}, cycles per second {CPS, cps}

褐 brown
褐色的 brown

【hēi】

黑 1)（黑色）black 2)（黑暗）dark 3)（秘密）secret, shady 4)（坏）wicked, sinister 黑白 black and white, right and wrong 黑色金属 ferrous metal 黑市 black market 黑市交易 off-the-books deal 黑市价格 black rate

黑白图形 black-and-white pattern
黑白影片 monochrome
黑板法 blackboard approach
黑板结构 blackboard structure
黑板模型 blackboard model
黑板系统 blackboard system
黑度 blackness
黑光 black light
黑光纤 dark fiber
黑盒
(电脑)黑客 hacker
黑体 bold face
黑体属性 boldface attribute
黑体字 bold, boldface (= bf), body face
黑体字符集 Gothic character set
黑体字型 boldface font
黑箱 black box
黑箱测试 black box testing
黑箱[黑盒]法 black box method
黑信号 black signal
黑噪声 black noise

【hén】

痕 痕迹 mark, trace, track

【hěn】

很 very, quite, awfully

狠 ruthless, relentless ◇ 凶狠 ferocious and ruthless 狠心 cruel-hearted, heartless

【hèn】

恨 1)（仇恨）hate 2)（悔恨）regret

【hēng】

亨 〈电气〉henry (H)

【héng】

恒 （持久）permanent,

lasting, constant eternal, everlasting ◇ 永恒
恒定 constant, invariable
恒心 perseverance
恒等 identity
恒等关系 identity relation
恒等函数 identity function
恒等律 identity law
恒等密码 identity cipher
恒等映像 identity mapping
恒定脉冲 isopulse
恒定线速度 constant linear velocity {CLV}
恒流电源 constant current source

横 (水平的) horizontal, transverse 横越 across, sideways
横表(键) tab
横排版 landscape
横条码 horizontal bar code
横向版面 landscape
横向表 horizontal table
横向磁记录 transverse (magnetic) recording
横向方式 horizontal mode
横向格式 horizontal format
横向回车 horizontal return
横向记录 transverse recording
横向接行 horizontal wraparound
横向进给 infeed
横向卷动 horizontal scrolling
横向卷绕 horizontal wraparound
横向控制 horizontal control
横向馈送 horizontal feed
横向奇偶性 transverse parity
横向扫描 transverse scan(ning)
横向校验 horizontal/transverse check
横向指令 horizontal instruction
横向指针 horizontal pointer
横向制表 horizontal tabulation
横向制表符 horizontal tabulation character {HT}
横向字符 horizontal character

衡 weigh 衡量 weigh, measure, judge 衡器 weighing apparatus

【hōng】

轰 rumble, bombard, boom 轰动 cause a sensation, make a stir

烘 dry or warm by the fire
烘干器 baker, drying apparatus 烘烤 toast, bake

【hóng】

红 red 红茶 black tea 红利 bonus, extra dividend 红绿灯 traffic light, traffic signal
红绿蓝三基色 red green blue {RGB}
红外遥控 infrared remote control
红线路 red circuit

宏 宏大 grand, great 宏图 great plan, grand prospect 宏伟 magnificent, grand
宏 macro
宏编程 macroprogramming
宏编码 macrocoding
宏变量 macro-variable
宏变元 macroargument
宏表达式 macro expression
宏参数 macro-parameter
宏操作符 macro-operator
宏程序库 macrolibrary {MACLIB}
宏处理指令 macroprocessing instruction

宏代码 macro, macrocode
宏单元 macrocell, macroelement
宏调用 macrocall
宏定义 macrodefinition
宏定义体 macro body of a definition
宏功能 macro, macro function/facility
宏功能名字 macro name
宏观结构 macro-structure
宏汇编 macroassembler
宏汇编语言 macroassembly language {MAL}
宏流程图 macro flowchart
宏逻辑 macrologic
宏嵌套 macro nest
宏数据 macro-data
宏说明 macro declaration
宏系统 macro-system
宏语句 macro-statement
宏元件 macroelement
宏(指令记录)原型 macroprototype
宏指令 macro instruction, macrofacility, macro, macros
宏指令表 skeleton table
宏指令库 macrolibrary {MACLIB}
宏组件 macroelement

洪

洪水 flood, floodwater

虹

rainbow

【hóu】

喉 throat, larynx

【hòu】

后 (以后)after, afterwards, later 后半 later half, second half 后备 reserve 后辈 younger generation 后代 later generations, descendants, posterity 后盾 backing, backup force 后果 consequence, aftermath 后记 postscript 后来 afterwards, later 后面 ①（位置）at the back, in the rear, behind ②（次序）later 后年 the year after next 后期 later stage, later period 后人 ①（后代之人）later generations ②（子孙）posterity, descendants 后天 ①（明天的明天）day after tomorrow ②（与先天相对）postnatal, acquired 后退 draw back, fall back, retreat 后援 back-up 后者 the latter
后板 back panel
后备存储器 backing storage, backing memory
后备(蓄)电池 battery backup
后备电源 battery pack
后备队列 pool queue
后备软盘 backup diskette
后备设备 backup facility
后备芯片 support chip
后备选路由 alternate routing
后变址 postindexing
后到先服务 last-come, first-served {LCFS}
后端 rear end, trailing end
后端(装置) back-end
后端处理机 back-end processor {BEP}
后端机 back-end machine
后端计算机 back-end computer
后端系统 back-end system
后根次序 postorder
后继表 successor list
后继地址 successor address
后继地址消息 subsequent address message {SAM}
后继顶点 descendant vertex, successor vertex
后继集合 successor set

后继节点 descendant node, successor node
后继块 successor block
后继站 successor
后继指令 next instruction
后进先出 last-in first-out {LIFO}
后台 background
后台程序 background program
后台处理 background processing, backgrounding
后台打印 background printing
后台方式 background mode
后台干扰 background noise
后台计算机 background computer
后台流 background stream
后台区 background partition, background region
后台任务 background task
后台用户 background user
后台终端(设备) background terminal
后台作业 background job
后文 postamble
后文件 epifile
后向传播 backpropagation
后向滚动 backscrolling
后向兼容 backward compatible {BC}
后向散射 back scatter
后向推理 back chinned inference
后向选择 backward option
后向自适应 backward adaptation
后效控制 residual control
后效作用 after-effect
后序 endorder
后序遍历 postorder traverse, endorder traversal
后压缩 rear compression
后援程序 support program
后援处理机 support processor
后援存储 backup store
后援电池 backup battery
后援设备 backup equipment
后援文件 file backup
后置集 post set
后缀 postfix, suffix
后缀表示(法) postfix notation
后缀表示法 suffix notation
后缀操作符 suffix operator
后缀算符 postfix operator

候
(等候) wait, await 候补 candidate, alternate 候选人 candidate

厚
1) (薄的反意) thick 2) (大) large, generous 厚利 large profits 厚度 thickness 厚薄 thickness 厚望 great expectations
厚膜电路 thick film circuit
厚膜封装 thick-film package

【hū】
呼 1) (叫) call 2) (大声喊) shout, cry out 3) (吐气) breathe out, exhale 呼唤 call, shout to 呼机 beeper
呼叫 ① (呼喊) call out, shout ② 〈电信〉call call for help 呼救信号 signal for help, SOS (Safe Our Souls) 呼吸 breathe, respire 呼应 echo, resound 呼吁 appeal, call on
呼叫保持 call hold
呼叫冲突 call collision
呼叫等待 call waiting
呼叫地址 call call(ing) address
呼叫方 calling party
呼叫管理 call control, call management
呼叫名称 call name
呼叫信号 alerting signal, call

呼叫者线路识别描述 caller line identification presentation {CLIP}
呼叫者线路识别限定 caller line identification restriction {CLIR}
呼叫指向码 call directing code {CDC}
呼叫中心 calling center
呼叫转发 call forwarding
呼叫转移 call (back) transfer
呼叫装置 calling device
呼叫状态图 calling state diagram

忽 忽略 ignore, neglect, overlook 忽然 suddenly, all of a sudden 忽视 ignore, overlook, neglect
忽略类 ignore class
忽略位 ignore bit

【hú】
弧 arc 弧形 arc, curve
弧有向图 arc-digraph

胡 胡说 talk nonsense 胡乱 carelessly, casually, at random

壶 1)(容器)kettle, pot 2)(瓶)bottle, flask

湖 lake

糊 1)(浆糊)paste 2)(粘住)stick with paste, paste

【hǔ】
虎 tiger

【hù】
互 mutual, each other 互访 exchange visit 互换 exchange, interchange 互惠 mutually beneficial, reciprocal 互利 mutually beneficial, mutual benefit 互相 mutual, each other 互助 help each other, mutual aid
互补触发器 complementing flip-flop
互补的 complemental, complementary
互补晶体管逻辑电路 complementary transistor logic {CTL}
互操作性 interactivity
互斥 mutual exclusion, mutually exclusive
互斥(性) exclusive
互斥存取 exclusive access
互斥方式 exclusive mode
互斥信息 exclusive message
互斥意图 exclusive intent
互斥引用 exclusive reference
互反 reciprocal
互反公式 reciprocity formula
互反关系 reciprocal relationship
互换通道 interexchange channel {IXC}
互换位置 transposition
互联网 internet(work), interconnection network
互连 interconnect(ion), interlink(age), nexus
互连费用 interconnection charge
互连函数 interconnection function
互连接口 nexus interface
互连网络 interconnection network
互锁(设备) interlock
互锁操作 interlocked operation
互相关 cross correlation
互相贯通 interpenetration

hù 户 护 huā 花 huá 华 划 滑 huà 化 划

户 1)（门）door 2)（住户）household, family 户数 number of household occupants ◇报户口 register one's residence, apply for residence ‖ 户口簿 (permanant) residence booklet 户头 (bank) account ◇开户头 open an account

护 （保护）protect, guard, shield 护理 nurse, tend and protect 护送 escort, convoy 护卫 protect, guard 护照 passport
护杆 guard bar

【huā】
花 花边 ①（边上的花纹）decorative border ②（编织物）lace 花朵 flower, blossom, bloom 花费 ①〈动〉spend, expend, cost ②〈名〉money spent, expenditure, expenses 花色 ①（花纹色彩）design and color ②（品种）variety 花纹 decorative pattern, figure 花样 pattern, variety 花园 (flower) garden
花瓣式打印机 petal printer

【huá】
华 1)（中国）China 2)（繁华）prosperous, flourishing bustling 3)（精华）best part, cream 4)（奢华）flashy, extravagant 华贵 luxurious, costly 华丽 magnificent, splendid

划 另见【huà】
（擦）scratch, cut the surface of 划水 paddle, row

滑 1)〈形〉slippery, smooth 2)〈动〉slip, slide 滑稽 funny, amusing, comical 滑翔 glide 滑翔机 glider, sailplane 滑行 slide, coast
滑动触头 slider
滑动窗口流程 sliding window flow
滑动窗口协议 sliding window protocol
滑动游标 scroll bar
滑架 carriage
滑架溢出 carriage overflow
滑块 slide
滑块臂 slider arm
滑块盒 slider box
滑块显示 slide show presentation

【huà】
化 1)（变化）change, turn, transform 2)（教化）convert, influence 3)（融化）melt, dissolve 化工 chemical industry 化合 chemical combination 化身 incarnation, embodiment 化石 fossil 化纤 chemical fiber 化学 chemistry 化验 chemical examination, laboratory test, assay
化验报告 analysis report 化验单 laboratory test report
化妆 put on makeup, make up

划 另见【huà】
1)（计划）plan 2)（划作标记）draw, mark, delineate 划定 delimit, designate 划分 ①（分成部分）divide, partition ②（区别）differentiate 划时代 epoch-making, very important 划一 standar-

huà 画话 huái 怀 huài 坏 huān 欢 huán 还环

dized, uniform
划分页面 paging
划线 scribe, scoring, dicing
划线尺 line ruler

画 1)〈动〉draw, paint 2)〈名〉drawing, painting, picture 画报 pictorial 画册 an album of paintings, picture 画家 painter, artist 画图 ①〈动〉draw designs, maps, etc. ②〈名〉picture 画像 ①〈动〉draw a portrait, portray ②〈名〉portrait, portrayal
画板 paintbrush
画草图 sketching
画面编辑 picture editing
画面平移 pan
画入 frame in

话 1)〈名〉word, talk ◇编者的话 editor's remark 2)〈动〉talk about, speak about 话题 subject of a talk, topic of conversation
话音通道 speech channel
话音系统 audio system
话音芯片 speech chip
话音信息 voice message
话音(语音,录音)邮件 voice mail
话音装置 audio unit
话语模型 discourse model
话语生成 discourse generation

【huái】

怀 怀抱 ①(抱在怀里)bosom ②(心里存有)cherish 怀疑 distrust, doubt, suspect

【huài】

坏 1)〈形〉bad 2)〈动〉go bad, spoil, ruin 坏处 harm, disadvantage
坏块表 bad block table
坏区 bad sector
坏扇区 bad sector

【huān】

欢 joyous, happy, delighted 欢度 spend (an occasion) joyfully 欢聚 happy get-together, happy reunion 欢快 happy, joyous, gay 欢庆 celebrate joyously 欢送 set off, send off 欢送会 farewell party 欢喜 ①〈形〉joyful, happy, delighted ②〈动〉like, fond of, delight in 欢迎 ①(高兴地迎接)welcome, greet ②(乐意接受)welcome, favorably receive

【huán】

还 另见【hái】
1)(回)go back, come back 2)(归还)give back, return, repay 还本 repayment of principal 还本付息 repay capital with interest 还价 counter-offer, counterbid 还清 pay off 还原 ①(恢复原状)return to the original condition, restore; recondition ②〈化学〉reduction, deoxidation 还原剂 reducing agent, reductant 还债 pay one's debt, repay a debt

环 ring, hoop, loop, circle, toroid, collar 环抱 surround, encircle, envelop 环顾 look about, look around 环节 link, segment 环境 environment, surroundings, circumstances, ambience 环球 ①(围绕地球)round the

world ②(整个地球)the earth, the whole world 环绕 surround, encircle, revolve around 环形 annular, ringlike
环保护 ring protection
环境保护 environmental protection
环境变量 environment variable
环境表 environment list
环境部 environment division
环境符号 environment symbol
环境控制表 environment control table {ECT}
环境列表 environment list
环境模块 environment module
环境模型 environment(al) model
环境问题 environmental problem
环境需求 environmental requirement
环境因子 environment factor
环境影响分析 environment impact analysis {EIA}
环路 loop, cycle
环路传输 loop transmission
环路功能部件 loop feature
环路控制器 loop control unit {LCU}
环路连接板 loop splice plate {LSP}
环路适配器 loop adapter, loop feature
环路增益 loop gain
环球网 web
环形表 ring list, circular list
环形磁头 ring head
环形缓冲区 ring buffer
环形寄存器 ring register
环形计数器 ring counter
环形结构 ring structure
环形累加器 ring accumulator
环形码 ring code
环形配置 loop configuration
环形[环式]网络 ring network
环形文件 ring file
环形线路 loop line
环形总线 ring bus

【huǎn】

缓 1)(慢,迟)slow, unhurried 2)(推迟)delay, postpone, put off 缓冲 buffer, cushion 缓和 relax, ease up, mitigate, alleviate 缓慢 slow 缓期 postpone a deadline, suspend
缓冲 buffering, damping
缓冲部件[单元] buffer unit
缓冲池 pool of buffer
缓冲存储 buffer store
缓冲单元 buffer cell
缓冲电路 buffer circuit
缓冲回路 buffer loop
缓冲技术 buffering technique
缓冲寄存器 buffer register
缓冲空间 buffer space
缓冲控制块 buffer control block {BCB}
缓冲器 buffer, buffer unit, cushion
缓冲区大小 buffer size
缓冲区段 buffer field
缓冲区分配 buffer allocation
缓冲区故障 buffer fault
缓冲区管理 buffer management
缓冲区控制块 buffer control block {BCB}
缓冲设备 buffered device
缓冲输出 buffer output
缓冲输入 buffered input
缓冲效应 buffer effect
缓存 buffer memory
缓存表 buffer list

【huàn】

幻 unreal, imaginary 幻想 illusion, fantasy
幻像 phantom image
幻像方式 phantom mode
幻像转移 phantom branch

患 1)(祸患)trouble, peril, disaster 2)(害病)contract (a disease), suffer from 患者 sufferer, patient, invalid

唤 call out 唤起 ①(使奋起)arouse ②(引起)call, recall

换 1)(交换)exchange, barter, trade 2)(变换)change 换班 ①(替换)change shift ②(交接班)relieve a person on duty 换取 exchange sth for, get in return 换算 conversion 换向 commutation, inverting, reversing
换档 shift
换档键 shift key {PSK}
换档锁 shift lock
换档字符 shift character
换行 line escapement, line feed, line advance
换行码 line feed code
换行字符 line feed character {LF}, new-line character {NL}, index character {INX}
换码 escape, escaping
换码代码 escape code
换码符 escape, escape character {ESC}
换码键 escape key {ESC key}, escaping key
换码消息 escape message
换码序列 escape sequence
换码指令 escape instruction
换名 by-name
换数字档 figure shift {FIGS}, numeric shift
换算表 conversion table
换算电路 scaling unit/system
换算因子 scaling factor
换页 page change, form feed {FF}, form advance
换页符 form feed character {FF}
换字母档 alphabetic shift

焕 焕发 shine, glow, irradiate

【huāng】

荒 (缺乏)shortage, scarcity 荒地 wasteland, uncultivated land 荒凉 desolate, barren 荒谬,荒唐 absurd, preposterous 荒疏 neglect, be out of practice 荒芜 waste

慌 慌乱 flurried, alarmed and bewildered 慌忙 in a great rush, in a flurry, hurriedly

【huáng】

黄 yellow 黄昏 dusk 黄金 gold 黄金储备 gold reserve 黄油 ①(奶油)butter ②(化学)consistent grease, consistent lubricant
黄页 yellow page {YP}

簧 (弹簧)spring 簧片 reed

皇 emperor, sovereign

惶 惶恐 terrified

【huǎng】

谎 谎话,谎言 lie, falsehood

【huàng】

晃 晃动 shake, rock, sway

【huī】

灰 灰白 greyish white, pale 灰色 grey 灰尘 dust, dirt 灰烬 ash 灰心 lose heart, be discouraged

灰度 density, gray scale
灰度等级 gray/grey scale
灰度划分 density slicing
灰度级 graylevel, grey level
灰度图像 gray scale image, tone image
灰色标度 gray scale
灰色条纹 gray bar
灰色图像 gray image

恢 恢复 ①〈变成原样〉resume, renew, restore, retrieve, restitute ②〈重新得到〉recover, regain ◇恢复健康 recover one's health

恢复按钮 restore button
恢复操作 undo
恢复程序 recovery program
恢复登记 recovery log
恢复地址 repair to address {RA}
恢复功能 recovery function
恢复管理 recovery management
恢复卷 recovery volume
恢复能力 recovery capability, resilience
恢复日志 recovery log
恢复删除 undelete, unerase
恢复图符 restore icon
恢复图像 restored image
恢复系统 recovery system
恢复中断 recovery interrupt

挥 〈指挥〉command (an army) 挥动 brandish, wave 挥发 volatilize 挥舞 wave, wield

辉 1)（闪耀的光彩）brightness 2)（照耀）shine 辉煌 brilliant, splendid, glorious

徽 emblem, badge, insignia ◇国徽 national emblem

【huí】

回 return 回报 ①（报告工作）report on what has been done ②（报答）repay, require, reciprocate 回避 evade, avoid 回程 ①〈返回的路程〉return trip ②〈机械〉return stroke, back stroke 回答 answer, reply, respond 回顾 look back, review 回绝 decline, refuse 回扣 rebate, (sales) commission 回来 return, come back, be back 回去 return, go back, be back 回升 rise again (after a fall), pick up 回收 retrieve, recover 回响 reverberate, echo, resound 回信 ①〈动〉write in reply, write back ②〈名〉a letter in reply 回旋 ①〈盘旋〉circle round ②〈进退〉(room for) maneuver 回忆 call to mind, recollect, recall 回音 ①（回声）echo ②（回信）reply 回执 receipt

回避冲突 collision avoidance
回波 echo
回波干扰 echo talker
回波衰减 echo attenuation
[回波[回音]消除 echo cancellation
回车键 enter key
回答 reply {REP, RPLY}, replication, return {RET}

回答模式 answer schema
回答时间 response time
回答字节 answer byte
回放 playback
回归 regression
回归法 method of regression
回滚 roll-back
回叫名 call back name
回路 circuit, loop
回路传输 loop transmission
回路电流 loop current
回路控制器 loop control unit {LCU}
回路矩阵 circuit matrix
回路向量 cycle vector
回路增益 loop gain
回绕测试 wrap test
回绕控制 rewind control
回扫 retrace
回扫时间 flyback, flyback time, retrace time
回声 echo, talker echo
回声畸变[失真] echo distortion
回声消除 echo cancellation
回送 echo, loopback, return {RET}
回送测试 echo test
回送测试[检查] loopback test
回送方式 echo-plex, echoplex mode, loopback mode
回送检查 echo test
回送检验[校验] echo check
回溯 backtrace, backtrack, backtracking, flashback
回溯程序 backtracking program
回溯点 backtracking point
回溯法 backtracking method
回溯功能 back track function
回溯控制 backtrack control
回退 backspace {BS}, backspacing, roll-back
回退带 backspace tape
回退校正 backspace correction
回退装置 backspace mechanism
回线 loop
回线测试 loop testing
回线集中器 loop wiring concentrator {LWC}
回线绞接板 loop splice plate {LSP}
回写 write back
回行 enter, carriage return {CR, cr}
回音取消 acoustic echo cancellation {AEC}
回应 answerback

【huǐ】

悔 regret, repent

毁 1)(破坏掉）destroy, ruin, damage 2)(焚烧掉）burn up 毁坏 destroy, damage, break 毁灭 destroy, exterminate 毁约 scrap a contract or treaty
毁坏程序 bomb

【huì】

汇 1)(聚集）gather together 2)(寄）remit 汇报 report, give an account of 汇编 assemble, compile 汇兑 remittance, exchange 汇费 remittance fee 汇合 converge 汇集 ①(聚集）collect, compile ②(集合）come together, converge, assemble 汇款 ①〈动〉remit money, make a remittance ②〈名〉remittance 汇款单 money order 汇款人 remitter 汇率 exchange rate 汇票 draft, bill of exchange, money order 汇总 gather, collect, accumulate
汇编程序 assemble program,

汇编缓冲器 assembler, assembly program/routine
汇编缓冲器 assembly buffer
汇编级 assembler level
汇编阶段 assembling/assembly phase
汇编控制 assembler control
汇编命令 assembler directive, assembly directive
汇编器 assembler, assembly unit
汇编系统 assemble/assembler system/system
汇编行 assembly line
汇编语句 assembly statement
汇编语言 assembler language/language, computer-dependent language
汇编指令 assembler/assembly instruction
汇点 sink, sink node
汇点树 sink tree
汇集时间 binding time

会 另见【kuài】
1) (能) can, be able to, be good at, be skil(l)ful in 2) (可能) be likely to, be sure to 3) (团体) association, society, union **会场** meeting-place, conference hall **会费** membership dues **会合** get together, assemble, join **会话** conversation **会籍** membership **会见** meet, see **会聚** assemble, flock together
会刊 ① (会议文件汇编) proceedings of a conference, etc. ② (协会的刊物) the journal of an association, society, etc. **会期** ① (开会日期) the time fixed for a conference, the date of a meeting ② (会议天数) the duration of a meeting **会谈** talks **会议** meeting, gathering, party, get-together, conference **会员** member **会员证** membership card **会章** (协会章程) the constitution of an association, society, etc. **会长** the president of an association or society

会话参数 session parameter
会话层 session layer
会话管理协议 session management protocol {SMP}
会话活动 session activation
会话伙伴 session partner
会话节点 session node
会话结构 session structure
会话目录 session directory {SD}
会话启动 session initiation
会话时间 talk time
会话说明协议 session description protocol {SDP}
会话通告协议 session announcement protocol {SAP}
会话限制 session limit
会话业务 session service
会话终端系统 conversational terminal system {CTS}
会话终止 session termination
会聚子层 convergence sublayer {CS}
会晤段 session segment
会晤管理器 session manager {SM}
会晤监控器 session monitor
会晤阶段 session stage
会晤路径 session path
会晤组 session group
会议呼叫[电话] conference call

绘 paint, draw **绘画** drawing, painting **绘图** map;

draw, draft, plot 绘图板 drawing board
绘画笔 brush pen
绘画菜单 paint menu
绘画程序 paint program
绘画工具 paint tool
绘画命令 paint command
绘画软件 painting software
绘画数据 paint data
绘图, paint(ing) tool
绘图板 plotting board, plotting/graphic tablet
绘图笔 needle pen
绘图程序 draw(ing)/plotting program
绘图处理机 drawing processor
绘图方式 plot(ting) mode
绘图工具 graphical tool
绘图机 graph(ic) plotter, draft(ing)/drawing machine
绘图[图形]软件 graphic software
绘图软件 drafting software
绘图数据 draw data
绘图速度 plot speed
绘图仪 graph(ic) plotter
绘图装置 plotting device, painter

贿 贿赂 bribe; bribery

慧 intelligent, bright ◇智慧 wisdom, intelligence

【hūn】
昏 1)（黄昏）dusk 2)（头脑迷糊）confused, muddled 3)（失去知觉）lose consciousness, faint 昏暗 dark, dim

婚 1)〈动〉wed, marry 2)〈名〉marriage, wedding 婚礼 wedding ceremony

【hún】
浑 浑浊 muddy, turbid
浑名 nickname

【hùn】
混 (蒙混)pass for, pass off as 混合 mix, blend, mingle, hybrid 混合物 mixture 混乱 confusion, chaos 混凝土 concrete 混同 confuse, mix up 混淆 obscure, blur, confuse, mix up 混杂 mix, mingle 混浊 muddy, turbid
混沌 chaos
混合操作系统 hybrid operating system
混合差错控制 hybrid error control
混合的 composite, compound
混合电路 hybrid circuit
混合对象关系模型 hybrid object relational model
混合方法 hybrid method
混合仿真 hybrid simulation
混合关联 mixed interconnection
混合光纤同轴电缆系统 hybrid fiber coax {**HFC**}
混合基数 radix mixed
混合集成电路 hybrid integrated circuit {**HIC**}
混合计算机 hybrid computer
混合监督器 hybrid monitor
混合接口 hybrid interface
混合纠错 hybrid error correction
混合局域网 hybrid local network
混合控制 hybrid control
混合模拟 hybrid simulation
混合模型 hybrid model
混合耦合 hybrid coupling
混合冗余 hybrid redundancy
混合冗余系统 hybrid redundancy system

混合软件 hybrid software
混合网络 mixed network, mixing net
混合系统 hybrid system
混合线圈 hybrid coil
混合相关 hybrid correlation
混合指令 mix instruction
混合终端机 hybrid terminal
混乱的 chaotic, garbled
混乱模型 chaos model
混乱状态 chaotic mode
混频 mixing
混频二极管 mixer diode
混洗 shuffle
混洗算子 shuffle operator
混洗图 shuffle graph
混洗网络 shuffling network

【huó】

活 1)(生存)live 2)(活着的) alive, living 3)(救活) save 4)(灵活) vivid, lively 5)(活动的) movable, moving 6)(工作) work 7)(产品) product **活动** ①〈动〉move about, exercise ②〈形〉movable, mobile, flexible ③〈名〉activity, maneuver
活力 vigor, vitality, energy
活泼 ① lively, vivid ②〈化学〉reactive **活期** current **活期储蓄** current deposit **活页** loose-leaf **活跃** ①〈形〉brisk, lively, vigorous ②〈动〉activate, invigorate
活动表 activity list
活动程序 active program, active level
活动窗口 active window
活动磁盘表 active disk table {ADT}
活动存储器 active storage
活动的 active, animatic
活动等待 active wait
活动队列 active queue, activity queue
活动分析 activity analysis
活动服务器页面 active server page
活动[激活]记录 activation record
活动节点 active node
活动界限 action limit
活动进程 active process
活动卷 active volume
活动空间 action space, playing space
活动模型 activity model
活动目录 activity content
活动盘卷 active volume
活动清单 activity inventory
活动区 active area
活动任务 active task
活动日志 activity logging
活动体 mobile
活动头 moving head
活动网络 activity network
活动向量 activity vector
活动页 active page
活动因子 activity factor
活动栈 active stack
活动站 active station
活动状态 active status
活动追踪 activity trace
活动字 active word
活化单元 active cell
活数据 live data
活锁 livelock
活网 live net
活系统 live system
活跃地址 active address
活跃段 active segment
活跃矩阵 active matrix
活跃面板 active pane
活跃配置 active configuration
活跃设备 active device
活跃网关 active gateway
活字带 type belt

活字箱 type case

【huǒ】

火 1)(火焰) fire, flame 2)(炮火) firearms, ammunition 火车 train 火光 flame, blaze 火急 urgent, pressing 火箭 rocket 火警 fire alarm 火线 ①(战场前沿) battle line ②〈电气〉live wire 火星 ①(小火花) spark ②〈天文〉Mars

伙 伙伴 partner, companion 伙食 mess, food, meals

钬 holmium (Ho)

【huò】

或 1)〈副〉perhaps, maybe, probably 2)〈连〉or, either ... or ... 或多或少 more or less, to a greater or lesser degree, in varying degrees 或许 perhaps, maybe
"或" logical OR, OR else, Boolean/logic(al) add
"或"操作 OR operation, inclusion-OR operation
"或非" NOR {NOT-OR}, nondisjunction, rejection, inclusive-NOR
"或非"门 neither-NOR gate, NOR element, negative OR gate, nondisjunction/ rejection gate

货 goods, commodity 货币 money, currency 货舱 (cargo) hold, cargo bay (of a plane) 货场 goods yard 货车 ①(货运列车) goods train, freight train ②(货运车皮) goods van, freight car ③(运货卡车) truck, lorry 货船 freighter, cargo ship, cargo vessel 货单 manifest, waybill, shipping list 货价 commodity price, price of goods 货款 money for buying or selling goods, payment for goods 货物 goods, commodity, merchandise 货样 sample goods, sample 货源 source of goods, supply of goods 货运 freight transport 货主 owner of cargo
货币符号 currency sign, currency symbol
货郎担问题 travelling salesman problem

获 获得 gain, obtain, acquire, win, achieve 获胜 win, victory, be victorious, triumph
获取 acquire, get, grab
获取操作 get operation

霍 霍尔效应 Hall effect
霍夫曼编码 Huffman coding
霍夫曼模型 Huffman model

惑 1)(迷惑) be puzzled, be bewildered 2)(使迷惑) delude, mislead

祸 misfortune, disaster, calamity ◇ 车祸 traffic accident, road accident 祸根 the root of the trouble, the cause of misfortune 祸害 ① disaster, curse, ② damage, distroy

豁 豁免 exempt, remit

J j

【jī】

几 另见[jǐ]
几乎 nearly, almost, practically 几率〈数学〉probability, chance

击 1) (攻击) attack, assault 2) (撞击) come in contact with, bump into 击败 defeat, beat, vanquish 击打 beat, hit, strike 击中 hit
击穿 breakdown
击穿点 yield point
击打部件 hammer bank
击打式打印机 impact printer
击键 click, type, key stroke (=keystroke), stroke
击中概率 hit probability

饥 饥饿 be hungry, starve
饥荒 famine, crop failure

机 机场 airport, airfield, aerodrome 机床 machine tool 机动 ① (机器开动) motor-driven, motorized ② (灵活) flexible, expedient, mobile ③ (备用的) keep in reserve, for emergency use
机动车 motor vehicle 机动时间 time kept in reserve 机房 generator room, motor room, computer room 机工 mechanic, machinist 机构 ① 〈机械〉mechanism ② (机关) organ, organization, institution, setup 机关 (组织机构) office, body, organization
机会 chance, occasion, opportunity 机警 alert, sharp-witted, vigilant 机密 ①〈形〉secret, classified, confidential ②〈名〉secret 机器 machine, machinery, apparatus 机器人 robot, roboting machine 机器人学 robotics 机体 ① housing; organism ② 〈航空〉airframe, hull ③〈生物〉organism 机械 ① (装置) machinery, machine, mechanism ② (控制的) machine-operated ③ (刻板) mechanical, inflexible, rigid 机械化 mechanize, motorize 机遇 favorable circumstances, opportunity 机智 quick-witted, resourceful 机制〈生物〉mechanism

机电一体化(技术) mechatronics {MEIS}
机电装置 electromechanical device
机顶盒 (TV) set top box {STB}
机读目录 machine-readable catalog {MARC}
机房 machine room, shop
机会节点 chance node
机架 bay, cage, chassis, cradle, frame(work), rack

机壳 envelope
机理 mechanics
机密性 confidentiality
机内表示 internal machine representation
机内测试 built-in test
机内工具 built-in tool
机器报警 machine alarm
机器编址 machine addressing
机器长度 machine length
机器程序 machine program
机器错误 machine error
机器代码 machine code
机器地址 machine address
机器对象 machine object
机器翻译 machine/ automatic/ mechanical translation
机器翻译系统 machine translation system {MTS}
机器方向 machine direction
机器辅助翻译 machine aided translation {MAT}
机器故障 machine error, machine stoppage
机器级 machine level
机器计算 machine computation
机器检查 machine check
机器接口 machine interface
机器结构 machine architecture
机器可读符号 machine-readable character
机器可读媒体 machine-readable medium
机器可读目录 machine-readable catalog {MARC}
机器可识别的 machine-recognizable
机器类别 machine class
机器零点 machine zero
机器逻辑 machine logic
机器码 machine code
机器码级[层次] machine code level

机器模型 machine model
机器配置 machine configuration
机器人 robot, bionic man
机器人臂 robotic arm
机器人传感器 robot sensor
机器人感觉 robot sense
机器人规划 robotic planning
机器人化 robotization
机器人视觉 robot vision
机器人学 robotics
机器视觉 machine vision
机器听觉 machine hearing
机器同步 machine timing
机器推理 machine inference
机器误差 machine error
机器学习 machine learning
机器语言 absolute language, computer language, machine language, mechanical language
机器指令 absolute instruction, machine instruction
机器指令集 machine instruction set
机器指令码 machine instruction code
机器状态寄存器 machine status register {MSR}
机器字长 machine word-length
机箱 equipment rack
机箱附件 cabinet assistance
机械电子学 mechatronics {MEIS}
机械工程 mechanical engineering
机械手 machine hand, (robot) manipulator, magic hand
机械鼠标 mechanical mouse
机载计算机 airborne computer, on-board computer
机载系统 mobile system
机(器辅)助编辑 machine-aided editing

机助翻译 machine-aided translation
机助检索 machine-aided retrieval
机助人译 machine-aided human translation {MAHT}
机助设计 machine-aided design

肌 muscle, flesh

鸡 chick, chicken 鸡蛋 egg

奇 另见【qí】
odd (number), uneven number
奇场[半帧] odd field
奇点 singular point
奇符号 odd symbol
奇函数 odd function
奇偶比特 parity bit
奇偶出错 parity error
奇偶单元 parity cell
奇偶发生器 parity generator
奇偶归并 odd-even merging
奇偶计数器 odd-even counter
奇偶检验中断 parity check interrupt
奇偶交叉(存取) odd-even interleaving
奇偶逻辑 parity logic
奇偶驱动 parity drive
奇偶数字 parity digit
奇偶位数 parity bit, parity digit
奇偶校验码 parity code
奇偶校验器 parity checker
奇偶校验状态 parity state
奇偶性 parity
奇偶性中断 parity interrupt
奇数 impair, odd number
奇数的 odd
奇数页 recto
奇字节 odd byte

迹 (痕迹)mark, trace 迹象 sign, indication

绩 (功绩)merits and achievements, contributions

积 (乘积)product 积存 store up, lay up, stockpile 积极 ①(正面的)positive ②(进取的) active, energetic, vigorous 积累 accumualte, store up, amass 积蓄 ①〈动〉put aside, save, accumulate ②〈名〉savings
积分 integral, integrate, integration
积分近似 integral approach
积分网络 integrating network
积分因子 integrating factor
积木化 modularization
积木结构 modular architecture/structure
积木块设计方法 building block design
积木式结构 building block architecture, modular construction
积木式系统 modular system

基 1)(基本的) basic, key, primary 2)〈化学〉radical 3)〈数学〉radix 基本 ①(根本的) basic, fundamental ②(主要的) main, essential ③(基础的) elementary, rudimentary ④(大体上)basically, in the main, on the whole, by and large 基本建设 capital construction 基本上 ①(主要)mainly ②(大体上) on the whole, in the main 基地 base 基点 basic point, staring point, center 基金 fund, foundation 基金会

foundation 基于 because of, in view of, on account of 基准 base, reference, datum, benchmark
基板 base plate
基本变量 basic variables, based variable
基本表达式 primary expression
基本[原始]操作 primitive operation
基本操作系统 basic operating system {BOS}, fundamental operating system
基本程序 base program
基本池 base pool
基本串 basic string
基本存储器 base memory
基本存取层[存取级] basic access level
基本存取法 basic access method {BAM}
基本单元 base location, base cell, elemental area
基本对象 basic object, elementary object
基本发送单位 basic transmission unit {BTU}
基本方式 basic mode
基本访问 basic access
基本分区 primary partition
基本符号 base notation
基本割集 fundamental cutset
基本格式 basic format
基本功能 primary function
基本规则 basis rule
基本和 elementary sum
基本合成器 base level synthesizer
基本回路 fundamental loop, fundamental cycle, fundamental circuit
基本会话 basic conversation
基本集 base set, basic set
基本记号 base notation

基本记录 base record, master record
基本键 base key
基本接口 basic interface
基本节点 fundamental node
基本结点 base node
基本卷 base volume
基本类 base class
基本链路单元 basic link unit {BLU}
基本路径 elementary path
基本(定)律 fundamental law
基本码 basic code
基本名 base name
基本命令 elementary command
基本命题 elementary sentence
基本模式 fundamental mode
基本模型 fundamental model
基本频带 baseband
基本区域 prime area
基本设备表 basic equipment list
基本设备单元 basic device unit {BDU}
基本数据 base data, basic data, master data
基本速率接口 basic rate interface {BRI}
基本通路 elementary path
基本系统 base system
基本项 base item, basic term, elemental term, elementary item, essential/ground term
基本信息单元(单位) basic information unit {BIU}
基本形式 elemental form
基本形状 base shape
基本行距 basic line space
基本循环 basic loop, elementary cycle
基本映像支持 basic mapping support {BMS}
基本元素 base element, basic element

基本指令 basic/elementary instruction
基本字符串 basic string
基本组 base group
基变量 basic variable
基标识符 base identifier
基表 base table, basic table
基参数 base parameter
基操作数 base operand
基础研究 fundamental research
基簇 base cluster
基带 baseband, substrate
基带传输 baseband transmission
基带网(络) baseband network
基带系统 baseband system
基带信号 baseband signal
基底 base, basis, substratum
基地址 base address
基段 base segment
基干通道 backbone channel
基干线路 basic trunk
基极 base
基极区 base region
基级 ground level
基卷 base volume
基群速率接口 primary rate interface {**PRI**}
基色 base/elementary color, color primaries
基数 base/basic number, cardinal number, radix, base, cardinality
基数分类 radix sort
基数据 base data
基数数字 radix digit
基数样条 cardinal spline
基数转换 radix transformation
基线 baseline, basis
基线范围 baseline extent
基线方向 baseline direction
基线角 baseline angle
基线校正 baseline correction
基线增量 baseline increment
基线轴 baseline axis
基向量 base vector
基页 base page
基优先级[数] base priority
基于规则(的)系统 rule-based system
基于模型系统 model base system
基于文本的 text based
基元 metaprimitive
基站 base station
基阵 basic matrix
基(地)址寄存器 base register
基址寻址 base addressing
基准程序 benchmark program
基准磁带 reference tape, standard tape
基准地址 presumptive/reference address
基准点 datum/data point
基准电平 reference level
基准电源 reference (power) supply
基准过程 baseline process
基准监控 reference monitor
基准例行程序 benchmark routine
基准时间 reference time
基准数据 reference data
基准题 benchmark problem, benchmark task
基准网络 baseline network
基准问题 benchmark problem
基准线 baseline, datum line, reference axis
基准信号 reference signal
基准音量 reference volume
基准噪声 reference noise
基准钟 reference clock

缉

缉拿 seize, arrest

畸

畸变 distortion, skewness

激

激 激变 violent change, cataclysm　激动 excite, stir, agitate　激发 ① arouse, stimulate, set off ②〈物理〉excitation　激光 laser　激化 sharpen, intensify, become acute　激励 ① encourage, impel, urge ②〈电子〉drive, excitation　激烈 intense, sharp, fierce, violent, acute　激增 increase sharply, soar, shoot up

激发规则　firing rules
激光唱片　compact disk {CD}
激光存储(器)　laser memory/storage
激光二极管　laser diode
激光跟踪　laser tracking
激光绘图仪　laser plotter
激光临界值　laser threshold
激光盘　compact disk {CD}, laser disk
激光扫描器　laser scanner
激光声纳　laser sonar
激光束　laser beam
激光通信　laser communication
激光系统　laser system
激光显示　laser display
激光印刷机　laser beam printer
激光印刷头　laser print head
激光印刷系统　laser printing system {LPS}
激光阈值　laser threshold
激光照排机　laser typesetter
激活　activate, activating, activation, sensitization
激活的窗口　active window
激活的单元　active cell
激活区　active region
激活态　active state
激活栈　activation stack
激活周期　activation cycle
激励表　excitation table
激励矩阵　excitation matrix

稽

稽 稽查 ①(检查)check, inspect, examine ②(检查人员)inspector, customs officer

【jí】

及

及 〈连〉and　及格 pass (a test, examination, etc.)　及时 ①(正赶上)timely, in time ②(立即)promptly, without delay　及早 as soon as possible, before it is too late

吉

吉 吉利, 吉祥 lucky, fortunate, auspicious

吉咖(千兆)　billion, kilomega
吉位　billibit, gigabit
吉字节(1024M字节)　gigabyte {Gbyte}

汲

汲 draw

级

级 1)(等级)level, rank, grade　2)(年级)course, grade, class 3)(台阶)step 4)〈物理〉cascade　级别 rank, level, grade, scale

级别控制表　level control table {LCT}
级工作区　level work area {LWA}
级间网络　interstage network
级控制表　level control table {LCT}
级联　cascading, cascade connection, tandem connection
级联表　cascade list, cascade table
级联菜单　cascade menu
级联过程　cascade process
级联控制　cascade control
级联逻辑　cascade logic
级联网络　cascade network

极

极 (两极) pole **极点** the utmost point, extreme **极度** extreme, exceeding, to the utmost **极端** ①(达到顶点)extreme ②(非常)extreme, exceeding **极力** do one's utmost, spare no effort **极其** extremely, utmost **极限** ①(最高限度)the limit, the maximum, the ultimate; critical, extreme ②〈数学〉limit
极大项 maxterm
极大元 maximal element, maximal member
极大值 maximum, maximal/maximum value
极点 extreme point, pole
极点配置 pole assignment
极端值 extremum
极化 polarization, polarize
极化电路 polar circuit
极图 extremal graph
极限地址 limiting address
极限点 limit point
极限分布 limit distribution
极限检验[检查] limit check
极限试验 marginal test
极限通路 limit path
极限优先级[权] limit priority, limit priority level
极限文件 limit file
极限值 limit value
极线 polar
极小(值) minimum
极性 polar, polarity
极值 extremal, extreme value, extremum, limit
极值点 extreme point
极值图 extremal graph

即 1)(当前)at present, in immediate future 2)(就是)be, mean; namely 3)(立即)promptly, at once, immediately, in no time **即将** be about to, be on the point of, soon **即使** even, even if, even though
即插即用 plug and play {PnP}

急 1)(急于)impatient, anxious, eager 2)(使着急)worry **急促** fast, rapid, violent **急件** urgent document, urgent dispatch **急救** first aid, emergency treatment **急剧** rapid, sharp, sudden **急忙** in a hurry, hurriedly, hastily **急迫** urgent, pressing **急需** ①〈动〉be badly in need of ②〈名〉urgent need **急躁** irritated, annoyed

疾 疾病 disease, sickness, illness **疾苦** suffering, pain **疾速** fast, quick

棘 棘手 thorny, troublesome, knotty

集 1)(集子)collection, anthology 2)(聚集)gather, collect, assemble 3)(书或分集)volume, partoog **集合** ① gather, assemble; integration, combination, collection ②〈数学〉set **集会** assembly, rally, gathering, meeting **集结** mass, concentrate, build up **集市** country fair, market **集体** collective **集团** group, clique, circle, bloc **集约经营** intensive management **集中** concentrate, centralize, focus, assemble, lump **集资** raise

funds, collect money, pool resources 集装 packaging
集成 integration
集成办公室系统 integrated office system {IOS}
集成磁盘 integrated disk
集成[整体]存储控制器 integrated storage control {ISC}
集成电路 integrated circuit {IC}
集成电路片尺寸 chip size
集成电源 integrated power supply
集成度 integrated level, integration degree, integration level
集成仿真器 integrated emulator
集成附件 integrated attachment
集成光学 integrated optics {IO}
集成化环境 integrated environment
集成化系统 integrated system
集成开发环境 integrated development environment {IDF}
集成配件 integrated attachment
集成器件 integrated component
集成适配器 integrated adapter
集成数据库 integrated database
集成通信适配器 integrated communication adapter {ICA}
集成系统 integrated system
集成注入逻辑 integrated injection logic {I²L, IIL}
集点块 collection point block {CPB}
集电器 current collector
集覆盖 set covering
集函数 set function
集合并 set union
集合差 set difference
集合符 set symbol
集合类型 set type, type set
集合论 set theory
集合体 aggregation, bank, complex, ensemble
集合运算 set operation
集结 aggregation
集结矩阵 aggregate matrix
集结模型 aggregate model
集名 set name
集思广益 brain storming {BS}
集系 set system
集线器 concentrator, hub
集线器板 hub board
集选择 set selection
集语句 set statement
集值 set occurrence, set value
集中保护电路 integrated protective circuit {IPC}
集中报文 concentrated messages
集中存储器控制 integrated storage control {ISC}
集中仿真 integrated emulation
集中绞接 mass splicing
集中控制 centralized control, pool
集中式配置 centralized configuration
集中式数据库 centralized database
集中式拓扑结构 centralized topology
集中式网(络) centralized network
集中式系统 integrated system
集中数据处理 centralized data processing, integrated data processing {IDP}
集中(式)刷新 centralized refresh
集中[内部]系统 in-house system
集子句 set clause

辑 1)〈动〉collect, compile, edit 2)〈名〉part, volume
辑要 summary, abstract

籍

籍贯 native place, home town, birthplace

【jǐ】

几 另见 jī

1)（询问数目）how many 2)（表示十以内的不定数）a few, several, some **几何** ① how much, how many ② 〈数学〉geometry **几时** what time, when

几何笔 geometric pen
几何处理 geometric processing
几何规划 geometric programming
几何级数 geometric progression, geometric series
几何结构 geometry
几何模型 geometric model
几何算法 geometric algorithm
几何图 geometric graph
几何推理 geometric reasoning
几何文本 geometric text
几何相关 geometric correlation
几何校正 geometric correction
几何序列 geometric sequence

己

1)（自己）oneself 2)（自己的）one's own, personal

挤

（拥挤）crowd, pack **挤开** jostle, push against **挤压** squeeze, press

给 另见【gěi】

supply, provide **给与** give, render, offer

【jì】

计

1)（主意）idea, plan 2)（仪器）meter, ga(u)ge **计划** ①〈名〉plan, project, program ②〈动〉map out, plan **计价** valuation **计件** count by the piece **计件工资** piece rate wage **计较** ①（在乎）bother about, fuss about ②（争论）argue, dispute ③（打算）think over, plan **计时** ① reckon by time **计时工资** payment by the hour, hourly wages, time wage ② timing, clocking, timekeeping **计算** calculate, compute, count, numerate, account, reckon

计步装置 step count set
计划更新 schedule regeneration
计划指标 planned target
计时[校时]带 timing tape
计时单元 timing unit
计时[定时]电路 timing circuit
计时卡片 timing sheet
计时器 calculagraph, clock {CLK}, clock register, time marker, timer, timing counter
计时器控制 timer control
计时文件 calendar file
计时中断 timer interruption
计时装置 timing service
计数 count(ing), scaling, tally(ing)
计数电路 access-control scheme, counting/scaling circuit
计数定时器 counter timer
计数分类 counting sort
计数寄存器 count(er) register, tally register
计[计算]控制 counting control
计数脉冲 count pulse
计数器 counter, counting device, scaler
计数区 count area, count block
计数图灵机 counting Turing machine {CTM}

计数型触发器 toggle flip-flop {T flip-flop}
计数循环 counting loop
计数元件 counting element
计数原理 counting principle
计数装置 counter unit, counting device
计算部件 evaluation unit
计算部件[元件] computing element
计算方式 account form, compute mode
计算费率 accounting rate
计算符号 compute sign
计算机 computer
计算机安置 computer installation
计算机安装 computer installation
计算机保密 computer privacy
计算机保险 computer insurance
计算机病毒 computer virus
计算机病毒学 computer virology
计算机程序 computer program
计算机代数 computer algebra {CA}
计算机捣乱者 hacker
计算机电话集成 computer telephony integration {CTI}
计算机动画片 computer generated animation {CGA}
计算机翻译 computer translation {CT}
计算机犯罪 computer crime
计算机辅助测试 computer-aided test {CAT}
计算机辅助分析 computer-aided analysis {CAA}
计算机辅助工程 computer-aided engineering {CAE}
计算机辅助工业 computer-aided industry {CAI}
计算机辅助管理 computer-aided management {CAM}
计算机辅助检索 computer-aided retrieval {CAR}, computer-assisted retrieval {CAR}
计算机辅助教学 computer-aided instruction {CAI}, programmed learning
计算机辅助教育 computer-aided education {CAE}
计算机辅助软件工程 computer-aided software engineering {CASE}
计算机辅助设计 computer-aided design {CAD}
计算机辅助制造 computer-aided manufacturing {CAM}
计算机工程 computer engineering
计算机管理教学 computer-managed instruction {CMI}
计算机和系统工程 computer and system engineering {CASE}
计算机化会议 computerized conference, computer-mediated conference/interaction
计算机会话 computer speak
计算机会议 computer conferencing/conference
计算机会议系统 computer conferencing system {CCS}
计算机绘图系统 computer plotting system
计算机集成制造 computer-integrated manufacturing {CIM}
计算机技术 computer technology
计算机加密 computer cryptography
计算机检索 computer search
计算机教学 computer instruc-

tion
计算机接口部件 computer interface unit {CIU}
计算机结构 computer architecture/organization/structure
计算机紧急响应组 computer emergency response team {CERT}
计算机科学 computer science
计算机科学网络 computer science network {CSNET}
计算机可读的 computer-readable
计算机控制 cybernate
计算机控制台 computer console, control console
计算机名 computer name
计算机模拟 computer simulation
计算机模式 computer patterns
计算机能力 computer capacity
计算机排版 computer typesetting
计算机配置 computer configuration
计算机认知 computer recognition
计算机X射线断层造影 computer tomography {CT}
计算机设计语言 computer design language {CDL}
计算机世代 computer generation, generation of computer
计算机视觉 computer vision
计算机体系结构 computer architecture
计算机通信 computer communication, telematique
计算机图像处理 computer image processing
计算机图形接口 computer graphics interface {CGI}
计算机图形元文件 computer graphics metafile {CGM}
计算机外围[外部]设备 computer peripheral apparatus
计算机网(络) computer network
计算机网络结构 computer network architecture
计算机网络设备 computer network facility
计算机网络协议 computer network protocol
计算机文化 computer culture
计算机文件 computer file
计算机文字处理 computerized word processing
计算机系列 computer series, family of computers
计算机系统 computer system, computing system
计算机系统安全 computer system security
计算机系统分析员 computer system analyst
计算机系统模拟 computer system simulation
计算机系统审计 computer system audit
计算机性能 computer performance/power
计算机应用 computer application
计算机硬件 computer hardware
计算机用户 computer user
计算机邮件 computer mail
计算机游戏 computer game
计算机语句 computer statement
计算机语言 computer language, computerese
计算机指令 computer instruction
计算机智能 computer mind
计算机中心 computer center
计算机终端(设备) computer terminal

计算机资源 computer resource
计算机字长 machine length
计算机字符 computer character
计算机字节 computer byte
计算机组织 computer organization
计算机组装 computer packaging
计算机作图 computer mapping
计算几何 computational geometry
计算技术 computing technology
计算空间 computation space
计算密度 bulk density
计算能力 computer power, computing capacity, computing power
计算器 calculator, calculating, machine
计算器芯片 calculator chip
计算器终端 calculator terminal
计算时间 computation time, computerization time
计算数学 computational mathematics, mathematics of computation/ computing, numerical mathematics
计算误差 calculation error, computational error, computing error, error of calculation
计算站 computer installation, shop
计算智能 computational intelligence {CI}
计算中心 computation center, computing center
计算装置 calculating apparatus/device

记 (标记)mark, sign 记分 ①(比赛用)keep the score, record the points ②(学校用)register a student's marks 记号 mark, sign, notation, symbol 记录 ①〈动〉write down, take notes, record ②〈名〉record, minutes, notes 记取 remember, bear in mind, commit to memory 记入 inscribe, log, entry, login 记事 ①〈动〉keep a record of events, make a memorandum ②〈名〉account, record of events, chronicles 记忆 ①〈动〉remember, recall ②〈名〉memory 记忆力 the faculty of memory, memory 记载 ①〈动〉put down in writing, record ②〈名〉record, notes, account 记帐 keep account, keep books 记者 reporter, correspondent, newsman, journalist
记分牌[板] score board
记录 record(ing), logging, log-on, log-in, registration, write-in
记录板 register bed
记录笔 stylus pen
记录标记 record mark
记录标题 record header, record heading
记录布局 record layout
记录槽 record slot
记录查找 record search
记录长度 length, record length
记录成分 record component
记录程序 logging program
记录传输 record transmission
记录磁头 (magnetic) recording head
记录访问块 record access block {RAB}
记录分隔符 record separator

{RS}, record separator character {RS}
记录分类 record sorting
记录分离符 record separator character {RS}
记录分区 record partitioning
记录格式 record format, record layout
记录更新 record updating
记录间隔 interrecord gap {IGP}, record gap
记录键 record key, write key
记录(间)结构 interrecord structure
记录结构 record layout, record structure
记录结束 end of record {EOR}
记录卡片 writer card
记录控制(表) log control table {LCT}
记录块 record block
记录类型 record type, type record
记录类型入口 log type entry
记录链 record chain
记录媒体 carrier {CARR}
记录密度 packing density, record density, recording density
记录描述符 record descriptor
记录模块 logging module
记录器 recorder, transcriptor, writer, inscriber, logger
记录区 field {FLD}, recording area
记录属性 record attribute
记录数目 record count
记录说明符 record lock
记录锁 record lock
记录锁定 record locking
记录替换 record replacement
记录通信 record communication
记录头 record head, recording head
记录文件 logfile
记录修改 record updating
记录选择 record option, record selection
记录因子 packing factor
记录引用 record reference
记录值 record occurrence
记录终止符 end of record {EOR}
记录[备注]字段 memo field
记日志 journaling, journalizing
记时 time stamp
记时标记 tick mark
记时卡片 time card
记数 number representation, numeration
记数法 notation, system of notation
记数系统 notation system, number (representation) system, numeration system
记忆电路 register circuit
记忆模型 memory model
记忆扫描 memory scanning
记忆系统 memory system
记帐文件 account file

纪
纪录片 documentary film
纪律 discipline 纪念 ①(怀念)commemorate, mark ②(纪念品)souvenir, keepsake ③(纪念日)commemoration day, anniversary 纪要 summary 纪元(时代)epoch, era

忌
忌妒 be jealous of, envy
忌怕 fear, dread

伎
伎俩 trick, intrigue, maneuver

技
技工 skilled worker,

mechanic, technician **技能** technical ability, skill **技巧** skill, technique, craftsmanship, feat **技师,技术员** technician **技术** technique, technology, skill, craft **技艺** skill, artistry

技术办公协议 technical office protocol {TOP}

技术储备 technical storage

技术规范 technical specification

技术评估[评价] technology/ technical assessment

技术验证 technical identification

系 另见【xì】
tie, fasten, do up, button up

季
season ◇淡季 dull season // 旺季 busy season **季度** quarter (of a year) **季节** season **季刊** quarterly (publication)

际
1) (边缘或分界处) border, boundary, edge 2) (相互之间) inter-, between, among

剂
1) (药剂,制剂) a pharmaceutical preparation, a chemical preparation 2) 〈化学〉agent ◇防腐剂 preservative // 干燥剂 drying agent 3) 〈量词〉(用于汤药) dose

济
1) (救济) give relief, aid, help 2) (有益) be of help, benefit ◇无济于事 not help matters, be of no help

既
(已经) already **既…又…**

both ... and, as well as **既成事实** accomplished fact **既定** set, fixed, established **既然** since, as, now that

继
1) (接续) continue, succeed, follow 2) (继而) then, afterwards **继承** inherit, succeed, carry on **继任** succeed sb in a post **继续** continue, go on (with), keep on, proceed

继承层次 inheritance hierarchies

继承码 inheritance code

继承推理 inheritance reasoning

寄
1) (递送) send, post, mail 2) (托付) entrust, deposit, place, park **寄存** deposit, leave with, check **寄件人** sender **寄卖,寄售** consign for sale on commission **寄宿** ①(借宿) lodge, put up ②(住校) board **寄宿生** resident student, boarder **寄宿学校** boarding schools, residential college

寄存器 register, box

寄存器窗口 register window

寄存器地址 register address

寄存器堆栈 register stack

寄存器分配 register allocation

寄存器结构 register structure

寄存器容量 register capacity

寄存器寻址 register addressing

寄存器指针 register pointer

寄存器转储 register dump

寄存器组 register block, register set

寄生电容 parasitic capacitance

寄生信号 alias, spurious signal

寄生型病毒 parasitic viruses

寄生元件 parasitic element

寂 寂静 quiet, still, silent 寂寞 lonely, lonesome, solitary

【jiā】

加 1)（相加）add, plus 2)（增加）increase, augment 3)（添上）put in, add, append 加班 work overtime, work an extra shift 加倍 double, be twice as much, redouble 加大 oversize 加法 addition, add 加工 ① process ②〈机械〉machining, working 加固 reinforce, strengthen, brace 加厚 thicken, intensify 加急 urgent 加紧 step up, speed up, intensify 加剧 aggravate, intensify 加快,加速 quicken, speed up, accelerate, pick up speed, boost 加宽 broaden, widen 加料 ①（进料）feed in raw material ②（添加或用优质原料制成）reinforced 加拿大 Canada 加拿大人 Canadian 加强 strengthen, enhance, reinforce, augment, stiffen 加热 heating 加入 ①（加上）add, mix, put in ②（参加）join 加深 deepen, speed up, accelerate 加以 in addition, moreover 加油 ①（加润滑油）oil, lubricate, grease up ②（加燃料油）refuel, dope ③（加劲）make a greater effort, make an extra effort 加重 ①（增加重量）make or become heavier, increase the weight of ②（增加程度）make or become more serious, give emphasis to 加注 filling-up, charging-up 加1 increment, tally up 加操作 add operation 加电 power on, power up 加电复位 power up reset, power-on reset 加电键 power-on key 加法 addition 加法操作 add operation 加法电路 additive/ summing circuit 加法器 adder, adding box, gauge, summer 加法速度 addition speed 加法算子 addition operator 加法幺元 additive identity 加法原理 addition principle 加法运算 add operation, additive cipher 加号 plus 加急报文处理 expedited message handling {EMH} 加减符 plus minus 加宽行距[字距] space out 加框 boxing 加密 encipher, encipherment, encrypt, encrypting, encryption, scramble 加密键 encryption key 加密密钥 enciphering key 加密术 cryptography 加密数据 enciphered data 加密算法 cryptographic/ encryption algorithm 加密网络 refined net 加权 weighted, weighting 加权二进制 binary weighted 加权法 weighted method 加权函数 weight(ing) function 加权和 weight(ed) sum 加权码 weighted code 加权平衡树 weighted balanced tree

加权校验 weighted check
加权有向图 weighted digraph
加载操作 load operation
加载错误 loading error
加载地址 load address
加载点 load point
加载故障 load fault
加载区 loading zone
加载时间 load time
加重电路 emphasizer

夹 夹缝 a narrow space between two adjacent things, crack, crevice 夹紧 clamp, grasp, fasten, grip 夹杂 mix, mingles, interperse 夹子 clip, clamp, folder 夹住 press from both sides, grip

佳 good, fine, excellent 佳音 welcome news, favorable reply 佳作 a fine piece of writing, an excellent work

家 1)(家庭)family, household 2)(住所)home 3)(专家)expert, a specialist in a certain field 家伙 ①(工具,武器)tool, utensil, weapon ②(人)fellow, guy 家教 family education, giving lessons at home 家具 furniture 家务 household duties 家务劳动 housework, household chores 家乡 hometown, native place 家用 domestic, household 家用电器 household appliances
家务管理 household management
家用计算机 home computer
家用录像系统 video home system {VHS}
家用终端 home terminal

镓 gallium (Ga)

嘉 1)(美好)good, fine 嘉宾 honored guest 2)(夸奖)praise, commend 嘉奖 commend, cite

【jiá】

铗 tongs

颊 cheek

【jiǎ】

甲 1)(第一)first 2)(指甲)nail 3)(装甲)armor 甲壳 shell, crust

钾 potassium (K), kalium

假 另见【jià】
1)〈形〉false, fake, sham, phoney, artificial 2)〈动〉borrow, avail oneself of, make use of 假扮,假充 disguise oneself as, pose as pretend to be 假定 suppose, assume, postulate 假借 make use of 假名 ①(非真名,笔名)pseudonym ②(日语字母)kana 假如 if, supposing, in case 假设 ①〈动〉suppose, assume, postulate, grant, presume ②〈名〉hypothesis, tentation 假使 if, in case, in the event that 假说 hypothesis 假想 ①(假设)imagination, hypothesis, supposition ②(假定的)imaginary, hypothetical, fictitious 假造 ①(伪造)forge, counterfeit ②(捏造)invent, fabricate 假装 pretend, feign, disguise

假 dummy, false
假报文 dummy message
假变元 dummy argument
假定 assumption, fiction
假定值 set value
假符号 false symbol
假负载 dummy load
假开始 false start
假命题 false proposition, false statement
假目标 decoy, false target
假输出 false output
假同步 false synchronization
假脱机 automatic spool
假脱机(输入输出) simultaneous peripheral operation on line {SPOOL}
假脱机对话 spool session
假脱机分区 spool partition
假脱机管理 spool management
假脱机卷宗 spool volume
假脱机容量 spool volume
假脱机输出 spool out
假脱机输入 spool in
假脱机文件 spool file
假脱机系统 spooling system
假脱机作业 spool job
假想工程 imagineering
假消息 dummy message
假信号 false/ ghost/ spurious signal, glitch
假言推理 modus ponens
假装入 dummy load

【jià】

价 1)(价格)price, tariff 2)〈化学〉valence 价值 value, cost; be worth 价钱 price
价格体系 price system
价值分析 value analysis
价值工程 value engineering
价值管理 value control, value management
价值系数 value coefficient

驾 驾驶 drive, pilot 驾驭 ①(驱使车马)drive ②(控制)control, master, dominate

架 架空 ①(离地)built on stilts, overhead, aerial ②(没有基础)impractical, unpractical 架设 put up, erect, mount 架子 ①(支架)frame, stand, rack, shelf ②(结构)framework, skeleton, outline

假 另见【jiǎ】
(休假)leave of absence 假期 holiday, vacation 假日 holiday, day off 假条 ①(请假条)application for leave ②(准假条)leave permit

嫁 1)(出嫁)marry 2)(转嫁)shift, transfer

【jiān】

尖 tip, apex, point 尖端 ①(尖) pointed end, tip, nib ②(最先进的)most advanced, sophisticated 尖端科学 most advanced branches of science, advanced science, top science 尖利 ①(刀锋)sharp, keen, cutting ②(声音)shrill, piercing
尖头 tip, tip side
尖头信号 pip

坚 hard, solid, firm 坚持 persist in, persevere in, insist on, stick to, adhere to 坚定 ①〈形〉firm, staunch, steadfast ②〈动〉strengthen 坚固 firm, solid, strong 坚决 firm, resolute, determined 坚强 ①〈形〉strong, firm, staunch ②〈动〉strengthen 坚韧 tough and tensile, firm and tenacious 坚实 solid, substantial 坚信 firmly believe, be firmly convinced, be fully confident of 坚硬 hard, rigid

间 另见【jiàn】
1) (中间) between, among 2) (一定空间或时间里) in, during 3) (房间) room

肩
1)〈名〉shoulder 2)〈动〉take on, undertake, shoulder, bear

艰
艰巨 arduous, formidable, extremely difficult 艰难 difficult, hard

监
(牢狱) prison, jail 监督 supervise, control, inspect 监督, 监视 ①〈动〉supervise, superintend, control ②〈名〉supervisor, inspect, watch 监工 overseer, supervisor 监禁 imprison, put in jail 监考 invigilate, monitor examinations 监牢, 监狱 prison, jail
监测器 monitor
监测系统 observation system
监督[监控]程序 monitoring program
监督程序 monitor, supervisor
监督程序调用 monitor call
监督反馈 monitoring feedback
监督过程 monitor procedure
监督控制 supervisory control
监督命令 monitor command
监督台 master console
监督显示(器) monitor display
监督序列 supervisory sequence
监督学习 supervised learning
监督训练 supervised training
监督终端 monitor terminal
监护变量 guardian variable
监控 monitoring, supervision
监控程序 monitor, supervisor
监控计算机 supervisory control computer
监控台 master/ supervisor/ supervisory console
监控系统 supervisory control system
监控装置 monitoring apparatus
监控状态[方式] monitor mode
监视部件 monitor unit
监视脉冲 watchdog pulse
监视器/控制面板 monitor/ control panel {MCP}
监听窗口 audit window
监听键 monitoring key
监听开关 listening key
监听项 audit entry

兼
兼备 have both ... and ...
兼并 acquire, annex (territory, companies, etc.) 兼顾 take account of two or more things 兼任,兼职 ①(同时任数职) hold a concurrent post ②(非专职) concurrent post, part-time job
兼容(的) compatible
兼容方式 compatibility mode
兼容关系 compatibility relation
兼容机 clone
兼容计算机 compatible computer
兼容模式 compatible pattern
兼容软件 compatible software
兼容式接口 compatible interface
兼容性集 compatibility set

兼容硬件 compatible hardware

笺 letter paper

缄 seal, close 缄默 keep silent

煎 1)(油煎)fry 2)(用文火煮)simmer in water, decoct

【jiǎn】

俭 俭朴 thrifty and simple, economical 俭省 thrifty, economical, frugal

拣 1)(挑选)choose, select, pick out 2)(拾取)pick up, collect, gather

捡 pick up, collect, gather

检 检测 detect 检索 retrieve, search, index 检修 maintenance, service; repair, overhaul 检验 check, inspect, examine, verify 检阅 review (troops, etc.), inspect
检测开关 sense switch
检测命令 sense command
检测模型 detection model
检测能力 detectability
检测器 detector, sensor
检测器保护装置 detector guard
检测设备 detecting device
检测响应 sense response
检测芯片 detection chip
检测噪声 detection noise
检查 auditing, censor, check up, checkout, detection, examine, inspection, look-up, observation, supervision, test
检查表 check table
检查[检验,试验]程序 test routine

检查程序 audit program, checking routine
检查[检验,校验]点 checkpoint
检查点程序 checkpoint routine
检查点记录 checkpoint record
检查点文件 checkpoint file
检查功能 audit function
检查和 check sum {CKS}
检查键 check key
检查盘 check disk
检查授权[特许]记录 check authorization record {CAR}
检查员 surveyor
检出 checkout
检错编码 error detecting code
检错码 error detecting code, error detection code
检错停机 check stop
检错与纠错 error checking and correction {ECC}
检错转储 error dump
检索表 search list
检索策略 search strategy
检索程序 retrieval/ search program
检索词文件 term file
检索地址 search address
检索工具 search engine
检索关键字 search key
检索过程 retrieval process
检索技术 retrieval technique
检索库 search library
检索链 search chain
检索率 recall ratio, recall
检索码 retrieval code
检索排序 retrieval ordering
检索试验 search test
检索数据 retrieval data
检索系统 retrieval system
检索项 search terms
检索信号 recall signal
检索性能 retrieval performance
检索因子 recall factor
检索语言 search language

检索阵列 index array
检索字 docuterm, search word
检索字段 search field
检误程序 debugger
检修周期 repair cycle
检验板 checker board
检验保护 check protect
检验标识 check tag
检验[练习,试验]程序 exerciser
检验程序 check program/ routine, checking program/ routine, checkout routine, inspector, subroutine test, test program
检验点记录 checkpoint record
检验点例程 checkpoint routine
检验点入口 checkpoint entry
检验[验证]方式 verification mode
检验核准记录 check authorization record {CAR}
检验和 check sum {CKS}
检验计算 checking computation
检验树 checking tree
检验数 check number
检验图 check plot
检验位 check bit
检验误差 verify error
检验行 check row
检验员 inspector
检验准备 inspection provision
检验准则 test criteria

减 (去掉)subtract 减产 decrease in output, drop in production 减低 reduce, lower, bring down, cut 减缓 retard, slow down 减价 reduce the price, mark down 减免 reduce, remit, exempt (taxation, etc.) 减轻 lighten, ease, alleviate, relieve; relaxation, abatement 减弱 weaken, attenuate, fade, deaden 减少 reduce, decrease, cut 减退 drop, go down, abate, decrease
减 minus, subtract
减1 decrement, tally down
减法 subtraction
减法器 subtracter
减量地址 decrement address
减量计数器 decrement counter
减量器逻辑 decremeter logic
减量指令 decrement instruction
减去 minus

剪 1)〈名〉scissors, shears, clippers 2)〈动〉cut (with scissors), clip 剪辑 ①〈电影〉montage, film editing ② (剪裁重编) editing and rearrangement, edit
剪裁 clipping, prune, pruning, tailor(ing)
剪辑室 editing room
剪切 clip, shear, shear cut
剪切和粘贴 cut and paste
剪取 clipping, scissor(ing)
剪贴板 clip board

简 simple, simplified, brief
简报 bulletin, brief report
简本 abridged edition 简便 simple and convenient, handy 简称 ①〈名〉abbreviation, shorter form ②〈动〉call sth for short 简单 ① simple, unsophisticated ② commonplace, ordinary 简短 brief, short 简化 simplify, reduce 简洁 succinct, concise 简介 brief introduction, synopsis 简历 biographical notes, curriculum vitae, resume 简炼 terse,

succinct, pithy 简陋 simple and crude 简略 abridged, brief, sketchy 简明 simple and clear, concise 简体字 simplified Chinese character 简讯 news in brief 简要 concise and to the point, brief 简易 simple and easy 简章 general regulation 简直 simply, at all, virtually
简便编译器 portable compiler
简单链 simple chain
简单名 simple name
简单命题 simple proposition
简单网络管理协议 simple network management protocol {SNMP}
简单邮件[信件]传输协议 simple mail[message] transfer protocol {SMTP}
简单值 plain value
简化表示 simplified representation
简化汉字 simplified Chinese character, simplified Hanzi
简化指令系统计算机 reduction instruction set computer {RISC}
简略符号 abbreviation
简码 brevity code
简图 schematic diagram
简易便携电话 personal handy phone {PHS}
简易性 ease, simplicity, simplification
简易终端 dumb terminal, simple data terminal equipment {simple DTE}

碱 1)〈化学〉alkali, base 2)(碳酸钠) soda

【jiàn】

见 1)(看见) see, catch sight of 2)(遇到) meet with, be exposed to 3)(参看) refer to, see 4)(会面) meet, call on, see 见解 view, opinion 见面 ①(相见) meet, see ②(接触) contact, link 见识 ①〈动〉widen one's knowledge, enrich one's experience ②〈名〉experience, knowledge 见闻 what one sees and hears, knowledge, information 见习 learn on the job, be on probation 见效 become effective, produce effect 见证 witness, testimony 见证人 eyewitness, witness

件 1)〈量词〉piece 2)(文件,信件) letter, correspondence, document ◇密件 confidential documents, secret papers

间 另见【jiān】
间断 be disconnected, break, be interrupted, intermit, discontinue 间隔 interval, intermission, space, gap 间接 indirect 间隙 ①(空隙) interval, gap, crack, interspace, intermittent ②〈机械〉clearance
间步 spacer step
间断序列 break sequence
间断字符 break character
间隔磁道 spacing track
间隔方式 interval mode
间隔符 gap character
间隔键 space key
间隔控制 interval control
间隔脉冲 spacing pulse
间隔偏差 spacing bias
间隔时钟 interval clock, interval timer
间接编址 indirect addressing

间接操作 indirect operation
间接地址 indirect address
间接递归 indirect recursion
间接调入[调用, 呼叫] indirect call
间接格式 remote format
间接共享 indirect sharing
间接寄存器 indirect register
间接控制 indirect control
间接输出 indirect output, off-line output
间接输入 indirect input
间接索引 indirect index
间接网络 indirect network
间接文件 indirect file
间接引用 dereference, indirect reference, indirect referencing
间接指令 indirect instruction
间接指示字 indirect pointer
间接指针 indirect pointer
间接周期 indirect cycle
间接转移 indirect branch
间距 separation distance, spacing
间距控制 pitch control
间隙大小 gap length
间隙符 gap character
间隙宽度 gap width
间隙损耗 gap loss
间歇故障 intermittent fault
间歇控制 intermittent control
间歇失效 intermittent failure
间歇现象 intermittency

建 建交 establish diplomatic relations 建立 establish, set up, found 建设 build, construct 建设性 constructive 建议 ① 〈动〉propose, suggest, recommend ② 〈名〉proposal, suggestion, recommendation 建造 build, construct, make 建制 organizational system 建筑 ①（建造）build, construct, erect ②（建筑物）building, structure, edifice ③（建筑学）architecture

建立程序 creation facilities program {**CFP**}
建立方式 create mode
建立模型 building model, model building
建立时间 built-up time, setting time, set-up time
建模 modeling
建模工具 modeling tool
建模技术 modeling technology
建模阶段 modeling phase
建网 networking

荐 recommend

舰 warship, naval vessel 舰队 fleet, naval force 舰艇 naval ships and boats, naval vessels

渐 渐渐 gradually, little by little 渐进 advance gradually, progress step by step ◇循序渐进 make progress in due order

渐近逼近法 asymptotic approximation
渐近表示 asymptotic representation
渐近操作(法) evolutionary operation {**EVOP**}
渐近法 asymptotic method, relaxation approach

贱 1)（价廉）low-priced, inexpensive, cheap 2)（地位低下）lowly, humble 3)（卑贱）despicable, mean

溅 splash, spatter

健 1)(强健)healthy, strong 2)(使强健)strengthen, toughen, invigorate 3)(善于)be strong in, be good at 健康 ①(指身体)in good health, sound, fit ②(情况正常)healthy, sound 健全 ①〈形〉sound, perfect, regular, perfect ②〈动〉perfect, improve, strengthen
健壮容错 robust fault tolerant
健壮性 robustness

鉴 鉴别 distinguish, differentiate, discriminate 鉴定 ①〈名〉appraisal (of a person's strong and weak points) ②〈动〉appraise, identify, determine, authenticate 鉴赏 appreciate 鉴于 in view of, seeing that, in consideration of
鉴别符 authenticator
鉴别服务器 authentication server {AS}
鉴定书 testimonial
鉴定文件 authenticated record
鉴权实体 authentication entity

键 1)〈机械〉key 2)(按键) key (of a typewriter, computer, etc.) 3)〈化学〉bound
键变元 key argument
键表 key table
键槽 keying slot, keyway
键插口 key jack
键窗口 key window
键存取 key access
键读出 key sense
键杆 keybar
键距 key pitch
键卡 keycard

键控波 keying wave
键控部件 keying unit
键控代码 key code
键控电平 keying level
键控范围 key range
键控脉冲 key pulse
键控器 keyer, keying unit
键控[按键]失真 keying loss
键控信号 key signal, keying wave
键码 key code, key
键码段 key field
键脉冲 key pulse
键盘 keyboard
键盘编码器 key encoder, keyboard encoder, keycoder
键盘程序 keyboard program
键盘发送/接收 keyboard send/receive {KSR}
键盘功能键 keyboard function key
键盘号 keyboard number
键盘缓冲区 keyboard buffer, type-ahead buffer
键盘换上下档[大小写] case shift
键盘接口 keyboard interface
键盘开关 keyboard switch
键盘控制台 keyboard console
键盘类型 keyboard type
键盘命令 keyboard command
键盘请求[询问] keyboard inquiry
键盘求助信息 keys help
键盘输入 key in, keyboard entry, keyboarding, key-entry
键盘中断 keyboard interrupt
键区 keypad
键入 type in, enter
键入动作 enter action
键元 key element
键组 keypad

箭 arrow
箭头 arrow head

箭头表示法 arrow notation
箭头键 arrow key
箭头图 arrow diagram

【 jiāng 】

江 river

浆 thick liquid

将 1)(将要)be going to, be about to, will, shall 2)(拿用)with, by 将近 close to, nearly, almost 将来 future

僵 僵持 refuse to give in (of both parties) 僵化 become rigid 僵局 deadlock, halt 僵滞 deadlocked 僵硬 ①(不能活动)stiff, numb ②(呆板的)rigid, inflexible

疆 boundary, border ◇边疆 frontier, borderland

【 jiǎng 】

讲 1)(说明)explain, make clear, interpret 2)(商量)discuss, negotiate 讲稿 ①(讲话稿)draft of a speech ②(讲课稿)lecture notes 讲话 speak, say, tell, talk about 讲解 explain, interpret, expound 讲解员 guide, interpreter 讲究 ①(重视)be particular about, pay attention to, stress, strive for ②(精美)exquisite, tasteful, elegant 讲课 teach, lecture 讲师 lecturer 讲述 tell about, give an account of, narrate, relate 讲台 platform, rostrum 讲坛 ①(讲台)platform, rostrum ②(讨论的场所)forum 讲学 give lectures, lecture on academic subjects 讲演 make a speech 讲义 teaching materials 讲座 a series of lectures 讲话器 talker

奖 1)〈动〉encourage, praise, reward, award 2)〈名〉award, prize, reward ◇得奖 win a prize // 得奖人 prize-winner, awardee 奖金 money award, bonus, premium 奖励 encourage and reward, award, commendation 奖牌,奖章 medal 奖品 prize, award, trophy 奖赏 award, reward 奖学金 scholarship 奖状 certificate of merit, certificate of award, citation

桨 ora, ①(短桨)scull ②(阔桨)paddle

【 jiàng 】

匠 craftsman, artisan ◇木匠 carpenter 匠心 ingenuity, craftsmanship ◇独具匠心 show ingenuity, have great originality

降 fall, drop, lower 降低 reduce, cut down, drop, lower 降价 depreciate, reduce the prices 降级 ①(降低级别)reduce to a lower rank, demote ②(留级)send to a lower grade 降临 befall, arrive, come

降级规则 collapsing rule
降级运行 degraded running
降序 descending
降序排列 descending order/sort

【jiāo】

交 1)(互相)mutual, reciprocal, each other 2)(时间、地点的相连)meet, join ◇杂交 crossbreed 3)(交易)deal, bargain, business, transaction ◇成交 strike a bargain, make a deal **交班** hand over to the next shift, turn over one's duty **交叉** ①(相互穿过)intersect, cross, intercross ②(重叠)overlapping ③(穿插)alternate, take turns **交错** interleave, crisscross, interlace, overlap **交代**,**交待** ①(移交)turn over, hand over, transfer ②(嘱咐)tell, leave words, order ③(说明)explain, make clear, brief ④(说清楚)account for, justify oneself ⑤(坦白)confess **交付** ①(付钱)pay ②(交给)turn over, hand in/over, deliver, consign **交割** complete a business transaction **交互** ①(相互)each other, mutual, interactive ②(替换)alternately, in turn **交换** exchange, swap, interchange, counterchange, commutate **交货** deliver **交货港** port of delivery **交际** social intercourse, communication **交接** ①(连接)join, connect ②(移交,接替)hand over and take over **交界** have a common border, have a common boundary **交流** exchange, interchange **交纳** pay, hand in **交配** mate, breed **交涉** negotiate, deal with, discuss terms with **交谈** talk with each other, converse, chat, have a conversation **交替** ①(接替)replace ②(替换着)alternately, in turn, alternate, reciprocate **交通** traffic, communications, transport(ation) **交往** friendship, association, contact **交易** business, deal, trade, transaction **交易会** (trade) fair ◇商品交易会 trade fair, commodities fair **交易所** exchange **交织** interlace, interleave, intertexture, interweave

交 intersection
交叉编译 cross compile
交叉部分 cross section
交叉操作 interlace operation
交叉场 crossed field
交叉程序 cross program
交叉存储 interleaved memory
交叉存取 interlacing, interleave
交叉存取[访问] interleaving access
交叉存取存储器 interlace memory
交叉存取方式 interlace mode
交叉点 crossover point, meeting
交叉调用 cross call
交叉方式 interleaved mode
交叉访问 cross referencing
交叉汇编 cross assembly
交叉检验 cross check
交叉开关网 crossbar network
交叉连接 cross connection
交叉模拟程序 cross simulator
交叉频率 crossover frequency
交叉奇偶校验 cross parity check, interlaced parity
交叉搜索 intersection search
交叉网络 cross network
交叉相加 cross addition
交叉校验 cross check

交叉引用 cross reference/referencing
交叉语言 cross language
交叉证实[确认] cross-validation
交叉制 crossbar system
交错码 interleave code
交错数组 interleaved array
交点 intersection
交合点 merge point
交互操作 interactive manipulation, interactive operation
交互查询 interactive query
交互查找 interactive searching
交互程序 interactive program
交互方式 interactive mode
交互仿真语言 interactive simulation language {ISL}
交互分区 interactive partition
交互干扰 crosstalk {XTALK}
交互工作 interworking
交互计算 interactive computing, interacting computation
交互式财务计划系统 interactive financial planning system {IFPS}
交互式电视 interactive television
交互式话音响应 interactive voice response {IVR}
交互式会话 interactive session
交互式活动 interacting activity
交互式机器人 interactive robot
交互式图表例程 interactive chart utility {ICU}
交互式系统 interactive system
交互式协议 interactive protocol
交互式语言 interactive language
交互式制图 interactive graphics {IG}
交互式终端 interaction terminal
交互视频 interactive video
交互视频磁盘系统 interactive videodisk system {IVS}
交互(式)系统 interactive system
交互(式)终端 interactive terminal
交互终端接口 interactive terminal interface {ITI}
交互终端装置 interactive terminal facility {ITF}
交互转换开关 seesaw switch
交互作用 interaction
交互作用区 interaction region
交互作用时间 interaction time
交互作用因子 interaction factor
交换标识 exchange identification {XID}
交换表 swap table
交换程序 swapper
交换处理 exchange processing
交换传输组 interchange transmission group {TG}
交换单元 crosspoint
交换等级 exchange class
交换点 interchange point
交换方式 swap mode
交换分机 branch exchange
交换服务网 switched service network
交换格式 interchange format
交换盒[开关] interchange box
交换机 switching system, exchanger, switchboard
交换机构 exchange mechanism
交换集 swap set, swapping set
交换记录分隔符 interchange record separator {IRS}
交换节点 switched/interchange node
交换局 exchange service
交换矩阵 switching array
交换控制 swapping control

交换控制记录 exchange control record {ECR}
交换律 commutative law, law of commutation
交换率 exchange rate
交换码 switch code, interchange code
交换区 exchange area
交换群 commutative group, Abelian group
交换时间 swap time
交换数据集[组] swap data set
交换算法 exchange algorithm
交换站 exchange station, switching center
交换[互换]通道 interchange channel
交换通信 switched communication
交换图 interchange graph
交换网络 flip/ swap/ switch network
交换线路 dial-up line, interchange/ switched circuit, switched line
交换信息 exchange message
交换虚连接 switched virtual connection {SVC}
交换虚电路 switched virtual circuit {SVC}
交换虚拟网络技术 switch virtual networking {SVN}
交换运作 commutative operation, exchange operation
交换中间寄存 exchange buffering
交换中心 switching center
交换组分隔符 interchange group separator {IGS}
交货付款 cash on delivery {COD}
交货日期 delivery date
交集 intersection set, intersection, intersect

交流电 alternating current {AC, ac}
交流区 communication region
交替的 alternating, alternate
交替法 alternative method
交替方式 alternate mode
交替工作 alternation
交替缓存 ping-pong buffer
交替恢复 alternate recovery {ACR}
交替逻辑 alternating logic
交替排序 oscillating sorting
交替区 alternate area
交替索引 alternate index
交图 intersection graph
交易[事务]文件 transaction file
交易流 transaction flow
交易数据 transaction data
交织图 intersection chart

郊

郊区 suburban district, suburbs, outskirts

胶

胶 glue, gum 胶结 cement, agglutinate 胶卷 film (strip) 胶片 film
胶件 jellyware
胶卷[片] film
胶卷小片 film chip
胶片记录器 film recorder
胶片扫描器 film scanner
胶片阅读器 film reader

浇

浇 1) (洒) pour liquid on, sprinkle 2) (浇灌) irrigate, water

娇

娇 (弱) fragile, delicate 娇嫩 tender, lovely, charming 娇气 squeamish

骄

骄 骄傲 ① (自大) arrogant, conceited ② (自豪) be proud, take pride in ③ (值得自豪的

人或事物) pride

教 另见【jiào】
teach, instruct

焦 (烧焦) burnt, charred 焦点 ①〈物理〉focal point, focus ②（注意点）focus of attention 焦急 worried, anxious 焦炭 coke
焦点窗口 focus window

蕉 (香蕉) banana

【jiáo】

嚼 masticate, chew

【jiǎo】

角 另见【jué】
1)（动物的角）horn 2)（号角）bugle, horn 3)（岬角）cape, promontory 4)〈数学〉angle 角度 ①〈数学〉angle, point of view 角落 corner

侥 侥幸 lucky, by luck

佼 handsome, beautiful 佼佼 above average, outstanding

狡 crafty, foxy, cunning 狡辩 quibble, resort to sophistry

皎 clear and bright 皎洁 (of moonlight) bright and clear

绞 绞动 wind 绞起 hoist, wind (up) 绞扭 twist, wring, entangle 绞刑 hang, strangle
绞合线 twisted pair {TP}
绞线(头) twist joint

铰 1)（剪）cut with scissors 2)〈机械〉ream

矫 矫正 correct, put right, rectify, level 矫直 straighten, level; reel
矫力 coercive, coercive force

脚 foot 脚步 step, pace 脚注 footnote, foot notation
脚本 script, scenario
脚本表示 script representation
脚本程序 shell script
脚本法 scenario method
脚本语言 scenario language

搅 搅拌 stir, mix 搅打 beat, beetle 搅和 ①（混合）mix, blend, mingle ②（扰乱）mess up, spoil 搅乱 confuse, throw into disorder, mess up

缴 pay, hand over, hand in 缴获 capture, seize 缴款通知 payment notice 缴纳 pay, hand in

【jiào】

叫 1)（招呼）call, greet 2)（预约）hire, order 3)（称为）name, call 4)（吩咐）ask, order, make 叫喊 shout, yell 叫唤 cry out, call out, shout 叫做 be called, be known as

轿 轿车 car, carriage, sedan

校 另见【xiào】
check, proofread 校订 check against the original text, re-

vise, redact 校对 ① 〈动〉proofread, proof, verify ② 〈名〉proofreader 校正 proofread and correct, rectify, update
校对员 proofreader, verifier
校验 check, checkout, verify
校验道 check track
校验符 check character
校验符号 check(ing) symbol
校验和 check sum {CKS}, gibberish total
校验码 check code
校验能力 checking feature
校验数位[数字] check digit
校验位 check bit, check digit
校验字 check word
校正公式 corrector/ updating formula
校正器 conditioner, corrector
校正增量 correction increment
校准 adjust {ADJ}, alignment, calibrate, calibration, graduation, orientation, synchronise
校准精度 alignment precision, calibration accuracy
校准器 aimer, calibrater, etalon

较 (相比)compare, as compared with, in comparison with 较量 have a contest, match

教 另见【jiào】
(宗教)religion 教案 teaching plan 教材 teaching material 教程 course (of study) 教导 ① 〈动〉instruct, teach, give guidance ② 〈名〉teaching, guidance, instruct 教改 educational reform 教科书 textbook 教练 ① 〈动〉train, drill, coach ② 〈名〉coach, instructor 教师,教员 teacher, instructor 教室 classroom, schoolroom 教授 ① 〈名〉professor ◇副教授 associate professor // 客座教授 visiting professor, guest professor ② 〈动〉instruct, teach 教学 teaching, education 教学大纲 teaching program(me), syllabus 教学法 pedagogy, teaching methodology 教训 ① 〈名〉lesson, moral ② 〈动〉teach sb a lesson 教研室 teaching and research section 教养 ① 〈动〉bring up, train, educate ② 〈名〉upringing, education, culture, breeding 教益 benefit gained through eduucation 教育 ① 〈名〉education ② 〈动〉teach, educate
教学软件 educational software, instructional software
教育机器人 educational robot

【jiē】

阶 1)(台阶)steps, stairs 2)(等级)rank 阶梯 a flight of stairs, ladder, staircase, cascade
阶 exponent, order
阶乘 factorial
阶段 phase {PH}, stage
阶符 exponent character
阶码下溢 characteristic underflow
阶码溢出 characteristic overflow
阶数 exponent number
阶梯形状 stair stepping
阶下溢 exponent underflow
阶跃变化 step change
阶跃高度 step height
阶跃响应 step response

jie 结接

结 另见【jié】

结实 ①（结出果实）bear fruit ②（坚固耐用）solid, sturdy, durable ③（健壮）strong, sturdy, tough

接 1)（连接）connect, join, put together 2)（承受）catch, take hold of 3)（迎接）meet, welcome **接触** ①（交往）come into contact with, get in touch with ②（碰着）contact **接待** receive, admit **接到** receive **接二连三** one after another, in quick succession **接管** take over **接合** joint, join, link, engage, connect **接见** receive, grant an interview to **接近** be close to, near, approach **接连** on end, in a row, in succession, running **接纳** admit (into), take in **接洽** consult with **接收** ①（收受）receive ②（接管）take over ③（接纳）admit **接受** accept, take, embrace **接替** take over, replace, succeed, take the place of **接头** ①（联接起来）connect, join, joint ②（找人联系）get in touch with ③〈机械〉connection, joint, connector, junction **接线**〈电气〉wiring, link **接应** come to sb's aid, coordinate with, reinforce **接着** ①（用手接）catch ②（紧接着）follow, carry on, go on (with), proceed
接插板 patch panel, patchboard
接插件 connector, connector assembly
接插件电缆 connector cable
接插头 patchplug
接插线 patch cord
接触点 contact point
接触电阻 contact resistance
接触端口 contact port
接触屏幕终端 touch screen terminal
接触式传感器 contact sensor
接触式打印机 contact printer
接地 ground {GND}, grounding, earth, earth connection
接地层 ground plane
接地线 ground earth line, earth connection
接卡器 receiver
接卡箱 card stacker, output magazine, output stacker, stacker
接口（一般指硬件）interface
接口插板 interface board
接口调试 interface debugging
接口控制信息 interface control information {ICI}
接口模块[组件] interface module
接口耦合 interface coupling
接口任务 interface task
接口软件 interface software
接口设备 interface unit
接口适配[转换]器 interface adapter
接口需求规范说明 interface requirements specification {IRS}
接口装置 interface equipment, interface unit, interfacer
接入方法 access method
接入控制 access control
接入收费 access charge
接入线路 access line
接收测试 acceptance test
接收超时 receive time-out
接收方式 receive mode

接收机 radio, receiver
接收挤塞[拥塞] reception congestion
接收器 receiver, recipient, sink
接收时钟 receive clock
接收数据 accepting of data, receive data
接收速度 inbound pacing
接收引线 receive leg
接收语句 receive statement
接收站 acception station, accepting station, destination
接收指示 receive data {RD}
接收中断 receive interruption
接收周期 receiving cycle
接收状态 accepting state, receive state, receive status
接收准备(好) receiver ready {RR}
接受标志 accepted flag
接受呼叫 call accepted
接受角 acceptance angle
接受器 acceptor (=accepter)
接受性 acceptance
接受者 recipient
接受状态 receive status
接通 switching-on, switch-on, turn-on, close, cut-in, energize, key on, make, unblock
接通地址 on address
接通开关 access switch
接通时间 cut in time, on time
接头 splice, tip, tip side, terminal
接头端 tip side
接线板 patch panel, connection box, terminal block, wire board, wiring board, wire board, board
接线瓣 wiring lobe
接线簿 wire list, wire chart
接线表 wire list

接线柜 wiring closet
接线夹[套] registered jack {RJ}
接线逻辑 wired logic
接线条 terminal strip
接线图 wiring diagram
接线中心 wire center
接续光纤 jointed fiber

揭 揭穿 expose, lay bare, show up 揭发, 揭露 expose, unmark, bring to light, lay open 揭开 uncover, reveal, open, disclose 揭幕 unveil, inaugurate 揭示 ①（公布）announce, promulgate, proclaim ②（使人看到）reveal, bring to light 揭晓 announce, make known, publish

街 street

【jié】

节 1)（段间相连处）joint, node, knot 2)（段落）division, part, section, paragraph 3)〈量词〉section, length 节俭 thrifty, frugal 节录 extract, excerpt 节目 program, item (on a program) 节能 energy saving 节日 festival, holiday 节省 economize, save, use sparingly, cut down on 节余 savings, sums of money saved 节食 practise thrift, curb expenditures 节制 ①（控制）command, administer, rule ②（限制）control, check, be moderate in ③（克制）temperance, abstinence
节点 node, node point
节点表 node table
节点初始化块 node initial-

节点处理机 node processor {NP}
节点分支 node branch
节点划分 node partition
节点基 node base
节点计算机 node computer
节点间 internode
节点路由选择 node routing
节点偏置 node bias
节点状态 node state
节点转换 node node switching
节距 pitch, step
节距调节[控制] pitch control
节名 section name
节拍 beat
节拍脉冲发生器 beat generator
节约空间 saving space

杰
杰出 outstanding, remarkable, prominent 杰作 masterpiece

洁
洁白 spotlessly white, pure white, snowy 洁净 clean, spotless, unstained; purity

结 另见【jie】
1)（编结）tie, knit, knot, weave 2)（凝结）congeal, form 3)〈电子〉junction 结成 form 结存 ①（指款项）cash on hand, balance ②（指货物）goods on hand, inventory 结构 ①（组成）structure, composition, construction, framework ②〈建筑〉structure, construction, architecture ◇钢结构 steel structure 结果 ①（结局）result, outcome, consequence ②（最终）finally, at last, in the end 结合（联合）link, connect, joint, combine, unite, integrate; associative, bonded 结婚 marry, get married 结晶 ①（析出晶体）crystallize ②（晶体）crystal ③（成果）crystallization, fruit, product 结局 final result, outcome, end 结论 conclusion, consecution 结束 end, finish, terminate, conclude, wind up, close 结束语 concluding remarks, summary, epilog(ue) 结算 settle accounts, close an account, wind up an account 结头 knot, node 结尾 ending, winding-up stage 结业 complete a course, wind up one's studies 结余 (cash) surplus, balance 结帐 settle accounts, square accounts, balance the books, close accounts
结 junction
结点 node, gateway node, junction point
结点管理 connection point manager {CPM}
结点加密 node encryption
结构测试 structured testing
结构成员 structure member
结构程序设计 structured programming
结构定义 structure definition, organization definition
结构访问 structure reference
结构分配部件 configuration assignment unit {CAU}
结构规则 formation rule
结构化编程 structured programming
结构化变量 structured variable
结构化布线 structured wring
结构化查询语言 structured

结构化程序 structured program
结构化程序设计 structured programming
结构化分析 structured analysis {SA}
结构化决策 structured decision
结构化框图 structured flowchart
结构化设计 structured design {SD}
结构化事物 structured object
结构化数据转移 structured data transfer {SDT}
结构化语言 structured language
结构建模 structural modelling
结构节点 structure node
结构类型 structure type, structured type
结构描述 structural description
结构名(字) structure name
结构模型 structural model, structured model
结构目录 structure category
结构设计 structural design, physical design
结构式查询语言 structured query language {SQL}
结构属性 structure attribute
结构数据模型 structured data model
结构数据设计 structuring data design
结构索引 structured index
结构特征 architectural feature
结构图 structure diagram {SD}, structure chart, structural graph, schematic diagram, diagram, pattern
结构(化)系统设计 structured system design
结构元素 structure element
结构指示器 structure pointer
结果标识符 result identifier
结果表 object list
结果调用 call by result, result call
结果文件 destination file
结果域 resultant field
结果元 result element
结果值 end value
结合点 articulation point
结合关系 marriage relation
结合律 associative law, associativity, law of association
结束标志 end mark
结束符 end mark, terminating symbol, terminator
结束符号 end symbol, ending character, stop code, termination symbol
结束栏 end column
结束时间 end time, finish-time
结束位 stop bit
结束语 conclusion, summary
结束帧 end frame
结束指令 end directive
结束中断 termination interrupt
结束字符 termination character
结算卡 debit card {DC}
结型激光器 junction laser

捷 1)(快) prompt, nimble, quick 2)(胜利) victory, triumph 捷径 shortcut

截 (阻拦) stop, check, stem, intercept 截断 cut off, truncate, intercept; chopping 截取 cut out 截然 sharply, completely, entirely 截至 by, up to 截止 ① 〈电子〉cut off ② (停止) end, close 截止期 deadline
截断操作 break-in operation
截断法 truncation method
截面 cross section, scarf
截舍 truncation

截听站 intercepted station
截止(点) cut-off
截止点 cut-off point
截止日期 expiration date
截止状态 cut-off state

竭

竭诚 wholeheartedly, with all one's heart 竭尽 use up, exhaust 竭力 do one's utmost, do one's heart, spare no efforts

【jiě】

姐 elder sister, sister

解
1)(分开)separate, divide 2)(减轻)allay, alleviate, dispel 3)(解释)explain, interpret 解除 remove, relieve, release, get rid of, exempt, free 解答 answer, explain, solve 解雇 discharge, dismiss, fire, sack 解开 untie, undo, disconnect 解决 solve, resolve, settle 解散 ①(分散) dismiss ②(取消) dissolve, disband 解释 interpret, explain 解说 explain orally, comment, narrate 解体 disintegrate, break up, knock down 解析 analyse, analysis; analytic(al) 解约 terminate an agreement, cancel a contract
解除编目 uncatalog
解除程序 destructor
解除中断 disarm, disarmed interrupt
解除状态 disarmed state
解调器 demodulator
解封锁 deblock
解链 unlink, delink
解码 decrypt, decode, decompiling
解(脉冲编)码器 demoder
解密 decryption, decipherment, decrypt, disclosure
解密密钥 deciphering key
解耦 decoupling
解释程序 interpretive program, interpret(er) program, interpreter
解释方式 interpretive mode
解释工具 explanation facilities
解释功能 explanation function
解释规则 interpretation rule
解释器 interpreter
解释系统 interpretive system
解释学习 explanation- based learning {EBL}
解释执行 interpretive execution, interpretation execution, interpreting
解锁 unlock, unblock
解图 solution graph
解析法 analytic method, analysis method
解析关系 analysis relationship
解析函数 analytic function
解析几何 analytic geometry
解析模型 analytic model, analytical modeling

【jiè】

介
(在两者中间)be situated between, interpose 介入 intervene, interpose, get involved 介绍 ①(使双方相识)introduce ②(推荐)recommend, suggest ③(使了解)let know, brief, provide information 介绍人 introducer, sponsor 介绍信 ①(介绍用)letter of introduction ②(推荐用)letter of recommendation 介意 take seriously, take to heart, mind
介质 medium, media

介质访问 medium access
介质访问控制 media-access control {MAC}
介质故障 media failure
介质兼容 media compatibility

戒
(警告) exhort, warn, admonish 戒备 guard against, be on the watch 戒除 give up, drop, stop

界
1) (一定范围) bounds, scope, extend ◇外界 external world 2) (社会各界) circle, world ◇学术界 academic circle 3) (动植物分类) primary division, kingdom 界面 interface, limiting surface 界限 ① (分界) demarcation line, dividing line, limits, bounds, margin, boundary ② (限度) limit, end 界线 ① (分界线) boundary line ② (分界) demarcation line, dividing line, limits, bounds, border
界标 boundscript
界地址 limit address
界对 bound pair
界分量 bound component
界面 (一般指软件) interface
界面构件 widget
界偶表 bound pair list
界限符 bound symbol
界限寄存器 bound register, limit register
界限控制模块 bound control module {BCM}
界限任务集 bound task set {BTS}

借
(凭借) make use of, take advantage of 借出 lend 借方 debit (side) 借故 find an excuse 借进 borrow 借鉴 use for reference, draw lessons from 借据,借条 receipt for a loan (IOU), certificate of indebtedness, evidence of debt 借口 excuse, pretext 借款 ①(借入) borrow money, ask for a loan ②(贷出) lend money, offer a loan ③(借用的钱) loan 借书证 library card, reader's card 借用 ①(借过来用) borrow, have the loan of ②(作别用) use sth for some other purpose, use as a substitute 借助 have the aid of, draw support from; with the help of
借位 borrow

届
届满 expiration, at the expiration of one's term of office 届时 when the time comes, at the appointed time, on the occasion

【jīn】

巾
a piece of cloth ◇餐巾 napkin ∥ 毛巾 towel

斤
jin (= 1/2 kilogram) 斤两 weight

今
(现在) modern, present-day, nowadays, now 今后 from now on, in the days to come 今年 this year 今天 today

禁
另见【jìn】
禁不住 ①(承受不住) be unable to bear or endure ②(抑制不住) cannot help

金
〈化学〉gold (Au) 金币

gold coin 金额 amount of money 金库 national (state) treasury, exchequer 金钱 money 金色的 golden 金融 finance, banking 金属 metal
金融服务 financial services
金融设备 finance device
金属氧化物半导体 metal-oxide-semiconductor {MOS}

津 津贴 subsidy, allowance

【jǐn】

仅 only, merely, barely, simply, solely

尽 另见【jìn】
尽管 though, even though, in spite of, despite, notwithstanding 尽可能, 尽量 as far as possible, to the best of one's ability 尽快 as quickly/soon/early as possible 尽先 give first priority to

紧 1)(不松)tight, taut, close 2)(牢固)fast, firm 3)(贴近)close 4)(拮据)short of money, hard up 紧凑 compact, terse, well-knit, tight 紧跟 follow closely, keep in step with, keep up with 紧固 fasten, bind, fix 紧急 urgent, pressing, critical 紧密 ①(密切)close together, inseparable ②(密集)thick and fast, rapid and intense 紧缩 reduce, tighten, cut down, retrench; compaction 紧要 critical, crucial, vital 紧张 ①(兴奋与紧张)nervous, high-strung ②(激烈)tense, intense, strained ③(供应不足)in short supply, tight
紧凑的 compact
紧急线法 critical path method {CPM}
紧密耦合系统 tightly coupled system {TCS}
紧缩模式 compact model
紧缩数字 packed numeric
紧缩数组 packed array

锦 锦标 prize, trophy, title 锦标赛 championship(s) contest

谨 (郑重)solemnly, sincerely 谨启 yours respectfully 谨致谢意 thank you earnestly, please accept my sincere thanks 谨防 guard against, beware of 谨上(书信具名)sincerely yours 谨慎 prudent, careful, cautious

【jìn】

尽 另见【jǐn】
尽力 do all one can, try one's best 尽情 to one's heart's content, as much as one likes 尽心 with all one's heart, put one's heart and soul into 尽早 with the least delay, at one's earliest convenience, as soon as possible
尽最大努力 best effort

进 1)(向前移动)advance, move forward, move ahead 2)(收进)receive 进货 lay in a new stock of goods 进步 ①〈动〉advance, progress, improve ②〈形〉progressive, advanced 进程 course, process, progress 进出 ①(进来和出去)pass in and out, get in and out ②(收入和支出) receipts and payments, turnover **进出口** ①(商品进出口) imports and exports ②(出入门口) exits and entrances **进度** ①(工作速度) rate of progress, rate of advance **进度表** progress chart ②(工作计划) planned speed, schedule **进化** evolution **进口** ①(船只进港) enter port, sail into a port ②(外贸进口) import ③(入口) entrance; intake, inlet **进来** come in, get in, enter **进取** keep forging ahead, be eager to make progress, be enterprising **进去** go in, get in, enter **进入** come into, go/get into, enter **进行** ①(开展) be in progress, be underway, go on ②(从事) carry on, carry out, conduct, make **进修** pursue further studies, take a refresher course **进一步** go a step further, further **进展** make progress, make headway, advance

进程调度 process scheduling
进程管理 management of processes
进程划分 process partition
进程间通信 interprocess communication {IPC}, process to process communication
进程控制块 process control block {PCB}
进程同步 process synchronization, synchronization between processes
进程状态字 process state word
进度表 schedule
进度访问组 process access group {PAG}
进度计划 scheduled plan
进度记录 progress record
进度控制 progress control
进化计算 evolutionary computation {EC}
进垃圾出垃圾 garbage in garbage out {GIGO}
进入 entry, income, entering
进入(系统) logon
进入点 entry point, enter point
进入日期 entry date
进入时间 entry time
进入系统 log-in
进位 carry digit, carry
进位标记[志] carry flag
进位传播 carry propagate
进位电路 carry circuit
进位寄存器 carry register
进位控制 carry control
进位类型 carry type
进位链 carry chain
进位逻辑 carry logic
进位门 carry gate
进位清除 carry reset
进位舍入 round up
进位时间 carry time
进位输出 carry out(put)
进位输入 carry in(put)
进位条件 carry condition
进位延迟 carry delay
进位状态字 carry status word
进栈 push on
进栈[推入,压栈]操作 push operation
进栈指令 push instruction
进纸 paper feed
进纸设备 paper feed aperture

近 1)(距离或时间接近) near, close, immediate 2)(大约为) approaching, approximately, close to 近

jin 浸禁晋 jing 茎惊

代 modern times 近海 coastal waters, inshore, offshore 近郊 outskirts of a city, suburbs, environs 近来 recently, lately 近邻 neighbor 近期 in the near future, short term 近似 approximate, similar 近因 immediate cause

近似规划 approximation programming

近似计算 approximate calculation, analog computation, approximate evaluation

近似推理 approximate reasoning

浸
soak, immerse 浸没 immersion, submersion 浸泡 soak, immerse 浸入 infusion, submergence, immersion 浸湿 soak, wet 浸透 soak, saturate, impregnate, sink

浸渗 impregnating

禁 另见【jīn】
1) (禁止) prohibit, inhibit, forbid, ban 2) (监禁) imprison 禁令 prohibition, ban, restriction 禁区 ①(禁止进入地区) forbidden zone, restricted zone ②(自然保护区) preserve, reserve, natural park 禁运 embargo

禁门 exclusion gate, except gate
禁写 write inhibit
禁用 forbidden
禁用词 stop word
禁用代码 forbidden code, non-permissible code, illegal code, unused code
禁用单元 forbidden cell
禁用开关 disabled switch
禁用数字 forbidden digit
禁用值 forbidden value
禁用指令 illegal instruction
禁用字符 forbidden character, illegal character, unallowable character, forbidden digit
禁止 exclusion, inhibited, inhibition, inhibit, disable, NOT-IF-THEN, quiescing
禁止打印 non-print, print inhibit, suppression
禁止电路 inhibit circuit
禁止规则 inhibition rule
禁止开关 disable switch
禁止脉冲 inhibit pulse
禁止门 exception gate, AND-NOT gate, except gate, A except B gate, inhibit gate, sine-junction gate, subjunction gate
禁止驱动器 inhibit driver
禁止输出 output disable
禁止输入 inhibit input, inhibiting input
禁止线 inhibit line, inhibit wire
禁止写入 write inhibit
禁止信号 inhibit signal, inhibiting signal, disable signal
禁止中断 disabled interrupt, disable interrupt, interrupt disable

晋
晋级 rise in rank 晋升 promote to a higher office

【jīng】
茎
stem (of a plant), stalk

惊
惊动 ①(使吃惊) startle, alarm, shock ②(使警惕) alert ③(惊扰) disturb, bother 惊奇 surprised,

amazed, astonished 惊 astonishing, amazing, alarming

经
1)(通过)as a result of, after, through 2)〈纺织〉warp 3)〈地理〉longitude ◇东经 east longitude 经常 ①(日常)day-to-day, everyday, daily ②(常常)often, frequently, constantly, regularly 经典 ①〈名〉classics ②〈形〉classical 经费 funds, expenditure 经管 in charge of; responsible for 经过 ①(从某处过)pass/go through, go by ②(通过)as a result of, after, through, via, by way of ③(过程)process, course 经纪人 broker, middleman, agent 经济 ①(经济学)economy ◇国民经济 national economy ②(与经济有关的)economic; of industrial value ③(个人经济状况)financial condition, income ④(节省的)economical, thrifty 经久 ①(长时间的)prolonged ②(耐用)durable, lasting 经理 ①〈动〉handle, manage ②〈名〉manager, director 经历 ①〈动〉go through, undergo, experience ②〈名〉experience 经商 engage in trade, be in business, go into business 经手 handle, deal with 经受 undergo, experience, withstand, endure 经售,经销 sell (on commission), deal in, distribute 经验 ①〈名〉experience ②〈动〉go through, experience ③〈形〉empiric(al), experimental, posterior 经营 manage, deal in, engage in
经典分析法 classical approach
经典网络理论 classical network theory
经济订货量 economic order quantity {EOQ}
经济规划 economic programming
经济模型 economic model
经济信息系统 economic information system {EIS}
经济预测 economic forecast
经济增长 economic growth
经验方法 empirical method
经验公式 empirical formula
经营管理 administrative operations
经营科学 management science {MS}

晶
1)(光亮)brilliant, glittering 2)(水晶)quartz, (rock) crystal
晶格 crystal lattice, pattern
晶格论 lattice theory
晶格模型 lattice model
晶片 chip
晶片规模集成电路 wafer-scale integration {WSI}
晶体 crystal(loid), X-tal
晶体点阵 crystal lattice, pattern
晶体管 transistor
晶体元件 crystal element
晶体组织 texture

精
1)(完美)perfect, excellent 2)(机灵)smart, sharp, clever, shrewd 精彩 brilliant, splendid, wonderful, marvelous 精打细算 careful calculation and strict budgeting 精干 ①(指人少而精)small in

number but very competent ②(精明强干)keen-witted and capable 精华 cream, essence 精简 simplify, cut, reduce 精炼 concise, succinct, terse 精良 excellent, superior; of the best quality 精美 exquisite, elegant 精密 precise, accurate; minuteness 精明 astute, shrewd, clever 精确 accurate, exact, precise, perfect 精辟 penetrating, incisive, profound 精巧 exquisite, ingenious 精神,精力 energy, spirit 精通 skilled, conversant, proficient 精细 meticulous, fine, careful, precise 精心 meticulously, painstakingly, elaborately 精选的 refined, picked, choice 精益求精 constantly improve, keep improving 精致 fine, exquisite, delicate 精制 make with extra care, refine, purify, refinish 精装 (of books) clothbound, hardback, hardcover

精度 accuracy, precision
精度损失 loss of significance
精简指令集计算(机) reduced instruction set computing {RISC}
精密仪器 precision instrument
精确定义 precise definition
精确度 accuracy
精确断点法 exact breaking method
精确回退 measured backspace
精确图像 exact image
精细排列 fine sort
精细图案 fine pattern

腈

〈化学〉nitrile 腈纶 acrylic fibers

【jǐng】

井 well ◇矿井 pit, mine // 油井 oil well

颈 (颈项)neck

景 (风景)view, scenery, scene 景况 situation, condition 景气 prosperity, boom 景色 scenery, view, scene, landscape 景象 scene, sight, picture, outlook

景物边界 scene border
景物变换 scene change
景物定义 scene definition
景物分割 scene segmentation
景物理解 scene understanding
景物识别 scene recognition

警 1)〈形〉alert, vigilant 2)〈动〉warn, alarm 3)〈名〉alarm 警报 alarm, warning, alert 警察 police, policeman 警告①〈动〉warn, caution, admonish ②〈名〉warning 警戒 warn, admonish; alert, guard, watch, security 警惕 be on guard against, watch out for, be vigilant, be on the alert 警卫(security) guard

警报(信息) alert
警告表 alert table
警告陷阱 warning trap

【jìng】

径 1)(小路)footway, path, track 2)(方法)way, means 3)(直径)diameter
径迹 trace, track
径向扫描 radial scan
径向伺服 radial servo

jìng 劲竞净竟敬静

劲 strong, powerful, tough

竞 compete, contest, vie
竞赛 contest, competition, emulation, race
竞争 competition, challenge, rivalry
竞争过程 contention procedure
竞争决策 decision under conflict
竞争网络 competition network
竞争学习 competition learning

净 clean, net
净利润 net profit
净值 net worth, net value
净带 raw tape
净化电源 power conditioner
净化室 clean room
净收入 net income
净效益 net contribution {NC}
净增益 net gain

竟 竟然 ① unexpectedly, to one's surprise, actually ② go so far as, go to the length of

敬 1)〈动〉〈名〉respect, honor 2)〈副〉respectfully
敬爱 respect and love
敬的 respected and beloved, esteemed
敬贺 congratulate
敬礼 ① (行礼) salute, give a salute ② (致敬意) extend one's greetings ◇此致敬礼 with best wishes, with kind regards
敬上 (用于书信结尾) truly yours, yours truly
敬意 respect, tribute, regards, salutions
敬赠 respectfully presented by
敬重 highly esteem
敬请光临 request the honor of your presence

静 1)(不动)still, calm, motionless 2)(不发声)silent, quiet 3)〈物理〉static
静点 dead point
静电 static electricity
静电存储器 electrostatic storage
静电防护 electrostatic protection
静电放电 electrostatic discharge {ESD}
静电复印 electrostatic printing (reproduction)
静电复印法[术] xerography
静电记录纸 electrostatic recording paper
静电屏蔽 electrostatic shield
静电摄影术 electrostatic photography
静电式绘图仪 electrostatic plotter
静电释放 electrostatic discharge {ESD}
静电图像 electrostatic image
静负荷 dead load
静键 dead key
静区 dead zone, fade zone, dead band, dead space, shadow
静态 static state, steady state deadly embrace, quiet, quieting
静态测试方式 static test mode
静态处理 static handling
静态MOS存储器 static MOS memory
静态存储器 static memory, static storage
静态打印 static dump, static printout, static typing
静态单元 static cell
静态的 inactive
静态调度 static scheduling
静态多功能流水线 static multi-

jìng 境镜 jiǒng 窘 jiū 究纠 jiǔ 九酒 jiù 旧

functional pipeline, static multifunction pipeline
静态分析 static analysis
静态规程 quiesce protocol
静态检查 static check
静态控制器 static controller
静态流水线 static pipeline
静态模型 static model
静态冗余 static redundancy
静态视频 still video
静态试验 captive test
静态算法 static algorithm
静态通信 quiesce communication
静态图 static map
静态图像 static image
静态显示 static status display
静态语义分析 static semantic analysis
静态语义规则 static semantic rule
静态(信息)转储 static dump
静线 dead line
静像 still video
静止 quiescent, quiescing, dwell, inaction
静止视频 still video
静止图像 stationary picture, still
静止帧 still frame

境 (疆界) border, boundary 境界 ①(地界) boundary ②(程度) state, realm, status 境况 condition, circumstances, situation

镜 1)(镜子) mirror 2)(光学器具) lens, glass, glasses
镜像 image, mirror image
镜像保护 mirrored protection
镜像对 mirrored pair
镜像干涉 image interference
镜像开关 mirror image switch
镜像匹配 image match
镜像语言 mirror language
镜像原理 image theory

【jiǒng】

窘 1)(窘困) poor, straitened 2)(为难) awkward, embarrassed, uncomfortable 3)(使为难) embarrass, discomfort 窘境 awkward situation, dilemma, predicament 窘迫 ①(十分为难) hard pressed, embarrassed, in a predicament ②(非常困难) poverty-stricken, very poor

【jiū】

究 究竟 ①(用于问句) actually, exactly ②(毕竟) after all, in the end

纠 1)(缠绕) entangle 2)(集合) gather, together 纠缠 ①(绕在一起) get entangled, be in a tangle ②(麻烦) worry, pester 纠纷 dispute, issue 纠正 correct, put right, rectify
纠错 debug, error correction
纠错程序 error correction routine/procedure
纠错规则 error-correction rule
纠错码 error-correction coding/code
纠错能力 error correcting capability

【jiǔ】

九 nine 九月 September

酒 wine, liquor, spirits

【jiù】

旧 1)(过去的) past, old,

outdated 2)(用过的)used, worn, old, secondhand 3)(以前的)former 旧货 secondhand goods, junk 旧货市场 junk market, flea market 旧历 the old Chinese calendar, the lunar calendar

咎 1)(过失)fault, blame 2)(责问)punish, reproach

救 1)(使脱险)rescue, save, salvage 2)(援助)help, relieve, aid 救护 give first aid, rescue 救火 fire fighting 救济 relieve, send relief to 救命 ①(救人性命)save sb's life ②(呼救声)Help! 救援 rescue, come to sb's help 救灾 send relief to a disaster area, relieve the victims of a disaster 救治 bring a patient out of danger, treat and cure 救助 help sb in danger or difficulty, succor

就 1)(凑近)come near, move towards 2)(开始从事)take up, undertake, engage in 3)(完成)accomplish, make 4)(将就)accommodate oneself to, suit 5)(按照)with regard to, concerning, in the light of 就此 at this point, here and now, thus 就地 on the spot, on site 就近 nearby, within reach, at close quarters 就任 take up one's post, take office 就是说 that is to say, in other words, namely 就位 take one's place 就绪 be in order, be ready 就要 be about to, be going to, be on the point of 就业 get a job 就职 assume office
就地控制 local control
就绪标志 ready flag
就绪表 ready list
就绪任务 ready task
就绪条件 ready condition
就绪位 ready bit
就绪显示器[指示符] ready indicator
就绪音 ready tone
就绪引线 ready line
就绪状态 ready state/ mode/ condition

舅 1)(舅父)mother's brother, uncle 2)(妻子的兄弟)wife's brother, brother-in-law

【jū】

居 1)(居住)reside, dwell, live 2)(住所)residence, house 3)(处于,在)occupy, hold, rank 居留 reside, live, inhabit 居民 resident, inhabitant 居然 ①(出乎意料)unexpectedly, to one's surprise ②(甚至)go so far as to 居中(mediate)between two parties, in the middle

拘 拘捕 arrest, capture 拘束 ①〈动〉restrain, restrict ②〈形〉constrained, ill at ease

【jú】

局 (机关)office, bureau 局促 ①(狭小)narrow, cramped ②(短促)short ③(拘谨)feel ill at ease 局部 part, section, portion 局面 phase, situation, phases 局势 situation 局限 limit, confine 局限性 limitations

局部变量 local variable
局部存储器[区] local memory, local storage
局部存储器映像 local memory image {LMI}
局部地址 local address
局部段 local segment
局部分布式数据接口 local distributed data interface {LDDI}
局部封锁 local lock
局部概念模式 local concept schema {LCS}
局部共享资源 local shared resources {LSR}
局部故障 local fault
局部化 localization
局部环境 local environ
局部回路 local loop
局部连通度 local connectivity
局部内模式 local internal schema {LIS}
局部判据 local criterion
局部旁路 local bypass
局部收敛 local convergence
局部数据集 locality set
局部数据库 local database
局部数据区 local data area
局部搜索[查找] local search
局部宿主 local host
局部外模式 local external schema {LES}
局部网络 local area network {LAN}, local network
局部性 locality
局部性相关 local association
局部性准则 local criterion
局部循环 local loop
局部运算 local operation
局部栈 local stack
局部诊断 local diagnosis
局部转储 partial dump
局部总线 local bus
局部组 local group

局部坐标 local coordinate
局间干线 interoffice trunk
局间通信 interoffice communication
局间中继线 interoffice trunk
局外交换 foreign exchange {FX}
局域群体 local group
局域网仿真 LAN emulation {LANE}
局域网仿真服务器 LAN emulation server {LES}
局域网仿真客户机 LAN emulation client {LEC}
局域网仿真配置服务器 LAN emulation configuration server {LECS}
局中人 player

菊

菊花轮打印机 daisy-wheel printer
菊花链 diasy chain

锔

锔 curium (Cm)

【jǔ】

举 1)(上举)lift, raise, hold up 2)(行为)act, deed, move 3)(推举)elect, choose 4)(列举)cite, enumerate 举办 conduct, hold, run 举动 movement, action, behavior 举荐 recommend (a person) 举例 give an example, cite an instance 举行 hold, give, host 举行会议 hold a meeting 举止 manner, behavior; air

矩 〈物〉moment ◇转矩 turning moment
矩量矩阵 moment matrix
矩形 rectangle

矩形波 square wave
矩形回线 squared loop
矩形框 bounding box
矩形图 histogram
矩形网格 rectangular mesh
矩形网络 rectangular net
矩形线圈 square coil
矩阵 matrix, matrices
矩阵编码器 matrix encoder
矩阵表示 matrix representation
矩阵乘法 matrix multiplication
矩阵代数 matrix algebra
矩阵地址 matrix-address
矩阵迭代(法) matrix iteration
矩阵对策 matrix game
矩阵范(数) matrix norm
矩阵方程 matrix equation
矩阵计算 matrix calculation
矩阵加法器 matrix adder
矩阵开关 matrix switch
矩阵模(量) matrix norm
矩阵式编码器 matrix encoder
矩阵式存储器 matrix storage
矩阵式加法器 matrix adder
矩阵文法 matrix grammar
矩阵显示板 matrix display panel
矩阵译码法 matrix-decoding method
矩阵运算 matrix operation

【jù】

句 sentence 句号 full stop, full point, period 句型 sentence pattern, sentential form
句柄 handle
句柄头 handle head
句柄尾 handle tail
句段 syntagma
句法 syntax
句法错误 syntactic distance
句法对象 lexical object
句法范围 lexical scope
句法分析 syntax/syntactic analysis
句法级 lexical level
句法剖析 syntax parsing
句法树 syntax tree, syntactic tree
句法语义分析 syntax-semantic parsing, paring
句文编辑 textual edit
句文扫描 textual scan
句型分析 parse of a sentential form

巨 huge, tremendous, gigantic 巨变 great change, radical change 巨大 huge, enormous, gigantic, tremendous 巨额 a huge sum, a large amount 巨型 giant, heavy, mammoth 巨著 monumental work, great work
巨型(计算)机 supercomputer, giant-scale computer, giant computer
巨型数据库 galactic database

拒 (抵抗)resist, repel
拒绝 reject {**REJ**}, refuse, reject(ion)
拒绝区 reject region
拒绝中断 disarm, disarmed interrupt

具 (用具)utensil, tool, implement 具备 possess, have, be provided with 具名 put one's name to a document, etc., affix one's signature 具体 concrete, specific, particular 具有 possess, have
具体编码 specific coding
具体编址 specific addressing
具体[绝对,特定]地址 specific address

具体化 embodiment, embody, visualize
具体[绝对](代)码 specific code
具体设备 embodiment
具体事务文件 transaction file
具体形式 concrete form
具体语法 concrete syntax

俱 all, complete, entire 俱全 complete in all varieties

惧 惧怕 fear, dread

剧 (戏剧) theatrical work, drama, play, opera 剧烈 acute, severe, intense, violent
剧本 script
剧本管理程序 script manager
剧本文件 script file

据 1)(占据) occupy, seize, take possession of, lay hold of 2)(凭借) rely on, depend on 3)(依据) according to, on the basis of 据此 on these grounds, in view of the above, accordingly 据说 it is said, they say 据悉 it is reported

距 (相距) be apart from, be away from, be at a distance from 距离 distance, range, space
距离矢量协议 distance vector protocol

锯 1)〈名〉saw 2)〈动〉cut with a saw, saw

聚 assemble, gather, get together 聚合 ① (聚集一起) get together ② 〈化学〉polymerization 聚会 get together, meet 聚积 accumulate, collect, build up 聚集 gather, assemble, collect, aggregate 聚精会神 concentrate one's attention
聚簇技术 clustering strategies
聚点 accumulation point
聚合功能 aggregate function
聚合关系 paradigmatic relation
聚合计算机 polycomputer
聚合体 aggregate entity
聚集分析 cluster analysis
聚集记法 aggregate notation
聚集运算 aggregate operation
聚焦 focus, focusing
聚焦伺服 focus servo
聚焦系统 lens system
聚类 clustering
聚类分析 cluster analysis
聚类流 clustering flow
聚类算法 clustering algorithm
聚类通道 clustering channel
聚类文件 clustered file, clustering file

【juān】

捐 1)〈动〉contribute money 2)〈名〉contribution, donation, subscription 捐献 contribute, donate 捐赠 contribute (as a gift), donate, present

【juǎn】

卷 另见【juàn】
卷起 roll up, coil, curl 卷曲 curl, crimp, warp 卷绕 wind, coil, wrap around 卷入 be drawn into, be involved in 卷走 sweep off, carry along 卷状物 cylindrical mass of sth, roll, reel
卷带电机 tape feed motor

卷动 roll, scroll, scrolling
卷动色带 scroll ribbon
卷痕 cinch mark
卷积 convolution, convolver
卷积码 convolution(al) code
卷积运算 convolution operation
卷盘轴 spool spindle
卷起窗口 scroll window
卷绕插头 wrap plug
卷纸(打印机用) stock form
卷轴 feed spool, reel spindle, scroll, squeegee roller
卷轴式记录纸 roll paper

【juàn】

卷 另见【juǎn】
1)(书本) book 2)(书籍册数) volume 3)(考卷) examination paper
卷标 volume (header) label
卷标的开始 beginning-of-volume label {VOL}
卷标题 volume header
卷布局 volume layout
卷测试 volume test
卷错误分析 error volume analysis {EVA}
卷错误统计 error statistics by volume {ESV}
卷登记项 volume entry
卷管理 volume management
卷结束 end of volume {EOV}
卷识别 volume recognition
卷索引 volume index
卷索引号 volume reference number
卷头 volume header, volume header label
卷尾 end of reel
卷终 end of volume {EOV}
卷宗 file, dossier
卷宗测试 volume test
卷宗集合 volume set
卷组 volume group

【jué】

决 (强调语气) definitely, certainly, under any circumstances
决策 ①〈动〉make policy ②〈名〉decision (making), policy decision, decision of strategic importance
决定 ①〈动〉decide, resolve, make up one's mind ②〈名〉decision, resolution ③〈形〉decisive, determinant
决断 ①〈动〉make a decision ②〈名〉resolution, decisiveness
决计 ①(主意已定) have decided, have made up one's mind ②(一定) definitely, certainly
决赛 finals ◇半决赛 semifinals
决算 final accounts, final accounting of revenue and expenditure
决心 determination, resolution
决议 resolution
决策点 decision point
决策点分支 act fork
决策反馈系统 decision feedback system
决策分析 decision analysis {DA}
决策功能 decision making function
决策规则 decision rule
决策过程 decision procedure
决策[判定]函数 decision function
决策基准 decision criterion
决策机制 decision mechanism
决策控制 decision-making control
决策论 decision theory
决策逻辑 decision logic
决策门 decision gate
决策模型 decision(-making) model

决策区域 decision region
决策[裁决,判定]树 decision tree
决策系统 decision-making system
决策箱 decision box
决策行动 decision action
决策者 decision maker
决策支持系统 decision support system {DSS}
决策指令 decision instruction
决策制定 decision making
决策质量 decision quality
决策中心 decision center
决策状况 decision situation
决策准则 decision criterion
决定性策略 deterministic policy
决定性集 decisive set
决定因子 determinant

诀
诀别 bid farewell, part
诀窍 knack, tricks of the trade ◇秘诀 secret of success, key to success

抉
抉择 choose ◇作出抉择 make one's choice

角 另见{jiǎo}
角色 role, part 角逐 contend, enter into rivalry
角色游戏 role playing game {RPG}
角色语言 actor language

觉
1)(感觉)sense, feel 2)(睡觉)wake (up), awake 觉察 detect, become aware of, perceive 觉得 feel, think, find 觉悟 become aware, become awakened

绝
1)(断绝)cut off, sever 2)(穷尽)exhausted, used up, finished 3)(无出路的)desperate, hopeless 4)(独一无二)unique, matchless 5)(极,最)extremely, most 绝对 absolute, unconditional; absolutely, definitely 绝迹 disappear, vanish 绝境 hopeless situation, impasse, blind alley 绝密 top-secret, most confidential
绝顶 tiptop
绝对边界 absolute bound
绝对编码 absolute coding, direct coding, actual coding, specific coding
绝对编址[寻址] absolute addressing
绝对尺度 absolute dimension
绝对代码 absolute code, direct code
绝对导数 absolute derivative
绝对的 absolute
绝对地址 absolute/ actual address
绝对二进制 absolute binary
绝对关键字 actual key
绝对规则 absolute rule
绝对极大[最大]值 absolute maximum
绝对极小值 absolute minimum
绝对界[限] absolute bound
绝对块 absolute block
绝对量 absolute magnitude
绝对偏差 absolute deviation
绝对收敛 absolute convergence
绝对数据 absolute data
绝对温标 absolute temperature scale
绝对温度 absolute temperature, Kelvin {K}
绝对误差 absolute error
绝对向量 absolute vector

绝对序列 absolute sequence
绝对压力 absolute pressure
绝对引用 absolute reference
绝对优先级 absolute priority
绝对值 absolute magnitude, absolute value
绝对指令 absolute instruction, absolute order
绝对转移 absolute jump/branch
绝对坐标 absolute coordinate
绝缘 insulation
绝缘的 insulated, isolated
绝缘体 insulator

崛 【jué】

崛起 ①(突起)rise abruptly, rise sharply ②(兴起)rise, spring up

【jūn】

军 军备 armament, arms 军队 armed forces, army, troops 军队的 military 军港 naval port 军工 ①(军事工业)war industry ②(军事工程)military project 军官 officer 军火 munitions, arms and ammunition 军人 soldier, serviceman, armyman 军事 military affairs 军事化 militarize 军械 ordnance, armament, weapon 军用 for military use; military

均 (全部)without exception, all 均等 equal, impartial, fair, even 均分 divide equally, share out equally 均衡 balanced, proportionate, harmonious, even; equalization, equilibrium 均匀 equal, even

均差 divided difference
均等共享 equitable sharing
均方 meansquare
均方差 meansquare deviation
均方根(法) root mean square {RMS}
均方偏移 meansquare deviation
均方误差 meansquare error, mean-squared error, error of mean square
均分负载组 load balancing group {LBG}
均衡价格 equilibrium price
均衡模型 equilibrium model
均衡系统 balanced system
均一性 homogeneous
均等性 equability
均匀(性) uniformity
均匀(线性)编码 uniform encoding
均匀处理机 uniform processor
均匀调整 stepless control
均匀分布 equidistribution, uniform distribution
均匀散列[杂凑] uniform hashing
均匀[一致]收敛 uniform convergence
均匀衰减 flat fading
均匀性 homogeneity
均匀需求 uniform demand
均值函数 mean value function
均值极限 limit in mean

【jùn】

峻 1)(高大) high, lofty 2)(严厉) harsh, severe

竣 complete, finish 竣工 (of a project) be completed

K k

【kā】
咖 咖啡 coffee

【kǎ】
卡 另见【qiǎ】
(热量单位) calorie 卡车 truck(美), lorry(英) 卡片 card 卡住 block, check
卡/分 cards per minute {CPM}
卡诺图 Karnaugh map
卡片槽 card slot
卡片程序 card program
卡片穿孔机 card puncher, punch
卡片存储器 card file, card storage
卡片叠 card pack, deck
卡片读出 card sensing
卡片分类 card sorting
卡片格式 card format, card form
卡片柜 card cabinet/file, card box
卡片盒 card box, card enclosure
卡片记录器 card recorder
卡片目录 card catalog
卡片容量 card capacity
卡片文件[目录] card file
卡片系统 card system, tabulating system
卡片阅读器 read-punch unit/overlap
卡片制 card system
卡片贮存器 card saver
卡片组名 deck name
卡通片 cartoon
卡纸 paper jam

【kāi】
开 1)(打开) open, turn on, be on 2)(打通,开辟) make an opening, open up 3)(发动,操纵) start, operate, drive, pilot, run, work 4)(写出) write out, make out ◇开支票 make out a check 5)(沸腾) boil 开办 open, set up, start, found, establish 开本 format, book size ◇八开本 octavo 开标 open sealed tenders 开采 mine, extract, exploit 开车 ①(开动车辆) drive, start ②(发动机器) set a machine going 开除 expel, discharge, dismiss, fire, sack 开创 start, initiate, found, set up, pioneer, open 开拓 exploit, exploiting 开动 start, set in motion, move, run, operate 开端 beginning, start 开发 develop, open up, exploit ◇经济开发区 economic development zone 开放 ①(开花) come into bloom ②(对外开放) open to the world, open-door 开放政策 open-door policy 开工

(开始生产)go into operation, start operation, be put into operation ②(开始修建)start, begin construction, begin building 开航 ①(开始通航)become open for navigation ②(船只启航)set sail 开户 open an account, establish an account 开会 hold a meeting, have a meeting, meet, attend a meeting 开架 open-shelf 开架阅览室 open-shelf reading room 开禁 lift a ban 开卷 open a book, read 开卷考试 open book examination 开课 give a course, teach a subject, deliver a course 开阔 ①〈形〉open, wide ②〈动〉widen 开路 ①(开辟道路)open a way, break a fresh path ②〈电气〉open circuit, open loop, open, disconnect 开幕 ①(演出开始)the curtain rises, begin the performance ②(会议、展览等开始)open, inaugurate 开幕词 opening speech, inaugural address 开幕式 opening ceremony, inaugural ceremony, inauguration 开辟 ①(打开道路)open up, hew out, break ②(创立、建设)open up, set up, establish ③(开发)open up, develop 开设 ①(设立)open, set up, found ②(设置)offer (a course in college) 开始 ①〈动〉begin, start, commence ②〈名〉initial stage, beginning, outset, inception, initiation 开水 ①(沸水)boiling water ②(开过的水)boiled water 开通 ①(打开道路)remove obstacles from

②(不守旧)open-minded, liberal, enlightened, broad-minded 开头 begin, start 开往 leave for, be bound for 开学 schools opens, term begins 开业 start business, open for business 开展 develop, launch, carry out 开张 ①(开始营业)open a business, begin doing business ②(第一笔交易)the first transaction of day's business 开支 ①〈动〉pay (expenses), spend ②〈名〉expense, expenditure, spending

开采问题 mining problem
开窗口 open window, window open, windowing
开发方法学 development methodology
开发软件 development software
开发时间 development time
开发系统 development system
开发[研制]周期 development cycle
开放(式系统)结构 open architecture
开放目标 open object
开放目录服务接口 open directory services interface {ODSI}
开放软件基金会 Open Software Foundation {OSF}
开放式操作系统 open operating system
开放式机房[计算站] open shop
开放式数据库管理系统 open database management system {ODBMS}
开放式数据链路接口 open datalink interface {ODI}
开放式体系结构 open architecture
开放式系统 open system

开放式系统结构 open system architecture {OSA}
开放数据库联接[连接] open database connectivity {ODBC}
开放数据链路接口 open data-link interface {ODI}
开放拓扑 open topology
开放网络 open network
开放系统互连 open system interconnection {OSI}
开放应用体系结构 open applications architecture {OAA}
开关 on-off, switch
开关电路理论 switching circuit theory
开关二极管 switching diode
开关方式 on-off mode
开关函数 switching function
开关机构 switching mechanism
开关级模型 switch-level model
开关寄存器 switch register {SR}
开关结构 switching configuration
开关矩阵 switch matrix
开-关控制 on-off control
开关理论 switching theory
开关设备 switch apparatus
开关时间 switching time
开关式 ping pong
开关式控制 bang-bang control
开关式伺服系统 on-off servo system
开关枢纽 switching tie
开关系数 switching coefficient
开关系统 switching system
开关虚拟电路 switched virtual circuit {SVC}
开关元件 switch element, switching element
开关值 switch value
开关指令 switch instruction, switch order

开关指示符 switch indicator
开关装置 switching device
开关状态测试 switch status test
开关状态条件 switch-status condition
开关字符 switch character {SW}
开关组合 switch combination
开关组件 switch block
开关组态 switching configuration
开环 open loop/cycle
开环策略[方案] open loop policy
开环电压增益 open loop voltage gain
开环过程控制 open loop process control
开环控制 open loop control
开环识别 open loop identification
开环增益 open loop gain
开集 open set
开口 opening, slot
开路接点 break contact
开路运行 open running
开启 open, turn-on, unblock
开启文件 file opening
开区间 open interval
开始(指令) sign-on
开始符号 begin symbol, starting symbol
开始栏[列] begin column
开始链 begin chain, beginning of chain
开始码 opening code
开始元素 start element
开式 open numbering
开锁 unlock
开-停系统 on-off service
开头大写字母 initial cap
开头符号 first symbol
开头项 first term
开头终结符 first terminal

开销时间 overhead time
开销通信量 overhead traffic
开型数据通路 open data path {ODP}
开型通路 open path
开型纹理结构 open texture
开域 open domain
开状态 on status

揩 wipe

锎 californium (Cf)

【kǎi】

楷 楷模 model, good example

慨 1)(愤激)indignant 2)(感慨)deeply touched 3)(慷慨)generous

【kān】

刊 1)(排印出版)print, publish 2)(定期或不定期出版物)periodical, publication ◇半月刊 fortnightly // 季刊 quarterly // 月刊 monthly // 周刊 weekly (publication)
刊登 publish in a newspaper/magazine, carry (in a publication)

看 另见【kàn】
(守护)guard, keep watch on

勘 1)(校订)read and correct the text of, collate 2)(探测)investigate, survey 勘察 ①(实地调查)reconnaissance ②〈地理〉prospecting 勘探 exploration, prospecting 勘误 correct errors in printing 勘误表 errata, corrigenda

【kǎn】

砍 cut, chop

【kàn】

看 另见【kān】
1)(观看)see, look at, watch 2)(阅读)read 3)(观察,判断)think, consider, view, observe, judge 4)(照料)look after 看成 look upon as, regard as, treat as, consider as 看出 make out, see, perceive, find out, be aware of 看待 look upon, regard, treat 看到 ①(看见)see, catch sight of ②(注意到)notice, be aware of 看法 view, opinion 看来 it seems, it appears, it looks as if 看起来 it seems, it appears, it looks as if 看轻 underestimate, look down upon 看透 ①(透彻了解)understand thoroughly, gain an insight into ②(透彻认识)see through 看望 call on, visit, go to see 看作 look upon, regard as

【kāng】

康 康复 be restored to health
康健 healthy, in good health

慷 慷慨 ①(激昂)vehement, fervent ②(不吝惜)generous

【káng】

扛 carry on the shoulder, shoulder

【kàng】

抗 (抵抗)resist, combat, fight 抗衡 contend with, match 抗拒 refuse, defy 抗

kàng 钪 kǎo 考拷烤 kào 靠 kē 苛钶科

议 protest, remonstrate, express opposition to
抗病毒产品 anti-virus product
抗毒(程序) virussafe
抗腐蚀性 corrosion resistance
抗干扰度 noise immunity
抗干扰装置 anti-intrusion device
抗扰度 noise immunity

钪 scandium (Sc)

【kǎo】

考 考查 examine, test, check 考察 ①(实地调查) inspect, investigate ②(仔细观察) observe and study 考古 arch(a)eology 考核 examine, check, assess (sb's proficiency) 考究 ①(查考,研究) observe and study, investigate, examine closely ②(讲究) care about, fastidious, particular ③(精美的) exquisite, fine 考卷 examination paper 考虑 think over, take into account, consider 考勤 attendance check 考勤簿 attendance record 考生 candidate for an examination, examinee, testee 考试 examination, test, exam 考题 examination questions, examination paper 考验 test, trial

拷 拷贝 copy, replica
拷贝操作 copy operation/function
拷贝程序 copy program, duplicate routine
拷贝机 copying machine
拷贝胶卷 print film
拷贝卷 copy volume
拷贝屏幕方式 copy screen mode
拷贝(件)群 copy group

烤 bake, roast, toast

【kào】

靠 1)(依着) lean against, rest against 2)(沿着) keep to, get near, come up to 3)(挨近) near, by 4)(依靠) depend on, rely on 5)(信赖) trust 靠近 ① near, close to, by ② draw near, approach 靠拢 draw close, go near
靠模装置 profile device

【kē】

苛 severe 苛待 treat harshly, be hard upon 苛刻 harsh 苛求 make excessive demands, be overcritical

钶 columbium (Cb)

科 1)(学科) branch of (academic) study 2)〈生物〉family 科班 regular professional training ◇科班出身的人 a person with professional training 科技 science and technology 科目 ①(学科) subject (in a curriculum), course ②(会计帐目) headings in an account book 科普 popular science 科室 department, section 科学 science, scientific knowledge 科学家 scientist 科学院 academy of sciences 科研 scientific research 科研机构 scientific research institution 科研人员 scientific research personnel 科研项

目 scientific research project
科学表示法 scientific notation
科学抽样 scientific sampling
科学管理 scientific management, research-on-research
科学计算 scientific calculation
科学计算机 scientific computer
科学计算可视化 visualization in scientific computing {VISC}
科学计算器 scientific calculator
科学计算语言 scientific language
科学记数法 scientific notation
科学可视化 scientific visualization
科学数据库 scientific database
科学用系统 scientific system

颗 **颗粒** pellet, particle, grain, granule

【ké】
壳 另见【qiào】
shell, case, housing, inclosure

咳 cough

【kě】
可 (同意)approve, permit 可变 variable 可拆 removable, detachable 可观 considerable, impressive, sizable 可见 it is thus clear/evident/obvious that 可靠 reliable, dependable, trustworthy 可能 ①〈形〉possible, probable ②〈副〉probably, maybe ③〈名〉possibility 可怕 fearful, terrible, frightening 可取 desirable, advisable, recommendable 可是 but, yet, however 可惜 what a pity, it's too bad; unfortunately, regretfully 可行 feasible, practicable, workable 可行性 feasibility 可以 can, may 可疑 suspicious, questionable, doubtful

可安装文件系统 installable file system {IFS}
可版本化对象 versionable object
可报警线程 alertable thread
可比集 comparable aggregate
可比较的 comparable
可比性 comparability, commensurability
可编程(序)除法器 programmable divider
可编程单位[单元] programmable unit
可编程功能[函数] programmable function
可编程(序)逻辑控制器 programmable logic controller {PLC}
可编程逻辑器件 programmable logic device {PLD}
可编程逻辑阵列 programmable logic array {PLA}
可编程(序)性 programmability
可编程优先中断 programmable priority interrupt
可编程只读存储器 programmable ROM {PROM}
可编译单位 compilable unit
可编址的 addressable
可编址性 addressability
可便携性 transportability
可变编号 variable numbering
可变标号 variable label
可变步长 variable step size
可变参量 variable quantity
可变长度 variable-length

可变长度(编)码 variable-length code {VLC}
可变长记录 variable-length record
可变长字 variable-length word
可变[修改]存储器 alterable memory
可变打字机 varitype
可变的 variable, changeable
可变地址 variable address, floating address
可变范围 variable range
可变符号 flexible symbol, flexional symbols, variable symbol
可变格式报文 variable-format message
可变结构计算机 variable structure computer
可变界限[约束] variable bound
可变控制块区 variable control block area {VCBA}
可变块 variable block
可变逻辑 variable logic
可变名 flexible name
可变时间 variable time
可变数据 variable data
可变文本 variable text
可变误差[错误] variable error
可变信息 variable information
可变因子 variable factor
可变语音速度控制 variable speech/speed control {VSC}
可变阈值逻辑电路 variable threshold logic circuit {VTL}
可变址的 indexable
可变指令 variable order
可变周期 variable cycle
可变装置 variset
可变字 variable word
可变字长 variable word-length, word with variable-length
可变字段 variable field
可变字符 variable character, variant character
可擦(除)的 erasable
可擦(除)存储器 erasable storage/memory
可擦光盘 erasable optical disk
可操作性 operability, manipuility, workability
可测试的 testable
可测试性 testability
可插入性 insertability
可程控软件 software programmable
可重[再]定位的 relocatable
可重[再]定位库 relocatable library
可重复读 repeatable read
可重入表 reentrant list
可重入程序 reenterable program, reenterable routine
可重入代码 reenterable code
可重入[再入] reentrant
可重入[再入]的 reenterable, reentrant
可重入[再入]性 reenterabilty
可重写(人) rewritable
可重新进入 reenterable
可重(复使)用的 reusable
可重(复使)用文件 reusable file
可重用性方法 reusability method
可重用资源 reusable resource
可重置码点 replaceable code point
可重装[重调,清除]的 resettable
可除掉的 deletable
可处理性 manipuility
可穿透性 penetrance
可穿透性 penetrance
可传递的 transitive
可串联[级联,连接] cascadable
可存储的 memorable
可达(到)的 accessible, reachable
可达点 accessible point, reachable point

可达状态 accessible state, reachable state
可调尺寸 adjustable dimension
可调节范围 adjustable extent
可调维数 adjustable dimension
可调用接口 callable interface
可调整的 adjustable
可定位 settable
可定义的 definable
可定义函数 definable function
可动性 mobility, transferability
可读性 readability, intelligibility
可访问[寻址]存储器 addressable memory
可访问[寻址]的 addressable
可访问[寻址]点 addressable point
可访问[寻址]位置 addressable position
可访问[寻址]性 accessibility
可分割的 diceable
可分(离)规划 separable programming
可分级的 classable
可分解的 decomposable
可分解对策 decomposable game
可分解模型 decomposable model
可分解算子 decomposable operator
可分解性 decomposability, subsetability
可分类 separate families
可分类的 classable
可分离代码 separable code
可分离[开] separable
可分特性 separable characteristic
可分图形 separated graphics
可分析性 analyzability
可分性 separability
可分页[调页]动态区 pageable dynamic area
可服务时间 serviceable time
可服务时间比 serviceability ratio
可服务性 serviceability
可浮动表达式 relocatable expression
可浮动的 relocatable
可浮动库 relocatable library
可浮动模块 relocatable module
可浮动区 relocatable area
可浮动性 relocatability
可覆盖性图 coverability graph
可复位 reset mode
可复位计数器 resettable counter
可复位数据库 resettable database
可复用性 reusability
可改编程序的 reprogrammable
可改写的只读存储器 read mostly memory {**RMM**}
可改写光盘 rewritable optical disk
可更新数据 updatable data
可工作时间 operable time
可工作性 workability
可共享的程序 shareable program
可共享映像 shareable image
可构造函数 constructable function
可观测[察]的 observable
可观测[察]性 observability
可管理性 manipuility
可归约性 reducibility
可互换的 replaceable
可换磁盘 exchangeable/ interchangeability/ removable disk
可换磁盘存储器 exchangeable disk storage
可换磁盘组 removable disk pack

可换存储器 changeable storage
可换的 changeable
可换环 commutative ring
可恢复(的)目录 recoverable catalog
可恢复事务 recoverable transaction
可恢复数据库 resettable database
可恢复同步 recoverable synchronization
可恢复性 recoverability
可恢复(的)资源 recoverable resource
可汇编段 assembly unit
可计数的 countable
可计数函数 countable function
可计算的 calculable, computable
可计算概率 computable probability
可记录的 writable
可记帐性 accountability
可加索引的 indexable
可加性 additivity
可检测错误 detectable error
可检测像素[元素] detectable element
可检测性 detectability
可检验性 testability
可见标签 visual tag
可见的 visible
可见读出 visual readout
可见度 visibility, visual density
可见发光二极管 visible light emitting diode {VLED}
可见区域 viewing area
可见属性 visual attribute
可见图形 eye diagram
可见文件 video unit files, visible file
可见性 visibility
可见[视]页[面] visible page
可见语言 visible speech
可见[眼球]字符 eyeball character
可降级系统 degradable system
可交换磁盘存储器 exchangeable disk store {EDS}
可交换的(页,段) swappable
可交换的实体 communicability objective
可交换矩阵 commutative matrix
可交换性 commutativity, interchangeability
可接受的输入 acceptable input
可接受的质量级别 acceptable quality level {AQL}
可接受使用策略 acceptable use policy {AUP}
可接受性 acceptability, credibility
可接受性使用 acceptable use
可接受字 accepted word
可解的 soluble
可解节点 solved node
可解码 decodable code
可解码性 decodability
可解释的 decipherable
可解性 solvability
可禁止[拒绝]的 inhibitable
可靠的数据报协议 reliable datagram protocol {RDP}
可靠度 reliability rate
可靠流协议 reliable stream protocol {RSP}
可靠数据报协议 reliable datagram protocol {RDP}
可靠系统 secure system
可靠性 reliability, credibility, responsibility
可靠性方法 reliability method
可靠性分析 reliability analysis
可靠性逻辑 reliability logic
可靠性模型 reliability model
可靠性能 unfailing performance

可靠性设计 reliability design
可靠性研究 reliability consideration
可靠性预测 reliability prediction
可靠性原理 reliability principle
可控对(偶) controllable pair
可控硅整流器 silicon-controlled rectifier {SCR}, thyristor
可控冗余 controlled redundancy
可控(制)性[度] controllability
可控制的 controllable
可控制块区 variable control block area {VCBA}
可扩[扩展]的 extendible, expandable, open-ended, scalable
可扩充的程序 open-ended program
可扩充的系统 open-ended system
可扩充系统 open-ended system
可扩充[扩展]性 expandability, extendibility, scalability
可扩充语言 extendible language, extensible language {EL}
可扩展门 expandable gate
可扩展设计 open-ended design
可理解性 understandability
可利用率 available rate
可连接程序 linkable program
可连续的 continuable
可连续重用资源 serially reusable resource {SRR}
可重用的 serially reusable
可满足的 satisfiable
可满足性 satisfiability
可枚举集 enumerable set
可能性 possibility
可能性函数 possibility function
可能性研究 feasibility study {FS}
可逆编码 reversible coding
可逆变换 reversible transformation
可逆的 reversible
可逆电路 reversible circuit
可逆过程 reversible process
可逆函数 invertible function
可逆矩阵 invertible matrix
可逆律 invertible law
可逆码 reversible code
可逆性 reversibility, invertibility
可逆语法 invertible grammar
可逆元 invertible element
可逆中断 reverse interrupt {RVI}
可判定性 decidability
可配置站 configurable station
可启动的(磁盘等) bootable
可嵌链 embeddable chain
可嵌入的 embeddable
可切割的 diceable
可清除[取消]的 cancellable
可清除计数器 resettable counter
可清除区 erasable area
可确定的 definable
可熔片 fuse
可熔性只读存储器 fusible read-only memory {FROM}
容许干扰 acceptable interference
可三态的 three-stateable
可删除的 deletable
可伸缩的 scalable
可伸缩性 scalability
可实现的 realizable
可识别模型 recognizable pattern
可识别性 discirimity, identifiability
可识别字符 recognizable character

可使用(数据)库 active bank
可视查询语言 visual query language
可视程序设计 visual programming
可视的 viewable
可视电话 picturephone, video telephone, viewphone, videophone
可视电话会议 teleconference, videoconference
可视化 visualization
可视化Basic编程工具 visual basic {VB}
可视化工作平台 visual workbench {VWB}
可视化黑板 visualization blackboard
可视化界面 visualization interface
可视化流水线 visualization pipeline
可视化系统 visualization system
可视计算机 visual computer
可视界面 visual interface
可视距离 visual range
可视命令 visual command
可视实时信息 real-time visual information
可视数据 teletel, telset, viditel, viewmax, viewtron
可视数据库 videotex data bank, visual database
可视图文 teletel, telset, videotex, viewdata
可视[目视]图像 visual image
可视外壳语言 visual shell language
可视文件 video file
可视显示部件 visual display unit {VDU}
可视现象 visual phenomena
可视信息 visual information
可视页(面) visible page
可视语言 visual language
可视运算 visualization
可视终端 video terminal
可输出 output enable
可数[列]的 countable, denumerable
可数[列]集 countable set, denumerable set
可刷新[复制] refreshable
可(计)算函数 computable function
可算谓词 computable predicate
可(计)算性 computability
可听[闻]度 audibility
可微的 differentiable
可维护[维修]性 maintainability, serviceability
可校错误 correctable error
可协调性 coordinability, tunability
可携带计算机 luggable computer
可写的 writable
可写控制存储 writable control store {WCS}
可写信息 writable information
可写性 writability
可写指令系统 writable instruction set {WIS}
可卸插接板 detachable plugboard
可卸磁盘 removable disk
可信 credibility
可信产品 trusted products
可信的 credible
可信度 confidence level
可信度因子 certainty factor {CF}
可信计算基 trusted computing base {TCB}
可信进程 trusted process
可信赖性 dependability, responsibility
可信路径 trusted path

可信软件 trusted software
可信系统 trusted system
可信性 credibility, dependability
可行程序[方案] feasible program
可行法 feasible method
可行分解 feasible decomposition
可行集 feasible set
可行解 feasible solution
可行区域 feasible region
可行算法 effective algorithm
可行性 feasibility
可行性分析 feasibility analysis
可行性估计 feasibility assessment
可行性试验 feasibility test
可行性研究 feasibility research {FR}, feasibility study {FS}
可修复数据库 repairable database
可修复性 repairability
可修改性 modifiability
可选集 option set
可选(部)件[单元] selectable unit {SU}
可选进程 eligible process
可选启动 flexboot
可选文件 optional file
可选项[件] option
可选字长 selectable-length word
可寻址存储器 addressable memory, addressable storage
可寻址的网络部件 network addressable unit {NAU}
可寻址光标 addressable cursor
可寻址计数器 addressable counter
可训练性 trainability
可压缩的 compressible
可压缩文本 suppressible text
可延拓的 continuable
可演绎的 deducible

可依赖性 dependability
可移动的 portable
可移动头 moving head
可移动性 portability
可移植的软件 portable software
可移植性 portability, transplantation
可移植语言 portable language
可以连接的 joinable
可以有版本的 versionable
可引导的 bootable
可引导文件 bootable file
可印刷区 printable area
可印项 printable item
可用比特率 available bit rete {ABR}
可用存储区表 available storage list
可用带宽 available bandwidth
可用的 available
可用点 available point
可用机时 available machine time
可用空间 available space
可用控制装置 availability control unit
可用区 usable area
可用容量 active volume
可用性 serviceability, availability, usability
可用性模型 availability model
可用性性能 availability performance
可(选)用状态 status available
可优化的 optimizable
可约算子 reducible operator
可约性 divisibility, reducibility
可运行性 performability
可再[重]定位代码 relocatable code
可再[重]定位的 relocatable
可再[重]定位地址 relocatable address
可再[重]定位模块 relocatable

module
可再[重]定位性 relocatability
可再用[重复使用]的 reusable, serially reusable
可暂停的 suspendable
可展开的 expandable
可诊断的 diagnosable
可诊断性 diagnosticability
可证(明)的 provable
可执行程序 executable program
可执行的 executable
可执行程段 executable segment
可执行文件 executable file
可执行性 performability
可执行映像 executable image
可执行语句 executable statement
可执行指令 executable instruction
可执行状态 executable state
可置位 set enable, settable
可中断的 interruptable, interruptible, suspendable
可中断性 interruptibility
可中断状态 interruptable state
可中止的 suspendable
可终止的 open-ended
可逐点访问的 all points addressable {APA}
可转接代码 switchable code
可转换驱动 convertible drive
可转移性 transitivity
可自动化的 antomatable
可阻止的 inhibitable

渴 thirsty 渴望 thirst for, long for, yearn for

【kè】

克 1) (攻克) overcome, subdue, capture 2) (重量、质量单位) gram (g) 克服 surmount, overcome, conquer 克制 restrain

刻 1) (雕刻) carve, engrave, cut 2) (一刻钟) quarter 3) (时刻) moment ◇此刻 at the moment 4) (形容程度深) in the highest degree ◇深刻 penetrating, profound 刻板 mechanical, stiff, inflexible 刻苦 assiduous, hardworking
刻度 scale, graduate
刻度(线) scale mark
刻度零点 scale zero
刻度盘 dial
刻蚀 etch, etching
刻图 needle drawing
刻字机 carving machine

客 1) (客人) visitor, guest 2) (旅客) traveller, passenger 3) (顾客) customer 客车 ① (铁路) coach, passenger train ② (大轿车) bus, coach 客观 objective 客机 passenger plane, airplane, airliner 客气 polite, courteous 客体 〈哲学〉object 客运 passenger transport, passenger traffic 客座教授 visiting/ guest professor
客观评价 objective rating
客观性 objectivism
客户 customer, client
客户/服务器计算模型 client/server computing model
客户安装 customer set-up {CSU}
客户标识[识别]号 customer identification number
客户窗口 client window
客户存取[访问]区 customer access area
客户代理 client agent
客户服务代理 customer service

representative {CSR}
客户服务器 client server
客户工程师 customer engineer {CE}
客户工作站 client workstation
客户化 customization
客户机 client
客户机/服务器计算 client/server computing
客户机进程 client process
客户接口 client interface, customer interface
客户可换部件 customer replaceable unit {CRU}
客户控制 customer control
客户码 customer number
客户模型 client model
客户平台 client platform
客户区 client area
客户软件 customer software
客户网络管理 customer network management {CNM}
客户信息控制系统 customer information control system {CICS}
客户虚存 guest virtual storage
客户选择键 customer option key
客户站点 client side
客户支持服务 customer support service {CSS}
客人特权 guest privilege
客人组 guest group

课 1)(科目)subject 2)(上课时间)class 3)(上课内容)lesson 4)〈动〉(征收)levy 课本 textbook, coursebook 课表 school timetable 课程 course, curriculum 课间休息 break, interval 课时 class hour, period 课税 levy duty, charge duty 课堂 classroom, schoolroom 课题 question or problem for study or research, topic 课外 extracurricular; outside class, after school
课文 text
课程编写语言(程序) course writer
课程开发系统 course development system {CDS}
课程软件 courseware
课件工程 courseware engineering {CE}
课题名 project name
课题研究 subject study

氪 krypton (Kr)

【kěn】

肯 1)(同意)agree, consent 2)(愿意)be willing to, be ready to 肯定 ①〈动〉affirm, confirm, approve ②〈形〉positive, affirmative, definite ③〈副〉certainly, undoubtedly, definitely
肯定 acknowledgement {ACK}
肯定符号[字符] acknowledge character {ACK}
肯定响应 positive response
肯定应答[字符] affirmative acknowledgement {ACK}, positive acknowledgement, positive response
肯定中断 acknowledge interrupt
肯定字段 acknowledge field

垦 cultivate (land), reclaim (wasteland)

恳 1)〈副〉earnestly, sincerely 2)〈动〉request, beseech 恳切 earnest, sincere 恳请 earnestly request, cordially invite 恳求 implore, entreat

【kēng】
坑 hole, pit

【kōng】
空 另见{kòng}
1)(空的) empty, hollow, vacant 2)(天空) sky, air 3)(白白地) for nothing, in vain 空洞 ①(物体内的窟窿) cavity ②(无实质内容) empty, hollow, devoid of content 空军 air force 空旷 open, spacious 空气 ①(大气) air, atmosphere ②(气氛) atmosphere 空前 unprecedented, unparalleled 空调 air-conditioning 空头(有名无实的) nominal, phony 空头支票 dud check, empty promise 空想 idle dream, fantasy 空心 hollow 空虚 hollow, void 空运 air transport, air freight 空中 in the sky, in the air 空转 ①(机器无负载运转) racing; run idle ②(轮子打滑) spin, skid

空 null {NUL}
空板 bare board
空变量 blank variable
空表 space list
空操作 do-nothing operation, operation blank
空操作[无操作]位 no-operation bit
空操作指令 do-nothing instruction, do-nothing operation, dummy instruction, skip
空插件 blank card
空插孔电路板 unpopulated board
空程序 dummy routine
空串 empty string, null string
空存储 empty store
空代码 blank code
空单元 dummy cell
空的 empty, dummy, vacant
空登记项 empty entry
空地址 address blank, null address
空调用 idle call
空队列 empty queue
空符号 empty symbol, null symbol, skip symbol
空关系 empty relation, void relation
空函数 empty function
空号 absentee, dead number, open number, vacant number
空集(合) empty set
空记录 empty record, null record
空间 space, spacing, interspace
空间编码 space encoding
空间分辨率(电视图像的) spatial resolution
空间分辨率可变性 spatial scalability
空间分析 spatial analysis
空间复杂性 space complexity
空间跟踪系统 space tracking system {STS}
空间共享 space-sharing
空间技术 space technology
空间监视系统 space surveillance system {SSS}
空间曲线 space curve
空间冗余 space redundancy
空间扇形区 space segment
空间授权 spatial authority
空间属性 space attribute
空间数据 spatial data
空间数据库 spatial database
空间索引 spatial index
空间通信网络 space communication network {SPAN}

空间图 spacegraph
空间拓扑关系 spatial topological relation
空间网络 space network
空间物理分析网络 space physics analysis network {SPAN}
空间序列 spatial sequence
空间域 spatial domain
空间指针 space pointer
空交换 switching blank
空进程 null process
空句子 empty sentence
空(白)卷 blank coil
空连接 null link
空码 vacant code
空名字 null name
空气冷却 air cooling
空设备 null device
空事件 null event
空数据集 null data set
空位 bit bare, gap digit, vacancy
空位环 vacancy loop
空位名 slot name
空位值 slot value
空位置 empty position
空位[转]字符 idle character
空文件 space file
空系统 donothing system
空线 dead line, dead wire, idle wire
空项 null term, void item
空行 empty string, null {NUL}, null line, null string, space
空穴 hole
空页 gutter
空语句 dummy statement, null statement
空(间)域法 spatial domain method
空运行 dry run, running open
空载传输 backhaul
空栈 empty stack
空占的 empty

空值 null {NUL}, null value, void value
空指令 blank instruction, do- nothing instruction, dummy/ idle instruction, null instruction, skip
空指示符 null indicator
空指针 nil pointer, null pointer
空置换 empty substitution
空(转)周期 null cycle
空资源 null resource
空字 null word
空字段 null field
空字符 null character {NUL}, null word
空走 nonprocess runout {NPRO}

【kǒng】

孔 hole, opening, cell, aperture
孔间距 tie
孔径 bore
孔径效应 aperture effect
孔距 pitch, row pitch
孔位 hole site
孔隙 aperture slot
孔屑箱 chip box

恐 fear, dread 恐吓 threaten, freighten 恐慌 panic, scare 恐惧 fear, dread 恐怕 ①(担心)I'm afraid, fear ②(估计)perhaps, probably; I think

【kòng】

空 另见【kōng】
1)(腾出空间) leave empty, leave blank, vacate 2)(未占用的) unoccupied, vacant, blank 空白 blank (space), null, vacancy, void 空缺 vacant position, vacancy 空

隙 gap, space **空余时间** free time, spare time
空白标号 blank label
空白表格 blank form, spacing chart
空白带 blank tape, skip tape
空白段 clear band
空白对话[会话] clear session
空白符号 blank symbol, clear character
空白符删除器 blank deleter
空白格式 blank form
空白公用(存储)区 blank common
空白关系 void relation
空白盒[箱] clear box
空白级 blanking level
空白记录 blank record, space record
空白间隙 blanking interval
空白矩阵 blank matrix
空白列 blank column
空白密码键 clear key
空白命令 blank command
空白区 blank, blanked region, clear area, clear band, space
空白数据 clear data
空白填充 blank fill
空白文件 null file
空白行 blank line, after space
空白语句 empty statement
空白域[字段] null field
空白子句 blank clause
空白字符 blank character
空格 blank, space, spacing
空格(键) tab
空格标记字符 indent tab character {IT}
空格点 vacancy
空格分配 space allocation
空格符号 space symbol
空格键 space bar, space key
空格拉杆 space bar
空格压缩 space suppression
空格制表符 indent tab character {IT}
空格[空白,间隔]字符 space character {SP, sp}
空缺策略 default strategy
空缺集 vacancy set
空闲表 idle list
空闲(例行)程序 idle routine
空闲池[库] free pool
空闲待用 standby
空闲空间 free space
空闲块 free block
空闲链路 idle link
空闲码 bell idles
空闲区 free area
空闲[停机]时间 floor time
空闲时间 free time, idle hour, idle time, off-time
空闲线(路) idle line
空闲线程 idle thread
空闲中断 idle interrupt
空闲字符 idle character

控

控告 charge, accuse, complain
控制 control {CTRL, CTL}, administer, manipulation, predominate, steering
控制板 control board, control panel
控制变换 control change
控制[限制]变量 dominated variable
控制拨号盘 control dial
控制部件[(程序)块] control block
控制部件[单元,装置] control unit {CU}
控制菜单 control menu
控制操作 control function, control operation
控制操作员 control operator
控制层次 control hierarchy, hierarchy of control

控制程序 control procedure, control program, control routine, controller
控制程序键 control program key
控制程序软件 control program facility {CRF}
控制处理机 control processor
控制窗口 control window
控制磁道 control track, cue track
控制存储器 control stor(ag)e {CS}
控制带 control band, control tape
控制单元终端 control unit terminal {CUT}
控制电路 control circuit/ electronics
控制动作[行动] control action
控制端口 control port
控制段 control section {CSECT}, control segment
控制(变化)范围 span of control
控制方式 control mode, control scheme
控制分组 control packet
控制符 control character {CTRL}, instruction character, operational character
控制杆 control lever/ stick, joy-stick, lever key
控制格式 control format
控制过程 control procedure, control process
控制函数[功能] control function
控制号 control number
控制环[回路] control loop
控制机 cybertron
控制级别 control hierarchy
控制间隔 control interval
控制键 control key

控制键盘 supervisory keyboard
控制件 cyberware
控制交换中心 control switching point {CSP}
控制接口 control interface
控制节 control section {CSECT}
控制结构 control structure
控制精度 control accuracy
控制卷 control volume
控制卡(片) control card
控制开关[切换]点 control switching point {CSP}
控制孔 control hole
控制(数据)库 control library
控制例程 control routine
控制流 control flow/ stream, flow of control
控制流程图 control flowchart
控制流计算机 control flow computer
控制流图 control flow diagram
控制路径系统 controlled path system {CPS}
控制论 cybernetics, kybernetics
控制论的 cybernetic
控制论方法 cybernetic approach
控制论环 cybernetic loop
控制论模型 cybernetic model
控制论优化 cyberculture
控制逻辑单元 control logical unit {CLU}
控制码 control code
控制面板[盘] control panel
控制命令 control command
控制模块 control module
控制目标 control objective
控制器 control block, control unit {CU}, controller
控制器功能[操作] controller function
控制器描述 controller description {CTLD}

控制器区域网络 controller area network {CAN}
控制区(域) control band, control region
控制驱动 control-driven
控制室 pulpit
控制数据集 control data set {CDS}
控制数据项 control data item
控制数字 planned target
控制台 console, control desk, operation board, pulpit
控制台电源 console supply
控制台调试 console debug
控制台调整(程序) console debugging
控制台堆栈 console stack
控制台功能 console function
控制台假脱机 console spooling
控制台请求 console request
控制台通信服务 console communication services {CCS}
控制台陷阱[自阱] console trap
控制台中断 console interrupt
控制台作业 console job
控制态 control state
控制条 control strip
控制条件 controlled condition
控制通路 control path
控制头栏[标器] control heading
控制尾栏[基础群] control footing group
控制位 control bit
控制线 control line, guide line, pilot wire
控制项 control item
控制向量 control vector
控制消除 controlled cancel
控制型指令 control-type instruction
控制序列 control/instruction sequence
控制循环 control loop
控制依赖 control dependence

控制用计算机 control computer
控制语句 control statement
控制域 control domain, control field
控制元件 pilot cell
控制元素 control element
控制栈 control stack
控制帧 control frame
控制指令 control instruction, steering order
控制中止层 control break level
控制周期 control cycle
控制转移指令 control transfer instruction
控制装置 control apparatus, control device
控制状态 control mode
控制准则 control criterion
控制(器)字 control word
控制字段 control field
控制字符 instruction character, control character
控制字节 control byte
控制总数 control total
控制总线 control bus
控制组[栏] control group

【kǒu】

口 1) (嘴) mouth 2) (容器口) mouth, rim 3) (出入口) opening, entrance, inlet, outlet, exit 4) (口子) cut, hole, opening 5) (刀口) the edge of a knife 口岸 port, harbor 口号 slogan 口径(圆物直径) bore, caliber 口令 ① (口头命令) word of command, command ② (识别暗号) password 口试 oral examination, oral test 口授 ① (口头传授) oral instruction, pass on (sth) through oral instruction ② (口述让别人代写) dictate 口头 ①

（用说话方式）oral, verbal ②（口头上）in words, in speech, on one's lips 口译 ①（口头翻译）oral interpretation, interpret ②（译员）interpreter 口语 colloquial/spoken language
口令(字) password
口令安全(保密)性 password security
口令保护 password protection, crack
口令认证 password authentication protocol {PAP}
口头协议 verbal protocol

【kòu】

扣 扣动 press, pull 扣留 detain, arrest 扣去 deduct, discount, take off, subtract 扣压 withhold 扣子 knot, button, buckle 扣住 button up, fasten

【kū】

哭 cry, weep, sob

枯 枯竭 dried up, exhausted, drained 枯萎 withered 枯燥 uninteresting, dry and dull

窟 窟窿 hole, cavity

【kǔ】

苦 1)（味苦）bitter 2)（痛苦）hardship, suffering, pain, bitterness 3)（使痛苦）cause sb suffering, give sb a hard time 4)（苦于）suffer from, be troubled by 5)（尽力地）painstakingly, doing one's utmost 苦干 work hard 苦功 hard work, painstaking effort 苦练 practice hard, drill diligently

【kù】

库 1)（仓库）warehouse, storehouse 2)〈计算机〉library, bank, pool 库藏 have in storage, have a storage of, have in store 库存 stock, reserve, inventory
库表 library list
库成员 library member
库程序 library program
库程序包 library package
库存管理 inventory control
库存控制 inventory control, stock control
库存模型 inventory model
库存品 stock
库存问题 warehouse problem
库单位 library unit
库调用 library call
库对象 library object
库分配 library allocation
库分区 library partition
库工作区 library work area
库关系 base relation
库管理 library management
库函数 library function
库名 library name (= libname)
库命令 library command
库模块 library module
库目录 library directory
库目录磁道 library track
库数据块 library block
库搜寻 library searching
库外模式 external schema
库文本 library text
库文件 library file
库项 library item

裤 trousers, pants

酷 1)（残酷）cruel, brutal, oppressive 2)（程度深的）

very, extremely, exceedingly **酷爱** ardently love, be very fond of **酷似** be the very image of, be exactly like, bear a strong resemblance to

【kuā】
夸 夸张 exaggerate, overstate

【kuǎ】
垮 collapse, break down

【kuà】
跨 (迈步) step, stride 跨国公司 transnational corporation 跨年度 go beyond the year 跨骑 bestride, straddle, ride astride 跨越 stride across, leap over, cut across, span ◇跨越时空 cut across, go beyond
跨接 jumper, bridging, crossing, crossover
跨接表 strapping table
跨接带 strap
跨接线 jumper, jumper wire, wire jumper, crossover
跨距 stride
跨距计算 spacing computation
跨平台能力 cross-platform ability
跨区记录 spanned record
跨网访问 outgoing access
跨线 jumper
跨越记录 spanned record
跨越树 spanning tree
跨跃值 spanning value

【kuài】
会 另见(huì)
会计 ①(会计学) accounting, accountancy ②(会计人员) accountant, bookkeeper 会计师 accountant
会计报告 accounting report
会计程序 accounting routine
会计(核算)方法 accounting method/procedure
会计信息系统 accounting information system {**AIS**}
会计形式 accounting form
会计语言 accounting language
会计(制表)系统 accounting system

块 piece, lump, chunk, block
块比较指令 block compare instruction
块编辑 block editing
块编码 block coding
块变量 block variable
块标志 block mark
块长(度) block length
块处理程序 block handler {**BH**}, block processor
块传送 block movement/transfer/transmission
块存储器 block storage
块存取 block access, clock access
块大小 block size
块地址 block address
块分隔 block separation
块分隔符 block separator
块分类 block sort
块复制 block replicate
块格式 block format
块级共享 block level sharing
块加密 block encryption, blocking encryption
块间隙 block gap
块结构 block structure
块结束 end of block {**EOB**}
块结束符 block terminator
块控制 block control
块控制单元[区] block control unit {**BCU**}

块控制头部 block control header {**BCH**}
块控制字 block control word
块控制字节 block control byte {**BCB**}
块链接 block chaining
块码 block code
块名字 block name
块排序[分类] block sort, block sorting
块奇偶性 block parity
块删除 block delete
块设备 block device
块输出 block output
块输入 block input
块体 block body
块图 block graph
块尾 block end
块文件 block file
块相加 block add
块校验 block check
块移动 block move, block movement
块帧 block frame
块指针 block pointer
块状态 block state
块字符 block character

快 1)（速度高）fast, quick, rapid, swift, speedy 2)（速度）speed 3)（赶快）hurry up, make haste 4)（灵敏）quick-witted, ingenious 5)（锋利）sharp, keen 6)（爽快）straightforward, forthright 7)（愉快）pleased, happy **快报** bulletin, newsflash **快餐** fast food, quick meal, snack **快车** express train, express bus, fast train, hotshot **快递** express delivery **快递邮件** express mail **快乐** happy, joyful, cheerful, gay **快信** express letter **快要** soon, before long, be about to
快读 express read
快门 shutter
快闪存储器 flash memory
快速编码 fast coding
快速查询 quick query
快速查找 browse
快速存储器 active memory, high-speed storage, rapid storage
快速存取 rapid access
快速的 expedited, fast-speed
快速地址 fast address
快速返回 fast-back
快速分组交换 fast packet switch {**FPS**}
快速傅里叶变换 fast Fourier transform {**FFT**}
快速感光片 fast film
快速进带 fast forward
快速卡片 flash card
快速连接 fast connect
快速路由协议 fast path protocol
快速排序[分类] quick sorting, quicksort
快速启动 quick start
快速扫描 fast scan
快速适应 fast adaptation
快速算法 fast algorithm
快速图像处理 rapid picture manipulation
快速图像生成 quick rendering
快速响应[反应] quick-response
快速循环 rapid cycle
快速以太网 fast ethernet
快速转储 high-speed dump
快速转换(控制位) fast turn around {**FTA**}
快速装入 fast load

【kuān】
宽 1)("窄"的反意) wide,

broad 2)(使宽松)relax, relieve 3)(放宽期限)extend 宽大,宽敞 roomy, spacious, wide 宽度 width, breadth 宽广 broad, extensive, vast 宽宏大量 generous, lenient 宽阔 broad, wide 宽容 tolerably off, lenient 宽裕 comfortably off, well-off

宽带 width tape, broad band, wide band

宽带传输 broad(band) transmission

宽带发射 wide band emission

宽带放大器 broadband/wideband amplifier

宽带交换(机) broadband exchange {BEX}

宽带交换业务 broadband exchange services {BEXS}

宽带接入网 broadband access network

宽带局域[部]网 broadband LAN, broadband local network

宽带设备 broadband equipment, wideband equipment

宽带通道 broad channel, broadband channel

宽带网络 broadband network

宽带信道 wideband channel

宽带噪声 broadband noise

宽带综合业务数字网 broadband integrated services digital network {BISDN}

宽地址总线 wide address bus

宽度优先搜索 breadth-first search

宽高比 aspect ratio

宽频 broadband, wide band

宽位字符 wide character

宽线 thick line

宽行打印机 line printer {LP}

【kuǎn】

款 1)(招待)receive with hospitality, entertain 2)(条款)section, item 款式 pattern, style, design 款项 a sum of money, fund

【kuāng】

框 另见【kuàng】

1)(框框)frame, circle 2)(加线框)circumscribe, draw a frame round 3)(约束)place sth under control

【kuáng】

狂 1)(疯狂)mad, crazy 2)(纵情地)wild, delirious 狂暴 violent, wild 狂妄 arrogant, overbearing

【kuàng】

旷 (空旷)vast, spacious 旷工 stay away from work deliberately 旷课 play truant, skip school work

矿 (开采场所)mine 矿产 mineral products, minerals 矿藏 mineral resources, mineral reserves 矿床 ore deposit, mineral deposit 矿井 mine, pit 矿泉 mineral spring 矿泉水 mineral water 矿山 mine, mining area 矿石 ore 矿物 mineral 矿业 mining industry

框 另见【kuāng】

框 box, framework
框表 frame table
框窗口 frame window
框符 box
框号 box number

框架 cage, frame, skeleton, trellis
框架表示 frame representation
框架化 skeletonizing
框架理论 frame theory
框架模型 frame model
框架系统 frame system, framework system
框图 block diagram/ graph, diagram, schematic, schematic diagram
框图符号 block diagram symbols
框图模式 flowchart schema
框图系统 block diagram system, block system
框图语言 block diagram language

况 况且 besides, in addition, moreover

【kuī】
亏 1)(受损失) lose (money, etc.), have a deficit 2)(欠缺) short of, deficient 3)(幸亏) fortunately, luckily, thanks to 亏本 lose money in business, lose one's capital 亏待 treat unfairly 亏空 ①(欠人财物) be in debt, be in the red, cannot make both ends meet ②(所欠的财物) debt, deficit 亏损 ①(支出超过收入) loss, deficit ②(身体虚弱) general debility

窥 窥测 spy out 窥视 peep at, spy on 窥探 spy upon, pry about, snoop
窥视孔 sight hole, wicket
窥探算法 mouse algorithm
窥探终端 snooper terminal

【kuì】
匮 匮乏 short (of supplies), deficient

溃 (水冲破堤坝) burst 溃败 be defeated 溃烂 fester, ulcerate

馈 馈赠 present (a gift), make a present of sth
馈带机构 tape feed
馈电电桥 feeding dridge
馈电电缆 feeder cable
馈电路由 feeder route
馈路 feeder line
馈送 feed, feeding
馈送道 feed track
馈送孔 feed hole
馈送孔间距 feed pitch
馈送率 feed rate
馈送器 feeder
馈送状态 feed status
馈线 feeder line
馈线链路 feeder link

愧 1)(惭愧) ashamed 2)(不安) embarrassed, uneasy

【kǔn】
捆 tie, bind 捆绑 truss up, bind, tie up 捆扎 tie up, bundle up

【kùn】
困 1)(疲乏) tired, weary, fatigued 2)(围困) surround, pin down, besiege 困惑 puzzled, bewildered, at a loss 困境 difficult position, predicament, dilemma 困苦 hardship, deep distress, deep poverty 困难 ①(事情难办) difficulty ②(生活穷困) fi-

【kuò】

扩 扩充 expand, enlarge, extend 扩大 enlarge, expand, extend, widen, broaden 扩建 extend, expand 扩散 spread, diffuse 扩展 expand, spread, extend, develop

扩充(电路)板 expansion board
扩充版[编辑] extended edition
扩充部件[单元] expansion unit
扩充操作码 augmented operation code
扩充插件板 expansion card
扩充存储管理程序 expanded memory manager {EMM}
扩充的 expanded, extensional
扩充[展]的二叉树 extended binary tree
扩充的数据库 extended database {EDB}
扩充的图形字符集 extended graphic character set {EGCS}
扩充地址 extend address
扩充功能 extended function
扩充机构 extension mechanism
扩充接口 extended interface
扩充[展]节点 expanding node
扩充能力 expansion capacity
扩充器插件 extender card
扩充器电路板 extender board
扩充(存储)区 extended area
扩充区服务 extended area service {EAS}
扩充体系结构 extended architecture {XA}
扩充性 extendibility
扩充语言 extended language, extension language
扩充域 extended range
扩充字符 extended character, extension character
扩散激光 diffused laser light
扩印机 projection printer
扩展操作 extended operation
扩展处理机部件 extended processor unit {EPU}
扩展存储器管理程序 extended memory manager {XMM}
扩展的二十进制码 extended binary-coded decimal
扩展的工业标准结构 extended industry standard architecture {EISA}
扩展电路 expander
扩展电路板 expander board
扩展范围 extended range
扩展符 escape character {ESC}
扩展工业标准结构 extended industry standard architecture {EISA}
扩展合成器 extended synthesizer
扩展卡 expansion card
扩展门(电路) expanded gate
扩展名 expanded name
扩展扫描 expanded sweep
扩展属性 extended attribute

括 include 括号 brackets ◇大括号 braces // 方括号 brackets // 圆括号 curves, parentheses
括号表达式 parenthesized expression
括号对 bracket pair
括号运算 bracket operation

阔 1) (宽广) wide, broad, vast 2) (有钱) rich, wealthy

L l

【lā】

拉 1)（朝自己方向移动）pull, draw, drag, tow 2)（用车运输）transport by vehicle, haul 3)（演奏）play 拉丁美洲 Latin America 拉开 ①（打开）pull open, draw back ②（增加距离）increase the distance between, space out 拉平 bring to the same level, even up 拉手 ①（握手）shake hands ②（把手）handle

拉出 zoom out

拉杆 bar

拉格朗日插值 Lagrange interpolation

【lā】

垃 垃圾 rubbish, garbage

【lǎ】

喇 喇叭 ①（管乐）brass-wind instruments ②（扬声器）loudspeaker

【là】

蜡 wax 蜡纸（包装用）wax paper

辣 （毒辣）vicious, ruthless 辣味 hot, peppery

【lái】

来 1)（来到）come, arrive 2)（发生）occur, take place 3)（未来的）future, coming, next 4)（以来）ever since 来不及 there isn't enough time (to do sth), too late to do sth 来得及 there's still time, have enough time to do sth 来电 ①〈名〉incoming phone call/ telegram, your massage ②〈动〉send a telegram, make a call here 来回 ①（往复一次）make a round trip, make a return journey ②（往复多次）back and forth, to and fro 来历 origin, source, background 来临 arrive, come, approach 来年 the coming year, next year 来往 ①（来和去）come and go ②（交际往来）dealings, contact 来文 document received 来信 ①〈动〉send a letter here ②〈名〉letter received 来源 ①〈名〉source, origin ②〈动〉originate, stem from

铼 rhenium (Re)

【lán】

拦 拦截 intercept 拦住 hold up, keep away 拦阻 block, hold back

栏 1)（栏杆）fence, railing 2)（畜圈）pen, shed 3)（部分版

lan 蓝篮镧,览揽缆懒,烂滥 lang 廊,朗,浪 lao 捞,劳牢

面)column ◇广告栏 advertisement column
栏眉 column heading
栏数 column number
栏题头 column heading

蓝 blue 蓝本 ①(原始材料) chief source ②(底本) original version (of a literary work)
蓝宝石 sapphire
蓝宝石硅(片) silicon on sapphire {SOS}
蓝图 blueprint
蓝牙技术 bluetooth technology

篮 basket 篮球 basketball

镧 lanthanum (La)

【lǎn】

览 1)(看) look at, view ◇游览 tour 2)(阅读) read 浏览 glance over, skim through, skim over

揽 1)(用胳膊围住) take into one's arms 2)(固定) fasten with a rope, etc. 3)(拉到自己一边) take on, take upon oneself

缆 hawser, mooring rope, cable, cord ◇钢缆 steel cable

懒 懒惰 lazy, indolent

【làn】

烂 1)(松软) sodden, mashed 2)(腐烂) rot, spoil, fester, decay 3)(破烂) worn-out 烂泥 mud, slush

滥 1)(泛滥) overflow, flood 2)(无节制) excessive 滥用 abuse, misuse

【láng】

廊 porch, corridor

【lǎng】

朗 1)(光线明亮) bright 2)(声音响亮) loud and clear 朗诵 recite

【làng】

浪 1)(波浪) wave 2)(放纵) unrestrained 3)(英国长度单位) furlong 浪潮 tide, wave 浪费 waste, squander, be extravagant

【lāo】

捞 1)(打捞) drag for, dredge up 2)(攫取) get by improper means

【láo】

劳 (功劳) meritorious deed, service 劳保 ①(劳动保险) labour insurance ②(劳动保护) labour protection 劳动 work, labor 劳动力 ①(人力) labor (force) ②(劳动能力) capacity for physical labor ③(有劳动能力的人) able-bodied person 劳苦 fatigue, toil 劳驾 ①(要求让路等) Excuse me. ②(要求别人做事) May I trouble you? 劳累 tired, overworked 劳模 model worker 劳务 labor services 劳资 labor and capital

牢 (监狱) jail, prison 牢固 firm, secure 牢记 keep firmly in mind, remember well

牢靠 ① (稳固) firm, strong, sturdy ② (可靠) dependable, reliable

铹 lawrencium (Lw)

【lǎo】

老 1) (年龄大) old, aged 2) (历史久) of long standing, old 3) (陈旧) outdated 老百姓 ordinary people, civilians 老板 boss, shopowner 老化 ageing 老练 veteran, experienced 老年 old age 老人 the old, the aged 老师 teacher 老实 ① (诚实) honest, frank ② (规矩) well-behaved, good 老手 old hand, veteran

老化缺陷[污点] aging blemish

铑 rhodium (Rh)

【lè】

乐 另见【yuè】
(快乐) happy, cheerful, joyful 乐观 optimistic 乐趣 delight, pleasure, joy 乐意 ① be willing to, be ready to ② pleased, happy 乐于 be glad to, enjoy doing sth

乐观方法 optimistic methods
乐观估计 optimistic estimate
乐观主义 optimism

勒 勒索 extort, blackmail

【léi】

累 另见【lěi】【lèi】
累赘 ① (多余) burdensome, cumbersome ② (多话) wordy ② (麻烦事) burden, nuisance

雷 (爆炸武器) mine ◇地雷 land mine 雷电 thunder and lightning 雷声 thunder 雷同 be identical 雷雨 thunderstorm

雷达 radar (= radio detection and ranging)
雷达捕捉 radar contact
雷达目标 obstacle
雷达探测 radar detection
雷达通信 radar communication
雷达图像 radar image
雷达陷阱 radar trap
雷达信号检测 radar signal detection
雷达中继站 radar link

镭 radium (Ra)

【lěi】

累 另见【léi】【lèi】
累及 implicate, involve, drag in 累计 ① <动> add up ② <名> accumulative total

累积估计 accumulative estimation
累积量 cumulant
累积频率 cumulative frequency
累计误差 accumulated error
累加 accumulate {ACC}, accumulation, summation, totalizing
累加存储器 sigma memory, sigma storage
累加和 accumulated sum
累加寄存器 accumulation/accumulator register
累加计数器 summary counter
累加器操作 accumulator operation
累加器地址 accumulator address
累加数组 summing array
累加态 accumulation mode

累加原理 accumulation principle

【lèi】

类 1)(种类) kind, type, class, category 2)(像) resemble, be similar to 类似 similar, analogous, like 类推 analogize, reason by analogy 类型 type, style (分)类包装 class wrapping
类比法 synectics
类比模型 analog model
类比驱动 analogy-driven
类比推理 analog reasoning, analogical inference, analogical reasoning
类比学习 analogical learning, learning by analogy
类变量 class variable
类别 category, class, grade, subsumption
类别代数 sorted algebra
类别名 class name
类别锁 class lock
类别条件 class condition
类操作 class operation
类程序包 generic package
类对象 class object
类函数 generic function
类库 class library
类属程序 generic routine
类属单位 generic unit
类属关系 generic relation
类属键 generic key
类描述符 categorical descriptor
类属性 class attributes, generic attribute
类似的 like, similar
类似模型 analog model
类图 class diagram
类型安全 type-safe
类型表 type list
类型参数 type parameter
类型等价 type equivalence
类型对象 type object
类型概念 type concept
类型过程 type procedure
类型兼容 type compatibility
类型结合 type association
类型论 type theory
类型属性 type attribute
类型说明 type specification, type specifier
类型相容性 type consistency
类型字段 type field
类性 genericity
类演算 class calculus
类要求 generic request
类指数 class index
类中断 class interrupt
类转换 class transition

累 另见【léi】【lěi】

1)(疲劳) tired, fatigued, weary 2)(使疲劳) tire, strain, wear out 3)(操劳) work hard, toil

【léng】

棱 1)(两个平面连接部分) arris, edge 2)(条状凸起部分) corrugation, ridge
棱镜 prism
棱形 lozenge

【lěng】

冷 cold 冷藏 keep in refrigeration, cold storage 冷淡 ①(不热情)cold, indifferent ②(接待不热情)treat coldly 冷冻 freezing 冷静 sober, calm, quiet 冷门 ①(职业等)a neglected profession or branch of learning ②(意外成功者)an unexpected winner, dark horse 冷僻

(偏僻) deserted, out of the way ②(不常见的) rare, unfamiliar **冷气** air conditioning **冷却** cooling
冷(却)板 cold plate
冷错误 cold fault
冷启动 cold start, cool start
冷引导 cold boot, cold bootstrap
冷自举 cold bootstrap

【lí】

厘 厘米 centimeter

离 1)(分离) leave, be parted from, be away from 2)(相距) off, away, from 3)(缺少) without, independent of **离别** part, farewell **离不开** ①(少不了) cannot do without ②(走不开) too busy to get away **离开** leave, depart from **离奇** odd, fantastic, queer **离题** digress from, stray from
离合器 clutch
离散变量 discrete variable
离散表示法 discrete representation
离散单元 discrete unit
离散地址 discrete address
离散对数 discrete logarithm
离散多音技术 discrete multitone technology
离散分布 discrete distribution
离散(型)傅里叶变换 discrete Fourier transform {DFT}
离散(型)规划 discrete programming
离散函数 discrete function
离散结构 discrete topology
离散卷积 discrete convolution
离散控制 discrete control
离散类型 discrete type
离散逻辑 discrete logic
离散模拟 discrete analog
离散模拟[仿真] discrete simulation
离散模型 discrete model
离散时间 discrete-time
离散事件 discrete event
离散数据 discrete data
离散数学 discrete mathematics
离散搜索 discrete search
离散拓扑 discrete topology
离散外形 discrete profile
离散问题 discrete problem
离散系统 discontinuous/discrete system
离散信号 discrete signal
离散信息 discrete message
离散信(息)源 discrete information source, discrete source
离散型问题 discrete-variable problem
离散形状 discrete shape
离散序列 discrete series
离散样元 discrete sample
离散音频 discrete tone
离散余弦变换 discrete cosine transform {DCT}
离散状态 discrete state
离线 off-line (=off line, offline), out-of-line
离线操作 off-line operation
离线处理 off-line process
离线系统 off-line system
离心 eccentric
离子注入 ion implantation

黎 黎明 dawn, daybreak

【lǐ】

礼 (仪式) ceremony, service **礼节** courtesy, etiquette, protocol, ceremony **礼品,礼物** gift, present **礼堂** assem-

里

1)（里边的）inner 2)（衣服衬里）lining, inside 3)（长度单位）li (=0.5 km) 4)（在里面）in, inside **里程碑** milestone, landmark **里面** inside, interior

理

1)（纹理）texture, grain 2)（道理）reason, logic, truth 3)（办理）manage, run 4)（整理）put in order **理睬** pay attention to **理解** understand, comprehend **理解力** faculty of understanding, comprehension **理科** (natural) science **理论** theory **理事** member of a council, director **理所当然** of course, naturally **理想** ideal **理由** reason, ground, argument **理智** reason, senses, judgment

理解力 comprehension, perception
理解器 understander
理想边界 ideal boundary
理想的系统 ideal system
理想点 ideal point
理想化模式 idealized pattern
理想化形式 idealized form
理想(计算)机 ideal machine
理想滤波器 ideal filter
理想码 ideal code
理想(化)值 idealized value
理想值 ideal value

锂

lithium (Li)

【lì】

力

1)（努力）effort, endeavour 2)（作用力）force **力量** ①（力气）physical strength ②（能力）power, force, strength **力气** physical strength **力求** make every effort to, do one's best to, strive to **力图** try hard to, strive to **力争** ①（极力争取）work hard for, do all one can to ②（极力争辩）argue strongly

力传感器 force sensor
力反馈 force feedback

立

1)（站）stand 2)（竖立）erect, set up 3)（直立的）upright, erect, vertical 4)（建立）found, establish, set up **立场** position, stand, attitude **立方** cube **立方米** cubic meter **立即、立刻** immediately, at once, promptly **立交桥** ① overpass, flyover ② motorway interchange **立体** three-dimensional, stereoscopic **立足** ①（站住脚）get a foothold ②（处于某立场）base oneself upon **立足点** ①（立脚点）foothold, footing ②（立场）standpoint, position

立方(体) cube
立方的 cubic
立方卷积 cubic convolution
立方体表示法 cubic notation
立方体管理器 cube manager
立方体网络 cube network
立即操作 immediate operation
立即操作数 immediate operand
立即存储 store immediate
立即存取[访问] instantaneous access, zero access, immediate access
立即打印 immediate printing
立即[直接]地址 immediate address
立即调度 no-wait schedule

立即加 immediate add
立即码 instantaneous code
立即命令 immediate command
立即任务 immediate task
立即数据 immediate data
立即跳转 instant jump
立即停机 hard stop
立即寻址方式 immediate addressing mode
立式箱体 vertical cabinet
立视 stereoview
立体存储器 three-dimensional storage
立体结构 three-dimensional structure
立体可视化 volume visualization
立体声的 stereophonic
立体视觉 stereo vision
立体图 spacegraph
立体系统 three dimension system
立体显示 stereo display
立体效应 stereoscopic effect
立体眼镜 polarized filter
立体影像 stereopsis
立体映射 stereomapping
立体照相 stereogram

历 (经历)go through, undergo, experience 历程 course 历次 all previous 历代 successive dynasties, past dynastics 历法 calendar ◇阳历 solar calendar ‖ 阴历 lunar calendar 历届 all previous 历来 always, consistently 历年 over the years 历时 last, take 历史 history, past records
历史版本 historical version
历史存储器 history memory
历史的类推 historical analogy
历史规则 historical rule
历史日志[运行记录] history log
历史数据 historical data, history data
历史数据库 historical database
历史数据装置 historical data device
历史文件 history file

厉 1)(严格)strict, rigorous 2)(严肃) stern, severe 厉害 ①(严厉的)severe, sharp, fierce ②(极度的)terrible 厉行 strictly enforce

励 encourage, urge

利 1)(锋利)sharp 2)(顺利) favorable 利弊 advantages and disadvantages, pros and cons 利器 ①(锐利武器)sharp weapon ②(有效的工具) useful tool, effective instrument 利润,利息 profit, interest 利息 interest 利益 advantage, interest, benefit, profit 利用 ①(使发挥作用) use, utilize, make use of ②(使为自己服务) take advantage of
利(息)率 interest rate

例 1)(例子)example, instance 2)(先例) precedent 3)(事例)case, instance 例会 regular meeting 例句 illustrative sentence, example sentence 例如 for instance, for example (e.g.), such as 例外 exception 例证 illustration, example, case in point
例程 routine
例程选择 routine select
例示 instantiation, oracle
例示变量 instance variable

例外条件 exceptional condition
例行程序 routine
例行程序包 routine package
例行程序名 routine name
例行试验 routine test
例行维护 routine/ scheduled maintenance
例行子程序 subroutine {SUB}
例因 instance

隶

隶属 be subordinate to, be under the jurisdiction of, be directly under

莅

莅临 arrive, be present ◇敬请莅临指导 Your presence and guidance are requested

粒

(颗粒) grain, granule, pellet 粒状 granular

【lián】

连 1)(包括在内) include 2)(甚至) even 连队 company 连贯 ①(连接贯通) link up, piece together ②(前后一致) coherent, consistent 连接 link, join, connect, bind, conjunct 连年 in successive years, for years running, for years on end 连任 be reappointed or reelected, renew one's term of office 连日 for days on end, day after day 连同 together with, along with 连续 continuous, successive, running, in succession 连载 publish in instalments, serialize 连字符 hyphen
连带的 associated
连贯性校验 continuity check
连环 interlink
连环图式 comic mode
连接(词) conjunction
连接(法) connection
连接按钮 link button
连接标识符 connection identifier {CID, connection ID}
连接表 chained list, linked list
连接部件[设备] link
连接操作 attended operation, chain operation
连接测试 join test
连接程序 join program, linker
连接词 connective
连接存储[装入] link load
连接单元 attaching unit
连接单元接口 attachment unit interface {AUI}
连接的单元 connected unit
连接地址 link address, chained address
连接点 joint point
连接点管理(程序) connection point manager {CPM}
连接电路[设备] interface
连接定义 link definition
连接段 link segment, linkage section
连接方式 attended mode, join system
连接访问 connected reference
连接分类 link sort
连接符 connector, connector symbol
连接故障 linkage fault
连接号 connection number
连接汇编 join assembly
连接建立 connection establishment
连接阶段 connect phase
连接[邻接]矩阵 adjacency matrix
连接控制块 thread control block {TCB}
连接库 link library

连接框 connect box
连接类 join class
连接路径 conjunctive path
连接名 link name, linkage name
连接命令 bind command
连接能力 connection capability
连接排序 link sorting
连接器 connection box, connector, junctor, hub
连接器件 interface unit
连接器接口 attachment unit interface {AUI}
连接器区 connector area
连接请求消息段 connection request segment
连接时间 link time, logged on time, connect time
连接(方)式 interconnection mode
连接式 interconnection system
连接释放 connection release
连接图 connected graph, join graph, link map
连接位 link bit
连接位置 connection location
连接文件 linked file, threaded file
连接系统 join system
连接陷阱 connection trap
连接线(路) tie line
连接相关[依赖] join dependency, joint dependency
连接项目 continuous item
连接信息 link information
连接型业务 connection service
连接学习 connectionist learning
连接溢出 link overflow
连接映像 bind image
连接映像表 bind image table
连接域 link field
连接原语 link primitive
连接约定 linkage convention
连接允许控制 connection admission control {CAC}
连接运算 concatenation operation
连接指令 bridging order, link, link order, linkage instruction, order
连接指示ం link indicator
连接指示字 link pointer
连接指针 link pointer
连接中断 linkage interrupt
连接中继线 tie trunk
连接装配(存储)区 link pack area {LPA}
连接子系统 connectivity subsystem {CSS}
连接字 connective word, link word
连接字段 join field, link field
连接组 link group
连结板 web
连路程序库 linker library
连体字 ligature
连通超图 connected hypergraph
连通的 connected
连通的有向图 connected directed graph
连通分量[分支] connected component
连通集 connected set
连通件 connectedness
连通图 connected graph
连通性 connectedness, connectivity
连通性对[偶] connectivity pair
连网 networking
连网设备 attaching device
连线表 net list, wire list
连续 contiguous, continuation, continuous
连续操作 consecutive operation, continuous function
连续处理 continuous processing

连续打印纸 continuous forms, continuous stationery
连续对策 continuous game
连续分布 continuous distribution
连续格式纸堆积箱 continuous forms stacker {CFS}
连续功能 continuous function
连续函数 continuous function
连续记录 continuous record
连续栏 continue column
连续路径 continuous path
连续色调 continuous tone
连续时钟 continuous clock
连续算子 continuous operator
连续图像表征 continuous image characterization
连续文件 contiguous file
连续行 consecutive line
连续性 continuity
连续性邮件 continuous mail
连续印刷 web
连续映射 continuous mapping
连续纸 continuous-form paper
连字 double letter
连字符 hyphen {HYP}

联 ally, unite, join, associate 联邦 federation, union, commonwealth 联合 ①〈动〉unite, ally ②〈名〉alliance, union ③〈形〉joint, combined, united 联合国 the United Nations (U.N.) 联合国大会 the United Nations General Assembly 联合会 federation, union 联结 bind, tie, join 联络 contact, get in touch with 联盟 alliance, league, union, coalition 联系 ①〈名〉contact, touch, connection ②〈动〉integrate, relate, link, get in touch with 联想 associate, association, connect in the mind 联营 joint operation

联邦式数据库系统 federated database system {FDBS}
联邦信息处理标准 federal information processing standard {FIPS}
联编规则 binding rule
联编程序 binder, binder program
联编实用程序 binder utility
联调 gang tuning
联动 ganging, linkage
联动开关 gang switch
联动控制 ganged control
联分类 cascade sort
联合安装 cooperative installation
联合标志 union tag
联合查询 conjunctive query
联合分布 joint distribution
联合分析 coalition analysis
联合规划法 unified program planning {UPP}
联合类型 union type
联合模式[图样] union pattern
联合目录 union, union catalog
联机 in-line
联机(设备) on-line (=on line, online)
联机备份[后缀] on-line backup
联机编码 in-line coding
联机操作 on-line operation
联机测试 on-line testing
联机测试系统 on-line test system {OLTS}
联机程序设计 on-line programming
联机处理 on-line processing
联机存取 on-line access
联机调试 debug on-line, debugging on-line, on-line debug

联机调试技术 on-line debugging technique {ODT}
联机对话 dialog on-line, on-line dialog
联机方式 on-line mode
联机仿真 in-circuit emulation
联机仿真程序 on-line simulator
联机分时系统 on-line time-shared system
联机分析处理 on-line analytical processing {OLAP}
联机服务 on-line service
联机复制 on-line backup
联机跟踪 on-line tracking
联机过程 in-line procedure
联机恢复 in-line recovery
联机检错 debug on-line
联机控制 on-line control
联机媒体 on-line media
联机命令 on-line order
联机求助 on-line help
联机设备 on-line unit
联机实时操作 on-line real-time operation {OLRT}
联机事务处理 on-line transaction processing {OLTP}
联机数据处理 in-line data process, on-line data processing
联机数据库 on-line database
联机算法 on-line algorithm
联机系统 on-line system, in-line system
联机信息 on-line information
联机询问 on-line query
联机应用 on-line application
联机用户 on-line user
联机杂志[刊物] on-line journal
联机诊断 on-line diagnostics
联机指示灯 on-line light
联机终端(装置) on-line terminal
联机状态 online state
联机作业 on-line job
联结点 connect node

联盟结构 coalition structure
联锁(设备) interlock
联锁操作 interlocked operation
联锁通信 interlocked communication
联锁系统 interlock system
联锁信号 interlocking signal
联锁中断 interlock interrupt
联系 associate, bind, relationship
联系集 relationship set
联系类 associate class
联想存储器[记忆] associative memory, content-addressable memory {CAM}
联想式汉字输入法 associated Chinese character input
联想输入 associating inputing
联想思维 associative thinking
联想网络 associative network

廉 (便宜) low-priced, inexpensive, cheap 廉价 low-priced, cheap ◇廉价出售 sell at a low price, sell cheap 廉洁 honest and clean
廉价(独立)磁盘冗余阵列 redundant array of independent or inexpensive disks {RAID}

【liǎn】
脸 face

【liàn】
练 练习 ①〈动〉practice, train, drill ②〈名〉exercise, drill

炼 1)(熔炼,精炼) smelt, refine 2)(锤炼) temper with fire

链 chain, link, catena
链编码 chain encoding

链表 chained list, link(ed) list
链表结构 list structure
链查询 chain query
链错误 chain error
链接 chain, (inter)link, link(age)
链接表 chained list, linked list
链接操作 chain operation
链接存储 chaining
链接地址 chained address
链接队列 linked queue
链接对象 linked object
链接方式 on-link mode {OLM}
链接关键字 concatenated key
链接特征 chain feature
链接位 link bit
链接文件 chained file, threaded file
链接指示器 link indicator
链结束(符) end of chain {EOC}
链开始 start-of-chain
链路 link
链路报头 link header
链路报尾 link trailer
链路编辑 link edit
链路变量 link variable
链路标题 link header
链路测试 link test
链路层 link layer
链路存取[访问]协议 link access protocol {LAP}
链路调度程序 link scheduler
链路服务接入点 link service access point {LSAP}
链路级 link level
链路加密 link encryption
链路接入进程 link access procedure {LAP}
链路控制 link control
链路失效 link failure
链路头 link header
链路尾 link trailer
链路项 link entry, link item
链路协议 link discipline, link protocol
链路协议转换器 link protocol converter {LPC}
链路一致性测试 link integrity verification tests {LIVT}
链路站 link station
链路支持层 link support layer {LSL}
链路装配区 link pack area {LPA}
链路状态 link status {LS}
链轮送载 sprocket feed
链轮 sprocket
链群 chain group
链式表 chained list
链式传送 chain delivery
链式打印机 chain printer
链式地址 chain address
链式调度 chain scheduling
链式队列 linked queue
链式法则 chain rule
链式记录 chained record
链式进位 chain carry
链式码 chain code
链式命令 chain command
链式输出 chaining output
链式输送[送能]机构 chain delivery mechanism
链式数据 chain data
链式索引 chain indexing
链式通道输出 chain-out
链式通道输入 chain-in
链式文件 chained file
链式栈 linked stack
链式字节 chain byte
链式作业 chain job
链首 first-in-chain {FIC}, first-of-chain
链索引 chain index
链头 begin chain, beginning-of-chain
链尾 last-of-chain
链形网(络) recurrent net(work)
链中第一单元 first-in-chain

liáng 良梁量粮 liǎng 两 liàng 亮量

{FIC}
链(锁)中断 chain break
链中间单元 middle-in-chain {MIC}, middle-of-chain

【liáng】

良 good, fine　良机 good opportunity
良好性能 superperformance
良好状态的 well-conditioned
良性病毒 benign viruses
良性的 well-behaved
良性网络 well-behaved net
良序 well order, well-ordering

梁 1)(房梁)(roof) beam, girder 2)(桥梁) bridge 3)(山梁) mountain ridge

量 另见【liàng】
1)(测量) measure 2)(称量) weigh

粮 粮食 grain, cereals, food

【liǎng】

两 1)(二) two 2)(双方) both (sides), either (side) 3)(不定数目) a few, some ◇过两天 in a few days 4)(重量单位) liang (=50 grams)　两倍 twofold, double, twice as much　两边 ①(两个边) both sides ②(两处) both places ③(两个方向) both directions ④(双方) both parties, both sides　两次 twice　两极 ①(地球的两极) the two poles of the earth ②〈物理〉(阴阳极) the two poles, anode and cathode　两可 either will do, either will do　两利 be good for both sides, benefit both　两面 ①(正反面) two sides, both sides, two aspects, both aspects ②(双重的) having a dual character, dual, double　两讫 the goods are delivered and the bill is paid　两全 be satisfactory to both parties　两样 not the same
两项计算 double-calculation
两道带 two-track tape
两分 dichotomy
两分插入法 binary insertion
两分法 dichotomy
两两独立 pairwise independence
两两正交 pairwise orthogonal
两面复印 double-sided copying
两维图 two-dimensional graphics
两位长字节 doublet
两用电键 combined key
两掷开关 two-throw switch
两字节指令 two-byte instruction

【liàng】

亮 1)(明亮) bright, light 2)(响亮) loud and clear 3)(开朗) enlightened 4)(发光) shine
亮点 luminous point
亮点大小 spot size
亮度 brightness, luminance, luminosity
亮度比 brightness ratio
亮度对比 luminance contrast
亮度分辨率 intensity resolution
亮度衰减 luminance decay
亮度信号 luminance signal
亮视觉 photopic vision
亮线 brilliant line

量 另见【liáng】
1)(容纳限度) capacity 2)(数量) quantity, amount, vol-

liàng 谅 liáo 聊寥僚缭 liǎo 了钌潦 liào 料 liè 列

ume 3)(估计，衡量)estimate, measure 量力 estimate one's strength or ability (and act accordingly)
量程 quantum, quanta
量程钟 quantum clock
量词 quantifier
量度 measurement
量纲 dimension
量规 gauge
量化 quantify, quantize
量化符号 quantification symbol, quantized symbol
量化命题 quantified statement
量化效应 quantization effect
量化信号 quantized signal
量化噪声 quantization noise
量子 quantum, quanta

谅 1)(原谅)forgive, excuse, pardon 2)(料想)I think, I suppose, I expect 谅必 most likely, probably 谅解 understanding

【liáo】

聊 1)(姑且)merely, just 聊表谢意 just a token of gratitude, just to show my appreciation 2)(略微)a little, slightly 3)(闲谈)chat
聊天室 chat

寥 1)(稀少)few 2)(静寂)silent, deserted

僚 official ◇官僚 bureaucrat 僚属 subordinates, staff

缭 缭乱 confused, in turmoil

【liǎo】

了 1)(明白)know clearly, understand 2)(完毕)end, finish, settle 3)(在动词后表示有可能)can ◇办得了 can manage it 了不起 amazing, extraordinary 了结 finish, settle, bring to an end 了解 ①(知道)understand, comprehend ②(打听)find out, learn

钌 ruthenium (Ru)

潦 潦草 ①(不工整)careless, illegible ②(不仔细)sloppy

【liào】

料 1)(预料)expect, anticipate 2)(原料)material, stuff 料理 arrange, handle, attend to, take care of 料想 expect, presume, estimate

【liè】

列 1)(排列)arrange, line up 2)(行列)row, rank, line 列车 train 列举 enumerate, list 列入 list, enter in a list 列席 attend as a nonvoting delegate, attend without voting right
列 column, train
列表 list, list up, tabulation
列表编目 listing
列表标题 table header
列表程序 list procedure, lister
列表的 tabular
列表法 tabulation method
列表机构 tabulator
列表结束 end of list {EOL}
列表框 list box
列表设置键 tabulator set key
列表数据 table data
列表顺序 tab sequential
列表优先级 list priority

列表元(素) list element
列长 column inch
列地址 column address
列访问 column access
列分割 column split
列格式 column format
列函数 column function
列计数 column count
列间距 column pitch
列矩阵 column matrix
列举法 enumeration method
列驱动线 column drive wire
列扫描 column scan
列扫描算法 column sweep algorithm
列式表征 aligned attribute
列式打印机 train printer, train type printer
列数 column number
列线图 nomogram, nomograph
列线图学 nomography
列向量 column vector
列选 column selection
列选通门 column gate
列译码 column decoding

劣 bad, inferior, of low quality 劣等 of inferior quality, low-grade, poor 劣势 disadvantageous position, unfavourable situation

烈 1)(强烈)strong, violent, intense 2)(暴烈)fiery 烈度 intensity 烈性 ①(性情刚烈)high-spirited ②(性质猛烈)strong, violent, destructive

猎 hunt 猎奇 hunt for novelty, seek novelty

裂 split, crack, break 裂缝 rift, crevice, crack, break 裂痕 rift, crack, fissure 裂开 split open 裂口 breach, gap, split 裂隙 crack, crevice, fracture 裂区 split plot 裂纹 crack

【lín】

邻 邻近 near, close to, adjacent to 邻近的 neighboring, near, adjacent 邻居 neighbor
邻层 adjacent layer
邻接 adjacency, contiguous
邻接表 adjacency list
邻接磁盘 contiguous disk
邻接的 contiguous
邻接顶点 adjacent vertex
邻接法 adjacent method
邻接关系 adjacency relation
邻接节点 adjacent node
邻接矩阵 adjacent matrix
邻接性 adjacency
邻接[相邻]字符 adjacent character
邻近 adjacency, proximity
邻近间距 adjacency
邻近控制点 adjacent control point
邻近区域 adjacent domain, proximity zone
邻域 neighborhood

林 (树林) forest, woods, grove 林产品 forest products 林场 forestry center, tree farm, forest farm 林带 forest belt 林立 stand in great numbers 林业 forestry
林氏交互语言 Lindenmayer language with interaction {**IL language**}

lín

临 1)(靠近) face, overlook 2)(来到) arrive, be present 3)(将要) on the point of, just before, be about to 临别 at parting, just before parting 临近 close to, close on 临时 ①(事到临头) at the time when sth happens ②(暂时的) temporary, provisional, for a short time 临时工 temporary worker

临界 crash
临界操作 critical operation
临界尺寸 critical dimension
临界错误 critical error
临界的 critical, marginal
临界点 crash/critical point
临界电流 critical current
临界负载 critical load
临界角 critical angle
临界竞争 critical race
临界区(域) critical area, critical region
临界熔化[停闪]频率 critical fusion frequency {CFF}
临界时间 crash time
临界条件 critical condition
临界通路测试 critical path test
临界图 critical graph
临界温度 critical temperature
临界线 critical line
临界值 critical value, marginal value
临界状态 critical state
临时报告 interim report
临时程序 transient program
临时窗口 secondary window
临时存储器 temporary memory
临时存储区 scratchpad area {SPA}
临时单元 temporary location
临时的 provisional, tentative, transitory
临时[暂用]电缆 patch cable
临时电路 patch
临时对象 temporary objects
临时工作空间 temporary working space
临时缓冲区 temporary buffer
临时交换机间信令协议 interin interswitch signaling protocol {IISP}
临时局部管理接口 interin local management interface {ILMI}
临时库 temporary library
临时名字 temporary name
临时盘 temporary disk {T-disk}
临时区 temporary area
临时数据集 temporary data set
临时[暂时]文本延迟符 temporary text delay {TTD}
临时文件 temporary file
临时用户 casual user

磷 phosphorus (P)

[lìn]

吝 吝啬 stingy, miserly, mean 吝惜 grudge, stint

赁 (租赁) rent, hire

[líng]

灵 灵感 inspiration 灵活 quick, clever, sharp 灵魂 spirit, soul, mind 灵敏 sensitive, keen, agile, acute 灵巧 skil(l)ful, ingenious 灵验 efficacious, effective

灵活存储 elastic store
灵活单元 flexible cell
灵活的控制台 smart console
灵活的终端设备 smart terminal
灵活设备 smart
灵敏传感器 smart sensor
灵敏度控制 conference control, sensitivity control
灵敏度自动控制 automatic

sensitivity control {ASC}
灵巧电缆 smart cable
灵巧卡 smart card
灵巧[智能]连接 smart linkage
灵巧外设 smart peripheral
灵巧终端(设备) smart terminal

铃 bell

龄 1)(岁数)age, years 2)(年限)length or time, duration ◇工龄 number of years of service

凌 1)(欺侮)insult 2)(逼近)approach 3)(升高)rise high, tower aloft 凌晨 in the small hours, before dawn 凌空 be high up in the air, soar or tower aloft 凌乱 in disorder, in a mess

零 零件 parts 零卖 ①(零售)retail, sell retail ②(零散地卖)sell by the piece or in small quantities 零钱 ①(币值小的钱)small change, coin ②(零用钱)pocket money 零售 retail, sell retail 零碎 ①(琐碎的)scrappy, fragmentary, piecemeal ②(琐碎事物)odds and ends, bits and pieces 零头 ①(零头数)odd ②(用剩部分)remnant
零 cypher, nil, null {NUL}, zero
零变换 null transformation
零变元 zero argument
零标号 zero label
零标记[志] zero flag
零标记符号 zero-marker
零标偏移 zero-scale offset
零博弈 zero game
零参考点 zero reference point

零除 zero divide
零道 zero track
零地址 zero address
零地址指令 zero-address instruction
零点 zero point
零点漂移 zero drift, zero wander
零点误差 zero point error
零电平 zero level
零电压 zero voltage
零调节 zero adjust
零调制 zero modulation {ZM}
零故障 zero-fault
零集 null set
零级地址 real-time address, zero-level address
零检查 zero check
零交叉点 zero cross point
零进程 null process
零校正 null correction
零阶保持 zero-order hold
零矩阵 null matrix, zero matrix
零空间 null space
零框架 zero frame
零码位 zero bit (= z, z-bit)
"零"门 null gate
零屏蔽 zero mask
零售商网 dealer net
零售通信 retail communication
零售终端系统 retail terminal system
零输出 zero output
零输出信号 zero output signal
零算符 zero operator
零图 null graph
零位 zero bit (= z, z-bit)
零位调整 zero adjustment, zeroing
零位读出器 zero reader
零位复位 zero reset
零位函数 zero-place function
零位检测 zero bit detection

零位频率 zero frequency
零位谓词 zero-place predicate
零位移 zero shift
零位(校)正 zero correction
零文件 zero file
零误差 zero error
零下的 subzero
零向量 null vector, zero vector
零形式 zero form
零行 top row
零序 null sequence, zero sequence
零循环 null recurrent
零压缩 zero compression
零页 page zero, zero page
零页定址[寻址] zero page addressing
零页方式 zero page mode
零抑制 null suppression
零元 null element
零指示器 zero indicator, null indicator
零指针 nil pointer
零中心 zero center
零转移 zero branch
零状态 nought state, null state, zero condition, zero state
零状态标志 zero status flag
零状态位 zero status bit
零字符 null character {NUL}

【lǐng】

令 另见【lìng】
ream (1 令 = 500 张纸)

领 1)(颈)neck 2)(衣领)collar 3)(要点)outline, main point 4)(带引)lead, usher, show around 领班 foreman 领带 tie, necktie 领导 ①〈动〉lead, exercise leadership ②〈名〉leadership, leader 领队 ①〈名〉lead a group ②〈动〉the leader of a group, sports team, etc. 领海 territorial waters, territorial sea 领航 navigate, pilot 领航员 navigator, pilot 领会 understand, comprehend, grasp 领空 territorial sky, territorial air space 领先 lead the way 领略 have a taste of, realize 领取 receive, draw 领事 consul 领事馆 consulate 领土 territory, domain, realm ②(范围)field, sphere, realm, area, domain
领域控制器 domain controller
领域名 domain name
领域名服务器 domain name server {DNS}
领域名系统 domain name system {DNS}
领域模型 domain model
领域搜索 domain search
领域知识 domain knowledge
领域专家 domain expert

【lìng】

另 other, another 另外 in addition, moreover, besides 另行安排 be arranged separately, make separate arrangement 另行通知 be notified later, till further notice 另议 be discussed separately

令 另见【lǐng】
1)(命令)command, order, decree, instruction 2)(使)make, cause 3)(时节)season
令牌 token
令牌[标记]环 token ring
令牌传递 token passing

令牌传送网 token passing network
令牌存取控制 token access control
令牌环 token ring
令牌环接口耦合器 token-ring interface coupler {TIC}
令牌(环)网 token ring (network)
令牌网络 token network
令牌协议 token protocol
令牌总线(网) token bus

【liū】

溜 1)(往下滑)slide, glide 2)(光滑)smooth 溜走 leave stealthily, slip away

【liú】

浏 浏览 glance over, skim through, browse
浏览器 browser, web browser web
浏览算法 viewing algorithm
浏览显示 browse display

流 1)(液体流动)flow, run 2)(移动不定)moving from place to place, drifting, wandering 3)(逐渐变坏)change for the worse, degenerate 4)(水流)stream of water 5)(等级)class, rate, grade 流产 ① (指胎儿) abortion ②(半途而废)miscarry, fall through 流畅 easy and smooth 流传 spread 流动 ①(流体移动)flow, drift ②(经常变换位置)going from place to place, on the move, mobile 流利 fluent, smooth 流派 school ◇学术流派 schools of thought 流失 run off, be washed away 流逝 pass, elapse, slip away 流通 circulate 流星 meteor, shooting star 流行 prevailing, popular, fashionable 流血 bleed, shed blood 流域 valley, river basin, drainage area 流于形式 be reduced to a mere formality
流, flow, stream
流编码 stream encryption
流部件 stream unit
流程 flow
流程表 flow table
流程分析 flow analysis
流程跟踪 flow trace
流程控制 flow control
流程模型 procedural model
流程判定 flow decision
流程算法 flow algorithm
流程图表示 flowcharting
流程图部件 flowchart package
流程图符号 flowchart symbol
流程图规则 flowchart convention
流程图模式 flowchart schema
流程图说明文件 flowchart text
流程序 string routine
流出 outflow, snap out
流出指令 escape instruction
流传输 stream transmission
流存取 stream access
流标签域 flow label field
流动路线 glide path
流动网络 flow network
流动系统 mobile system
流动信息 flowing information
流动性 mobility
流方式 stream mode
流控制单位 flit (=flow-control units)
流量 flow
流量控制 flow control
流(密)码 stream cipher

流式播放协议 streaming protocol
流式处理 stream processing
流式磁带 streaming tape
流式磁带机 streamer
流式文件 stream-oriented file
流水传送 piping
流水生产线 flow process line
流水式车间 flow shop
流水线 pipeline
流水线操作 pipelining, streamline operation
流水线处理 pipeline processing, pipelining processing
流水线处理机 pipeline processor
流水线单元 pipeline element {PLE}
流水线调度 pipeline schedule
流水线段 pipelining segment
流水线寄存器 pipeline register
流水线计算机 pipeline computer
流水线间隔时间 pipeline interval
流水线结构 pipeline architecture/organization
流水线控制 pipeline control
流水线链接 pipeline chaining
流水线图 pipeline graph
流水线系统 pipeline system, pipelined system
流水线效率 pipeline efficiency
流水线硬件 pipeline hardware
流水线周期 pipeline cycle
流水选择 pipeline option
流说明 flow specification
流体(性)的 fluidic
流体网络 fluid network
流体学 fluidics
流(程)图 chart, diagram, flow diagram/ graph, flow process chart/ diagram, flowchart, flowsheet, process chart

硫 sulphur (S) 硫酸 sulfuric acid

留 1)(不离去) stay, remain 2)(使留) ask sb to stay 3)(保留) reserve, keep, save 4)(收下) accept, 留存 ①(保存) preserve, keep ②(存放) remain, be extant 留任 retain a post, remain in office 留神 be careful, take care, mind 留心, 留意 be careful, look out, take care 留学 study abroad ◇归国留学生 returned student 留言 leave one's comments, leave a message 留意 be careful, look out, keep one's eyes open 留用 continue to employ, keep on
留空 run around
留守 left-in
留言电话 leave word call

【liù】
六 six 六月 June

【lóng】
龙 dragon 龙卷风 tornado 龙头 ①(旋塞) faucet, tap, valve, cock (tap) ②(自行车把) handlebar

聋 deaf, hard of hearing 聋哑 deaf and dumb, deaf-mute

隆 1)(兴盛) prosperous, thriving 2)(深厚) intense, deep 隆起 swell, bulge 隆重 grand, solemn, ceremonious

【lǒng】

垄 垄断 monopolize

笼 笼统 generally, sweeping, broadly, on the whole 笼罩 envelop, cover, wrap 笼子 a large box or chest, trunk

【lóu】

楼 楼层 story, floor, storey 楼板 floor 楼房 a storied building 楼上 upstairs 楼梯 stairs, staircase 楼下 downstairs

【lòu】

镂 镂刻 engrave, carve

漏 1) (渗漏) leak 2) (泄露) divulge, leak 3) (遗漏) miss, leave out by mistake 漏洞 ① (空隙) leak ② (破绽) flaw, hole, loophole 漏税 evade payment of a tax, evade taxation

漏电 inleakage
漏极 drain
漏检错误 undetected error
漏检故障率 residual error rate
漏码 missing code
漏行 line dropout

陋 1) (不好看) plain, ugly 2) (狭小) humble, mean 3) (不文明) bad, corrupt, undesirable 陋规 corrupt practices 陋习 corrupt customs, bad habits

【lú】

卢 卢比 rupee 卢布 rouble

炉 stove, furnace, oven

【lǔ】

卤 1) (盐卤) bittern 2) 〈化学〉halogen

鲁 dull, blunt, stupid 鲁莽 rash, indiscreet

镥 lutecium (Lu), lutetium, cassiopeium

【lù】

陆 陆地 (dry) land 陆路 land route 陆续 one after nother, in succession

录 1) (记录, 抄录) record, write down, copy 2) (任用) employ, hire 录取 enroll, recruit, admit 录音,录像 record

录入与退出 log-in and log-out
录像 video recording
录像磁带 video tape
录像磁盘系统 video disk system
录像磁片[磁盘] video sheet
录像机 video recorder
录像盘 viewdisk
录像系统 video system
录音 sound recording
录音磁带 audio tape
录音磁带存储器 audio tape storage unit
录音合成 layback
录音机 recorder
录音邮件系统 voice mail system

路 1) (道路) road, path, way 2) (途径) way, means 3) (条理) sequence, line, logic 路程 journey, distance, route, course 路径 ① (道路) route, way ② (门路)

method, ways, means 路人 passerby, pedestrian, stranger 路线 ①（经过的道路）route, itinerary ②（思想政治路线）line, guideline

路径 path, route, leg
路径表 routing table, path table
路径表达式 routing expression
路径长度 path-length
路径矩阵 path matrix
路径扩充 route extension {REX}
路径[通路]敏化 path sensitization
路径名 pathname
路径[路由]选择 routing
路径选择策略 routing strategy
路径[路由]选择控制 routing control
路径选择算法 routing algorithm
路径状态表 path state table
路线 route
路线标记 routing flag
路线表 route sheet
路选表 routing table
路线代码 routing code
路线通路 routing path
路由 path, route
路由表 routing list/table
路由拨号 route dialing
路由处理器 route processor
路由队列 routing queue
路由服务器 route server
路由交换器 routing switcher
路由矩阵 route matrix
路由控制 path control {PC}
路由器 router
路由器接口 router interface
路由(选择)器 router
路由入口 routing entry
路由算法 routing algorithm
路由(选择)信息 routing information

路由信息协议 routing information protocol {RIP}
路由选择 route planning, routing select, route selection
路由选择程序 routing program
路由选择服务 route selection services {RSS}
路由选择关键字 routing key
路由选择逻辑 routing logic
路由选择码 routing code
路由延伸 route extension {REX}
路由最佳化 route optimization
路站 way station

露
（饮料）syrup, juice 露出 show, reveal 露水 dew

【lǚ】

铝
alumin(i)um (Al), aluminous

旅
旅伴 travelling companion, fellow traveller 旅程 route, itinerary 旅费 travelling expenses 旅馆 hotel, inn 旅客 tourist, traveller, passenger 旅途 journey, trip 旅行 travel, journey, tour 旅游 tour, tourism

屡
屡次 time and again, repeatedly

履
1)（鞋）shoe 2)（踩，踏）tread on, walk on 3)（脚步）footstep 履历 personal details, antecedents 履历表〈法语〉résumé, curriculum vitae 履行 perform, fulfil, carry out 履约保证 pèrformance bond, performance guarantee

【lǜ】

律 1)(法律)law, statute 2)(规律)law, rule 律师 lawyer

绿 green 绿化 make green by planting trees, flowers, etc., afforest
绿色电源 green power supply
绿色监视器 green monitor

率 另见〖shuài〗
rate, proportion, ratio

虑 1)(思考)consider, ponder, think over 2)(担忧)concern, anxiety, worry

氯 chlorine (Cl)

滤 strain, filter
滤波 filtration
滤波器 filter
滤光 optical filtering
滤光器 glare filter, optical filter
滤色器 color filter

【luán】

孪 孪生儿 twins
孪生的 twin
孪生指针 twin pointer

【luǎn】

卵 ovum, egg, spawn

【luàn】

乱 1)(秩序乱)in disorder, in a mess 2)(心情乱)be confused, be upset, be disturbed 3)(使混乱)confuse, upset 4)(任意)random, arbitrary 5)(骚乱)disorder, upheaval, chaos, riot, unrest, turmoil

乱读 dirty read
乱码(现象) clobber

【lüè】

略 1)(简单)brief, sketchy 3)(简叙)summary, brief account, outline 略去 omit, delete, leave out, discard
略微 slightly, a little, somewhat
略图 contour, outline map, rough draft, schema, schematic drawing, sketch (pad)

【lún】

纶 1)(青丝带子)black silk ribbon 2)(合成纤维)synthetic fiber

轮 轮班 in shifts, in relays, in rotation 轮船 steamboat, steamer 轮换 rotate, take turns 轮廓 outline, contour, profile 轮流 take turns, in turn 轮训 training in rotation
轮子 wheel
轮叫探询 roll-call polling
轮廓报告 profile report
轮廓模型 skeleton pattern/ model
轮廓图 line drawing
轮廓图像 contour image
轮廓字体(字型) outline font
轮流服务 round-robin service
轮流复用 round-robin
轮流探询 roll polling
轮式打印机 flying printer, wheel type printer
轮形图 wheel
轮询 poll, roll polling
轮询比 polling ratio
轮询表 polling list
轮询操作 polling operation

轮询次数 wrap count
轮询电路 polling circuit
轮询方案 polling scheme
轮询方式 polling mode
轮询间隔 polling interval
轮询模型 polling model
轮询系统 polling system
轮询中断 polling interrupt
轮询周期 polling cycle

【lùn】

论 1)（谈论）discuss, talk about, discourse 2)（看法，说法）view, opinion, statement 3)（学说）theory 4)（提及，看待）mention, regard, consider 5)（衡量）decide on, determine **论点** argument, point of view **论证** view, argument **论断** inference, judgment, thesis **论及** touch upon **论据**(grounds of) argument **论理** normally, as things should be **论述** discuss **论坛** forum, tribune **论文** thesis, dissertation, paper, article **论文集** symposium, colloquium, proceedings **论证** ①〈名〉demonstration, proof ②〈动〉expound and prove **论著** treatise, work, book
论点 issue
论据 datum, fact
论题 subject matter, topic
论域 discourse domain
论域理论 domain theory

【luó】

罗 1)（张网捕）catch (birds) with a net 2)（计量单位）gross (=12 dozen) **罗列** ①（陈列）spread out, set out ②（列举）enumerate, list **罗**网 net, trap
罗马数字 Roman numeral
罗马体 roman
罗马字(符) Roma character

逻 逻辑 logic; logistic

逻辑安全 logical security
逻辑报文 logical message
逻辑比较 logic comparison
逻辑编程语言 programming in logic {PROLOG}
逻辑编号 logical number
逻辑编辑 logical edit
逻辑变量 logic variable, switching variable
逻辑表达式 logic expression
逻辑补 logical complement
逻辑部件 logic unit {LU}
逻辑部件号 logical unit number
逻辑操作[运算] logical operation
逻辑测试 logic test
逻辑层次 logical level
逻辑常数 logical constant
逻辑乘 conjunction, intersect, logic multiply, multiply
逻辑乘(积) logic product
逻辑乘门 logic product gate
逻辑程序 logic program, logic sequence
逻辑出错条件 logic fault condition
逻辑磁道 logical track
逻辑词 logical word
逻辑存储结构 logical storage structure
逻辑存取[访问]层 logical access level
逻辑存取级 logical access level
逻辑错误 logic error, logical mistake
逻辑代数 algebra of logic, Boolean algebra, logic alge-

bra

逻辑代数符 boolean operator

逻辑单元 logical block, logical unit {LU}

逻辑单元阵列 logic cell arrays {LCA}

逻辑的 logical, logistic, boolean

逻辑等价 logical equivalence

逻辑低(电平) logic low

逻辑地址 logic address

逻辑电路 logic circuit

逻辑电路板 logic card

逻辑电平 logic level

逻辑方程 logical equation

逻辑仿真[模拟] logical simulation

逻辑访问控制 logical access control

逻辑非门 logic inverter

逻辑分类 logical classfication

逻辑分区[划分] logical partition

逻辑分析 logic analysis, logical analysis

逻辑分页 logical paging

逻辑符号 logic symbol, logical symbol

逻辑覆盖 logical overlay

逻辑父辈 logical parent

逻辑高(电平) logic high

逻辑跟踪 logical tracing

逻辑功能[函数] logic function

逻辑公式 logical formula

逻辑故障 logic fault

逻辑关系 logic relation

逻辑和 logic sum

逻辑合成 logic synthesis

逻辑划分 logic partition, logical division

逻辑环 logical ring

逻辑基元 logic primitive

逻辑积 logic product

逻辑级 logic level

逻辑记录 logic record

逻辑记录存取法 logical record access {LRA}

逻辑记录型 logical record type

逻辑加 Boolean add, logic add, logical OR

逻辑兼容性 logical compatibility

逻辑接点 logic node

逻辑接口 logic interface

逻辑结构 logical structure

逻辑矩阵 logic matrix

逻辑卷 logical volume

逻辑决策 logical decision

逻辑开关 logic switch

逻辑空间 logical space

逻辑库 logic base

逻辑块 logical block

逻辑块号 logical block number {LBN}

逻辑框 logic box

逻辑框图 logic diagram

逻辑类型 logical type

逻辑联结 logical join

逻辑联系[关] logical relationship

逻辑连接 logical joint

逻辑连接符 logical connector

逻辑链路控制 logical link control {LLC}

逻辑流程 logic flow

逻辑论 logic theory

逻辑冒险 logic hazard

逻辑门 logic gate

逻辑描述符 logical descriptor

逻辑名表 logical name table

逻辑模块 logic module

逻辑模拟 logic simulation

逻辑模式 logical schema

逻辑模型 logic model

逻辑判定表 logic decision table

逻辑求反 Boolean complementation

逻辑驱动器 logical drive

逻辑柔性 logic flexibility
逻辑设备,logical device, logical unit {LU}
逻辑设备表 logical device table {LDT}
逻辑设备地址 logical device address {LDA}
逻辑设备名 logical unit name
逻辑设计 logic design
逻辑时钟 logical timer/clock
逻辑实体 logic entity
逻辑事件 logic event
逻辑视图 logical view
逻辑收信端[方] logical destination
逻辑(型)数据 logical data
逻辑数值数据计算机 logic numeric data computer {LND}
逻辑数组[阵列] logic array
逻辑思维 logical thinking
逻辑算子 logic operator
逻辑探头[针] logic probe
逻辑特性[行为] logic behaviour
逻辑条件 logic condition
逻辑通道 logical channel {LC}
逻辑通道队列 logical channel queue {LCH}
逻辑通道号 logical channel number {LCN}
逻辑通道组 logical channel group
逻辑图 logic map
逻辑(流程)图 logic chart/flowchart
逻辑推理 logical reasoning, logical-inference
逻辑推理机 logic inference machine
逻辑网络 logical net
逻辑文法 logical grammar
逻辑文件 logic file
逻辑系统 logic system
逻辑线路组 logic line group {LLG}
逻辑相关(性) logical dependency
逻辑项 logical term
逻辑消息 logical message
逻辑芯片 logic chip
逻辑信息 logic information
逻辑型 logical type
逻辑形式 logical form
逻辑行 logical line
逻辑学 logistics
逻辑演算 Boolean calculus
逻辑页(面) logical page {LPAGE}
逻辑页(编)号 logical page number {LPN}
逻辑移位 logic shift, unsigned shift
逻辑右移 logic shift right
逻辑元件 functor, logic element, logical element
逻辑运算 logic operation
逻辑运算符 logic operator
逻辑运算指令 logic operation instruction
逻辑暂驻程序区 logical transient area {LTA}
逻辑炸弹 logic bomb
逻辑(永)真(式) logical truth
逻辑阵列 logic array
逻辑值 logic value
逻辑指令 logic instruction
逻辑终端 logical terminal {LTERM}
逻辑转义符 logical escape symbol
逻辑装置 logic device, logical unit {LU}
逻辑状态 logic state
逻辑追踪 logical tracing
逻辑资源 logical resource
逻辑字 logical word
逻辑字符 logical character
逻辑综合 logic synthesis

逻辑组件 logic module

螺 spiral shell, snail 螺丝钉 screw
螺帽型开关 nut switch
螺线扫描 helical scan

【luǒ】
裸 bare, naked, exposed
裸计算机 bare computer, bare machine

【luò】
洛 洛氏硬度 Rockwell hardness

落 1)(掉下)fall, drop 2)(下降)go down, set 3)(使下降)lower 4)(衰败)decline, come down, sink 5)(留下)leave behind, stay behind 落成 completion 落成典礼 inauguration ceremony 落后 ①〈动〉fall behind, lag behind ②〈形〉backward 落空 come to nothing, fail 落入 fall-in 落实 ①(切实的)practicable, workable ②(实现)carry out, fulfil, implement, put into effect 落伍 fall behind the ranks, straggle, drop behind, drop out

M m

【mā】

妈 mother

抹 另见【mǒ】wipe

【má】

麻 1)(麻类植物)fiber crops 2)(芝麻)sesame 3)(不光滑)rough, coarse 麻痹 ①(使丧失警惕)lull, blunt ②(疏忽)be off one's guard, relax one's vigilance 麻烦 ①〈形〉troublesome, inconvenient ②〈动〉trouble, bother

【mǎ】

马 horse 马虎 careless, casual 马克(德国货币)mark 马路 road, street, avenue 马上 at once, immediately, straight away, right away 马力 horsepower
马达 motor
马尔可夫链 Markov chain
马尔可夫模型 Markov model

码 1)(数目符号)number 2)(英制长度单位)yard ◇尺码 size // 价格 marked price // 页码 page number 码头 wharf, dock, pier
码长[度] code length
码间干扰 intersymbol interference
码距 code distance
码页转换 code page switching
码元 code element
码元偶 bit pair
码重 code weight
码字 code word
码组 code block, code group

【mà】

骂 1)(咒骂)curse, swear, call names 2)(斥责)condemn, scold, reproach

【mái】

埋 cover up, bury 埋藏 ①(藏在土中)hide in the earth, bury ②(隐藏)hide, conceal
埋层 buried layer

【mǎi】

买 buy, purchase 买方 the buying party, buyer 买价 buying price 买卖 buying and selling, business, deal, transaction 买主 buyer, customer

【mài】

迈 1)(向前进)step, stride 2)(老)old 迈进 stride forward, advance with big strides

卖 1)(出售)sell 2)(背叛)betray 卖方 the selling party,

seller 卖价 selling price 卖弄 show off, parade 卖主 bargainer, seller

脉 1)(动脉和静脉)arteries and veins 2)(像血管的东西)vein 脉搏 pulse
脉冲 imp, impulse, pulse
脉冲编码 impulse coding, pulse code
脉冲编码调制 pulse code modulation {PCM}
脉冲编码装置 moder
脉冲变压器 pulse transformer
脉冲串[系列] burst, pulse string, pulse train
脉冲串式 burst mode
脉冲代码 pulse code
脉冲电路 pulse circuit
脉冲发生器 pulse generator
脉冲放大器 pulse amplifier
脉冲分离器 pulse separator
脉冲分配器 pulse distributor
脉冲检测 impulse testing
脉冲宽度 pulse length
脉冲扩展器 pulse stretcher
脉冲上升时间 pulse rise time
脉冲通道 pulse channel
脉冲下降时间 pulse fall time
脉冲响应 impulse response
脉冲序列 impulse train
脉冲再生 pulse regeneration
脉冲噪声 impulse noise
脉冲整形 pulse shaping
脉冲周期 pulse period
脉动 ripple
脉动[波纹]放大器 ripple amplifier
脉动神经计算机 systolic neural computer
脉动算法 systolic algorithm
脉动阵列结构 systolic array architecture
脉[冲]宽 pulse length, pulse width

【mán】

蛮 (野蛮) rough, fierce, unreasoning 蛮干 act rashly or recklessly

瞒 hide the truth from

【mǎn】

满 1)(全部充满) full, filled, packed 2)(使满) fill 3)(全) completely, entirely, perfectly 满额 fulfil the quota 满分 full marks 满期 expire, come to deadline 满意 satisfied, pleased 满员 ①(人数满)at full strength ②(坐满)all seats taken 满载 loaded to capacity, fully loaded, overall loaded 满足 ①〈形〉satisfied, content ②〈动〉satisfy, meet
满标 full scale
满标度 full range
满标值 full scale
满二叉树 full binary tree
满刻度 full scale
满屏处理 full-screen processing {FSP}
满屏幕 flooding
满射 epimorphism
满同态 epimorphism

【màn】

漫 1)(溢出) overflow, flood 2)(到处都是) all over the place, everywhere 漫笔 informal essay, literary notes 漫长 very long, endless 漫谈 informal discussion
漫画 cartoon
漫游 roam, browse, navigate

màn 慢 mang 忙茫盲,莽 mao 毛矛锚,铆,茂冒帽

慢
1)(速度慢)slow 2)(从缓)postpone, defer 慢车 slow train 慢慢 ①(速度慢)slowly, leisurely ②(逐渐地)gradually

慢动作 slow motion
慢进 jog
慢速 slow
慢速扫描 slow scan

【máng】

忙
1)(事情多)busy, fully occupied 2)(匆忙)hurry, hasten 忙碌 be busy, bustle about 忙乱 do one's work in a hasty and disorderly manner

忙标记 busy tag
忙等待 busy waiting
忙碌标记(记号) busy token
忙碌标志 busy flag
忙碌位 busy bit
忙碌信号 busy signal
忙线 busy line
忙音中继线 busy tone trunk
忙状态 busy status

茫
茫然 ignorant, in the dark, at a loss

盲
blind 盲目 blind 盲目性 blindness

盲触 blind touch
盲点 unreachable position
盲键盘 blind keyboard
盲区 blind, dead spot, fade zone, shadow
盲搜索 blind search

【mǎng】
莽
(鲁莽)rash

【máo】
毛
1)(皮上的毛)hair, feather 2)(羊毛)wool 毛笔 writing brush 毛病 ①(疾病)illness, disease ②(故障)trouble 毛糙 crude, coarse, careless 毛发 hair 毛巾 towel 毛利 gross profit
毛条版面 body matter

矛
lance, spear, pike 矛盾 contradictory, contradiction
矛盾否定 contradictory opposite
矛盾论点 paradox
矛盾命题 contradictory proposition

锚
anchor

【mǎo】
铆
铆工 ①(工种)riveting ②(工人)riveter 铆接 riveting

【mào】
茂
茂盛 luxuriant, flourishing

冒
1)(冒出来)emit, send out, discharge 2)(不顾)risk, brave 冒充 pretend to be, disguise as 冒犯 offend, violate 冒险 ①〈动〉take a risk, take chances ②〈名〉adventure, gamble, hazard, venture 冒号 colon 冒名 go under sb else's name, assume another's name 冒牌 a counterfeit of an established trade mark 冒用商标 infringement of trade-mark

冒充程序 masquerader
冒号分类法 colon classification
冒泡排序 bubble sorting

帽
帽子 hat, cap 帽状物

cap-like cover

贸
贸然 rashly, hastily, without careful consideration
贸易 trade, trading

貌
looks, appearance 貌似 seemingly, in appearance

【méi】

没 另见【mò】
没法子 can do nothing about it, cannot help it 没关系 it doesn't matter, it's nothing, that's all right, never mind
没有 ①(无)not have, there is not ②(不及,不如)not so ... as ... ③(不到)less than ④(未)not yet
没有定义的 undefined
没有发现错误 no fault found {NFF}

眉
(眉毛)eyebrow, brow

媒
媒介 intermediary, medium, vehicle
媒件 middleware
媒介语言 intermediate language {IL}
媒体 media, medium
媒体播放器 media player
媒体存储器 media bank
媒体[介质]存取[访问]控制 medium access control {MAC}
媒体存取控制协议 medium access control protocol
媒体返回 carrier return
媒体返回字符 carrier return character {CRE}
媒体控制接口[界面] media control interface {MCI}
媒体[介质]连接单元 medium attachment unit {MAU}
媒体模型 media model
媒体抹除器 media eraser
媒体驱动器 media drive
媒体室 media room
媒体图 medium map
媒体托架 carrier {CARR}, media carriage
媒体文件 media files
媒体转换 media conversion
媒质代码 media code
媒质类型 media type

煤
(煤炭)coal 煤灰 coal ash 煤矿 coal mine, colliery 煤渣 coal cinder

酶
enzyme, ferment

锚
americium (Am)

枚
枚举 enumerate
枚举标量类型 enumerated scalar type
枚举标志 enumeration tag
枚举常数 enumeration constant
枚举法 enumeration method
枚举类型 enumeration type
枚举排序 enumeration sorting
枚举数据类型 enumerated data type
枚举算法 enumeration algorithm

【měi】

每
(各个)every, each, per
每当 whenever, every time
每每 often 每时每刻 all the time, at all times
每道扇区数 sectors per track {SPT}
每分钟行数 lines per minute {LPM, lpm}
每分钟字数 word(s) per minute

{WPM, wpm}

每个像素的位数 bits per pixel {BPP}

每秒比特数 bits per second {BPS}

每秒分组数 packets per second {PPS}

每秒吉(咖)次浮点运算 gigaflops

每秒吉(咖)位 gigabits per second {Gbps}

每秒千位 kilobits per second {Kbps}

每秒千字节数 kilobytes per second {KBPS}

每秒事务[交易]数 transaction per second {TPS}

每秒太(拉)位 terabits per second {Tbps}

每秒行(数) lines per second {lps}

每秒兆位 megabits per second {Mbps}

每秒指令数 orders per second

每秒周期数 cycles per second {CPS, cps}

每秒字节数 bytes per second (=bps, bytes/s)

每页行数 lines per page {lpp}

每英寸比特数 bits per inch {BPI}

每英寸磁道数 tracks per inch {TPI}

每英寸点数 dot per inch {bpi, dpi (=dot per inch)}

每英寸多点数 dots per inch {DIP}

每英寸行 lines per inch {LPI, lpi}

每帧字符数 characters per frame

美 1)(好)very satisfactory 2)(得意)be pleased with oneself 美德 virtue, moral excellence 美感 aesthetic feeling, sense of beauty 美工 ①(美术工作)art designing ②(美术工作者)art designer 美观 pleasing to the eye, beautiful to look at 美国 the United States of America (U.S.A) 美好 fine, glorious, bright 美化 beautify, prettify 美丽 beautiful, pretty 美妙 beautiful, splendid, wonderful 美术 ①(造型艺术)the fine arts, art ②(绘画)painting 美学 aesthetics 美元 American dollar, U.S. dollar 美洲 America

美国标准学会 United States of America Standards Institute {USASI}

美国国家标准学会 American National Standards Institute {ANSI}

美国信息交换标准代码 USA Standard Code for Information Interchange {USASCII}

美元符号 dollar mark, dollar sign

镁 magnesium (Mg)

【mèi】

妹 younger sister

魅 魅力 attraction, charm, enchantment, fascination

【mén】

门 1)(出入口)entrance, door, gate 2)(开关)valve, switch 3)(类别)field, sphere, branch 门把 door knob, door handle 门径 way to do sth 门槛 threshold

门口 entrance, doorway 门类 class, kind, category 门市 retail sales 门市部 retail department, sales department, salesroom 门卫 extrance guard
门(电路) gate
门电路 gate circuit
门级逻辑模拟 gate level logic simulation
门控制块 gate control block {GCB}
门脉冲 gate pulse
门数 gate count
门限 threshold
门延迟 gate delay
门阵列 gate array

【měng】
蒙 另见【méng】
蒙骗 cheat, deceive

【méng】
萌 萌发 sprout, shoot forth 萌芽 ①(植物生芽)sprout, shoot, bud ②(新生事物)rudiment, shoot

蒙 另见【měng】
1)(盖)cover 2)(受)receive, meet with 蒙蔽 hoodwink, deceive, fool 蒙昧 ①(未开化的)uncivilized, uncultured ②(无知)ignorant, uneducated 蒙受 suffer, sustain

盟 (同盟)alliance 盟邦,盟国 allied country, ally 盟友 ally 盟约 oath of alliance, treaty of alliance

【měng】
猛 (突然)suddenly, abruptly 猛烈 fierce, vigorous, violent, energetic

锰 manganese (Mn)

梦 dream 梦幻 illusion, dream, reverie 梦境 dreamland, dreamworld, dream 梦想 ①(妄想)dream of, vainly hope ②(渴望)earnest wish

【mí】
弥 弥补 make up, remedy, compensate 弥漫 fill the air

迷 1)(沉醉)be fascinated by, be crazy about 2)(爱好者)fan, enthusiast 3)(使看不清)confuse, perplex 迷航 drift off course, lose one's course, get lost 迷惑 puzzle, confuse, perplex, baffle 迷路 lose one's way, get lost 迷人 charming, fascinating, enchanting 迷失 be confused, be lost
迷宫法 maze method
迷宫算法 labyrinth algorithm

谜 (未弄清的事物)mystery, puzzle 谜语 riddle

糜 糜烂 rotten to the core, corrupted, profligate, debauched

醚 ether

【mǐ】
米 1)(稻米)rice 2)(长度单位)metre, meter 米色 cream-colored

【mì】

觅 look for, hunt for, seek

秘 1)〈形〉secret, confidential 2)〈动〉keep sth secret, hold sth back 秘方 secret formula 秘诀 secret 秘密 secret, confidential 秘书 secretary 秘书处 secretariat 秘书长 secretary general
秘密保护 privacy protection
秘密键 secret key

密 1)(距离近,空间小)close, dense, thick 2)(亲密)intimate, close 3)(秘密)secret 密闭 airtight, hermetic 密布 densely covered 密度 density, thickness 密封 ① seal up ② seal airtight 密集 concentrated, crowded together 密件 a confidential paper or letter, classified material 密谋 conspire, plot, intrigue 密切 ①(关系近)close, intimate ②(仔细)carefully, intently, closely
密报 cryptogram
密电 confidential telegram
密度 density, density scale
密度函数 density function
密封层 sealant, sealer
密封接头 sealed head
密封电流 sealing current
密封器 sealer
密级数据 classified data
密级信息 security information
密码(的) cipher, cryptogram, cryptographic, cypher, password, security key
密码保护 cryptoguard
密码变换 cryptographic transform
密码传真 cifax
密码电报 ciphertext
密码电文 cryptotext
密码对话[会话] cryptographic session
密码分析 code breaking, cryptoanalysis, cryptographic analysis
密码关键字数据集 cryptographic key data set {**CKDS**}
密码键 cryptographic key
密码控制 cryptographic control
密码器 scrambler
密码设施 cryptographic facility
密码使用者 cypherpunk
密码术 cryptography
密码算法 cryptographic algorithm
密码体制 cipher system, cryptographic system, cryptosystem
密码通信 cryptographic communication
密码文件 ciphertext
密码系统 cryptographic system, cryptosystem
密码验证 cryptographic authentication
密码主键 cryptographic master key
密码转换 cryptographic transformation
密文 ciphertext, cryptogram
密文空间 cryptogram space
密钥 cryptographic key, key
密钥词组 key phrase
密钥管理 key management
密钥加密技术 key encryption technology
密钥结构 key structure
密钥流 key stream
密钥数据集 cryptographic key data set {**CKDS**}

幂 〈数学〉power, exponent

幂等 idempotent
幂等变换 idempotent transformation
幂等(定)律 idempotent law
幂等元 idempotent element
幂函数 power function
幂集 power set
幂论域 powerdomain
幂数 power of number

【mián】

棉 (棉花)cotton 棉布 cotton (cloth) 棉纱 cotton yarn 棉线 cotton thread, cotton 棉絮(棉毛纤维)cotton fiber

绵 绵延 continuous

眠 (睡眠)sleep

【miǎn】

免 1)(去掉)excuse sb from sth, exempt, dispense with 2)(避免)avoid, escape 3)(不可)not allowed, forbidden ◇闲人免进 No admittance except on business 免除 ① (免去)prevent, avoid ② (免掉)remit, excuse, exempt, relieve 免得 so as not to, avoid 免费 free of charge, free 免税 exempt from taxation, tax-free, duty free 免验 exempt from customs examination 免验放行 pass without examination (P.W.E.) 免验证 laissez-passer
免错 fault avoidance
免费软件 free software, freeware
免费软件组织 free software foundation {FSF}

勉 (努力)exert oneself, strive 勉强 ①(尽力)manage with an effort, do with difficulty ②(不情愿)reluctantly ③(强迫)force sb do sth ④(牵强)inadequate, unconvincing ⑤(刚刚够)barely enough
勉励 encourage, urge

【miàn】

面 1)(脸)face 2)(向着)face 3)(表面)surface, top, face 4)(当面)personally, directly, face to face 5)(外皮)the right side, cover, outside 6)〈数学〉(平面)surface 7)(方面)side, aspect 8)(全面)entire area 9)(范围)extend, range, scale, scope 面包 bread 面对 face, confront 面对面 face facing each other, face-to-face 面额〈经贸〉denomination 面粉 (wheat) flour 面积 area 面临 be faced with, be confronted with 面貌,面目 ① (相貌) face, features, looks ②(面目)appearance, look, aspect 面前 face of, in front of, before 面试 interview 面谈 speak to sb face to face, discuss in person 面条 noodles 面向 ① (朝着)turn one's face to, turn in the direction of, face ②(使适合)be geared to the needs of, cater to 面值 ① (票面价格)par value, face value, nominal value ②(纸币单位)denomination
面板. faceplate, panel
面板编号 panel number
面板标题 panel title
面板插座 panel jack
面板开关 panel switch

miáo 描

面板区 panel area
面板设备 face equipment
面板显示 panel display
面板组件 panel assembly
面存储密度 areal packing density, areal storage density
面积元素 surface element
面记录密度 areal recording density
面密度 areal density
面图 surface chart
面向比特的协议 bit oriented protocol
面向表达式的语言 expression oriented language
面向表系统 list-oriented system
面向程序的语言 program-oriented language
面向…的 oriented
面向对象 object oriented {OO}
面向对象表示 object-oriented representation
面向对象的编程语言 object oriented programming language {OOPL}
面向对象的模型 object oriented model
面向对象的数据库管理系统 object oriented database management system {ODBMS}
面向对象的体系结构 object-oriented architecture
面向对象分析 object-oriented analysis {OOA}
面向对象技术 object oriented technology
面向对象设计 object-oriented design {OOD}
面向对象数据库系统 object-oriented database system {OODBS}
面向对象数据模型 object-oriented data model {OODM}
面向服务器的网络 server oriented network
面向规则的系统 rule-oriented system
面向过程的 procedure-oriented
面向机器的 machine-orientated
面向控制的功能 control-oriented function
面向框架的 frame oriented
面向连接的通信 connection oriented communication
面向目标的 goal-oriented
面向软件的 software-oriented
面向商业的通用语言 COBOL (=common business-oriented language)
面向事件的 event-oriented
面向事件模拟 event-directed simulation
面向事务的系统 transaction oriented system
面向位(比特)的 bit-oriented
面向文件的系统 file-oriented system
面向问题的语言 problem-oriented language
面向信息的语言 information oriented language {INFOL}
面向应用的软件 application oriented software
面向用户的 user-oriented
面向知识的对象语言 knowledge-oriented object language {KOOL}
面向字节的 byte-oriented

【miáo】
描 1)(照底样画) trace, copy 2)(重复涂抹) touch up, retouch 描画 draw, paint, depict, describe 描绘 depict, describe, portray 描述 describe 描图 tracing 描图员 tracer 描写 describe, depict, portray

miao 瞄,秒渺藐 妙 miè 灭蔑 min 民,敏 míng 名

描绘单元 delineation unit
描绘的 rendered
描绘器 plotter
描述表 description list
描述词[符] descriptor
描述符表 descriptor table
描述符语言 descriptor language
描述函数 describing function
描述环境 describe environment
描述模型 descriptive model
描述语言 descriptive language
描图器 drafter

瞄 take aim
瞄准 aim, collimation
瞄准点 gunsight aiming point
瞄准符 aiming symbol
瞄准器 aiming circle

【miǎo】

秒 second

渺 渺茫 far and obscure, vague 渺小 tiny, negligible, insignificant

藐 藐视 despise, look down upon

【miào】

妙 1)(美妙)wonderful, excellent, fine 2)(奇妙)ingenious, clever, subtle 妙计 excellent plan, brilliant scheme 妙论 extraordinary argument, covincing discourse, sparkling discourse

【miè】

灭 1)(熄灭)go out 2)(使熄灭)extinguish, put out, turn off 3)(淹没)drown 4)(消灭)destroy, wipe out 灭迹 destroy the evidence 灭绝,灭亡 become extinct, die out, destroyed

蔑 蔑视 despise, disdain, scorn

【mín】

民 1)(人民)the people 2)(非军人)civilian 民办 run by the local people 民法 civil law 民航 civil aviation 民间 ①(人民之间的)among the people, folk ②(非官方的)nongovernmental people 民间的 of the people, folk 民权 civil rights, democratic rights 民事 issues relating to civil law 民用 for civil use, civil 民众 the masses of the people, the common people, the populace 民主 ①〈名〉democracy, democratic rights ②〈形〉democratic 民族 nation, nationality

【mǐn】

敏 敏感 sensitive, susceptible 敏捷 quick, nimble, agile 敏锐 sharp, acute, keen
敏感器件 sensing device
敏感数据 sensitive data
敏感性 susceptibility
敏感元件 pickoff, sensing unit, sensitive pick-up, sensor (element)
敏感元件阵列 sensor array
敏化 sensitization

【míng】

名 1)(名字)name, title 2)(有名的)famous, well-known 名册 register, roll 名次 position in a name list, place in a competition 名单 name list 名额 the number of people assigned, quota of people 名副其实 the name matches the reality, be worthy of the name 名贵 famous and precious, rare 名目 names of things, items 名牌 famous brand 名片 visiting card, calling card 名气 reputation, fame, prestige 名人 famous person, celebrity 名声 fame, reputation, repute, renown 名胜 famous scenic spots, well-known places for sighseeing 名义 ①（名称）name ②（表面上）nominal, in name 名誉 ①（名声）fame, reputation ②（名义上的）honorary 名誉顾问 honorary advisor 名著 famous book, famous work

名表 name entry
名称 designation, name
名称参数 name parameter
名词 noun
名空间 name space
名录服务 directory service
名人口 name entry
名字标识符 name identifier
名字表 name table
名字参数 name parameter
名字常数 name constant {NCON}
名字代码 name code
名字代码 name replacement
名字服务器 name server
名字管理协议 name management protocol {NMP}
名字鉴别 name resolution
名字块 name block {NAM}
名字栏[域, 段] name field
名字替换 name substitution
名字转换 name resolution

明 1)（亮）bright, brilliant, light 2)（清楚）clear, distinct 3)（公开的）open, overt, explicit 4)（眼力好）sharp-eyed, clear-sighted 5)（光明正大的）aboveboard, honest 6)（视觉）sight 7)（懂得）understand, know 明白 ①（清楚）clear, obvious, plain ②（懂得）know, understand 明朗 ①（光亮）bright and clear ②（明显）clear, obvious ③（开朗）forthright, bright and cheerful 明亮 ①（光线足）light, well-lit, bright ②（发亮的）bright, shining 明了 ①〈动〉clearly understand, be clear about ②〈形〉clear, plain 明年 next year 明确 ①〈形〉clear and definite, clear-cut, explicit ②〈动〉make clear and definite 明天 ①（明日）tomorrow ②（不远的将来）the near future 明显 clear, obvious, evident, distinct 明证 proof 明星 star 明智 sensible, wise

明暗度 intensity
明度对比 brightness contrast
明码 evident code, plain
明码对话[会话] clear session
明码通信报文 clear text
明码文本 plaintext
明文 clear text, plaintext
明晰度 perspectivity
明细表 specification (=spec.)
明细数据 detail data
明线 open line, open wire
明线布线 front wiring
明线图像 clear-line-image

鸣 鸣谢 express gratitude,

express one's thanks formally

铭 铭刻 ①（刻在器物上的文字）inscription ②（铭记）engrave on one's mind

【míng】

命 （生命）life 命令 order, command 命名 name; designation, denomination 命题 ①（出题目）assign a topic, design test items ②〈逻辑〉〈数学〉proposition 命运 lot, fate, destiny 命中 hit the target, score a hit
命令 command {CMD, CMND}, directive, internal command, order, prescript
命令编码 command code
命令标识符 command identifier
命令表 command list {CLIST}, command table
命令菜单 command menu
命令参数 command parameter
命令操作 command operation
命令处理程序 command processor
命令串 command string
命令定义表 command definition table {CDT}
命令段 command frame, command phase
命令方式[模式,状态] command mode
命令格式 command format
命令函数 command function
命令级 command level
命令键 command key
命令接口 command interface
命令阶段 command phase
命令解释 command interpretation
命令拒绝 command reject {CMDR}
命令(语)句 command/ imperative tatement
命令开关 command switch
命令控制块 command control block {CCB}
命令框 command format
命令链(路) command chain, command link
命令列表 command list {CLIST}
命令流 command stream
命令名(称) command name
命令权限 command authority
命令授权 command authority
命令特权级 command privilege class
命令提示符 command prompt
命令位 command bit
命令行 command line
命令序列 order sequence
命令语言 command language, scripting language
命令状态 command phase/state/status
命令字段 command field
命令字符 command character
命令总线 command bus
命名的 named
命名法 nomenclature
命名符 designator
命名管道 named pipe
命名权 naming authority
命题变元 propositional variable, statement variable
命题常量 propositional constant
命题公式 propositional formula, statement formula
命题量词 statement quantifier
命题逻辑 propositional logic, statement logic
命题逻辑式 well-formed formula {WFF, wff}

命题树 proposition tree
命中率 hit ratio
命中文件 hit file

【miù】

谬 wrong, false 谬论 fallacy, false theory, falsehood 谬误 falsehood, error, mistake

【mō】

摸 (接触)touch, feel, finger 摸索 grope, feel for/about, search, fumble
摸感屏 touch screen
摸感显示器 touch-sensitive display

【mó】

模 另见【mú】
(规范)pattern, standard 模范 model 模糊 ①(不清楚) dim, vague, indistinct ②(混淆)blur ③〈数学〉fuzzy
模特儿 model 模型 ① model ② mold, matrix, pattern
模 mod, modulo, modulus
模板 platen, template, templet)
模板比较[匹配] template matching
模板图像 template image
模板罩 platen cover
模(绘)版 stencil
模仿 emulate, imitate, impersonate, impersonation, mimicking
模仿的 mimic
模分离器 mode stripper
模2和 modulo-two sum
模糊闭集 fuzzy closed set
模糊变量 fuzzy variable
模糊表达式 fuzzy expression
模糊测度 fuzzy measure
模糊处理机 fuzzy processor
模糊代数 fuzzy algebra
模糊点 ambiguity
模糊动态规划 fuzzy dynamic programming
模糊度 fuzzy degree
模糊对策 fuzzy game
模糊范畴 fuzzy category
模糊方程 fuzzy equation
模糊概率 fuzzy probability
模糊概念 fuzzy concept
模糊关系 ambiguity relation, fuzzy relation
模糊规划 fuzzy programming, fuzzy scheduling
模糊规则 fuzzy rule
模糊过程 fuzzy process
模糊函数 fuzzy function
模糊划分 fuzzy partition
模糊积分 fuzzifying integral, fuzzy integral
模糊集[合] fuzzy set
模糊集合论[理论] fuzzy set theory
模糊计算机 fuzzy computer
模糊检索 fuzzy search
模糊矩阵 confusion matrix, fuzzy matrix
模糊聚类 fuzzy aggregation
模糊决策 fuzzy decision
模糊控制 fuzzy control
模糊控制器 fuzzy controller
模糊理论 fuzzy theory
模糊联想记忆 fuzzy associative memories {FAM}
模糊量词 fuzzy quantifier
模糊逻辑 fuzzy logic
模糊命题 fuzzy proposition
模糊模型 fuzzy model
模糊区间 fuzzy interval
模糊权 fuzzy weight
模糊群 fuzzy group
模糊熵 fuzzy entropy
模糊神经网络 fuzzy neural

network
模糊神经元 fuzzy neuron
模糊识别 fuzzy recognition
模糊数 fuzzy number
模糊数据库 fuzzy database
模糊数学 fuzzing mathematics
模糊算法 fuzzy algorithm
模糊特性 fuzzy behaviour
模糊推断 fuzzy assertion
模糊推理 fuzzy reasoning
模糊推理语言 fuzzy inference language {FIL}
模糊拓扑 fuzzy topology
模糊系统 fuzzy system
模糊线性规划 fuzzy linear programming
模糊相关 fuzzy correlation
模糊性 fuzzification, fuzziness
模糊隐含[蕴涵] fuzzy implication
模糊映射 fuzzy mapping
模糊语法 fuzzy grammar
模糊状态 fuzzy state
模件 modular unit, module
模块 modular, module
模块板 module board
模块化 modular, modularity, modularization
模块化程序设计 modular programming
模块化的 modularized
模块化结构 modular structure
模块化设计 modular design
模块结构 modular construction
模块模式 template pattern
模块耦合 module coupling
模块体 module body
模块性 modularity
模块组织 modular organization
模拟 analogy, emulate, emulation, imitate, imitation, simulate, simulation
模拟(物理量) analog

模拟板 perfboard
模拟程序 imitator, simulation program, simulator
模拟程序设计语言 simulation programming language {SPL}
模拟存储器 analog memory
模拟蜂窝无线系统 analogue cellular radio
模拟环境 simulation environment
模拟幻像 simulation phantom
模拟计算 analog computation, analogy calculation
模拟计算机 analog computer
模拟开关 analog switch
模拟控制 analogi(cal) control, simulating control
模拟命令 simulation command
模拟器 emulator, imitator, simulator
模拟设备 analog device, simulation device, simulation equipment
模拟设置终端 analog facility terminal {AFT}
模拟神经元 analog neuron
模拟时间 simulated time
模拟视频 analog video
模拟输出 analog output
模拟数据 analog data, simulated data, simulation data
模拟-数字转换器 analog-digital converter
模拟退火 simulated annealing {SA}
模拟网络 analog network
模拟信道 analog channel
模拟信号 analogue signal
模拟语言 artificial voice, simulation language {SIMULA}
模拟装置 analog device
模式 mode, module, pattern, schema

模式版本 schema version
模式变换 schema conversion
模式捕获 schematic capture
模式串 pattern string
模式对话框 modal dialog box
模式管理 schema management
模式基元 pattern primitive
模式敏感故障 pattern sensitive fault
模式名 schema name
模式匹配 pattern matching
模式[图形]识别 pattern recognition {PR}
模式图 schema chart
模式项目 schema entry
模式映像 schema mapping
模数 modular, modulo (=mod), modulus
模数校验 modulo check
模-数转换 analog- to- digital conversion {ADC}
模态 modality
模同态 module homomorphism
模校验 modulo check
模型 model, pattern
模型分析 model analysis
模型结构 model building
模型控制 model control
模型库 model base, model library
模型理论 model theory
模型匹配 model matching
模型驱动 model driven
模型软件 modeling soft
模型设计 model-design
模型设计(图) pattern layout
模型文件 model file

膜 film, pellicle
膜元 membrane element

摩 摩擦 ① rub, wear ② friction 摩天大楼 skyscraper

磨 另见 {mò}
1) (折磨) wear down, wear out 2) (纠缠) trouble, worry 3) (拖时间) dawdle, waste time 磨光 polish 磨练 temper oneself, steel oneself 磨灭 wear away, obliterate 磨碎 grind
磨光函数 smoothing function
磨光样条 smoothing spline
磨损[退化]失效 deterioration failure

魔 魔力 magic (power), charm

【mǒ】
抹 另见 {ma}
1) (涂抹) put on, apply, spread 2) (擦去) wipe off 抹除 erase, delete, cross out
抹除方式 erase mode
抹除头 erase head
抹掉 remove
抹去 efface, knockout

【mò】
末 1) (最后) end, last stage ◇周末 weekend 2) (粉末) power, dust 末了 last, finally, in the end 末期 last phase, final phase, last stage 末梢 tip, end 末叶 last years
末端 end, endpoint, tag end
末端程序 extremity routine
末端节点 end station, endpoint node
末端块 end block
末端装置 distal
末尾 omega
末行 terminal row
末元素 last element
末状态 last current state

末字符 last character

没 另见【méi】
1)（沉没）sink, submerge 2)（高过）overflow, rise beyond 3)（隐没）disappear, hide
没收 confiscate, expropriate
没顶 be drowned

莫
（不）no, not 莫过于 nothing is more ... than, nothing is better than 莫名其妙 ① be baffled ② without rhyme or reason, inexplicable 莫如 would be better, might as well

漠
1)（沙漠）desert 2)（冷淡地）indifferent, unconcerned
漠视 ignore, overlook, pay no attention to

墨
（黑）black, dark 墨块 China ink, ink stick 墨水 ink 墨西哥 Mexico
墨带盒 ink ribbon cartridge
墨喷印刷头 ink jet printing head
墨水 ink
墨水均匀性 ink uniformity
墨水容器 ink tank
墨嘴 nose

磨 另见【mó】
磨碎 mill, grind 磨子 mill, millstone

默
（不说话）silent, tacit 默契 ①（心照不宣）tacit agreement, tacit understanding ②（秘密协定）secret agreement 默认 give tacit consent to, tacitly approve 默示 imply 默写 write from memory

默认(值) default
默认[缺省]标记 default label
默认[缺省]参数 default parameter
默认[缺省]格式 default form
默认[缺省]规则 default rule
默认[缺省]条件 default condition
默认值 default value

【móu】

牟
牟利 seek profit 牟取 seek (to gain), obtain

谋
（主意）stratagem, plan, scheme 谋划 plan, scheme, try to find a solution 谋利 profit, turn something to profit 谋略 strategy 谋求 work for, seek, plot 谋取 try to gain, seek, obtain

【mǒu】

某
certain, some 某某 so-and-so 某些 certain, a few

【mú】

模 另见【mó】
（模子）mold, pattern, matrix ①〈建筑〉shuttering, formwork ②〈机械〉(模型板) pattern plate 模样 ① appearance, look ② approximately, about, around

【mǔ】

母
1)（母亲）mother 2)（雌性）female 母公司 parent company 母校 one's old school, Alma Mater 母语 mother tongue
母板 master mask, masterboard, mother board

母表 matrix, matrices
母体 population
母图 supergraph
母线 highway, trunk
母语 native
母语言 superlanguage

【mù】

木 (树木) tree 木材 wood, timber, lumber 木工 ①(工种) woodwork, carpentry ②(工匠) woodworker, carpenter 木工机械 woodworking machinery 木头 timber, wood, log 木制的 made of wood, wooden

目 1)(眼睛) eye 2)(看) look, regard 3)(项目) item 4)〈生物〉order 目标 ①(对象) target, objective ②(目的) goal, aim, objective 目的 purpose, aim, goal, objective, end 目睹 see with one's own eyes, witness 目光 sight, vision, view 目击 see with one's own eyes, witness 目击者 eyewitness, witness 目录 ①(事物名目) catalogue, list, directory ②(篇章名目) table of contents, contents 目前 present, at the moment
目标变量 object variable, target variable
目标(程序)表 object list
目标表 object table
目标捕获 target acquisition
目标插板 target board
目标程序 object program/routine, objective/target program
目标程序结构 object configuration
目标程序库 object base, object library, text library
目标池 object pool
目标磁盘 target disk
目标代码 destination code
目标定义 object definition
目标[实体]定义表 object definition table {ODT}
目标符号 aiming symbol
目标服务访问点 destination service access point {DASP}
目标格式 object format
目标函数 object(ive) function, result function
目标机 object machine, target machine
目标节点 destination node
目标库 object library, target libraries
目标路径 target path
目标(代)码 object code, target code
目标描述 object description
目标实体名 object name
目标模式 object schema, target pattern
目标驱动系统 goal-driven system
目标软盘 target diskette
目标识别 target discrimination, target identification, target recognition
目标事件 object event
目标树 goal tree, object(ive) tree
目标特征 target signature
目标图 object map
目标位置显示器 target position indicator
目标文件 destination file, file destination, object file, target file
目标系统 target system
目标显示 object display

目标语句 object statement, target statement
目标语言 catalanguage, object(ive) language, target language
目标栈 goal stack
目标指令 target instruction
目标指针 object pointer
目标状态 goal state
目标字段 aiming field
目测 visual inspection, visualize
目的[地址]域 destination field
目的地 destination
目的端口号 destination port number
目的地元字段 destination element field {DEF}
目的地址字段 destination address field {DAF}
目的分析 goal analysis
目的论 teleology
目的名 destination name
目的网络 destination network
目的系统 destination system
目的站 destination station
目的字段 destination field
目录表 catalog listing, contents list, directory table, table of contents {TOC}
目录表管理 directory management
目录菜单 directory menu
目录查找系统 directory lookup system {DLS}
目录窗口 directory window
目录的层次结构 hierarchical structure of directory
目录登记项 directory entry
目录段 directory section
目录服务 directory service(s) {DS}
目录高速缓存 directory caching
目录函数 catalog function

目录恢复区 catalog recovery area {CRA}
目录记录 catalog record, directory record
目录检索 catalog search, contents retrieval
目录结构 directory structure
目录控制项 directory control entry {DCE}
目录链 directory chain
目录路径 directory path
目录码 directory code
目录名 directory name
目录区 directory area
目录文件 catalog file, directory file
目录系统代理 directory system agent {DSA}
目录信息库 directory information Base {DIB}
目录信息树 directory information tree {DIT}
目录用户代理 directory user agent {DUA}
目录字典 catalog directory, contents dictionary, contents directory
目前文件 current file
目前状态 current state
目视调准 visual alignment
目视检查 visual check, visual test
目视控制 eyeball control
目态 problem mode, problem state

钼

molybdenum (Mo)

募

募集 raise, collect 募捐 solicit contributions, collect donations

幕

幕布 curtain, screen

N n

【ná】

拿 1)(取物)hold, take, fetch, get 2)(夺取)seize, capture

镎 neptunium (Np)

【nǎ】

哪 1)(疑问)which, what 2)(泛指)any 哪个 ①(指物)which ②(指人)who 哪里, 哪儿 ①(问住处)where ②(泛指任何处所)wherever, anywhere 哪能 how can 哪怕 even, even if, even though, no matter how 哪些 which, who, what 哪样 ①(用于问话)what kind of, which ②(泛指)any kind of

【nà】

那 (指较远的人或事物)that 那个 that 那里 that place, there 那么 ①like that, in that way ②then, in that case 那时 at that time, then, in those days 那些 those 那样 of that kind, like that, such, so

纳 1)(放进来)receive, admit 2)(接受)accept, take in 3)(交纳)pay, offer 纳入 bring in, fit into 纳税 pay taxes

纳(诺)(单位前级) nano-(=10^{-9}), billi
纳米 nanometer (=nm)
纳米技术 nanotechnology
纳秒电路 nanosecond circuit
纳诺程序级 nanoprogram level

钠 sodium, natrium (Na)

【nǎi】

氖 neon (Ne)

【nài】

耐 be able to bear or endure, resistant 耐烦 patient 耐寒 cold-resistant 耐久, 耐用 lasting, durable 耐劳 able to endure hard work 耐力 endurance

萘 naphthalene

【nán】

南 south 南半球 the Southern Hemisphere 南北 ①(南边和北边)south and north ②(从南到北)from north to south 南方 ①(南)south ②(南部地区)the southern part of the country 南风 south wind 南极 Antarctic, the South Pole, the Antarctic pole

男 (儿子)sun, boy 男性

male, man, the men sex 男[雄]性的 male

难 另见【nàn】
1) (困难的) difficult, hard, troublesome 2) (不好) bad, unpleasant 难得 ① (不易得到) hard to come by, rare ② (不常发生) seldom, rarely 难点 difficult point, difficulty 难懂 difficult to comprehend, hard to understand 难度 degree of difficulty 难怪 (怪不得) no wonder 难过 ① (不易过活) have a hard time ② (难受) feel sorry, feel bad, be grieved 难免 hard to avoid, unavoidable 难受 ① (身体不舒服) feel sick ② (心里不痛快) feel unhappy, feel bad 难题 difficult problems, a hard nut to crack 难听 ① (不悦耳) unpleasant to hear ② (刺耳) offensive, nasty ③ (不体面) scandalous 难忘 unforgettable, memorable 难住 baffle, bewilder

难 另见【nán】
1) (灾难) catastrophe, disaster, calamity 2) (质难) blame, reproach

【náng】
囊 1) (口袋) bag, pocket 2) (口袋样物) something shaped like a bag 囊括 include, embrace

【nǎo】
恼 1) (生气) angry, annoyed, furious 2) (烦闷) unhappy, worried

脑 brain 脑筋 ① (指思考、记忆等能力) mind, thinking ② (指意识) ideas, conception 脑力劳动 mental work 脑件 brainware

【nào】
闹 1) (喧哗) noisy 2) (吵) make a noise, stir up trouble 闹市 busy shopping center, downtown area

【nèi】
内 inner, inside, within 内部 inside, internal, interior 内地 inland, interior, hinterland 内涵 intension, connotation 内行 expert, adept, hands-on 内河 inland river 内陆 inland, interior, landlocked 内容 content, substance 内外 inside and outside, domestic and foreign 内心 heart, innermost being 内因 internal cause 内在 inherent, intrinsic 内政 internal affairs
内部表征 internal attribute
内部查找 internal searching
内部传感器 internal sensor
内部存储器 internal memory/ storage
内部代码 internal code
内部地址 home/ internal address
内部调用 intrinsic call
内部对象 internal object
内部格式 internal format
内部固件 internal firmware
内部函数 intrinsic function
内部检查 built-in check
内部交换通道 interexchange channel {**IXC**}

内部接口 internal interface
内部结点 internal node
内部块 internal block
内部描述 internal description
内部命令 built-in command, internal command, intrinsic command
内部模式[模型] internal model
内部目标 internal object
内部排序 internal sort
内部适配器 built-in adapter
内部属性 built-in attribute, internal attribute
内部通信 intercommunication
内部网 intranet
内部网关协议 interior gateway protocol {IGP}
内部文本 internal text
内部校验 built-in check
内部信息 internal information
内部中断 internal interrupt
内部字体[字型] built-in font, internal font
内部总线 internal bus
内插 interpolate
内插板 add-in board
内插法 interpolation (method)
内插式附件 add-in
内插式软件 add-in soft
内处理 in-line processing
内存 internal memory/storage/store, memory
内存保护 memory protect
内存变量 storage variable
内存布局 memory mapping
内存常驻区 core memory resident
内存储器 built-in storage
内存储信息位置图示 topogram
内存多路数据链 memory multiplex data link {MMDL}
内存分级体系 memory hierarchy
内存分配 memory allocation
内存覆盖 memory overlay
内存故障 memory fault
内存管理单元 memory management unit {MMU}
内存节点 memory node
内存控制器 memory controller
内存扩充[扩展] memory expansion
内存区 memory field
内存释放 memory deallocation
内存数据寄存器 memory data register {MDR}
内存闲置 memory idle {MI}
内存芯片 memory chip
内存栈 memory stack
内存争用 memory collision
内存驻留病毒 memory-resident viruses
内存转储 memory dump
内分类 internal sort, key sort
内符 insymbol
内过程 internal procedure
内含成员 include member
内含子 intron
内函数 intrinsic function, in-line function
内核 kernel
内积 inner product, scalar product
内建函数 built-in function
内建自测电路 build-in self-test {BIST}
内接符 inconnecter
内节点 interior node
内结构 internal structure
内径 bore
内菊花链 internal daisy chain
内联图像 inline image
内联网 intranet
内目录 in-list
内容表 table of contents {TOC}
内容列表 contents list
内容目录 contents directory

内容耦合 content coupling
内容清除 flush out
内容视图 content view
内扫描 interscan
内时钟 internal clock
内推法 interpolation
内务操作 bookkeeping/housekeeping operation
内务的 in-house
内校验 in-line check
内行操作 hands-on operation
内循环 inner loop
内移位 internal shift
内元素 interior element
内蕴函数 intrinsic function
内蕴状态 intrinsic state
内在故障 indigenous fault
内在函数 intrinsic function
内在效力 internal validity
内系统 built-in system
内状态 internal state
内自陷 internal trap
内总线 internal bus

【nèn】

嫩 1)(娇嫩)tender, delicate 2)(烹调时间短)underdone, tender 3)(色浅)light, delicate 4)(阅历浅)inexperienced, immature, green

【néng】

能 (有能力的)able, capable 能动 active, dynamic, vigorous 能动性 dynamic role, activity, initiative 能干 able, capable, competent 能够 can, be able to, be capable of 能量 energy 能力 ability, capability, skill 能手 expert 能源 the source of energy, energy resources, 能带 energy band

能(量损)耗 energy loss
能级 energy level, level
能级图 energy level diagram
能力 ability, capability, power
能力测试[测验] ability test, aptitude test
能力库 ability base
能量扩散 energy dispersal
能删除的文件 delete-capable file
能态 energy state
能用目录的网络 directory enabled network {DEN}

【ní】

尼 尼龙 nylon

泥 泥巴 mud, mire, clay 泥土 ①(土壤)earth, soil ②(粘土)clay 泥状物 mash

铌 niobium (Nb)

【nǐ】

你 1)(指对方)you 2)(泛指任何人)you, one 你们

拟 1)(起草)draw up, draft 2)(打算)intend, plan 拟定 draw, draft, work out 拟订 draw up, draft, work out 拟稿 make a draft 拟议 ①(初步考虑)proposal, recommendation ②(草拟)draw up, draft
拟变量 quasivariable
拟合 fit
拟合平滑法 adaptive smoothing method
拟人机器人 anthropomorphic type robot
拟图 graphoid
拟语言 quasi-language

【nì】

逆 1)（方向相反）contrary, counter, adverse, converse, inverse 2)（抵触）go against, disobey 逆差 adverse balance of trade, trade deficit 逆境 adverse circumstances 逆流 adverse current, countercurrent 逆转 take a turn for the worse, reverse, become worse, deteriorate
逆编译 decompiling
逆变换 inverse transformation
逆波兰表示法 reverse Polish notation {RPN}
逆插值法 inverse interpolation
逆传网络 counterpropagation network
逆代码 inverse code
逆迭代 inverse iteration
逆读 read backward
逆访问 reversed access
逆关系 converse of relation
逆矩阵 inverse matrix
逆邻接表 inverse adjacency list
逆推理 inverse inference
逆相 antiphase
逆向产生式系统 backward production system
逆向地址解析协议 reverse address resolution protocol {RARP}
逆向链 chaining backward
逆向推理 reasoning backward
逆向显示 inverse video
逆信道 inverse channel
逆行原理 retrogression principle
逆序 inverted sequence, reverse order
逆序词典 backward dictionary
逆映像图 converse digraph
逆元（素）inverse element
逆转力矩 stall torque

匿 hide, conceal 匿名 anonymous
匿名变量 anonymous variable

【nián】

年 1)（时间单位）year 2)（每年的）annual, yearly 3)（岁数）age, year 年报 annual report, annual, annals 年表 chronological table 年初 the beginning of the year 年代 ①（时代）age, years, time ②（十年的时期）a decade of a century 年度 year ◇财政年度 financial year, fiscal year 年会 annual meeting 年级 grade, year 年纪 age 年鉴 yearbook, almanac 年刊 annals, annual 年利 annual interest 年龄 age 年年 every year, year after year, year by year 年青 young 年轻 young 年息 annual interest 年限 fixed number of years 年薪 yearly salary 年终 the end of the year, year-end

黏（粘）sticky, glutinous 黏附 adhere 黏附力 adhesion 黏附■剂 binder, adhesive, bonding agent 黏结 cohere 黏结力 cohesion, cohesive force 黏结性 cohesiveness 黏土 clay 黏性 stickiness, viscosity

【niǎn】

捻 twist, lay, twine

碾 1)（谷物去壳）grind or

【niàn】

念 (想念) think of, miss 念头 thought, idea

【niǎo】

鸟 bird 鸟瞰 ① (从高处往下看) get a bird's-eye view ② (概括描写) general survey of a subject, bird's-eye view

【niē】

捏 捏造 fabricate, fake, make up

【niè】

啮 啮合 ① (上下咬紧) clench the teech ② (轮的啮合) mesh, engage, gear, mate

镍 nickel (Ni)

镊 镊子 tweezers

【níng】

宁 另见【nìng】
宁静 peaceful, tranquil, quiet

拧 另见【nìng】
1) (绞扭) twist, wring 2) (捏) pinch, tweak

凝 (注意力集中) focus one's attention 凝固 solidify 凝结 ① (气体变为液体) condense ② (液体变为固体) coagulate, congeal ③ (结合) cement 凝视 gaze fixedly, stare at

【nǐng】

拧 另见【níng】

(旋转) twist, screw, turn around, wrench, wring

【nìng】

宁 (would) rather 宁可, 宁愿, 宁肯 would rather

【niú】

牛 ox, cow, cattle (总称)
牛奶 milk 牛肉 beef
牛顿插值 Newton interpolation

【niǔ】

扭 (拧) twist, wrench 扭伤 sprain, wrench 扭转 ① (掉转) turn round, turn about ② (纠正) turn back, reverse 扭转 turn round
扭接头 twist joint

纽 纽带 link, tie, bond

钮 钮扣 knob, button

【nóng】

农 农产品 agricultural products, farm produce 农场 farm 农村 rural area, countryside, village 农历 the traditional Chinese calender 农民 peasant, farmer 农田 farmland, cropland, cultivated land 农业 agriculture, farming 农作物 crops

浓 1) (稠密) dense, thick, concentrated 2) (味道浓) strong, rich 浓度 density, concentration 浓厚 ① (很浓) dense, thick ② (色彩浓重) deep, strong, profound ③ (程度深) strong 浓密 dense, thick
浓淡程序 shading program

浓淡处理 shade
浓淡度 gradation
浓淡模型 shading model
浓淡图像 shading image, shading pattern
浓度控制 density control
浓缩集合 upgrade set

【nòng】

弄 1)(戏耍)play with, fool with, trifle with 2)(做,干)do, make, handle 3)(设法取得)get, fetch

【nǔ】

努 努力 make great efforts, try hard, exert oneself

【nù】

怒 (愤怒)angry, rage, fury

【nǚ】

女 女儿 daughter, girl 女士 lady 女王 queen 女性 ①(性别)the female sex ②(妇女)woman 女子 woman, female

钕 neodymium (Nd)

【nuǎn】

暖 1)〈形〉warm 2)〈动〉warm up 暖流 warm current 暖气(central) heating

【nüè】

虐 虐待 maltreat, ill-treat

【nuó】

挪 挪动 move, shift 挪用 ①(把钱移作别用)divert ②(私自动用)misappropriate, embezzle
挪用[窃用]总线 steal bus

【nuò】

诺 (许诺)promise, assent 诺贝尔奖金 Nobel Prize 诺言 promise
诺模术 nomography
诺模图 nomogram, nomograph
诺维尔网络 Novell Netware

锘 nobelium (No)

懦 懦夫 coward, craven 懦怯 cowardly

O o

【ōu】

欧 欧盟(欧洲联盟) European Union 欧美 Europe and America, Western, the West 欧洲 Europe 欧洲经济共同体 the European Economic Community (E.E.C)
欧几里得空间 Euclidean space
欧拉常数 Euler constant
欧拉回路 Euler loop
欧拉循环 Euler cycle/loop
欧拉有向图 Eulerian digraph
欧拉坐标 Eulerian coordinate
欧姆(电阻单位) ohm
欧姆表 ohmmeter
欧洲标准化委员会 European Committee for Standardization {CEN}
欧洲电工标准化委员会 European Committee for Electrotechnical Standardization {CENELEC}
欧洲电信标准学会 European Telecommunications Standards Institute {EISI}
欧洲计算机制造商联合会 European Computer Manufacturers Association {ECMA}
欧洲信息网 European Information Network {EIN}

【ǒu】

偶 1)(双数)even, in pairs 2)(配偶)mate, spouse 3)(力偶,电偶)couple, duplet 偶合 coincidence 偶然 ① accidental, fortuitous ② accidentally by chance ③ once in a while 偶像 image, idol ◇木偶 wooden image, puppet
偶代换 even substitution
偶对称 even symmetry
偶分支 even component
偶函数 even function
偶然[偶发]故障 chance failure
偶然失效率 constant failure rate {CFR}
偶然事故 accident
偶数 even number
偶数奇偶校验 even parity (check)
偶数域 even field
偶图 bipartite graph, bigraph, dual graph
偶校验 even parity check
偶置换 even permutation

耦

耦合 couple, coupling
耦合变量 coupling variable
耦合度 coupling degree
耦合矩阵 coupled matrix
耦合器 coupler
耦合位 coupling bit
耦合系数 coupling coefficient
耦合因数 coupling factor

P p

【pá】

爬 (攀登) climb, clamber 爬行 crawl, creep

【pà】

怕 1) (害怕) fear, dread, be afraid of 2) (估计) I'm afraid, I suppose, perhaps 3) (担心) for fear, fear 怕羞 shy, bashful

【pāi】

拍 拍板 ① 〈经贸〉rap the gavel ◇拍板成交 strike a bargain, clinch a deal ② (做出决定) have the final say, give the final verdict 拍打 clap, pat 拍卖 ① (当众出售) auction, sell sth at auction ② (减价抛售) selling off goods at reduced prices, sale 拍摄,拍照 take a picture, photograph, shoot 拍子 bat, racket
拍(它) (单位前缀) peta- (=10^{15})
拍符号 flip symbol, flop symbol
拍节·syllable
拍摄脚本 shooting script

【pái】

排 1) (按次排列) arrange, put in order 2) (排成的行列) row, line, rank 3) (军队) platoon 4) (竹排,木排) raft 排斥 repel of, exclude, reject 排除 get rid of, remove, exclude, eliminate 排队 form a line, line up, queue up 排放 emission, discharge 排列 ① arrange, range, put in order ② 〈数学〉permutation 排演 rehearse
排版 compose, type set
排出 eject, snap out, squeeze out
排错 fault avoidance
排队表 queuing list
排队对话 queued session
排队分析 queuing analysis
排队机构 queuing mechanism
排队论 queu(e)ing theory, waiting line theory
排队模型 queuing model, waiting line model
排队时延 queuing delay {QD}
排队网络 queuing network
排队文件 queue file
排列 arrangement, marshalling, permutation, reorder, sequence
排他锁 exclusive lock
排他性访问 exclusive access
排序 collate, order(ing), reorder, collating (sequence), rank, sequencing, sort(ing)
排序标记 key sequencing, tag along sort

排序标志 sort flag
排序策略 ordering policy/strategy
排序程序 sequencer, sorter
排序分类 collating sort
排序归并 sort merge
排序键 sequencing key
排序偏移 ordering bias
排序算法 sort algorithm, sorting algorithm
排序网络 sorting network
排序字段 sort(ing) field

徘 徘徊 ①(来回走)pace up and down, walk back and forth ②(犹豫不决)hesitate, waver, hover ③〈经贸〉fluctuate

牌 1)(标志牌)plate, tablet, board 2)(商标)brand 3)(娱乐用品)cards ◇扑克牌 playing cards 牌号 ①(商店字号)shop sign ②(商标)trademark, mark 牌价 ①(标出价格)set price ②(市价)market price 牌照 license plate, license tag

【pài】
派 (委派)send, dispatch, assign, appoint 派别 group, school, faction 派生 derivation, variant, fork 派生词 derivative 派头 style, manner and air
派遣 dispatch
派生类比 derivational analogy
派生树 derivation tree
派生指令 fork instruction

【pán】
盘 盘点 check, make an inventory of 盘绕 coil, wind, twist 盘算 calculate, figure, plan 盘旋 spiral, circle, wheel, hover, convolve 盘子 tray, plate, dish 盘状物 sth shaped like or used as a tray, plate
盘 disk, disc
盘卷 reel
盘面区带 disk bands
盘片 platter
盘式打字机 type disk typewriter
盘伺服机构 reel servo
盘用开关 panel switch
盘阵列 disk array

【pàn】
判 判定,判断 judge, decide, determine 判决 court decision, judgment 判明 distinguish, ascertain, draw a clear distinction 判断 judge, judgment, decide, determine
判别 discrimination, distinguish
判别路径[通路]法 critical path method {CPM}
判别指令 decision instruction, discriminating order, discrimination instruction
判别准则 decision criterion
判定边界 decision boundary
判定标准 criterion, criteria
判定表 critical table, decision(al) table
判定分析 decision analysis {DA}
判定规则 criterion rule, decision rule
判定框 criteria frame, decision box
判定框图 decision box
判定算法 decision algorithm
判定图 decision graph

【 pàn 】

判定系统 decision making system
判定验证 decision verification
判定指令 decision/ discrimination instruction
判定装置 decision mechanism
判断时间 think time
判据 criterion, criteria
判决表 decisional table
判优 arbitration
判优程序 arbiter

盼 盼望 hope for, long for, look forward to

【 páng 】

庞 庞大 huge, colossal, gigantic, immense 庞杂 numerous and disorderly

旁 (其他)other, else 旁边 side 旁观 look on, be an onlooker 旁听 be a visitor at a meeting, in a school class, audit 旁听生 audit
旁路 bylink, bypass, shunt
旁路电容器 bypass capacitor
旁通 bypass

【 pàng 】

胖 fat, obese, plump 胖子 a fat person, fatty

【 pāo 】

抛 1)(扔)throw, toss, fling 2)(丢下)leave behind, cast aside 抛锚 ①(停船下锚)drop anchor, cast anchor ②(车辆故障)break down, be out of order 抛弃 abandon, cast aside, discard 抛售 undersell, dump
抛光 lap, polishing

刨 另见(bào)
(挖掘)dig, excavate

【 pǎo 】

跑 (逃走)run away, escape, flee 跑步 run 跑道 ① runway ② track

【 pào 】

泡 1)(气泡)bubble 2)(泡状物)sth shaped like a bubble 3)(浸泡)steep, soak 泡沫 foam, froth
泡形图 bubble chart

炮 gun, cannon, artillery
炮轰,炮击 bombard, shell
炮火 artillery fire, gunfire

【 péi 】

培 培训 train 培训班 training class 培养 foster, train, develop, educate, cultivate 培育 cultivate, foster, breed, nurture, rear 培植 cultivate, foster, train, educate

陪 accompany 陪伴 keep company with 陪审 serve on a jury 陪同 accompany, be in the company of
陪集 coset

赔 赔本 run a business at a loss 赔偿 compensate, pay for 赔款 ①(赔偿损失)pay an indemnity, pay reparations ②(赔偿费)indemnity, reparations, amends 赔礼 offer/ make an apology, apologize 赔偿 compensate, pay for

锫 berkelium (Bk)

【pèi】

佩 佩带 wear, bear 佩服 admire

配 1)(按比例调合) blend, compound, mix ◇配颜色 mix colors 2)(相称) match 3)(配得上) deserve, be worthy of, be qualified 配给 distribute according to plan, apportion 配齐 fit out, complete ◇配成一套 complete the set // 配零件 replace parts 配备 ①(根据需要分配) allocate, provide, fit out ②(布置兵力) dispose (troops, etc.), deploy ③(成套的器物等) outfit, equipment 配额 quota 配合 coordinate, cooperate, ration, allot, distribute 配套 form a complete set
配电 distribution
配电板 power board
配电盒 power-supply box
配电盘 panel
配电系统 distributed system
配对 conjugate, pairing
配墨色带打字机 typewriter with carbon ribbon
配套工具 kit
配套软件 software kit
配线架 distribution frame
配线面板 distribution panel
配置 configuration, configure, coordination, dispersal, distribution, layout, set-up, profile
配置报告程序 configuration report program {CRP}
配置部分 configuration section
配置程序 configurator
配置方案 allocation plan
配置方法 collocation method
配置管理程序 configuration manager
配置机制 configuration facility
配置控制 configuration control
配置器 configurator
配置数据 layout data
配置文件 configuration file
配置状态 configuration state

【pēn】

喷 喷出 spurt, spout 喷洒 spray, sprinkle 喷射 spray, spurt, jet
喷墨的 ink-jet
喷墨绘图机 ink jet plotter
喷墨印刷[打印]机 ink jet printer
喷墨嘴 ink nozzle

【pén】

盆 basin, tub, pot

【pēng】

烹 boil, cook 烹饪 cooking, cuisine

【péng】

朋 朋友 friend

硼 boron (B), boracium

蓬 蓬勃 vigorous, flourishing

膨 膨胀 expand, swell, dilate

【pěng】

捧 (用双手托) hold or carry in both hands

【pèng】

碰 touch, bump 碰见 meet

unexpectedly, run into, encounter, come across 碰巧 by chance, by coincidence, happen to 碰撞 ①（猛然碰上）collide, run into, crash, bump, knock ②〈物理〉collision, impact

碰撞检测 collision detection {CD}

【pī】

批 批驳 ①（否决）veto an opinion or a request ②（批评）refute, criticize 批次 batch (of aircraft, etc.) 批发 ①（成批销售）wholesale ②（批准发布）be authorized for dispatch 批号 lot number, batch number 批判 criticize, repudiate 批评 ① criticize ② criticism 批示 ①〈名〉written instructions or comments ②〈动〉make comments and instructions 批语 remarks on a piece of writing 批注 ①〈动〉annotate and comment on ②〈名〉annotations and commentaries, marginalia, head-note 批准 ratify, approve, sanction

批保留与恢复 batch save/restore
批报文处理 batch message processing {BMP}
批操作 batch operation
批程序 batch program
批处理 batch process(ing)
批处理程序 batch facility, batch processing program
批处理方式 batch mode, batch processing mode
批处理环境 batch environment
批处理系统 batch processing system
批方式 batch mode
批功能 batch facility
批检查点/再启动 batch checkpoint
批量 batch, lot size
批量表 batch table
批量打印 bulk print
批量调度 lot size scheduling
批量接口文件 batch interface file {ITF}
批量库存 lot size inventories
批量作业 batch of jobs
批流量 batch stream
批命令 batch command
批命令文件 batch command file
批启动 batch initiation
批式作业队列 batch job queue
批通信 batched communication
批文件传输 batch file transmission
批文件控制 batch file control
批执行 batch execution
批作业 batch job, batched job

坯 坯件 base, semifinished product 坯模 mold

披 披露 ①（发表）publish, announce, make public ②（表露）reveal, show, disclose

【pī】

纰 纰漏 careless mistake, small accident, slip

劈 另见[pǐ]
劈开 split, chop, cut 劈雷 strike

【pí】

皮 1)（外皮）skin 2)（毛皮）fur 3)（封皮）cover, wrapper

4) (表面) surface 皮带 ① (腰带) leather belt ② (传动带) belt, strap 皮肤 skin 皮革 leather, hide 皮毛 ① (带皮的兽皮) fur ② (表面的知识) smattering, superficial knowledge 皮鞋 leather shoes

皮(可) (单位前缀) pico- $(=10^{-12})$
皮可程序语言 picoprogramming language
皮可处理器 picoprocessor
皮可计算机 picocomputer
皮可计算机结构 pico architecture
皮秒 picosecond (= ps, psec)

毗 毗连,毗邻 adjoin, be adjacent to

铍 beryllium, berillium (Be), glucin(i)um

疲 疲劳 ① (劳累) tired, fatigued, weary ② (反应迟缓) fatigue, strain ③〈物理〉fatigue ◇弹性疲劳 elastic fatigue 疲软 ① (疲乏无力) fatigued and weak ②〈经贸〉weak, slump 疲惫 tired, weary

【pǐ】

匹
匹配 marriage, match(ing)
匹配[配对]程序 matcher
匹配[器]调整 marriage adjustment
匹配规则 unification rule
匹配过程 matching process
匹配技术 matching technique
匹配滤波器 matched filter, matching filter
匹配数据 matcher data
匹配条件 match condition
匹配置换 match substitution

劈 另见【pi】
(分开) divide, split

【pì】

辟 1) (开辟) open up, start 2) (透彻) penetrating, incisive ◇精辟 profound, incisive 3) (驳斥) refute, repudiate

媲 媲美 compare favorably with, rival

譬 譬如 for example, for instance, such as

【piān】

片 另见【piàn】
片子 ① (电影胶片) a roll of film ② (影片) film, movie ③ (唱片) gramophone record, disc

偏 (偏向) inclined to one side, slanting, leaning 偏爱 have a preference for, be partial to 偏差 ① (偏离角度) deviation, declination ② (工作差错) deviation, error 偏废 do one thing and neglect another, emphasized one thing at the expense of another 偏见 prejudice, bias, preconception 偏离 deviate, diverge 偏僻 remote, out-of-the-way 偏袒 show partiality for, take sides with 偏向 ① (不正确的倾向) erroneous tendency, deviation ② (袒

护)be partial to 偏心(不公正)partiality, bias 偏重 lay particular stress on, one-sidely emphasize
偏差 bias, deflexion, departure, deviation, variance
偏磁电平 bias level
偏函数 partial function
偏离 bias, departure, skew
偏离差错 bias error
偏离磁道 off-track
偏离角 deflection angle
偏离率 bias ratio
偏离失真 bias distortion
偏离数据 bias data
偏离误差 biased error
偏斜 skew
偏序 partial order
偏序集 partially ordered set
偏压 bias
偏压电平 bias level
偏移 bias, dispersion, displacement, offset
偏移量 displacement
偏移数据 offset data
偏移位 offset bit
偏移误差 offset error
偏移字节 displacement byte
偏置 offsetting
偏置零 offset null
偏置逻辑 bias logic, biasing logic
偏转角 deflection angle

篇 〈量词〉piece, sheet 篇幅 ①(文章长短)length (of a piece of writing) ②(指刊印的篇幅)space ◇限于篇幅 due to the limited space 篇目 table of contents, contents
篇章 discourse, writings

【pián】
便 另见【biàn】
便宜 ①(价钱低)cheap, inexpensive ②(使得到便宜)let sb off lightly

【piàn】
片 另见【piān】
(薄片)piece, slice 片段 part, extract, fragment 片刻 a short while, an instant, a moment 片面 ①(单方面的)unilateral, one-sided ②(不全面)one-sided, lopsided
片标 trimmer
片段 fragment, segment
片段标识符 segment identifier {SID}
片段模式 fragment schema
片段匹配 segment match
片段前缀 segment prefix
片段扫描 segment scan
片内定时器 on-chip timer
片内时钟振荡器 on-chip clock oscillator
片选 chip enable {CE}, chip select {CS}, chip selection
片选线 chip select line
片总线 chip bus

骗 (欺骗)deceive, fool, hoodwink 骗局 fraud, hoax, deception 骗子 swindler, trickster

【piāo】
剽 剽窃 plagiarize, lift

漂 另见【piǎo】【piào】
漂浮 ①(漂动)float ②(工作不踏实)showy, superficial
漂流 ①(漂浮)be driven by the current, drift about ②(漂泊)lead a wandering life, rove, drift
漂移 drift, shift, swim

漂移(频率) creeping
漂移编辑 drifting editing
漂移点 shift point
漂移符号 drifting symbol
漂移误差 drift error

飘 wave to and fro, float (in the air), flutter

【piǎo】

漂 另见【piāo】【piào】
(用水冲干净)rinse 漂白 bleach

【piào】

票 1)(车票等)ticket ◇来回票 round trip ticket 2)(钞票)bill, bank note 票额 the sum stated on a check or bill, denomination, face value 票价 the price of a ticket, admission fee, entrance fee 票据 ①(有金额的单据)bill, note ②(出纳或货运凭证)voucher, receipt 票面 face value, par value, nominal value 票面值 denomination
票据(计算)机 billing machine
票据、收帐、销售分析 billing, accounts receivable, sales analysis {BARSA}

漂 另见【piāo】【piǎo】
漂亮 ①(好看)handsome, good-looking, pretty, beautiful ②(出色)smart, remarkable, brilliant, splendid, beautiful

【piē】

氕 light hydrogen, protium (H^1)

撇 另见【piě】
(抛弃)cast aside, throw overboard, neglect 撇开 leave aside, bypass 撇沫 skim

【piě】

撇 另见【piē】
撇号 apostrophe

【pīn】

拼 拼合 put together, piece together 拼命 be ready to risk one's life, go all out in work 拼错 misspell, transliterate 拼音 combine sounds into syllables, spell
拼错 misspelling
拼法检查 spell check
拼接 concatenation, paste-up, splicing
拼接器 splicer
拼图 paste-up
拼写方式 spell mode
拼写检查 spell check
拼写模式 spell mode
拼装区 build-up area

【pín】

贫 poor ①(穷)poor, impoverished ②(缺少)be deficient in, be poor in, be scanty of 贫乏 poor, short, lacking 贫穷 poor, needy

频 (频繁)frequently, repeatedly
频带 band, frequency band
频带宽度 bandwidth {BW}, frequency bandwidth
频道 band, frequency channel
频道管理员 channel operator
频分多路传输 frequency division multiplexing {FDM}
频分多路复用技术 frequency

division multiplexing {FDM}
频率 frequency
频率调制 frequency modulation {FM}
频率法 frequency method {FM}
频率分多路复用 frequency division multiplexing {FDM}
频率分配 allocation of frequence, frequency allocation
频率分片 frequency slicing
频率分析仪 frequency analyzer
频率复用 frequency reuse
频率计 cymometer
频率计数器 frequency counter
频率漂移 creep, frequency deviation
频率失真 frequency distortion
频率图 frequency diagram
频率校正电路 emphasizer
频率协调 frequency coordination
频谱 frequency spectrum, spectrum
频谱学 spectroscopy
频谱仪 spectrometer
频移 carrier shift
频域 frequency domain

【pǐn】
品 (物品) article, product 品德 moral character, morality 品级 grade, class, rank 品名 the name of an aritcle, the name or description of a commodity 品评 judge, assess 品种 〈生物〉breed, strain, variety 〈产品种类〉variety, assortment 品质 character, quality

【pìn】
聘 聘请,聘任 appoint, invite, employ 聘书 letter of appointment, contract 聘用 employ, engage, appoint to a position

【pīng】
乓
乒乓病毒 ping pong virus
乒乓法 ping-pong procedure
乒乓开关 toggle, toggle switch

【píng】
平 1)(使平) level, even 2)(高度相同) be on the same level, be on a par, 3)(公平) fair, impartial 4)(安定) calm, peaceful, quiet 平安 safe and sound, without mishap, well 平常 ①(普通) ordinary, common ②(平时) generally, usually, ordinary, as a rule ③(不出色) average, mediocre 平常的 average, common 平淡 flat, insipid, dull 平等 equally 平定 put down, suppress 平凡 ordinary, common, mediocre 平分 divide equally, go halves 平静 calm, quiet, tranquil 平局 draw, tie 平均 average, mean 平时 at ordinary times, usually 平坦 flat, level, even, smooth 平稳 smooth and steady, smooth, stable, equable 平行 ①(等级相同) of equal rank, on an equal footing ②(同时进行的) simultaneous, parallel ③〈数学〉parallel; collateral 平原 plain 平整 ①〈动〉level ②〈形〉neat, smooth
平板 flat
平板绘图机 flat-bed plotter
平板扫描器 flat-bed scanner

平板式数字化仪 tablet digitizer
平板式显示器 panel display
平板数据装置 panel data set
平版胶印术 offset lithography
平版印刷 lithography
平凡图 trivial graph
平凡文法 trivial grammar
平方 quadrate, square
平方根 square root
平方器 squarer
平分按钮 cascade button
平衡 balance, equalization, equilibration, equilibrium
平衡超图 balanced hypergraph
平衡点 equilibrium point
平衡二叉树 balanced binary tree
平衡放大器 balanced amplifier
平衡分类 balanced sort
平衡概率 equilibrium probability
平衡归并排序 balanced merge sort
平衡合并 balanced merge
平衡环 gimbal
平衡路由 balanced routing
平衡器 counter poise
平衡算法 balanced algorithm
平衡网络 balanced network, compromise net
平衡制 balanced system
平衡状态 equilibrium state
平滑 smooth, smoothing
平滑电路 smoothing circuit
平滑过程 smoothing process
平滑算法 smoothing algorithm
平滑线路 smoothline
平均操作时间 average operation time
平均查找时间 average search time
平均成本 averaging cost
平均的 averaging, equable, mean, medial

平均等待时间 average latency, average waiting time
平均分类法 mean sort
平均负载 average load
平均故障间隔时间 mean time between failures {MTBF}
平均故障检测时间 mean time to detection {MTD}
平均恢复时间 mean time recovery {MTTR}, mean time to recover {MTTR}
平均加权 average weighted
平均检查 average test
平均密度 average density
平均偏差 mean deviation
平均失效间隔时间 mean time to failure {MTTF}
平均寿命 mean life
平均数 average
平均速度 average rate
平均替换间隔时间 mean time between replacement {MTBR}
平均维修响应时间 mean time to respond to repair {MTTR}
平均无故障时间 mean free error time, mean time between failures {MTBF}, mean time to failure {MTTF}
平均误差 average error, mean error
平均修复时间 mean repair time, mean time to repair
平均寻(找)磁)道时间 average seek time
平均诊断时间 mean time to diagnose {MTTD}
平均值 mean, mean value
平均指令数/秒 average instructions per second {AIP}
平面 face, nodal plane, plane, two-dimension
平面部件 planar
平面封装 flat pack

平面工艺 planar process, planar technology
平面屏幕 flat screen
平面树 plane tree
平面图 planar graph, plane graph
平面网络 planar network
平面像素 planar pixel
平面元 flat element
平铺 cascade, tiling
平铅字 flat type
平台 platform
平台集成 platform integration
平稳点 stationary point
平稳分布 stationary distribution
平稳区 stable zone
平稳性 stationarity
平稳状态 stationary state
平行板(绘图用的) clinograph
平行搜索 parallel sweep
平行子句 parallel-clause
平移 pan, translating, translation
平移变换 translation transformation

评
评比 appraise through comparison, compare and assess 评定 judge, evaluate, assess 评分 mark, grade, score 评估 ① assessment, evaluation, estimation ② evaluate 评级 grade, rate 评价 appraise, evaluate, assess, estimate 评介 review (a new book, etc.) 评论 ①〈动〉comment on, discuss ②〈名〉comment, commentary, review 评判 pass judgment on, judge 评审 examine and appraise 评选 choose through public appraisal, discuss and elect 评议 appraise 评语 comment, remark 评阅 read and appraise 评注 ①〈动〉make commetary and annotation ②〈名〉notes and commentary
评价报告 evaluation report
评价测试程序 evaluation test program
评价插板 evaluation board
评价函数 evaluation function
评价模块 evaluation module
评价模型 evaluation model, evaluative model
评价系统 evaluation system
评价准则 evaluation criterion
评论员 commenter, observer
评判题 benchmark problem, benchmark task
评述 survey

苹
苹果 apple

凭
1)(靠着) lean on, lean against 2)(依靠) rely on, depend on 3)(证据) certification, evidence, proof 4)(根据) go by, base on, take as the basis 凭单 voucher, indenture, a certificate for drawing money, goods, etc. 凭借 rely on, depend on 凭空 out of the void, without foundation; groundless 凭证 proof, evidence, certificate, voucher
凭单编号 order number
凭证到期时间 certificate expiration
凭证管理 certificate management
凭证扩展 certificate extension
凭证列表 certificate chain
凭证签发 certificate issuance
凭证申请 certificate applicant

píng 屏瓶 pō 钋泊坡泼 pó 婆 pǒ 钷 pò 迫破

凭证申请过程 enrollment
凭证申请人 end user subscriber
凭证体制 certificate hierarchy
凭证序列号 certificate serial number

屏 另见【bǐng】

屏障 protective screen, shield, shelter
屏蔽 mask(ing), screen(ing), shield(ing)
屏蔽传输线 strip (transmission) line
屏蔽的 disabled, masked
屏蔽法 screening
屏蔽级 level of masking, mask level
屏蔽寄存器 mask(ing) register
屏蔽码操作数 mask operand
屏蔽冗余 masking redundancy
屏蔽双绞线 shielded twist(ed) pair {STP}
屏蔽位 mask bit
屏蔽线 shield line
屏蔽值 mask value
屏蔽指令 mask(ing) instruction
屏蔽状态 masked state
屏蔽字 mask word
屏蔽字段 mask field
屏蔽字节 mask byte
屏蔽总线 mask bus
屏面格式 screen format
屏面号 panel number
屏幕 screen
屏幕编辑 on-screen editing
屏幕菜单 screen menu
屏幕打印键 PrtSc key
屏幕分割 split screen
屏幕符号 screen symbol
屏幕光标 screen cursor
屏幕缓冲区 screen buffer
屏幕空间 screen space
屏幕屏蔽区 screen mask
屏幕色调 screen tone
屏幕闪烁 screen flicker
屏幕设计工具 screen design aid {SDA}
屏幕生成程序 screen generator
屏幕图像 screen image
屏幕元件 screen element
屏幕转储 screen dump
屏幕状态区 screen status area
屏幕字体 screen font
屏幕坐标 screen coordinates

瓶 bottle, vase, jar, flask
瓶颈 bottleneck

【pō】

钋 polonium (Po), dvitellurium

泊 另见【bó】 poise (unit of dynamic viscosity)

坡 1)(斜坡)slope 2)(倾斜) slopping, slanting

泼 (泼出)sprinkle, splash, spill

【pó】

婆 1)(老年妇女)old woman 2)(丈夫的母亲)husband's mother, mother-in-law

【pǒ】

钷 promethium (Pm)

【pò】

迫 1)〈动〉compel, force, press 2)〈形〉urgent, pressing 迫切 urgent, pressing
迫使 force, compel, coerce

破 1)(使损坏)break (down), damage 2)(突破)break, break through 3)(打败)defeat, capture 4)（揭穿）expose the truth of, lay bare 破产 ①（丧失全部财产）go bankrupt, become impoverished ②（失败）go bankruptcy, fall through 破除 do away with, get rid of, destroy 破格,破例 break a rule, make an exception 破坏 ①（毁损）destroy, damage ②（使受到损害）do great damage to, damage, disrupt ③（违反）violate, break, breach 破旧 broken, damaged, torn, wornout 破开 break, split, cut 破烂 ①（残破的）tattered, ragged, worn-out ②（破烂物）junk, scrap 破裂 burst, split, rupture, crack 破碎 ①〈形〉tattered, broken ②〈动〉smash sth to pieces, break into pieces, crush 破损 damaged, worn, torn; damage, breakage 破晓 dawn, daybreak 破绽 ①（衣服开线）a burst seam ②（漏洞）flaw, weak point 破折号 dash

破坏程序 hacking
破坏程序的用户 hacker
破坏读出 destructive read out {DRO}
破坏性测试[试验] destructive testing
破坏性存储器 destructive memory
破坏性竞争 destructive competition
破坏性试验 destructive test
破坏者 cracker
破译 decrypt

魄 魄力 daring and resolution, boldness

【pōu】
剖 1)（破开）cut open, rip open 2)（分析）analyse, examine 剖析 analyse, dissect
剖分 subdivision
剖面 cross section, orthography, profile
剖视 section

【pū】
扑 1)（冲向）throw oneself on, pounce on 2)（全力以赴）devote 3)（拍打）flap, flutter 扑打 rush at, attack 扑灭 stamp out, put out, extinguish, wipe out

铺 另见[pù]
铺路 ①（铺设道路）pave a road, pave the way ②（排除障碍）pave the way for 铺平 spread, extend, unfold 铺设 pave, lay 铺张 extravagant 铺张浪费 extravagance and waste

【pǔ】
朴 朴素 simple, plain

普 general, universal 普遍 universal, general, widespread, common 普查 general investigation, general survey 普及 ①（推广）popularize, spread ②（传遍）universal, popular 普通 normal, common, ordinary, average 普通话 common spoken Chinese

普通变量 ordinary variable
普通标识符 ordinary identifier
普通的 general, generic

普通二进制　normal binary, pure binary, straight binary
普通符号　ordinary symbol
普通文件传输协议　trivial file transfer protocol {TFTP}
普通划分　trivial partition
普通[正规]状态　normal state

谱　spectrum
谱窗　spectral window
谱分析　spectral analysis

镨　praseodymium (Pr)

【pù】

铺　另见【pū】
1)(店铺)shop, store 2)(床铺)plank bed

瀑　瀑布　waterfall, falls

Q q

【qī】

七 seven 七月 July

欺 欺骗 deceive, cheat, defraud, take in

期 1)（一段时间）a period of time, phase, stage 2)（规定期限）designated time, scheduled time 3)〈量词〉issue, number, term ◇最近一期杂志 current issue of the journal 期待 anticipate, await, expect, look forward to 期货〈经贸〉futures ◇做期货交易 deal in futures 期间 time, course, duration, interval 期刊 periodical, magazine, journal 期满 expire, run out, come to an end 期望 hope, expectation 期限 allotted time, time limit, deadline 期终考试 term examinatiom, final examination

期待值 expected value
期满检验[校验] expiration check
期望变量 expecting variable
期望货币价值 expected monetary value {EMV}
期望收益 expected revenue
期望数据 expected data
期望值 desired/ expected value, expectation

漆 1)〈名〉lacquer, paint 2)〈动〉paint, coat with paint (lacquer) 漆黑 ①（光线很暗）pitch-dark ②（非常黑）pitch-black, jet-black

戚 1)（亲戚）relative 2)（悲哀）sorrow, woe

妻 wife

【qí】

齐 1)（整齐）neat, even, uniform 2)（与…一样高）be level with 3)（一块儿）together, simultaneously 齐备 all ready, all present 齐名 enjoy equal popularity, be equally famous 齐全 complete, all in readiness

齐次方程 homogeneous equation
齐次规划 homogeneous program
齐次函数 homogeneous function
齐次型网络 homogeneous network
齐次性 homogeneity

其 1)（他的，她的，它的，他们的，她们的，它们的）his, her, its, their 2)（他，她，它，他们，她们，它们）he, she, it, they 其次 ①（较后）next, secondly, then ②（次要的）secondary 其间 between them, between which, among them, among which 其实 actually, in fact, as a matter of fact, really 其他, 其它 other, else 其余 the others, the rest, the remainder 其中 among which/them, in which/it

祈
（祈祷）pray 祈求 pray for, entreat 祈望 hope, wish

奇 另见【jī】
1)（奇怪的）strange, queer, rare 2)（出乎意料）unexpected, unpredictable 3)（惊奇）surprise, wonder, astonish 4)（非常）extremely, exceedingly 奇迹 miracle, wonder, marvel 奇妙 marvellous, wonderful 奇特 peculiar, queer, weird
奇迹 miracle
奇异点 singular point
奇异方程 singular equation
奇异覆盖 singular cover
奇异集[络,系,组] singular set
奇异解 singular solution
奇异矩阵 singular matrix
奇异算子 singular operator
奇异值 singular value

歧
（不一致）divergent, different 歧路 fork, branch 歧途 wrong road 歧义 different meanings, various interpretations, ambiguity
歧点 ambiguous point, spinode
歧义性误差 ambiguity error

崎
崎岖 rugged, uneven

骑
ride, sit on the back of

棋
chess

旗
flag, banner

【qǐ】

企
企求 desire to gain, strive 企图 attempt, seek, try 企业 enterprise, business, corporation
企业范围网络 enterprise-wide network
企业管理 management of enterprise
企业管理系统结构 enterprise management architecture {EMA}
企业模式 enterprise model
企业内网 intranet
企业网(络) enterprise network(s)
企业系统规划 business system planning {BSP}
企业信息门户 enterprise information port {EIP}
企业银行 enterprise bank
企业资源计划 enterprise resources planning {ERP}

启
1)（开启）open 2)（开始）start, initiate 启程 set out, start on a journey 启发 enlighten, inspire, make aware 启封 ①（去封）unseal, break the seal, remove the seal ②（拆包）open an envelop or wrapper 启蒙（入门）impart rudimentary knowledge to beginners, initiate 启示 enlightenment, inspira-

tion 启事 notice, announcement
启闭信号 key signal
启动 activate, start up, boot up, enable(ment), initiate, trigger
启动按钮 start button, activate button, initialize button, initiate button
启动标记 start mark
启动程序 bootleg program, initiator, starter
启动地址 start address, enabling address
启动点 starting point
启动方式 initiate mode
启动过程 starting procedure
启动键 activate key, start key
启动控制字 initiate control word
启动逻辑 enable logic
启动脉冲 starting pulse
启动门 enable gate
启动命令 start command
启动请求 initiate
启动区病毒 boot virus
启动任务 activate task, initiating task, initiator task
启动时间 startup/attack time, start(ing) time
启动输入 enable input
启动数据 log-on data
启动算法 starting algorithm
启动位 start bit
启动位置 enable position
启动向量 start vector
启动信号 actuating signal, start(ing) signal
启动序列 start-up sequence
启动用户 activate user
启动与停止[启停] start stop {SS}
启动帧 start frame
启动指令 enabled instruction

启动/终止程序 initiator/terminator
启发[试探]函数 heuristic function
启发能力 heuristic power
启发式规则 heuristic rule
启发式推理 heuristic inference
启发性算法 heuristic algorithm
启停距离 start/stop distance
启用状态 initiate mode

起 1)（起来）rise, get up, stand up 2)（取出）draw out, remove, extract, pull 3)（开始）start, begin 起草 draft, draw up 起程 leave, set out, start on a journey 起初 originally, at first, at the outset, in the beginning 起落 rise and fall, up and down 起码 ①（最初的）minimum, rudimentary, elementary ②（至少）at least 起讫 the beginning and the end 起先 at first, in the beginning 起因 cause, origin 起源 ①〈名〉origin ②〈动〉originate from, stem from, come from 起子 ①（开瓶盖的）bottle opener ②（螺丝刀）screwdriver 起作用 ①（起影响）play a part (in) ②（产生效果）take effect
起点 initial point, origin, originate
起动操作 start-up function
起动程序 start-up routine
起动电平 start level
起动电源 start-up source
起动级 start level
起动器 starter
起动源 start-up source
起泡 blister
起始程序 initializer routine

起始磁道号 starting track number
起始带 initial tape
起始单元 home cell, start element
起始单元字段 origin element field {OEF}
起始地 home
起始地址 initial address, origin
起始地址段 origin address field {OAF}
起始地址空间 home address space
起始地址伪指令 origin directive
起始地址信息 initial address message {IAM}
起始点 start point, starting point
起始方式 initial mode
起始符(号) start symbol, starting symbol
起始和 initial sum
起始回车 initial carriage return
起始记录 home record
起始节点 initial node, start node
起始空白(边) start margin
起始树 initial tree
起始条件 starting condition
起始条件码 initial condition code
起始位 start bit
起始位置 home position, starting location, top of file {TOF}
起始线 start line
起始信号 start signal
起始信号单元 initial signal unit {ISU}
起始信息 start information
起始行 initial row
起始序列 homing sequence
起始页[主页] home page
起始语句 start statement
起始指令[命令] initial order
起始置"1" initial set
起始状态 start state, starting state
起始字符 beginning character
起停 start stop {SS}
起停方式 start-stop mode
起停控制 stop/start control
起停时间 start-stop time
起停式设备 start-stop device
起停(式)系统 start-stop system
起停字符 start-stop character
起止式系统 start-stop system
起止式终端 start-stop terminal

岂

岂有此理 preposterous, outrageous

【qì】

气 1)(空气) air 2)(习气) airs, manner, style 3)(使人生气) make angry, enrage 4)(自己生气) get angry 气候 climate 气流 air current, airflow, airstream 气体 gas 气味 smell, odor, flavor 气味 smell, odor 气温 air temperature, atmospheric temperature 气象 ①(天气现象) meteorological phenomena ②(气象学) meteorology 气息 breath 气压 atmospheric pressure, barometric pressure
气动计算机 pneumatic computer
气动控制器 pneumatic controller
气动模拟 pneumatic analog
气阀 pneumatic valve
气体放电显示器 gas discharge

display
气体(放电)显示屏 gas panel
气体影影 gaseous development

讫
1) (完结) settled, completed, done ◇收讫 received in full ◇验讫 checked, examined ‖ 银货两讫 delivered and paid 2) (截止) end

迄
迄今 up to now, to this day, to date, so far

汽
vapor, steam 汽车 automobile, motor vehicle, car ◇公共汽车 bus 汽车库 garage 汽车旅馆 motel 汽水 soft drink, soda (water) 汽油 petrol, gasoline, gas

弃
throw away, discard, abandon, give up 弃权 ①(放弃投票) abstain from voting ②(体育) waive the right (to play) 弃置 discard, throw aside

契
契合 agree with, suit 契机 (事物转化的关键) turning point, juncture 契约 contract, deed, charter

砌
build by laying bricks or stones

器
器材 equipment, material 器具 appliance, instrument, utensil, implement, furniture 器皿 household utensils or containers 器械 apparatus, appliance, instrument 器重 think highly of
器件 device
器件库 component library
器件面积 device area
器件模拟 device simulation
器件模型 device model
器件设计 device design

【qiǎ】
卡 另见【kǎ】
1) (夹住) wedge, get stuck 2) (关卡) checkpost 卡子 clip, fastener
卡口 bayonet
卡盘 cartridge
卡盘字体 cartridge font

【qià】
恰
恰当 proper, suitable, appropriate 恰好 just right 恰恰 just, exactly 恰如其分 apt, oppropriate, just right

洽
1) (融洽) be in harmony, agree 2) (接洽) consult, arrange with 洽谈 make arrangements with, talk over with

【qiān】
千
thousand, kilo- 千方百计 by every possible means
千 kilo {K, k}
千比特每秒 kilobits per second {Kbits/s}
千波特 kilobaud
千分之一 milli
千伏安 kilovolt-ampere (kVA)
千赫 kilohertz (kHz)
千克 kilogram (kg)
千米 kilometer (km)
千瓦 kilowatt (kW)
千(二进制)位 kilobit
千位/每秒 kilobits per second {Kbps}
千字节 kilobyte {K byte, KB}

迁
(变迁) change 迁就 yield to 迁移 move, remove, migrate, migration, transport
迁移机构 travelling mechanism
迁移卷 migration volume

牵
(拉) lead (along), pull 牵挂 worry, care 牵连 involve (in trouble), implicate, tie up with 牵强 forced (interpretation, etc.), farfetched 牵涉 concern, invlove 牵引 tow, draw, haul 牵制 pin down, tie up, check

铅
lead (Pb), plumbum 铅笔 pencil
铅字 fount, type
铅字尺寸 body size
铅字宽度 set width
铅字盘 fount disk
铅字条 slug
铅字外缘斜面 beard
铅字箱 type case

签
(标签) label, sticker, tag 签到 sign in, check in 签订 conclude and sign 签订合同 sign a contract 签发 sign and issue (a document, etc.) 签名 sign, autograph 签收 sign after receiving sth, sign for 签署意见 subscribe 签证 visa, visé 签字 sign, affix one's signature
签到命令 sign-on command
签到验证 sign-on verification
签名分析 signature analysis
签名分析器 signature analyzer
签名区 sig block
签名文件 signature file, authenticated record
签名验证 signature verification
签署者 subscriber

谦
谦虚 ① modest, self-effacing ② make modest remarks

【qián】

前
1)(正面的) front 2)(向前) forward, ahead 3)(以前) ago, before, preceding 4)(以前的) former; formerly 5)(次序在先的) first 前边 in front, ahead ② above, preceding 前程 future prospect 前方 ①(前面) ahead ②(前线) the front 前后 ①(时间接近) around, about ②(自始至终) from start to finish, from beginning to end ③(前面和后面) in front and behind 前进 advance, go forward, forge ahead 前景 prospect, vista, perspective 前例 precedent 前列 front row, front rank, forefront 前门 front door 前面 ①(位置靠前) in front, at the head, ahead ②(次序靠前) above, preceding 前年 the year before last 前期 earlier stage, early days 前任 predecessor 前日、前天 the day before yesterday 前身 predecessor 前所未有 never existed before, unprecedented 前提 ①〈逻辑〉premise ②(必要条件) prerequisite, presupposition 前途 future, prospect 前往 go to, leave for, proceed to 前夕 eve 前言 preface, foreword, introduction 前兆 omen, forewarning 前者 the former
前部[前端]压缩 front compression

前处理与后置处理 pre-and-post-processing
前导[引导]空格 leading space
前导页 leading page
前端 front-end, leading end, nose
前端编辑 front-end edit
前端处理 front-end processing
前端处理机 front processor
前端处理器 front-end (processor) {FEP}
前端分析 front-end analysis
前端计算机 front computer, front-end computer
前端软件 front-end software
前端通信处理机 front-end communication processor
前端系统 front-end system
前端应用程序 front-end application
前端预处理系统 front-end preprocessing system
前端网络处理机 front-end network processor
前发脉冲 preliminary pulse
前后[上下]文关系 context
前景色 foreground color
前景问题 horizon problem
前馈 feed forward
前馈控制 feed-forward control
前馈网络模型 feed-forward network model
前馈原理 feed forward principle
前列地址 top address
前(导)零 leading zero
前驱 predecessor
前台 foreground
前台部分 foreground partition
前台程序 foreground program
前台处理 foreground processing, foregrounding
前台方式 foreground mode
前台监控程序 foreground monitor
前台进程 foreground process
前台启动 foreground initiation
前台任务 foreground task
前台设置 foregrounding
前台图像 foreground image
前台作业 foreground job
前向 forward direction
前向递归 forward reduction
前向纠错 forward error correction
前向连接 feed forward connection
前向链 forward chaining
前向搜索 forward search
前沿 frontier, front edge, leading edge
前沿科学 frontier science
前页屏幕 previous screen
前置代码 prefix code
前置控制 predictor control
前置区 prefix area
前置输出 preout
前置条件 precondition
前置位 preamble bit
前置型 prefix type
前置组件 prebox
前缀 prefix
前缀表 prefix table
前缀表示法 prefix notation, Lukasiewicz notation
前缀次序 preorder
前缀区 prefix area
前缀型 prefix type
前缀性质 prefix property

乾 乾坤 heaven and earth, the universe

钱 (款项)fund, sum 钱包 wallet, purse 钱币 coin, cash 钱财 money, wealth

钳 1)〈名〉pincers, pliers,

tongs 2)〈动〉grip, clamp 钳工 ①(工种)benchwork ②(工人)fitter 钳子 pliers, pincers

潜
1)(隐藏)latent, hidden 2)(秘密)secretly, stealthily 潜藏 hide, go into hiding 潜力 latent capacity, potential, potentiality 潜入 ①(偷偷地进入)slip into, sneak into, steal in ②(钻入水中)dive into, go under water, submerge 潜水 dive 潜在 latent, potential
潜伏期 incubation
潜伏时间 latency
潜伏性 incubation

【qiǎn】
浅 1)("深"的反意)shallow 2)(交情不深)not intimate, not close 3)(颜色淡)light 浅薄 superficial 浅见 superficial view, humble opinion 浅显 simple, easy
浅层知识 shallow knowledge, superficial knowledge
浅度推理 shallow reasoning

谴
谴责 condemn, denounce, criticize

【qiàn】
欠 1)(未还)owe, be in debt 2)(不够)insufficient, not enough 欠款 balance due, debt 欠缺 ①(不够)be deficient in, be short of ②(不够的地方)shortcoming, deficiency 欠妥 not proper 欠债 ①〈动〉owe a debt, run into bebt ②〈名〉debt, due, outstanding accounts
欠资(邮费) postage due

嵌
inlay, embed
嵌入 imbed(ding), insertion, embed(ding)
嵌入的字体 built-in font
嵌入法 insertion method
嵌入空白 embedded blank
嵌入控制 embedded control
嵌入码 embedded code, imbedded code
嵌入命令 embedded command
嵌入式操作系统 embedded OS
嵌入式结构查询语言 embedded structured query language {ESQL}
嵌入式软件 embedded software
嵌入式实时操作 embedded real-time OS {RTOS}
嵌入式语言 embedded language
嵌入系统 embedded system
嵌入映像 embedding mapping
嵌入指针 embedded pointer
嵌入字体 embedded font
嵌套 nest, nesting
嵌套层次 level of nesting
嵌套过程 nested procedure
嵌套宏调用 nested macrocall
嵌套宏定义 nested macrodefinition
嵌套级 nest level
嵌套结构 nested structure
嵌套循环 nest loop, nested loop
嵌套映射 embedding mapping
嵌套语句 nest statement

歉
歉收 crop failure, poor harvest 歉意 apology, regret

【qiāng】
枪 rifle, gun, pistol 枪弹

cartridge, bullet 枪械 firearms

【qiáng】

强 另见【qiǎng】

1)(力量大)strong, powerful
2)(略多些)slightly more than, plus ◇三分之一强 slightly more than one third
强大 (big and) powerful 强调 stress, emphasize, underline 强度 intensity, strength 强固 strong, solid 强化 strengthen, intensify, consolidate 强加 impose, force 强烈 strong, intense, violent 强迫 by force 强盛 powerful and prosperous 强硬 strong, tough, stiff 强制 (brute) force, coerce, compel 强壮 strong, robust, stout
强调符 bullet
强功能的 powerful
强构件 strong component
强函数 major function
强类型 strong type, strong typing, strongly-type
强连通性 strong connectivity
强耦合系统 strongly coupled system
强相容 strongly consistent
强行断开 forced disconnect
强行显示 forced display
强行写 force-writing
强循环 strong loop
强依赖性 strong dependency
强引用 strongly reference
强有向图 strong digraph
强占算法 preemptive algorithm
强制操作 imperative operation
强制函数 coercive function, forcing function
强制决策法 forced decision {FD}
强制启动 force start
强制时间 force time
强制退出 force quit
强制性的 mandatory
强制语句 imperative statement

墙 wall

【qiǎng】

强 另见【qiáng】

强迫 force, compel 强求 insist on, impose
强迫响应 forced response
强迫中断 compulsive interrupt, involuntary interrupt

抢 (赶紧)rush 抢夺 snatch, grab, seize 抢救 rescue, save, salvage 抢劫 rob, loot 抢时间 race against time 抢先 vie for, scramble for 抢险 rush to deal with an emergency 抢修 rush to repair, make urgent repair on; first-aid
抢先 preemption
抢先调度 preemptive schedule, preemptive scheduling
抢先输入 anticipated input
抢先算法 preemptive algorithm
抢先优先权 preemptive priority

【qiāo】

悄 悄悄 ①(低声)quietly ②(不让人知道)without being noticed

锹 spade, hoe, grafting tool

敲 knock, beat, strike
敲诈 extort, blackmail

【qiáo】

乔 乔姆斯基范式 Chomsky nor-

qiáo 侨桥 qiǎo 巧 qiào 俏窍翘撬壳 qiè切 qiě且 qiè切

mal form

侨 侨民 a person living abroad 侨居 live abroad

桥 (桥梁)bridge 桥洞 bridge opening 桥墩(bridge) pier
桥接 bridging
桥接故障 bridge fault, bridging fault
桥接件 bridgeware
桥(接电)路 bridge circuit
桥路器 brouter
桥式放大器 bridging amplifier
桥式网络 lattice network

【qiǎo】

巧 1)(灵巧)skil(l)ful, ingenious, clever 2)(恰巧)opportunely, coincidentally, as it happens 巧合 coincidence 巧计 clever plan, artful scheme 巧匠 clever artisan, skilled workman 巧妙 ingenious, clever

【qiào】

俏 1)(俊俏)pretty, smart, good-looking, handsome 2)(销路好)sell well, be in great demand

窍 (孔洞)aperture 窍门 key to sth, knack, dodge ◇诀窍 knack, trick of a trade

翘 warp, buckle

撬 prize, pry

壳 另见【ké】
sell
body case

壳体[外壳]理论 shell theory

【qiē】

切 另见【qiè】
cut, slice 切开 cut open, cut apart 切片 cut into slices 切碎 cut up
切标 trimscript
切除 excision
切(线)点 tangent point
切断 cut-out, lock-out, key-off, shut-off, disconnecting, interruption
切断电源开关 power disconnect switch
切断电源状态 power-off condition
切断信号 disconnect signal
切断序列 shutoff sequence {SO}
切割标记 cut mark
切割线 cutting lines
切换 switchover
切换窗口 switch window
切换键 toggle button
切换载波 switched carrier
切角 corner cut
切口 slot
切口编码法 direct coding
切面 chamfer
切片 slab, slice, slicing
切去部分 cut-off
切线 tangent

【qiě】

且 1)(暂且)just, for the time being 2)(尚且)even 3)(并且)both ... and ..., as well (as)

【qiè】

切 另见【qiē】
1)(迫切)eager, anxious 2)(务必)be sure to 切合 correspond to, be close to 切忌

must guard against, avoid by all means 切实 ①(切合实际)feasible, practical, realistic ②(实实在在)conscientiously, earnestly 切题 keep to the point, be relevant to the subject 切勿 be sure not to

窃 1)〈动〉steal, shoplift 2)〈副〉secretly, stealthily 窃听 wiretap, bug 窃取 steal, grab
窃取信道信息 passive wiretapping
窃取信息 scavenging
窃听机 detectophone

【qīn】
侵 侵犯 invade, violate 侵害 encroach on, make inroads on 侵略 aggression, invasion, intrusion 侵权行为 tort 侵入 invade, intrude into, make incursions into 侵蚀 corrode, erode, corrupt 侵吞 ①(暗中非法占有)embezzle, peculate ②(用武力吞并)swallow up, annex 侵袭 make inroads on, invade and attack, hit 侵占 invade and occupy, seize
侵犯版权 piracy

亲 1)(父母)parent 2)(血缘近)blood relation, next of kin 亲爱的 dear, beloved 亲笔 in one's own handwriting, in one's own hand 亲口 personally 亲密 close, intimate 亲切 cordial, kind. 亲热 affectionate, intimate 亲手 with one's own hands, personally 亲属 relative, kinsfolk 亲眼 with one's own eyes, personally 亲自 in person, oneself

钦 钦佩 admire, esteem

【qín】
勤 (经常)often, frequently, regularly 勤奋 diligent, industrious 勤俭 hardworking and thrifty 勤劳 diligent, industrious, hardworking 勤务 duty, attendance, service ◇考勤 check on work attendance

【qǐn】
寝 (睡)sleep 寝室 bedroom, dormitory

【qīng】
青 1)(青色)blue or green 2)(年轻)young (people) 青春 youth, youthfulness 青年 youth, young people 青少年 youngsters, teenagers

轻 1)(重量小)light 2)(数量少)small in number/ degree etc. 3)(不重要)not important 4)(用力小)gently, softly, lightly 轻便 light, portable 轻工业 light industry 轻巧 ①(灵巧,轻便)light and handy ②(轻松灵巧)deft, dexterous 轻轻 lightly, gently, softly 轻声 in a soft voice, softly 轻视 despise, look down on, underestimate 轻松 light, relaxed 轻率 rash(ly), hasty, reckless 轻微 light, slight 轻型 light-duty, low-duty; lightweight 轻易 ① easily

② lightly 轻音乐 light music 轻重 ①(重量大小)weight ②(事情的主次)degree of seriousness, relative importance

轻便打字机 lightweight typewriter

氢 hydrogen (H)

倾 1)(歪斜)incline, lean, bend 2)(倒塌)collapse 3)(全部倒出)overturn and pour out, empty 倾向(趋势) tendency, trend, inclination, deviation 倾向性 tendentiousness 倾向于 be inclined to, prefer 倾销 dump 倾斜 tilt, incline, slope, slant, oblique

倾斜度 obliquity
倾斜轨道 inclined orbit

清 1)(纯净)pure, clear, clean 2)(结清)settle, clear up 清白 pure, clean, stainless 清查 check, investigate 清仓 make an inventory of warehouses 清偿 pay out, clear off 清除 clear away, eliminate, get rid of 清楚 ①(容易辨认)clear, distinct ②(不糊涂)clear, lucid 清单 detailed list, bill, detailed account, specification, inventory 清点 check, make an inventory 清洁 clean 清理 put in order, check up, clear, sort/ clean out 清算 clear (accounts) 清晰 distinct, clear 清洗 raise, wash, clean

清除(存储器) sanitizing
清除按钮 reset button
清除包[分组] clear packet
清除标志 clear flag
清除表(格) erase list
清除表目 erase entry
清除冲突 clear collision
清除打印[转储] memory dump
清除发送(信号) clear to send {CTS}
清除键 cancel key, clear key, clearing key
清除控制逻辑 clear control logic
清除脉冲 clear pulse, reset pulse
清除门 reset gate
清除条件 cleared condition, reset condition
清除显示 clear display
清除信号 clear signal
清除指令 clear instruction, clearance order
清除指示符 clear indicator
清存储器 clear memory, clear storage
清单文件 inventory file
清洁磁带 clean tape
清洁基 clean base
清洁盘 cleaning diskette
清洁区 clear area, clear band
清零 clear, reset
清零电路 clear circuit
清零开关 reset switch
清零状态 cleared condition
清屏 blanking
清晰度 articulation, clearness, definition, readability, resolution, sharpness
清晰区域 clear area
清洗残余 erase residual
清洗卷筒 cleaning web
清洗器 eraser
清洗头 erase head
清(除)中断 clear interrupt, clearing interrupt

【qíng】

情 1)(感情)feeling, sentiment, emotion 2)(爱情)love, passion, affection 情报 intelligence, information 情感 emotion 情节 ①(内容)plot, story ②(事实经过)circumstances 情景 scene, sight, circumstances 情况, 情形 circumstances, situation, condition, case, state of affairs 情理 reason, sense, logic 情面 favor, kindness, sensibilities, feelings 情绪 ①(心理状态)morale, mood, sentiments ②(心情不好)depression, moodiness 情愿 ①(愿意)be willing to ②(宁愿)prefer, would rather, had rather

情报安全性 information security
情报处理 information handling
情报分析中心 information analysis centre
情报服务 information service
情报检索 information retrieval {IR}
情报科学 information science
情报提供者 information provider {IP}
情报源 information source
情况变量 situation variable
情况子句 case clause

晴 fine, clear 晴天 fine day, sunny day

【qǐng】

顷 (公顷)hectare 顷刻 moment, instant, a little while

请 1)(请求)request, ask 2)(邀请)invite 3)(敬语)please 请便 do as you wish, please youself 请假 ask for leave 请柬, 请帖 invitation (card) 请教 ask for advise, consult 请示 request/ask for instructions 请问 ①(用于请对方回答问题)excuse me, please ②(向对方提出问题时用)we should like to ask, it may be asked, one may ask 请勿 please don't 请勿入内!No admittance 请勿吸烟!No smoking 请愿(present a) petition

请求 call, demand, invoke, request {RQE}, solicit
请求标题 request header {RH}
请求表 required list
请求参数表 request parameter list {RPL}
请求操作 solicit operation
请求测试报文 test request message {TRM}
请求处理 demand processing, request stacking
请求单元[装置] request unit {RU}
请求调页 demand paging
请求读(数) demand reading
请求堆积 request stacking
请求队列 request queue
请求方式 demand mode
请求服务 request service
请求会话 queued session
请求控制块 request control block {RCB}
请求联机/脱机 log on/off
请求轮询 demand poll
请求排队 request queue
请求启用 request enable
请求任务 request task
请求式系统 on-demand system
请求首部 request header {RH}

【qìng】

庆 庆典 celebration, a ceremony to celebrate 庆典日 occasion for celebration 庆贺 congratulate, celebrate 庆祝 celebrate, congratulate

【qióng】

穷 1)(贫穷)poor, poverty 2)(穷尽)limit, end 3)(彻底)thoroughly 4)(极端)extremely 穷人 poor people, the poor

穷举 exhaustivity
穷举调试 exhaustive testing
穷举法 exhaust algorithm, exhaustive method, method of exhaustion
穷举搜索法 exhaustive search algorithm
穷举索引 exhaustive index

穹 穹顶 dome 穹形 vaulterd, arched

【qiū】

秋 autumn, fall 秋收 autumn harvest

【qiú】

囚 囚犯 prisoner, convict 囚禁 imprison

求 1)(请求)ask, beg, request, entreat, beseech 2)(寻求)strive for, seek, try 3)(需求)demand 求教 ask for advice 求救 ask sb to come to rescue, cry for help 求全 ①(要求完美无缺)demand perfection ②(希望事情成功)try to round sth off 求学 ①(在学校学习)go to school, attend school ②(探求学问)pursue one's studies, seek knowledge 求知 seek knowledge 求知欲 desire for knowledge 求助 turn to sb for help, seek help

求并运算 cup
求补 complementing
求补器 two's complementer
求补指令 negate instruction
求部分和 subtotaling
求反 complementation, complementing, negate
求反程序 negate routine
求反算符 complementary operator
求反运算 complementary operation
求负 negate
求根 extract, extract a root
求和 summation, totalization
求和法 summation
求和检验 summation check
求交 intersect
求逆 inversion
求值 evaluate, evaluation
求助菜单 help menu
求助程序 help program, helper

求助窗口 help window
求助管理程序 help manager
求助键 Help key
求助视图 help view
求助文本 help text
求助支持 help support

球 1)〈数学〉sphere 2)〈体育〉ball 3)(地球)the globe, the earth
球-栅形封装 ball grid array {BGA}
球面天线 spherical antenna
球式打印机 character-ball printer
球型病毒 ball-type virus
球型[球形]打字机 ball printer
球型(打印)头 spherical type head
球形的 spherical

【qū】

区 区别 ①〈动〉distinguish, differentiate, make a distinction between ②〈名〉difference 区分 differentiate, distinguish
区(域)变量 area variable
区标 trim
区别符 diacritic
区别记号 diacritical mark, diacritical sign
区别树 distinguishing tree
区别状态 distinguishing state
区地址 regional address
区段 section, sector
区段尺寸[大小] sector size
区段方式 sector mode, segmented mode
区段格式 zone format
区段寄存器 sector register
区段界限 segment limit
区段链接 sector chaining
区段排队 sector queuing
区段入口 segment entry
区段数 sector number, zone digit
区段位 section bit, zone bit
区段文件 sectored file
区分部分 specification part
区分符 specificator, specifier
区分类 region class
区间 interval
区间变换 interval mapping
区间查询 interval query
区间图 interval graph
区间线性规划 interval linear programming
区间映像 interval mapping
区交换 area exchange
区结束(符) end of extent {EOE}
区(域)搜索 area search
区位 zone bit
区位记录 zone bit recording {ZBR}
区位宽度 zone width
区位码 region-position code
区位字段 zoned field
区域 area, circumscription, extent, field {FLD}, range, realm, region, section, sphere, zone, domain
区域边界 zone boundary
区域编号方案 area numbering plan {ANP}
区域表 region list
区域操作员 domain operator
区域地址 regional address
区域电话局 area exchange
区域对象 section object
区域分割 region segmentation
区域合并 region merging
区域级 region class
区域间呼叫 interzone call
区域检查 range check
区域交换中心[交换站](电话的) zone switching center

区域聚类 region clustering
区域宽度 zone width
区域(代)码 area code
区域描述 region description
区域名(称) domain name
区域请求 area request
区域设置 region-setting
区域填充 area fill, area in fill, region fill
区域头部 zone header
区域图 area chart
区域制 zone system
区域中心 regional center {RC}
区域转移 area transfer
区域作图机 area composition machine {ACM}

曲 另见【qū】
1)(弯曲) bent, crooked 2)(弯曲处) bend 3)(理号) wrong, unjustifiable 曲解 (deliberately) misinterpret, twist 曲线 curve 曲折 ①(弯曲) winding ②(复杂情节) complications 曲直 right and wrong
曲面 curved surface
曲面拟合 surface fitting
曲面造型 surface modelling
曲线(板) curve
曲线拟合 curve fitting
曲线系统 contouring systems {CS}

驱
驱使 compel, order about 驱逐 drive out, expel, banish
驱动 drive, driving
驱动程序 driver, driver routine
驱动电流 drive current
驱动电路 drive circuit
驱动功率 driving power
驱动脉冲 drive pulse
驱动器 drive, driver, bootstrap driver
驱动器编号 drive number
驱动器部件 driver module
驱动器电平 driver level
驱动器检测 drive sense
驱动器诊断程序 drive diagnostic program {DDP}
驱动器字母[字符] drive letter
驱动软件 driver software
驱动实用程序 driver utility
驱动文件 drive file
驱动信号 driving signal
驱动源 drive source
驱动装置 drive

屈
屈从 submit to, yield to
屈服 surrender, yield

祛
祛除 dispel, get rid of, drive out

躯
躯干 trunk, torso 躯体 body

趋
趋势 trend, tendency 趋向 ①〈动〉tend to, incline to ②〈名〉trend, direction

【qú】
渠 canal, ditch, channel
渠道 ①(灌溉水道) irrigation ditch, canal, channel ②(途径) medium, channel

【qǔ】
曲 另见【qū】
1)(歌曲, 曲调) song, tune, melody 2)(乐谱) music

取
1)(拿取) take, get, fetch 2)(采取) adopt, assume, choose 取代 replace, substitute for, displace 取得 gain,

acquire, obtain 取决 be decided by, depend on 取舍 accept or reject, make one's choice 取证 obtain evidence
取操作 load operation
取操作数 fetch operand
取出 fetch
取出码 code fetch
"取出"位 fetch bit
取出序列 fetch sequence
取得信号 get signal
取景变换 viewing transformation
取景方向 viewing direction
取景角度 viewing angle
取景器光 filter light
取景向量 viewing vector
取逻辑 fetch logic
取码 code fetch
取幂 exponentiation
取数 load, peek
取数保护 fetch protection
取数[存取]方式 access mode
取数据 data fetch, fetch data
取数孔 access hole
取数[存取]时间 access time
取数[访问]位 access bit
取消 cancel(lation) {CANCL}, kill, undo, cross off/out, revoke, backout
取消符 erase character
取消命令 countermand
取消[作废]字符 cancel character {CAN}
取样 sample
取样读出 sampling read out
取样机构 sampling mechanism
取样间隔 sample interval
取样设备 sample device
取样时钟 sampling clock
取整 ceiling
取指令 fetch instruction, instruction fetch
取指令阶段 fetch phase, instruction fetch phase
取指周期 fetch phase
取周期 fetch cycle

【qù】

去 1)(去某处) go, leave, depart 2)(除去) remove, get rid of 去处 ①(去的地方) place to go, whereabouts ②(场所) place, site 去年 last year 去世 die, pass away 去污 decontamination 去向 direction in which sb or sth has gone, whereabouts
去磁 degauss
去磁器 degausser
去磁头 erasing head
去抖动 debouncing
去抖动电路[器] debouncer
去卷积 deconvolution
去卷曲 decurl
去模糊 defuzzification
去耦 decouple
去(分)配 deallocate
去启动 deactivation
去同步 desynchronizing
去相关 decorrelation

趣 1)(趣味) interest, delight 2)(有趣的) interesting

【quān】

圈 1)(环形) circle, ring, loop 2)(范围) circle, group, rang 3)(围) enclose, encircle 4)(画圈儿) make with a circle, circle
圈电流 loop current
圈向量 cycle vector

【quán】

权 权衡 weigh 权利 right 权力 power, authority 权且 temporarily, for the time be-

权势 power and influence
权威 authority 权限 limits of sb's authority, competence, extent of power
权益 rights and interests
权 〈数学〉weight
权标 token
权标[令牌]环 token ring
权标传递 token passing
权标传送网 token passing network
权标总线网 token bus network
权函数 weight function, weighting function
权限操作 limiting operation
权限检查 authorization checking, scope check
权向量 weight vector
权值 weighted value

全 1)(齐全)complete 2)(保全)make perfect or complete, keep intact 3)(整个)whole, entire, full, total 4)(完全,都)entirely, completely 全部 all, whole, complete, total, without exception 全才 a versatile person, all-rounder 全程 whole journey, whole course 全方位 omnibearing 全国 nationwide, throughout the country 全会 plenary meeting, plenary session 全集 ① complete works, collected works ② universal set 全景 full view, whole scene, panoramic view, group shot 全局 overall situation, situation as a whole 全力 with all one's strength, all-out, sparing no effort 全力以赴 go all out, spare no effort 全貌 complete picture, full view 全面 overall, comprehensive, all-round 全民 the whole people, the entire people, all the people 全名 full name
全年 annual, yearly 全盘 overall, comprehensive, wholesale 全球 the whole world 全权 full powers, plenary powers 全然 completely, entirely 全日制 full-time 全盛 flourishing, in full bloom 全体 all, entire, whole 全文 full text
全心全意 wholeheartedly, heart and soul
全安装 full install
全部清除 clear all
全部占线 all trunks busy {ATB}
全彩色 full color
全称闭包 universal closure
全称量词 universal quantifier
全称域名 fully qualified domain name {FQDN}
全程[全局]变量 global variable
全程单元 global location
全程[全文]搜索 global search
全程引用 global reference
全程值 global value
全等角 congruent angle
全等线 congruent line
全地址 full address
全点可寻址的 all points addressable {APA}
全电子化的 all electronic
全对称函数 totally symmetric function
全服务网 full service network {FSN}
全负载 full load
全割集 all cut-set
全功能网络 fully functional network
全函数 total function
全互连网络 fully-connected

全缓存 global buffer
全混洗 perfect shuffle
全机清除键 all clear key
全加器 full adder, one-position adder, three-input adder
全进程 full process
全局变量 global variable, global change
全局参数 global parameter
全局操作 global operation
全局查询 global query
全局存储(器) global memory, global storage
全局代码 global code
全局段 global section, global segment
全局方式 global mode
全局分布模式 global distributed schema {GDS}
全局分块模式 global partition schema {GPS}
全局符号 global symbol
全局符号表 global symbol table {GST}
全局概念模式 global concept schema {GCS}
全局共享资源 global shared resource {GSR}
全局关系 global relation
全局管理 global administration
全局空间 global extent
全局名 global name
全局命令 global command
全局命名服务 global naming service
全局模式 global schema
全局目标 global object
全局目录 global dictionary
全局区 global zone
全局区域 global area
全局时钟(脉冲) global clock
全局实体 global entity
全局输出 global output

全局数据 global data
全局死锁 global deadlock
全局网络 global network
全局性相关 global association
全局性准则 global criterion
全局序列 global sequence
全局页表 global page table
全局引用 global reference
全局优化 global optimization
全局字符 global character
全局坐标 world coordinate {WC}
全空间 total space
全空字段 all blank field
全零信号 all-zero signal
全零状态 all-zero state
全路径名 full path name
全逻辑控制 full logic control
全码 full code
全旁路 total bypass
全屏幕 full screen
全屏幕编辑 full-screen editing
全屏幕处理 full-screen processing {FSP}
全屏幕方式 full-screen mode
全屏幕图像 full screen image
全屏幕形式 full-screen form
全清 all clear, clear all
全球地址 global address
全球定位系统 global/globe] position(ing) system {GPS}
全球跟踪网 global tracking network
全球互联网络 Internet
全球数字移动通信系统 global system for mobile communication {GSM}
全球卫星系统 global star
全色视频图像打印机 video full color printer
全色原件 full-tone original
全数字仿算 all-digital simulation
全数字呼叫 all-number calling

{ANC}
全数字显示 all-digital display
全数字相关 all-digital correlation
全数组 whole array
全双工 full duplex {FD, FDX}
全双工操作 full-duplex operation
全双工传输 full-duplex transmission
全双工方式 full duplex mode
全双工链路 full-duplex link
全双工通信 full-duplex communication
全双工线路 full-duplex line
全双工信道 full-duplex channel
全双工终端 full-duplex terminal
全双工主站 full-duplex primary station
全双向的 full duplex {FD, FDX}
全速 full speed
全套 full set
全通路名 full path name
全通网络 all pass network
全同部件 identity unit
全同操作[运算] identity operation
全同门 identity gate
全同元(件) identity element, identity unit
全图 total graph
全网 catanet
全文检索 full text retrieval, full-text search
全息透镜 hololens
全息图 hologram
全息显示 holographic display
全息照相 total hologram
全系统 total system
全相联映射 fully associative mapping
全向码 omnidirectional code
全写入 full write
全信息函数 full-information function
全行方式 full-line mode, full-mode
全序 total order, total ordering, simple order, linear order
全序集 simply ordered set, totally ordered set
全选脉冲 full-read pulse
全选择 fullselect
全页显示 full-page display
全因子 total divisor
全语言 full language
全域 universe, universe set
全域关系 universal relation
全域理论 population theory
全帧速率(电视) full motion
全值变量 full value variable
全主元 complete pivot
全转换 full conversion
全转接 total bypass
全转移 total transfer
全状态 total state
全自动编译技术 fully automatic compiling technique {FACT}
全自动处理 full automatic processing
全字 full word
全字二进制 fullword binary
全字符串 complete chain
全字界 full-word boundary
全字空格 em space
全字体 omnifont
全组合键 full compound key

痊 痊愈 fully recover from an illness, regain health

泉 spring ◇矿泉 mineral spring 泉水 spring water, spring 泉源 ①(水源) fountainhead, springhead

② (来源) source

蜷 蜷曲 curl, coil, twist 蜷缩 roll up, huddle up, curl up

拳 拳曲 curl, twist, bend 拳头 fist

【quǎn】

犬 dog, canine

【quàn】

劝 (勉励) encourage 劝告 advise, urge 劝架 mediate, make peace between, bring people together 劝解, 劝导 help sb to get over his worries, etc. 劝说 advise, urge, try to persuade

券 certificate, ticket ◇入场券 admission ticket

【quē】

炔 〈化学〉alkyne

缺 (残缺) imcomplete, imperfect 缺点 shortcoming, defect, weakness, drawback 缺乏 be short of, lack 缺货 be in short supply, be out of stock 缺课 be absent from school, miss a class 缺口 ① (缺缘) breach, gap ② (缺额) insufficiency 缺勤 absence from duty/work 缺勤率 absence rate 缺席 absent (from a meeting, etc.) 缺陷 defect, drawback, flaw, deficiency, disadvantage, shortage
缺带 low tape
缺段中断 missing segment interrupt
缺码 missing code
缺少变元 missing argument, missing variable
缺省(值) default
缺省值 default value
缺席者 absentee
缺页率 page fault rate
缺页中断 missing page interrupt, missing page interruption
缺纸带 low tape
缺纸检测 low paper detection
缺纸指示灯 low paper indicator

【què】

却 1) (退却) set back, fall back 2) (使退却) drive back, repulse 3) (然而) but, yet

确 1) (符合事实) true, reliable, authentic 2) (坚定) firmly 确保 ensure, guarantee 确定① (使确定) define, fix, determine, ascertain ② (明确而肯定) definite, certain, for sure 确立 establish 确切 definite, exact, precise 确认 affirm, confirm, acknowledge 确实① (真实可靠) true, reliable ② (的确) really, indeed 确信 firmly believe, be convinced, be sure 确凿 conclusive, authentic, irrefutable
确定 definition, detrimination, establish, settlement
确定的表达式 deterministic expression
确定的堆栈自动机 deterministic stack automaton
确定的有穷[限]自动机 deterministic finite automaton

{DFA}
确定系统 definite system
确定响应 definite response
确定型下推自动机 deterministic push down automaton {DPDA}
确定性 certainty, definiteness, determinacy, determinism
确定性博弈 deterministic game
确定性调度 deterministic schedule
确定性仿真[模拟] deterministic simulation
确定性模型 deterministic model
确定性算法 deterministic algorithm
确定性图灵机 deterministic Turing machine, unambiguous Turing machine {UTM}
确定性文法 unambiguous grammar
确定性自动机 deterministic automaton
确定因素 certainty factor {CF}
确定[确切]应答 definite response
确认 acknowledge(ment) {ACK}, confirm(ation)
确认标识符 commit identifier
确认点 commit point
确认(字)符 acknowledge character {ACK}
确认功能 commitment function
确认号 acknowledgement number
确认收到 (affirmative) acknowledge(ment) {ACK}
确认协议 acknowledge protocol
确认原语 confirm primitive
确实性 validity
确信度 certainty factor {CF}

【qún】

群 1)〈聚在一起〉crowd, group 2)〈量词〉group, herd, flock 群岛 archipelago, islands 群体 ①〈生物〉colony ②（社会）group 群众 the masses
群读出器 group reader
群分离符 group separator character {GS}
群集 swarm
群集(器) cluster
群集计算机 cluster computer
群集控制器 cluster control unit, cluster controller
群集控制器节点 cluster controller node {CCN}
群集控制装置 cluster control unit
群集模型 cluster model
群集系统 cluster systems
群集终端 cluster terminal
群件 groupware
群聚 clustering
群决策 group decision making
群控 group control
群控节点 cluster controller node {CCN}
群控器 cluster control unit, cluster controller
群论 group theory
群码 group code
群速度 group velocity
群体决策支持系统 group decision support system {GDSS}
群体智能 swarm intelligence
群同步 group synchronization
群网络 group network
群组支持系统 group support system {GSS}

R r

【rán】
然 然而 yet, but, however 然后 then, after that, afterwards

燃 （点燃）ignite, light, set fire to 燃料 fuel 燃烧 burn; 〈化学〉combustion, inflammation

【rǎn】
染 1)（着色）dye 2)（感染）catch (a disease) 3)（沾染）acquire (a bad habit, etc.), contaminate
染色 coloration, coloring, decoration, render
染色问题 coloring problem

【rǎng】
壤 （土壤）soil

【ràng】
让 1)（听任）let, allow, make 2)（让利于人）give way, give ground, yield 让步 step back, give way, yield 让开 get out, step aside, make way 让路 make way, give sb the right of way 让位 ①（让出地位）abdicate, give up an official position ②（让座）offer one's seat to sb ③（转向）yield to, give way to, change into

【ráo】
饶 （富饶）rich, plentiful 饶恕 have mercy on, let sb off, forgive

【rǎo】
扰 扰乱 harass, perturb, disturb
扰动参数 disturbance parameter
扰动控制 disturbed control
扰动理论 perturbation theory

【rào】
绕 1)（缠绕）wind, coil ◇绕线 wind thread 2)（围着转动）move round, circle, revolve
绕带时间 rewind time
绕回 wrap, wraparound
绕线电路 wire-wrapped circuit
绕接法 wrapped connection
绕线 wire wind

【rě】
惹 1)（引起）cause, ask for, induce 2)（触动对方）offend, provoke, tease 惹事 stir up trouble

【rè】
热 1)〈物理〉heat; thermal 2)（温度高）hot 3)（加热）heat up, warm (up) 4)（体温

高) fever, temperature 5) (情意深厚) warm-hearted 6) (受欢迎的) in great demand, popular 7) (风行) craze, fad, fever ◇ 旅游热 travel craze 热爱 ardently love, have deep love for 热潮 great development, upsurge 热诚 warm and sincere, cordial 热带 the torrid zone, the tropics 热度 ①(冷热程度) degree of heat, heat ②(体温高) fever, high temperature 热量 quantity of heat 热烈 warm, enthusiastic, ardent 热流 ①〈气象〉thermal current ②(激奋) warm current flows in great demand, popular 热闹 ①〈形〉lively, bustling with noise and excitement ②〈动〉liven up, have a jolly time ③〈名〉a scene of bustle and excitement, a thrilling sight 热情 ①〈名〉enthusiasm, zeal, warmth ②〈形〉warm, fervent, enthusiastic, warm-hearted 热心 enthusiastic, ardent, earnest, warm-hearted 热中 ①(急切想得) hanker after, crave ②(十分爱好) be fond of, be keen on
热报警 thermal warning
热备份 hot backup, hot standby
热备用(系统) warm standby
热成像 thermal imaging
热处理 heat treat
热存储器 hot memory
热打印 hot print
热(传)导模块 thermal conduction module {TCM}
热点 hot spot
热电效应 thermoelectric effect
热关键点 warm key point
热键 hot key
热门课题 heat subject
热门题目 hot topic
热敏打印头 thermal printer head
热敏过程 thermographic process
热敏印刷法 thermal printing
热敏印刷机 heat-sensitive printer
热敏印图机 thermal graphics printer
热敏元件 thermal sensor
热敏纸 thermal paper
热启动 warm boot, warm start
热线 hot-wire, red circuit
热线服务 hot line service
热修复 hot fix
热再启动 warm restart

【rén】

人 1)(泛指人) man, person, people, human being 2)(成年人) adult, grown-up 3)(某种人) a person engaged in a particular activity ◇工人 worker 4)(别人)(other) people 5)(每人) everybody, each, all 人才 a person of ability, a talented person, talent 人次 person-time, man-time 人工 ①〈形〉man-made, artificial ②〈名〉manual work, work done by hand 人类 humankind 人日(工作量) manpower, man-day 人口 ①(某地总人数) population ②(一家人数) number of people in a family 人类 mankind, humanity 人力 manpower, labor power 人们 people, man, the public

人民 the people 人民币 Renminbi (RMB) 人权 human rights, rights of man 人群 crowd, throng 人身 ① 〈名〉 person ② 〈形〉 personal, physical 人身安全 personal safety 人生 life 人事 personnel matters 人手 manpower, hand 人寿保险 life insurance 人体 human body 人为 artifical, man-made 人文科学 the humanities, humane studies 人物 ① (杰出的人) figure, personage ② (作品中的人) character 人像 portrait, image, figure 人行道 pavement, sidewalk 人行天桥 pedestrian overpass 人选 person selected, choice of persons 人员 personnel, staff, faculty 人造 man-made, artificial, synthetic

人工[手动操作] manual operation

人工初启 manual start

人工翻译 human translation

人工分析 manual analysis

人工校验 desk checking

人工神经网络 artificial neural network {ANN}

人工神经元 artificial neuron

人工识别 artificial recognition, artificial perception, artificial cognition

人工视觉 artificial vision

人工输入键 manual load key

人工输入设备 manual input unit

人工数据输入 manual data input {MDI}

人工网络 artificial network

人工纹理 artificial texture

人工语言 artificial language, fabricated language, formal language, synthetic language

人工智能 artificial intelligence {AI}, intellect, silicon-intelligence

人工智能方法 artificial intelligence approach

人工智能识别 artificial intelligence recognition

人工中断 force interrupt

人机对话 (hu)man-computer dialogue/ interaction, man-machine conversation, interactive dialog

人机仿真 man-machine simulation

人机会谈 man-machine discourse

人机交互 man-machine interaction, human-computer interaction, user interaction

人机交互系统 man-machine interactive system

人机接口[界面] (hu)man-machine interface

人机联系[交互] man-machine interaction, man-machine interface, man-computer interaction

人机模拟 man-machine simulation

人机软件包 man-machine package {MMP}

人机(关系)图 man-machine chart

人机系统 man-machine system

人机语言 man-machine language

人可读的 human-readable

人类语言 human language

人力分配方法 manpower allocation procedure {MAP}

人力规划 manpower planning

人力资源部 department of hu-

人力资源信息系统 human resource information system {HRIS}
人为差错 human incurring error
人为错误 personal error
人为干扰 jamming, man-made noise
人为故障 man-made fault
人为误差 human error
人员配备 orgware
人造的 artificial, man-made
人造语言 synthetic language
人助机器译 human-aided machine translation {HAMT}

【rěn】

忍不住 unable to bear, cannot help (doing sth) 忍耐 exercise patience, restrain oneself 忍受 bear, endure, tolerate

【rèn】

刃 the edge of a knife, sword, etc., blade

认 〈承认〉admit, recognize 认错 acknowledge a mistake, admit a fault, make an apology 认得 know, recognize 认定 firmly believe, maintain, assert 认购 offer to buy, subscribe 认可 approve, accept, confirm 认识 ①〈动〉know, understand, recognize ②〈名〉understanding, knowledge, cognition 认输 admit defeat 认为 think, consider, hold, reckon 认真 ①（当真）take seriously, take to heart ②（不马虎）conscientious, earnest, serious 认知〈心理〉cognition
认可测试 acceptance testing
认识论 epistemology
认识[识别]系统 recognition system
认证 certification
认证密码 verification key
认证图样 verification pattern
认证中心 issuing authority {IA}
认知的 epistemic, cognitive
认知机 (neo)cognitron
认知经济 cognitive economy
认知科学 cognitive science
认知模拟 cognitive simulation
认知模式 cognitive modeling
认知模型 cognitive model
认知图 cognitive maps
认知系统 cognitive system
认知心理学 cognitive psychology
认知性智能 cognitive intelligence

任 〈担任〉assume a post, take up a job 〈任何〉any, whatever, whichever 任免 appoint and remove 任命 designate, appoint 任凭 ①（听凭）at one's convenience, at one's discretion ②（不管）no matter (what, how, etc.) 任期 term of office, tenure of office 任务 assignment, mission, task, job 任意 wantonly, arbitrarily, willfully 任用 appoint, assign sb to a post 任职 hold a post, be in office
任务变量 task variable
任务表 task list, task table
任务程序库 task library
任务调度 task schedule, mission/task scheduling

任务调度程序 task dispatcher/scheduler
任务调用 task call
任务定义表 task definition table
任务队列 task queue
任务分配 allocation in task, allocation of task, task allocation
任务概述 mission profile
任务挂起[暂停] task suspension
任务管理 task control, task management
任务号 task number
任务集[组] task set
任务检查点 task check point
任务建立[启动] task start
任务开关[转换] task switch
任务开始 task initiation
任务控制表 task control table
任务控制块 task control block {TCB}
任务库 task library
任务类型 task type
任务流程图 mission flow diagram
任务名 task name
任务模型 task model
任务排队 task queue
任务启动 task start
任务嵌套 task nest
任务输入队列 task input queue {TIQ}
任务映射 task mapping
任务执行区 task execution area
任务执行状态 task state
任务转储 task dump
任务转换 task switch
任务状态 task status/state
任务族 task family
任选 optional
任选板 option board
任选(程序)包 option package
任选表 option table
任选参数 optional parameter
任选成分[成员] optional member
任选单元 option unit
任选点 optional point
任选调用 call option
任选功能 optional feature
任选接口 option interface
任选空白 option blank
任选名 option name
任选特点 optional feature
任选文件 optional file
任选项 option
任选中断 optional interrupt
任选字段 optional field
任意的 arbitrary, discretional, voluntary
任意方式 any mode
任意截听 wilful intercept
任意曲线 free curve
任意位 don't-care bit
任意选择 discretionary

韧 tough, tenacious

【rēng】
扔 1)(抛)throw, cast 2)(抛弃)throw away, cast aside

【réng】
仍 仍旧 ①(不变)remain the same ②(仍然)still, yet 仍然 still, yet

【rì】
日 1)(太阳)sun 2)(白天)daytime, day 3)(一昼夜)day 4)(每天)daily, every day, with each passing day
日班 day shift 日报 daily (paper) 日本 Japan ◇日本人 Japanese 日常 day-to-day, everyday, daily, routine 日程 program, schedule

日戳 ①(戳子)date stamp, dater ②(印下的戳记)datemark 日光 sunlight, sunbeam 日光灯 fluorescent lamp, daylight lamp 日记 diary, log 日期 date 日夜 day and night, night and day, round the clock 日益 increasingly, day by day 日用 ①(日常费用)daily expense ②(日常用的)of everyday use 日用品 daily necessities 日语 Japanese (language) 日元 Yen 日照 sunshine 日志 daily record, journal, log ◇工作日志 daily record of work

日报表 daily activity report {DAR}
日备份卷 daily backup volume
日常软件 utility software
日初始(化)软盘 daily initialization diskette
日历 calendar, time-of-day {TOD}
日历程序 calendar program
日历时间 time-of-day {TOD}
日历时钟 calendar clock
日历视图 calendar view
日期字段 date field
日时组 date-time group
日用备份卷 daily backup volume
日志报表 journal sheet
日志操作 journalizing
日志[日记]打印机 journal printer
日志[日记]缓冲器 journal buffer
日志记录 journal log
日志卷后退 journal roll-back
日志卷前进 journal roll forward
日志任务 log task
日志输出 journal output
日志[日记]文件 journal file
日志项 journal entry
日志[日记]阅读器 journal reader
日钟 day clock

【róng】

荣 1)(茂盛)flourish 2)(光荣)honor, glory 荣获 have the honor to get or win 荣幸 be honored, have the honor 荣誉 honor, credit, glory

容 (表情)facial expression 容积 volume 容貌 appearance, looks 容纳 hold, contain 容器 container, vessel 容忍 tolerate, put up with 容许 permit, allow 容易 easy

容差 allowance, fault-tolerant, process allowance, tolerance
容差分析 tolerance analysis
容错 fault-tolerance/tolerant
容错操作 fault-tolerant operation
容错操作系统 fault-tolerant operating system
容错超方立体 fault-tolerant hypercube
容错程序 fault-tolerant
容错处理机 fault-tolerant processor
容错动态 fault-tolerant dynamic
容错方法 fault-tolerance approach
容错概念 fault-tolerant concept
容错技术 fault-tolerant technique
容错计算 fault-tolerant/tolerance computing
容错计算机 fault-tolerant computer

róng 溶熔融 rǒng 冗 róu 柔 ròu 肉 rú 如

容错(体系)结构 fault-tolerant architecture
容错控制系统 fault-tolerant control system
容错逻辑 fault-tolerant logic
容错匹配 permissive matching
容错软件 fault-tolerant software
容错设计 fault-tolerant design
容错算法 tolerant fail algorithm
容错系统 fault-tolerant system, fault-tolerant
容错性能 fault freedom
容量 capacity, content, volume
容量分配 capacity assignment
容量字段 size field
容许函数 admissible function
容许控制 admissible control
容许误差 admissible error, permissible error

溶 溶化 dissolve 溶解 dissolve 溶蚀 corrosion 溶液 solution

熔 melt, fuse, smelt
熔丝 fuse
熔丝模式 fuse pattern
熔丝图[映像] fuse map
熔性只读存储器 fusible ROM {FROM}

融 融合 blend, fuse, be in harmony 融化 melt, thaw
融洽 harmonious, on friendly terms
融合算法 fusion algorithm

【 rǒng 】
冗 冗长 tediously long, lengthy 冗余 redundancy
冗余(技术) redundancy
冗余测试 redundancy testing
冗余程序设计(法) redundant programming
冗余环 redundancy loop
冗余记录 redundant recording
冗余检验[校检] redundancy check
冗余节点 redundant node
冗余码[位,项] redundancy (=redundance)
冗余设备 redundant equipment
冗余位 redundancy bit
冗余线路 redundant circuit
冗余项 superfluous term
冗余校验 redundancy check, redundant check
冗余运算 redundant operation
冗余状态 redundant state

【 róu 】
柔 1)(柔软) soft, supple, flexible 2)(使变软) soften 3)(柔和) gentle, yielding, mild
柔顺性 flexibility, compliance
柔性管理 flexible management
柔性网络 flexible network
柔性制造 flexible manufacturing
柔性制造系统 flexible manufacturing system {FMS}

【 ròu 】
肉 1)(人或动物肉) meat, flesh 2)(果肉) pulp, flesh (of fruit) 肉眼 naked eye

【 rú 】
如 1)(依照) in compliance with, according to 2)(比得上) can compare with, be as good as 3)(比如) for instance, such as, as 如此 so, such, in this way, like

that 如果 if, in case, in the event of 如何 how, what 如今 nowadays, now 如期 as scheduled, by the scheduled time, on schedule 如上 as above 如上所述 as stated above, as mentioned above 如实 strictly according to the facts, as things really are, exactly 如数 exactly the number or amount 如同 like, as, as if 如下 as follows
如果一则规则 if-then rule

蠕 蠕虫 worm 蠕动 wriggle, squirm
蠕虫程序 worm

【rǔ】

乳 (奶汁) milk 乳白 milky white, cream color 乳房 breast
乳胶片 emulsion sheet
乳状(膜) emulsion

辱 1)(耻辱) disgrace, dishonor 2)(使受辱) bring disgrace to, insult 辱骂 abuse, call sb names

【rù】

入 1)(进入) enter 2)(参加) join, be admitted into, become a member of 3)(收入) income, means 入场 entrance, admission 入股 buy a share, become a shareholder 入伙 enter into partnership with 入籍 naturalization 入境 enter a country 入境签证 entry visa 入口 ①(进嘴中) enter the mouth ②(进入的门) entrance 入库 be put in storage, be laid up 入门 ①(初步学会) cross the threshold, learn the rudiments of a subject ②(初级知识) elementary course, ABC 入迷 be fascinated, be attracted 入手 start with, begin with 入选 be selected, be chosen 入学 enter a school 入帐 enter an item in an account, enter into the account book

入口 entry, entrance, inlet, intake
入口表达式 entry expression
入口常数 entry constant
入口程序 entry program
入口处理机 gateway processor {GWP}
入口处理器 gateway
入口地址 entry address
入口点 entry point, access point
入口点向量 entry point vector {EPV}
入口符号 entry symbol
入口过程 entry procedure, entry process
入口级别 entry level
入口键 entry key
入口交换 gateway exchange
入口结合 entry association
入口名 entry name
入口数据 entry data
入口顺序 entry sequence
入口台 entry platform
入口条件 entry condition
入口位置 entry position
入口引用 entry reference
入口语句 entry statement
入口值 entry value
入口指令 entry instruction
入口指针 entry reference
入侵型病毒 intrusive viruses

入树 in-tree
入文件队 infile
入选表 eligible list
入站 inbound

【ruǎn】

软 1)(质地不硬)soft, flexible, supple, pliable 2)(柔和)soft, mild, gentle **软管** flexible pipe or tube, hose **软化** soften **软木** cork **软弱** weak, feeble, flabby **软饮料** soft drinks

软错(误) soft error
软代数 soft algebra
软地址 software address
软返回 soft return
软分段 soft sectoring
软故障 graceful degradation, soft failure
软宏元 soft macro
软回车 soft return
软计算 soft computing
软键 soft key
软键盘 soft keyboard
软件 software
软件安全性 software security
软件版权 software copyright
软件包 software kit, software package, canned software, package, package of software
软件保护 software protection
软件保密 software privacy
软件变换 software mapping
软件操作 software operation
软件策略 software strategy
软件测试 software test, software measurement
软件产品 software product
软件产业 software industry
软件车间 software house
软件成本 software cost
软件成本估计 software costing
软件成分 software component
软件程序 software program
软件出版 software publishing
软件错误 software bug, software error
软件盗窃 software piracy
软件调试 software debugging
软件(设计)方法学 software methodology
软件仿真[模拟] software emulation
软件复杂性 software complexity
软件跟踪 software trace
软件工程 software engineering {SE}
软件工程方法 software engineering method
软件工程环境 software engineering environment {SEE}
软件工程师 software engineer
软件工具 software tool
软件功能 software function
软件故障 software failure
软件/固件包 software/firmware package
软件关联 software context
软件管理 software management
软件规格说明 software specification
软件过程 software process
软件环境 software environment
软件恢复功能 software recovery facility {SRF}
软件技术 software technique
软件计划[项目] software project
软件记录设备 software recording facility {SRF}
软件加密 software cryptography
软件兼容性 software compatibility

软件检验	software testing, soft check
软件健壮性	software robustness
软件接口	software interface
软件结构	software structure
软件开发	software development
软件开发包	software development kit {SDK}
软件开发工具	software development tool, software development kit {SDK}
软件开发环境	software development environment
软件开发计划	software development plan
软件开发阶段	software development stage
软件开发系统	software development system
软件开销	software overhead
软件科学	software science
软件可靠性	software reliability
软件可理解性	software understandability
软件可维护性	software maintainability
软件可移植性	software portability
软件可重用性	software reusability
软件控制	software control
软件库	software library, library of software
软件模块	software module
软件模拟程序	software simulator
软件模型	software model
软件评价	software evaluation
软件驱动程序	software driver
软件缺陷	software bug
软件人才(人件)	software human resource
软件冗余(法)	software redundancy
软件设计	software design
软件设计方法	software design approach
软件设计工具	software design tool
软件设计描述	software design description {SDD}
软件生产语言	software production language {SPL}
软件失效	software failure
软件实现	software implementation
软件实用程序	software utility
软件说明书[文档]	software document
软件套件	software suites
软件维护	software maintenance
软件文档	software document
软件系统	software system
软件项目	software project
软件效率分析	software performance analysis {SPA}
软件信号	software signal
软件性能	software performance
软件研究	software study
软件用户手册	software user's manual
软件优化	software optimization
软件支撑环境	software support environment
软件支持	software support
软件质量	software quality
软件中断	software interrupt
软件资料	software document
软拷贝	soft copy
软拷贝文件	screen file
软拷贝终端	soft copy terminal
软科学	soft science
软控键	soft key

软面板 soft front panel
软(磁)盘 diskette (=discette), flexible disk, floppy disk, flipping
软盘操作系统 floppy disk/diskette operating system
软盘初始状态 diskette initialize
软盘存储器 diskette storage, flexible disk memory
软盘存储驱动器 diskette storage drive(r)
软盘传送 floppy disk facsimile
软盘格式化 diskette formatting
软盘盒 library case
软盘机 diskette drive, flexible disk drive/ unit, flippy (=floppy)
软盘接口 floppy disk interface
软盘控制器 diskette controller, floppy disk controller {FDC}
软盘目录 diskette directory
软盘片 diskette sheet
软盘驱动器 diskette drive, flexible disk driver, floppy disk drive {FDD}
软盘数据格式 floppy disk data format
软盘文件 diskette file, floppy (disk) file
软盘文件目录 diskette file directory
软(磁)盘组 flexible disk pack
软扇区(记录)格式 soft-sectored format
软停机 soft stop
软线 flexible wire
软性永久虚信道 soft permanent virtual circuit {SPVC}
软硬件 soft hardware
软中断 software (generated) interrupt, trap

软字体 soft font

【ruì】

锐 锐利 sharp, keen 锐气 vigor, fighting spirit

瑞 瑞典 Sweden 瑞典人 Swede, the Swedish 瑞士 Switzerland 瑞士人 Swiss

【rùn】

闰 闰年 leap year, intercalary year

润 润色 polish, finish

【ruò】

若 1)(好像)like, seem, as if 2)(如果)if 若非 if not, were it not for 若干 ①(一些)a certain number or amount ②(多少)how many, how much

弱 1)(软弱)weak, feeble 2)(年幼)young 3)(能力差)inferior 4)(略少)a little less than ◇弱三分之一 a little less than one-third 弱点 weakness, weak point, deficiency 弱小 small and weak
弱连通的 weakly connected
弱连通图 weaked/ weakly connected graph
弱密钥 weak key
弱耦合 loose coupling
弱推理 weakly inference
弱位 weak bit
弱循环 weak loop
弱引用 weak reference
弱有向图 weak digraph

S s

【sǎ】

撒 1)(散布) scatter, sprinkle, spread 2)(洒落) spill, drop

洒 sprinkle, spray, splash

【sāi】

塞 1)〈动〉fill in, squeeze in, stuff 2)〈名〉stopper, cork, plug, spigot
塞孔 pin hole, receptacle
塞入脉冲 stuff pulse

【sài】

赛 1)(比赛) match, game, competition, contest 2)(胜过) be comparable to, surpass 赛跑 race
赛博空间 cyberspace

【sān】

三 three 三班制 three-shift system 三角 ①(三角形物) triangle ②〈数学〉trigonometry 三月 March
三倍 tripling
三倍字 triple word
三层板 three-ply
三层格式 three-level scheme
三重的 ternary, three-ply, triple, triplet
三重访问 triple access
三重结构记录 triple-structured record
三重链接 triply linked
三重内积 triple scalar product
三重投影 triple plane
三重性 ternary
三重序 ordered triple
三次样条函数 cubic splines
三地址 three-address, triple address
三地址结构 three-address architecture
三地址系统 three-address system
三地址指令 three-address instruction
三级编址 three-level addressing
三级地址 third-level address, three-level address
三级记录 three-level record
三角函数 trigonometric function
三角级数 trigonometric series
三角矩阵 triangular matrix
三角网格 triangular mesh
三角形 triangle
三角形网络 triangle network, triangular net
三角学 trigonometry
三进制 ternary notation, ternary system
三进制乘法 ternary multiplication
三进制存储单元 ternary cell, ternary memory element
三进制代码 ternary code

三进制计数器 ternary counter
三进制记数法 ternary notation
三进制逻辑电路 ternary logic circuit
三进制全加器 ternary full adder
三进制数 ternary number
三进制数位 trit
三进制运算 ternary arithmetic
三模冗余 triplication redundancy
三模冗余(表决系统) triple modular redundancy {TMR}
三输入端加法器 three-input adder
三索引符号 three-index symbol
三态控制信号 three-state control signal
三态逻辑电路 tri-state logic {TSL}
三态门 three-state gate, tristate gate
三态启动 three-state enable
三态驱动器 three-state driver
三态使能 three-state enable
三态总线 three-state bus, tri-state bus line
三维存储器 three-dimensional storage
三维的 three-dimensional
三维结构 three-dimensional structure
三维轮廓仪 contourgraph
三维模型 three-dimensional model
三维数组 three-dimensional array
三维图 three-dimensional graphics
三维图示技术 three-dimensional graphics
三维系统 three dimension system
三维像素体 voxel volume
三维组装 three-dimensional package
三位编码 tri-bit encoding
三稳态设备 three-stable state device
三线电缆 triaxial, tri-line cable
三元 ternary
三元代数 ternary algebra
三元级 triplet
三元组 three-bit byte, three-tuple, triad, triple, triplet
三元组表 triple table
三原色的 trichromatic
三原色值 tristimulus values
三值逻辑 ternary logic
三值模拟 three-value simulation
三字母(组) trigram

【sǎn】

伞 umbrella

散 另见【sàn】

1) (松开，无约束)come loose, fall apart, not hold together
2) (分散的)scattered 散装 bulk, in bulk
散列 hash, hashing, scatter
散列编址 hash addressing
散列表类 hash class
散列表项 hash table entry
散列表元 hash table bucket
散列查找 hash look-up
散列存储技术 scatter storage technique
散列地址 hash address
散列法 hash method, hashing
散列函数 hash function, hashing function
散列技术 hashing technique
散列码 hash code
散列数据 hash data
散列[杂凑]算法 hashing algorithm

散列向量 hash vector
散列信息 hash information
散射 scatter
散射图 point chart, point diagram

【sàn】
散 另见【sǎn】
（排除）dispel, let out 散布 distribute, scatter, spread 散发 ①（发出）send out, send forth, diffuse, emit ②（分发）distribute, issue, give out 散会 (of a meeting) be over, break up 散开 break up, disperse 散失 ①（分散遗失）scatter and disappear, be lost, be missing ②（消散失去）(of moisture, etc.) be lost, vaporize, dissipate, evaporate
散光器 scrim
散焦数据 defocus data
散热孔 louver
散热器 heat sink, sink

【sāng】
丧 另见【sàng】
funeral, mourning 丧葬 burial, funeral

【sàng】
丧 另见【sāng】lose 丧失 lose, forfeit

【sāo】
搔 scratch

骚 骚乱 disturbance, riot, chaos, unrest 骚扰 harass, disturb

【sǎo】
扫 1)（打扫）sweep 2)（很快地移动）pass quickly along or over, sweep 扫除 ①（清除）cleaning, cleanup ②（清除）clear away, remove, wipe out 扫兴 feel disappointed
扫出 scan-out
扫描 scan, scanning, sweep, pass
扫描变换 scan conversion
扫描查找 scanning search
扫描程序 scanner, scanning program
扫描电子束 scanning beam
扫描分辨率 scan resolution
扫描光点 scanning spot
扫描机 scanning machine
扫描机构 scanning mechanism
扫描记录 sweep record
扫描界限 scan limit
扫描控制 scanning control
扫描宽度 sweep width
扫描路径 scan path, scanning pattern
扫描码 scan code
扫描面 sweep plane
扫描模式 scan pattern
扫描频带 scan band
扫描区域 scanning area
扫描软件 scanning software
扫描设备 scanning device
扫描输出 scan-out
扫描输入 scan-in
扫描速度 scanning speed, sweep speed
扫描算法 scan(ning) algorithm
扫描头 scan head
扫描图案 scanning pattern
扫描文件 scanning file
扫描线 scan line
扫描选择器 scanner selector
扫描仪(器) scanner
扫描域 scanning field
扫描周期 scan(ning) period
扫频 frequency sweep

sǎo 嫂 sè 色 铯 sēn 森 sha 杀沙纱刹,傻,厦 shāi 筛

扫入 scan-in
扫视程序 scanner

嫂 elder brother's wife, sister in law

【 sè 】

色 1)(颜色)color 2)(脸色)look, countenance, expression 3)(景色)scene, scenery
色彩 color, hue, tint, shade
色斑的 stained
饱和 color saturation
色饱和强度 hue saturation intensity {HSI}
色标 color stripe/code
色标数 color code number
色表 color table
色彩成份 hue component
色彩浓度 color saturation
色彩图 chromaticity diagram, color map
色彩映射 color mapping
色差 chromatic aberration, color difference
色带盒 ribbon carriage, ribbon cartridge
色带架 ribbon carriage
色带卷 ink donor roll, ribbon spool
色带提升导向(器) ribbon lift guide
色调 hue, shade, tone
色调、饱和度、亮度 hue-saturation-brightness {HSB}
色调分离 tone separation
色调控制 toning
色调图 tone illustration
色调线 tone line
色度 chroma, chromaticity, chrominance
色度键控 chroma-keying
色度信号 chroma signal
色度学 colorimetry
色空间 color spacing
色匹配 color matching
色散补偿 dispersion compensation
色散位移单模光纤 dispersion shifted single mode fiber {DSSMF}
色数 chromatic number
色条 color stripe, streak
色同步 color burst
色图 color graph
色线 color bars

铯 cesium (Cs), caesium

【 sēn 】

森 1)(树多)full of trees 2)(阴暗)dark, gloomy 森林 forest 森严 stern, strict, forbidding

【 shā 】

杀 kill, slaughter

沙 sand 沙发 sofa, settee 沙漠 desert

纱 (线)yarn 纱布 gauze

刹 put on the brakes, stop, check, curb 刹车 ① brake ② turn off a machine ③ stop a vehicle by applying the brakes

【 shǎ 】

傻 傻子 fool, idiot, blockheads

【 shà 】

厦 tall building, mansion

【 shāi 】

筛 1)〈名〉sieve, sifter,

screen 2)〈动〉sift, sieve, screen
筛法 sieve method
筛选 fallout, screen, screening, sifting
筛选分类法 sifting sort
筛选模块冗余 sift-out modular redundancy {SMR}
筛选试验 screening test

【shài】
晒 (日照) shine upon 晒干 dry in the sun 晒图 make a blueprint, blueprint 晒印纸 blueprint paper
晒板台纸 flat

【shān】
山 hill, mountain 山顶 the summit of a mountain, hill top 山峰 mountain peak 山谷 mountain valley 山脉 mountain range, mountain chain

钐 samarium (Sm)

扇 另见【shàn】
1) (扇风) fan 2) (鼓动) incite, instigate, fan up, stir up
扇出 fan-out (=fanout)
扇出率 fanout ratio
扇出/扇入网络 fan-out/fan-in network
扇出特点 fanout feature
扇出转移[分枝] fan-out branch
扇入 fan-in

删 delete, leave out 删改 delete and change, revise, finalize 删节 abridge, abbreviate
删插功能 insert/delete capability
删除 delete, deletion, cancel {CANCL}, erasure, kill, pruning, removal, suppress
删除标记 delete flag
删除标志 deleted marker
删除表 delete list
删除部分 deletion
删除程序 killer program, killer
删除代码 delete code
删除符 cancellation mark, delete character {DEL}, deletion mark, erase character
删除键 cancel key, delete key
删除码 cancel code
删除权 delete rights
删除位 delete bit, deletion bit
删除文件 delete(d) file
删除无用的 space brooming
删除项 deleted entry
删除异常 delete anomaly
删除语句 cancel statement, delete statement
删除字符 delete character {DEL}
删改记录 deletion record
删去 crossing off, dash-out, delete, efface, rub-out
删行符号 line delete symbol
删行命令 line delete command

【shǎn】
闪 闪电 lightning 闪光 ①〈名〉flash of light, glare ②〈动〉gleam, glisten, glitter, glimmer 闪现 flash before one's eyes 闪耀 glitter, shine, radiate
闪光插座 flashing jack
闪光记录卡 flash card
闪烁 blinking, flicker(ing), scintillation
闪烁计(数器) scintillometer
闪烁扫描图 scintiscan

闪烁信号 wink signal

【shàn】

扇 另见【shān】 fan 扇形 ①〈形〉fan-shaped ②〈名〉sector, sectional form
扇段 sector
扇面长度 sector length
扇面磁盘 sector disk
扇面读出 sector read
扇面缓冲器 sector buffer
扇区 sector
扇区标号 sector label
扇区标识符 sector marker
扇区传感器 sector transducer
扇区(存储)单元 sector location
扇区地址 sector address
扇区格式 sector format
扇区环 sector ring
扇区孔 sector hole
扇区脉冲 sector pulse
扇区伺服 sector servo
扇区图 sector map
扇形扫描 sector display, sector scanning, sectoring
扇形图 pie chart
扇形显示 sector display

擅 擅长 be good at, be expert in, be skilled in 擅自 do sth without authorization, act at will

嬗 嬗变 ①(演变)evolution ②〈物理〉transmutation

善 1)(友善)kind, friendly 2)(易于)be apt to 善恶 good and evil 善后 cope with the aftermath of a disaster 善良 good and honest, kindhearted 善意 goodwill, good intentions 善于 be good at, be expert in

缮 (修缮)repair, mend 缮写 copy(out)

膳 meals, board 膳费 board expenses 膳食 meals, food 膳宿 board and lodging

赡 (赡养)support, provide for

【shāng】

伤 1)〈名〉wound, injury 2)〈动〉injure, hurt 伤害 injure, harm, hurt 伤亡 injuries and deaths, casualties 伤心 sad, grieved, sorrowful

商 商标 trade mark, brand (mark) 商标法 trademark law 商场 market, bazaar 商店 shop, store 商定 decide through consultation, agree 商界 business circles, commercial circles 商量 discuss, consult 商品 commodity, goods, merchandise 商洽 talk and arrange with sb 商榷 discuss, deliberate 商人 merchant, trader, businessman, dealer 商数〈数学〉quotient 商谈 exchange views, discuss, negotiate 商讨 discuss, deliberate over 商务 commercial affairs, business affairs 商业 trade, commerce, business 商议 confer, discuss
商品空间 commodity space
商品目录 inventory
商群 factor group, quotient group
商图 quotient graph
商务处理 business process

商业软件 business software
商业数据处理 business data processing
商业通信卫星 commercial communication satellite
商业图表 business graphic
商业信贷 commercial loan
商业在线服务 commercial online service
商用计算机 business computer, commercial computer
商用软件 business soft

熵 〈物理〉entropy
熵编码 entropy coding

【shǎng】
赏 1)（奖赏）grant a reward, award 2)（奖品）reward, award 3)（欣赏）admire, enjoy, appreciate

【shàng】
上 1)（上方）upper, up, upward 2)（上等）high, superior, better 3)（在前的）first (part), preceding, previous ◇上半年 the first half of the year 4)（登上）go up, mount, board, get on ◇上船 go on board, go abroad a ship 5)（安上）place sth in position, set, fix 上班 go to work, start work, be on duty 上报 ①（登载）appear in the newspapers ②（向上级报告）report to a higher body, report to the leadership 上当 be taken in, be fooled 上级 higher level, higher autorities 上交 hand in, turn over to the higher authorities 上届 previous term or session, last 上进 go forward, make progress 上课 ①（学生听课）attend class, go to class ②（教师讲课）conduct a class, give a lesson 上列 the above-listed, the above 上面 ①（位置较高处）above, over, on top of, on the surface of ②（前面）above-mentioned, foregoing 上任 take up an official post, assume office 上升 rise, go up, ascend 上市 go/ appear on the market 上述 above mentioned 上司 superior, boss 上诉 appeal (to a higher count) 上午 forenoon, morning 上下文 context 上学 go to school, attend school, be at school 上旬 the first ten- day period of a month 上涨 rise, go up
上边界 coboundary
上边缘 upper edge
上（角）标 superscript
上标字符 superscript character {SPS}
上层 father
上层节点 father of node
上道 upper track
上滚 rolling-up, roll-up
上滑（显示屏上信息）roll(ing) up
上划线 overline
上界 upper bound
上界表达式 upper bound expression
上界操作数 high operand
上卷 scroll
上卷程序 scroll program, scroller
上卷定时 scroll timing
上卷键 scroll key
上卷区域 scroll area
上拉菜单 pull-up menu

shàng 尚 shāo 烧稍 sháo 勺 shǎo 少 shào 少

上确界 least upper bound {LUB}, supremum (=sup)
上色 color coat, fuser, paint
上色动画 paint animation
上色工具 paint tool
上升时间 rise time
上升沿 rising edge
上态 upper state
上通路 uplink
上推 push-up
上推分类[排序]法 bubble sort
上推排序 shifting sort, shifting sorting
上托 pop, pop up
上下段位移 case shift
上下界 bound
上下文(关系) context
上下文编辑程序 context editor
上下文检查 context check
上下文检索 context indexing
上下文结构 context architecture
上下文开关 context switch
上下文控制块 context control block
上下文树 context tree
上下文说明 contextual declaration
上下文搜索 contextual search
上下文条件 context condition
上下文图 context diagram
上下文外关键词 keyword out context {KWOC}, keyword out-of-context {KWOC}
上下文无关的 context free
上下文无关语言 context-free speech
上下文相关 context-dependent
上下文有关(的) context-sensitive
上下文有关语法 context-sensitive syntax
上下限 bound
上限 upper bound
上行部分 ascender
上行链路 uplink
上行线 upline, uplink
上移 page-up, shift up, supershift (=SS, ss), upper shift
上溢 overflow
上载 upload
上止机构 upstop

尚 (还)still, yet 尚且 even

【shāo】
烧 1)(燃烧)burn 2)(加热)cook, prepare, boil 3)(发烧) run a fever, have a temperature 烧毁 burn out, burn down

稍 稍微 a little, a bit, slightly

【sháo】
勺 scoop, spoon

【shǎo】
少 另见【shào】
1)(数量少) few, little, less 2)(缺少) be short, lack 3)(丢失)lose, be missing 少量 a small amount, a little, a few 少数 small number, few, minority 少许 a little, a few, a modicum 少有 rare, exceptional, seldom

【shào】
少 另见【shǎo】(年轻)young 少年 ①(10～16岁的时期) early youth ②(10～16岁的人)juvenile, young teenagers

【shē】

奢 奢侈 luxurious, extravagant, wasteful 奢望 extravagant hopes, wild wishes

赊 赊欠 buy or sell on credit, give or get credit 赊帐 on credit, on account

【shé】

舌 (舌头)tongue
舌簧开关 reed switch

蛇 snake, serpent 蛇形 snakelike, S-shaped

【shě】

舍 1)(舍弃)give up, abandon 2)(施舍)give alms, dispense charity 舍得 be willing to spend, not grudge
舍入 half-adjust, rounded, rounding, round-off
舍入方式[过程] rounding procedure
舍入符号 round-off symbol
舍入位 rounding bit
舍入误差 rounding error, round-off error
舍位 truncation

【shè】

社 (集体组织)organized body, agency, society 社会 society 社论 editorial, leading article, leader 社团 mass organizations, community
社会工程学 social engineering
社会模型 social model
社会性认知 social cognition

设 1)(设立)set up, establish, found 2)(筹划) work out 3)(假设)given, suppose 设备 equipment, installation, facilities 设法 try, endeavor 设计 design, plan, outline, layout 设施 installation, facilities 设想 ①〈动〉imagine, envisage, conceive, assume ②〈名〉tentative plan/idea 设置 set up, put up, install
设备标记 device token
设备标识符 device ID, device identifier
设备标志 device flag, device identification
设备部件 device unit, equipment unit
设备参数表 device parameter list
设备操作结束 device-end {DE}
设备差错登记 device error log
设备处理程序 device handler, device processor
设备代码 device code
设备电源 device power supply {DPS}
设备队列 device queue
设备仿真 device emulation
设备分配 device/facility allocation, facility assignment
设备更新 equipment replacement
设备故障 equipment failure
设备管理 device management, facility management
设备管理器 device manager
设备号 device number
设备级别 facility level
设备架 equipment rack
设备监督器 hardware monitor
设备兼容(性) device/equipment compatibility
设备接口 device/equipment/unit interface

设备节点 device node
设备空间 device space
设备控制 device/unit control
设备控制单元 device control cell
设备控制块 device control block {DCB}
设备控制面板 device control panel
设备控制字(符) device control character/word
设备跨展 device spanning
设备扩充 device/ equipment augmentation
设备类型 device type
设备连接 device attachment
设备轮询 device polling
设备码 device code
设备描述块 device descriptor block {DDB}
设备名 device name
设备目录 facility inventory
设备能力 plant capacity
设备排队 device queue
设备配置 device configuration
设备请求 facility request
设备驱动器[程序] device driver
设备删除 unit deletion
设备失效 device failure
设备时钟 equipment clock
设备输出格式 device output format {DOF}
设备输入格式 device input format {DIF}
设备数据块 device data block
设备特性表 device characteristics table {DCT}
设备头 device head
设备维修 equipment maintenance
设备位 unit bit
设备位置 device location
设备文件 device file
设备无关位图 device independent bitmap {DIB}

设备无关性 device independence
设备误差 equipment error
设备相关位图 device dependent bitmap {DDB}
设备相关[依赖]性 device dependence
设备相似 unit affinity
设备向量表 device vector table {DVT}
设备信息[消息]处理程序 device message handler {DMH}
设备信息行 device line
设备虚址 virtual unit address
设备询问 equipment selection
设备选择码 device selection code
设备选择器 device selector
设备询问 environment inquiry
设备异常 unit exception
设备应答 device ack
设备优先级 device priority, priority facility
设备支持程序 device support routine {DSR}
设备支持软件 device support facilities
设备智能 device intelligence
设备中断 device interrupt
设备种类 device class
设备状态 device state
设备状态表 device status table {DST}
设备状态域 device status field
设备状态字 device status word {DSW}
设备状态字段 device status field
设备状态字节 device status byte
设备字段 device field {DFLD}
设定回答 default reply
设计版本 design version
设计参数 design parameter

设计策略 design strategy
设计差错 design error
设计程序 layout procedure
设计工具 design tool
设计故障 design fault
设计差错说明 design specification
设计阶段 design phase, design stage, planning phase, project stage
设计科学 design science
设计目的 design target
设计[详细,形式]说明 spec. (=specification)
设计图 scaling system
设计文档[资料] design documentation
设计文件 design file
设计语言 design language
设计原则 design principle
设计员 designer
设计者 composer, designer
设计周期 design cycle
设计自动化 design automation {DA}
设置断点 set breakpoint
设置模式 allocation schema
设置时间 set-up time

涉
涉及 involve, relate, concern 涉足 set foot in

射
1)(射击) shoot, fire 2)(喷射) discharge in a jet 3)(放出) send out (light, heat, etc.)
射击对策 firing game
射极耦合单元 emitter-coupled cell
射流技术 fluidics
射频 radio frequency
射频调制器 radio frequency modulator
射频发射 radio frequency emission {RFE}
射频放大器 radio-frequency amplifier
射频干扰 radio frequency interference {RFI}
射束存储器 beam storage
射束记录 beam recording
射束偏转 beam deflection

摄
摄取 absorb, assimilate
摄影 take a photograph of, shoot
摄动 disturbance, perturbation
摄动理论 perturbation theory
摄氏(的) Celsius {C}
摄像处理机 camera processor
摄影(技术) photography
摄影处理 photographic processing

【shēn】

申
(说明) state, express, explain 申报 ①(向上报告) report to a higher body ②(向海关申报纳税) declare sth (to the customs) 申辩 defend oneself, explain oneself, argue one's case 申斥 reprimand, reproach 申明 declare, state 申请 apply for 申述 state, explain in detail 申诉 appeal

伸
stretch, extend 伸长 elongation 伸缩 ①(伸长和缩短) stretch out and draw back, expand and contract, lengthen and shorten ②(变动) flexible, elastic, adjustable 伸展 spread, extend, stretch

砷
arsenic (As), arsenium

身

身 1)（生命）life 2)（自身）oneself, personally 3)（物体的主要部分）body ◇汽车车身 the body of a motor car 身材 stature, figure 身份（社会地位）status, capacity, identity 身份证 identity card, identification card, certificate of identification 身高 height 身上 ①（身体上）on one's body ②（随身）(have sth) on/with one 身体 body 身体健康 health 身心 body and mind

身份验证[鉴定] accreditation, identity authentication

深

深 深奥 difficult, profound 深沉 ①（程度深）dark, deep ②（沉沉）deep, heavy, dull ③（性情含蓄）concealing one's real feelings 深度 depth, deepness 深厚 close, intimate 深化 deepen 深究 go into (a matter) seriously, get to the bottom of (a matter) 深刻 deep, profound, deepgoing 深浅 depth, depth 深入 go deep into, penetrate into 深色 dark 深夜 late at night 深远 profound and lasting, far-reaching

深层结构 deep structure
深层知识 deep knowledge
深度缓存 depth buffer
深度排队 depth queuing, depth-queued
深度图 depth map
深度推理 deep reasoning

【shén】

什 另见 [shí]
什么 what, anything 什么人 ?Who? 什么地方?Where? 什么时候?When?

神 （精神）spirit, mind 神经 nerve 神经紧张 be nervous 神灵 god, deity, divinity 神秘 mysterious, mystical 神妙 wonderful, marvellous, ingenious 神奇 supernatural, magical 神气 ①（神情）expression, air, manner ②（精神饱满）spirited, vigorous ③（骄傲得意）putting on airs, cocky, overweening 神情 expression, look 神速 marvellously quick, with amazing speed 神志 consciousness, senses, mind

神经处理机 neuroprocessor
神经单元 neural unit
神经动力学 neurodynamics
神经堆 neuropile
神经仿真程序 neuron emulator
神经(元)计算机 neural computer
神经计算技术 neural computing
神经计算 neurocomputing
神经模糊逻辑 neural fuzzy logic
神经模拟 neuron simulation
神经器件 neuristor
神经网络 neural net(work)
神经网络计算机 neural network computer
神经细胞 nerve/neural cell
神经芯片 neurochip
神经信息学 neuroinformatics
神经元 neuron
神经元连接 neural connectionism
神经元学习 learning of neuron
神经专家系统 neural expert system

【shěn】

审 审查 examine, investigate 审订 examine and revise 审定 examine and approve 审核 examine and verify 审计 audit 审美 appreciation of the beauty 审判 bring to trial, try 审批 examine and approve 审问 interrogate, question, examine, hear, try 审议 consideration, deliberation, discussion; consider 审阅 check and approve

审查 auditing, censor
审查程序 audit program
审查命令语言 audit command language {ACL}
审计窗口 audit window
审计区域 audit area
审计员 auditor

【shèn】

肾 kidney

甚 1)(很,极)very, extremely 2)(超过)more than, exceed, surpass 甚至 even, (go) so far as to
甚低频 very-low frequency {VLF}
甚高频 very-high frequency {VHF}

渗 ooze, seep, leak 渗透 ①〈物理〉osmosis ②(透过) permeate, soak, percolatie ③(逐渐渗入)penetrate, infiltrate
渗漏 bleed
渗墨 ink bleed
渗入 inleakage

慎 careful, cautious 慎重 cautious, prudent, discreet

【shēng】

升 1)(升高)rise, hoist, go up, ascend 2)(升级)promote 3)(容量单位)liter (l,L) 升级 ①(晋升)upgrade ②(学生升级)go up (one grade, etc.) 升学 go to a school of a higher grade, enter a higher school 升值〈经贸〉revalue
升级(版本) upgrade
升序 ascending, ascending order
升序键 ascending key
升序排列 ascending order, ascending sort
升序序列 ascending sequence

生 1)(出生)be born 2)(活的) living ◇生物 living things 3)(产生,发生)get, have 4)(未熟)unripe, green 5)(未煮熟的)raw, uncooked 6)(未加工的) unprocessed, unrefined, crude 生病 fall ill, be sick 生产 ①(制造)produce, manufacture, fabricate ②(生孩子) give birth to a child 生产力 productive forces 生产率 productivity 生词 new word 生存 exist, live, survive 生动 lively, vivid 生活 ①〈名〉life ②〈动〉live 生命 life 生命力 life force, vitality 生命线 lifeblood 生僻 uncommon, rare 生平 all one's life, biography 生气 take offence, get angry 生日 birthday 生手 green hand, new hand 生疏 ①(不熟悉) not familiar ②(不熟练)out of practice, rusty 生态

ecology, organism's habits 生物 living things, organisms 生效 go into effect, become effective 生意(买卖) business, trade 生硬 stiff, rigid, unnatural 生育 give birth to, bear 生长 ①(长大)grow ②(成长)grow up, be brought up

生产成本 first cost, production cost
生产程序 production program/routine
生产管理 production management
生产过程 production process
生产计划 production planning, productive planning
生产监督系统 manufacturing monitor(ing) system {MMS}
生产模型 production model
生产线 production line
生产数据管理 production data mangement {PDM}
生产周期 production cycle
生产资料 capital equipment
生产自动化协议 manufacturing automation protocol {MAP}
生长模型 population model
生长树算法 spanning tree algorithm
生成 generate, generating, span, spanning
生成程序 generator, generating/generative program
生成多项式 generating polynomial
生成函数 generation function
生成空间 spanning space
生成树 generating tree, generation tree, spanning tree
生成数据组 generation data group {GDG}
生成算法 span algorithm
生成文法 generative grammar
生成文件 generation file, spanned file
生存对策 survival game
生存期费用 life cycle cost {LCC}
生存时间 time to live {TTL}
生活质量法[水平] quality of life {QOL}
生理学 physiology
生命型软件 life type software
生态学 ecology
生物传感器 biosensor
生物电子学 biological electronics
生物电子装置 bioelectronic device {BED}
生物反馈 biofeedback
生物工程 bioengineering, biological engineering
生物[仿生]计算机 biocomputer
生物晶片 biochip
生物控制论 biocybernetics
生物模型 living model
生物能量学 bioenergetics
生物数学 biomathematics
生物芯片 biochip, biological chip
生物信息学 bioinformatics
生物学 biology
生物学信息遥控术 biological telemetry
生物预测(数据库) biosis previews
生物钟 living clock

声 1)〈名〉sound, voice 2)〈动〉make a sound 声称 claim, assert 声调(音调) tone, note 声明 ①〈动〉state, declare, announce ②〈名〉statement, declaration 声望 popularity, prestige

声音 sound, voice 声誉 reputation, fame, prestige
声波 acoustic wave, speech waveform
声波分析 acoustic wave analysis
声波文件 wave file
声场 acoustic field
声存储器 acoustic store, sonic memory
声导引系统 acoustic homing system
声道 audio track, sound track, voice tract
声调制解调器 acoustic modem
声对抗 acoustic countermeasure
声发射 acoustic emanation
声反馈 acoustic regeneration
声仿真 acoustic simulation
声光介质 acousto-optic medium
声光效应 acousto-optic effect
声光仪 acoustooptic {AO}
声迹 audio track
声级表 sound level meter
声接收机 acoustic receiver
声卡 sound card
声码器 sounder, voice coder (= vocoder)
声纳 sonar
声耦合器 acoustic coupler
声频存储器 audio memory
声频系统 audio system
声频询问 audio inquiry
声谱图 sonograph
声全息图 acoustic hologram
声全息照相术 acoustic holography
声失真 acoustic distortion
声(音)输入装置 acoustic input device
声数据耦合器 acoustic data coupler
声速 acoustic velocity
声探测 acoustic detection
声特征 acoustic signature
声图 sonogram
声图文系统 picture-character-speech system
声图远程会议 audio graphics conferencing
声纹 voice print
声纹机 voiceprinter
声相容性 acoustic compatibility
声效 sound effects {SFX}
声信号识别 acoustic signal recognition
声学 acoustics
声学处理 acoustic treatment
声学抖动 audio dithering
声学工程 acoustic engineering
声学技术 acoustic technique
声(音)延迟线 acoustic delay line
声(音编)码器 sounder, voice coder (= vocoder)
声音操作继电器 voice-operated relay {VOR}
声音操作开关 voice-operated switch
声音带宽 sound bandwidth
声音单元 voice unit {VU}
声音的识别 sound recognition
声音点播 audio on demand
声音段 audio segment
声音合成 audio systhesis
声音合成器 audio mixer, sound synthesiser, voice synthesizer
声音缓存区 sound buffer
声音激活 voice activation
声音监控 acoustic surveillance, voice guard
声音库 voice bank
声音脉冲 acoustic impulse

声音耦合 acoustic coupling
声音频带 voiceband
声音生成器 sound generator
声音[语音]识别 voice recognition
声音识别输入 acoustic recognition input
声音识别系统 sound recognition system
声音[语音]输入 voice input
声音输入设备 voice input device
声音数据库 audio database
声音数据输入 voice data entry
声音通信 audio communication
声音文件 audio file
声音响应 audible feedback, voice response
声音压缩 voice compression
声音应答装置 audio response unit {ARU}, voice answer back {VAB}
声音邮件服务 voice mail service
声音终端 audio terminal
声音踪迹 audio track
声印机 voiceprinter
声再生 acoustic regeneration

牲 (家畜)domestic animal

甥 sister's son, nephew

【shéng】
绳 (绳子)rope, cord, string

【shěng】
省 1)(节约)economize, save 2)(免掉)omit, leave out
省份 province 省会 provincial capital 省力 save effort, save labor, economize 省略 ①(除去)leave out, omit ②(语言)ellipsis 省钱 save money, be economical 省事 ①(少麻烦)save trouble, simplify matters ②(方便) it's more convenient to
省略(符号) cross out, ellipsis, omission
省略功能 omit function
省字符 apostrophe

【shèng】
圣 1)(最崇高的)sage, saint 2)(神圣的)holy, sacred 圣诞 the birthday of Jesus Christ 圣诞节 Christmas Day 圣经 the (Holy) Bible
圣诞节病毒 christmas virus
圣诞节引导病毒 christmas boot virus
圣诞树病毒 christmas tree virus

胜 胜败,胜负 victory or defeat, success or failure 胜利 ①〈名〉victory, triumph ②〈副〉successfully 胜利者 victor, winner 胜任 competent, qualified, equal to 胜似 be better than, surpass 胜诉 win a lawsuit, carry the cause 胜仗 victorious battle, victory

盛 另见【chéng】
1)(繁盛)flourishing, prosperous 2)(旺盛)vigorous, energetic 3)(深厚)abundant, plentiful 盛大 magnificent, grand 盛典 grand ceremony 盛会 distinguished gathering, grand meeting 盛况 grand occasion, spectacular event 盛名 great reputation 盛夏 the height of summer, midsummer 盛行 popular,

common, wide-spread 盛意 great kindness, generosity 盛誉 great fame, high reputation

剩 surplus, remnant, leave (over) 剩下 be left (over), remain 剩余 surplus, remainder, residue
剩余群 residual group
剩余码 residue code
剩余校验 residue check
剩余值 residual value

【shi】

失 1)(丢失)lose 2)(错过) miss, let slip 3)(过失) defect, mistake, error 失败 be defeated, lose, fail 失策 unwise, inexpedient 失常 abnormal, odd 失当 improper, inappropriate 失火 catch fire, be on fire 失礼 breach of etiquette, impoliteness, discourtesy 失利 suffer a loss, undergo a defeat 失灵 not work properly, be out of order 失眠 (suffer from) insomnia 失明 lose one's sight, go blind 失窃 have things stolen 失实 inconsistent with the facts 失事 (have an) accident, wreck 失算 miscalculate, misjudge 失望 lose hope, feel disappointed 失物 lost article, lost property 失误 fault, muff, slip, error 失效 ①(药物)lose effect, cease to be effective ②(条约)be no longer in force, become invalid 失信 break one's promise, fail to keep one's word 失修 be in bad repair, fall into disrepair 失言 make a slip of tongue 失业 lose one's job, be out of work, be unemployed 失职 neglect one's duties 失主 owner of lost property 失踪 disappear, absence, be missing
失调 detune, misalignment
失控 out of control, runaway
失配 mismatch
失缺[遗漏]位 missing bit
失误规则 mal-rule
失效磁道 dead track
失效存储器 fail memory
失效机理 failure mechanism
失效节点 failure node
失效类别 fail category
失效率 failure rate
失效模式分析 failure mode analysis {FMA}
失效判据 failure criterion
失效树分析 fault tree analysis {FTA}
失效数据 fail data
失效位 fail bit
失效终端 dead terminal
失效状态 failure state
失真 distortion, aberration, aliasing, deformation
失真度 degree of distortion, distortion factor
失真分析仪 distortion analyzer
失真胶片 jam
失真图像 scrambled image
失真仪 distortion set

师 (教师)teacher, instructor 师范 teacher-training 师范大学 teachers/ normal university 师范学校 normal school 师父,师傅 master (teacher) 师资 teaching personnel, teachers

诗 poetry, verse, poem

施 1)(实行)execute, carry out 2)(给予)bestow, grant, hand out 施工 carry out construction 加施 exert, impose 施行 ①(执行)put into force, execute, apply ②(实行)perform

湿 wet, damp, humid 湿度 humidity 湿润 moist

狮 lion

【shí】

十 ten 十二月 December 十分 very, fully, utterly, extremely 十全十美 be perfect in every way, leave nothing to be desired 十一月 November 十月 October 十足 ①(纯粹的)100 per cent, out-and-out, pure ②(十分充足)full of, absolutely solid
十年[年,进,卷] decade
十的补码 ten's complement
十间距 ten pitch
十进编码的 decimal-coded
十进法 denary scale
十进记数制 decimal numeration system
十进(制代)码 decimal code
十进数制 decimal number system
十进位信号 decadic signal
十进制 decimal, decimalism
十进制标记 decimal marker
十进制除法 decimal division
十进制单元 decimal location
十进制符号 decimal symbol
十进制计数器 decade counter, decimal counter
十进制记数法 decimal notation
十进制记数制 decimal base, decimal number system
十进制进位 decimal carry
十进制数 decimal number
十进制数位[数字] decimal digit
十进制算术运算 decimal arithmetic operation
十进制小数 decimal fraction
十进制小数部分 decimal part
十进制小数点 decimal point
十六进制(的) hexadecimal {HEX, hex, sexadecimal}
十六进制格式 hexadecimal format
十六进制基数 hexadecimal base
十六进制记数法 hexadecimal/sexadecimal notation
十六进制字节 hexadecimal byte
十五迷宫 fifteen puzzle

什 另见【shén】
什物 articles for daily use, odds and ends

石 (岩石)stone, rock 石刻 stone inscription 石油 petroleum, oil
石印原版 litho master
石英晶体 quartz crystal

时 1)(时间)time 2)(计时单位)hour 时差 time difference 时常 often, frequently 时代 ①(时期)time, age, era, epoch ②(生命中的某个时期)a period in one's life 时而 ①(有时候)from time to time ②(叠用)now ... now ..., sometimes ... sometimes ... 时候 time, moment 时机 chance, opportunity 时节 season 时刻 ①(时间里的某一点)time, hour,

moment ②(每时每刻)constantly, always **时髦** fashionable, stylish, in vogue **时期** period **时区** time zone **时时** often, constantly **时事** current events, current affairs **时态(语言)** tense **时限** time limit
时变 time-varying
时变媒体 time-varying media
时变模型 time-varying model
时变网络 time-varying network
时标 clock {CLK}, time mark, time scale, time stamp, timing mark
时标相位 clock phase
时标因子 time-scale factor
时不变系统 time invariant system
时(间)差 time difference
时差调整 skew adjustment
时迟系统 time lag system
时分 time division
时分多路复用(技术) time-division multiplex(ing) {TDM}
时分复用交换 time multiplexed switching {TMS}
时分交换 time-division switching
时分通道[信道] time-derived channel
时分网络 time devided network
时分系统 time-division system
时基 time base
时基[时标]电容 timing capacitor
时基模块 time base module
时基误差 time base error
时基校正器 time base corrector {TBC}
时准确度 time base accuracy
时间编码 time (en)coding
时间标记 time stamp
时间表 time schedule/ sheet/ table
时间步 time step
时间槽 time slot
时间常数 time constant
时间窗(口) time window
时间戳 time stamp
时间单位 time unit
时间单元 time cell
时间段 time quantum
时间范围 time frame
时间分辨率 time resolution
时间分片 time slicing
时间复杂性 time complexity
时间共享 time share
时间划分 time division
时间间隔 time interval
时间角色 time case
时间竞争 race
时间[时态,时序]逻辑 temporal logic
时间片 slot time, time slice, time slicing, time slot
时间片仿真 time slice simulation
时间片环 slotted ring
时间片间隔 time slice interval
时间驱动 time driven
时间冗余 time redundancy
时间图 time/timing chart
时间相关 time correlation
时间压缩 time compression
时间延迟 time delay
时间依赖 time-dependent
时间映射 time mapping
时间帧 time frame
时间指示器 time marker
时空图 space-time diagram
时空折衷 time-space trade-off
时码信号 time code signal
时飘 time drift
时态数据 temporal data
时态图 temporal diagram
时态信息 temporal information
时态语义学 temporal semantics

时系列 time series
时限 quantum (=quanta)
时效日期 aging date
时序 sequence, sequence in time, time sequence, timing sequence
时序标记 gomma
时序操作 sequencing/ sequential operation
时序电路 sequential circuit
时序机 sequential machine
时序控制 sequential control, time-oriented sequential control
时序逻辑 sequential logic
时序逻辑电路 sequential logic circuit
时序脉冲发生器 sequence timer
时序图 sequence chart, timing diagram
时序推理 temporal reasoning
时序网络 sequential network
时序险态 sequential hazard
时序相关段 sequential dependent segment
时序组织 sequential organization
时延 delay, time delay, time lag
时延差 delay difference
时延常数 delay constant
时延电路 time delay circuit
时延畸变 delay distortion
时延网络 time delay network
时域 time domain
时域反射 time domain reflectometry {TDR}
时域分析 analysis in time-domain, time-domain analysis
时域响应 time-domain response
时滞 skew
时滞系统 time lag system

时钟 clock {CLK}, time clock
时钟版本 clock version
时钟比较器 clock comparator
时钟步进 clock step
时钟程序 timing routine
时钟窗(口) clock window
时钟代数 clock algebra
时钟单位 clock-unit
时钟(磁)道 clock track
时钟电路 clock circuit
时钟发生器 clock generator
时钟放大器 clock amplifier
时钟恢复 clock recovery
时钟链 clock chain
时钟脉冲 clock {CLK}, clock pulse, sprocket pulse
时钟(同步)脉冲门 clock gate
时钟脉宽 clock pulse width
时钟(脉冲)频率 clock frequency
时钟频率[速率] clock rate
时钟时间 clock time
时钟(脉冲)系统 clock system
时钟(脉冲)限制器 clock qualifier
时钟(脉冲)相位 clock phase
时钟(脉冲)信号 clock signal
时钟信号发生器 clock signal generator
时钟(脉冲)源 clock source
时钟振荡器 clock oscillator
时钟指针 clock pointer
时钟中断 clock/timer interrupt
时钟周期 clock cycle/ period/ tick

识 1)(认识) know, recognize 2)(知识) knowledge 识别 discriminate, distinguish, identify, discern 识破 see through, penetrate
识别程序 recognizer
识别(字)串 identification string

识别段 identification burst
识别符 identifier {ID}
识别矩阵 recognition matrix
识别逻辑 recognition logic
识别码 identify code
识别器 recognizer
识别设备 recognition device
识别算法 recognition algorithm, recognizer
识别项 identification item

实 1) (真实) true, real, factual 2) (果实) fruit, seed **实地** on the spot **实话** truth **实际** ①〈名〉reality, practice ②〈形〉realistic, practical, actual, real **实价** actual price **实践** ①〈名〉practice ②〈动〉put into practise, carry out, live up to **实据** substantial evidence/proof **实况转播** live broadcast, live telecast **实力** (actual) strength **实例** (living) example **实权** real power **实施** put into effect, implement, carry out **实事求是** seek truth from facts, be practical and realistic **实物** material object **实习** practice, training **实现** realize, achieve, implement perform, bring about **实效** actual effect, substantial results **实心** solid **实行** put into practice, carry out, practise, implement **实验** experiment, test **实业** industry (and commerce) **实业家** industrialist **实用** practical, pragmatic, functional **实在** ① (真实) true, real, honest, dependable ② (的确) indeed, really, honestly ③ (其实) in fact, as a matter of fact **实质** substance, essence

实变函数 real variable function
实变元 actual argument, real argument
实部 real part
实参数 actual parameter, real parameter
实存(储器) real storage
实存储器管理 real storage management {RSM}
实存管理 real storage management {RSM}
实存页(面)表 real storage page table {RSPT}
实存(储器)转储 real memory dump
实代码 true code
实地址 real address
实地址空间 real address space
实分区 real partition
实分析 real analysis
实符号 real symbol
实函数 real function
实际 practice
实际编码 actual coding
实际变元 actual argument
实际表 actual list
实际部件 physical unit {PU}
实际代码 actual code
实际地址 actual address, real address
实际费用 actual cost
实际符号 actual symbol
实际关键字 actual key
实际[有效]寄存器 actual register
实际块处理机 actual block processor {ABP}
实际媒体 physical medium
实际人口 actual entry
实际设备 physical/real device
实际时间 actual time
实际输出 actual output
实际损失 real loss

实际误差 actual error
实际显示 real display
实际资源 real resource
实例变量 instance variable
实例方法 instance method
实例关系查询 relational query by example {RQBE}
实例化 instantiate
实例学习 case based learning
实模式 real pattern
实驱动 real drive
实施计划 starting plan
实时 actual time, current time, real-time {RT}, true time
实时保护 real-time guard
实时并发性 real-time concurrency
实时操作系统 real time operating system {RTOS}
实时处理 real-time application/processing
实时传输协议 real time transport protocol {RTP}
实时的 real-time {RT}
实时动画(制作) real-time animation
实时仿真[模拟] real-time simulation/emulation
实时分析 real-time analysis
实时工作 real-time working
实时核心 real-time kernel
实时监控程序 real-time monitor {RTM}
实时接口 real-time interface
实时进程 real-time process, time critical process
实时控制 real-time control
实时控制器 real-time controller
实时控制协议 real time control protocol {RTCP}
实时流放协议 real time streaming protocol {RTSP}
实时批处理 real-time batch processing
实时任务 real-time task
实时视频 real-time video {RTV}
实时数据采集 real-time data acquisition
实时数据处理 real-time data processing
实时数据传输 real-time data transmission
实时协议 real-time protocol {RTP}
实时寻址 real-time addressing
实时约束 real-time constraint
实时执行程序 real-time executive {RTE}
实(时)时钟 real-time clock {RTC}
实时作业 real-time job
实数 real, real number
实数类型 type real
实体 entity, incarnation, reality, solid object
实体定义 object definition
实体段 entity section
实体功能 entity function
实体关系模型 entity relationship model
实体集 entity set
实体记录 entity record
实体接口 entity interface
实体类型 entity type, object type
实体联系[关系]图 entity relationship diagram {ERD}
实体模型 physical model
实体[目标]权限 object authority
实体事例 entity instance
实体属性 entity attribute
实体图 stereogram
实体完整性 entity integrity, entity-integrity property
实体系统 physical system

实体型 entity type
实体验证 object authentication
实体映像 solid mapping
实体元数据 entity metadata
实体造型 solid modeling
实现程序 implementater
实像 real image
实心部分 solid section
实心集 solid set
实型 real, real type
实验电路板 breadboard
实验[试验]误差 experimental error
实验性系统 pilot system
实用程序 utility, utility program/routine
实用程序控制设施 utility control facility {UCF}
实用处理程序 utility processor
实用功能 utility function
实用会话 utility session
实用模型 utility model
实用软件 utility software
实用软件包 utility software package
实用设备程序 utility facilities program {UFP}
实用系统 live system, utility system
实用装置 utility unit
实在参数表 actual parameter list
实在参数结合 actual parameter association
实质等价 essentially equivalent
实质性 essentiality
实质蕴涵 material implication

拾
pick up (from the ground), collect

食
1)(吃) eat 2)(饲料) feed 3)(天体现象) eclipse **食品** foodstuff, food, provisions **食宿** board and lodging **食堂** dining room, canteen, cafeteria **食物** meal, food **食言** break one's promise **食油** edible oil, cooking oil **食欲** appetite **食指** index finger, forefinger

蚀
1)(损失) lose 2)(腐蚀) erode, corrode 3)(天体现象) eclipse **蚀本** lose one's capital

【shǐ】

史
history **史料** historical data, historical materials **史前** prehistoric

矢
矢量 vector, vector quantity
矢量化 vector quantization {VQ}
矢量检索 vector search
矢量数据 vector data
矢量图 arrow diagram, phaser diagram, vector diagram (= vectogram)
矢量显示 vector display
矢量字型 vector font
矢线图 arrow diagram

使
1)(派遣) send, tell sb to do sth 2)(用) use, employ, apply 3)(致使) make, cause, enable **使馆** diplomatic mission, embassy **使节** (diplomatic) envoy **使命** mission **使团** diplomatic corps **使用** make use of, use, employ, apply **使者** envoy, messenger
使能 enable
使平滑 smoothing
使同步 synchronize

使脱开 unlink
使用参数控制 usage parameter control {**UPC**}
使用寿命 service life, working life
使用授权 use authority
使用数据 service data
使用位 usage bit, use bit
使用总线 utility bus

始 beginning, start 始发站 starting station 始末 beginning and end, the whole story 始终 from beginning to end, all along, throughout
始端系统 origin system
始发方式 originating mode
始发站[者] originator

驶 1)(开动)sail, drive, ride 2)(飞驶)speed, rush, race

【shi】

士 士兵 the rank and file, soldier

氏 (姓氏)family name, surname

示 show, notify, express, instruct 示范 set an example, demonstrate, illustrate 示例 give typical examples, give a demonstration 示意图 ① sketch map ② schematic diagram, schematic drawing
示波器 oscilloscope (=scope), electrograph, oscillograph, oscillometer
示波图 oscillogram
示例变量 instance variable
示例法 instance method
示例空间 instance space
示例目标 instance object
示例生成 instance generation
示例属性 instance attribute
示例修改 instance modification
示振器 vibrograph

世 1)(一辈子)lifetime, life 2)(一代)generation 3)(时代)age, era 世代 for generations, from generation to generation 世纪 century ◇ 二十一世纪 the 21th century 世界 world 世界博览会 World's Fair 世界纪录 world record 世界水平 world standard, world level, international level
世代数据组 generation data group {**GDG**}
世代文件 generation file
世界贸易组织 World Trade Organization {**WTO**}

市 (城市)city, municipal(ity) 市场 market, marketplace, bazaar 市价 market price 市郊 suburb, outskirts 市区 city proper, urban district 市长 mayor 市镇 town 市政 municipal administration
市场调查 market research
市场经济 market economy
市场模型 market model
市场学 marketing

式 1)(样式)type, style, model 2)(格式)pattern, form 3)(仪式)ceremony, ritual 4)(公式)formula
式样 fashion
式样设计 fashion design

侍 侍候 wait upon, look after, attend 侍者 waiter

势 1)(趋势)momentum, tendency 2)(形势)situation, state of affairs, circumstances 3)(姿势)sign, gesture **势必** certainly will, be bound to **势力** force, power, influence **势头** ①(情势)impetus, momentum ②(形势)tendency, the look of things

势能 potential energy
势态控制 situation control

事 1)(职业)job, work 2)(责任)responsibility, involvement **事端** disturbance, incident **事故** trouble, accident **事后** after the event, afterwards **事迹** deed, achievement **事件** incident, event **事例** example, instance ◇典型事例 a typical case **事前** before the event, in advance, beforehand **事情** matter, affair, thing, business **事实** fact, truth **事实上** in fact, as a matter of fact, actually **事事** everything, state of affairs **事态** state of affairs, situation **事务** ①(事情)work, routine ②(总务)general affairs **事物** thing, object, matter **事先** in advance, beforehand, prior **事项** item, matter **事业**(从事的活动)cause, undertaking **事业单位** nonprofit establishments, institution **事由** ①(事情的原委)the origin of an incident, particulars of a matter ②(公用语)main content

事故性[灾难性]转储 disaster dump
事后编辑 post-edit
事后处理程序 postprocessor
事件报告 event report
事件变量 event variable
事件标志 event flag, event notice
事件表 event list
事件程序 event routine
事件处理 event handling, event processing
事件处理程序 event handler
事件登记 event posting
事件调度程序 event schedule
事件队列 event queue
事件发生器 event generator
事件方式 event mode
事件跟踪 event trace
事件管理器 event manager
事件记录 event recording, incident record, logging
事件监督 event monitoring
事件控制块 event control block {ECB}
事件类 event class
事件例程 event routine
事件链 event chain
事件名 event name
事件模型 event model
事件驱动 event driven
事件驱动程序设计 event-driven programming
事件驱动语言 event driven language {EDL}
事件驱动执行程序 event driven executive {EDX}
事件任选(项) event option
事件扫描 event scanning
事件设备 event device
事件属性 event attribute
事件数据 event data
事件相关 fact correlation
事前估计 prior estimate
事实检索 fact retrieval
事实库 fact base

事实校正 fact correction
事务(处理) transaction
事务标识器 transaction identifier
事务处理 transaction processing {TP}
事务处理程序 transaction program
事务处理机制 transaction processing facility {TPF}
事务处理文件 transaction file
事务处理系统 transaction processing system {TPS}
事务处理终端 transaction terminal
事务处理装置 transacter
事务[交易]文件 transaction file
事务管理接口 administration interface
事务(处理)记录 transaction record
事务记录[日志] transaction journal, transaction log
事务(处理)卡 transaction card
事务流 transaction flow
事务流程图 clerical flowchart
事务密钥 transaction key
事务驱动系统 transaction driven system
事务日志 transaction journal
事务数据 transaction data
事务系统 transaction system
事务显示 transaction display
事务用计算机 office computer, office machine
事务终端系统 administrative terminal system {ATS}

饰 1)(装饰)decorate, ornament 2)(修饰)adorn, dress up, polish, cover up 3)(扮演)play the role, act the part of

试 1)(尝试)try, test, attempt 2)(考试)examination, test 试点 make experiments, launch a pilot project 试卷 examination paper, test paper 试探 sound out, probe, explore 试题 examination questions, test questions 试图 attempt, try 试销 trial marketing, trial sale 试行 try out 试验 trial, experiment, test 试用 test, try out, on trial 试制 trial-produce, trail-manufacture
试探的 heuristic
试验床[台] test bed
试验电路板 perfboard, breadboard
试验片 test piece
试验设计 experiment design
试验条 test bar
试验性系统 pilot system
试验性项目 pilot project
试样 proof sample
试用版 beta
试用程序 hello program
试运行 test run, trial run, preoperation

拭 wipe (away)

视 1)(看)look at 2)(看待)regard, look upon 3)(考察)inspect, watch 视察 inspect 视角 angle of view, visual angle, viewing angle 视力 vision, sight, view 视线 line of vision, line of sight, visual line 视野 field of vision
视窗 window
视窗系统 windows system
视见区 viewing area
视觉 vision
视觉处理机 vision processor

视觉传感器 vision sensor
视觉反馈 visual feedback
视觉分析器 vision analyzer
视觉机器 visual machine
视觉机器人 vision robot
视觉接口 visual interface
视觉模型 vision model
视觉识别 visual recognition
视觉系统 vision system
视口管理器 view manager
视口转换 viewport transformation
视盘 video disk
视频 video
视频(线路)板 video board
视频编码器 video encoder
视频拨号音 video dial-tone
视频存储器 video memory
视频带宽 video bandwidth
视频点播 video on demand {VOD}
视频电缆 video cable
视频段 video segment
视频发生器 video generator
视频方式 video mode
视频分析器 video analyzer
视频服务器 video server
视频缓冲(区) video buffer
视频会议 video conference
视频混合 video mixing
视频集成 video integration
视频检波器 video detector
视频控制器 video controller
视频快表 video lookup table {VLT}
视频盘 video disc
视频扫描 video scan
视频适配器 video adapter
视频数据库 video database
视频数字化仪 video digitizer
视频头 video head
视频图像适配器 super VGA {SVGA}
视频图形卡[板] video graphics board
视频图形[图像]阵列 video graphics array {VGA}
视频显示界面 visual interface
视频显示卡 video display card
视频显示器 video display, video display unit {VDU}, video display tube
视频显示适配器 video display adapter {VDA}
视频显示输入 video display input {VDI}
视频显示终端 video display terminal {VDT}, visual display terminal {VDT}
视频显示装置 visual display unit {VDU}
视频效应 visual effect
视频[可视]信号 visual signal
视频信号 video signal
视频信号编码器 video coder
视频压缩 video compression
视频增益 video gain
视平面 view plane
视平线 eye level
视区 viewpart, viewport
视体 view volume
视听的 audiovisual
视听教材 audiovisuals
视图 view
视图操作 view operation
视图处理器 viewing processor
视图等价 view equivalent
视图定义 view definition
视图点 viewpoint
视图流水线 viewing pipeline
视图区 view area
视像管 videocon
视像文本系统 video text
视野 visual field {VF}, prospects
视域 field of view

是 1)〈系词〉be 2)(对)correct, right 3)（应答词）yes 4)（表示存在）be, exist 是的 yes, right, that's it 是非 right and wrong 是否 whether or not, whether, if

适 1)（恰好）right, just 2)（舒服）comfortable, well 适当 fit, suitable; proper 适度 appropriate measure, moderate degree 适合 suit, fit 适时 at the right moment, in good time, timely 适宜 suitable, fit, appropriate 适应 suit, adapt, fit 适用 suit, apply to 适中 ①（适度）moderate, just right ②（位置适中）well-situated
适合性[度] fitness, suitability
适配器 adapter
适配器控制块 adapter control block {ACB}
适应测试 adaptive testing
适应算法 adaptive algorithm
适应性 adaptability, flexibility
适应性机构 homeostatic mechanism
适应性学习系统 adaptive learning system

室 room, chamber 室内 indoor 室外 outdoor, outside
室内电缆 house cable
室内网络 internal home network
室外的 exterior {EXT}

铈 cerium (Ce)

释 1)（解释）explain, expound 2)（消除）clear up, dispel 释放 let go, release, set free
释放报警 release alarm
释放命令 release command
释放时间 release time, take-down time
释放语句 free statement
释放占用 release busy
释放指令 release command, release order

逝 1)（过去）pass 2)（死）die, pass away

誓 （发誓）swear, vow, pledge 誓言 oath, vow, pledge

【shōu】

收 收藏 collect, store up 收成 harvest, crop 收到 receive, get, achieve, obtain 收费 collect fees, charge 收购 purchase, buy 收回 ①（取回）get back, call in, regain, recall ②（取消）withdraw, countermand 收获 harvest; results, gains 收集 collect, gather 收件人 addressee, consignee 收据 receipt 收款人 payee 收拢 take in, put away 收取 collect 收入 ①〈名〉income, revenue, earnings ②〈动〉take in, include 收缩 ①（缩小,缩短）contract, shrink, retract ②（紧缩）concentrate one's forces, draw back 收条 receipt 收听 listen in 收尾 ①（结束）stop, quit, wind up ②（文章末尾）ending (of an article, etc.) 收效 yield results, produce effects, bear fruit 收信人 the recipient of a letter, addressee 收益 income, profit, earnings, gains, avails 收音机 radio (set), wireless set 收支 income and expenses

收编 incorporation, incorporate
收带盘 take-up reel
收发键盘装置 send/receive keyboard set {RSK}
收发两用机 receiver-transmitter
收发器 transceiver
收费器 rater
收集器 trap
收集日志 collector journal
收集时间 acquisition time
收集站 collection station
收卷 wrapup
收敛 contraction, converge
收敛(性) convergence
收敛程度 degree of convergence
收敛速度 speed of convergence
收敛因子 convergence factor
收缩阵列 systolic array
收缩算法 contraction algorithm
收缩映射 shrinking mapping
收听方式 listening mode
收听器 listener
收听者地址 listener address

【shǒu】

手 1)(人的手)hand 2)(亲手)personally 手臂 arm 手边 on hand, at hand 手表 (wrist) watch 手段 ①(方法)way, method ②(不正当的方法)trick, scheme 手法 ①(技巧)skill, technique ②(不正当的方法)trick, intrigue 手感 feel, handle 手稿(original) manuscript 手工 ①(手做的工作)handwork ②(用手操作)done by hand, manual 手工业 handicraft (industry) 手工艺 handicraft (art) 手帕 handkerchief 手枪 pistol 手势 gesture, sign, signal 手套 gloves, mittens 手提箱 suitcase 手推车 handcart, wheelbarrow 手续 procedures, formalities 手指 finger

手册 handbook, manual, booklet
手持光标 puck
手持式计算机 hand-hold computer {HHC}
手动开关 manual switch
手动输入 manual input
手稿编辑 manuscript editing
手稿文件 script file
手工操作 hand operating
手工呼叫 manual calling
手工计算 hand computation
手工检查 desk checking
手工排字 hand composition
手工输入 by-hand input
手工送入 manual entry
手工送纸 threading
手画 free-form
手控 hand control, manual control
手控方式 manual mode
手提式计算机 portable computer
手写笔画识别 handwritten stroke recognition
手写汉字 handprinted chinese character
手写入方式 handprinted system
手写体 script handwriting
手写体汉字识别 handwritten Hanzi recognition
手写图形输入板 script graphics tablet
手写字符 hand-written character
手写(体)字符识别 hand-print-

守

守法 abide by the law, keep the law
守候 ① (等待) wait for, expect ② (看护) keep watch
守卫 guard, defend
守信 keep one's word, abide by one's word
守则 rules, regulations
守护程序 d(a)emon
守护进程 d(a)emon process

首

首 1) (头) head 2) (第一) first
首倡 initiate, start
首创 initiate, originate for the first time, first
首都 capital
首领 leader, head, chief
首尾 ① (始末) the head and the tail, the beginning and the end ② (始终) from beginning to end
首先 ① (最先) first ② (第一) in the first place, first of all, above all
首相 prime minister
首要 of the first importance, first, chief
首长 leading cadre, senior officer
首标 header label {HDR}
首标卡 header card
首标开始 start of header {SOH}
首标签 header label {HDR}
首部记录 leader
首部信息 header message
首部指示符 head pointer
首符 first symbol
首尾相连 end to end
首尾压缩方法 front-rear compression method
首席信息官 chief information officer {CIO}
首席执行官 chief excution officer {CEO}
首项 first term
首项表 first item list
首要的 prime, principal
首页标题 headline

【shòu】

寿 1) (长命) longevity 2) (年岁) life, age
寿命 life time, age limit, lifespan
寿命分布 age distribution
寿命函数 life time function
寿命曲线 life time curve
寿命试验 life test, endurance test
寿命终止 end of life

受 1) (接受) receive, accept 2) (遭受) suffer, be subjected to 3) (忍受) stand, endure
受潮 become damp
受罚 be punished
受害 fall victim, be ruined
受奖 be rewarded
受苦 suffer (hardships)
受累 ① (受到牵累) get involved on account of sb else ② (受劳累) be put to much trouble, be inconvenienced
受骗 be deceived, be taken in
受热 be heated
受伤 be injured, be wounded
受托 be commissioned, be entrusted (with a task)
受益 profit by, benefit from
受援 receive aid
受保护单元 protected location
受保护区域 protected field
受保护资源 protected resource, locked resource
受感染磁盘 infected disk
受管理节点 managed node
受管理系统 managed system

受叫方 called party
受控变量 manipulated variable
受控参数 controlled parameter
受控窗口 managed windows
受控对象 managed objects, controlled plant
受控访问单元 controlled access unit {CAU}
受控扫描 directed scan
受控条件 controlled condition
受控[被控]系统 controlled system
受控载波 controlled carrier
受控装置 controlled device
受限变量 restricted variable
受限语言 restricted language, controlled language

授 1)(交付)award, vest, confer, give 2)(传授)teach, instruct 授奖 award a prize 授课 give lessons, give instruction 授权 empower, authorize, warrant 授意 prompt sb to do sth, inspire, suggest 授予 confer, award, grant, endow

授权表 authorization list
授权代码 authorization code
授权区 zone of authority
授权文件 authorization file
授权信息 authorization message
授权验证 authority checking
授权拥有者 authority holder

售 (卖)sell 售货 sell goods 售货机 vending machine 售货员 shop assistant, salesclerk 售价(selling) price

兽 1)(哺乳动物的通称)beast, animal 2)(野蛮)beastly, bestial, brutal

瘦 1)(肉少)thin, skinny, bony 2)(脂肪少)lean

【shū】

书 1)(信)letter 2)(文件)document 书报 books, newspapers and magazines 书橱 bookcase 书店 bookshop, bookstore 书房 study 书号 book number ◇国际标准书号 ISBN, International Standard Book Number 书籍 books, works, literature 书记 ①(党团负责人)secretary ②(文牍员)clerk 书面 written, in written form, in writing 书面语 written language 书名 the title of a book, title 书目 booklist, title catalogue ◇参考书目 bibliography 书评 book review 书写 write 书页 page

书签 bookmark
书式报文 book message
书式复制 book copying
书式消息 book message
书写行 writing line

枢 枢纽 pivot, axis, key position

枢列 pivot column
枢纽的 nodal
枢行 pivot row
枢元 pivot entry

叔 uncle

殊 1)(不同)different 2)(特殊)outstanding, special, remarkable

舒 舒畅 happy, cheerful, in

good spirits 舒服 ①（舒适）comfortable ②（无病）be well 舒适 comfortable, cosy 舒适噪声 comfort noise

疏 1)（关系远）(of family or social relations) distant 2)（不熟悉）not familiar with 疏忽 carelessness, negligence, oversight 疏浚 dredge (a river, etc.) 疏落 thin, sparse, scattered 疏通 ①（疏浚）dredge ②（沟通）mediate between two parties 疏远 drift apart, become distant

蔬 蔬菜 vegetables, greens

输（失败）lose, be beaten, be defeated 输出 ①（往外运）export ②〈电气〉output 输入 ①（往里运）import ②〈电气〉input, feed-in, entering 输送 transport, convey, carry

输出比较器 output comparator
输出变量 output variable
输出表 output list/table
输出参数 output parameter
输出程序 output program/routine, written-out program
输出处理[输出进程] output process
输出存储区 output storage/block
输出电平 output level
输出端 output terminal/wire
输出端口 output port
输出端数 fan-out
输出队列 output queue
输出反馈 output feedback
输出范围 output bound
输出符号 outsymbol
输出格式 exported form
输出过程 output procedure/process
输出缓冲器[区] output buffer
输出缓冲区 output area
输出回路 output loop
输出记录 output record
输出假脱机 output spool
输出接口 output interface
输出开关 output switch
输出量 output quantity
输出列表 output listing
输出流 output/efferent stream
输出媒体 output medium/media
输出门 out gate
输出能力 output capability/capacity
输出排队 output queue
输出请求 output request
输出区 output area/storage
输出设备 output equipment/device/unit, out-device
输出数据 output data
输出速度 output speed
输出锁存器 output latch
输出特性 output characteristic
输出通道 output channel, efferent stream
输出通路 outbound path
输出文件 outfile
输出线 output line
输出信号 output signal
输出延迟 output delay
输出优先权 output priority
输出语句 output statement
输出指令 output instruction/order
输出质量等级 outgoing quality level {OQL}
输出种类 output class
输出装置 output device/unit
输出状态 output state/mode
输出总线 output bus
输出阻抗 output impedance
输入板 tablet

输入保护 input protection
输入笔 stylus
输入编辑 input edit(ing)
输入变量 input variable
输入标题 input header
输入参数 input parameter
输入操作 load operation
输入程序 input procedure/routine
输入处理 input process
输入处理程序 input handler
输入串 input string
输入存储区 input area/storage
输入点 enter point
输入电平 input level
输入端 input wire/header, in-fan
输入端数 fan-in
输入方式[形式] input/enter mode
输入符号 incoming symbol
输入[入口]格式 entry format
输入格式 input pattern
输入过程 input procedure/process
输入函数 input function
输入缓冲 input buffering
输入缓冲器[缓冲区] input buffer
输入加载 input loading
输入键 enter/entry/load key
输入接口 input interface
输入阶段 input phase
输入介质[媒体] input medium
输入禁止 input inhibit
输入井 input well
输入口 input port
输入块 input block
输入码 input code
输入门 in-gate
输入模块 input module
输入屏蔽码 entry mask
输入请求 input request
输入区 input area/field/region
输入驱动器 input driver
输入确认 input validation, entry approval
输入任务 incoming task
输入任选 input option
输入设备[装置] input equipment/device/unit
输入输出 input/output {I/O}, in-out
输入输出变量 input/output variable
输入输出程序库 input/output library
输入输出的 import/export
输入输出端(口) input/output port
输入输出法 input/output method
输入输出分析 input/output analysis
输入输出过程 input/output procedure
输入输出寄存器 input/output register
输入输出开关[转接] input/output switching
输入输出控制块 input/output control block {IOCB}
输入输出控制器 input/output controller {IOC}
输入输出控制系统 input/output control system {IOCS}
输入输出流控制 input/output stream control
输入输出模型 input/output model
输入输出特性 input/output characteristic, input/output property
输入输出通道 input/output channel
输入输出外围设备 input/output peripheral
输入输出指令格式 input/out-

put instruction format
输入输出装置 input/output unit
输入输出总线 input/output bus, input/output trunk
输入属性 input attribute
输入数 input number, input digit, input
输入数据 input/incoming data
输入数据错误 input data error
输入数据集 input data set
输入数据流 input stream
输入数据验证 input data validation
输入说明 input specification
输入台[站] input station
输入特性 input characteristic
输入提示(符) input prompt
输入通道 input channel
输入图像 input image
输入图形 input pattern
输入图元 input primitive
输入位 input digit
输入文本模型 input text type
输入文档[资料] input document
输入文件 input file
输入显示屏 input panel
输入线 input line
输入相关 input dependence
输入向量 input vector
输入信息 input information/message
输入信息流 input steam
输入形式 input form
输入游标 input cursor
输入语句 enter statement
输入原语 input primitive
输入源 input source
输入中继线 incoming trunk
输入终端 input terminal
输入重定向 input redirect
输入状态 input state/mode
输入自变量 input argument
输入字 input word
输入字段 input field
输入字母(表) input alphabet
输入作业 input job
输入作业流 input (job) stream
输入作业排队 input work queue
输送机构 delivery mechanism
输送孔 sprocket, sprocket hole
输送轮 delivery wheel/roller
输送托盘 delivery tray
输送系统 transport system
输送纸带 carriage tape
输送状态 feed status
输纸部件 tractor feeder, paper feed unit
输纸机构 page drive mechanism
输纸孔 track hole, tractor hole(s)
输纸器 paper transport, tractor
输纸设备 tractor feeder
输纸装置 paper carrier

【shú】

赎 (弥补) pay for, make amends for 赎回 redeem, ransom, buy back

熟 1)(成熟) ripe 2)(煮熟) cooked, done 熟记 learn by heart, memorize, commit to memory 熟练 skilled, proficient, experienced 熟识 be well acquainted with, know well 熟悉 know well, be familiar with

【shǔ】

属 1)(隶属) be under, subordinate to 2)(归属) belong to 3)(亲属) family members,

dependents, relatives 4)(类别)category 属性 attribute, quality, characteristic, property 属于 belong to, be part of
属性表 attribute list/table
属性分析 attribute analysis
属性集 attribute set
属性块 attribute block
属性名 attribute name
属性模拟 attribute simulation
属性文法 attribute grammar
属性元数据 attribute metadata
属性字段 attribute field

鼠 mouse, rat
鼠标(器) mouse
鼠标阀值 mouse threshold
鼠标器按钮 mouse button

数 另见【shǔ】(清点)count

暑 heat, hot weather 暑假 summer vacation

署 1)(办公处所)(a government) office 2)(布置)make arrangements for 署名 sign, put one's signature to

曙 daybreak, dawn 曙光 first light of morning, dawn

【shù】

术 1)(技艺)art, skill, technique 2)(方法)method, tactics, strategy 术语(technical) terms, terminology
术语控制 terminological control
术语库 terminology bank
术语学 orismology

束 1)(捆)bind, tie 2)〈量词〉bundle, bunch, cluster 3)(约束)control, restrain 束缚 tie, bind up, hamper

述 state, narrate, recount, relate 述评 review, commentary

恕 (饶恕)forgive, pardon, excuse

树 tree 树立 set up, establish 树林 woods, forest
树叉 tree branch
树查询 tree query
树处理 tree processing
树的遍历 tree traversal
树的二元形 tree binary form
树根 root of tree, tree root
树节点 tree node
树结构 tree structure
树理论 tree theory
树名 tree name
树模式 tree schema
树排序 tree sort(ing)
树搜索 tree searching
树搜索算法 tree search algorithm
树形 tree form/like
树形表示 tree representation
树形布局 tree topology
树形层次 tree hierarchy
树形结构 tree structure
树形排序 tree ordering
树形图 tree diagram, arbore/scence
树形网络 tree network, tree type network, tree
树形线路 tree circuit
树叶 tree leaf
树域 tree domain
树枝 tree branch
树指示字[指针] tree pointer
树桩电缆 stub cable

树桩网 stub network
树状 arborescence

竖 1)〈形〉vertical, upright, perpendicular 2)〈动〉set upright, erect, stand
竖式[纵向]打印机 column printer
竖式监视器 portrait monitor
竖式印刷 portrait mode

数 另见【shǔ】
number, digit, figure 数词 numeral 数额 number, amount 数据 number, digital information 数量 quantity, amount, magnitude, scalar 数目 number, amount 数学 mathematics 数字 ① numeral, figure, digit ② quantity, amount
数表 tables
数传机 data set {DS}, data loop transceiver {DLT}
数点处理 digital point processing
数格式 number format
数根 radix
数基 number base, number system base
数积 scalar product
数记号 number token
数据安全(性) data security
数据安全软件包 data security package
数据[报文]包 packet
数据包 data packet, package, data pack, data capsule
数据包装 data wrap
数据保护 data protection, protection of data
数据保密 data scramble
数据保密性 data privacy
数据报 datagram {DG}
数据报头 datagram header, data message
数据笔 data pen
数据编辑 data editing/edition
数据编码格式 data encoding format
数据编码系统 data encoding system, data-coding system
数据编址 data addressing
数据变换 data transformation/conversion, conversion of information
数据变换[映像] data map
数据标记 data tagging
数据标识符 data identifier
数据标志 data label
数据表 data list table/ sheet/ /book
数据表块 table block
数据表示 data expression
数据捕获[捕捉,获取] data capture
数据布局 data layout
数据采集 data gathering/ acquisition
数据采集和控制 data acquisition and control {DAC}
数据采集器 data acquisition unit {DAU}
数据采集设备 data acquisition equipment {DAE}
数据采集适配器 capture adaptor
数据采集文件 capture file
数据采样 data sampling
数据仓库 data warehouse/warehousing
数据操作语言 data manipulation language {DML}
数据测试设备 data test set
数据层次 data hierarchy
数据查找 data search
数据常量 data constant
数据长度 data length

数据冲突 data collision
数据抽象 data abstraction
数据初始化 data initialization
数据处理 data processing {DP}, data handling
数据处理程序 data processor/handler
数据处理过程 data handling procedure
数据处理技术 data processing technique
数据处理能力 data handling capacity
数据处理权 data rights
数据处理事务 data transaction
数据传输方式 data transfer mode
数据传输速率 data rate
数据传输装置 data line
数据传送 data transfer
数据传送方式 data mode
数据传送换码 data link escape
数据传送码 data transmission code
数据传送状态 data transfer state
数据串 data string
数据窗 data window
数据磁带 data tape
数据磁道 data track
数据磁盘 data disk
数据存储 data storage
数据存储层 data store layer
数据存储器 data memory/storage
数据存取层 data access layer
数据存取对象 data access object {DAO}
数据存取方法 data access method {DAM}
数据存取规程[协议] data access protocol {DAP}
数据存取寄存器 data access register {DAR}
数据存取路径 data access path
数据存取图 data access diagram
数据存取系统 data access system
数据存取语言 data access language
数据存取装置 data access arrangement {DAA}
数据打印格式 data layout
数据打字机 data typewriter
数据代码 data code
数据单元 data cell/unit/location
数据的合法性 data validation
数据登录器 data logger
数据地址 data address
数据点 data point
数据电报 datagram
数据电话 data telephone, dataphone
数据电缆服务接口标准 data over cables service interface specification {DOCSIS}
数据电路 data circuit
数据电路终端设备 data circuit terminating equipment {DCE}
数据调制解调器 data modem
数据定界符 data delimiter
数据定位 data registration
数据定义 data definition {DD}
数据定义语言 data definition/define language {DDL}
数据独立性 data independence
数据段 data segment/division/field
数据队列 data queue
数据对齐 alignment of data
数据对象 data object
数据方式 data mode
数据访问 data access
数据访问法 data access method {DAM}
数据访问寄存器 data access register {DAR}

数据访问控制 data access control
数据访问路径 data access path
数据访问语言 data access language {DAL}
数据分布 data distribution
数据分层 data hierarchy
数据分叉 data fork
数据分拆 data striping
数据分隔符 data separator
数据分级[法] data staging
数据分级结构 data hierarchy
数据分解 data resolution
数据分类 data sorting/class
数据分析 data analysis
数据封锁 data locking
数据封装 data encapsulation, digital envelop
数据服务 data services
数据服务管理程序 data services manager {DSM}
数据服务命令处理器[程序] data services command processor {DSCP}
数据服务任务 data services task {DST}
数据服务设备 data services unit {DSU}
数据副本[转录] data transcription
数据附录 data appendix
数据格式 data format/layout
数据格式化 data formatting
数据跟踪网络 tracking-data network
数据共享 data share, data sharing
数据管理 data management/administration
数据管理块 data management block {DMB}
数据管理器 data manager
数据管理软件 data management software {DMS}
数据管理系统 data management system {DMS}
数据管理语言 data management language {DML}
数据管理员[装置] data administrator
数据规则 data rule
数据归并 data merge
数据盒式磁带(机) data cartridge
数据互操作 data interoperation
数据互调[互用,交换] data exchange
数据互换 data interchange
数据划分 data division, data partitioning
数据缓冲区 data buffer
数据换码符 data escape character
数据恢复 data recovery, data retrieval
数据汇集 data collection, data gathering
数据汇总 data summarization
数据基空间 dbspace
数据集 data set {DS}
数据集成 data integration
数据集定义 data set definition {DSD}
数据集概貌 data set profile
数据集控制块 data set control block {DSCB}
数据集名 data set name (=dsname)
数据集市 data mart
数据集中 data concentration
数据集组 data set group {DSG}
数据级 data level, data staging
数据寄存器 data register
数据计数字段 data count field {DCF}
数据记录 data record
数据记录控制 data recording

control {DRC}
数据记录媒体 data carrier
数据记录器 data logger, data recorder
数据记录区 data recorded area
数据记录设备[装置] data recording device {DRD}
数据加密 data encryption
数据加密标准 data encryption standard {DES}
数据加密密钥 data encryption/encrypting key {DEK}
数据兼容[互换]性 data compatibility
数据检测 data detection
数据检查 data check(ing), data examination
数据检索语言 data retrieval language {DRL}
数据建模 data modeling
数据交换 data switching, data interchange
数据交换(机) data switching exchange {DSE}
数据交换格式 data interchange format {DIF}
数据交换接口 data exchange interface {DXD}
数据交换设备 data switching equipment {DSE}, data exchange unit
数据交换系统 data exchange system
数据交换中心 data switching center
数据接收机[器] data receiver
数据阶段 data phase
数据截断 data truncation
数据结构 data structure {DS}
数据结构图 data structure diagram {DSD}
数据结束(指示)符 end of data {EOD}, end of data delimiter, end of data indicator

数据解析论 datalogy
数据界限保护 datum limit protection
数据矩阵 data matrix
数据聚合 data aggregate
数据卡(片) data card/deck
数据开关 data switch
数据可视化 data visualization
数据空间 data space
数据控制 data control
数据控制块 data control block {DCB}
数据控制系统 data control system
数据控制语言 data control language {DCL}
数据库 database {DB}, data library/bank/pool
数据库安全性 database security
数据库保护 database protection
数据库部件[成分,组分] database component
数据库操作 database manipulation
数据库查询 database inquiry, database query
数据库程序设施 database facility {DBF}
数据库程序员 database programmer
数据库处理机 database processor
数据库处理器 database handler
数据库存储器 database memory
数据库存取 database access
数据库调用 database call
数据库定义 database definition
数据库段 database segment
数据库对象 database objects
数据库方案 database scheme
数据库仿真器 database system

simulator

数据库分析员 database analyst

数据库服务 database service

数据库服务器 database server

数据库工程 database engineering

数据库管理 database management, database administration {DBA}

数据库管理[控制]系统 database control system {DBCS}

数据库管理系统 database management system {DBMS}

数据库管理语言 database administration language {DAL}

数据库管理员 database manager, database administrator {DBA}

数据库环境 database environment

数据库恢复 database roll-back, database recovery

数据库活动图 database action diagram {DAD}

数据库机(器) database machine

数据库集 data bank

数据库级 database level

数据库计算机 database computer {DBC}, database machine

数据库记录 database record

数据库检索 database search

数据库建立 database creation

数据库结构 database structure

数据库开发生命周期 database development life cycle {DDLC}

数据库可靠性 database reliability

数据库控制 database control

数据库链路 database link

数据库略图 database profile

数据库描述 database description {DBD}

数据库模式 database schema

数据库模型 database model

数据库目录 database directory

数据库评价 database evaluation

数据库设备[设施] database facility {DBF}

数据库设计辅助工具 database design aid {DBDA}

数据库设计员 database designer

数据库实现 database implementation

数据库实用程序 database utility

数据库事务 database transaction

数据库数据模型 database data model

数据库说明 database description {DBD}, database specification

数据库体系结构 database architecture

数据库完整性 database integrity

数据库维护 database maintenance

数据库文件 database file

数据库系名 database set name

数据库系统 database system, data bank system

数据库引导程序 database engine

数据库用户 database user

数据库语言 database language {DBL}

数据库语义 database semantic

数据库元数据 database metadata

数据库运行记录法 database logging

数据库诊断 database diagnostics

数据库重建 database recreation

数据库转储	database dump
数据库装入	database load
数据库状态	database state
数据库资源	database resource
数据库组织	database organization
数据块	data block {DBLK}, block of data, block data
数据块传送	block transfer
数据块复制	block copy
数据块缓冲	data block buffering
数据块间隔	interblock gap {IBG}
数据块检验	block check
数据宽度	data width
数据馈送装置	feed
数据类	data class
数据类型	data type
数据连接器	data connector
数据链控制	data link control {DLC}
数据链路	data link
数据链路层	data link layer
数据链路协议	data link protocol
数据量	data quantity/volume
数据列表	data list
数据流	data stream
数据流程图	data flow diagram, data flowchart
数据流程序	data flow program
数据流处理机	data flow processor
数据流分析	data flow analysis
数据流格式	data flow format, data stream format
数据流计算机	data flow computer
数据流接口	data stream interface {DSI}
数据流结构	data flow structure
数据流控制	data flow control {DFC}, data stream control
数据流模式	data flow model
数据流驱动器	streamer
数据流扫描器	data flow scanner
数据流设计	data flow design
数据流系统	data flow system
数据录入	data entry
数据码	data code
数据密度	data density
数据描述	data description
数据描述符	data specificator, data descriptor
数据描述语言	data description language {DDL}
数据名(称)	data name
数据模型	data model
数据模型质量	data model quality
数据目录	data directory/content/inventory
数据内容	data content
数据耦合	data coupling
数据品质	data quality
数据屏蔽	data mask
数据迁移	data migration
数据窃用	abuse
数据清理	data purging
数据请求	data request
数据区	data area/field/region/space, datastore
数据区分隔符	field tab {FTAB}
数据驱动	data driven
数据驱动计算机	data driven computer/machine
数据驱动设计法	data-driven design
数据驱动推理	data-driven reasoning
数据驱动系统	data-driven system
数据群聚	data clustering
数据冗余(性)	data redundancy
数据筛选	data filtering
数据设备控制块	data/device

control block {DCB}
数据设计 data design
数据生成 data generation
数据识别符 data identifier
数据适配器 data adapter
数据视频 digital video
数据收集 data collection/gathering/capture/aggregate
数据收集终端 data collector terminal, data capture terminal
数据收集装置 transacter
数据手册 data (hand)book
数据授权 data authority
数据输出 data output, data-out
数据输出端口 data-out port
数据输出寄存器 data output register
数据输出开关 data output switch
数据输出控制 data-out control
数据输入 data input, data-in
数据输入板 data tablet
数据输入程序 data entry program
数据输入端口 data-in port
数据输入寄存器 data input register, data-in register
数据输入控制 data-in control
数据输入系统 data entry system
数据输入站 data input station, data entry station
数据输入终端 data entry terminal
数据输入总线 data input bus {DIB}
数据属性 data attribute
数据数量 data quantity/volume
数据数字音频磁带 data digital audio tape {DAT}
数据数组 data array
数据顺序号 data sequence number {DSN}
数据说明 data specification/declaration
数据宿主节点 data host node
数据锁 data lock
数据提取 data extract
数据条 stripe
数据通道 data channel
数据通路[径] data path
数据通信 data communication {DC}, communication, datacom, digicom
数据通信多路复用器 data communication multiplexer {DCM}
数据通信管理程序 data communications manager
数据通信控制器 data communications control unit
数据通信设备 data communications equipment {DCE}
数据通信网(络) data communication network
数据通信网络体系 data communication network architecture {DCNA}
数据通信线路 data line, tie line
数据通信协议 data communication protocol
数据通信学 data communications
数据通信站 data communication station
数据头 data head
数据挖掘 data mining
数据完整性 data integrity
数据网络 data network
数据网络识别码 data network identification code {DNIC}
数据维护 data maintenance
数据位 data bit
数据位流 bit stream

数据文本 data text
数据文件 data file, document file
数据文件实用程序 data file utility {DFU}
数据文件指针 data file pointer
数据无关 data independence
数据无线电 data radio
数据误差 data error
数据误码率 data error rate
数据误用 abuse
数据系统接口 data system interface
数据显示 data display
数据显示模件 data display module
数据显示装置 data display unit
数据线 data wire
数据线路终端 data line terminal •
数据相关 data correlation/ dependency
数据相关图 data dependence graph
数据相位 data phase
数据项 data element/ item
数据项分隔符 data item separator
数据项描述 data item description {DID}
数据芯片 data chip
数据信道 data channel
数据信号 data signal
数据信息处理机 data handler
数据信息量 data traffic
数据形式 data form
数据序列号 data sequence number {DSN}
数据选通 data strobe
数据选择 data select(ing), data selection
数据寻址 data addressing
数据压缩 data compression, compaction of data

数据延迟 data delay
数据掩码 data mask
数据一致性 data consistency
数据依赖 data dependence
数据移动 data movement, staging
数据移位寄存器 data shift register
数据易变性 data volatility
数据异常 data exception, data abnormal
数据映像装置 data mapping unit
数据有效性 data validity
数据语言 data language
数据语义学 data semantics
数据域 data field
数据元 data element
数据元链 data element chain
数据元素 data element/ component
数据元组 data tuple
数据源 data source, information source, origin, data pool
数据约束 data constraint
数据阅读机[器] data reader
数据栈 data bank
数据站 data station
数据阵列 data array
数据争用 data collision
数据整理 data reduction
数据帧 data frame
数据值 data value
数据指针 data pointer
数据质量 data quality
数据中心 data center/mart
数据终端就绪 data terminal ready {DTR}
数据终端装置[设备] data terminal equipment {DTE}, data terminal installation
数据转储 data dump
数据转换器 data converter

shù 数

数据转接交换机 data switching exchange {DSE}
数据转接中心 data switching center
数据转义字符 data escape character
数据装置 data set {DS}
数据状态 data state/mode
数据准备 data preparation
数据准备状态 data ready
数据资源 data resource
数据自动化 data automation, datamation
数据自由通路 data free way
数据字 data word
数据字长 data word length, data word size
数据字典 data dictionary {DD}
数据字典目录 data dictionary directory {DDD}
数据字典系统 data dictionary system {DDS}
数据字段 data field
数据总库 data bank
数据总线 data bus
数据组 data array/field/group
数据组标志 group mark {GM}
数据组分 data component
数据组织 data organization
数控 numerical control {NC}, digital control
数控编程 numerical control programming
数控带 numerical control tape
数控单元 digital control unit
数控机床 digital controlled machine
数控机器 numerically controlled machine
数控机器人 digital control robot
数理逻辑 mathematical logic
数理统计 mathematical statistics
数量级 magnitude
数量特征 quantitative attribute
数列 sequence, series
数论 number theory
数码 figure
数码管 nixie tube, nixie light
数码影碟 digital video disk
数码总线 number bus
数码组 number group
数-模译码器 digital-analog decoder
数-模转换器 digital-(to-)analog converter {D/A converter, DAC}
数位 numerical digit
数位符号 digit sign, numerical character
数位脉冲 pulse digit
数位位置 digit position/place, bit site, column
数位选择器 digit selection
数位压缩 digit compression
数位延迟 digit delay
数位周期 one-digit time
数位组 digroup
数学变换 mathematical manipulation
数学表征 mathematical characterization
数学处理 mathematical manipulation/treatment
数学定义 mathematical definition
数学方法 mathematical method/approach
数学分解 mathematical decomposition
数学分析 mathematical analysis
数学关系 mathematical relation
数学规划 mathematical programming
数学归纳法 mathematical induction

数学模型 mathematic(al) model
数学算符 mathematical operator
数学同构 mathematical isomorphism
数学系统 mathematical system
数学语义模型 mathematical semantic model
数学证明学习系统 mathematics proving learning system {MPLS}
数域 number field
数值 numeric(al) value, value, amount, magnitude
数值变量 numeric(al) variable
数值表达式 mathematical expression, numeric(al) expression
数值表示法 numeric representation
数值参数 mathematical parameter
数值程序 mathematical program/routine
数值程序包 mathpak
数值处理 numeric process
数值代数 numerical algebra
数值读出 numerical readout
数值范围 number range
数值放样 mathematical lofting
数值分析 numeric(al) analysis
数值估计 numerical estimate
数值函数 mathematical/numeric function
数值函数库 mathematical function library
数值积分 numerical integration
数值计算 numerical computation/calculation
数值检查[校验] numerical check
数值键 value key
数值孔径 numerical aperture {NA}
数值控制 numeric(al) control {NC}
数值栏 numeric field
数值数据处理 numerical data processing
数值搜索 numerical search
数值文字 numeric literal
数值项 numeric item
数值协处理器 numeric(al)/math coprocessor
数值芯片 math(ematical) chip
数值移位 numeric shift
数值运算符 numeric operator
数值字 numeric(al) word
数值字段 numeric field
数制 numeric(al) system, numeration system, number representation system
数制系统 number system
数字 digit, number, numeral, figure
数字编辑程序 numeric editor
数字编码 digital coding, numerical coding, figure code
数字编码器 digital encoder
数字变量 digital variable
数字表 numeration table
数字表示法 digital/number/numeric representation
数字部分 numeric portion
数字常数 numeric constant
数字乘法器 digital multiplier
数字处理 crunch
数字穿孔 digit punch
数字传输 digital transmission
数字传送总线 digit/number transfer bus, digit transfer trunk
数字串 numeric string
数字窗口 numeric window
数字磁记录 digital magnetic recording
数字打印 print numerically {PRN}
数字打印机 digital printer

数字代码 digital/numeric code
数字的 digital, numeric(al)
数字地球 digital earth
数字地图 digital map
数字地形模型 digital terrain models {DTM}
数字电话 digital telephone
数字电话网 digital telephone network
数字电路 digital circuit
数字电路复用设备 digital circuit multiplication equipment {DCME}
数字电视 digital television
数字电压表 digital voltmeter {DVM}
数字读出 digital readout
数字多(功)能光盘 digital versatile disc {DVD}
数字多路复用 digital multiplexing
数字发生器 number generator
数字发送器 digit emitter
数字仿真[模拟] digital simulation
数字犯罪 digital crime
数字分隔符 thousands separator
数字分类 digital sort(ing)
数字蜂窝无线系统 digital cellular radio
数字符号 numerical symbol, numeric character
数字服务单元 digital service unit {DSU}
数字格式 digital format
数字故障模拟 digital fault simulation
数字光记录 digital optical recording {DOR}
数字光盘 digital optical disk, optical data disk
数字广播声音 digital broadcast audio {DBA}
数字化 digitization, digitize, digitizing, numeralization
数字化板 digitizer tablet
数字化唱片 digital audio disk {DAD}
数字化话音 digitized speech
数字化开关 digitizing switch
数字化声音交换设备 digital voice exchange {DVX}
数字化视频 digitized video
数字化图像 digitized image
数字化仪 digitizer
数字化音频 digitized audio
数字化终端系统 digital termination system {DTS}
数字换档 numeric shift
数字绘图仪 digital plotter
数字基群 digroup
数字集成电路 digital integrated circuit
数字集中器 digital concentrator
数字计数器 digit(al) counter
数字计算 digital computing/ calculation
数字计算机 digital computer
数字记录 cruncher
数字记录 digital recording
数字加法器 digital adder
数字间隔[空格]符 numeric space character {NSP}
数字检测 digital detection
数字检查 digit check
数字键区 numeric keypad
数字交叉连接系统 digital cross connect {DXC} system
数字交换[转接] digital switching
数字交换机 digital switch
数字接口[界面] digital interface
数字解码器[译码器] digital decoder
数字开关 numerical switch
数字控制 numeric(al) control {NC}, digital control

数字量　digital quantity
数字列　digit column
数字路径　digital path
数字录音带　digital audio tape {DAT}
数字逻辑　digit(al) logic
数字滤波器　digital filter
数字码　digital/ numerical/ number code
数字密码　digit-cypher
数字模式　figure pattern
数字匹配　digital matching
数字签名[签字]　digital signature
数字嵌套　digital nest
数字区分符　digit specifier
数字声音磁带　digital audio tape {DAT}
数字时钟　digital clock
数字识别系统　digit-recognition system
数字式光计算机　digital optical computer {DOC}
数字式交互装置　digital interactive facility
数字式扫描　digital scanning
数字事件　digital event
数字视盘　digital video disc {DVD}
数字视频接口　digital video interactive {DVI}
数字视频效果　digital video effect {DVE}
数字输入　digital input
数字数据　digital data, numeric(al)/ numeral data
数字数据代码　number data code
数字数据记录　digital data record
数字数据交换　digital data switching
数字数据库　numeral database
数字数据流　digital data flow
数字数据网　digital data network {DDN}
数字数据业务　digital data service
数字数据源　digital data source
数字锁定键　Num Lock key
数字通路　digital path
数字通信　digital communications
数字图表　digiography
数字图片　digital picture
数字图书馆　digital library
数字图像[影像]　digital image
数字图像合成　digital image synthesis
数字网(络)　digital network
数字网结构[体系]　digital network architecture {DNA}
数字位　digit bit
数字文字　numeric literal
数字系统　digital/ number system
数字显示　digital display
数字显像　digital scene
数字线路　digital line
数字项　numeric item
数字校验　digit check, digital proof
数字信道库　digital channel bank
数字信号　digit(al)/figure signal
数字信号处理　digital signal processing {DSP}
数字信号方式　digital signalling
数字信息　digital/ numerical information
数字信息处理器　digital signal processor {DSP}
数字型数据　digital data
数字行　numeral row
数字序列　number sequence
数字压缩　digit(al) compression
数字移动　numeric move
数字音乐光盘标准格式

compact disc digital audio {**CD-DA**}
数字音频 digital audio
数字音频磁带 digital audio tape {**DAT**}
数字影像分析 digital image analysis
数字用户线(路) digital subscriber line {**DSL**}
数字域 numeric field
数字运算 digit(al) arithmetic/operation
数字照相机 digital camera
数字指令 digital command
数字[显示]钟 digital clock
数字专用小交换机 digital private branch exchange
数字转换 digital conversion, digitization, quantize
数字字符发生器 digital character generator
数字字符集 numeric character set
数字字体 digital font
数字作图 digiplot
数组 array
数组变量 array variable
数组标识符 array identifier
数组表 array list
数组成分[分量] array component
数组处理 array processing/manipulation
数组处理器 array processor
数组定义 array defining
数组分配 array allocation
数组赋值 array assignment
数组复写子程序 array copy subroutine
数组函数 array function
数组赋址 array architecture
数组界 array bound
数组类型 array type
数组流水线 array pipeline
数组名(字) array name
数组排序 array sort
数组说明 array declaration
数组维数 array dimension, dimensionality of array
数组下标 array subscript
数组项 array item
数组引用 array reference
数组元素 array element, element in array
数组运算 array operation

【shuā】

刷 1)〈名〉brush 2)〈动〉brush, scrub, daub
刷新 flush, refresh
刷新电路 refresh circuit
刷新间隔 refresh interval
刷新请求 refresh request
刷新周期 refresh period/cycle

【shuāi】

衰 衰败 decline, wane 衰落 decline, ebb, fade 衰弱 weak, feeble 衰退 decline and fall, die out
衰减 decay, degeneracy, degeneration, damping, loss
衰减比 decay ratio
衰减常数 decay constant
衰减模型 decay model
衰减因子 decay factor, degeneration factor
衰老故障[失效] wear-out failure
衰落边际 fade margin

摔 1)(下落)plunge 2)(打破)cause to fall and break 3)(扔)cast, throw, fling 摔交 fall, tumble

【shuǎi】

甩 1)(扔)throw, fling, toss

2)(抛开)leave sb behind, throw off

【shuǎi】
率 另见 lǜ
1)(轻率)rash, hasty 2)(直爽)frank, straightforward
率领 lead, command, direct
率先 take the lead in doing sth, be the first to do sth

【shuān】
闩 bolt, lacth
闩锁 locking
闩锁触发器 flip-latch, latch flip-flop
闩锁装置 latch unit, locking device

【shuāng】
双 1)(两个)two, twin, both, dual 2)(量词)pair 3)(偶数的)even 4)(加倍)double, twofold **双边** bilateral, mutual **双层** double layer; double-deck, double-ply, double-skin **双重** double, dual, twofold **双方** both sides, the two parties **双料** of reinforced material, extra quality **双面** two-sided, double-edged, double-faced **双数** even numbers **双月刊** bimonthly **双周刊** biweekly, fortnightly
双倍长表示法 double-length notation
双倍长寄存器 double(-length) register
双倍长数 double-length numeral/number
双倍长字 double-length word
双倍乘积 double product
双倍积 double product
双倍字 double-word
双笔记录 two-pen record
双臂式绘图机 dual arm plotter
双边[双方]控制 bilateral control
双变量 bivariate
双层磁带 two-layer magnetic tape
双重端口 twin port
双重否定 double negation
双重进位 double carry
双重控制 duplex control
双重链接 double linkage
双重material double acknowledge
双重系统 duplex(ed) system
双重校验 twin check
双处理机[器] dual processors
双处理机系统 dual processor system
双道转接器 biplexer
双地址 double-address
双调排序 bitonic sort(ing)
双端口存储器 dual port memory
双端口总线 dual port bus
双端设备 two-end device
双耳的 binaural
双耳效应 binaural effect
双二重的 duo-duplex
双分量 bicomponent
双份 dupleting
双份编码 dual coding
双缝磁头 dual-gap head
双缝重写头 dual-gap rewrite head
双工[双向]操作 duplex operation
双工传输 duplex transmission
双工器 duplexer
双工通信 duplex communication
双工线路 duplex circuit
双工运行 duplex running
双工制[系统] duplex system,

duplexed system
双股的 bifilar
双股电缆 twinaxial cable
双机系统 dual (processor) system, duplex machine system
双极晶体管电路 bipolar transistor circuit
双极逻辑 bipolar logic
双极器件 bipolar device
双极型存储器 bipolar memory
双极型晶体管 bipolar transistor
双极型微处理机 bipolar microprocessor
双极性 bipolarity
双极性芯片 bipolar chip
双极性信号 polar signal
双计算机 duplex computer
双记录 double recording, dual log
双间距打印机 dual-pitch printer
双绞软线 twisted cord
双绞线 twisted-pair (wiring) {TP}
双绞线电缆 twisted-pair cable
双绞线以太网 twisted-pair Ethernet
双(倍)精度 double-precision
双精度变量 double-precision variable
双精度常数 double-precision constant
双精度计算 double-precision computation
双精度数 double-precision number/quantity
双精度运算 double-precision arithmetic/operation
双卡片 double-card, dual card
双口网络 two-port network
双连接站 dual attached station {DAS}
双链表 double linked list
双链环 doubly linked ring

双链树 double chained tree
双列处理 dual column
双列直插式封装 dual in-line package {DIP}
双路传输 two-way transmission
双路交替传输 two-way alternate {TWA}
双码 dicode
双码信号 dicode signal
双码制 dicode system
双密度 double dense, double/dual density
双密度磁盘 double density disk
双密度记录 double-dense/density recording
双密度设备 dual-density device
双面磁盘 double-sided disk
双面复印 double-sided/ duplex copying
双面媒体 double-sided media
双面软盘 dual floppy, two-sided diskette
双面双密度 double-sided double-density {DSD}
双模拟 bisimulation
双模冗余 duplication redundancy
双模态的 bimodal
双目成像 binocular imaging
双目立体视觉 binocular stereo vision
双目视觉系统 stereo vision
双纽线电缆 paired/ twining cable, twisted-pair cable
双排直插封装 dual inline package {DIP}
双频道 double channel
双频制记录 double-frequency recording {DF}
双谱处理 dual spectrum process
双亲 parent
双亲关系 parentage
双亲链 parent's chain

双入口 twin port
双三进制 biternary
双色 two-tone color
双色图 bicolorable graph
双输入 double entry
双速打印机 dual-mode printer
双态 bifurcation, binary state
双态存储元件 bimorph memory cell
双态的 bimorph, binary
双态信号 binary signal
双态元件 binary element, toggle
双体型病毒 binary viruses
双条件 bicondition, biconditional
双通道 double channel
双通道系统 dual channel system
双同步的 binary synchronous (=bisynchronous, bisync)
双同步方式 bisync mode
双同步通信 binary synchronous communication {BISYNC, BSC}
双同步协议 bisync protocol
双图 bipartite graph, bigraph
双位错误 double bit error
双稳触发器 bistable flip-flop
双稳器件 bistable device
双稳态电路 bistable circuit, trigger pair
双稳元件 bistable component/ element
双系统 dual system
双线的 bifilar
双线电路 two-wire circuit
双线逻辑 double-rail logic
双线信道 two-wire channel
双线性型 bilinear form
双相 biphase
双相编码 biphase code
双相电平 biphase level
双向操作 bidirectional/ both-way operation
双向传播 two-way propagation
双向传输 bidirectional/ bipolar/ duplex/ two-way transmission
双向打印 bidirectional/ two-way printing
双向打印机 bidirectional printer
双向的 bidirectional, bipartite, duplex
双向端口 bidirectional port
双向队列 double-end queue, deque
双向环 two-way ring
双向缓冲器 bidirectional buffer
双向寄存器 bidirectional register
双向晶体管 bidirectional transistor
双向连接 two-way linkage
双向连接表 doubly-linked list
双向连通图 disconnected graph
双向链表 doubly-linked list
双向流 bidirectional flow
双向逆函数 two-sided inverse
双向输入读头 two-way input head
双向数据总线 bidirectional data bus
双向搜索[查找] bidirectional search
双向通道 duplex channel, two-way/two-wire channel
双向同步传输 bisynchronous transmission
双向推理 bidirection reasoning, bidirectional inference
双向网络 bilateral network
双向线路 two-way circuit
双向信道 duplex/ two-way channel
双向总线 bidirectional bus
双压电晶片 bimorph
双页检测器 double sheet

shuāng 霜 shuǎng 爽 shuí 谁 shuǐ 水 shuì 税 睡 shùn 顺

detector
双页输送器 double sheet ejector
双叶 double leaf
双音调制 two-tone keying
双音多频 dual tone multi-frequency {DTMF}
双用卡片 dual purpose card
双优先 double priority
双钥密码系统 two-key crypto-system
双值的 bilevel, dyadic
双值化 binarization
双值逻辑 two-valued logic
双值图像 bilevel image
双值运算 dyadic operation
双轴电缆 twinaxial
双字 double-word
双(倍)字长 double-length
双字长数 double-length number
双字节 double byte
双字界 double-word boundary
双字母 bigram
双字数据 double-word data
双字整数 double-word integer
双坐标绘图仪 X-Y plotter

霜 frost

【shuǎng】
爽 1)(天气)bright, clear, crisp 2)(直率)frank, straight forward

【shuí】
谁 1)(什么人)who 2)(任何人)someone, anyone

【shuǐ】
水 water 水果 fruit 水库 reservoir 水利 ①(资源利用) water utilization, irrigation ②(工程) irrigation works, water conservancy project 水龙头 (water) tap, faucet 水路 waterway, water route 水泥 cement 水平 level 水域 waters, water area, body of water 水源 the source of a river, source of water 水运 water transport
水平并行处理 horizontal parallelism
水平回扫 horizontal flyback/retrace
水平间距调整 horizontal spacing
水平控制 horizontal control
水平微指令 horizontal microinstruction
水平线 horizon, level line
水印磁性处理 watermark magnetics

【shuì】
税 tax, duty ◇纳税 pay taxes 税法 law of tax, tax law 税率 tax rate, rate of taxation, tariff rate 税收 tax revenue 税则 tax regulations 税制 tax system, taxation
睡 sleep
睡眠程序 sleep program
睡眠方式 sleep mode
睡眠过程 sleeping process
睡眠状态 hibernation

【shùn】
顺 (沿着)along 顺便 in passing, by the way, incidentally 顺差 favorable balance, surplus 顺次 in order, in succession, in proper sequence 顺从 obey, yield to, submit to 顺利

smoothly, successfully 顺向 in the same direction as, with
顺序 ① (次序) sequence, order ② (依次) in proper order, in turn
顺排文档 linear file
顺排文件 normal file
顺向的 directed
顺序表示法 sequential notation
顺序表征 sequential attribute
顺序操作 consecutive/sequential operation
顺序测试 sequential test
顺序查找 sequential search
顺序处理 sequential process(ing)
顺序存储器 continuous memory
顺序存取 sequential access
顺序包交换(协议) sequential packet exchange {SPX}
顺序等价 sequence equivalence
顺序读取 serial read
顺序法 sequential method
顺序访问 sequential access
顺序分配 sequential allocation
顺序符号 sequence symbol
顺序关系 ordinal relation
顺序号 sequence number
顺序集 sequence set
顺序检测 sequential detection
顺序检索 sequential retrieval, sequential search
顺序结构 sequential structure
顺序进程 sequential process
顺序控制 sequence/sequencing/sequential control
顺序控制器 sequence controller
顺序链设备优先级 daisy chain device priority
顺序码 sequence code
顺序扫描 progressive/sequential scanning
顺序文件 sequential file
顺序校验 sequence check
顺序寻址 sequential addressing
顺序映射 sequence map
顺序域 sequence field
顺序子句 serial clause

瞬
瞬息 twinkling 瞬息之间 in the twinkling of an eye
瞬变现象 transient
瞬时错误 transient error
瞬时故障 transient fault
瞬时接收图像 instant vision
瞬时值 instantaneous value
瞬态 simultaneous, transient state, transition condition
瞬态的 transient
瞬态分析 transient analysis
瞬态偏差 transient deviation
瞬态特性 transient behaviour
瞬态条件 transient condition
瞬态响应 transient response
瞬态转储 snapshot dump
瞬息有取法 evanescent access method
瞬像 snapshot

【shuō】
说 1)(说话)speak, talk, say 2)(解释)explain 3)(学说)theory, teachings, doctrine 4)(批评)scold, reproach
说法 ① (措词) way of expressing sth, wording ② (意见) opinion, view, version
说服 persuade, convince
说谎 tell a lie, lie
说理 argue, reason, debate
说明 ①〈动〉explain, illustrate, show ②〈名〉explanation, directions, caption
说明书 ①(文字说明)direction ②(技术说明)instruction, specification, (technical) manual
说明表 specification sheet

说明部分 declarative part, specification part
说明词 declarer
说明段 declaration section
说明符 declarator, declare, descriptor, specificator, specifier
说明符脚注 declarator subscript
说明符名 declarator name
说明功能 explanation function
说明记号 declaration token
说明属性 declared attribute
说明位 declared bit

【shuò】

硕 硕果 rich fruits, great achievements 硕士 Master ◇理学硕士 Master of Science (M.S.) ∥ 文学硕士 Master of Arts (M.A.) ∥ 硕士学位 Master's degree

【sī】

司 1)(负责)take charge of, attend to, manage 2)(部门)department, bureau, board 司法 administration of justice, judicature, jurisdiction 司机 driver

丝 silk, filament 丝毫 the slightest amount or degree, a bit

私 1)(个人的)personal, private 2)(非法的)illicit, illegal 私产 private property 私事 privacy, private affairs, personal affairs 私下 secret, private 私心 selfish 私营 privately owned, privately operated 私有 privately owned, private 私有财产 private property 私自 privately, secretly, without permission
私人密匙 private key
私人数据 private data
私人信件 private mail
私有键[密钥] private key
私有类型 private type

思 思潮 trend of thought, ideological trend 思考 think, consider 思路 train of thought, thread of thought 思念 think of, long for, miss 思索 think deeply, ponder 思维 thought, thinking 思想 thought, thinking, idea, ideology
思维法 mentality
思维机器 thinking machine
思维科学 noetic/ thinking science
思维模型 mental model
思维行为 thinking behavior
思想库 think bank/ factory/ tank

撕 tear, rip 撕毁 tear up, break, violate

【sǐ】

死 1)(死亡)die, death, pass away 2)(拼死)to the death 3)(达到极点)extremely, to death 4)(不可调和的)deadly 5)(不能通过)impassable, closed 死板 fixed, rigid, inflexible 死角 dead angle, blind angle, dead space 死路 ①(不通的路)blind alley, dead end ②(毁灭的途径)the road to ruin 死者 the dead, the deceased, the departed
死道 dead track

死点 dead point, dead spot
死端 dead end
死机 lock up, down
死区 dead band, dead zone
死区单元 dead zone unit
死锁 deadlock, deadly embrace
死锁防止 deadlock prevention
死锁恢复 deadlock recovery
死锁检测 deadlock detection
死锁诊断 deadlock diagnosis
死停 dead halt
死线 dead wire
死循环 closed loop, endless loop

【sì】

四 four 四处 in all directions, everywhere 四方 ① (各处) the four directions (north, south, east, west), all sides, all quarters ② (正方形) square ③ (立方体的) cubic 四季 the four seasons 四面 (on) four sides, (on) all sides 四月 April 四周 all around
四边形 quadrangle, quadrilateral
四叉树 quad tree
四地址 four-address, quadruple address
四端电路 quadripole
四方的 quartic
四工的 quadruple
四工系统 quadruplex system
四色猜想 four-color conjecture
四色处理 four-color process
四色定理 four-color theorem
四舍五入 half-adjust
四声道的 quadriphonic
四位 four-digit, quadbit
四位字节 nib (= nibble), nybble, quartet

四位组 quadbit, tetrad
四线电路 four-wire circuit
四线信道 four-wire channel
四芯(导)线 quad
四元 quad
四元的 quadruple
四元树 quad tree
四元数 quaternion
四元组 quadruple
四值逻辑 quaternary logic

似 (像) similar, like 似乎 it seems, as if, seemingly
似规则原理 rule-like principle

伺 watch, await
伺服 servo (= servomechanism)
伺服臂机器人 servo arm robot
伺服标记 servo mark
伺服部件 servocomponent
伺服道录写器 servo track writer **STW**
伺服电动机 servomotor
伺服交换 servo swap
伺服控制 servo control
伺服理论 servo theory
伺服逻辑 servo logic
伺服扇区 servo sector
伺服头 servohead
伺服系统 follow-up system, servosystem

饲 饲料 forage, fodder, feed
饲养 raise, rear

肆 肆意 wantonly, recklessly, willfully

【sōng】

松 1) (松树) pine tree 2) (松散) loose, slack 3) (使松) loosen, relax, slacken 松弛 ① (不坚实) limp, flabby, slack ② (不紧) lax 松紧 ①

sōng 耸 sòng 宋送 sōu 搜 sū 苏 sú 俗 sù 夙诉素

(松或紧的程度) degree of tightness ②(伸缩) elasticity
松软 soft, spongy, loose
松散 ①(结构不紧密) loose ②(精神不集中) inattentive ③(使轻松舒畅) relax, take one's ease 松手 loosen one's grip, let go
松弛变量 slack variable
松弛表 loose list
松弛参数 relaxation parameter
松弛路径 slack path
松散耦合网络 loosely-coupled network {LCN}
松散同步 loose synchronization

【sǒng】
耸 (使人吃惊) alarm, shock
耸立 towering, lofty

【sòng】
宋 (响度单位) sone

送 1)(拿东西给人) deliver, carry 2)(陪送) see sb off, accompany, escort 送还 give back, return 送货 deliver goods 送交 deliver, hand over 送礼 give (as a present)
送带机构 tape feed
送卡箱 card hopper, card input magazine, hopper
送入 load
送指令 load instruction
送纸 paper feed
送纸器 sheet feeder

【sōu】
搜 search 搜集 collect, gather 搜索 ①〈动〉search for, hunt for, scout around ②〈名〉search, hunting, recon(naissance) 搜寻 search for, look for, seek
搜索策略 search strategy
搜索串 search string
搜索窗 search window
搜索对策 search game
搜索法 search method
搜索范围 hunting zone
搜索规则 search rule
搜索空间 search space
搜索模型 search model
搜索树 search tree
搜索算法 search algorithm
搜索条件 search condition
搜索图 search graph
搜索系统 searching system
搜索引擎 search engine

【sū】
苏
苏格拉底论证 Socrates argument

【sú】
俗 1)(风俗) custom, convention 2)(通俗) popular, common 3)(庸俗) vulgar
俗语 common saying, proverb

【sù】
夙 夙愿 long-cherished wish
诉 诉说 tell, relate, recount
诉讼 lawsuit, litigation

素 1)(本来的) native 2)(白色,本色) white 3)(颜色单纯) plain, simple, quiet 4)(基本物质)(basic) element
素菜 vegetable 素材 (source) material, raw data 素来 usually, habitually, always
素质 nature, quality, per-

formance, level of competence
素数 prime, prime number
素数键 prime key
素数下标 prime index
素图 prime graph
素项 prime implicant
素信息 prime information
素域 prime field
素蕴涵 prime implicant

速 (迅速)fast, rapid, quick, speedy 速度 ①〈物理〉speed, velocity ②(快慢的程度)speed, rate, pace,〈意大利语〉tempo 速记 shorthand, stenography 速决 quick decision 速率 speed, rate
速查表 zoom table
速成原型 rapid prototype
速度传感器 tachosensor, velocity sensor
速度控制器 speed control
速度矢量 velocity vector {VV}
速度图 tachogram
速率测试 rate test
速率反馈 rate feedback
速率矩阵 rate matrix
速率控制 rate control
速率图 rate diagram

宿 put up for the night, stay overnight, lodge 宿舍 hostel, living quarters, dormitory 宿愿 long-cherished wish
宿主表 host table
宿主地址 host address
宿主机 host
宿主结构 host structure
宿主名 hostname
宿主系统 host-based system

塑 model, mold 塑料 plastics 塑像 ①〈动〉mold a statue ②〈名〉statue 塑造 ①(造型)model, mold ②(描写)portray
塑料封装 plastic package
塑料光 plastic optical fiber {POF}

溯 1)(逆水行进)go against the stream 2)(追溯)trace back, recall 溯源 trace to the source

【suān】

酸 1)(心酸)sick at heart, grieved, distressed 2)〈化学〉acid, acidum 酸痛 tingle, ache 酸味 sour, tart 酸雨 acid rain

【suàn】

算 1)(计算)calculate, count, compute, figure 2)(谋划)plan, calculate 3)(推测)think, suppose 4)(当作)consider, regard as, count as 算入 include 算盘 abacus 算术 arithmetic 算数 count, hold, stand 算帐 ①(计算帐目)do accounts, balance the books ②(算清)square accounts with sb, get even with sb
算出 figure out
算错 miscalculation, miscount
算法 algorithm, algorithmic
算法逼近 algorithmic approach
算法比较 algorithm comparison
算法表示法 algorithmic notation
算法程序 algorithm routine, algorithmic procedure

算法调度 algorithmic dispatching/scheduling
算法翻译 algorithmic translation
算法分析 algorithm analysis
算法复杂性 algorithm(ic) complexity
算法级 algorithm level
算法库 algorithm library
算法理论 algorithm theory
算法例程 algorithm routine, algorithmic routine
算法逻辑 algorithmic logic
算法问题求解 algorithmic problem solving
算法形式 algorithm pattern
算法图 algorithm chart
算法语言 algorithm(ic) language {ALGOL}
算法语言学 algorithmic linguistics
算法证明 algorithm proof
算符 functor, operator
算符表 operator table
算符分类 operator class
算符优先文法 operator precedence grammer
算术表达式 arithmetic expression
算术函数 arithmetic function
算术和 arithmetic sum
算术加法 arithmetic addition
算术逻辑部件[单元] arithmetic logic unit {ALU}
算术平均 arithmetic average/mean
算术权 arithmetic weight
算术数 arithmetic number
算术误差 arithmetic error
算术项 arithmetic term
算术移位 arithmetic shift
算术右移 arithmetic shift right
算术运算 arithmetic operation
算术运算符 arithmetic operator
算术左移 arithmetic shift left, shift left arithmetic
算态 computing mode, problem mode, problem state
算子 operator
算子符号 operator notation
算子(定义)域 operator domain

【suī】

虽 虽然 though, although, even if

【suí】

随 1)(跟)follow 2)(顺从)comply with, adapt to 3)(任凭)let (sb do as he likes) 4)(顺便)along with 随便 ①(不加限制) casual, random, informal ②(不拘礼) do as one pleases ③(不加考虑) careless ④(任性)wanton, willful, arbitrary ⑤(无论) anyhow, any 随带 ①(随同带去) going along with ② (随身携带) have sth taken along with one 随地 anywhere, everywhere 随后 soon afterwards 随即 immediately, presently 随时 at any time, at all times 随手 conveniently, without extra trouble 随同 follow, accompany 随意 at will, as one pleases 随着 along with, in pace with
随动系统 follow-up system, servo (＝servomechanism), servosystem
随附信息组 trailer block
随机变量 random/stochastic variable
随机采样 random sample
随机测试 random testing

随机产生式 stochastic production
随机常数 arbitrary constant
随机抽样 random sample, stochastic sampling
随机存取 arbitrary access, random access
随机存取[访问]存储器 random access memory {RAM}
随机调度 random schedule
随机多址访问 random multiple access {RMA}
随机访问 arbitrary access, random access
随机故障 random failure
随机过程 random process, stochastic process
随机活动 stochastic activity
随机控制 arbitrary control
随机逻辑 random logic
随机码 random code
随机模型 stochastic model
随机扫描 random scan/sweep
随机失真 random distortion
随机事件 random event
随机数 random number
随机数发生器 random number generator, randomizer
随机算子 stochastic operator
随机图灵机 stochastic Turing machine {STM}
随机推理 stochastic reasoning
随机文法 stochastic grammar
随机文件 random access file, random file
随机误差 accidental error, random error
随机系统 stochastic system
随机向量 random vector
随机序列 random sequence
随机学习 stochastic learning
随机因素 stochastic factor
随机有限状态自动机 stochastic finite state automaton

【suì】

碎 1)〈动〉break to pieces, smash 2)〈形〉broken, fragmentary

碎片 fragment

遂 遂意 to one's liking

隧 隧道 tunnel
隧道二极管 tunnel diode
隧道效应 Esaki effect

【sūn】

孙 孙女 granddaughter 孙子 grandson

【sǔn】

损 （减少）decrease, lose 损害 harm, damage 损耗 ①（损失消耗）loss, wear and tear ②〈经贸〉wastage, spoilage 损伤 ①〈动〉damnify, harm, damage, injure ②〈名〉loss, damnification 损失 ①〈动〉lose ②〈名〉loss

损耗矩阵 loss matrix
损坏 casualty, damage
损坏形状 deform
损失函数 loss function
损失矩阵 loss matrix

【suō】

缩 1)（收缩）contract, shrink 2)（退缩）draw back, withdraw, recoil 缩短 shorten, curtail, cut down, contract 缩减 reduce, cut, condense, shrink, contract 缩小 reduce, lessen, contract, narrow, shrink 缩写 ①（语法）abbreviation ②（缩短篇幅）abridge

缩比[图像,形象]模型 iconic model
缩词 acronym
缩放控制 zoom control
缩放系数 zoom factor
缩合词 acronym
缩回 retraction
缩减指令集计算机 reduced instruction set computer {RISC}
缩略名 mnemonic name
缩排 hanging indent
缩微包 microfolio
缩微出版 micropublishing
缩微传真 microfacsimile
缩微底片 master microform
缩微复制品 microcopy
缩微复制print microprint
缩微黑卡 microopaque
缩微绘图 micrographics
缩微记录 microrecording
缩微胶卷 microfilm
缩微胶卷机 microfilmer
缩微(照相)胶片 microfiche
缩微胶片格式 microfiche format
缩微胶片输出 microfilm output
缩微胶片书 microfiche book
缩微胶片帧 microfiche frame, microfilm frame
缩微介质 microform
缩微卡(片) microcard
缩微胶片阅读台 stage
缩微品 microform
缩微平片 microfiche
缩微摄影术 microphotography
缩微图形学 micrographics
缩微图像(数据) microimage
缩微文件 microfile
缩微影像 microform
缩微原文 microtext
缩微照片 microcopy
缩微照相机 microfilm camera
缩微照相术 micrographics

缩位拨号 abbreviated dialing, short code dialing
缩位拨号 abbreviated dialing
缩位呼叫 abbreviated calling
缩小的 necked
缩小的系统 minisystem
缩小化 downsizing
缩小率 reduction
缩写标记 abbreviated notation
缩写句 acronym
缩写规则 contraction rule
缩写名 mnemonic name

【 suǒ 】

所 1)(处所)place 2)(机构)bureau, agency ◇ 研究所 (research) institute 所得 income, earnings, gains 所谓 ①(所说的)what is called ②(某些人所说的)so-called 所以 so, therefore, as a result 所有 ① own, possess ② possessions ③ all 所有权 proprietary rights, ownership, title 所有制 ownership, system of ownership 所在 ①(处所)place, location ②(存在的地方)where
所见即所得(法) what you see is what you get {WYSIWYG}
所有者类型 owner type
所有中继线忙 all trunks busy {ATB}

索 1)(粗绳)large rope 2)(搜寻)search 索赔 claim (indemnity) 索取 ask for, demand, claim 索引 index, concordance, directory ◇ 标题索引 subject index // 书名索引 title index
索引标记 index mark
索引标识符 index identifier {IID}

索引表 concordance/ index(ed) list, index table
索引表示法 index notation
索引表部分 index component
索引层 index level
索引词 index term
索引存取方法 indexed access method {IAM}
索引存取控制块 indexed access control block {IACB, ICB}
索引带头 index tape head
索引点 index point
索引法 indexing method
索引集 index set
索引记录 index record
索引检索 indexed search
索引结构 index(ed) structure
索引卡 index card
索引孔 index hole
索引口 index slit
索引块 index block
索引脉冲 index pulse
索引名 index name
索引生成 index generation
索引升级 index upgrade
索引输出 index output
索引输入 index input
索引输入/输出 indexed I/O
索引数据库 index database
索引数据名 index data-name
索引数据项 index data item
索引顺序存取法 indexed sequential access method {ISAM}
索引顺序文件 index(ed) sequential file
索引条 index slip
索引文件 index(ed) file
索引文件位图 index file bit map
索引文件组织 indexed file organization
索引系统 index system
索引项 index entry
索引信号 index

索引栈 index stack
索引帧 index frame
索引值 index value
索引纸条 index slip
索引重复 index replication
索引字 index term
索引字符 index character {INX}

琐 琐事 trifles, trivial matters
琐碎 trivial, petty

锁 1)（锁具）lock ◇挂锁 padlock // 弹簧锁 spring lock 2)（上锁）lock up
锁步 lock-step
锁查找 lock search
锁存 latching, latch-up
锁存[闩锁]电路 latch
锁存电路 latch circuit
锁存故障 latch fault
锁存寄存器 latch register
锁存[闩锁]逻辑 latch logic
锁存器 flip-latch, latch, latch unit
锁存状态 latch mode
锁定 latch-up, locking, lock-on, lock-out, synchronize
锁定表 lock table
锁定方式 lock mode
锁定级 lock hierarchy
锁定设备 locking device
锁定转义 locking escape
锁定状态 lock state
锁定字节 lock byte
锁分层[层次]结构 locked hierarchy
锁管理 lock management
锁键 lock key
锁推演 lock deduction
锁相振荡器 phase-locked oscillator
锁-钥匙式保护 lock-and-key protection

tā 它他她铊踏 tǎ 塔 tà 踏 tái 台抬 tài 太态

T t

【tā】

它 it 它们 they

他 1)(第三人称阳性)he 2)(另外的,其他的)other, another, some other 他方 ①(另一方)the other party ②(别的地方)other places 他们 they 他人 another person, other people, others

她 she 她们 they

铊 thallium (Tl)

踏 另见【tà】
踏实 ①(不浮躁)dependable, steady ②(安心)free from anxiety

【tǎ】

塔 1)(佛教的塔)pagoda 2)(塔形物)tower

【tà】

踏 另见【tā】
step on, tread, stamp

【tái】

台 1)(桌子)table, desk 2)(平台)platform, stage, terrace 3)(座子)stand, support, bed 台灯 desk lamp, table lamp, reading lamp 台历 desk calendar
台板 plate
台阶 step
台式出版系统 desk publishing system {DPS}
台式复印机 desk-top copier
台式机管理任务组 desktop management task force {DMTF}
台式计算机 desk computer, desk-size machine, desk-top computer
台式计算器 desk calculator, desk-top calculator

抬 1)(举起)lift up, raise 2)(用手或肩搬运)carry

【tài】

太 1)(过分)too, over 2)(极)highest, greatest, remotest 3)〈副〉too, extremely 太空 outer space 太平 peace and tranquility 太平洋 the Pacific (Ocean) 太阳 the sun, solar 太阳能 solar energy
太(拉)(单位前缀)femto- (=10⁻¹²){T}
太拉赫 terahertz
太阳能电池 solar cell
太字节 terabyte {TB}

态 1)(状态)form, shape, condition 2)(语态)voice 3)

〈物理〉state ◇固态 solid state ‖ 气态 gaseous state ‖ 液态 liquid state 态度 ①（神态）manner, bearing ②（看法）attitude, approach

钛 titanium (Ti)

泰 （平安）safe, peaceful 泰国 Tailand

【tān】

坍 坍塌 collapse, fall down

贪
贪心树 greedy tree
贪心算法 greedy algorithm

摊 1)（铺平）spread out, unfold 2)（分担）take a share in 摊派 apportion, allot, allocate 摊子 vendor's stand, booth, stall

【tán】

谈 talk, chat, discuss 谈到 speak of, talk about, refer to 谈话 ①（聚谈）conversation, talk, chat ②（发表见解）statement, talk 谈论 discuss, talk about 谈判 negotiations, talks 谈起 mention, speak of

弹 另见【dàn】
（有弹性）elastic 弹回 leap, spring 弹射 shoot, send forth, eject 弹跳 bounce, spring 弹奏 play, pluck
弹出 pop, pop up, pull
弹出操作 pull operation
弹出式窗口 pop-up window
弹出式菜单 pop-up menu
弹出指令 pull instruction
弹球病毒 bouncing ball
弹性 elasticity, resilience
弹性存储 elastic store

【tǎn】

坦 （平坦）level, smooth 坦白 ①（坦率）honest, frank, candid ②（实说）confess, admit, recount 坦然 calm, composed, at ease

钽 tantalum (Ta)

【tàn】

探 （看望）visit, pay a call on 探测 survey, sound, probe, explore 探究 make a thorough inquiry, probe into 探明 ascertain, verify 探求 seek, pursue, search after 探索 try to find out, explore, examine 探讨 inquire into, probe into 探险 explore, make explorations
探测点 exploring spot, probe point
探测能力 detectability
探测器 seeker
探试法 heuristic approach
探试分析 heuristic analysis
探试规则 heuristic rule
探试技术 heuristic technique
探试控制 heuristic control
探试算法 heuristic algorithm
探索的 heuristic
探头 probe
探向器 direction finder {DF}
探询 interview, polling
探询表 polling list
探询电路 polling circuit
探询周期 polling cycle
探寻 seek
探针 needle, probe

tàn 碳 tang 汤,堂膛糖,倘躺 tao 逃淘陶,讨,套 tè 特

碳 carbon (C)

【tāng】

汤 (热水,开水) hot water, boiling water 汤汁 soup, broth

【táng】

堂 1)(大厅) hall 2)(堂兄弟、姐妹) relations between cousins

膛 1)(胸膛) thorax, chest 2)(器物的中空部分) chamber, bore

糖 1)(食糖) sugar 2)(糖果) candy, sweets

【tǎng】

倘 倘若 if, supposing, in case

躺 lie, recline

【táo】

逃 逃避 evade, dodge, shirk, escape 逃跑 run away, escape, flee, take flight 逃税 evade a tax; tax evasion

淘 淘汰 replace, replacement, weed out

陶 (陶器) pottery, earthenware
陶瓷,陶器 ceramics
陶瓷封装 ceramic packaging

【tǎo】

讨 (索取) demand, ask for 讨伐 take punitive action 讨还 get sth back 讨价 ask a price, name a price 讨价还价 bargain, haggle 讨教 ask for advice 讨论 discuss, talk over 讨论会 symposium, workshop, discussion 讨厌 ①(惹人厌烦) disagreeable, disgusting ②(事情难办) hard to handle, troublesome ③(厌恶) dislike, hate 讨债 demand repayment of a loan

【tào】

套 1)(罩上) cover with, slip on 2)(量词) set, suit, suite ◇一套衣服 a suit of clothes 套子 cover, case, jacket
套管 sleeve
套接表示符 socket
套接号 socket
套接字 socket
套接字地址 socket address
套圈 ferrule
套筒打印机 thimble printer
套印 overpaint
套用 nesting

【tè】

特 特别 ①(与众不同) special, particular, out of the ordinary ②(格外) especially, particularly ③(特地) specially 特产 special local product, specialty, speciality 特长 what one is skilled in, (one's) line, speciality, strong point 特出 outstanding, prominent, extraordinary 特此 hereby 特大 especially big, the most 特等 special grade, top grade 特点 characteristic, distinguishing feature, peculiarity, trait 特定 ①（特别指定的）specially appointed, specially designated ②（某一个）given, specified, specific 特级 special grade, superfine 特急 extra urgent 特价 special offer, bargain price 特刊 special issue, special 特快 express 特快列车 express train 特例 special case 特派 specially appointed 特权 privilege, special authority 特色 characteristic, distinguishing feature 特殊 special, specific, particular, peculiar 特效 special good effect 特写 ①（文学）feature article or story, feature ②（电影）close-up 特异 ①（特别优异）exceptionally good, excellent, superfine ②（特殊）peculiar, distinctive 特有 peculiar, characteristic 特约 engage by special arrangement 特约维修店 special repair shop 特征 characteristic, feature, trait 特指 refer in particular to 特制 specially made, made to order 特种 special type, particular kind

特别指令 special instruction
特大芯片 jumbo chip
特定轮询 specific poll(ing)
特定性能 particular characteristic
特级 flash override {FO}, special-grade
特级码 supercode
特解 special solution
特权程序 privileged program
特权方式 privilege(d) mode
特权访问[存取] privileged access
特权过程 privileged procedure
特权级 privilege class, privilege level
特权进程 privileged process
特权命令 privileged command
特权任务 privileged task
特权输入 privileged input
特权用户 privileged user
特权指令 privileged instruction
特权状态 privileged mode/ state
特殊变量 special variable
特殊电路 special hardware
特殊符号 special sign, special symbol
特殊功能部件 special feature
特殊函数 special function
特殊记号 special token
特殊名称表 onomasticon
特殊名字项 special names entry
特殊文件 special file
特殊形 special form
特殊行 special row
特殊硬件 special hardware
特殊用途 special purpose
特殊字符 additional character, special character
特效生成器 special effects generator {SEG}
特性 characteristic, distinction, feature, performance, property
特性表 property list
特性分类 property sort
特性继承 property inheritance
特性曲线 characteristic curve, curve, pattern, response
特许 authorization, authorize, concession, grant authorize, license, privilege
特许材料 licensed material
特许程序 authorized/ licensed program
特许代码 authorization code
特许方式 privilege mode

特许分类 privilege class
特许检查 authorization checking
特许命令 authorized command
特许输入 privileged input
特许数据 authorization data, privileged data
特许文档[资料] licensed documentation
特许文件 authorization file, licensed publication
特许消息 authorization message
特许用户 authorized user
特许证 authorization credentials, license
特许状态 authorized state, privileged state
特异[异性]条件 diversity condition
特异元素 distinguished element
特征编码 feature coding
特征变量 characteristic variable
特征标记 signature
特征表 property table, tag list
特征长度 characteristic length
特征尺寸 feature size
特征抽取[提取] feature extraction
特征处理机 tagged processor
特征[特性]点 significant point
特征动画片 character animation
特征方程 characteristic/secular equation
特征分析 feature/ signature analysis
特征根 characteristic root, latent root
特征函数 characteristic/ proper function, eigenfunction
特征检测 feature detection
特征解 characteristic solution
特征空间 feature space
特征码 condition code
特征数据库 property database
特征搜索 signature search
特征体系结构 tagged architecture
特征位 flag, flag bit, sign
特征位(操作码中的) stencil bit
特征向量 characteristic/ feature/ latent/ proper vector
特征选择 feature selection
特征映射 proper map
特征值 characteristic/ proper value, eigenvalue
特征值分析 signature analysis
特征总线字节 tag bus byte
特征阻抗 characteristic impedance {Z}
特制[定制] custom circuit

铽 terbium (Tb)

【téng】

疼 (疼痛) ache, pain, sore

腾 1)(跑或跳) gallop, jump, prance 2)(使空出) make room, clear out, vacate 腾飞 soar, exceptionally fast growth 腾越 jump over

誊 誊写 transcribe, copy out 誊清 make a fair copy of

【tī】

剔 (刮) clean with a pointed instrument, pick 剔除 pick out and throw away, reject

梯 梯级 stair, step 梯子 ladder, steps, stairs ◇电梯 elevator, lift ∥电动扶梯 escalator

梯度 gradient
梯度法 gradient method
梯度搜索 gradient search
梯度算符 gradient operator
梯度线 gradient line
梯度相关 gradient related
梯式打字机 ladder printer
梯形法则 trapezoidal rule
梯形畸变波形 keystone waveform
梯形滤波器 trapezoidal filter
梯形失真 keystoning
梯形图 ladder chart/diagram
梯形网络 ladder network

锑 antimony, stibium (Sb), stibonium

【tí】

提 另见【dī】
1) (手提) carry in one's hand
2) (往上提) lift, raise, promote 提案 motion, proposal, draft resolution 提拔 promote 提倡 advocate, promote, encourage 提成 deduct a percentage (from a sum of money) 提出 put forward, bring up, raise, pose (货) 提单 bill of lading (B/L) 提到 mention, refer to, bring up 提防 be cautious or watchful, be in the alert, guard against 提纲 outline, compendium 提高 raise, increase, improve 提供 provide, supply, furnish, offer 提货 pick up goods, take delivery of goods 提炼 extract and purify, abstract, refine 提名 nominate 提交 commit, submit, present 提前 ① (往前移) shift to an earlier date, move up, advance ② (事先) in advance, ahead of time, beforehand 提取 (取出) draw, pick up, collect ② (提炼) extract, abstract, refine 提升 ① (提级) promote, advance ② (提高) hoist, elevate 提示 point out, prompt(ing) 提问 put questions to, quiz 提醒 remind, warn, call attention to 提要 summary, abstract, synopsis 提议 ① 〈动〉propose, suggest, move ② 〈名〉proposal, motion 提早 be earlier than planned
提出疑问 challenge
提纯 purification, refinement
提纯判据 refinement criterion
提存 drawing
提法 synectics
提法注意表 attention table
提纲式询问 skeletal query
提高质量 upgrade
提供方 provider
提交表 commit list
提交操作 commit operation
提交点 commit point
提交定义 commitment definition
提交清单 commit list
提交时间 submission time
提交文件 submit file
提交状态 submit state
提交作业 submit job
提款 withdrawal
提前写 log write ahead
提前[正向]作业 forward job
提取 abstract, extract
提升电平 enhance level
提示磁道 cue track
提示方式 prompt mode
提示符 prompt
提示功能 prompt facility

提示图灵机 oracle Turing machine {OTM}
提示项 reminder
提示信号 cue signal
提示行 prompt line
提问词 question term
提问电路 quiz circuit
提醒装置 attention device

题 （写上）inscribe 题材 subject matter, theme 题词 ① 〈动〉write an inscription ② 〈名〉inscription, foreword 题解 key to exercises or problems 题目 ①（标题）title, subject, topic, problem ②（习题）exercise, problem, examination questions
题标栏 title bar
题目定义 problem definition
题目描述 problem description
题目数据 problem data
题目说明 problem definition/ description
题目文件 problem file, problem folder, run book

【tǐ】

体 1)（身体）body, part of the body 2)（物体）substance 体裁 style, form 体会 ① 〈动〉know from experience, realize ② 〈名〉experience, understanding 体积 volume, bulk 体力 physical strength, physical power 体力劳动 physical labor 体例 stylistic rules and layout, style 体系 system, type, formalism 体现 embody, reflect, give expression to 体型 form, figure, build 体验 learn through practice, experience 体育 physical culture/ education/ training, sports 体制 system, organization, structure
体绘制 volume rendering
体基元 volume primitive
体视 volume viewing
体视的 stereoscopic
体视化 volume visualization
体数据位 volume data sets
体素场 voxel field
体素分割 voxel dice
体素化 voxelization
体素记录 voxel record
体素结构 voxel architecture
体素生成 voxel spanning
体素数据 voxel data
体素索引 voxel index
体素线 voxelized line
体图 volume map (=voxmap)
体图形学 volume graphics
体图元 volume primitive
体外层 volume surrounding
体纹理 solid texture
体纹理函数 solid texture function
体纹理化 solid texturing
体系结构模型 solid texture model
体系结构 architectural structure, architecture, organization, system architecture
体系数 hierarchy number
体系特征 architectural feature
体映射 volume imaging
体元，体素 voxel, vox element
体阵列 volume array

【tì】

剃 shave, cut

替 （为）for, on behalf of 替代 take the place of, replace, substitute for, displace 替工 ① 〈动〉work as a substitute ② 〈名〉temporary substitute

(worker) 替换 replace, substitute for, displace, take the place of
替补磁带机 alternate tape
替代串 substitution string
替代方式 substitute mode
替代路由 alternate route/routing, alt-route
替代字符 alternate character
替换变量 substitution variable
替换表 substitution table
替换策略 replacement policy
替换程序 alternative routine
替换磁道 alternative track
替换代码 alternate code
替换方式 substitute mode
替换规则 substitution rule
替换键 alternate key
替换路径 alternate route/routing, alt-route
替换码页 alternate code page
替换名称 alternate name
替换入口 alias
替换扇区 alternative sector
替换设备 alternate device
替换属性 alternative attribute
替换算法 replacement algorithm
替换物 alternative
替换线路 alternative line
替换原理 paramodulation principle
替换阵列 replacement array
替换值 override
替换字符集 alternate character set

【tiān】

天 (一昼夜,白天)day 天才 ①(才能)genius, talent, gift ②(有天才的人)genius, gifted person 天地 ①(天和地)heaven and earth, universe, world ②(活动范围)field of activity, scope of operation, horison 天赋 ①〈形〉inborn, innate, natural, endowed by nature ②〈名〉natural gift, talent, endowments 天空 sky, heaven 天亮,天明 daybreak, dawn 天气 weather 天桥 overline bridge, platform bridge 天然 natural 天然气 natural gas 天生 born, inborn, inherent, innate 天天 every day, daily, from day to day 天文 astronomy

天体力学 celestial mechanics
天线 antenna, aerial
天线电缆 aerial cable
天线定位系统 antenna positioning system {APS}
天线共用器 diplexer
天线耦合器 antenna coupler

添 add, increase, have more
添加 add, addition, add-on, augment
添加窗口 supplemental windows
添加法 additive process
添加模块 addition module
添加属性 additive attribute

【tián】

田 field, farmland, cropland

甜 sweet, sugary

填 填表 fill in a form 填补 fill (in, up) 填充,填空 ①(填补)fill a vacant position, fill a vacancy ②(填空测验)fill in the blanks 填平 fill up, stuff 填写 fill in, write
填补寄存器 fill register
填充程序 filler

填充剂 coupler
填充区 fill area, filling area
填充位 filler, padding bit
填充字符 fill(er)/ filling/ pad(ding) character
填充字节 file byte
填空白 space filling
填零 zero fill, zeroise
填满 padding

【tiāo】

挑 另见【tiǎo】
挑担 carry on the shoulder with a pole, shoulder 挑选 choose, select, pick out

【tiáo】

条 bar, stripe 条件 ①（客观因素）condition, term, factor ②（主观要求）requirement, prerequisite 条款 clause, article, provision, term, item 条理 proper arrangement or presentation, regular sequence 条例 regulations, rules, stipulations 条目 ①（规章中的）clauses and subclauses ②（词典中的）entry 条文 article, clause 条纹 stripe, streak, band 条约 treaty, pact
条件编译 conditional compilation
条件变量 conditional variable
条件标记 condition flag
条件表达式 condition(al) expression, expression of condition, IF expression
条件表征码 condition mask
条件捕获 conditional capture
条件操作 conditional operation
条件返回 conditional return
条件方差 conditional variance
条件盒 condition box
条件汇编 conditional assembly
条件结合 conditional association
条件矩 conditional moment
条件句 conditional sentence
条件开关 condition switch
条件框 condition box
条件逻辑 conditional logic
条件码 condition(al) code
条件名 condition name
条件屏蔽 condition mask
条件熵 average conditional information content, conditional entropy
条件式 conditionals
条件收益 conditional profit
条件数 condition number
条件停机 optional stop
条件同步 conditional synchronization
条件位 condition bit
条件无关 conditional independence
条件域 condition field
条件运算 conditional operation
条件指令 conditional instruction, conditional order
条件指示符 condition indicator
条件转储 conditional dump
条件转移 conditional branch/ jump/transfer, jump if not
条件子句 conditional clause, conditional phrase, IF clause
条式打印机 bar printer
条纹记录器 strip-chart recorder
条纹图形 striate pattern
条型缓冲区 strip buffer
条形[码]码 bar coding
条形标识[标记] bar mark
条形段 bar segment
条形码 bar code
条形码读入器 wand, wand reader
条形码扫描器 bar code scanner

条形码识别 bar code recognition
条形码阅读器 bar code reader
条形图 bar chart, bar graph

调 另见【diào】
1)(配合适当)suit well, fit in perfectly 2)(使配合均匀)mix, adjust **调和** ①(配合适当)be in harmony ②(调解)mediate, reconcile ③(妥协)compromise, make concessions **调解** mediate
调停 mediate, make peace
调整 adjust, regulate, balance
调幅 amplitude modulation {AM}
调幅制 amplitude modulation system
调和程序 reconciliation procedure
调和共轭 harmonic conjugate
调和函数 harmonic function
调和级数 harmonic series
调和数 harmonic number
调焦 focus
调节 adjust {ADJ}, adjustment, regulation, conditioning
调节器 regulator, setter
调节作用 regulating action
调解 conciliation, reconciliation
调解法 paramodulation
调零 zero modulation {ZM}, zero adjust, zeroing
调频数据 frequency modulation data {FM data}
调频制 frequency modulation {FM}, frequency modulation system
调色板 (color) palette
调色表 palette table

调试 debug, debugging
调试步 debugging step
调试部件 debugging unit
调试成分 debugging component
调试程序 debugged program, debug routine, debugger, debugging program/routine
调试方式 debug mode
调试工具 debug(ging) tool/aids
调试功能 debug function
调试过程 debugging process
调试回路 debug loop
调试活动 debugging activity
调试检查 bug check
调试阶段 debug phase, debugging stage
调试节 debugging section
调试命令 debug(ging) command
调试软件包 debugging software package
调试系统 debug system
调试行 debug(ging) line
调试语句 debug(ging) statement
调试周期 debug cycle
调态 debugging mode
调相 phase modulation {PM}
调谐控制 tuning control
调行器 aligner
调压器 voltage regulator
调整 adjust {ADJ}, adjustment, justify, regulation, settle, trade-off, tuning
调整电平 levelling
调整扭斜 adjust skew
调整器 adjuster
调整事项 adjustment
调制 modulate, modulation
调制定理 modulation theorem
调制方式 modulation mode
调制解调器 modulator-demodulator {MODEM}
调制码 modulation code

调制速率 modulation rate
调制系数 modulation factor
调准分贝 adjusted decibel {dBa}
调准器 aligner

【tiǎo】

挑 另见【tiāo】
挑拨 stir up, instigate, provoke 挑起 put sth up with a pole or stick, raise 挑战 ①(挑衅)challenge to battle ②(提出竞赛)challenge to a contest

【tiào】

跳 (越过)skip, omit, drop 跳动 move up and down, beat 跳级 skip a grade 跳舞 dance 跳跃 jump, leap, spring, bounce, hop
跳步测试 galloping test, leapfrog test
跳步指令 skip
跳动 beat, jitter, jumping
跳过 kill, skip
跳线 wire jumper
跳线电缆 jumper cable
跳线块 jumper block
跳(换)行 skip line
跳行打印机 skip printer
跳行符 skip symbol
跳跃标记 skip flag
跳跃表 skip list
跳跃函数 jump function
跳跃链 skip link
跳跃码 skip code
跳跃区 skip zone
跳跃扫描 skip scan
跳跃(计)数 hop count
跳跃条件 jump/skip condition
跳跃转移 jump if not, jump transfer
跳跃字 skip word
跳纸 paper skip
跳转 jump
跳转程序 jump routine
跳转[转移]指令 jump instruction
跳转踪迹 jump trace

【tiē】

贴 1)(粘贴)paste, stick, glue 2)(紧挨)close to, against 3)(津贴)subsidies
贴补 subsidize, help (out) financially 贴换 trade sth in, trade in 贴切 apt, suitable, appropriate, proper 贴现 discount 贴现率 discount rate
贴入 paste

【tiě】

铁 iron (Fe), ferrum 铁路 railroad, railway
铁笔 stylus pen
铁磁材料 ferromagnetic material
铁磁学 ferromagnetics
铁心 core
铁氧体 ferric oxide, ferrite
铁氧体薄膜磁盘 ferrite film disk

【tīng】

厅 1)(大房间)hall 2)(部门)office, department

听 1)(耳听)listen, hear 2)〈量词〉tin, can ◇一听饼干 a tin of biscuits 听便 as one pleases, please yourself 听从 obey 听候 wait for, pending 听讲 listen to a talk, attend a lecture 听觉 sense of hearing 听课 attend a lecture, sit in on a lesson 听凭 allow,

let 听取 listen to 听说 be told, hear of/ about 听众 audience, listeners
听力[听觉]的 aural
听力计 audiometer
听者 auditor
听诊耳机 stethophone

【tíng】

亭 (亭子)pavilion, kiosk

停 停车 ①(车辆停止行驶) stop, pull up ②(停放车辆) park ③(机器停止转动) stall, stop working 停顿 ①(停止)stop, halt, pause ◇处于停顿状态 be at a standstill ②(说话的间歇)pause 停放 park, place 停工 stop work, shut down 停刊 stop publication 停课 suspend classes 停留 stay for a time, stop over, remain 停业 stop doing business, close down; stop, cease 停职 suspend sb from his duties 停止 stop, cease, halt, pause 停滞 stagnate, be at a stand-still
停笔 pen-off
停电控制 power down control
停机 closedown, down, halt, hang-up, stop
停机按钮 stop button
停机方式 halt mode
停机函数 halting function
停机号 halt number
停机键 stop key
停机开关 halt switch, stop key
停机码 stop code
停机挪用 halt steal
停机时间 downtime, shutdown/signal
停机输入 halt input
停机信号 halt signal, stopping signal
停机指令 halt/stop instruction
停机状态 halt mode, halting state
停用键 dead key
停用卡片 dead card
停用文件 dead file
停止单元[位,比特] stop bit, stop element
停止(字)符 stop character 〈STP〉
停止符号 stop element
停止规则 stop rule
停止(代)码 stop code
停止码元 stop element
停止脉冲 stop pulse
停止时间 stopping time
停止位置 stop position
停滞时间 dead time
停滞位置 dead position
停滞状态 dead state
停转 stalling

庭 1)(庭院)front courtyard, front yard 2)(法院)law court

【tǐng】

挺 1)(硬而直)straight, erect, stiff 2)(伸直) straighten up, stick out, make upright 3)(勉强支持) endure, stand, hold out

艇 boat, ship, craft, watercraft

【tōng】

通 1)(可以通过)open, through 2)(疏通)open up, clear out 3)(相通)connect, communicate, link 4)(使知道)notify, tell 通报 ①〈动〉circulate a notice ②〈名〉circular, bulletin, journal, report **通常** general, usual, normal **通畅** ①〈运行无阻〉clear, unblocked ②〈流畅〉easy and smooth **通车** ①〈开始行车〉be open to traffic ②〈有车来往〉have transport service **通称** ①〈通常叫做〉be generally called, be generally known as ②〈通常的名字〉a general term, common name, popular name **通道** channel, path, passage(way) **通风** ventilate **通告** ①〈动〉give public notice, anounce, inform ②〈名〉public notice, announcement **通过** ①〈穿过〉pass through, get past, traverse ②〈同意议案〉adopt, pass, approve ③〈用,经过〉by means of, by way of, by, through ④〈征得某人同意〉ask the approval of **通话** ①〈通电话〉communicate by telephone ②〈彼此交谈〉converse, talk with, hold conversation **通货膨胀** inflation **通例** general rule, usual practice **通商** have trade relations **通顺** logical, coherent **通俗** popular, common **通向** lead to, go to **通宵** throughout the night **通晓** thoroughly understand, be well versed in, be proficient in **通信** communicate by letter, correspond **通行** ①〈通过〉pass through ②〈通用〉current, general **通行证** pass, permit **通讯** ① communication ② news report, correspondence, newsletter **通用** ①〈普通使用〉in common use, current, general, universal ②〈可换用〉interchangeable **通则** general rule, general provisions **通知** ①〈动〉notify, inform, give notice, let know ②〈名〉notice, circular, message

通报板 bulletin board
通代(符) unifier
通道标志(符) channel flag
通道布线算法 channel routing algorithm
通道程序 channel program
通道处理机 channel processor
通道传输率 channel capacity
通道传送装置 channel unit
通道到通道 channel-to-channel {CTC}
通道地址字 channel address word {CAW}
通道调度程序 channel scheduler
通道方式 channel mode
通道分配 channel allocation
通道服务单元 channel service unit {CSU}
通道号 channel number
通道划分 channeling, channelize
通道缓冲器 channel buffer
通道结构 channel architecture, channel design
通道开销 path overhead {POH}
通道控制块 channel control block
通道控制器 channel control unit, channel controller
通道控制向量 channel control vector {CHCV}
通道宽度 channel width
通道链接 channel link
通道轮询 channel polling
通道忙碌 channel busy
通道门 channel gate

通道命令 channel command
通道命令字 channel command word {CCW}
通道屏蔽 channel mask
通道请求 channel request
通道请求优先级 channel request priority {CRP}
通道[信道]容量 channel capacity
通道容量 channel volume
通道适配器 channel adaptor
通道探询 channel polling
通道协议 channel protocol
通道许可 channel grant {CG}
通道掩码 channel mash
通道指令 channel instruction
通道指示器 channel pointer {CHP}
通道指示字 channel indicator
通道状态 channel mode/status
通道状态字 channel state/status word {CSW}
通道组 channel set
通电 power on
通过键 pass key
通话 telephony
通话单位 unit call
通话地址 talk address
通话[对讲]电路 talking circuit
通话回声 talk echo
通话质量 speech quality
通孔 feed-through, via hole
通灵系统 turnkey
通路 chain, channel, gangway, passage, path
通路分类 way sort
通路控制 path control {PC}
通配符 wild card, wildcard character
通俗音乐 pop music
通俗性 popularity
通信标识符 communication identifier {CID}
通信参数 communication parameter
通信程序 communicator
通信处理 communication processing
通信电缆 communication cable
通信电路 communication circuit
通信端口 communication port
通信段 communication section
通信队列 comm-queue, communication queue, comm-device queue
通信方式 communication mode
通信分类 traffic class
通信服务(程序) communication services {CS}
通信服务核准 communication service authorization {CSA}
通信服务器 communication server
通信(中继)干线 communication trunk
通信格式 communication format
通信光缆 fiber-optic telecommunication cable
通信过程 communication process, correspondent process
通信缓冲区 communication buffer
通信伙伴 communication partner
通信寄存单元 communication register unit {CRU}
通信计算机 communication computer, teleputer
通信接口 communication interface
通信接口适配器 communication interface adapter
通信节 communication section
通信节点 traffic node
通信进程 communication process
通信竞争者 bidder

通信距离 haul
通信卡 communication card
通信控制程序 communication control program {CCP}
通信控制符 communication control character
通信控制码 communication control code
通信控制器[部件,装置] communication controller/control unit
通信联结 communication cohesion
通信链 communication link
通信路由表 communication routing table
通信区 communication area, communication region
通信任务 communication task
通信软件 communication software
通信扫描器板 communication scanner base {CSB}
通信设备 communication device/facility
通信实体 communication entity
通信识别符 communication identifier {CID}
通信网 communication(s) network, net
通信网络管理 communication network management {CNM}
通信网络(体系)结构 communication network architecture {CNA}
通信卫星 communication satellite
通信文件 communication file
通信系统 communication system
通信线 order wire
通信线路 communication line, communication link
通信线路适配器 communication line adapter {CLA}
通信线路终端 communication line terminal {CLT}
通信协议 communication protocol
通信信道 communication channel
通信业务 communication service
通信硬件 communication hardware
通信原语 intercommunication primitive
通信员 communicator
通信源(点) communication(s) source
通信质量 correspondence quality
通信终端(装置) communication terminal
通信转接器 communication adapter
通信装置 communicator
通信状态字 communication status word
通信子网 communication subnet
通信字处理机 communicating word processor {CWP}
通信字段 communication field
通信总线 tie bus
通行字 password
通用报文事务协议 versatile message transaction protocol {VTMP}
通用标题 global title
通用标志 conventional sign
通用查询 general poll
通用程序 general (purpose) program, general(ized) routine
通用程序库 general library
通用(存储)池 general pool
通用处理机 general (purpose) processor

通用串行总线 universal serial bus {USB}
通用存储卷 general use volume
通用存取 generic access, universal access
通用地址 universal address
通用电气 general electric {GE}
通用端口 universal port
通用仿真系统 general purpose simulation system {GPSS}
通用符号 conventional sign, ordinary symbol
通用格式识别符 general format identifier {GFI}
通用跟踪[追踪]程序 generalized trace facility {GTF}
通用函数 universal function
通用汇编程序 general assembly program {GAP}
通用寄存器 general purpose register {GPR}
通用计算机 universal/ general computer, general purpose computer {GP computer, GPC}, general purpose machine, all-purpose computer
通用键 universal key
通用建模语言 unified modeling language {UML}
通用接口 general purpose interface, general-use interface
通用控制器 general-purpose controller
通用(程序)库 general-purpose library
通用例程 general purpose routine
通用逻辑组件 universal logic module
通用模拟系统 general purpose simulation system {GPSS}
通用模式 general pattern
通用日志 general journal
通用软件 general purpose software, common software
通用数据访问 universal data access
通用数据链路控制 universal data link control {UDLC}
通用数据流 general data stream {GDS}
通用算法 universal algorithm
通用网络 universal network
通用微处理机 general purpose microprocessor
通用文件 general file, universal file
通用系统 general purpose system, universal system
通用信息(处理)系统 generalized information system {GIS}
通用性 generality
通用移动电话系统 universal mobile telecommunications system {UMTS}
通用异步接收发送器 universal asynchronous receiver/ transmitter {UART}
通用硬件 common hardware
通用语言 common language, general purpose language, all-purpose language
通用阵列逻辑(电路) generic array logic {GAL}
通用指令集 universal instruction set
通用终端 general terminal
通用资源定位器 universal resource locator {URL}
通用字符集 universal character set {UCS}
通知单 notification, requisition
通知目标 notify object
通知信息 notify message
通知者 informant

【tóng】

同 1)(相同)same, alike 2)(跟…相同)be the same as 3)(共同)together, in common
同等 of the same class/rank/status, on an equal basis
同类 of the same kind, similar
同盟 alliance, league
同期 the corresponding period
同情 sympathize with
同上 ditto, 〈拉丁语〉idem
同时 ①(在同一时候)at the same time, simultaneously, meanwhile, in the meantime ②(并且)moreover, besides, furthermore
同事 ①〈动〉work in the same place, work together ②〈名〉colleague, fellow worker
同学 ①〈动〉study in the same school ②〈名〉fellow student, schoolmate
同样 same, equal, similar
同一 same, identical
同义词 synonym
同意 agree, consent, approve
同步 synchronization (=sync, synch), synchronous, in-sync, in-phase, clocking, timing
同步[通道] sync channel
同步比特 synchronization bit
同步操作 synchronization/synchronous operation
同步传输 synchronous/asymmetrical transmission
同步传输接收器 synchronous transmitter/receiver {STR}
同步传输模式 synchronous transfer mode {STM}
同步道 clock/timing track
同步点服务 sync point services {SPS}
同步点管理器 sync point manager {SPM}
同步电路 sync circuit
同步调制解调器 synchronous modem
同步读出器 synchro reader
同步多媒体集成语言 synchronized multimedia integration language {SMIL}
同步分析器 synchro resolver
同步光纤网(络) synchronous optical network {SONET}
同步恢复 clock recovery
同步机 synchro, synchronous machine
同步级 synchronous level
同步计数器 coincidence counter
同步接口 synchronous interface
同步接收器 synchronous receiver
同步空转字符 synchronous idle character {SYN}
同步控制 synchronous control
同步流 synchronous flow
同步脉冲 clock {CLK}, synchronization pulse, sync pulses
同步耦合器 genlock
同步时序电路 synchronizing sequential circuit
同步时钟 synchronous clock
同步收发机 synchronous receiver-transmitter, synchronous transmitter/receiver {STR}
同步输入 synchronous input
同步数据链路控制(协议) synchronous data link control {SDLC}
同步数字层次化 synchronous digital hierarchy {SDH}
同步数字体系 synchronous digital hierarchy {SDH}

同步刷新 synchronous refresh
同步双工 synchro duplexing
同步通信 synchronous/synchronization communication
同步位 sync bit
同步卫星 synchronous satellite
同步系统 synchronous system
同步协议 synchronous protocol
同步信号 sync(hronizing) signal, clock pulse
同步信号单元 synchronization signal unit {SYU}
同步序列 synchronizing sequence
同步原语 synchronization primitive
同步执行 synchronous execution
同步装置 synchrobox, synchronizer
同步(信号)字符 synchronous idle character {SYN}
同步字节 sync byte
同构 isomorph, isomorphic, isomorphism
同构图 isomorphic graph
同构问题 isomorphism problem
同构映射 isomorphic mapping
"同或" exclusive-NOR {XNOR}, inclusive OR
同机种网络 homogeneous network
同级节点 brother node
同级树 brother tree
同类 cognate
同类结构 homogeneous structure
同胚 homeomorphism
同胚的 homeomorphic
同谱图 cospectral graph
同时(性) concurrency (=concurrence)
同时操作 simultaneous operation
同时处理 simultaneous processing, symbiont
同时(发生)的 concurrent, simultaneous
同时进位 simultaneous carry
同时控制 simultaneous control
同时事件 concurrent
同时双向的 full duplex {FD, FDX}
同时性 simultaneity
同态 homomorphism
同态过滤器 homomorphic filter
同态像 homomorph, homomorphic image
同态学 morphology
同态映射 homomorphism mapping
同位素 isotope
同相 same phase
同形 isomorph
同形的 isomorphic
同性 homogeneity, homogeneous
同性质的 cognate
同一律 identity law, law of identity
同义链 synonym chain
同义名 alias, synonym
同义名字链 synonym chain
同义性 synonymity
同余法 congruential method
同余数 congruent number
同余序列 congruential sequence
同域 same area
同真 identically true
同轴 coaxial, ganging
同轴控制 gang control
同轴电缆 coaxial cable {CC}, concentric cable {C/C}

tóng 铜童 tǒng 统桶 tòng 痛 tōu 偷 tóu 头

同轴电缆电视 coaxial television {CATV}
同轴电缆网络 coax network
同轴电缆信息系统 coaxial cable information system {CCIS}
同轴线 coaxial line
同轴线接插件 coaxial connector

铜 copper (Cu)
铜箔板 copper foil laminate, copper-clad laminate

童 (儿童) child

【tǒng】

统 1) (全部) all, together 2) (总括) gather into one, unite 统筹 plan as a whole 统筹安排 overall arrangement 统计 ①〈名〉statistics ②〈动〉add up, count 统统 all, completely, entirely 统一 ①〈动〉unify, unite, integrate ②〈形〉unified, unitary, centralized
统计编码 statistical coding
统计查询 statistical query
统计方法 statistical method
统计仿真[模拟] statistical simulation
统计分布 statistical distribution
统计分析 statistical analysis
统计过程 statistical process
统计检验 statistical test
统计控制 statistical control
统计模型 statistical model
统计取样 statistical sampling
统计生成程序 statistics generation program {SGP}
统计数据库 statistical database
统计图表 pictogrph
统计文件 account file
统计误差 statistical error
统计学 statistics
统计质量管理 statistical quality control {SQC}
统一操作 unified operation
统一程序 consolidator
统一规划法 unified program planning {UPP}
统一数据库语言 unified database language {UDL}
统一文件 unified file
统一性 integrity
统一资源标识符 uniform resource identifier {URI}
统一资源地址[定位器] uniform resource locator {URL}
统一总线 unified bus

桶 1) (容器) tub, bucket, barrel, pail 2) (容量单位) barrel (= 31.5 加仑)
桶排序 bucket sort
桶形开关 barrel switch

【tòng】

痛 1) (疼痛) ache, pain 2) (悲伤) sorrow, sadness, grief 痛苦 pain, suffering, agony

【tōu】

偷 (瞒着干) stealthily, secretly
偷窃 steal, thieve, snitch

【tóu】

头 1) (脑袋) head 2) (物体顶端) top, end 头等 first-class, first-rate 头号 ① (第一号) number one, size one ② (最好的) first-rate, top quality 头脑 ① (思想能力) brains, mind ② (头绪) main threads, clue 头衔 title

头部标号 header label {HDR}
头部符号 head symbol
头部卡片 header card
头地址 header address
头端器 headend
头盘组合件 head disk assembly {HDA}
头文件 header file

投 1)(投、扔) throw, fling, hurl 2)(投入) put in, drop 3)(跳进去) throw oneself into 投保 insure 投产 go into operation, put into production 投递 deliver 投放 throw in, put in 投放资金 put money into circulation
投稿 submit a piece of writing for publication, contribute
投考 sign up for an examination 投票 vote, cast a vote
投射 ①(扔,掷) throw, cast ②(光线等) project, cast
投掷 throw, hurl 投资 ①〈动〉invest ②〈名〉investment
投标 bid, bidding, proposal
投标活动 proposal activity
投递清单 mailing list
投票规则 voting rule
投票请求 call for votes {CFV}
投影 project(ion)
投影变换 projection transformation
投影操作 projection operation
投影定理 projection theorem
投影函数 projection function
投影平面 projection plane
投影区 projected area
投影图 skiagraph
投影仪 projector
投影纸 projection paper
投资成本 capitalized cost
投资费用 investment cost

【tòu】

透 透彻 fully, thoroughly, in a penetrating way 透过 penetrate, pass/seep through
透露 disclose, reveal 透明 transparent, glassy 透明度 transparency, diaphaneity, penetrability, pellucidity 透支 overdraw, make an overdraft
透光错误 light transmission error {LTE}
透镜 lens
透明传送 transparent transfer
透明方式 transparency mode
透明胶 glassine
透明接口 transparent interface
透明码 transparent code
透明区 clear area
透明网关 transparent gateway
透明网桥 transparent bridge
透明性 transparency, penetrability, pellucidity
透明原件 transparent original
透视 perspective, show-through, penetrate
透视变换 perspective transformation
透视景物 perspective scene
透视深度 perspective depth
透视投影 perspective projection
透视图 perspective view, rendering, skeleton view
透视性 perspectivity
透析码 transparent code

【tū】

凸 1)〈形〉protruding, raised 2)〈名〉(凸出物) convex, prominence
凸包 convex closure/hull
凸轮 cam

凸轮操纵开关 cam switch
凸轮盘 cam disk
凸模糊决策 convex fuzzy decision
凸系统 convex system
凸线 facet
凸形卡 embossed card
凸性 convexity
凸域 convex domain
凸缘 flange, lip, lug

突 (猛冲) dash forward, charge **突出** ①(鼓出来) protruding, projecting, sticking out ②(出众) outstanding, prominent ③(强调) stress, highlight, give prominence to **突破** ①(打开缺口) break through, make a breakthrough ②(打破) surmount, break, overcome **突然** suddenly, abruptly, unexpectedly

突变现象 jumping
突出特征 salient features
突出显示 emphasis
突触 synapse
突发差错 error burst
突发错误[差错] burst error
突发恢复[更新] burst refresh
突发型 burst mode
突防 penetration
突防装置 penetration aids
突破点 break-through point
突然失效 sudden failure

【tú】

图 1)(谋划) scheme, plan, attempt 2)(贪图) pursue, seek 3)(意图) intention, intent **图案** pattern, design **图表** chart, diagram, graph **图画** picture, drawing, chart, map **图片** picture, photograph **图书馆** library **图章** seal, stamp **图纸** blueprint, drawing

图案填充 pattern fill
图标 icon
图标符号 legend
图标格 chart scale
图标界面 iconic interface
图标模式 icon pattern
图标模型 iconographic model
图标题 graph title
图标资源 icon resource
图表布局 chart layout
图表法 diagram method
图表分解 diagrammatic decomposition
图表格式 chart format
图表技术 table technique
图表接口 drawing interface
图表框 chart frame
图表模型 schematic model
图表区 chart area
图表示 graph representation
图表数据库 graph table database
图表语言 diagram language
图表帧 chart frame
图操作 graphic operation
图度 graph order
图段 segment
图符 icon, pictogram
图符菜单 icon menu
图符框 icon box
图合并 graph merge
图解 graphic analysis/solution, scheme, iconography
图解法 diagram method, graphic method, graphology
图解分析 graphic analysis
图解计算 graphic calculation
图解结构 graphic entity
图解零件目录 illustrated parts catalog {**IPC**}
图解模型 graphic model,

iconographic model
图解实体 graphic entity
图解数据 graphic data
图解算法 graph algorithm
图解学 iconography
图景 presentation
图块 segment
图例 legend
图灵机 Turing machine
图论 graph theory
图枚举 enumeration of graph
图胚 graphoid
图片的 pictorial
图片库 clip art library
图片描述符 picture descriptor {PD}
图片序列 portfolio
图示法 diagrammatic representation, graphic method
图示符 glyph
图示光标 graphic cursor
图示面板 graphic panel
图示形式 graphic form
图示[图形]字符 graphic character
图书馆自动化 library automation
图书目录 library catalog
图搜索 graph search, graphic searching
图(像元)素 picture element {PEL, PIXEL, pel, pixel}
图算法 nomography
图同构 graph isomorphism
图文电视 video text, teletext
图文段 boilerplate
图文法 graph grammar
图文重叠 overlap
图像 picture, image
图像逼真(度) image fidelity
图像比例尺 image scale
图像编码 image (en)coding, picture coding
图像编排 image arrangement

图像变换 image transformation
图像变焦 image zoom
图像表示 iconic representation, presentation image
图像捕捉 picture-capture
图像部分 image area
图像采集设备 image capture device
图像插入 graphics insertion
图像产生 image generation
图像处理 image/picture processing, graphic process
图像传感器 image sensor
图像[模式]存储库 pattern library
图像[图形]存取法 graphic access method {GAM}
图像打印机 video printer
图像单元 elemental area, image cell
图像底片 image master
图像电平 iconic level, picture level
图像调整 picture control
图像对象 image/picture object
图像反转 image reversal
图像方式 image mode/map
图像放大 image magnification, blow back
图像分辨率 image resolution, resolution ratio
图像分割 image segmentation
图像分类 presentation class
图像符号 picture character
图像符号集 image symbol set {ISS}
图像覆盖 image overlay
图像复原 image restoration
图像干涉 image interference
图像工作站 image workstation
图像光电变换管 image converter
图像混合 image/video mixing
图像机构 picture mechanism

图像畸变[失真] image/ pattern distortion
图像计算 image computing
图像检测 image/ picture detection
图像接口 visual interface
图像卡 image card
图像开始 start of image {SOI}
图像空间 image/ picture space
图像控制 image control
图像库 image library
图像理解 image understanding
图像亮度 image intensity
图像滤波 imaging filtering
图像描述 image description
图像明暗法[浓淡法] dither
图像模糊 fog
图像模式识别 image pattern recognition
图像模型 image model
图像目录 image directory
图像内容 image content
图像排字机 imagesetter
图像匹配 image match(ing)
图像平滑化 image smoothing
图像平面 image plane
图像切割 image cut
图像清晰度 image resolution, picture sharpness
图像区 image area
图像取样 image sampling
图像扫描 image scanning
图像扫描器 image scanner
图像生成 image generation
图像失真 image distortion
图像识别 image/ picture recognition
图像输出设备 image output device
图像属性 picture attribute
图像数据库 image database
图像数据压缩 image data compression
图像数字化仪 image digitizer

图像[写照]说明 picture specification
图像搜索 picture search
图像缩小 image contract
图像锁定 image lock, pixlock
图像特征抽取 image feature extraction
图像图形 image graphic
图像位图 image bit map
图像文法 picture grammar
图像文件 image/screen file
图像系统 image system
图像显示 image/ pictorial/ picture display
图像信号 image/picture signal
图像形状 image geometry
图像序列 image sequence
图像旋转 image rotation
图像学 iconography
图像压缩 image/ picture compression, cramping
图像语言 graphic/ picture/ figurative language
图像元 image primitive
图像载波 picture carrier
图像再生[再现] image regeneration
图像增亮 fade-up
图像质量 image quality
图像滞留 image retention
图像重复 image repetition
图像重构 image reconstruction
图像重现 image repitition, pattern playback
图像转换 image transfer
图形 graph, figure, chart, diagram, pattern
图形板 graphical board, graphics pad
图形(软件)包 graphics package
图形边界 graphic limit
图形变比 zoom
图形标记 dingbat

图形捕获 frame grab
图形捕捉 schematic capture
图形采集设备 graph capture device
图形操作语言 graphics manipulating language {GML}
图形(数据)处理 graphic processing
图形处理装置 graphic processing facility {GPF}
图形传输网 graphnet
图形窗口 graphical/ graphics window
图形存储器 picture memory
图形打印机 graphic printer
图形断面 pattern profile
图形对象 graphic object
图形发生器 graphic generator
图形符号 graphic(al) symbol, graphic
图形覆盖 graphic overlay
图形工作站 graphics workstation
图形光标 graphical cursor
图形核心系统 graphic(al)/ graphics kernel system {GKS}
图形基元[原语] graphic primitive
图形记录器 chart recorder
图形加速器 graphic accelerator
图形键 graph key
图形交换格式 graphic(al) interchange format {GIF}
图形接口[界面] graphic(s) interface
图形结构 picture structure
图形(端)口 graphics port
图形口 grafport
图形(程序)库 graphical library
图形理论 graph theory
图形码 graphic code
图形描述指令 picture description instruction {PDI}
图形命令 graphic command

图形模式 graphic mode
图形设备 graphics device
图形设备界面[接口] graphics device interface {GDI}
图形设计 schematic layout
图形失真 aliasing
图形式菜单 icon menu
图形[作图]适配器 graphics adapter
图形输出板 plotting board
图形输出设备 graphical output device
图形输入装置 graphic input device
图形数据显示管理程序 graphical data display manager {GDDM}
图形数据字典 graphic data dictionary
图形数字化 graphic digitizer
图形图像格式 graphics image format {GIF}
图形外部设备 graphics peripheral
图形[字符]网格 character grid
图形文本 graphics text
图形文档 graphic document
图形文件 picture file
图形文件格式 graphic file format
图形显示控制器芯片 graphic display controller {GDC}
图形显示器 plotter
图形显示终端 graphic display terminal {GDT}
图形信息 graphical information
图形学 graphics
图形用户接口[界面] graphical user interrace {GUI}
图形语言 graphic language
图形元 pattern primitive
图形元素 graphical elements,

pictorial character
图形阅读器 chart/ pattern reader
图形转义字符 graphic escape character
图形字符集 graphic character set
图形字体 graphical character font
图形作业处理程序 graphic job processor {GJP}
图序 graph order
图样 drawing
图元 primitive
图元属性 primitive attribute
图元文件调色板 metafile palette
图纸设计 layout design
图注 legend

徒 1)(空的)empty, bare 2)(仅仅)merely, only 徒步 on foot 徒弟 apprentice, pupil 徒劳 futile effort, fruitless labour 徒然 in vain
徒手草稿 free sketch

涂 1)(抹去)cross out, rub out, delete 2)(乱写)scribble, scrawl 涂改 alter, markover 涂抹 spread on, apply, smear, coat
涂层 blanket, coating
涂层夹 blanket clip
涂敷层 blanket
涂色 color coat, paint
涂色工具 paint roller

途 way, road, route, course 途经 by way of, via 途径 way, channel, means

【tǔ】

土 1)(土壤)soil, earth 2)(地方性的)local, native 土产 local product 土地 ①(田地)land, soil, ground ②(疆域)territory 土星 Saturn

吐 spit 吐露 reveal, tell

钍 thorium (Th)

【tù】

兔 hare, rabbit

【tuán】

团 1)(圆形的)round, circular 2)(揉成球形)roll (sth into a ball) 3)(一堆圆形物)lump, mass 团结 unite, rally 团体 group, society, organization
团图 clique graph

【tuī】

推 1)(使向前移动)push, shove, thrust 2)(使事情开展)push forward, promote, advance 推测 infer, conjecture, guess 推迟 put off, postpone 推动 push forward, promote, give impetus to 推翻 ①(武力打垮)overthrow, overturn ②(根本否定)overrule, cancel, reverse 推断 infer, deduce 推广 popularize, spread, extend 推荐 recommend 推进 push on, carry forward, advance, propel 推理 inference, reasoning 推论 inference, deduction 推销 promote sales, market 推行 carry out, practice, exercise, pursue 推卸 push away, shirk, shift 推选 elect, choose 推移 ①(时间上)elapse, pass ②(形

势变化)develop, evolve
推 push
推测 guess, conjecture, speculate, abduct
推测的 abductive, speculative
推出 popping, release
推导 derivation, parsing, development, reasoning
推导规则 derivation rule
推导树 derivation tree
推导图 derivation graph
推断 infer(ence), extrapolation
推广规则 generalization rule
推荐 recommendation, propose
推进系统 propulsion system
推近 zoom in
推理 deduction, inference, reason, reasoning
推理策略 inference strategy
推理方法 inference method
推理规则 inference rule, inferential rule
推理机 inference engine, inference machine
推理模型 inference model
推理网络 inference network
推理知识 inference knowledge
推论 inference, consequence, consequent, extrapolation
推销员问题 travelling salesman problem
推延 restard

【tuǐ】
腿 1)(人腿) leg 2)(腿形支撑物) leglike support

【tuì】
退 1)(向后移动) move back, retreat 2)(使向后移动) cause to move back, withdraw, remove 3)(减退) decline, recede, ebb 4)(撤消) cancel, break off 退后 ①(落后) lag behind, retrogress ②(退路) room for maneuver, leeway 退出 withdraw from, secede, quit 退回 ①(退还) return, send back ②(返回原地) go back 退还 return, give back, refund 退货 return of goods, returned purchase 退赔 recompense, compensate 退让 make a concession, yield, give in 退休 retire 退学 leave school, stop schooling
退步 regression
退步原理 retrogression principle
退出 exit, quit, sign-off, logout
退出配置 deconfiguration
退出系统 log-off
退磁 degauss
退磁函数 degausser function
退磁装置 demagnetizer
退格 backspace {BS}
退化 degradation, degeneration, extinction, degeneracy
退化变量 degenerate variable
退化故障 degradation failure
退化函数 degenerate function
退化矩阵 degenerate matrix
退化空间 reduced space
退化网络 degenerate network

【tūn】
吞
吞吐量 throughput capacity
吞吐率 throughput rate

【tuō】
托 1)(向上承受) hold in the palm, support with the hand or palm 2)(委托) ask, entrust 3)(推托) plead, give as

a pretext 4)（依赖）rely upon, owe to 托管 trusteeship 托拉斯〈经贸〉trust, monopoly 托运 hand over for shipment, check

托板 pallet
托架 carriage, tray, backstop
托盘 tray, tile

拖
（牵引）pull, drag, haul 拖拉 dilatory, slow, sluggish 拖欠 be behind in payment, be in arrears 拖延 delay, put off, hold off, drag on

拖动 drag, dragging
拖动机构 tractor

脱
1)（取下）take off, cast off 2)（漏掉）miss out 脱节 come apart, be disjointed, be out of line with 脱离 separate oneself from, break away from, escape from, be divorced from, get out of 脱落 drop, fall off, come off 脱险 be out of danger, escape danger 脱销 out of stock, sold out

脱机 off-line (=off line, offline), out-of-line
脱机操作 off-line operation
脱机处理 off-line process, off-lining
脱机方式 off-line mode
脱机检索 off-line retrieval, off-line search
脱机输出 off-line output, out-line output
脱机输入 off-line input
脱机诊断 off-line diagnostics
脱机作业 off-line job

【tuǒ】

妥 妥当 appropriate, proper 妥协 come to terms, compromise 妥善 appropriate, proper

椭 椭圆 ellipse

【tuò】

拓 open up, reclaim, develop

拓扑 topology
拓扑次序 topological ordering
拓扑和路由服务 topology and routing services {**TRS**}
拓扑检索 topological searching
拓扑结构 topological structure
拓扑排序 topological sorting
拓扑属性 topological attribute
拓扑数据库 topology database
拓扑图 topological graph
拓扑优化 topological optimization

W w

【wā】

挖 挖掘 dig, excavate, unearth

【wǎ】

瓦 瓦解 disintegrate, crumble, collapse 瓦片 tile
瓦片式系统 tiled system
瓦片型窗口 tiled window
瓦特 watt {W}

【wà】

袜 socks, stockings, hose

【wāi】

歪 (不正当的) devious, underhanded, dishonest 歪曲 distort, misrepresent, twist 歪斜 crooked, inclined, skew, slanting
歪斜字符 skew character

【wài】

外 1) (外边) outer, outward, outside 2) (另外) besides, in addition, beyond 外币 foreign currency 外表 outward appearance, exterior, surface 外宾 foreign guest, foreign visitor 外部 ① (某一范围以外) outside, external ② (表面) exterior, outside, surface 外观 outward appearance, exterior 外国 foreign country 外国人 foreigner 外行 ① (外行的人) layman, nonprofessional ② (不懂或没经验) lay, unprofessional 外汇 foreign exchange 外加 more, additional, extra 外交 diplomacy, foreign affairs 外交关系 diplomatic relations 外来 outside, external, foreign 外力 ① (外部力量) outside force ② 〈物理〉external force 外贸 foreign trade, external trade 外貌 appearance, exterior, looks 外面 ① (外表) outward appearance, exterior, surface ② (外边) outside, out 外人 ① (局外人) stranger, outsider ② (外国人) foreigner, alien, outlander 外商 foreign tradesman 外事 foreign affairs, external affairs 外套 overcoat, coat, jacket, outer clothing 外围 periphery, edges 外向型经济 export-oriented economy 外销 export, for sale abroad or in other parts of the country 外形 appearance, external form, contour, figuration, profile 外因 external cause 外语 foreign language 外援 foreign aid, outside help, external assistance 外债 external debt, foreign debt 外资 foreign capital

外部变量 external variable
外部表 out list
外部参考 external reference {EXTRN}, extern
外部操作 auxiliary operation
外部查找 external search(ing)
外部程序 external subroutine
外部存储器 external memory
外部代理 foreign agent
外部的 exterior {EXT}, external, outside, superficial
外部地址 external address
外部调用 external reference {EXTRN}, external call
外部发送 outboard
外部符号 external symbol, exterior label
外部符号字典 external symbol dictionary {ESD}
外部过程 external procedure, out-of-line procedure
外部函数 external function {XFCN}
外部函数引用 external function reference
外部呼叫 external call
外部环境 external environment
外部记录程序 outboard recorder {OBR}
外部接口 peripheral interface
外部节点 external node, peripheral node
外部开关 external switch
外部可达地址 exterior reachable address
外部控制 outside control
外部链路 exterior link
外部媒介 external medium
外部描述 external description
外部名 external name
外部命令 external command {XCMD}
外部模型 external model
外部目标 external object
外部目录 out list
外部耦合 external coupling
外部排序 external sort
外部请求 external request
外部围设备 peripheral device/equipment
外部设备标识符 external unit identifier
外部设备控制 external device control
外部设备码 external device code
外部设备中断 external device interrupt, peripheral interrupt
外部设备状态 external device status
外部事件 external event
外部输入 external input
外部属性 external attribute
外部数据表示 external data representation {XDR}
外部数据项 external data item
外部数组 out array
外部网关协议 external gateway protocol {EGP}
外部线路 external line, external scheme
外部页面表 external page table {EXPT}
外部引用 external reference {EXTRN}
外部噪声 outer noise
外部中断 external/ peripheral interrupt, external/ attention interruption
外层 external level
外层循环 outer/ surrounding loop
外存 external memory/storage
外符 outsymbol
外加符号 extra symbol

外界 outboard
外界的 exterior {EXT}
外局交换(电话) foreign exchange {FX}
外壳 shell, container, body case, skin, can
外壳变量 shell variables
外壳程序 shell program
外壳过程 shell procedure
外壳进程 shell process
外壳提示(符) shell prompt
外壳型病毒 shell virus(es)
外联图像 external image
外联网 extranet
外(部)模式 external schema
外排序 external ordering/sort(ing)
外设插槽 peripheral slot
外同步方式 external sync mode
外推法 extrapolated/extrapolation method
外围操作 peripheral operation
外围处理机[器] peripheral processor
外围存储器 peripheral storage
外围记录器 outboard recorder {OBR}
外围节点 peripheral node
外围控制器 peripheral controller
外围设备 peripheral, peripheral apparatus
外围设备互连 peripheral component interconnect {PCI}
外线 external line
外项(数) extreme
外向 outgoing
外形图 outline drawing
外形字体 outline font
外循环 output/outside loop
外延 extent, extensive, epitaxy
外法 abduction
外页表 external page table {EXPT}

【wān】

弯 1)〈形〉curved, tortuous, crooked, bent 2)〈动〉bend, flex 弯曲 winding, meandering, zigzag, crooked, curved, bending
弯曲角 bend angle

湾 1)(河湾) river bend 2)(海湾) gulf, bay

【wán】

完 1)(完整) intact, whole, unharmed 2)(用完) exhaust, finish, use up, run out 完备 complete, perfect 完成 accomplish, complete, finish, fulfil 完工 complete a project, etc., finish doing sth, get through with sth 完美 perfect, ideal 完全 ①(齐全) complete, whole ②(全部) completely, fully, wholly, entirely, absolutely 完善 perfect, consummate 完整 complete, integrated
完备的二叉树 complete binary tree
完备集 complete set
完备码 perfect code
完成位 completion/done bit
完全安装 full install
完全保密 perfect secrecy
完全混洗网络 complete shuffle network
完全加密 pretty good privacy {PGP}
完全偶图 complete bipartite graph
完全数据库语言 complete database language
完全停机 drop-dead halt, dead halt, clean stop

wán 顽 wǎn 挽晚 wàn 万 wáng 亡 wǎng 网

完全图 complete graph
完全问题 complete problem
完全性 integrity
完整性 integrity, completeness
完整性数据块 data integrity block {**DIB**}

顽 (愚笨) stupid, dense, insensate 顽固 stubborn 顽皮 naughty, mischievous 顽强 staunch, unbending

【wǎn】

挽 1) (拉) draw, pull 2) (向上卷) roll up 挽回 retrieve 挽救 save, rescue

晚 (时间靠后的) late 晚安 good night 晚餐 supper, dinner 晚会 evening party 晚上 (in the) evening, (at) night

【wàn】

万 1) (数目) ten thousand 2) (很多) a very great number, myriad 3) (绝对) absolutely, by all means 万恶 extremely evil, absolutely vicious 万分 very much, extremely 万能 ① (无所不能) all-powerful ② (多用途) universal, all-purpose 万千 ① (绝对,用于否定) absolutely, wholly ② (亿) hundred million 万一 ① (可能性极小的假设) just in case, if by any chance ② (可能性极小的意外) contingency, eventuality ③ (极小的一部分) one ten thousandth, a very small percentage
万维网 world wide web, Web {**WWW**}

万维网服务器 web server
万维网协会 World Wide Web consortium {**W3C**}
万维网站 website
万位存储器 myriabit memory

【wáng】

亡 1) (逃跑) flee, run away 2) (失去) lose, be gone, be missing 3) (死) die, pass away 4) (死去的) deceased, departed

【wǎng】

网 1) (网类物) net 2) (系统) network ◇ 国际互联网 internet ‖ 万维网 World Wide Web (WWW)
网表 net list
网点 gateway node, web site, implet
网格 grid, grill, net
网格边界 mesh/net boundary
网格尺寸 grid size
网格单元 grid cell
网格点 net point
网格节点 grid node
网格图形 grid pattern
网格阵列 mesh array
网关 gateway
网关到网关协议 gateway to gateway protocol {**GGP**}
网关接口 gateway interface
网关节点 gateway node
网关宿主机 gateway host
网管区 network domain
网管员 network administrator
网际协议 Internet protocol {**IP**}
网间地址 Internet address
网间分组交换 internetwork packet exchange {**IPX**}
网间网[互联网] internetwork
网间协议 Internet protocol {**IP**}

网间选路 internetwork routing
网件 netware, web ware
网景公司 Netscape
网景通信器 Netscape communicator
网景网络会议 netscape conference
网景消息中心 netscape message center
网景浏览器 netscape navigator
网卡 network card
网卡检测 net card detection
网络 network, mesh, cross-domain communication
网络安全(性) network security
网络编址[寻址]单元 network addressable unit {NAU}
网络标识符 network identifier {NetID}
网络部件 network element/component
网络参数控制 network parameter control {NPC}
网络操作系统 network operating system {NOS}
网络操作中心 network operations center {NOC}
网络层 network level/ layer, network control layer
网络冲浪 surfing
网络传输层 transport network layer
网络存取控制 network access control
网络存取设备 network access facility {NAF}
网络打印机 network printer
网络导航器 netscape
网络到网络接口 network to network interface {NNI}
网络地址 network address
网络地址翻译 network address translation {NAT}
网络电话 internet phone {IP}
网络端口 network port
网络方式 network mode
网络仿真 network simulation
网络分区 network partition
网络分析 network analysis {NA}
网络分析器 network analyzer
网络服务 network service {NS}
网络服务公司 network service provider {NSP}
网络服务器 network server
网络服务提供者 network service provider {NSP}
网络服务协议 network service protocol {NSP}
网络工程师 network engineer
网络供应商 network service provider {NSP}
网络共享资源 network shared resource
网络管理 network management {NM}
网络管理层 network management layer
网络管理代理 network management agent
网络管理器[程序] network manager {NM}
网络管理网关 network management gateway {NMG}
网络管理系统 network management system
网络管理协议 network management protocol {NMP}
网络管理员 network administrator
网络管理站 network management station
网络规划 network planning
网络规模 network size
网络互联[互连] internetwork, network interconnect
网络互连包交换 internetwork packet exchange {IPX}

网络货币 cybercash
网络基本输入输出系统 network basic input output system {**NetBIOS**}
网络级 network level
网络计算机 network computer {NC}
网络加密 network encryption
网络监视 network monitoring
网络交换中心 network switching center {NSC}
网络接口层 network interface layer
网络接口卡 network interface card {NIC}
网络接入层 network access layer
网络节点处理器 network node processor
网络节点接口 network-node interface {NNI}
网络结构 plex structure
网络经济 network economy
网络控制层 network control layer
网络控制协议 network control protocol
网络控制语言 network control language {NCL}
网络控制中心 network control center {NCC}
网络狂热者 cyberholic
网络扩展设备[连接器] network extension unit {NEU}
网络老手 net head
网络类 network class
网络理论 network theory
网络连接 internetwork connection, network connect
网络领域 network domain
网络路由 network route
网络名 network name
网络模块 network module
网络模式 network schemer/schema
网络谋利者 netcropper
网络目录 network directory
网络配置 network configuration
网络驱动器[程序] network driver
网络驱动器[设备]接口规范 network driver interface specification {NDIS}
网络日志 network log
网络冗余(度) network redundancy
网络软件 network software
网络设备驱动器 network device driver
网络设施 network facility
网络识别 network awareness, grid recognition
网络识别符 network identifier
网络适配器[卡] network adapter
网络数据库 network database
网络数据模型 network data model
网络体系结构 network architecture
网络通信 internetwork communication
网络透明性 network transparency
网络图 network chart
网络拓扑 net(work) topology, topology of networks
网络网关记帐 network gateway accounting {NGA}
网络文件 network file
网络文件服务器[程序] network file server
网络文件系统 network file system {NFS}
网络线路 net line, network circuit
网络向外拨号 network out dialing

网络协议 network(ing) protocol
网络新闻 network news
网络新闻传输协议 network news transfer protocol {NNTP}
网络信息服务 network information service {NIS}
网络信息中心 network information center {NIC}
网络性能 network performance
网络虚拟终端机 network virtual terminal {NVT}
网络许可证 network license
网络延迟 network delay/slowdown
网络演示 network drill
网络业务接入点 network service access point {NSAP}
网络营销策略 net marketing strategy
网络拥挤[阻塞] network congestion
网络用户标识符 network user identifier {NUI}
网络用户地址 network user address {NUA}
网络邮政服务器 network mail server
网络语言 net speak
网络运行服务 netrun service
网络运行中心 network operating center {NOC}
网络诊断 network diagnosis
网络智能 network intelligence
网络资源 network resource
网络阻塞 network congestion
网膜 retina, web
网膜版 half-tone
网膜读出器 retina character reader {RCR}
网膜屏幕 half screen
网屏 half-tone screen
网桥 bridge
网桥[桥式]路由器 brouter
网上服务 online service
网上礼仪 netiquette
网上聊天 cyberchat
网上庞克族 cyberpunk
网上行销 cyber-selling
网上银行 internet banking
网头 nethead
网纹衬底 textured substrate
网页[主页] home/web page
网域 network domain
网元 network element {NE}
网元功能 network element function {NEF}
网站 web side
网址栏 web site entry
网状结构 lattice-like structure, net/reticular structure
网状模型 network model
网状[网络]数据库 network database
网状数据模型 network data model
网状网络 mesh network
网状物 reticulation, web

往 另见【wǎng】
1)(到,去)go 2)(向某处去) in the direction of, towards 3)(过去的)former, past, previous 往常 habitually in the past 往返(来回) go there and back 往复 move back and forth, reciprocate 往来 ①(来去) come and go ②(交际) contact, dealings 往事 past events, the past 往往 often, frequently
往复寻道 accordion seek

【wàng】
忘 (忽略)overlook, neglect
忘记 overlook, neglect, forget

往 另见{wǎng}
to, toward 往后 from now on, later on, in the future

旺
旺季 peak period, rush season 旺盛 vigorous

望
1)(向远处看)gaze into the distance, look over, look far ahead 2)(探望)call on, visit 3)(希望)hope, expect, look forward to, anticipate 望远镜 telescope

【wēi】

危
危害 harm, endanger, jeopardize 危机 crisis 危及 endanger, imperil 危急 critical, crucial 危险 ① dangerous, perilous ② danger, peril
危险竞争 critical race

威
威风 ①〈名〉dignity, majesty, power and prestige ②〈形〉imposing, impressive 威力 power, might, force 威望 prestige, repute 威胁 threaten, menace 威信 prestige, credit, reputation

微
(衰落)decline 微薄 meager, scanty 微观 microcosmic 微妙 delicate, subtle 微弱 faint, feeble, weak 微小 little, minute, small, tiny 微笑 smile 微型 miniature
微 (单位前缀) micro- (=10^{-6})
微比特 micro bit
微编码 microcoding
微波传输 microwave transmission
微波通信 microwave communication
微操作 microoperation
微程序 microprogram
微程序编制器 microprogrammer
微程序部件 microprogram unit
微程序存储器 microprogram memory
微程序地址寄存器 microprogram address register
微程序调试 microprogram debugging
微程序仿真 microprogram emulation
微程序缓存 microcache
微程序级 microprogram level
微程序结构 microprogram structure
微程序控制 microprogram(med) control
微程序控制逻辑 micrologic
微程序控制器 microprogram control unit {MCU}
微程序模块 micromodule
微程序软件 microprogram software
微程序设计 microcoding, microprogramming
微程序实现 microprogram implementation
微程序体系结构 microprogram architecture
微程序只读存储器 microm
微程序中断 microprogram interrupt
微处理机 microprocessing unit, microprocessor
微处理机板 microprocessor board
微处理机插件卡 microprocessor card
微处理机仿真 microprocessor emulation

微处理机检测 microprocessor testing
微处理机开发系统 microprocessor development system {MDS}
微处理机通信 microprocessor communication
微处理机系统 microprocessor system {MPS}
微处理机阵列 microprocessor array
微处理机智能 microprocessor intelligence
微处理机终端 microprocessor terminal
微处理机装置 microprocessor unit {MPU}
微处理器 microprocessor, microprocessor unit {MPU}
微处理器芯片 microprocessor chip, microprocessor slice, processor chips
微存储器 micro memory, microstorage
微存储器字 micro memory word
微代码 microcode
微单元 microcell
微地址 micro address
微电路 microcircuit
微电脑 microcomputer
微电子电路 microelectronic circuit
微电子技术 microelectronic technique, microelectronics
微电子学 microelectronics
微电子组件 micromodule
微电子组装 microelectronic packaging
微调 fine tuning, matching
微调控制 fine control
微动[微调]开关 inching switch
微冻结 microfreeze
微分的 differential

微分电路 differentiator
微分法 differential approach, differentiation
微分方程式 differential equation
微分分析器 differential analyzer
微分模时延 differential mode delay {DMD}
微分器 differentiator
微分算符[算子] differential operator
微分学 differential calculus
微封装 micropackage
微伏(特) microvolt
微观的 microscopic
微光 glimmer
微(型计算)机 microcomputer
微机测试 microcomputer testing
微机插件箱 microcomputer card cage
微机成套件 micro(computer) kit
微机程序库 microcomputer program library
微机底板 microcomputer backplane
微机点 micropoint
微机辅助测试 microcomputer aided testing
微机接口 microcomputer interfacing
微机接口套件 micro(computer) kit, microcomputer interfacing kit
微机开发系统 microcomputer development system {MDS}
微机控制 microcomputer control
微机扩展卡 PC card
微机模件 microcomputer module
微机软件 microcomputer

software
微机套件 micro(computer) kit
微机系列 microcomputer family
微机系统 microcomputer system
微机芯片 microcomputer chip
微机应用 microcomputer application
微机终端 microcomputer terminal
微积分(学) calculus, differential and integral calculus
微寄存器 micro register
微件 microware
微结构 microarchitecture, microstructure
微控制器仿真器 microcontroller simulator
微控制台 microconsole
微例(行)程(序) microroutine
微逻辑 micrologic
微码 microcode
微米 micron (μm)
微秒 microsecond
微命令 microcommand, microorder
微内核 microkernel
微软件 microsoftware
微软视窗 microsoft windows
微软视窗新技术 microsoft windows new technology {MWNT}
微体系结构 microarchitecture
微通道结构 micro channel architecture {MCA}
微位 micro bit
微芯片 microchip
微型[小型]磁盘 minidisk
微型存储器 micro memory
微型电池 microcell
微型工作站 microstation
微型盒带 microcassette
微型机 micro-machine
微型机器人 microrobotics

微型驱动器 microdrive
微型软盘 compact floopy disk {CFD}, microfloppy (disk)
微型鼠标器 micromouse
微型体系结构 microarchitecture
微型网(络) micronet
微型温盘 micro Winchester
微型显示屏 microscreen
微型芯片 microchip
微型语声器 microspeech
微型诊断 micro terminal
微型主机 micromainframe
微型组件 micromodule
微影像 microimage
微(型)邮件 micromail
微语言 microlanguage
微诊断 microdiagnosis, microdiagnostics
微诊断的 microdiagnostic
微指令 microcode, micros, microinstruction, microorder
微指令操作 microinstruction operation
微指令格式 microinstruction format
微指令寄存器 microinstruction register
微指令宽度 microcode/microinstruction width
微指令模拟 microinstruction simulation
微指令周期 microinstruction cycle
微指令字 microinstruction word
微中断 microinterrupt
微周期 microcycle
微字 micro word
微字模 microfont
微总线 microbus

【wéi】

为 另见【wèi】
1)(做)do, act 2)(作为)act as, serve as 3)(成为)be-

come 为首 with sb as the leader, headed by, led by 为限 be within the limit of, not exceed, be good for ... only 为止 up to, till 为主 give first place to, give priority to

违 违背 violate, go against, run counter to 违法 break the law, be illegal 违反 violate, run counter to, breach 违禁 violate a ban 违禁品 contraband (goods) 违约 ① (违反约定) break a contract, violate a treaty ② (失约) break one's promise, break off an engagement 违章 break rules and regulations

围 1) (环绕) enclose, surround 2) (四周) all round, around 围绕 ① (绕…转动) revolve round ② (以…为中心) center on
围栏 rail

唯 only, alone 唯恐 for fear that, lest 唯一 only, sole, unique
唯一解 unique solution
唯一索引 unique index
唯一性 uniqueness

维 维持 keep, maintain, safeguard, preserve 维护 safeguard, defend, uphold 维(数)〈数学〉dimension ◇三维空间 three-dimensional space 维修 keep in (good) repair, service, maintain 维持时间 standby time
维护 attention {ATTN}, maintenance, service working
维护成本 maintenance cost
维护程序 maintenance program/routine
维护处理 maintenance process
维护费用 maintenance cost
维护分析程序[过程] maintenance analysis procedure {MAP}
维护工程分析 maintenance engineering analysis {MEA}
维护记录 service log
维护阶段 maintenance phase
维护空间 service clearance
维护控制部件 maintenance control unit {MCU}
维护(控制)面板 service panel
维护屏幕 maintenance screen
维护设计 maintenance design
维护时间 service hours, servicing time
维护[维修]手册 service book
维护系统 servicing system
维护指令 maintenance instruction
维数 dimension, number of dimension, dimensionality
维数界限 dimension bound
维说明 dimension specification
维修时间 maintenance time

【wěi】

伪 1) (虚假的) false, fake, forged 2) (不合法的) puppet, unlawful, illegal 伪造 forge, falsify, fabricate, counterfeit
伪 pseudo-
伪编码 pseudo-coding
伪变量 pseudo-variable
伪标量 pseudo-scalar
伪表 dummy list
伪彩色 pseudo-color
伪操作 **pseudo-** operation (=pseudo-op)

伪程序 dummy, pseudo-program
伪处理机 pseudo-host
伪传递性 pseudotransitivity
伪传送 dummy transfer
伪串 dummy string
伪代码 pseudo-code, p-code, false code
伪单调函数 pseudo-monotone function
伪单元 dummy unit
伪地址 dummy address, pseudo-address
伪定时器 pseudo timer
伪对策 pseudo-game
伪符号 pseudo symbol
伪光标 pseudocursor
伪会话 pseudo conversational
伪机器 pseudomachine
伪计时器 pseudo timer
伪记录 dummy record
伪结构 pseudo-structure
伪命令 pseudo command
伪目标 false target
伪穷举测试 pseudo-exhaustive testing
伪设备 pseudo-device
伪时钟 pseudo-clock
伪输入 dummy input
伪数组 pseudo-array
伪随机 pseudo-random
伪随机序列 pseudorandom sequence
伪同步 pseudo-clock
伪图 pseudograph
伪脱机作业 spool job
伪线性 pseudolinear
伪向量 pseudo-vector
伪校验 dummy check
伪语言 pseudolanguage, quasi-language
伪指令 dummy instruction, pseudo command, pseudo/quasi-instruction
伪终端输入 dummy terminal input
伪装入 dummy load
伪装置 pseudo-device
伪字 dummy word

伟 big, great 伟业 great cause, exploit

尾 1)(尾巴)tail 2)(末端)end 3)(未了结的事物)remaining part, remnant
尾随 ①(跟在后面)tail behind, tag along after ②(跟踪)tail
尾部 postlude, trail(er), trailing end
尾部符号 tail symbol
尾部记录 trailer record
尾部字段 trailer field
尾端 trailing end
尾卡 trailer card
尾数 mantissa
尾文件 epifile
尾帧 tail frame

纬 纬度 latitude 纬线 weft

委 委派 appoint, delegate, designate 委托 entrust, appoint 委任 appoint 委员 committee member, member of a committe 委员会 committee, commission, council
委托(代理权)代理 proxy agent
委托(代理权)关系 proxy relationship
委托窗口 client window
委托代理 proxy agent
委托方 clients
委托接口 client interface
委托进程 client process
委托模型 client model
委托事件 commit event

【wèi】

卫 defend, guard, protect 卫生 hygiene, health, sanitation 卫生间 toilet 卫星 satellite, moon
卫星处理机 satellite processor
卫星导航 satellite navigation
卫星跟踪 satellite tracking
卫星机 subhost
卫星接收机 satellite receiver
卫星链路 satellite link, uplink
卫星频带[波段] satellite band
卫星数据 satellite data
卫星通信 satellite communication {SATCOM}
卫星通信线路 satellite line
卫星网络 satellite network
卫星邮政 intepost
卫星站 satellite station
卫星终端 satellite terminal
卫星作图系统 satellite graphics system

为 另见【wéi】
1)(给,替)for, for the benefit of 2)(因为)because, for, on account of 为此 to this end, for this reason, for this purpose 为了 for, for the sake of, in order to 为何 why, for what reason 为什么 why

未 1)(没)have not, did not, not yet 2)(不)not, no 未必 may not, not necessarily 未定 uncertain, undecided, undefined 未付 outstanding, unpaid 未婚 unmarried, single 未来 ①〈形〉coming, approaching, future ②〈名〉future, tomorrow 免 rather, a bit too, truly 未完 unfinished 未完待续 to be continued 未详 unknown
未保护 unprotect
未饱和树 unsaturated tree
未定义 undefinition
未对齐 unjustified
未发现错误 no defect found {NDF}
未分块文件 unblocked file
未分配 unallocate
未感染程序 uninfected program
未格式化[无格式]软盘 unformatted diskette
未接通的呼叫 lost call
未就绪状态 not-ready state
未来事件 future event
未确认数据 outstanding data
未收到字符 negative acknowledge character {NAK}
未印出 print miss
未用号码 unassigned number
未占用[空]段 empty segment
未知参数 unknown parameter
未知站 unknown station
未装配设备 unpacked device

位 1)(地点)place, location, site 2)(职位)position 3)〈数学〉figure ◇三位数 three figure number 位于 to be located, be situated, lie 位置 ①(所在地方)seat, place, site, location ②(地位)place, position
位 binary digit {bit}
位比较 bit comparison
位编码 bit encoding
位标 indexer
位/秒 bits per second {BPS}
位/英寸 bits per inch {BPI}
位并行 bit parallel
位操作 bit operation/grinding/manipulation
位测试 bit test
位常数 bit constant

位串 bit string
位串算符[算子] bit string operator
位串行 bit serial
位存储 bit storage
位存储桶 bit bucket
位错阵列 dislocation array
位带 bit strip
位单元 bit cell, bit location, bit position
位道 bit track
位地址 bit address
位点 bit point
位读出线 sense digit line
位符 bit symbol
位符号 bit sign
位号 bit number
位寄存器 bit register
位间距 column pitch
位检测器 bit detector
位结构 bit architecture/configuration/structure
位矩阵 bit matrix
位开关 bit switch
位控制块 bit control block {BCB}
位块传送 blit
位块传送器 blitter
位宽 bit wide
位垒 potential barrier
位流 bit stream
位脉冲 digit pulse
位密度 bit density
位面 bit plane
位/秒 bits per second (=bits/second) {bps}
位模式 bit pattern
位偶 bit pair
位片 bit slice
位片处理器 bit-slice processor
位片式存储器 bit slice memory
位片式微处理机 bit slice microprocessor
位片系列 bit slice family

位片系统 bit slice system
位片系统[方式] bit-slicing system
位屏蔽 bit mask
位驱动 bit drive
位时间 bit time
位时钟 bit clocking
位试验 bit test
位数 bit number, number of bits
位速率 bit rate
位填充 bit stuffing
位同步 bit synchronization
位桶 bit bucket
位图 bit map
位图文件 bitmap file
位图文件头 bitmap file header
位图像 bit image
位图资源 bitmap resource
位置 bit location, bit site
位向量 bit vector
位校验 bit check
位序列 bit sequence
位寻址 bit addressing
位移 bit shift, offset, offsetting
位移变量 offset variable
位移[偏移]地址 offset address
位移方式 displacement mode
位移分支 offset branching
位移角 displacement angle
位移量 displacement
位移算子 displacement operator
位移映像 displacement map
位溢[溢出]寄存器 overflow register
位影像图 bitmapped graphic
位/英寸 bits per inch {bpi}
位映像 bit map, bit map image, bit mapping
位映像图 bit map graphic
位拥挤 bit crowding
位域 bit field

位元 switch cell
位指令 bit instruction
位指针 bit pointer
位置检测器 position detector
位置变量 locator variable
位置控制块 station control block {SCB}
位置名 location name
位置偏差信号 position error signal {PES}
位置迁移网[变迁网] place/ transition net
位置向量 position vector
位置值 position value
位置指针 position pointer
位周期 bit period
位状态 bit status
位字 bit word
位字段 bit field
位总线 bit bus

胃 stomach

喂 (招呼)hello, hey 喂养 feed, raise

谓 (所谓)so-called
谓词 predicate
谓词公式 predicate formula
谓词逻辑 predicate logic
谓词演算 predicate calculus

【wēn】

温 1)(不冷不热)warm, lukewarm 2)(加温)warm up, heat up 温带 temperate zone 温度 temperature 温度表[计]thermometer ◇华氏温度表 Fahrenheit thermometer // 摄氏温度表 centigrade thermometer, Celsius thermometer 温和 ①(天气)temperate, mild, moderate ②(态度)gentle, mild ③(温度适中)lukewarm, warm 温暖 ①〈形〉warm ②〈名〉warmth, kindness 温习 review, revise
温度控制系统 temperature control system
温(切斯特)盘 Winchester disk
温切斯特技术 Winchester technique/technology

【wén】

文 (语言)language 文稿 manuscript, draft 文告 proclamation, statement, notice 文化 ①(精神)civilization, culture ②(知识)education, culture, literacy 文集 collected works, anthology 文件 ①(公文)(official) documents, papers ②(计算机的) file 文具 stationery 文科 liberal arts, the humanities 文明 〈名〉civilization, culture ②〈形〉civilized 文凭 diploma 文体 ①(体裁)type of writing, literary form, style ②(文娱体育) recreation and sports 文献 document, literature 文选 selected works, literary selections 文摘 abstract, digest, extract 文章 ①(短篇论著) essay, article ②(著作) literary works, writings 文字 characters, script, writing, literal
文本 text
文本编辑 text editing, text editor, TextEdit, textual edit
文本处理 text processing
文本窗口 text window
文本端口 textport
文本段落 fragment of text
文本方式 text mode

文本格式化程序 text formatter
文本管理 text management
文本滚卷 text wrap
文本缓冲器 text buffer
文本检索 text retrieval
文本结构 text structure
文本结束符 end-of-text {ETX}, end-of-text character {ETX character}
文本开始符 start of text {STX}, start-of-text character {STX}
文本控制(字段) text control
文本库 text library
文本框 text box
文本模式 text pattern
文本识别 text recognition
文本视图 text view
文本输入 text input
文本属性 text attribute
文本数据 text data
文本数据库 text database
文本锁 text lock
文本文档 text document
文本文件 text file
文本行 text line
文本压缩 text compression
文本帧 text frame
文本字体 text font
文档 document, documentary
文档标记[志] document mark
文档处理 document handling, document processing
文档窗口 document window
文档存储体 document bank
文档对准 document alignment
文档格式 document format
文档合并 document merge
文档汇编 document assembly
文档汇总 documentation book
文档机 document machine
文档级 document(ation) level
文档[文献,资料]检索 document retrieval

文档卡片 document card
文档库 document library
文档类 document class
文档内容结构 document content architecture {DCA}
文档区 document area
文档索引 document index(ing)
文档文件 document file
文档信息管理 documentation information management {DIM}
文法 grammar, syntax
文法分类 grammar class
文法分析 grammatical analysis
文法规则 grammar rule, grammatical rule
文化帝国主义 cultural imperialism
文件 file
文件安全 file safety
文件安全性 file security
文件保护 file protect(ion)
文件保护方式 file protect mode {FPM}
文件保护环 file protect(ion) ring
文件爆炸[碎裂] file fragmentation
文件备份 file backup
文件编辑 file edit
文件标号 file label
文件标记 file mark
文件标题 file header/title
文件标准 file standard
文件表达式 file expression
文件布局 file layout/placement
文件操作 file manipulation, file operation
文件插入 file insertion
文件查找服务 archie
文件长度 file length
文件成分 file component
文件尺寸 file size
文件重构 file restructure

文件处理 file handling, file manipulation, file processing
文件处理[归档, 编排] fil(l)ing
文件处理机 file processor
文件传输 file transfer
文件传输协议 file transfer protocol {FIP}
文件传送 file transfer
文件传送支持 file transfer support {FTS}
文件存储器 file memory/storage
文件存储桶 file bucket
文件存取 file access
文件打印 file print
文件大小 file size
文件定义 file definition
文件对象 file object
文件对象模型 document object model {DOM}
文件分割 file splitting
文件分隔符 file separator (character) {FS}
文件分配 file allocation
文件分配表 file allocation table {FAT}
文件服务器 file server
文件副本 file copy
文件格式 file format/layout
文件更新 file maintenance, file update/updating
文件共享 file sharing
文件关闭 file closing
文件管理 document management
文件管理程序[管理器] file manager
文件管理系统 file management system {FMS}
文件规范说明书 file specification
文件号 file number
文件合并 file merge
文件缓冲 file buffering

文件恢复 file recovery
文件活动 file activity
文件集 cartulary, file set
文件夹 file binder, folder, portfolio
文件加密 file encryption
文件间隔 file gap
文件检索 file search
文件检验 file check
文件建立 file creation
文件交换 file swapping
文件节 file section
文件结构 file structure
文件结束标志 end-of-file mark {EOF}
文件卷 file reel, file volume
文件卡 file card
文件开始 beginning-of-file {BOF}
文件空间 file space
文件空间分配 file space allocation
文件空间管理 file space management
文件空间目录 file space catalog
文件控制 file control
文件控制表 file control table {FCT}
文件控制段 file control paragraph
文件控制块 file control block {FCB}
文件控制模式 file control mode
文件控制区 file control area {FCA}
文件控制项 file control entry
文件库 files library
文件馈送 file feed
文件类型 file type
文件流 file stream
文件轮廓文件 file profile
文件媒体 file medium
文件描述 file description
文件名 file name

文件名字表 file name table
文件目录 file catalog(ue), file directory
文件排序 file ordering, file sort
文件清理 file clean-up
文件区 file area
文件扫描 file scan
文件属性 file attribute
文件树 file tree
文件说明 file description
文件索引 file/citation index
文件锁定 file lock, file lockout
文件特征 file characteristic
文件头 file header, top of file {TOF}
文件维护 file maintenance
文件位置 file position
文件系统 file system
文件系统控制块 file system control block {FSCB}
文件向后恢复 backward file recovery
文件向前恢复 forward file recovery
文件修改 file update
文件选择框 file selection box
文件压缩 file compression
文件验证 file verification
文件引用 file include/reference
文件映像 file map
文件拥有者 file owner, owner
文件争用 file contention
文件整理 file clean-up, file consolidation, file tidying
文件指针 file pointer
文件种类 file class
文件转储 file dump
文件转换 file conversion, file translation
文件状态表 file status table {FST}
文件组 file group, file set
文卷结束 end of volume {EOV}
文首(字)符 start-of-text (character) {STX}
文图 boilerplate
文献管理 documentation management
文献检索 documentation retrieval, literature search
文献结构 document structure
文献聚类 document clustering
文献类目 document category
文献目录 bibliography, document directory
文献数据库 document database
文终(字)符 end-of-text (character) {ETX}
文字表 literal table
文字表达式 literal expression
文字参数 text parameter
文字常数 literals
文字池[库] literal pool
文字处理 word processing {WP}
文字串 literal string, text string
文字电视 telescan
文字描述符 letter descriptor
文字型数据 literal data
文字原子 literal atom
文字指令 literal order
文字字段 literal field

纹 纹理 veins, grain, texture
纹理编码 texture coding
纹理分析 texture analysis
纹理合成 texture synthesis
纹理模式 texture pattern
纹理模型 texture model
纹理识别 texture recognition
纹理图像 texture image
纹理像素 texel (=texture elements)
纹理映像 texture mapping

闻 1)(听见) hear 2)(听到的消息) news, story ◇要闻

important news 3)（嗅）smell
闻名 well-known, famous, renowned

【wěn】

吻 吻合 be identical, match, coincide

紊 紊乱 disorder, chaos, confusion

稳 稳当 steady, firm, reliable, secure, safe 稳定 ①〈形〉stable, steady, equable, safe ②〈动〉stabilize, steady ③〈名〉equability, stabilization 稳固 firm, stable 稳妥 sure, certain, safe, reliable
稳定策略 stable strategy
稳定解 stable solution
稳定器 stabilizer
稳定区 stable zone
稳定系统 stabilization system, stable system
稳定性 stability, stationarity
稳定性理论 stability theory
稳定装置 detent
稳定状态 stable/steady state
稳流器 current regulator, current stabilizer
稳态 stable, stationary
稳态分析 steady-state analysis
稳态过程 steady-state process
稳态控制 stable control
稳态险态 steady-state hazard
稳压电路 voltage regulator
稳压电源 stabilized voltage supply
稳压[齐纳]二极管 Zener diode
稳压器 voltage regulator

【wèn】

问 1)（询问）ask, inquire 2)（讯问）interrogate, examine 问好，问候 say hello to, ask after, enquire after 问号 ①（标点符号）question mark, interrogation mark (?) ②（疑问）unknown factor, unsolved problem 问世 be published, come out, be presented to the public 问题 ①（待回答的）question, problem ②（待研究解决的）problem, matter ③（事故或意外）trouble, mishap, accident ④（关键处）the point, the crux of a problem 问讯 enquire, ask 问讯处 enquiry office, information desk
问答机 interrogation responsor, interrogator-transponder
问候屏幕 hello screen
问题定义 problem definition
问题范围 problem scope
问题分解 problem decomposition
问题归约 problem reduction
问题空间 problem space
问题类 problem class
问题描述 problem description
问题判定 problem determination
问题求解 problem solving
问题特征 problem characteristic
问题诊断 problem diagnosis
问题状态 problem state

【wō】

涡 涡流 eddy
涡流卡片存储器 eddy card memory
涡式通信访问法 vortex telecommunication access method

【wǒ】

我 I 我们 we

【wò】

卧 1)(躺下)lie 2)(动物趴)crouch, sit 卧室 bedroom
卧式箱体 low boy cabinet

握 hold, grasp 握手 shake hands, clasp hands
握手(方式) handshaking, handshake
握手协议 handshaking protocol

【wū】

污 (玷污)stain, sully, smear 污点 stain, spot 污垢 dirt, filth 污染 pollute, contaminate ◇环境污染 environmental pollution // 噪声污染 noise pollution 污秽 dirty, filthy, foul

钨 tungsten, wolfram (W)

屋 1)(房子)house 2)(房间)room

【wú】

无 1)(没有)nothing, nil; not have; without 2)(不)not 3)(不论)regardless of, no matter whether, what, etc. 无比 incomparable, unparalleled, matchless 无补 of no help, of no avail 无不 all without exception, invariably 无偿 free, gratuitous 无法 unable, incapable 无非 nothing but, no more than, simply, only 无故 without cause or reason 无关 have nothing to do with, be unrelated 无害 harmless, do no harm to 无理 unreasonable, unjustifiable, irrational 无论 no matter what/ how etc., regardless of 无论如何 in any case, at any rate, at all events 无名 ①(无名称)nameless ②(不为人知)unknown ③(说不出道理的)inexplicable, indescribable 无能 incompetent, unskil(l)ful 无穷 infinite, endless, inexhaustible 无人 ①(驾驶)unmaned ②(居住)depopulated 无视 ignore, disregard, defy 无数 ①(难以计算)innumerable, countless, incalculable ②(吃不准)be uncertain 无双 unparalleled, unrivaled, matchless 无条件 unconditional, without preconditions 无畏 fearless, dauntless, courageous 无限 infinite, boundless, unlimitless, endless 无限期 indefinite duration 无效 of no avail, invalid, null and void 无形 invisible 无须 need not, not have to 无疑 doubtless, beyond doubt, undoubtedly 无异 not different from, the same as 无益 unprofitable, useless no good 无意 ①(不愿)have no intention (of doing sth) ②(偶然)accidentally 无用 useless, of no use 无噪声 noiseless, silent 无知 ignorant 无止境 have no limits, know no end

无 nil, null {NUL}
无保护 unprotect
无报警 alarm free
无比的 almighty
无比例型 ratioless type
无笔绘图仪 penless plotter

wú 无

无边 sideless
无编码 codeless
无变化 no change {NC}
无变量的 non-variant
无标号的 nonlabeled
无标题的 untitled
无操作(指令) no-operation {NOP, no-OP, no-op, nop}
无层网络 layerless network
无差错 error-free
无差异类 indifference class
无程序语言 programless language
无冲突 conflict-free
无窗算法 windowless algorithm
无磁盘工作站 diskless workstation
无磁盘系统 diskless system
无磁盘簇 diskless cluster
无错操作 error-free operation
无错的 trouble-free
无(磁)带控制 tapeless control
无代码 codeless
无登记 no logging
无地址指令 addressless instruction, no-address instruction
无反馈网络 feedback free network
无缝的 seamless
无符号移位 unsigned shift
无符号整数 signless integer, unsigned integer
无干扰的 aliasing free, noiseless
无感应的 inductionless
无格式 nonformat
无格式记录 unformatted record
无格式输入 formatless input
无格式数据 unformatted data
无格式图像 unformatted image
无根树 unrooted tree
无故障 fault-free, no defect found {NDF}

无关变量 irrelevant variable
无关的 independent
无关非门 negative ignore gate
无关条件 don't-care condition
无关性 independence
无关状态 don't-care state, extraneous state
无管脚芯片载体 leadless chip carrier {LCC}
无光栅 grating null
无环路的 loop-free
无回路的 loop-free
无记忆的 memoryless
无记忆系统 memoryless system
无监督学习 unsupervised learning
无间隙 gapless
无结果的 resultless
无进位 no-carry
无孔插件板 plain module board
无控制的 uncontrolled
无栏 column free
无理的 irrational
无理函数 irrational function
无理数 irrational number
无连接 connectionless
无连接服务 connectionless service
无连接通信 connectionless communication
无连接网络服务 connectionless network service {CLNS}
无连接网络协议 connectionless network protocol {CLNP}
无连接业务 connectionless service
无零数 roundness
无冒险的 hazardless
无冒险电路 hazard-free circuit
无媒体 medialess
无名管道 anonymous pipe, unnamed pipe
无名文件传输协议 anonymous

无 file transfer protocol {FTP}
无墨的 inkless
无目录 directoryless
无偏 without bias
无偏测试 unbiased test
无屏蔽 exposure, unmask
无屏蔽双绞线 unshielded twisted pair {UTP}
无屏蔽双扭线 unshielded twisted pair
无歧义图灵机 unambiguous Turing machine {UTM}
无歧义文法 unambiguous grammar
无歧义性 unambiguity
无穷大 infinitely great
无穷环 infinite loop
无穷集 infinite set
无穷级数 infinite series
无穷树 infinite tree
无穷小 infinitely small, infinitesimal
无穷语言 infinite language
无圈图 acyclic graph
无人工厂 unmanned factory
无冗余电路 nonredundent circuit
无冗余覆盖 irredundant cover
无色的 colo(u)rless
无扇出电路 fanout-free circuit
无(噪)声打字机 noiseless typewriter
无声印刷[打印]机 silent printer
无时间延迟 non-time delay
无时性 achrony
无顺序 out-of-order
无死锁的 deadlock-free
无损的 non-derogatory
无损读出元件 nondestructive read element
无损耗网络 lossless network
无损检测 nondestruction testing
无锁定方式 lock free system

无条件的 categorical, discretional, unconditional
无条件跳转 unconditional jump
无条件选择 unconditional selection
无通道 channel free
无下标变量 unsubscripted variable
无限性 infinity
无限规划 infinite program, infinite programming
无限集 infinite set
无限图 infinite graph
无限序列 infinite sequence
无限循环 endless loop, infinite loop
无限制语言 unrestricted language
无线的 wireless, cordless
无线电 radio
无线电电传 radio teletype {RTTY}
无线电电话 radio telephony
无线电控制 radio control
无线电链路 radio link
无线电频带 radio-frequency band
无线电频率 radio frequency {RF}
无线电设备 radio set
无线光笔 wireless light pen
无线局域网 wireless local area network {WLAN}
无线数据传输链路 wireless data link {WDL}
无线通信 wireless communication
无线网络 wireless network
无线终端 wireless terminal
无响应 no response
无向边 undirected edge
无向图 indirected/non-oriented/undirected graph
无效 unavailability

无效存取块 invalid access block	无应答 no response
无效存取区 invalid access area	无用部分 nonuseable part
无效的 effectless, illegal, inert, invalid	无用单元区 garbage area
无效地址 invalid address	无用的 extinct, void, idle
无效电平 inactive level	无用输出 garbage-out
无效呼叫 lost call	无用输入 garbage-in
无效键 invalid key	无用输入无用输出 garbage-in garbage-out {GIGO}
无效码 invalid code	无用数据 gibberish, hash data, ignore data
无效命令 invalid command	无用数据[信号] junk
无效请求 invalid request	无用信息 gibberish, hash information
无效数据 dirty/invalid data	无源电路 passive circuit
无效数位 insignificant digit, invalid digit	无源端头 passive headend
无效锁 invalidate lock	无源设备 passive device
无效下标 invalid index	无源网关 passive gateway
无效行数 invalid line number	无源元件 passive element
无效页 dead page	无源站 passive station
无效页面 invalid page	无约束变量 unrestricted variable, variable free
无效引用 no-valid reference	无约束任务集 unbound task set {UTS}
无效用 disutility	无载波调幅调相 carrierless amplitude phase {CAP}
无效作用 invalidate	无载的 empty
无信号区 dead space	无噪声的 noiseless
无信号状态 nonsignaled state	无终止的 open-ended
无性传输 neutral transmission	无状态协议 stateless protocol
无休止的 nonstop	无阻塞 nonblocking
无序 disorder, out-of-order	
无序表 unordered table	
无序链 nonsequenced chain	
无序模型 chaos model	【wǔ】
无序神经网络 chaos neural network	午 noon, midday 午饭 lunch 午后 afternoon, p.m. 午前 forenoon, before noon, morning, a.m. 午夜 midnight
无序神经元模型 chaos neuron model	
无页码 without foliation/pagination	
无意泄密 inadvertent disclosure	五 five 五金(the five) metals, hardware 五年计划 five-year plan 五月 May
无意义 nonsense	五单元码 five-unit code
无因果关系 causal independence	五-二码 quibinary code
无引脚芯片 leaderless chip carrier {LCC}	五子棋 five-in-a-row

武 (军事) military 武断 arbitrary decision, judge subjectively 武力 force, fight

舞 (跳舞) dance 舞弊 irregularities, fraudulent practices 舞动 brandish, wave 舞台 stage, arena

【wù】

务 1)(事务) affair, business 2)(从事) be engaged in 务必 must, be sure to

恶 另见【è】 dislike, hate

物 thing, matter, object 物产 products, produce 物价 (commodity) prices 物理 physics 物力 material resources 物品 article, goods 物体 body, substance, object 物质 matter, substance, material 物资 goods, materials, commodities
物理报文[信息] physical message
物理部件 physical unit {PU}
物理层 physical layer {PHY}
物理存储器 physical storage
物理(学)的 physical
物理登录[记录,录入] physical logging
物理结构 physical structure
物理介质 physical medium
物理卷 physical volume
物理连接 physical connection
物理链路 physical link
物理模块 physical module
物理模拟 physical analog, physical simulation
物理模型 physical model
物理设备 physical device, physical unit {PU}
物理映像 physical image/map
物体 object

误 1)(错误) mistake, error, fault 2)(耽误) miss, fail to seize the right moment 3)(使受害) harm 4)(不是故意) by mistake, by accident 误差 error 误解 ①〈动〉misread, misunderstand, mistake ②〈名〉misunderstanding
误操作 misoperation
误差 error {ERR}
误差比 error ratio
误差传播 error propagation
误差范围 error range
误差分析 error analysis
误差估计 error estimate
误差函数 error function
误差检测 error detecting
误差控制 error control
误差系数 error coefficient
误差系统 error system
误差校正 error correction
误打印 misprint
误导 mislead
误动作 malfunction
误读 misread
误检 false drop/retrieve
误馈送 misfeed
误码率 bit error rate {BER}, error rate
误码字 error code word
误组(块)率 block error rate {BER}

雾 fog, mist

X x

【xī】

西 (方向)west 西班牙 Spain 西班牙语 Spanish (language) 西半球 the Western Hemisphere 西北 northwest 西餐 Western-style food 西方(方向)the west, westward 西方国家 the Western countries 西服 Western-style clothes 西文草体 cursive

吸 吸入(体内)inhale, breathe in, draw 吸收 absorb, suck up 吸烟 smoke 吸引 attract, draw, appeal to
吸墨性 absorbency
吸墨纸 blotter
吸收 absorb, absorption, assimilate, incorporate, incorporation, sink
吸收电流 sink current
吸收集 absorbing set
吸收律 absorption law, law of absorption
吸收率 absorptivity
吸收器 absorber
吸收作用 absorption

希 希罕 rare, scarce, uncommon 希腊 Greece 希腊人 Greek 希奇 rare, strange, queer 希望 hope, wish, expect

矽 silicon (Si)

析 1)(分散)divide, separate 2)(分析)analyse, resolve, dissect
析取 disjunction, extract, extraction, unpack
析取范式 disjunction/disjunctive normal form, normal disjunctive form
析取概念 disjunctive concept
析取搜索 disjunctive search
析取字 extractor
析像管 image dissector
析像器 dissector, image sensor

牺 牺牲 ①(舍弃生命)sacrifice one's life ②(放弃利益)sacrifice, give up, do sth at the expense of

硒 selenium (Se)

悉 1)(全,尽)all, entirely 2)(知道)know, learn, be aware of 悉数 ①(列举)enumerate in full detail ②(全部)all, every single one

稀 稀少 rare, scarce, uncommon, rarefaction 稀疏 sparse, scattered, thin 稀薄 (含水多)watery, thin
稀薄空间 thin space

稀疏集 sparse set
稀疏向量 sparse vector
稀疏阵列[数组] sparse array

锡 tin (Sn)

熄 熄灭 extinguish, put out, go out, die out

膝 knee
膝上型的 laptop

【xí】

习 1)(练习) practice, exercise, review 2)(熟习) get accustomed to, be used to 习惯 ①〈动〉be accustomed to, be used to, be familiar with ②〈名〉habit, custom 习俗 custom, convention 习题 exercises (in school work)
习惯的 conventional

席 席卷 sweep across engulf

袭 袭用 take over

【xǐ】

喜 (快乐) happy, delighted, pleased 喜欢 feel happy, become delighted 喜爱 like, love, be fond of, be keen on 喜事 happy event (esp. wedding), occasion for celebration

【xì】

戏 1)(游戏) play, show 2)(开玩笑) make fun of, joke
戏剧 drama, play, theater
戏院 theater

系 另见 {jì}
1)(高校院系) department (in a college), faculty 2)(栓,绑) tie, fasten 系列 series, set, family 系统 system, series 系统工程 systems engineering
系列插件板 family board
系列处理机 family processor
系列化 seriation
系列计算机 family computer
系列器件 family device
系列芯片 family chip
系内噪声 inner noise
系数 coefficient, factor, modulus
系数矩阵 coefficient matrix
系统安全性 system security
系统安全有效度 system safety effectiveness {SSE}
系统安装 system install
系统板 system board
系统(软件)包 system package {SP}
系统保护 system protection
系统饱和 system saturation
系统报文 system message
系统崩溃 system crash
系统变量 system variable
系统变量表 system variable table {SVT}
系统标准 system standard
系统部件 system unit
系统菜单 system menu
系统参数表 system parameter table {SPT}
系统参数记录 system parameter record {SPR}
系统操作 system operation
系统测试 system testing
系统层次结构 system hierarchy
系统(程序)产品 system product {SP}
系统常驻 system residence {SYSRES}
系统程序 system program {SP}
系统程序控制器 system

program controller {SPC}
系统程序库 component library, system library
系统程序员 system programmer
系统池 system pool
系统抽样[采样] systematic sampling
系统处理器 system processor
系统磁盘 system disk {S-disk}
系统错误 system mistake
系统错误登记[记录] system error log
系统打印机 system printer
系统带 system tape
系统登录[登记,记录] system log {SYSLOG}
系统等待 system wait
系统地址表 system address list
系统地址空间 system address space
系统地址总线 system address bus
系统电源 system power supplies
系统调度(程序)表 system scheduler table {SST}
系统调试 system debug
系统调用 system call
系统定义 system define/definition
系统队列区 system queue area {SQA}
系统对象模型 system object model {SOM}
系统方法 system approach, system method
系统方法论 system methodology
系统方式 system mode
系统仿真[模拟] system simulation
系统分类 system classification/taxonomy
系统分区 system partition

系统分析 system analysis
系统分析员 system analyst
系统封锁 system lock
系统服务 system service
系统服务程序 system service program {SSP}
系统服务工具 system service tools {SST}
系统服务控制部件 system service control point {SSCP}
系统复原[位] system reset
系统负载[加载] system load
系统概念 system concept
系统更新 system update
系统更新[再生] system refresh
系统工程 system engineering
系统工程师 system engineer
系统功能 system function
系统故障 system down/failure
系统固件 system firmware
系统关闭(时刻) system shutdown
系统管理 system management
系统管理表 system table
系统管理程序 system supervisor
系统管理软件 system managment software
系统管理员 administrator, system administrator/manager
系统规划 system planning
系统核心 system kernel
系统核心程序 system nucleus
系统合成环境 system composite environment
系统环境 system environment
系统缓冲区 system buffer
系统恢复表 system recovery table
系统基址寄存器 system base register {SBR}
系统集成 system integration
系统集成商 system integrator
系统级别 system level

系统级模拟 system level simulation
系统记录 system record
系统监视 system monitoring
系统间隔 system interval
系统兼容性 system compatibility
系统剪裁 system tailoring
系统键 system key
系统接口 system interface
系统结构 system architecture, system structure, systematic structure
系统进程 system process
系统矩阵 system matrix
系统卷 system volume
系统决策 system decision
系统开发[研制] system development
系统开发生命周期 systems development life cycle {SDLC}
系统开销 overhead
系统可靠度 system dependability
系统可靠性 fail-safety, system reliability
系统可扩充性 system expandability
系统可维护性 system maintainability
系统可维修性 system repairability
系统可行性 system feasibility
系统可移动性 system movability
系统可用性 system availability
系统空间 system space
系统控制 system control
系统控制程序软件 system control programming {SCP}
系统控制器 system controller
系统控制区 system control area {SCA}
系统控制台 system console
系统控制语言 system control language {SCL}
系统口令文件 system password file
系统库 system library
系统框架 system framework
系统框图 block diagram of system, system chart/ diagram/ flowchart
系统逻辑 system logic
系统略图 system outline
系统模拟 system emulation/simulation
系统模型 system model
系统默认值 system default
系统目标 system objective
系统目录表 system directory list {SDL}
系统内容目录 system contents directory {SCD}
系统排队区 system queue area {SQA}
系统盘 system disk {S-disk}
系统判优器 system arbiter
系统配置 system configuration
系统平衡 system balancing/balance
系统评价 system assessment/evaluation
系统屏蔽 system mask
系统求助 system help
系统缺省值 system default
系统任务 system task
系统日期 system date
系统日志 system journal, system log {SYSLOG}
系统容错(技术) system fault tolerance {SFT}
系统容量 system capacity
系统软件 system software
系统设备 system device
系统设定值 default, default value, system default

系统设计 system design
系统设计工具[手段] system design aid
系统设计员 system designer
系统生成 system generation {SYSGEN, sysgen}
系统升级 system upgrade
系统失效 system failure
系统时钟 system clock
系统实用程序 system utility, system utility program
系统识别 system identification
系统适用性 system applicability
系统视图 system view
系统手册 system handbook
系统输出 system output {SYSOUT}
系统输入 system input {SYSIN}, system loading
系统数据 system data
系统说明书 system description/specification
系统死锁 system deadlock
系统算法 system algorithm
系统锁(定) system lock
系统提示 system prompt
系统停机 system halt
系统通信 system communication
系统通信表 system communication table {SCT}
系统图 system diagram
系统退化 system degradation
系统完整性 system integrity
系统网络(体系)结构 system network architecture {SNA}
系统维护 system maintenance
系统位 system bit
系统文法 systemic grammar
系统文件 system file
系统文件管理员 system librarian
系统文件夹 system folder

系统误差 system(atic) error
系统显示 system display
系统校验 system check
系统效能 system effectiveness {SE}
系统信号 system signal
系统信赖度 system dependability
系统信息 system information, system message
系统信息服务 system information service {SIS}
系统形成 system generation {SYSGEN, sysgen}
系统性能 system feature, system performance
系统性能指标 system performance index
系统修复时间 system repair time
系统修改 system modification
系统需求 system requirement
系统询问 system interrogation
系统验证 system verification
系统页表 system page table {SPT}
系统业务控制点 system service control point {SSCP}
系统印证 system validation
系统应用体系结构 system application architecture {SAA}
系统硬件 system hardware
系统映像 system image
系统用户 system user
系统优化 system optimization, system optimize
系统有效能 system effectiveness {SE}
系统有效性 system availability
系统元件 system element
系统原理 system philosophy
系统运行 system operation
系统运行记录 system log {SYSLOG}

系统再启动 system restart
系统噪声 system(atic) noise
系统诊断 system diagnosis
系统值 system value
系统中断 system interrupt
系统终端 system terminal
系统重运行 system roll-back
系统重置 system reset
系统仲裁器 system arbiter
系统驻留(卷) system residence {SYSRES}
系统转储 system dump
系统转换 system conversion
系统装入 system loading
系统资源 system resource
系统字体 system font
系统总线 system bus
系统作业队列 system job queue
系序 set order

细 1)(颗粒小)in small particles, fine 2)(精细)fine, exquisite, delicate 3)(仔细)carefully, closely **细节** details, particulars **细目** detailed catalogue, specific item, detail **细微** slight, fine, subtle **细小** minute, trifling, tiny **细心** careful, attentive **细则** detailed rules and regulations **细条** thin, slender, slim **细致** careful, meticulous
细胞表 cellular list
细胞逻辑 cellular logic
细胞式链 cellular chain
细胞式自动机 cellular automata
细胞网络 cellular network
细胞阵列 cellular array
细胞阵列处理机 cellular array processor
细窗显示 thin window display
细调 fine tuning, tweak
细分类 fine sort
细分图 subdivision graph
细化 detailing, thinning
细节特征 minutia
细缆以太网 thin Ethernet
细目栏 detail group
细目文件 detail file, transaction file
细网络 refined net
细线条 hairline

隙 隙封 gap seal

【xiá】

匣 匣子 a small box/case, casket

狭 narrow **狭义** narrow sense **狭窄** narrow, cramped

瑕 瑕疵 flaw, blemish

辖 (管辖)have jurisdiction over, administer, govern

【xià】

下 1)(低处的)below, down, under, underneath ◇零下十度 ten degrees below zero 2)(等级低的)lower, inferior 3)(次序或时间在后的)next, latter, second 4)(向下)downward, down 5)(往低处)降, get off 6)(形成)form (an idea, opinion, etc.) **下班** come or go off work **下边** ① below, under, underneath ② next, following **下层**(指机构等)lower levels **下沉** sink, submerge **下次** next time **下级**(指组织)lower level ②(指人员)subordinate **下降** descend, go or come down,

drop, fall, decline 下课 get out of class, finish class 下来 come down 下列 listed below, following 下面 ①（位置较低的地方）below, under, underneath ②（次序靠后的部分）next, following 下属 subordinate 下水道 sewer, drainage 下同（用于附注）similarly hereinafter, the same below 下午 afternoon 下旬 the last ten-day period of a month
下笔 pen-down
下（角）标 subscript, inferior figure
下标变量 index variable, subscript(ed) variable
下标表达式 subscript expression
下标范围 subscript range
下标计算 subscripting
下标界 subscript bound
下标类型 index type
下标名 index name
下标偶[对] subscript pair
下标数组 index array
下标值 subscript value
下部的 inferior
下层流 lower stream
下带 lower bound
下道 lower track
下划线 underline, underscore
下划线显示 underscore display
下降法 descent method
下降时间 fall time
下降沿 falling/negative edge
下界 lower bound
下卷 roll down
下拉 drop, pulldown
下拉(式)菜单 drop-down menu, pull-down menu
下拉(式)列表 drop-down list
下拉(式)组合框 drop-down combination box
下盘字模库 lower magazine {LM}
下确界 greatest lower bound {GLB}, infimum, inf
下舍入 round down
下推 push-down
下推自动机 push-down automation {PDA}
下限 lower bound, lower limit
下限寄存器 lower limit register
下行 fallthrough
下行部分 descender
下行链路 down link
下行线 downline
下一代因特网 next generation internet {NGI}
下一个 next
下一语句 next statement
下移 page-down, shift-down
下溢 underflow
下载 unmount, download
下载字体 download font

吓

吓唬 frighten, scare, intimidate

夏

夏季，夏天 summer

【xiān】

先 1)（在前）first, earlier, before 2)（祖先）elder generation, ancestor 先导 guide, forerunner, precursor 先后 ①（先和后）early or late, priority, order ②（前后相继）successively, one after another 先进 advanced 先决条件 prerequisite, precondition 先例 precedent 先期 earlier on, in advance 先前 before, previously 先驱 pioneer, forerunner 先生 ①（老师）teacher ②（称呼）mis-

ter (Mr.), gentleman, sir
先到先服务 first-come first-served
先根次序 preorder
先结束先送 first-ended first-out {FEFO}
先进后出 first-in last-out {FILO}
先进后出表 push-down list
先进科学计算机 advanced scientific computer {ASC}
先进先出 first-in first-out {FIFO}
先进先出表 push-up list
先进制造技术 advanced manufacturing technology {AMT}
先来先服务法 first come first service {FCFS}
先听без讲 listen before talk {LBT}
先行 antecedent, look ahead
先行地址 predecessor address
先行调度 anticipatory paging
先行分析 look-ahead analysis
先行规则 antecedent rule
先行进位 carry look ahead, look ahead carry
先行进位逻辑 carry look ahead logic
先行控制 control with look-ahead capability, look ahead control
先行零 leading zero
先行设备 look ahead device
先行序列 go-ahead sequence {GA}
先于 precede

纤 (细小) fine, minute 纤维 fiber, staple 纤细 very thin, slender, fine, tenuous
纤维光学 photonics
纤维色带 fabric ribbon

氙 xenon (Xe)

掀 lift (a cover, etc.) 掀起 throw 掀起 ① (揭起) lift, raise ② (翻腾) (cause to) surge ③ (大规模兴起) set off, start

鲜 (新鲜) fresh 鲜花 (fresh) flowers 鲜美 delicious, tasty 鲜明 bright, distinct 鲜血 blood 鲜艳 bright-colored, gaily-colored

【xián】

闲 1) (不忙) not busy, idle, unoccupied 2) (搁置中) not in use/operation 3) (空闲) spare time, free time, leisure 闲谈 chat 闲置 leave unused, let sth lie idle, set aside
闲码 bell idles
闲置的 idle
闲置时间 shelf life

弦 1) (弓弦) bowstring, string 2) (钟表发条) spring 3) (圆周两点连线) chord 4) (直角三角形斜边) hypotenuse

贤 1) 〈形〉virtuous, praiseworthy, high-minded 2) 〈名〉an able and virtuous person

咸 (咸味) salted, salty

衔 1) (含在嘴里) hold in the mouth 2) (级别) rank, title
衔接 link up, join, connect

嫌 (厌恶) dislike, mind, complain of 嫌疑 suspicion

【xiǎn】

显 (明显) apparent, obvious, evident 显得 look, seem, appear 显而易见 obviously, evidently, clearly 显见 obvious, self-evident, apparent 显然 obvious, evident, clear 显微镜 microscope 显示 show, display, demonstrate, manifest 显著 outstanding, marked, remarkable

显定义 explicit definition
显函数 explicit function
显式引用 explicit reference
显式路径[路由] explicit route {ER}
显示板 display board/panel
显示报警 display alarm
显示背景 display background
显示表 display list
显示部件[元件] display component
显示菜单 display menu
显示程序 display routine
显示处理部件(器) display processing unit {DPU}
显示窗口 display window
显示存储器 display memory
显示打印转接器 display printer adapter {DPA}
显示代码 display code
显示灯 tutorial light
显示方式(模式) display mode
显示仿真(程序) display emulation
显示访问 display access
显示分辨率 display resolution
显示符号 display symbol
显示工作站 display workstation
显示管 display tube
显示光标 display cursor
显示行 device line, display line
显示画面滚动 display rolling, roll-and-scroll technique
显示缓冲存储器 display buffer memory/storage
显示缓冲器[缓冲区] display buffer
显示寄存器 display register
显示监视器 display monitor, video monitor
显示接口 display interface
显示卡 display card
显示列 display column
显示屏 panel
显示屏幕 display screen, video screen
显示器 display
显示区 display space
显示设备 display device
显示(器)属性 video attribute
显示数据终端 video data terminal
显示图像 display image, videograph
显示位置 display position
显示文件 brougt-forward file, display file, display list
显示像元 display element
显示域 display field
显示帧 display frame
显示中心 display center
显示终端 display terminal, video terminal
显示装置 display unit
显示字符发生器 display character generator
显示字符集 display character set
显微全息术 microholography
显微投影 microprojection
显微投影器 microprojector
显微照片 photomicrograph
显像 development, picture display, video picture, visualization
显像管 picture tube

显像锁定 display lock
显影 activating, develop(ing), development
显影剂 developing agent
显影系统 toning system
显影液 activator

险 (危险) danger, risk

【xiàn】

宪 宪法 constitution, charter
宪章 charter

现 1)(表现出) show, appear, reveal 2)(现在) now, at present, at this moment, current 3)(当场)(do sth) in time of need, on the spot 现场 ①(出事地点)scene ②(工作地点)site, spot 现成 ready-made 现代 ①〈名〉modern times, the contemporary age, up-to-date ②〈形〉modern, contemporary 现代化 modernize, modernization 现货 merchandise on hand 现价 present price 现金, 现款 ready money, cash 现实 ①〈名〉reality ②〈形〉realistic 现象 phenomenon 现行 ①(正在施行的) currently in effect/ force/ operation ②(正在犯罪的)active 现有 now available, existing 现状 present/ current situation, existing state of affairs
现场 field {FLD}, on site
现场操作员 site operator
现场测试 field testing
现场工程设计 field engineering {FE}
现场工程师 customer engineer {CE}, field engineer {FE}
现场可编程门阵列 field-programmable gate array {FPGA}
现场可编程序逻辑阵列 field programmable logic array {FPLA}
现场可变控制元件 field-alterable control element {FACE}
现场升级 field upgrade
现场维护 on-scene care
现场维修 field maintenance, field service
现场写入控制芯片 field-alterable control element {FACE}
现场总线控制系统 fieldbus control system {FCS}
现存量 stock on hand
现代的 living, up-to-date
现代控制理论 modern control theory
现代字体 modern typeface
现金管理 cash management
现金交货 cash on delivery {COD}
现金卡 cash card
现金流出 cash outflow
现金流入 cash in flow
现任务 current task
现实空间 realistic space
现实世界 real world
现实性 reality
现行当前窗口 current window
现行磁盘 current disk
现行方式 current mode {curmod}
现行驱动器 current drive
现行事件 active event, present event
现行页面寄存器 current page register {CPR}
现行优先级 current priority (level)
现行值 current value

现行指令 current order
现行[当前]状态 current state
现役表 active list
现用窗口 active window
现用监督程序 active monitor
现用卡片 active card
现用区域 active partition
现用文件表 active file table {AFT}
现值分析 present analysis

限 限定 set a limit to, restrict 限度 limit, limitation, extent, boundedness 限额 norm, limit, quota 限量 limit the quantity of, set bounds to 限期 ①〈动〉set a time limit/ deadline (for sth) ②〈名〉time limit, deadline 限于 be confined to, be limited to, due to 限制 place restrictions on, restrict, limit, confine
限定词 bound terms, determiner, qualifier
限定关系 qualified relation
限定名 qualified name
限定区 limiting zone
限定子句文法 definite clause grammar {DCG}
限幅 clip, clipping, slice
限幅电路 clipper, limiter circuit
限幅器 amplitude limiter, limiter
限界法 bound method
限流器 current limiter
限位器 limiter
限制电路 limiter circuit
限制器 eliminator, limiter, restrictor
限制性操作 limiting operation

线 1)(各种线)thread, string, wire 2)(交通路线) route, line 3)(交界线) boundary, border 4)〈数学〉line 线路 ①〈电气〉circuit, line ②〈交通〉route, line 线索 clue, thread 线条 line
线程 thread
线程调度 thread scheduling
线程调用 thread dispatching
线程对象 thread object
线程化 threading
线程描述表 thread context
线存储器 wire storage
线对 pair
线缓冲器 line buffer
线回扫 line flyback
线"或" wire-OR
线夹 clip, fastener
线架 line set
线接口库 line interface base {LIB}
线框 wire frame
线框模 line mask
线缆 wire cable {WC}
线连通度 line-connectivity
线路代码 line code
线路电平 line level
线路电压 line voltage
线路调节器 line regulator
线路封锁 line lock
线路负荷[负载] line load, circuit load
线路跟踪 line trace
线路故障 line out, wire fault
线路规程 line discipline
线路集中 line concentration
线路交叉 crossing
线路交换网(络) circuit switched network {CSN}, switched circuit network {SCN}
线路接口板 line interface base {LIB}
线路接收器 line receiver
线路均衡器 line equalizer

线路开关 line switching
线路控制规程 line control discipline
线路控制机[控制器] line control unit
线路控制块 line control block {LCB}
线路类别 circuit grade
线路频率 line frequency
线路冗余级 line redundancy level
线路扫描器 line scanner
线路设计 line layout
线路通信量 line traffic
线路协议 line protocol
线路质量监测 line quality monitoring {LQM}
线路中继 line relay
线路周转 turnaround
线路转接 circuit switch, line switching
线路阻抗 line impedance
线密度 linear density
线驱动器 line driver
线圈架 former
线式打印机 wire printer
线束 harness
线数/英寸 lines per inch {LPI, lpi}
线搜索 line search
线索树 threaded tree
线条画 calligraphic drawing
线图 line graph
线型 line style, line type
线性 linear, linearity
线性变换 linear transformation
线性表 linear list
线性表示(法) linear representation
线性插值 linear interpolation
线性查找 linear search
线性程序设计 wire programming, linear program(ming) {LP}
线性代数 linear algebra
线性地址空间 flat address space
线性电路 linear circuit
线性调频脉冲 chirp
线性调制 linear modulation
线性方程 linear equation
线性关系 linear relation
线性规划 linear planning, linear programming {LP}, mathematical programming
线性规则 linear rule
线性函数 linear function
线性回归 line flyback, linear regression
线性检测 linear detection
线性结构 linear organization, linear structure
线性空间 linear space
线性连接表 linear list, linked linear list
线性流水线 linear pipeline
线性模糊系统 linear fuzzy system
线性模型 linear model
线性扫描 linear scanning
线性视频 linear video
线性树 linear tree
线性图 linear graph
线性网络 linear network
线性文法 linear grammar
线性无关 linearly independent
线性相关 linear dependence, linearly dependent
线性序 linear order(ing), simple/total order
线性优化 linear optimization
线性有界自动机 linear bounded automaton {LBA}

线性有限自动机 linear finite automaton/automata
线性语言 linear language
线性组合 linear combination
线性最优控制 linear optimal control
线延迟 wire delay
线有向图 line digraph
线状 striation

陷
陷入 sink into, fall into, be caught in, get bogged down in
陷波器 wave trap
陷阱标记 trap flag
陷阱断点 trap breakpoint
陷阱屏蔽 trap mask
陷阱请求 trap request
陷阱指令 trapped instruction

献
1)(奉献)offer, present, dedicate, donate 2)(表现)show, put on, display 献计,献策 offer advice, make suggestions

【xiāng】

香
香蕉 banana 香烟(卷烟) cigarette

相
(互相)each other, one another, mutually 相比 compare with 相差 differ; difference between 相称 match, suit 相当 ①(配得上) match, balance, correspond to, be equivalent to ②(适当)suitable, fit, appropriate ③(程度高)quite, fairly, rather 相当好 fairly good 相等 be equal, equality 相抵 offset, balance, counterbalance 相对 ①(面对面)opposite, face to face ②(非绝对的)relative ③(比较的)relatively, comparatively 相反 opposite, contrary, adverse, reverse 相仿 similar, quite alike, more or less the same 相符 conform to, agree with, correspond to 相隔 be separated by, be apart, be at a distance of 相互 mutual, reciprocal, each other 相继 in succession, one after another 相近 ①(距离近)close, near ②(相似)be similar to 相距 apart, at a distance of, away from 相连 be linked together, be joined 相商 consult with, talk over with 相似 resemble, be similar, be alike 相通 communicate with each other, be interlinked 相同 identical, the same, alike 相信 believe in, be convinced of, have faith in 相应 corresponding, relevant
相伴 associate
相比拟的 comparable
相补 complement
相称的 proportional
相对编址[寻址] relative addressing
相对代码 relative code
相对地址 displacement, relation/relative address
相对路径名 relative pathname
相对论 relativity theory
相对位置 relative position
相对稳定性 relative stability
相对误差 fractional error, proportional error, relative error
相对性 relativity
相对移动[运动] relative movement

相对值 relative magnitude
相对指令 relative instruction, relative order
相对转移指令 jump relative instruction, relative jump instruction
相对字节地址 relative byte address {RBA}
相反的 opposed
相反命题 contrary proposition
相干 coherent
相干光束 coherent (light) beam
相干滤波 coherent filtering
相干脉冲 coherent pulse
相干效应 coherent effect
相干信号 coherent signal
相关 correlation, interfix
相关(性)[依赖(性)] dependence
相关变量 correlated variable, dependent variable
相关存储器 relational memory
相关带宽 correlation bandwidth
相关的 correlative, pertinent, related
相关函数 correlation function
相关矩阵 correlation/relevance matrix
相关联锁 interlock
相关实体 dependent entity
相关树 relevance tree
相关索引 coordinate indexing, correlative index, manipulation indexing
相关体 acquaintance
相关图 correlogram
相关推理 correlation reasoning
相关完整性 association integrity
相关线路 interlock circuit
相关性 coherence, correlation, interdependency
相互调用 cross call
相互独立 mutual independence

相互关系 interrelationship
相互控制 interacting control
相互流 interflow
相互性 interactivity
相互作用 interact, interaction, mutual effect
相互作用模型 interactive model
相交 crossing, intersect, intersection, meet
相角 phase angle
相空间 phase space
相联查找 associative lookup
相联存取[访问] content access
相联地址空间 associated address space
相联关键字 associative key
相联寄存器 associative register
相联数组寄存器 associative array register
相联文件 associated file
相联字母表 contiguous alphabet
相邻 adjacent
相邻层 adjacent layer
相邻节点 adjacent node
相邻信道 adjacent channel
相邻信道[通道] adjacent channel
相逻辑 phase logic
相容的 compatible, consistent
相容访问[引用] inclusive reference
相容[兼容]关系 compatible relation
相容关系 compatibility relation
相容性[一致性] consistency, consistence
相容性矩阵 compatibility matrix
相容元 conforming element, consistent element
相容约束 consistent bindings
相似表示 similar representation

相似功能 intimate fuction
相似矩阵 similar matrix
相似性 likeness, similarity
相同表 identical table
相位 phase {PH}
相位编码 phase encoding/encode {PE}
相位差 phase difference
相位调制 phase modulation {PM}
相位计 phasemeter
相位监视器 phase monitor
相位检波器[检测器] phase detector
相位角 phase angle
相位失真 phase distortion
相位误差 phase error
相异[不同]的 variant
相异性 diversity

箱 chest, box, case, trunk
箱式分类 bin sort
箱式排序 bin sort

镶 (嵌入) inlay, set, mount
镶边 fringe, fringing

【xiáng】

详 详尽 detailed, exhaustive, thorough 详细 detailed, minute 详细情况 details, particulars
详细[详图] detail
详细记录 detail record
详细流程图 detail chart, detail flowchart
详细设计 detail(ed) design

翔 circle in the air, fly 翔实 full and accurate, detailed and accurate

【xiǎng】

响 (发出声音) make a sound, sound, ring 响亮 loud, noisy 响声 sound, noise 响应 respond, answer
响铃 ringdown
响应 reply {REP, RPLY}, response
响应窗口 response window
响应单元 response unit {RU}
响应方法 response method
响应方式 response mode
响应分析程序 response analysis program {RAP}
响应时间 response time, response duration
响应原语 response primitive
响应帧 action/response frame
响应指示器 response indicator

享 enjoy 享有 enjoy

想 1)(思考)think 2)(认为) suppose, reckon, think, consider 3)(打算) want to, would like to, feel like (doing sth) 想必 presumably, most probably 想到 think of, call to mind 想法 ①(想办法) think of a way, find a solution ②(意见) idea, opinion 想念 miss, long to see again 想起 remember, recall, call to mind, think of 想象 ①〈动〉imagine, fancy, visualize ②〈名〉imagination, conception, visualization

【xiàng】

向 1)(方向) direction 2)(对着) face, turn towards 3)(偏袒) favor, side with, take the part of, be partial to 向导 guide 向后 towards the back, backward 向来 always, all along 向前 forward, onward, ahead 向上 upward, up 向外 outward 向往 yearn for, look forward to 向下 downward, down 向右 towards the right 向左 towards the left

向导信号 go ahead

向导序列 go-ahead sequence {GA}

向后差分法 backward difference/ differentiation method {BDF}

向后传播 backpropagation

向后调度 backward scheduling

向后方程 backward equation, retrospective equation

向后恢复 backward recovery

向后链接 back(ward) link

向后引用 backward reference

向量 vector, vector quantity

向量变量 vector variable

向量表 vector table

向量表达式 vector expression

向量表示 vector representation

向量参数 vector parameter

向量乘法 vector multiplication

向量处理 vector processing

向量地址 vector address

向量范围 vectorscope

向量方式 vector mode

向量分析 vector analysis

向量符号集 vector symbol set {VSS}

向量格式 vector format

向量归并 vector merge

向量和 vector sum

向量化 vector quantization {VQ}, vectorization, vectorize

向量绘图[制图, 图形] vector graphics

向量机 vector machine

向量积 vector product

向量记法 vector notation

向量结构 vector architecture, vector structure

向量矩阵 vector array

向量巨型机 vector supercomputer

向量空间 vector space

向量块 vector block

向量量化 vector quantization {VQ}

向量屏蔽 vector mask {VM}

向量起始地址 vector start address

向量扫描器 vector scanner

向量设备[设施] vector facility

向量势 vector potential

向量属性 vector attribute

向量算子 vector operator

向量图 arrow diagram, vector diagram (= vectogram)

向量相图 vector phasor

向量循环 vector loop

向量映像 vector mapping

向量优化 vector optimization

向量优先级 vector priority

向量域 vector field

向量运算 vector arithmetic, vector operation

向量增量 vector increment

向量指令 vector instruction

向量中断 vector interrupt, vectored interrupt {VI}

向量转移 vector jump

向量总线 vector bus

向前版本管理 forward version management

向前滚动 roll forward

向前恢复 forward recovery

向前计划[调度] forward scheduling

向前链 chaining forward

向前推理 forward reasoning

向上兼容的 up-compatible

向上兼容性 compatibility forward, upward compatibility

向上引用[访问] upward

向外访问 outgoing access
向下发送 down load
向下兼容 downward compatibility
向下引用 down(ward) reference
向右对齐 right justify
向左调节[对齐]的 left-justified
向左移位 left shift

项
1)（颈后部）nape (of the neck) 2)（条目）item, term 3)（款项）sum 4)〈数学〉〈物理〉term 项目 item, project, entry
项表 term list
项目分隔符 item separation symbol
项目分类 item sorting
项目符号 item mark
项目[条目,表目]格式 entry format
项目管理 project management
项目经理 project manager
项目控制 project control
项目块 entry block
项目名 project name
项目说明 item description, project specification
项目文件 project file

象
1)（大象）elephant 2)（形状）appearance, shape 3)（仿效）imitate 象征 ①〈动〉symbolize, signify, stand for ②〈名〉symbol, emblem, token
象限 quadrant
象形符 glyph
象形图 pictogram
象形文字 pictogrph

像
1)（图像,人像）image, likeness (of sb), portrait, picture 2)（相像）be like, resemble, take after 3)（好像）seem, look as if, appear
像场 image field, picture-field
像点 image (point), picture dot/point
像空间 image space
像平面 image plane
像区 image area
像素[元] elemental area, image element, picture dot, picture element {PEL, PIXEL, pel, pixel}, picture point, pixel, image cell
像素表[图] pixel map, pixmap
像素层次 pixel layer
像素化 pixellation
像素矩阵 pel matrix, picture element matrix {PEL matrix}
像素区 pixel region
像素值 pixel value

橡
橡胶 rubber

【xiāo】

削 另见【xuē】
削波电路 clipper
削波器 chopper, wave clipper

消
消除 eliminate, remove 消费 consume 消耗 consume, use up, expend 消极 ①（反面的）negative ②（消沉的）passive, inactive 消灭 ①（消亡）perish, die out, pass away ②（除掉）eliminate, abolish, wipe out 消磨 ①（逐渐消耗）wear down, fritter away ②（度过）idle away 消磨时间 kill time, pass the time 消失 disappear, vanish, dissolve 消遣 pass the time in a leisurely way 消息 ①（报

消除抖动 debouncing
消除多义 disambiguation
消除器 eliminator
消磁器 degausser, demagnetizer
消磁头 erase/erasing head
消链 chain destroy
消去 elimination
消去动作 erasing move
消去法 elimination method, subtractive process
消色 achromatic color
消失区 fade zone
消息标题 message header
消息处理服务(系统) message handling service {MHS}
消息处理机制 message processing facility {MPF}
消息传递代理 message transfer agent {MTA}
消息格式 message format
消息管理中心 message center
消息截取 message intercept
消息控制系统 message control system {MCS}
消息框 message box
消息模式 message pattern
消息求助信息 message help
消息日志 message log
消息收到符号 acknowledge character {ACK}
消息文件 message file
消息行 message line
消元法 elimination (method), elimination of unknown
消元算法 elimination algorithm

销 1)(除去) cancel, annul ◇注销 write off, cancel 2)(销售) sell, market 3)(固定用小零件) pin, dog 销毁 destroy by melting or burning
销路 sale, market 销售 sell, market
销售点(系统) point of sale {POS}
销售模型 marketing model
销售数据 sales data

【xiǎo】

小 1)(与"大"相反) small, little, petty, minor 2)(年纪小的) young 小册子 booklet, pamphlet 小刀 pocket knife 小规模 small-scale 小结 ①〈名〉brief summary ②〈动〉summarize briefly 小姐 ①(称呼) Miss ②(少女) young lady 小康 well-to-do, fairly well-off 小麦 wheat 小时 hour 小事 trifle, petty thing, minor matter 小说 novel, fiction 小写 small letter 小心 take care, be careful, be cautious 小型 small-size, miniature 小学 primary school, elementary school 小传 brief biography, biographical sketch, profile 小组 group
小波 wavelet
小波图像 wavelet image
小程序块 blockette
小工具 widget
小规模集成电路 small-scale integrated circuit {SSI}, small-scale integration {SSI}
小规模系统 minisystem
小号大写字母 small capital
小号大写字母 small caps
小计 subtotal, subtotaling
小键盘 keypad, pad, small keyboard
小巨型计算机 mini-super-computer
小配件 gadget

小球病毒 bouncing ball, ping pong virus
小软盘 minifloppy
小数 decimal, fractional (part)
小数表示(法) fractional representation
小数部分 fractional part
小数的循环节 repetend
小数点 arithmetic point, base/radix point
小数定点制 fractional fixed point
小数位 fractional digit
小写字母 lower case letter, small letter
小芯片尺寸 chip size
小信息块 blockette
小型操作系统 small-scale operating system
小型仿真器[程序] miniemulator
小型号 small/ting model
小型盒式磁带机 minicartridge, minicassette
小型机 minimicro
小型计算机 minicomputer, small computer
小型计算机系统 small computer system {SCS}
小型计算机系统接口 small computer system interface {SCSI}
小型开关 nut switch
小型控制台 consolette
小型软盘 minifloppy diskette, minidiskette, minifloppy
小于 less-than {LT}
小于或等于 less-than or equal to {LE}
小组进位 group carry

【xiāo】

肖
肖特基二极管 Schottky diode

肖像方式 portrait mode
肖像格式 portrait format

笑 1)(欢笑)smile, laugh 2)(讥笑)ridicule, laugh at

效 (仿效)imitate, follow the example of 效果 effect, efficient, purpose, result 效力 effect 效益 beneficial result, benefit 效用 effectiveness, usefulness, utility
效果系统图 effect system diagram
效率 ability, effectiveness, efficiency
效能 effect, efficiency

校 另见【jiào】
(学校)school, college, university 校刊 school magazine, college journal 校友(男)alumnus, (女)alumna 校园 campus, school yard 校长 ①(中小学) headmaster, principal ②(大专院校) president, chancellor
校园网络 campus network
校园综合信息服务系统 campus wide information system {CWIS}

【xiē】

楔 wedge, key

歇 1)(休息)have a rest 2)(停止)stop, knock off 歇业 close a business, go out of business

【xié】

挟 1)(用胳膊夹住)hold sth under the arm 2)(挟制)force sb to submit to one's will, coerce

协

1) 〈形〉joint, common 2) 〈动〉assist 协定 agreement, treaty, deal 协会 society, association 协力 joint/concerted efforts 协商 consult and discuss 协调 coordinate, concert, harmonize 协同 work in coordination with, cooperate with 协议 ① 〈动〉agree on ② 〈名〉agreement, protocol 协助 assist, help 协作 ① 〈动〉cooperate, coordinate, work jointly ② 〈形〉cooperative, synerg(ist)ic ③ 〈名〉cooperation, coordination, collaboration

协(同)处理器 coprocessor
协方差 covariance
协方差函数 analysis function
协方差矩阵 analysis matrix
协调[一致性]公式 consistent formula
协调元 conforming element, consistent element
协同操作模式 cooperative mode
协同程序 co(-)routine
协同处理 coprocessing
协同的 synergistic
协同进程 cooperating process
协同控制 cooperative control
协同性 cooperativity
协同驻留 coresident
协议边界 protocol boundary
协议标准 protocol standard
协议层 layer protocol
协议窗口 protocol window
协议错误 protocol error
协议独立多目标广播(协议) protocol independent multicast {PIM}
协议端口 protocol port
协议堆 protocol stack
协议仿真程序[仿真器] protocol emulator
协议分析 protocol analysis
协议规范 protocol specifications
协议级 protocol levels
协议控制 protocol control {PC}
协议模型 protocol model
协议数据单元 protocol data unit {PDU}
协议栈 protocol stack
协议转换器 protocol converter
协作处理 cooperative processing
协作模式 collaboration mode
协作图 collaboration diagram

斜

oblique, slanting, inclined, tilted 斜坡 slope
斜的 skew
斜面 cant, chamfer, scarf, slant
斜视图 oblique view
斜体 italic, oblique
斜体罗马字 sloped Roman
斜体字 italic, italic font
斜线 skew line, slash, oblique line

谐

谐波(的) harmonic
谐波失真 harmonic distortion
谐振 resonance

携

携带 carry, take along, bring along 携手 hand in hand
携带式微计算机 portable microcomputer

【xiě】

写

1) (用笔写) write 2) (描

写) describe, depict 3) (画) paint, draw 写字台(writing) desk 写作 writing
写 write {W}, writing
写-写相关 write-write association
写保护 write protect(ion)
写保护标签 write-protection label
写保护格式 copy-protected format
写保护开关 write protection switch
写保护器 write protector
写保护区 write-protected zone
写保护缺口 notch
写保护软盘 write-protected diskette
写保护贴片 write protect tab
写保护信号 write protect signal
写补偿电路 writing compensate circuit
写操作 write operation
写冲突 write conflict
写出错 write error
存存储器 memory write
写错误 write error
写电路 write circuit
写读串扰 cross feed, write-to-read crossfeed
写访问 write access
写分配 write allocate
写管 writing tube
写后读 read-after-write {RAW}
写后检测 check-after-write
写后直接读出 direct read after write {DRAW}
写集 writeset
写寄存器 write register
写控制字符 write control character {WCC}
写脉冲 write pulse
写屏蔽 write mask
写请求 write request

写驱动器 write driver
写入 load, write {W}, write-in, writing
写入磁带 write magnetic tape
写入封锁 write lockout
写入间隔 write interval
写入键 write key
写入门 write gate
写入时直接读出 direct read during write {DRDW}
写入头 write head
写入装置 writer
写头 record/ write/ writing head
写响应 write response
写选择线 write select line
写指令 write instruction
写装置 write device

【xiè】

泄 1) (排出) let out, discharge, release 2) (发泄) give vent to 泄漏 let out, leak 泄露 let out, reveal, betray 泄密 disclose a secret

卸 1) (搬下) unload, discharge 2) (拆卸) remove, strip 3) (推卸) get rid of, shirk 卸车 unload (goods, etc. from a vehicle) 卸货 unload cargo, discharge cargo, unload 卸任 be relieved of one's office
卸出 dump out, unload
卸下 demount, dismount, downloading, take-down, unload(ing), unmount
卸下时间 take-down time
卸载 downloading, down load, off-loading
卸载区 unload zone

械 1)(器械)tool, instrument

2)(武器)weapon

屑
1)(碎末)bits, scraps, fragments 2)(琐碎)trifling

谢
1)(感谢)thank 2)(道歉)apologize, make an apology 3)(谢绝)decline, refuse 谢意 gratitude, thankfulness

【xīn】

心
1)(思想感情)heart, mind, feeling 2)(中心)center, core 心情 state of mind, mood 心思 ①(念头)thought, idea ②(脑筋)thinking, thoughts 心愿 cherished desire, aspiration, wish 心脏 heart
心动的 systolic
心动[脉动]式计算机 systolic computer
心动[脉动]网格 systolic network
心动[脉动]网络 systolic mesh
心理电子学 psychotronics
心理效应 psychological effect
心理学 psychology

芯
core
芯件 chipware
芯片 chip, chip die
芯片布设 chip layout
芯片测试 chip testing
芯片级 chip level
芯片计算机 transputer
芯片检测[检验] chip inspection
芯片设计 chip layout
芯片直接电路板 chip on board {COB}

辛
1)(辣)hot (in taste, flavor, etc.) 2)(痛苦)suffering 辛苦 hard, laborious, toilsome 辛劳 pains, toil 辛勤 industrious, hardworking

欣
glad, happy, joyful 欣赏 appreciate, enjoy, admire 欣慰 be gratified 欣欣向荣 thriving, flourishing, prosperous

锌
zinc (Zn)

新
new, fresh, up-to-date 新版 new edition 新纪元 new era, new epoch 新加坡 Singapore 新近 recently, lately, in recent times 新年 New Year 新奇 strange, novel, new 新式 new type, latest type, new-style 新手 new hand, green hand, new recruit 新闻 news 新鲜 ①(清新的)fresh ②(新生的)new, novel, strange 新兴 new and developing 新型 new type, new pattern 新颖 new and original, novel
新版本 redaction
新媒体 new media
新识别机 neocognitron
新同步 new sync
新闻组 newsgroup
新行字符 new-line character {NL}
新一代计算机系统 future generation computer system {FGCS}
新组合 new pack

薪
薪金 salary, pay 薪水 salary, pay, wage

【xīn】

信
1)(书信)letter, mail 2)(相信)believe 3)(确实)true

4) (信奉) believe in 信贷 credit 信服 completely accept, be convinced 信汇 mail transfer (M/T) 信件 letters, mail 信赖 trust, count on, have faith in 信念 faith, belief, conviction 信任 trust, have confidence in 信守 abide by, stand by 信托 trust, entrust 信箱 ①(信筒)letter box, mailbox ②(邮局供租用的) post-office box (P.O.B) 信心 confidence, faith 信仰 belief, faith, conviction 信用 ①(信任)confidence, trust, faith, trustworthiness, credit ②〈经贸〉credit 信用卡 credit card 信誉 prestige, credit, reputation

信标 beacon
信标跟踪 beacon tracking
信标帧 beacon frame
信道 channel
信道编码 channel coding
信道带宽 channel bandwidth
信道调制 channel modulation
信道服务单元 channel service unit {CSU}
信道规划 channel plan
信道库 channel bank
信道宽度 channel width
信道(调度)排队 channel queue
信号 signal
信号比 signal ratio
信号编码 signal encoding
信号变换 signal conversion/transformation
信号标准化 signal normalization/standardization
信号处理程序 signal handler
信号传输 signal transmission
信号带宽 signal bandwidth
信号单元 signalling unit {SU}
信号灯 semaphore, sign lamp

信号电缆 signal cable
信号电平 signal level
信号调制 signal modulation
信号丢失 loss of signal {LOS}
信号发生器 signal generator
信号反馈系统 signal feedback system
信号放大器 signal amplifier
信号分离 demultiplex
信号分析器 signalling analyzer
信号计算系统结构 signal computing system architecture {SCSA}
信号间干扰 intersymbol interference {ISI}
信号间距 signal distance
信号检测 signal detection
信号交换 handshake, handshaking
信号禁止 signal-inhibiting
信号旗 semaphore
信号滤波 signal filtering
信号码元 signal element
信号器 annunciator
信号强度 signal strength
信号设备 signalling
信号时序 signal sequence
信号衰减 signal attenuation
信号速率 signal(ling) rate
信号网络 signalized network
信号显示板 signal panel
信号(传输)线 signal wire
信号相关 signal correlation
信号压缩 companding, signal compression
信号掩蔽比 signal to mask radio {SMR}
信号源 source
信号再生[整形] signal regeneration
信号噪声比 signal-to-noise ratio {S/N, SNR}
信号整形 signal shaping, signal normalization

信号转换 signal conversion/transformation
信号装置 annunciator
信号组 signal set
信件结束 end of letter {EOL}
信令 signaling, signalling
信令点 signaling point {SP}
信令转接点 signaling transfer point {STP}
信念区间 belief interval
信念系统 belief system {BS}
信任路径 trusted path
信头差错控制 header error control {HEC}
信息 information, message
信息安全性 information security
信息包 information packet, packet, message
信息包交换机 packet switch
信息包交换网络 data network
信息爆炸 information explosion
信息编码 information (en)coding
信息编组 message blocking
信息变换 conversion of information, information conversion
信息表示 information representation
信息采集[获取] information acquisition
信息仓库 information warehouse
信息查询系统 inquiry system
信息查询站 koisk
信息产业 information industry
信息处理 information handling/processing, message handling/processing
信息处理程序 message processing program {MPP}
信息处理中心 information handling center
信息传输 information transmission, trans(fered)-information
信息传输应用编程接口 messaging application programming interface {MAPI}
信息串 string
信息簇 informational cluster
信息存储(器) information storage
信息存储密度 information storage density
信息单位[单元] information unit
信息段 message block/segment
信息发生器 information generator
信息反馈 information/message feedback, loop checking
信息分隔符 information separator {IS}
信息服务提供商 information service provider {ISP}
信息干线 information trunk
信息港 infoport
信息高速公路 information superhighway
信息革命 information revolution
信息工程 information engineering
信息管理系统 information management system {IMS}
信息柜 data frame
信息化 informatization
信息化社会 information society
信息环境 information environment
信息技术 information technique/technology {IT}, telematics
信息检索 information retrieval {IR}
信息交换 information exchanging/interchange

信息交换体系结构 information interchange architecture {IIA}
信息交换网络 switched message network
信息接收 information reception
信息结构 information structure
信息[消息]结束码 end-of-message code {EOM}
信息经济学 information economics
信息科学 informatics, information science
信息控制程序 message control program {MCP}
信息控制块 message control block
信息库 information base
信息块 block of information, information/message block
信息链路 information link
信息量值 information magnitude
信息流 flow (of information), information flow/stream, message flow, stream
信息流程图 information flowchart
信息路径 information path
信息论 information theory
信息率 information rate
信息密度 information density
信息模式 information pattern
信息取样 message sample
信息容量 data capacity, informational capacity
信息冗余 information redundancy
信息商业 informacial
信息熵 message entropy
信息社会 inforcosm
信息社会学 information sociology
信息世界 information world

信息树 information tree
信息宿 information sink
信息提供者 information provider {IP}
信息体 informosome
信息通道 information channel
信息通路 information path, trunk
信息位 information bit, message digit
信息系统 information system
信息系统工程 information system engineering
信息项 information entry
信息学 informatics
信息要求[需求] information requirement
信息业务 information service
信息引导[导航]器 information navigator
信息元 information element
信息源 information/message source, source of information
信息载体 information carrier
信息中心 information center
信息转储 core dump, memory dump
信息资源词典 information resource dictionary {IRD}
信息资源共享 information resource sharing
信息资源管理 information resource management {IRM}
信息组 field {FLD}, field of words, information group, message block
信息组记录 block record
信用卡 credit card
信用卡购货 cashless shopping
信用卡系统 debit card system
信用量 credit {CR, CRD}
信元差错率 cell error rate {CER}

信元中继 cell relay
信噪比 signal noise ratio, signal-to-noise ratio {S/N, SNR}, speech/noise ratio

【xīng】

兴 另见【xìng】
（使盛行）encourage, promote 兴办 initiate, set up 兴建 build, construct 兴起 rise, spring up 兴盛 rise, prosper, prevail 兴旺 prosperous, flourishing, thriving

星 （明星）star 星号 asterisk (*) 星际 interplanetary, interstellar 星期（一周）week 星期日 Sunday 星期一 Monday 星期二 Tuesday 星期三 Wednesday 星期四 Thursday 星期五 Friday 星期六 Saturday 星球 star, heavenly body
星环网 star/ring network
星际链路 intersatellite link {ISL}
星际通信 interstellar communication
星形电路 star circuit
星形环 star ring
星形级链网络 cascaded star
星形交换网 switched star
星形结构 star structure
星形连接 star connect(ion)
星形配置 star configuration
星形树 star tree
星形拓扑 star topology
星形网络 star network, Y-network

【xíng】

行 另见【háng】
1)（走）go on foot, walk 2)（旅行）travel 3)（流行）be current, prevail, circulate 4)（做,办）do, perform, carry out, engage in 行程 ① route of travel ②〈机械〉stroke, throw 行动 ①（走动）move about, get about ②（活动）act, take action ③（行为,动作）action, operation 行使 exercise, perform 行驶 (of vehicle, ship, etc.) go, travel 行为 behavior, conduct, action 行政 administration
行程编码 run coding, run-length encode/encoding
行程长度编码 run length coding {RLC}
行程计数 trip count
行程开关 limit switch
行为空间 action space
行为模拟 behavioural simulation
行为模式 behaviour scheme, pattern of behaviour
行为模型 behavioural model
行政管理程序 administrative management {ADM}
行政管理控制 administrative control
行政管理支持系统 executive support system {ESS}
行政系统 administrative system

刑 刑法 penal code, criminal law

形 形成 take shapes, (take) form 形容 ①（形貌）appearance, countenance ②（描述）describe 形式 form, format, shape 形势 ①（地势）terrain, topographical features ②（事物发展情况）situation, circumstances

形态 form, shape, pattern
形象 image, form, figure
形体 body, entity, physique
形状 form, appearance, shape
形成规则 formation rule
形迹 evidence
形式变量 formal variable
形式参数 form(al) parameter
形式地址 formal address
形式定义 formal definition
形式规则 formal rule
形式化 formalization
形式检测 formal detection
形式检验 formal/ format check, formal testing
形式类 formal class
形式理论 formal theory
形式论 formalisms
形式逻辑系统 formal logical system
形式描述[说明] formal description
形式说明 formal specification
形式推导 formal deduction
形式推理 formal inference/ reasoning
形式文法 formal grammar
形式系统 formal system
形式下推自动机 formal push-down automaton
形式语法 formal syntax
形式语言 form(al) language
形式语言理论 formal language theory
形式语言文法 formal language grammar
形式语言学 semiotics
形式蕴涵 formal implication
形象思维 thinking with mental imagery
形音编码法 shape- phonetic encode method
形状表 shape table
形状分析 shape analysis
形状识别 shape recognition
形状原语 shape primitive

型 (模型)mold 型号 model, mode, type, form, pattern
型[类型] type

【xǐng】
醒 1)(恢复知觉)regain consciousness, come to 2)(睡醒)wake up, be awaken 3)(清醒)be clear in mind 醒目 striking

【xīng】
兴 另见【xìng】
兴高采烈 in high spirits, in great delight 兴趣 interest, taste

幸 幸存 survive 幸福 ①〈名〉happiness, well-being ②〈形〉happy
幸好 fortunately, luckily
幸亏 luckily, fortunately
幸免 have a narrow escape
幸运 good fortune, good luck

性 性格 nature, character
性别 sexual distinction, sex
性能 function, performance, property 性质 quality, character, nature, property
性状 shape and properties, character
性能规格 performance requirements
性能价格比 cost performance, performance/ cost ratio, price performance
性能评价 performance evaluation
性能优化 performance optimization

性质实体 property entity

姓 surname, family name 姓名 surname and personal name, full name

【xiōng】

凶 1)(不吉利)ominous 2)(利害)serious, terrible, fearful 凶恶 fierce, ferocious 凶猛 violent, ferocious

兄 elder brother 兄弟 ①(哥哥和弟弟)brothers ②(兄弟般的)fraternal, brotherly
兄弟树 brother tree

胸 1)(胸部)chest, bosom 2)(心胸)mind, heart

【xióng】

雄 (公的)male 雄厚 rich, solid, abundant 雄伟 grand, imposing, magnificent 雄心 great ambition, high aspiration

熊 bear 熊猫 panda

【xiū】

休 (停止)stop, cease, end 休会 adjourn 休假 have a holiday, take a vacation, be on leave 休息 have a rest, take a rest 休学 suspend from schooling 休业 suspend business, close down
休止状态 dormant state
休止协定 standstill agreement

修 1)(学习)study, cultivate ◇进修 pursue one's studies // 自修 study by oneself 2)(兴建)build, construct 修补 mend, patch up, repair, revamp 修辞 rhetoric 修订 revise 修复 repair, restore, renovate 修改 revise, modify, amend, alter 修建 build, costruct, erect 修理 repair, mend, fix 修缮 renovate 修饰 ①(装饰)decorate, adorn, embellish ②(打扮)make up and dress up 修养 ①(指知识水平)learning, training, mastery ②(涵养)ways of behaviour 修业 study at school 修业年限 length of schooling 修正 revise, amend, correct, modify 修筑 build, construct, put up
修补程序 patch program
修订[版本]号 revision number
修复动作 repair action
修复率 repair rate
修复时间 repair time, time to repair
修改的 updated
修改方式 alter/update mode
修改记录 amendment record
修改检测码 modification detection code {MDC}
修改量 modifier
修改区域 modifier area
修改位 modified/modifier bit
修剪 cut-off, prune, pruning
修剪操作 cut operation
修理等待时间 repair delay time
修正编辑 revised edition

【xiù】

秀 1)(清秀)elegant, beautiful, pretty 2)(优秀)excellent, outstanding

袖 sleeve 袖珍 pocket-size, pocket 袖珍本 pocket edition
袖珍计算机 hand-hold computer {HHC}, pocket computer
袖珍计算器 pocket calculator
袖珍键盘 keypad
袖珍式电子计算机 pocketronic

锈 1)〈名〉rust, stain 2)〈动〉become rusty

臭 另见【chòu】
odor, smell

嗅 smell, scent, sniff

溴 bromine (Br)

【xū】

须 (胡须)beard, mustache
须要 must, have to 须知 points for attention, notice

虚 1)(空虚)void, emptiness 2)(空着)empty, void, unoccupied 3)(心虚)timid, unconfident 虚报 make a false report, false declaration 虚构 fabricate, make up 虚假 false, unreal 虚弱 weak, in poor health, debilitated 虚心 open-minded, modest
虚变量 dummy variable, virtual argument
虚变元 virtual argument
虚表 virtual table
虚机构 virtual memory mechanism
虚存技术 virtual memory technique {VMT}
虚存系统 virtual storage system
虚空间 imaginary space
虚电路 virtual circuit
虚调用 virtual call
虚构的 fictitious
虚呼叫方式 virtual call mode {VCM}
虚活动 dummy activity
虚(拟)机控制块 virtual machine control block {VMBLOK}
虚节 dummy section
虚拟作业 virtual job
虚拟按钮 virtual push-button
虚拟变元 dummy argument
虚拟仓库 visual warehouse
虚拟处理机[器] virtual processor
虚拟磁盘 virtual disk
虚拟存储 virtual storage {VS}
虚拟存储存取法 virtual storage access method {VSAM}
虚拟存储法 virtual memory technique {VMT}
虚拟存储管理 virtual storage management {VSM}
虚拟存储器 virtual memory, virtual storage {VS}
虚拟存储系统 virtual storage system
虚拟存取[访问]法 virtual access method
虚拟等待时间 virtual wait time
虚拟地址空间 virtual address space
虚拟地址转换 virtual address translation
虚拟电路 virtual circuit
虚拟段 virtual segment
虚拟方式 virtual mode
虚拟分区 virtual partition
虚拟管理状态 virtual supervisor state
虚拟机 virtual machine
虚拟机管理器 virtual machine manager {VMM}

虚拟机器 virtual machine
虚拟级 virtual stage
虚拟计算机系统 virtual machine system
虚拟节 dummy section
虚拟节点 virtual node, v-node
虚拟局域网 virtual local area network {VLAN}
虚拟卷 virtual volume
虚拟空间 virtual space
虚拟控制段 dummy control section {DSECT}
虚拟连接 virtual connection
虚拟路径[路由] virtual route {VR}
虚拟路由节点 virtual routing node
虚拟区域 virtual region
虚拟驱动(器) virtual drive
虚拟设备 virtual device
虚拟设备地址 virtual unit address
虚拟设备接口 virtual device interface {VDI}
虚拟设备名字 virtual device name
虚拟设备中介文件 virtual device metafile {VDM}
虚拟神经计算机 virtual neurocomputer
虚拟输入设备 virtual input device
虚拟数据集 dummy data set
虚拟数据类型 virtual data type
虚拟数据网 virtual data network
虚拟数据项 virtual data-item, virtual field
虚拟隧道协议 virtual tunneling protocol {VIP}
虚拟态 virtual state
虚拟通道 virtual channel
虚拟通道逻辑 virtual channel logic
虚拟通道网络 virtual channel network
虚拟外(围)设(备) virtual peripheral
虚拟文件系统 virtual file system
虚拟系统 virtual system
虚拟现实 virtual reality {VR}
虚拟现实造型语言 virtual reality modeling language {VRML}
虚拟线路网络 virtual circuit network
虚拟寻址 virtual addressing
虚拟样机 virtual prototype
虚拟页 virtual page
虚拟银行 virtual banking
虚拟语言 pseudolanguage
虚拟远程通信存取法 virtual telecommunication access method {VTAM}
虚拟指令 virtual instruction
虚拟终端(机) virtual terminal
虚拟终端管理器 virtual terminal manager {VTM}
虚拟终端数据 virtual terminal data {VTD}
虚拟终端协议 virtual terminal protocol {VTP}
虚拟专用网(络) virtual private network {VNP}
虚拟专用线 virtual private line
虚拟装置 virtual device
虚拟字段 virtual field
虚拟作业 dummy activity
虚偶对 virtual pairing
虚盘 minidisk, virtual disk
虚盘目录 minidisk directory
虚区 virtual region
虚容器 virtual container {VC}
虚设备 dummy/virtual device
虚设的 dummy
虚设字符 dummy character
虚实方式 virtual real mode
虚实区 virtual-real area

虚数 imaginary number
虚通道 virtual path
虚通道标识符 virtual path identifier {VPI}
虚通道链路 virtual path link {VPL}
虚线 dashed/ dotted/ dummy/ imaginary line
虚协议 virtual protocol
虚信道 virtual channel {VC}
虚信道标识符 virtual channel identifier {VCI}
虚信道连接 virtual channel connection {VCC}
虚信道链路 virtual channel link {VCL}
虚行 virtual row
虚(拟)映像 virtual image
虚元素 ghost element
虚源 virtual source
虚终端协议 virtual terminal protocol {VTP}
虚主机 virtual host
虚作业 dummy activity

需 需求 requirement, demand 需要 need, want, require 需用物品 necessaries, needs
需求 requirements, demand
需求定义 requirement definition
需求分析 requirement(s) analysis
需求计划 requirements planning
需求预测 demand forecasting

【xú】
徐 徐徐 slowly, gently

【xǔ】
许 1)(称许) praise 2)(允许) allow, permit 3)(也许) maybe, perhaps, possibly 许多 many, much, a great deal of, a lot of 许久 for a long time, for ages, for long
许可 permit, allow, grant
许可证 licence, permit 许诺 promise
许可级别 clearance level
许可权 permission

【xù】
序 1)(次序) order, sequence 2)(排次序) arrange in order
序言 preface, foreword, introduction
序号 ordinal number, rank
序列 line-up, sequence, series
序列长度 sequence length
序列发生器 sequencer
序列号 serial number
序列检验 sequence check(ing), serial test
序列元素 sequential element

绪 绪论, 绪言 introduction

续 1)(连续不断) continuous, successive 2)(接在后面) continue, extend 3)(添,加) add, supply more 续集 continuation (of a book), sequel
续页入口 page entry

蓄 (积蓄) store up, save up
蓄电池 accumulator {ACC}

叙 叙述 narrate, recount, relate
叙述语句 descriptive statement

【xuān】
宣 宣布 declare, proclaim, announce 宣称 assert, de-

clare 宣传 propagate, publicize 宣读 read aloud (in public) 宣告 declare, proclaim 宣判 pronounce the judgement 宣誓 take/swear an oath, make a vow 宣言 declaration, manifesto 宣扬 publicize, propagate, advocate, advertise

【xuán】

玄 玄妙 mysterious, bewildering

悬 悬案 ①(未决案件)unsettled law case ②(未决问题) outstanding issue, unsettled question 悬挂 hang, suspend 悬空 hang in the air, suspend in midair 悬殊 great disparity, wide gap
悬挂节点 hanging node
悬挂线 suspended line
悬架 pendant

旋 (旋转) revolve, rotate, circle, spin, whirl
旋转[接头,轴承] swivel
旋转拨号盘 rotary dial
旋转磁头 rotary/rotating head
旋转的 rotational
旋转矩阵 spin matrix
旋转位置感传[检测] rotational position sensing {RPS}
旋转中心 pivot
旋转周期 cyclic convolution

【xuǎn】

选 选拔 select, choose 选定 make a choice of 选集 selections, anthology, selected works 选举 elect 选派 select and appoint 选票 vote, ballot 选修 take as an elective course 选用 select for use 选择 select, choose, pick
选出 choice-out, pick
选单[菜单] menu
选路表 routing table
选路网络 route selection network, routing network
选路信息协议 routing information protocol {RIF}
选取 access, selection
选取中继线 lunk
选台 selective calling
选通 gating, strobe
选通窗口 strobe window
选通电路 gating circuit
选通脉冲 gate/ strobe pulse, strobe, strobe window
选通门 strobing gate
选通信号 strobe signal
选项 option
选用指令 optional directive
选择笔 selector pen
选择表 option/picking table
选择程序 option program
选择调用 selective calling
选择对象 alternative
选择方式 selector mode
选择功能 option function, select function
选择光标 selection cursor
选择键 option key
选择开关 option switch
选择码 option code
选择门[电路] select gate
选择排序 selection sort(ing)
选择器 chooser, selector
选择设备 choice device
选择树 selection tree
选择提示 selective prompting
选择通道 selector channel
选择系数 selectance, selection factor
选择线 select line
选择信号 selection signal

xuàn 炫 xuē 削 xué 学 xuě 雪 xuè 血 xún 旬寻

选择优先级[权] selection/selecting priority
选择指令 select order, selection instruction
选择(性)转储 selection dump, selective dump
选择装置 option unit
选择子句 choice-clause
选址 site selection
选中(状态) true
选主元 pivoting

【xuàn】

炫 炫目 dazzle 炫耀 make a display of, show off

【xuē】

削 另见[xiāo]
削价 cut prices, lower the price 削减 cut (down), reduce, whittle down 削弱 weaken

【xué】

学 (模仿) imitate, mimic 学报 learned journal 学分 credit 学分制 the credit system 学风 style of study 学会 ① (学成) learn, master ② (团体) learned society, institute 学科 branch of learning, subject (of study), discipline, course 学会 institute, institution 学历 record of schooling, educational background 学年 school year, academic year 学派 school (of thought) 学期 (school) term, semester 学生 student, pupil 学生会 student union 学生证 student's identity card 学时 class hour, period 学识 learning, knowledge 学士 ① (文人) scholar ② (学位) bachelor ◇理学士 Bachelor of Science (B.S) ‖ 文学士 Bachelor of Arts (B.A.) 学术 academic learning, science 学术交流 academic exchanges 学术界 academic circles 学说 theory, doctrine 学位 (academic) degree 学问 learning, knowledge 学习 study, learn 学衔 academic rank, academic title 学校 school, educational institution, college 学业 one's studies, school work 学员 student, trainee 学院 college, academy, institute 学者 scholar, learned man, man of learning 学制 ① (教育制度) educational system, school system ② (学习年限) length of schooling
学科间的 interdisciplinary
学习程序 learning program
学习功能 learning function
学习规则 learning rules
学习机 learning machine
学习控制 learning control
学习系统 learning system {LS}

【xuě】

雪 snow 雪白 snow-white, snowy white

【xuè】

血 blood

【xún】

旬 a period of ten days ◇上旬 the first ten days of a month

寻 search, seek, look for 寻常 ordinary, usual, common 寻求 seek, explore, go in quest of

寻道 seek, track seeking
寻道时间 step-rate time, track seek time
寻径程序 routed
寻找 hunt, hunting, quest, search, seek
寻址 addressing
寻址操作 address operation, addressing operation
寻址范围 addressing range
寻址方式 address(ing) mode
寻址格式 address format
寻址机构 addressing mechanism
寻址级 addressing level
寻址技术 addressing technique
寻址能力 addressable capacity, addressing capability

巡
巡回检测 loop detection
巡回售货员问题 travelling salesman problem

询
（询问）ask, enquiry (=inquiry) {ENQ}, interrogation, query, enquire (=inquire) ◇查询 make enquiries (about)
询问(字)符 inquiry character {ENQ}, who- are- you {WRU}
询问符 interrogation mark
询问回答 inquire answer, query reply
询问器 interrogator
询问时间 query time
询问台 inquiry station
询问信号 request signal
询问站 inquiry station
询问中断 interrogate interrupt
询问装置 inquiry unit
询问字符 enquiry character {ENQ}

循
follow, abide by 循环 circulate, loop, cycle 循序 in proper order or sequence
循环半群 cyclic semigroup
循环变量 cyclic variable/variate, for-loop variable
循环变址 cycle/loop index
循环表 circular list, cyclic table, for list, loop table
循环操作 loop function, loop operation
循环[回路]测试 loopback test
循环测试 loop test(ing), sequence test
循环查询 cyclic query
循环程序 cyclic/loop program
循环存取 cyclic access
循环代码 loop code
循环迭代法 cyclic iterative method
循环读出 cycle/cyclic readout
循环方式 loop mode
循环复位 cycle reset
循环规则 cyclic rule
循环寄存器 circulating register
循环计数 counting loop, cycle count
循环计数器 cycle/loop counter
循环检查 loop test(ing)
循环检索 chaining/ cyclic search
循环结构 for- loop structure, loop construct, loop structure
循环矩阵 cyclic matrix
循环控制 cycle/loop control
循环链表 circular linked list
循环链接 circular linkage
循环码 chain/ cycle/ cyclic/ loop/ reflected code, modified binary code
循环门 cyclic gate
循环排队 circular queue,

cyclic queuing
循环排列 cyclic permutation
循环排序 cyclic ordering, rotational ordering
循环器 circulator
循环嵌套 loop nesting
循环群 cyclic group
循环冗余(码)校验 cyclic redundancy check {CRC}
循环时间 cycle/ cycling time, end-cycle time
循环数据 for data, repeating data
循环(本)体 loop body
循环通道 cycle channel
循环通路 cyclic path
循环图 cyclic graph
循环图表 cyclogram
循环网络 loop network, recirculation network
循环小数 recurring decimal
循环移位 around/ circular/ circulating/ cycle/ cyclic/ nonarithmetic/ ring shift
循环右移 rotate shift right, shift right circular

循环语句 DO statement, loop(ing) statement
循环指令 circulate instruction
循环周期 loop cycle
循环状态 loop/ recirculating/ recurrent state

【xùn】

训 训诫 lecture, teach, train 训练 train, drill 训练班 training class, training course
训练仿真系统 training simulation system
训练模式 training pattern

迅 迅即 immediately, at once 迅捷 fast, agile, quick 迅猛 swift and violent 迅速 rapid, swift, speedy, prompt

讯 (消息) message, dispatch, news 讯问 interrogate, question

逊 逊色 be inferior

Y y

【yā】

压 1)(加压) press, push down 2)(使稳住)(keep under) control 压倒 overwhelm, overpower, prevail over 压低 bring down, lower, reduce 压力 ①(精神上的) overwheming force ②〈物理〉pressure, compressive force 压平 flatten, even 压缩 compress, condense, reduce, cut down; compact, condensed; packed 压弯 bend

压板 platen, pressure plate
压带轮 pinch roller
压电材料 piezoelectric material
压电晶体 piezoelectric crystal
压电效应 piezoelectric effect, piezo-electricity
压轮式绘图仪 pinch-roller plotter
压敏纸 impact paper
压入 push
压缩程式 packing routine
压缩的文件 compressed file
压缩格式 packed format
压缩格式[形式] compressed format
压缩还原 decompaction
压缩卷文件 compressed volume file {CVF}
压缩[组合]十进制 packed decimal
压缩视频 compressed video
压缩图像数据 compressed image data
压缩字符 condensed character
压缩字距 kern, kerning
压印滚筒 impression cylinder
压栈 stack push-down
压纸尺 paper holder
压纸滚筒 platen

押 1)(抵押) give as security, mortgage, pawn 2)(扣押) detain, take into custody 3)(押送) escort 4)(签字) signature, mark in lieu of signature 押金 deposit, security 押款 ①〈动〉borrow money on secuirity ②〈名〉a loan on security

鸭 duck

【yá】

牙 (象牙) ivory 牙齿 tooth

【yǎ】

哑 mute, dumb
哑变量 dummy argument/variable
哑变量名 dummy variable name
哑变元数组 dummy argument array
哑表 dummy table
哑定义 dummy definition
哑工作站 dumb workstation
哑过程 dummy procedure

yǎ 雅　yà 轧亚氩　yān 烟淹　yán 言延

哑节 dummy section
哑节点 dummy node
哑控制节 dummy control section {DSECT}
哑设备 dummy device
哑卫星 dark satellite
哑终端 dumb terminal

雅
(高雅) refined, elegant, graceful 雅致 refined, tasteful
雅可比迭代法 Jucobi iterative method
雅可比定理 Jacobi's theorem

【yà】

轧
另见【zhá】
(滚压) roll, run over 轧碎 crush to pieces

亚
1) (较差) inferior, second 2) (次于) sub- 亚军 second place, runner-up 亚热带 subtropical zone, subtropics, semitropics 亚洲 Asia 亚洲人 Asian
亚对策 metagame
亚结构 metastructure
亚纳秒 subnanosecond
亚稳态 metastable state

氩
argon (Ar)

【yān】

烟
烟草 tobacco, cigarette
烟气 smoke, fume 烟雾 mist, vapor, smog

淹
淹没 submerge, flood, drown

【yán】

言
1) (话) speech, word 2) (说) say, talk, speak 言论 opinion on public affairs, speech 言行 words and deeds, statements and actions 言语 spoken language, speech

延
延长 prolong, extend, lengthen 延缓 delay, postpone, put off 延期 postpone, defer, put off 延伸 extend, stretch, elongate 延误 incur loss through delay 延续 continue, go on, last
延迟 deference, delay, lag, postpone, restard, slowdown
延迟变量 lagged variable
延迟补偿 delay compensation
延迟部件 delay unit
延迟策略 delay policy
延迟程序 delay routine
延迟触发器 delay flip-flop
延迟电缆 delay cable
延迟电路 delay circuit
延迟故障 delay fault
延迟过程调用 deferred procedure call {DPC}
延迟回声 deferred echo
延迟进位 delay carry
延迟链 delay chain
延迟启动 delayed start
延迟确认时间 unacked time {UAT}
延迟人口 deferred entry
延迟失真 delay distortion
延迟时间 delay time, lag time
延迟网络 delay network
延迟系统 delay system
延迟线 delay line
延迟响应[应答] delayed response
延迟向量 delay vector
延迟因素 delay factor
延迟元件 delay element, delay unit
延迟约束 deferred constraint

yán 严岩沿研盐颜 yǎn 衍掩眼

延迟装置 delay unit
延迟状态 defer/delaying state
延期出口 deferred exit
延期时间 defer time
延伸器 extender
延伸性 scalability
延时保护 timed guard
延时电路 time delay circuit
延时畸变 delay distortion

严 严防 take strict precautions against 严格 strict, rigid, rigorous, stringent 严禁 strictly forbid 严厉 stern, severe 严密 tight, close 严肃 ①（令人敬畏）serious, solemn ②（认真）serious, earnest, grave 严重 serious, grave, critical
严格博弈 rigid game
严格代码 severity code
严格定义的 well-defined
严重错误 severe error
严重失效 major failure

岩 岩石 rock

沿 1)（顺着）along 2)（依照）follow 3)（边缘）edge, border 沿革 evolution, the course of change and development

研 研究 ①（探索）study, research ②（商讨）consider, discuss, deliberate 研究生 postgraduate (student) 研究所 (research) institute 研磨 ①（研成粉末）grind, pestle ②（磨光）abrade, polish 研讨 deliberate, discuss 研讨会 seminar, symposium, workshop 研制 prepare, manufacture, develop

研究网 research network
研制系统 development system
研制周期 lead time

盐 salt

颜 颜料 pigment, color, dyestuff
颜色 colo(u)r
颜色菜单 color menu
颜色分辨率 color resolution
颜色深度 color depth
颜色视觉 color vision
颜色数 color number
颜色噪声 color noise
颜色值 color value

【 yǎn 】

衍 衍变 evolution

掩 （关闭）shut, close 掩蔽 screen, mask, shelter, cover 掩盖 cover, conceal 掩饰 cover up, gloss over
掩码 mask
掩码程序 mask program
掩模框 mask frame
掩模原版 master reticle
掩膜设计 mask design
掩膜原图 mask artwork

眼 1)（眼睛）eye 2)（小洞）small hole, aperture 眼光 ①（视线）eye, look, gaze ②（洞察力）sight, foresight, insight ③（观点）view, way of looking at things 眼界 field of vision, outlook, view 眼镜 glasses, spectacles 眼泪 tears, eyedrop 眼力 ①（视力）eyesight, vision ②（辨别力）judgment, discrimination 眼前 ①（跟前）before one's eyes ②（目前）at the

yǎn 演 yàn 厌验焰谚赝 yāng 央殃 yáng 羊扬

moment, at present, now
眼脑系统 eye-brain system
眼视仪 eyephone
眼图 eye pattern

演
(表演)perform, play, act 演变 develop, evolve 演出 perform, show, put on a show 演化 evolution 演讲 give lecture, make a speech 演示 demonstrate, play 演说 ①〈动〉deliver a speech, make an address ②〈名〉speech 演算 perform mathematical calculation 演习 drill, practice 演绎 deduction
演化病毒 evolutionary virus
演示程序 demonstration program
演绎 deduce, deduction
演绎定理 deduction theorem
演绎法 deduction, deductive approach, deductive method
演绎规则 deduction rule
演绎逻辑 deduction logic
演绎模拟 deductive simulation
演绎能力 deductive capability
演绎树 deduction tree
演绎数据库 deductive database
演绎推理 deduction reasoning, deductive inference
演绎推理规则 deductive inference rule
演绎学习 deductive learning

【yàn】

厌 厌恶 be disgusted with 厌烦 be sick of, be fed up with 厌倦 be weary of, be tired of

验 1)(察看)examine, check, test 2)(应验)come true, get the expected effect
验货 examine goods 验收 check and accept, check before acceptance, check upon delivery 验证 test and verify, prove
验错 error-checking
验卡机 card verifier
验收测试 acceptance testing
验收区域 acceptance region
验收试验 acceptance test
验收准则 acceptance criteria
验证测试 verification test
验证机制 examination mechanism
验证密钥 authentication key
验证时间 proving time
验证算法 authentication algorithm
验证套件 validation suite
验证员 verifier

焰 flame, glow, glare

谚 谚语 proverb, saying

赝 赝品 counterfeit, fake, sham

【yāng】

央 央求 beg, plead, appeal to

殃 1)(祸害)calamity, disaster, misfortune 2)(使受害)bring disaster to

【yáng】

羊 sheep 羊毛 sheep's wool, fleece

扬 1)(高举)raise, wave 2)(往上撒)throw up and scatter, winnow 3)(传播)spread, make known 扬名 become famous, gain publicity

yáng 洋阳 yǎng 养氧 yàng 样 yāo 要腰邀幺 yáo 摇遥

扬声器控制 loudspeaker control

洋 1)(盛大)vast, tremendous 2)(海洋)ocean 3)(外国的)foreign

阳 the sun 阳光 sunlight, sunshine 阳性 positive, male

【yǎng】

养 1)(供养)support, provide for 2)(饲养或培植)raise, keep, grow, rear 3)(生育)give birth to 4)(培养)form, acquire, cultivate

氧 oxygen (O) 氧化 oxidize, oxidate

【yàng】

样 (模样)shape, form 样品 sample, model, pattern, specimen 样式 pattern, type, style, form 样子 ①(形状)appearance, shape ②(神情)manner, air, mood, expression ③(样品)sample, model, pattern
样板[品] template (=templet)
样本 sample, example, exponent, specimen, test driver
样本点 sample point
样本范围 sample range
样本方差 sample variance
样本均值 sample average/mean
样本空间 sample space
样本设计 sample design
样本输入 sample input
样本树 sample tree
样本文件 sample file
样本误差 sample error
样本协方差 sample covariance
样机 model, prototype, prototype model
样机板 prototype board
样机操作系统 prototyping operating system
样机开发系统 prototype development system
样机研制 prototype design
样片 sample wafer
样片测试 prototype test
样条 spline
样条函数 spline function
样条拟合 spline fit
样条曲线 spline curve

【yāo】

要 另见【yào】
要求 ask, demand, require, claim
要求图 claim graph

腰 waist

邀 邀请 invite, request

幺
幺环 identity ring
幺图 identity graph

【yáo】

摇 shake, wave, rock, turn
摇摆 sway, swing, rock, vacillate 摇晃 rock, shake

遥 遥控 remote control, telecontrol, distant control
遥远 distant, remote, far-away
遥测 remote measurement, telemeter(ing), telemetry
遥测参数 telemetry parameter
遥测计 telemeter
遥测术 telemetering
遥测系统 telemetry system
遥测线路 telemeter link
遥测信号 telesignalling

遥测组件 telepack
遥感 remote sensing
遥感器 remote sensor
遥控操作 teleoperation
遥控操作器 teleoperator
遥控机器人 telepresence robot
遥控监视系统 remote control monitoring system
遥控设备 remote control equipment
遥控台 remote console, remote control board
遥控系统 remote control system
遥控指令 remote control command, telecommand
遥控指令装置 telecommander
遥控装置 teleequipment
遥远的 remote

【yào】

药 medicine, drug, remedy

要 另见【yāo】
1)(重要)important, essential 2)(希望得到)want, ask for, wish, desire 3)(请求)ask sb to do sth 4)(想做)want to, wish to 5)(必须)must, should 6)(将要)shall, will, be going to 要点 main points, essentials, gist 要害 ① (致命部分)vital part, fatal spot ② (重要部门)strategic point 要价 ask a price, charge 要紧 ① (重要)important, urgent ② (严重)critical, serious, severe 要领 main points, essentials, gist 要求 claim, expect, postulate, quest, requirement 要人 very important person (V.I.P.), important personage 要是 if, suppose, in case 要素 essential factor, key element 要闻 important news, front-page story

钥 钥匙 key

【yě】

也 (同样)also, too, as well, either 也许 perhaps, probably, maybe

冶 冶金 metallurgy 冶炼 smelt (metal)

野 野生 wild, uncultivated 野外 open country, the open

【yè】

业 1)(行业)line of business, trade, industry 2)(职业)occupation, profession, employment, job 3)(学业)course of study 4)(事业)cause, enterprise 5)(已经)already 业已证明 have already been proved 业绩 outstanding achievements, performance 业务 service, professional work, business 业余 ① (工作时间以外的)sparetime ② (非专业的)amateur 业主 owner, proprietor
业务管理系统 service management system {SMS}
业务交换点 service switching point {SSP}
业务接入点 service access point {SAP}
业务卡 transaction card
业务控制点 service control point {SCP}
业务类别 class of service {COS}

业务量 traffic
业务生成环境 service creation environment {SCE}
业务通信 newsletter
业务信息系统 operational information system {OIS}

叶 leaf
叶对象 leaf object
叶节点 leaf node
叶类 leaf class

页 1)(张)leaf, sheet 2)(面) page 页边 margin
页边[边缘]空白 margin
页边文本 margin text
页编号 page number
页标题 page heading
页标志 footers
页表 page table
页表项 page table entry
页槽号 slot number
页(面)池 page pool
页方式 page mode
页故障 page fault
页号 page number
页基 page base
页(面)寄存器 page register
页检查 page check
页脚注释 footnote
页结点 page node
页界 margin for page, page boundary
页拷贝 page copy
页控制块 page control block
页框(架) page frame
页框表入口 frame table entry {FTE}
页框号 frame number
页码机 paginating machine, paging machine
页面 page, hume page
页面标志 page marker
页面布局 page layout
页面长度 page length
页面出错 page fault
页面大小 page size
页面调出 page-out
页面调度程序 pager
页面分割 page break
页面控制 page control
页面挪用 page stealing
页面入口 page entry, page-in
页面设计[图案] page layout portrait
页面碎片 page breakage
页面替换 page replacement
页面显示 page display
页面寻址(法) page addressing
页式存储管理 paged storage management
页式存储系统 page memory system
页式控制 page control
页式终端 paging terminal
页首 page heading
页映像(图) page map
页帧 page frame
页指针 page pointer

夜 night, evening
夜班 night shift 夜半 midnight
夜间 at night

液 liquid, fluid, juice 液体 liquid
液晶 liquid crystal
液晶显示(器) liquid-crystal display {LCD}
液晶印刷机 liquid crystal printer
液芯光纤 liquid core fiber

【yī】
一 1)(数目)one 2)(同一)same, one 3)(另一)also, otherwise 4)(全)whole, all, throughout 一年到头 all

the year round 一般 ①(同样)same as, just like ②(普通)general(ized), normal, ordinary, common 一半 (one) half 一边 ①(一方)one side, aside ③(旁边)by the side, aside ③(动作同时发生)while, as, at the same time, simultaneously 一并 along with all the others, in the lump 一次 once 一打 a dozen 一旦 once, in case, now that 一道 together, side by side 一点(儿)a bit 一定 ①(确定的)fixed, established, regular ②(固定不变的)definite, constant ③(必定)surely, certainly, be bound to ④(特定的)certain, specific, given 一度 ①(一次)once, at one time, for a time ②(有过一次)on one occasion 一对 a pair, a couple 一方面 one side, for one thing, on the one hand 一方面…一方面 on the one side … on the other side 一副 a pair, a set 一概 one and all, without exception, totally 一共 altogether, in all 一贯 consistent, persistent, all along 一览表 table, schedule, inventory 一连串 a succession of, a series of, a string of, a chain of 一律 ①(一个样子)same, alike, uniform ②(无例外)all, without exception 一面 ①(一个面)one side ②(一个方面) one section, one aspect ③(动作同时发生)at the same time, simultaneously 一批 a batch, a shipment 一起 ①(同在一处)in the same place

②(一同)together, in company 一切 all, every, everything 一生 all one's life, throughout one's life 一时 ①(短时间)for a short while, temporary, momentary ②(一个时期)a period of time 一同 together 一系列 a series of 一些 some, certain, a little, a number of, a few 一心 ①(专心)wholeheartedly, heart and soul ②(齐心)of one mind, at one 一样 the same, equally, alike 一月 January 一再 time and again, again and again, repeatedly 一直 ①(不拐弯的)straight ②(始终)continuously, always, all along, all the way 一致 showing no difference, identical, unanimous, consistent
一百 centi-, hecto-
一般程序 general procedure
一般递归谓词 general recursive predicate
一般格式 general format
一般规则 general rule
一般算法 general algorithm
一般优先权 normal priority
一般语法分析 general parsing
一步 one-step, single step
一步迭代 single-step iteration
一次重叠 one overlap
一的补码 one's complement
一地址指令 one- address instruction
一堆 crowd
一对多(的) one-to-many
一对一(的) one-to-one
一对一关系 one- one relationship
一对一映射[映照] one- to- one mapping

一级编址[寻址,定址] direct addressing
一级变量 level-one variable
一级存储器 first/one/single level storage/store/memory
一级代码 one-level code
一级地址 direct address, first/one/single level address
一级中断 one-level interrupt
一阶 single order
一阶理论 first order theory
一阶逻辑 first-order logic
一阶模型 first order modeling
一阶谓词 first-order predicate
一阶系统 first-order system
一览 summary
一览表 compendium, directory, spec(ification)
一览表(数据) catalog(ue)
一目布尔运算 monadic Boolean operation
一目减算符 unary minus operator
一目算子 monadic operator
一目运算 monadic operation, unary operation
一目[一元]运算符 unary operator
一排 tier
一批 batch, party
一群 crowd
一束 batch
一套字符 fount
一维表示(法) one-dimensional representation
一维数组 one-dimensional array
一维搜索[寻查] unidimensional search, linear search, one-dimensional search
一位 single order
一位代码 unitary code
一行代码 line code
一一对应 monogamy, one-to-one (correspondence)
一元表达式 unary expression
一元操作 unary operation
一元查询 unary (sub)query
一元的 monadic
一致(性) uniformity, conformity
一致接口 uniform interface
一致界(限) uniform bound, union bound
一致[相干]网络 coherent network
一致性 coherency, conformance, consistency/consistence
一致性操作 consistency operation
一致性测试 conformance texting
一致性处理 consensus processing
一致性检查(程序) consistency check
一致性约束 consistency constraint
一组 party

衣
（衣服）clothing, clothes, garment

医
医生 doctor, physician
医学 medical science, medical service, medicine 医药 medicine 医院 hospital 医治 cure, treat, heal
医疗图像 medical image
医学 medicine
医学成像 medical imaging
医学科学 medicine science
医学数据库 medical database
医学信息系统 medical information system

依
（按照）according to, in the light of 依此类推 and so

on and so forth **依次** in proper order, successively **依从** comply with, listen to, yield to **依附** depend on, attach oneself to, become an appendage to **依旧,依然** as before, still **依据** ①（根据）in accordance with, on the basis of ②（基础）basis, evidence, foundation **依靠** depend on, rely on **依赖** rely on, be dependent on **依照** according to, in the light of
依附图 adjoint
依赖(性) dependency, depending
依赖边 dependence edge
依赖关系 dependency relation
依赖关系图 dependence graph
依赖图 dependency graph
依赖性码 dependent code
依赖于硬件的 hardware-dependent

铱 iridium (Ir)

【yí】
仪 **仪表**(外貌)appearance **仪式** ceremony, rite, funcion
仪表化[设备] instrumentation
仪器 apparatus, instrument, meter

宜 1)（合适）suitable, appropriate, fit 2)（应当）should, ought to

贻 贻误 affect adversely, bungle

姨 1)（姨母）aunt 2)（妻子的姐妹）sister-in-law

移 （改变）change, alter **移动** (re)move, shift, travel **移交** turn over, transfer, hand over
移出 shift out
移出(字)符 shift-out character {SO}
移动笔 move pen
移动臂磁盘 moving arm disk
移动计算 mobile computing
移动[活动]窗口 moving window
移频键控(调制) frequency shift keying {FSK, fsk}
移去 remove
移入 immigrate, shift-in
移入(字)符 shift-in character {SI}
移数 shift
移位 dislocation, shift
移位(操作) shifting
移位寄存器 shift(ing)/ stepping register
移位计数值 shift count
移位键 shift key {PSK}
移位矩阵 shift matrix
移位控制 shift control
移位链 shift chain
移位逻辑 logic with shift
移位码 shift code
移位脉冲 shift pulse
移位器 shifter
移位数 carry digit
移位算子 shift(ing) operator
移位锁定 shift lock
移位网 shift network
移位位置 shift position
移位运算 shift operation
移位指令 shift order, shifting instruction
移位字典 relocation dictionary {RLD}
移相器 phase shifter
移行 carryover, division into syllables, division of words,

overrun line
移植 implantation, porting, transplatation
移植能力 transferability

遗
（遗失的东西）something lost 遗憾 regret, pity 遗留 leave over, hand down 遗漏 omit 遗失 lose, miss 遗忘 forget 遗作 posthumous work
遗传密码 genetic code
遗传算法 genetic algorithm
遗传学 genetics
遗传学控制理论 genetic control theory
遗传学习 genetic learning
遗漏错误 missing error

疑
doubt, disbelieve, suspect 疑点 doubtful point 疑惑 feel uncertain, not be convinced 疑虑 misgivings, doubt 疑难 difficult, knotty 疑问 query, question, doubt
疑题 paradox
疑问符 interrogation mark, question mark

【yǐ】

乙
second 乙等 the second grade, Grade B

已
（停止）stop, cease, end 已故 deceased, late 已经 already 已往 before, previously, in the past
已编号的 numbered
已变更记录 changed record
已存数据 canned data
已分配变量 allocated variable
已分配的存储器 allocated storage
已激发的 excited
已确认状态 committed state
已加框 open box
已知量 known quantity
已知数 datum, known number
已知状态 known state

以
1)（用，拿）use, take 2)（依照）according to 3)（因）because of that, in order to, so as to 以此 for this reason, on this account 以次 ① （依次序）in proper order ②（某处以下）the following 以后 after, afterwards, later 以及 as well as, along with, and 以来 since 以免 in order to avoid, so as not to, lest 以内 within, less than, inside of 以前 before, ago 以求 in order to, in an attempt to 以上 ①（某点以上）more than, over, above ②（前面的）above, the foregoing, the above-mentioned 以外 beyond, outside, other than, except 以往 before, formerly, in the past 以为 think, believe, consider 以下 ①（在某一点以下）below, under ②（指下面的）the following 以至 ①（表示延伸）down to, up to ②（表示结果）so ... as to ..., so ... that ...
以致 so that, as a result, consequently
以计算机为基础的教育 computer-based education {CBE}
以数据为中心 data-centric
以太网 Ethernet
以太网电缆 Ethernet cable
以太网接口 Ethernet interface

以太网协议 Ethernet protocol

倚 1)(靠)lean on/against, rest on/against 2)(仗恃)rely on, count on

椅 椅子 chair

【yì】

义 1)(正义)justice 2)(正义的)righteous, just 3)(意义)meaning, significance 4)(人造的)artificial, false 义肢 artificial limb 义务 ①(责任)duty, obligation ②(不要报酬的)volunteer, voluntary

亿 a hundred million

艺 1)(技能)skill 2)(艺术)art

亦 also, too

议 1)〈名〉opinion, view 2)〈动〉discuss, exchange views on, talk over 议程 agenda 议定书 protocol 议论 comment, talk, discuss 议题 subject under discussion, topic for discussion

异 1)(不同)different 2)(奇异)strange, unusual, extraordinary 3)(惊奇)surprise 异常 ①(不同寻常)unusual, abnormal ②(非常)extremely 异同 similarities and differences 异性 ①(不同性别)the opposite sex ②(性质不同)different in nature 异议 objection, dissent 异步 asynchronization

异步操作 asynchronous operation/working
异步出口 asynchronous exit
异步传输 asynchronous transmission
异步传输[传送]模式 asynchronous transfer mode {ATM}, asynchronous transmission mode
异步串行数据 asynchronous serial data
异步存储器 asynchronous memory
异步的 asynchronous, heterochromous
异步断路方式 asynchronous disconnected mode {ADM}
异步机 asynchronous machine
异步计时器 asynchronous timer
异步计算机 asynchronous computer
异步结构 asynchronous structure
异步均衡方式 asynchronous balanced mode {ABM}
异步控制 asynchronous control
异步(数据)流 asynchronous flow
异步请求 asynchronous request
异步设备 asynchronous device
异步时序电路 asynchronous sequential circuit
异步时序网络 asynchronous sequential network
异步事件 asynchronous event
异步输入 asynchronous input
异步数据传送 asynchronous data transfer
异步数据收集 asynchronous data collection
异步刷新 asynchronous refresh
异步通信 asynchronous com-

异步通信服务器 asynchronous communication server {ACS}
异步通信接口适配器 asynchronous communication interface adapter {ACIA}
异步通信控制附件 asynchronous communication control attachment {ACCA}
异步通信控制适配器 asynchronous communication control adapter {ACCA}
异步网络 asynchronous network
异步应答方式 asynchronous response mode
异步终端 asynchronous terminal
异步转移模式 asynchronous transfer mode {ATM}
异步装置 asynchronous device
异步总线 asynchronous bus
异常报告 exception report(ing)
异常报文 exception message
异常表征 abnormal attribute
异常出口 exception exit
异常(情况)处理 exception handling
异常回答[应答] exception response
异常结束[中止] abnormal ending {ABEND}, abort
异常例程 exception routine
异常请求 exception request {EXR}
异常条件 exception(al) condition
异常停机 cancel closedown
异常响应 exception response
异常项 exception item
异常向量 exception vector
异常性 abnormality
异常中止模式 abort pattern
异常中止事件 abort event
异常终止 abnormal termination
异常终止[结束] abnormal end {ABEND}
异常转储 abnormal dump
异构事务 heterogeneous transaction
异构网络 heterogeneous network
异构型多处理机 heterogeneous multiprocessor
"异或"电路 anticoincidence circuit
"异或"门 exclusive-OR gate, nonequivalence element, partial sum gate
"异或"运算 nonequivalence operation
异类结构 heterogeneous structure
异体汉字 variant Chinese character, variant Hanzi
异体字 variant
异元性 incongruity

屹
屹立 stand towering like a giant, stand erect

抑
抑制 choke, inhibit, jamming, suppress(ion), abatement
抑制摆动 debounce
抑制器 eliminator
抑制性神经元 inhibitory neuron
抑制语句 suppress statement
抑制振动 debounce
抑制字符 suppression character

疫
疫 plaque, pestilence
疫苗程序 vaccine program

译
译 translate, interpret
译名 translated term or name
译文

translation 译员(口译)interpreter, (笔译)translator
译成密码 encipher, encrypt
译码[解码] decode, decoding, decrypt, decryption, interpretation
译码操作 decod(ed) operation
译码机 decode machine
译码级 decode stage
译码逻辑 decode/decoding logic
译码器 decoder, code translator, decipherer, demultiplexer, function table
译码算法 decoding algorithm
译码图文件 decode map file
译码译密 decipher
译码装置 code translator

易 1)(容易)easy 2)(平和)amiable, good-natured 3)(改变)change 4)(交换)exchange 易碎 breakable, fragile
易变的 labile, variant, versatile
易变计算 mobile computing
易变文件 volatile file
易变性 mobility, volatility
易测性设计 testability design
易处理的 tractable
易读的 self-reading
易读性 legibility
易裂性 fragibility, fragility
易失(性)存储器 volatile memory/storage
易失动态存储器 volatile dynamic storage
易失属性 volatile attribute
易失显示 volatile display
易失性 volatility
易失性测试 volatility test
易碎的 fragile
易碎性 fragibility, fragility

益 1)(好处)benefit, profit 2)(增加)increase 3)(更加)all the more, increasingly 4)(有益的)beneficial

逸 逸出 overswing

意 (心意)wish, desire, intention 意大利 Italy 意大利语,意大利人 Italian 意见 ①(看法或想法)judgement, idea, view, opinion, suggestion ②(反对或不满意)objection, complaint 意料 anticipate, expect 意念 idea, thought 意识 ①〈名〉consciousness ②〈动〉be conscious of, be aware of, realize 意思 ①(意想,构思)meaning, idea, sense ②(愿望)opinion, wish, desire 意图 intention 意外 ①(意料之外)unexpected, unforeseen ②(不幸事件)accident, mishap 意味着 signify, mean, imply 意向 intention, purpose 意义 ①(意思)meaning, purpose, sense ②(价值)significance, importance 意愿 wish, desire, aspiration
意外的 fortuitous
意外事件 chance
意外停机 unexpected halt
意外中断 involuntary interrupt, unexpected halt

溢 溢出 overflow, out-of-range, spill
溢出标记 overflow flag
溢出表 overflow table
溢出处理 overflow handling, spill process
溢出检测器 overflow detector

溢出检查[检验] overflow check
溢出卷 spill volume
溢出类型 overflow type
溢出清除 overflow clear
溢出区 overflow/spill area
溢出条件 overflow condition
溢出位 overflow bit, overflow position
溢出项 overflow entry
溢出异常 overflow exception
溢出指示 overflow indication
溢出状态 overflow status
溢出自陷 overflow trap

毅 firm, resolute 毅力 willpower, will

翼 1)(翅膀) wing 2)(侧) flank

臆 臆测 conjecture, surmise, guess 臆断 assume, suppose

镱 ytterbium (Yb)

【yīn】

因 (原因) cause, reason 因此 therefore, for this reason, consequently 因而 thus, as a result 因公 on duty, on business 因公出差 take an official trip, go somewhere on business 因果 cause and effect 因果关系 causality 因素 factor, element 因为 because of, as a result of, for
因变量 dependent variable
因果 cause and effect
因果(性) causality
因果分析 causal(ity) analysis
因果分析法 causal method
因果链图 cause and effect chain diagram
因果逻辑 causal logic
因果模型 causal model
因果推理 causal reasoning
因果性网络 causal network
因式分解 factoring, factorization
因特网 Internet
因特网编号分配管理机构 internet assigned number authority {IANA}
因特网标准通讯协议 internet protocol {IP}
因特网打印协议 internet printing protocol {IPP}
因特网打印协议工作组 internet printing protocol working group {IPPWG}
因特网对象请求代理间协议 internet inter ORB protocol {IIOP}
因特网服务提供商 internet service provider {ISP}
因特网工程备忘录 internet engineering notes {IEN}
因特网工程任务组 internet engineering task force {IETF}
因特网工程指导组 internet engineering steering group {IESG}
因特网号码分配局 internet assigned numbers authority {IANA}
因特网活动委员会 internet activities board {IBA}
因特网控制消息协议 internet control message protocol {ICMP}
因特网平台提供商 internet presence provider {IPP}
因特网体系结构委员会 internet architecture board {IAB}
因特网网虫 internet worm
因特网网络操作中心 internet network operations center

因特网协会 internet society
因特网协议 internet protocol {IP}
因特网协议安全性 internet protocol security {IPSec}
因特网信息访问协议 internet message access protocol {IMAP}
因特网研究任务组 internet research task force {IRTF}
因特网中继闲谈 internet relay chat {IRC}
因特网浏览器软件 internet explorer {IE}
因子 divisor, factor
因子分解[分析] factor analysis
因子设计 factor design

阴 1)(天气)overcast, cloudy 2)(无阳光处)shade 3)(带负电的)negative 阴暗 dark, gloomy 阴历 lunar calendar 阴谋 plot, scheme, conspiracy 阴险 sinister 阴性 negative, female 阴影 shadow, shade
阴极 cathode
阴极射线 cathode ray
阴极射线管 cathode ray tube {CRT}
阴影层次 shadow level
阴影处理程序 shadow handler
阴影区 shadow region/zone
阴影图 shadow map
阴影线 hatch

音 1)(声音)sound 2)(消息)news, tidings, information 音标 phonetic symbol, phonetic transcription 音调 ① 〈音乐〉tone ②〈物理〉pitch 音节 syllable 音强 ①〈音乐〉the loudness of a sound ②〈物理〉intensity 音素 phoneme 音乐 music
音触终端 voice-actuated terminal
音调控制 tone/toning control
音控开关 voice switch
音乐病毒 music virus
音乐虫 musicbug
音乐箱 jukebox
音量 volume
音量单位 voice unit {VU}, volume unit {VU}
音量级 volume level
音量控制器 volume control
音频 audio/voice frequency
音频传输设备 voiceband facility
音频带 voic band
音频电报 tonal telegraphy
音频放大器 audio amplifier
音频功率放大器 audio power amplifier
音频盒(盒式磁)带记录 audio cassette recording
音频输出 audio output
音频线路 voiceband line, voice-grade line
音频响应 audio response
音频信道 voice channel, voice-grade channel
音频信号方式 voice-frequency signalling
音频应答器 audio response unit {ARU}
音圈电机 voice coil motor
音像多媒体业务 audio/visual multimedia services {AMS}
音效耦合器 acoustic coupler
音质 acoustics

铟 indium (In)

【yín】

银 (金属)silver (Ag) 银币

silver coin 银行 bank 银幕 (motion-picture) screen, projection/ viewing screen 银牌 silver medal 银色的 silver-colored

银行出纳机 teller's machine
银行信用卡 bank credit card {BCC}
银行业务联机系统 banking on-line system
银行业务系统 banking system

【yīn】

引 (牵引) draw, stretch 引导 lead(ing), booting, guiding, homing, induct, pilot, vectoring 引号 quotation marks 引见 introduce, present 引荐 recommend 引进(进口) import, introduce, recommend 引起 give rise to, lead to, cause, arouse 引人注目 noticeable, conspicuous 引入 lead into, draw into 引入 lead-in, import, induct(ion), inlet, insert, gather 引起 cause, make 引文 quoted passage, quotation 引言 foreword, introduction 引用 quote, quoting, instancing, refer to, reference 引证 quote, cite

引出次数 out(-)degree
引出线[部分] leader, outlet
引出组 outgoing group
引导[自展]程序 bootstrap
引导程序 boot (program), bootstrap program/ routine, director
引导代码 guidance code
引导段 boot segment
引导分区 boot partition
引导技术 bootstrap technique
引导记录 boot/ home/ leader record
引导块 boot(strap) block
引导模型 pilot model
引导驱动器 bootstrap driver
引导扇区 boot sector
引导扇区病毒 boot sector virus
引导算法 bootstrap algorithm
引导指令 bootstrap driver, bootstrapping, key instruction {ATTN}
引脚 lead, pin
引脚分配 pin assignment
引脚图 pinout
引起注意的信号 attention {ATTN}
引头microfiche lead microfiche
引线 lead, leg, terminal
引线电缆 drop cable
引用参数 reference parameter
引用层 reference level
引用程序 reference program
引用调用 call by reference
引用频率 reference frequency
引用完整性 reference/ referential integrity

饮 drink 饮料 drink, beverage 饮食 food and drink, diet 饮用水 drinking water

隐 (潜伏的) latent, dormant, lurking 隐蔽 conceal(ment), hide, take cover, wrapup 隐患 hidden trouble, hidden danger 隐匿 hide, go into hiding, lie low 隐性 recessiveness

隐(式) implicit
隐蔽设备 privacy device
隐蔽信道 covert channel
隐变量 hidden variable/ variable
隐参数 implicit parameter

隐藏 hide
隐藏单元 hidden unit
隐藏式文件 hidden file
隐藏字符 hidden character
隐地址 implicit/ implied address
隐定义 implicit definition
隐方式 implicit mode
隐含 imply
隐含表 implication table
隐含关系 implication relation
隐含门 implication gate
隐含数 implicant
隐含项 between-the-line entry
隐匿位 hidden bit
隐请求 implicit request
隐去 crossfade, unposting
隐式存储 implicit storage
隐式方法 implicit method
隐式类型 implicit type
隐式属性 implicit attribute
隐式说明 implicit declaration
隐式系统 implicit system
隐式选择 implicit selection
隐式寻址 implied addressing
隐式引用 implicit reference
隐选择 default option
隐字段 hidden field

【yin】

印 1)（图章）seal, stamp, chop 2)（痕迹）print, mark 3)（付印）put sth into print 印度 India 印度人 Indian 印度洋 the Indian Ocean 印度尼西亚 Indonesia 印度尼西亚人 Indonesian 印发 print and distribute 印花 ①（税票）stamp ②〈纺织〉printing 印象 impression 印证 confirm, corroborate, verify
印错 print miss
印记签署 endorser
印刷 print(ing), imprinting
印刷格式 print format
印刷速度 print(ing) speed
印刷体 block letter
印刷头 print head
印刷网格 print grid
印刷位置 imprint position
印图机 terminal graphics printer
印制板 printed board
印制电路插件 printed-circuit card
印制线 track
印制线路 printed wiring
印字 lettering
印字锤 hammer
印字故障 ink trouble
印字机 inkwriter
印字头 print head

【yīng】

应 另见【yìng】
1)（答应）answer, respond 2)（答应做）promise, agree, accept 应得 deserved, due 应该 should, ought to 应届毕业生 this year's graduates 应有 due, proper, deserved 应允 assent, consent

英 英磅 pound 英镑 pound, sterling 英才 gifted people 英国 Britain, England 英国人 the British, Englishman or Englishwoman 英国英语 British English 英明 wise, brilliant, intelligent 英亩 acre 英雄 hero ◇女英雄 heroine 英语 English ◇美国英语 American English
英特尔公司 INTEL Corp.
英制尺寸 inch size

【yíng】

迎 （对着）move towards, meet face to face 迎接 go to

ying 荧盈营赢 yǐng 影 yìng 应

meet, greet, welcome, receive

荧 burning faintly, flickering, glimmering
荧光屏 screen
荧光显示器 fluorescence display

盈 1)(充满)be full of, be filled with 2)(多余)have a surplus of **盈利** profit, gain **盈余** surplus, profit
盈利分析 profitability analysis

营 1)(谋求)seek 2)(经营)operate, run, manage 3)(军队编制单位)battalion 4)(军队驻地)camp, barracks **营救** rescue, save, aid **营利** seek profits, make money **营业** do business **营造** construct, build

赢 1)(胜)win 2)(获利)gain, obtain, profit **赢余** surplus, profit

【yǐng】

影 1)(模糊的形象)trace, vague impression, sign 2)(照片)photograph, picture **影片** film, movie, picture **影响** ①〈动〉influence, affect ②〈名〉influence, effect, impact **影像** reflection, image **影院** cinema, movie theater **影子** d(a)emon, shadow
影片(式的)图像 cine-oriented image
影视点播 video on demand {VOD}
影响分析 impact analysis
影响函数 Green function, influence function
影响数 influence number
影响线 influence line
影像 image, phantom
影像放大 zoom
影像副本 image copy
影像数据 photographic data
影像数据系统 viewdata
影像文件 image file
影音电碟 digital video disc {DVD}
影子存储器 shadow memory

【yìng】

应 另见【yīng】
1)(回答)answer, respond, echo 2)(满足要求)comply with, accept 3)(适应)suit, repond to **应变** ①(应付突发事情)meet an emergency ◇随机应变 adjust to changing circumstances ②〈物理〉strain **应付** ①(对付)meet, cope with, deal with, handle ②(敷衍了事)do sth perfunctorily ③(将就)manage, make do **应急** meet an urgent need, meet an emergency **应急计划** emergency plan **应考** take an examination **应聘** accept an offer of employment **应邀** at sb's invitation, on invitation **应用** apply, application, use **应战** (接受挑战)accept a challenge **应征** (响应某种征求)answer to calls, answer to requests
应答 acknowledgement {ACK}, answer(back), answering, feedback, reply {REP,RPLY}, response
应答报文 reply message
应答标题 response header {RH}

应答表 answer list
应答部件[单元] response unit {RU}
应答超时 acknowledge timeout
应答电话 answerphone
应答队列元素 reply queue element {RQE}
应答方式 answer/response mode
应答分析程序 response analysis program {RAP}
应答过程 answer
应答码 answer-back code
应答模式 answer mode
应答信号 acknowledge(ment) signal, off-hook signal
应答延迟 answer delay
应答字符 acknowledge character {ACK}
应急(运行)方式 emergency mode
应急开关 emergency/intervention switch
应急维修 emergency maintenance, maintenance emergency
应急转储 panic dump
应力 stress
应力分析 stress analysis
应力矩阵 stress matrix
应力图 stress diagram, stress pattern
应用报文处理程序 application message handler {AMH}
应用编程接口 application programming interface {API}
应用层 application layer
应用程序 application, application program/routine, utility
应用程序接口[界面] application program interface {API}
应用程序接口联合会 application program interface association {APIA}

应用程序设计 application programming
应用程序装入表 application load list {ALL}
应用处理功能 application processing function {APF}
应用窗口 application window
应用范围 application domain
应用分析 application analysis
应用进程 application process {AP}
应用进程 application process {AP}
应用开发生命周期 application development life cycle {ADLC}
应用控制表 application control table
应用类 application class
应用逻辑 applied logic
应用配置访问协议 application configuration access protocol {ACAP}
应用软件 application software
应用软件包 application software package
应用软件工具 application software tools
应用设备 utility unit
应用手册 application manual
应用数学 applied mathematics
应用文件 application file
应用系统 application system {AS}
应用小程序 Applet
应用性 utility

映 (反映)reflect, mirror
映射[映像] image, map(ping)
映射存储器 mapping memory
映射存取 mapped access
映射功能[函数] mapping function
映射[映像]缓冲区 mapped buf-

fer
映射流水线 mapping pipeline
映射逻辑 mapping logic
映射[映象]算法 mapping algorithm
映射位图 mapped bitmap
映射文件 mapped file
映射系统 mapped system
映射装置 mapping device
映像编辑程序 map editor
映像程序 map/image program, mapper
映像处理程序 image processor
映像存储区 image store
映像段 image section {ISECT}
映像方式 image mode
映像分析 image analysis
映像会话 mapped conversation
映像名 image name
映像说明库 map specification library {MSL}
映像图形学 image graphics
映像信号 image signal
映像语句 image statement
映像语言 mapping language

硬 1) (坚硬) hard, stiff, tough 2) (刚强) strong, firm, tough 硬币 coin, specie 硬化 harden, stiffen 硬件 hardware 硬通货 hard currency
硬插件板 hard card
硬磁盘 hard disk, rigid/solid disk
硬磁盘存储器 hard disk memory
硬磁盘控制器 hard disk controller
硬磁盘片叠 hard disk pack
硬磁盘驱动器 hard disk driver, hard drive
硬错(误) hard error
硬的 hard

硬度 hardness, solidness
硬分段 hard sectoring
硬格式 hard format
硬故障 hard fault
硬核 hard core
硬宏元 hard macro
硬回车 hard return
硬键 dongle, hardware key
硬件安全 hardware security
硬件表示(法) hardware representation
硬件部件 hardware component
硬件常驻 hardware resident
硬件成分 hardware component
硬件抽象层 hardware abstraction layer {HAL}
硬件单元 hardware cell
硬件调试 hardare debugging
硬件堆栈 hardware stack
硬件仿真程序 hardware emulator
硬件封锁 hardware lockout
硬件复位 hardware reset
硬件故障[失效] hardware failure
硬件关联 hardware context
硬件管理 hardware management
硬件兼容 hardware compatibility
硬件检查 hardware check
硬件校验 hardware check
硬件接口 hardware interface
硬件结构 hardware structure
硬件开发 hardware development
硬件控制 hardware control
硬件连接的 hardwired
硬件路由选择器 hardware router
硬件逻辑图 hardware logic diagrams {HLDS}
硬件密码 hardware encryption
硬件配置 hardware configura-

yōng 佣拥 yǒng 永勇 yòng 用

tion
硬件平台 hardware platform
硬件评价 hardware evaluation
硬件冗余法 hardware redundancy
硬件设计 hardware design
硬件实现 hardware implementation/realization
硬件锁[钥匙] hardware key
硬件体系结构 hardware architecture
硬件通 hacker
硬件网络 hardware net
硬件维修 hardware maintenance
硬件系统 hard system
硬件性能 hardware performance
硬件优化 hardware optimization
硬件诊断程序 hardware diagnostic
硬件支持[支援] hardware support
硬件中断 hardware interrupt
硬件资源 hardware resource
硬拷贝 hard copy
硬拷贝打印机 hard copy printer
硬拷贝任务 hard copy task {HCT}
硬拷贝输出 hard copy output
硬拷贝终端 hard copy terminal
硬壳式机身[结构] monocoque
硬连线逻辑(电路) hardwired logic
硬连字号 hard hyphen
硬逻辑阵列 hard array logic {HAL}
硬盘 hard disk
硬盘盒 hard disk cartridge
硬盘卡 hard disk card
硬盘类型 hard disk type
硬盘系统 hard disk system
硬盘柱(面) hard disk cylinder
硬盘面盘 hard sectored disk

硬扇区 hard sector
硬扇区分段[划分] hard sectored
硬扇区(记录)格式 hard sectored format
硬设备 hardware
硬设备校验 hard machine check
硬设施 hard facility
硬停机 hard stop

【yōng】

佣 另读【yòng】
1)(雇用)hire 2)(仆人)servant

拥 拥抱 embrace, hug, hold in one's arms 拥挤 crowd, be crowded, congestion 拥有 possess, have, own
拥挤[拥塞]控制 congestion control
拥塞缓解 congestion collapse

【yǒng】

永 forever, always 永不 never 永存 eternal, lasting forever, remain forever 永久 permanent, perpetual, everlasting, forever 永远 always, forever, ever
永久存储器 non-leak memory
永久错误[误差] permanent error
永久消除 superzapping
永久虚连接 permanent virtual connection {PVC}
永久虚拟电路 permanent virtual circuit {PVC}

勇 勇敢 brave, courageous

【yòng】

用 1)(使用)use, employ,

apply 2)（费用）expense, cost 用处 usefulness, use 用法 use, usage 用功 hardworking, diligent 用户 consumer, user, subscriber 用劲，用力 exert oneself, use one's strength 用尽 exhaust, use up 用具 utensil, apparatus, tool 用器 appliance, tool 用品 articles, goods 用途 purpose, application, use(fulness) 用意 intention, purpose 用语 ①（措词）choice of words, wording ②（专业词语）phraseology, term
用户 user, consumer, subscriber, party
用户安装程序 installed user program {IUP}
用户变量 user variable
用户标号 user label
用户标记 user flag
用户标识码 user identification code {UIC}
用户表 user table
用户测试 user test
用户程序 user program, user routine
用户程序方式 job program mode
用户处理机 user processor
用户存储器 user memory
用户代理 user agent {UA}
用户地址表 user address list
用户地址空间 user address space
用户电报 teleprinter exchange service {TEX, Telex}, Telex {TEX}
用户调查 user survey
用户端 user side
用户对象 user object
用户服务[业务] user service
用户服务设施 user facility
用户概述 user profile
用户干线拨号 subscriber trunk dialling {STD}
用户工作站 user work station
用户功能 user facility
用户(代)号 user number {UID}
用户化 customization
用户环境 user environment
用户环路 customer loop
用户级 user level/class
用户级安全性 user-level security
用户级协议 user level protocol
用户级指令 user level instruction
用户记帐 user-account
用户接口[界面] user interface
用户接口程序 user interface program {UIP}
用户接口工具箱 user interface toolbox
用户结构 user structure
用户界面管理系统 user interface management system {UIMS}
用户界面开发工具 user interface development tool
用户卷(宗) user volume
用户可选项 user option
用户空间 user space
用户控制存储器 user control storage {UCS}
用户口令 user password
用户(程序)库 user library
用户块 user block
用户链 user chain
用户轮廓 user profile
用户名(字) user name
用户命令 user command
用户目录 user catalog
用户盘 user disk
用户请求[需求] user requirement
用户区 user area {UA}

用户区段 user segment
用户群 user group {UG}
用户热线 user hotline
用户软件 customer software
用户软件工程 user software engineering {USE}
用户设备 customer premises equipment {CPE}
用户视图处理系统 view processing {VP}
用户手册 user manual, user handbook
用户属性 user attribute
用户数据 user data
用户数据报协议 user datagram protocol {UDP}
用户数据空间 user data space
用户说明 user specification
用户特权 user privilege
用户提示 user prompt
用户网络 user network
用户网络连接 user-network interface {UNI}
用户文本 user version
用户文件 user file
用户箱 user kit
用户需求 user requirements
用户友好的 user-friendly, genial
用户站 user station
用户指南 user/user's guide
用户终端[设备] user terminal
用户状态[方式] user state, user mode
用户组[群] user(s) group {UG}

佣 另见【yōng】
佣金 commission brokerage, middleman's fee

【yōu】
优 (优良) fine, good, excellent 优待 give preferential treatment, award a privilege 优等 high-class, first-rate, excellent 优点 merit, strong point, advantage, virtue 优惠 preferential, favorable 优美 graceful, fine, exquisite 优胜 winning, superior 优势 superiority, advantage 优先 give priority to, take precedence 优秀 outstanding, excellent, splendid, fine 优异 excellent, outstanding 优越 superior, advantageous 优越性 superiority, advantage 优质 high quality/grade
优化 optimization, majorization
优化编译程序 optimising compiler
优化程序[优化器] optimizer
优化(方)法 optimization method
优化功能[函数] optimizational function
优化过程 optimization procedure
优化阶段 optimizing/ optimize phase
优化链 optimized chain
优化树 optimal tree
优化图 optimization graph
优化序列 majorizing sequence
优路线 major path
优先表 precedence table, priority list
优先程序 priority routine
优先(级)调度程序 priority scheduler
优先法 precedence/ priority method
优先方式 priority mode
优先符号 priority symbol
优先关系 precedence relation
优先规则 precedence/ priority rule
优先函数 precedence function

优先号 priority number
优先级 precedence/ priority level
优先级数 priority number
优先级中断 priority interrupt
优先级最高 shortest job first {SJF}
优先矩阵 precedence matrix
优先开放最短路径 open shortest path first {OSPF}
优先逻辑 priority logic
优先(代)码 precedence code
优先排队 priority queuing
优先权 priority, precedence/ preference priority
优先权编码器 priority encoder
优先说明 priority declaration
优先网络 priority network
优先文法 precedence grammar
优先线路 priority line
优先选择 priority selection/option
优先用户线 priority line
优先阈值 priority threshold
优先值 priority value
优先指示符 priority indicator
优先中断 priority interrupt
优先中断级 priority interrupt level
优先作业 priority job

忧 忧愁 sad, worried, depressed 忧虑 worried, concerned, filled with anxiety

悠 悠久 long-standing, long, age-old 悠闲 leisurely and carefree

幽 幽默 humorous 幽雅 quiet and tastefully laid out

【yóu】

尤 尤其 especially, particularly, heartfelt

由 1)(原因)cause, reason 2)(经过)by, through 3)(顺从)follow, obey 由此 from this, thus 由此可见 thus it can be seen, this shows, that proves 由来 origin 由于 owing to, thanks to, as a result of, because of 由衷 from the bottom of one's heart, sincere, heartfelt
由媒体而定的接口 medium dependent interface {MDI}
由底向上设计 bottom up design

犹 犹可 still all right 犹如 just as, like, as if 犹豫 hesitate, be irresolute

邮 post, mail 邮递 post delivery 邮递员 postman, mailman 邮费 postage 邮购 mail-order 邮汇 remit by post 邮寄 send by post, post 邮件 postal matter, post, mail 邮局 post office 邮票 (postage) stamp 邮筒 pillar-box, postbox, mailbox 邮运 deliver by mail, mail transportation 邮政 postal service 邮政编码 postcode, zip code 邮资 postage
邮递电报 mailgram
邮件程序 mailer
邮件登录 mail log
邮件队列 mail queue
邮件方式 lettergram mode {LTM}
邮件分发器 mail exploder
邮件服务器 mail server
邮件归并 mail merge

邮件夹 mail folder
邮件连网机[网关] mail gateway
邮件路径 mail path
邮件网桥[邮桥] mail bridge
邮件炸弹 letter bomb, mailbomb
邮箱 mail box
邮箱[信箱]服务 mailbox service
邮箱[信箱]系统 mailbox system
邮政服务 mail service
邮政协议 post office protocol {POP}
邮政信箱 postbox

油 1)(脂肪,油脂)oil, fat, grease 2)(用油涂抹)apply tung oil or paint 3)(被油弄脏)be stained with oil or grease 油画 oil painting 油墨 printing ink 油漆 ①〈名〉paint ②〈动〉cover with paint, paint 油田 oil field 油桶 oil drum 油污 greasy dirt

铀 uranium (U)

游 1)(旅游)travel, tour 2)(河段)part of a river, reach ◇上游 the upper reaches 游览 go sight-seeing, tour, visit 游戏 ①(娱乐活动)recreation, game ②(玩耍)play 游行 parade, march, demonstration 游艺 entertainment, recreation, amusement 游闲 stroll around, wander 游泳 swim 游泳池 swimming pool
游标 cursor, puck, slider
游程检验 runs test
游动变量 running variable
游动下标 running subscript
游戏棒 paddle

游戏包 games pack
游戏程序 game program
游戏杆 joy(-)stick
游戏盒(带) game cartridge
游戏卡 game card
游戏控制适配器 game control adapter
游戏(端)口 game port
游戏树 game tree

【yǒu】

友 1)(朋友)friend 2)(友好的)friendly 友谊 friendship

有 1)(具有)have, possess 2)(存在)there is, exist 有待 remain, await 有毒 poisonous 有关 about, concerned, related, relevant, regarding, concerning 有害 harmful 有机 organic 有计划 in a planned way, according to plan 有理 ①(有道理)reasonable, justified, right ②〈数学〉rational 有力 strong, powerful, forceful, energetic, vigorous 有利 advantageous, beneficial, favorable 有名 well-known, famous, renowned 有钱 rich, wealthy 有趣 interesting, fascinating, amusing 有色 colored 有色人种 colored race 有色金属 nonferrous metal 有时(候)sometimes, at times, now and then 有限 limited, finite, definite 有线 wired 有效 effective, valid, active, actual 有些 ①(有的)some ②(有一些)somewhat, rather 有益 profitable, beneficial, useful 有意 ①(想要)have a mind to, want, desire ②(故意)

intentionally, deliberately, purposely 有用 useful 有余 ① (有剩余) have a surplus, have enough and to spare ② (有零头) odd ◇10年有余 10-odd years 有助于 help, contribute to 有资格 capable, qualified

有保障的帧速率 guaranteed frame rate {GFR}
有标号的 labelled
有槽环形(网络) slotted-ring
有符号数 signed number
有根树 rooted tree
有根图 rooted graph
有关的 related
有关联的 correlative
有关系的 relative
有界变量 bounded variable
有界函数 bounded function
有界集(合) bounded set, bounded aggregate
有界平衡树 bounded-balanced tree {BB tree}
有界算符[算子] bounded operator
有界限的 definable
有界线性泛函 bounded linear functional
有界序列 bounded sequence
有界整数 bound integer
有理(的) rational
有理分式 rational fraction
有理数 rational number
有名的 named
有名公用区 named common area
有名管道 named pipe
有穷的 finite
有时效的 dated
有双重性的 amphibolous
有限表 finite table
有限表示(法) finite representation
有限差分 finite difference
有限对策 finite game
有限集[有穷集] finite set
有限计算 limited compute
有限控制器 finite control
有限链 finite chain
有限目标 finite goal
有限区域 finite region
有限群 finite group
有限图 finite graph
有限拓扑 finite topology
有限序列 finite sequence
有限域 finite field
有限元分析 finite element analysis {FEA}
有限元建模 finite element modeling
有限元空间 finite element space
有限元模型 finite element model
有限元系统 finite element system
有限值 limited value
有限状态 finite state
有限状态时序机 finite state sequential machine
有限子集 finite subset
有限自动机 finite automaton {FA}
有线电视 cable television {cable TV, CATV}
有线广播 cablecast
有线通信线路 wire communication line
有向边 directed edge
有向的 oriented
有向二叉树 oriented binary tree
有向回路[路径] oriented path
有向树 directed/oriented tree
有向图 digraph, directed/oriented graph
有效变元 valid argument

有效操作 valid/live operation
有效地址 effective/ valid address
有效电平 active level
有效范围 effective range
有效功率 actual power, real power
有效卷 active volume
有效控制 active control
有效全向辐射功率 effective isotropically radiated power {EIRP}
有效时间 active session, operational use time, up-time
有效数(位,性) significance
有效数(字) significand
有效数据 valid data, data valid
有效数字 significant digit/ figure
有效(数)位 significant digit
有效(数字)位 significant figure
有效位(数,数字) significant bit, valid bit
有效性 effectiveness, validity
有效性检查 validity check
有效域 effective domain
有效值 active value
有效字 active word
有序表 ordered table/list
有序对 ordered pair
有序集 ordered set
有序树 ordered tree
有序数 sequential number
有序文件 order file
有序向量 ordered vector
有序帧 sequenced frame
有源边 active edge
有源网络 active network
有源星形网络 active star
有源元件 active element

【yòu】

又 1)(重复)again 2)(再加上)and ◇一又二分之一 one and a half

右 right 右边 the right side, the right
右边缩进[缩格] right- hand indent
右乘 postmultiplication
右调节 right-align
右对齐 right justify, right-adjust
右截断 right truncation
右逆元 right inverse
右陪集 right coset
右移 right shift, shift right, right

幼 (小)young 幼儿 child, infant 幼年 childhood, infancy 幼稚 ①(年龄小)young ②(头脑简单)childish, naive
幼网络 thinnet

诱 诱发 bring out, induce, cause to happen
诱发故障 induced failure

釉 glaze, enamel

【yū】

迂 迂回 circuitous, tortuous, roundabout
迂回信程 backhaul

【yú】

于 1)(在)in, at, on 2)(对于,for, to 3)(自,从)from 4)(表示比较)than ◇多于 more than 于是 hence, consequently, as a result

余 1)(剩下)surplus, spare, remaining, residue 2)(整

后的零头) more than, odd, over 余地 leeway, margin, room 余额 ①(余下的空额) vacancy, room, unfilled job, etc. ②(帐目余额) remaining sum, balance 余量 margin 余 complement
余3代码 excess-three code
余集 complementary set
余码 excess code
余数 remainder, excess

鱼 fish

娱 娱乐 fun, recreation, entertainment

渔 fishing

逾 1)(逾越) exceed, go beyond 2)(更加) even more 逾期 exceed the time limit, be overdue

舆 舆论 public opinion

愚 愚蠢,愚笨 stupid, foolish, silly, clumsy 愚弄 deceive, fool, dupe 愚人 fool

愉 愉快 happy, joyful, delighted

【yǔ】

与 另见【yù】
1)(给) give, offer, grant 2)(跟) with, against 3)(和) and, together with 与此同时 ① in the meantime, simultaneously ② moreover, besides 与其 rather than, better than
"与" coincidence, collation operation, inclusive AND, intersection, logic multiply, logical multiply
"与/操作[运算]" conjunction
"与非" NAND {NOT·AND}, NOT-AND {NAND}
"与或非"门 AND- OR- NOT gate
"与或"树 AND-OR tree
"与或"图 AND-OR graph
与机器无关的 machine-independent
与机器相关的 machine-dependent
与上下文无关的关键词 keyword out-of-context {KWOC}
与设备无关的 device-independent
与设备相关的 device-dependent
与业务无关的构件 service independent building block {SIB}
与硬件相关的 hardware-dependent

予 予以 give, grant

宇 宇宙 universe, cosmos

雨 rain 雨季 rainy season 雨量 rainfall 雨伞 umbrella 雨天 rainy day, wet day 雨衣 raincoat

语 1)(说话) speak, say 2)(谚语) set phrase, proverb, saying 语调 intonation 语法 grammar 语汇 vocabulary 语句 statement, sentence 语录 recorded utterance, quotation 语态 voice 语序 word order 语言学 linguistics, philology 语义 semanteme, meaning, semantic 语义学

semantics **语音** ①（说话的声音）articulation, speech sounds ②（发音）pronunciation **语音学** phonetics
语法差错 syntax error
语法单位 syntactic unit
语法定义 syntax definition
语法分类 syntactic category
语法分析 syntactic/syntax analysis, parse, parsing
语法分析器 syntactic parser
语法分析树 pasing tree
语法概要 syntax summary
语法规则 syntactic/ syntax/ grammar rule
语法记号 syntax notation, syntactic token
语法检查 grammar testing
语法控制 syntax control
语法类型 syntactic type
语法树 syntax tree
语法图 syntax chart/diagram, syntax diagram form {**SDF**}, syntax graph
语法元语言 syntactic metalanguage
语根 radix
语句体 statement body
语谱图 spectrogram
语言板 language board
语言[语音]编码 language coding, speech encoding
语言变量 linguistic variable
语言变体 language variant
语言场 linguistic field
语言定义 language definition
语言翻译 language translation
语言分析 speech analysis
语言合成(器) speech synthesizer
语言结构 language structure/ construct
语言空间 language space
语言扩声系统 speech reinforcement system

语言理解 language understanding
语言描述 language description
语言模式 speech pattern
语言模型 language/linguistic/ verbal model
语言生成 language generation
语言[语音]识别系统 speech recognition system
语言输出(设备) speech output
语言输入 speech input
语言特点 language feature
语言形式化 language formalization
语言转换程序 language conversion program
语义处理 semantic processing
语义分析程序 semantic analyzer
语义检查 semantic check
语义模型 semantic model
语义树 semantic tree
语义完整性 semantic integrity
语义网 semantic net, C-network
语义学 language theory semantics, semantics
语义语法 semantic grammar
语音处理 speech processing
语音合成 voice synthesis speech
语音识别 speech recognition
语音系统 speech system
语音芯片 voice chip
语音应答器 voice answer back {**VAB**}
语音应答设备 audio response unit {**ARU**}
语音邮件服务 voice mail service
语音邮件设备 voice mail device

【yù】
与 另见【yǔ】
take part in 与会 participate

玉 玉石 jade

狱 (监狱) prison, jail

育 1) (生育) give birth to 2) (养育) rear, raise, bring up, breed 3) (教育) educate

浴 bath, bathe 浴室 bathroom, shower room

欲 (欲望) desire, wish, lust

裕 abundant, plentiful

域 territory, region, area, field, domain
域变量 area/domain variable
域标 field tag
域表 field list
域长度 field length
域界定符[分隔符] field delimiter, field separator
域对象 field object
域返回 field return
域控制 field control
域名 domain name {DN}, field name, realm name
域名地址 domain name address
域名服务器 domain name/naming server {DNS}
域字段描述符 field descriptor
域数据 field data
域说明体 field declarator
域提示 field prompt
域演算 domain calculus

预 in advance, beforehand
预报 forecast 预备 prepare, get ready 预测 forecast, predict(ion), figure out, predetermination, oracle, look ahead 预订 subscribe, book, place an order 预定 fix in advance, predetermine, schedule 预防 prevent, precaution, guard against 预付 payment in advance 预告 ① 〈动〉announce in advance, herald ② 〈名〉advance notice 预购 purchase in advance 预计 calculate in advance, estimate 预见 ① 〈动〉foresee, predict ② 〈名〉foresight, prevision 预期 expect, predict, anticipate 预示 betoken, indicate, presage, forebode 预算 budget, estimation 预习 prepare lessons before class 预先 in advance, beforehand 预想 anticipate, expect 预言 ① 〈动〉prophesy, predict, foretell ② 〈名〉prophecy, prediction 预约 ① (预定时间) make an appointment ② (预订) order, subscribe, reserve 预展 preview 预兆 omen, presage, sign, harbinger 预祝 congratulate beforehand

预编辑 pre(-)edit
预编译 precompile
预测法 predicted method
预测分析 look-ahead analysis, predictive analysis
预测模型 forecasting/ predictive model
预充电 precharge
预处理 preprocessing
预存储 prestore
预定[预置]参数 preset parameter
预定义的 predefined
预读磁头 preread head
预防死锁 prevent deadlock
预分类 presort

预分配 preassign, pre-allocation
预汇编 preassembly
预进位 precarry
预排序 presort
预期的 expected
预取 prefetch
预热时间 time warm-up, warm-up time
预设定 preset, presetting, initialize
预填充 prefill
预先估计 look ahead, prior estimate
预先写的 write-ahead
预校正 precorrection
预约表 reservation table
预占线 camp, camp on
预置(位) preset, presetting, initialize
预置窗口 default window
预置功能 preparatory function
预置码 preparatory code
预置目录 default directory
预置时间 preset time
预置实用程序 initialize utility
预置文件 default file
预置选项 default option
预置值 default, prevalue
预转换 supershift (=SS, ss)

阈 threshold
阈门 threshold gate
阈元件 threshold element
阈值 threshold, threshold value
阈值操作 threshold operation
阈值电压 threshold voltage
阈值函数 threshold function
阈值逻辑 threshold logic
阈值逻辑电路 threshold logic circuit {TLC}

寓 寓所 residence, abode, dwelling place 寓意 implied meaning

誉 (名声)reputation, fame

愈 1)(痊愈)recover 2)(越…越…) the more ... the more, more and more 愈加 increasingly, even more, all the more

遇 1)(相逢)meet 2)(对待) treat, receive 3)(机会) chance, opportunity 遇到 run into, encounter, come across 遇见 meet, come across

【yuān】
渊 渊博 broad and profound, erudite 渊源 origin, source

【yuán】
元 1)(开始的)first, primary 2)(为首的)chief, principal 3)(基本)basic, fundamental 4)(货币单位)yuan 元旦 New Year's Day 元素 element
元编译 metacompilation
元变量 metavariable, element variable
元产生式 metaproduction
元成员 metamember
元程序 metaprogram
元代码 metacode
元定理 metatheorem
元符号 metasymbol
元概念 metanotion
元规则 meta-rule
元环境 metaenvironment
元汇编程序 metaassembler
元级推理 meta inference, metalevel reasoning

元计算机科学 meta-computer science
元件 cell, element, component
元件可靠性 component reliability
元件失效效果分析 component failure impact analysis {CFIA}
元件引线 component lead
元控制 meta-control
元类 meta class, element class
元逻辑 metalogic
元媒体 metamedia
元模型 metamodel
元启发式 meta-heuristics
元任务 metatask
元认知 metacognition
元数据 metadata
元数据库 metadatabase
元推理 metareasoning
元文件 meta file
元文件层 metafile level
元文件描述符 metafile descriptor {MD}
元系统 metasystem
元信令 meta signaling
元语言 metalanguage
元知识 meta-knowledge
元注解 metacomment
元字符 metacharacter
元字模 metafont
元组 tuple
元组标识符 tuple identifier {TID}

员
员工 staff, personnel

园
garden, plantation
园区网 campus network

原
1) (最初的) primary, original, former 2) (没加工的) unprocessed, raw 3) (平原) level, open country, plain
原版 original edition, original negative 原本,原稿 original manuscript, master copy
原告 ①(民事的)plaintiff ②(刑事的) prosecutor 原件 script 原来 ①(原先)original, former ②(原来是…)so, turn out to be 原理 principle 原谅 excuse, pardon, forgive 原料 raw material 原始 ①(最初的)original, firsthand ②(未开发的)primitive, primeval 原书 the original 原文 soure text, the original 原物 the original 原先 former, original 原形 original shape, true colors
原意 original intention/idea
原因 cause, reason 原油 crude oil 原则 principle 原著 original (work) 原状 original state, previous condition, status quo ante
原子 atom 原子能 atomic energy
原版 first generation, master, original
原版本 original/prototype version
原操作数 primary operand
原点 origin
原理图 function/schematic diagram
原码(原码形式) true form
原始菜单 primitive menu
原始成分 primitive component
原始符号 original symbol
原始副本 clean copy, raw copy
原始立方 primitive cube
原始令牌 primitive token
原始逻辑单元 origin logical unit {OLU}

原始设备制造厂家 original equipment manufacturer {OEM}
原始索引 primitive index
原始文件 original/primary/primitive/source file
原始线程 primary thread
原图 original, original pattern
原线圈 primary winding
原信息 prime information
原型[机] original, prototype
原型复制 prototyping
原型系统 protosystem, prototype system
原语 primitive
原装母盘[主盘] original master

圆 1)(圆形的)round, circular, spherical 2)〈数学〉circle 圆规 compasses 圆满 satisfactory 圆珠笔 ball-point pen, ball-pen
圆片 wafer
圆片规模集成 wafer-scale integration {WSI}
圆形 roundness
圆周 circumference
圆柱面 cylinder

援 援救 rescue, save, salvage 援引 quote, cite 援助 help, support, aid

缘 (边缘)edge, fringe, brink, brim 缘分 predestined relationshop 缘故 cause, reason

源 1)(水源) source, fountain-head 2)(来源) source, cause 源泉 source, fountainhead
,源点,源程序,源代码 originating, source

源本 source book
源变量 source variable
源操作数 source operand
源程序 original program, source book/code/program/routine
源程序库 source library, source program library
源程序列表[清单] source listing
源程序形式 source program form
源窗口 source window
源磁盘 source disk
源代码 source, source code
源代码控制系统 source code control system {SCCS}
源地址 origin/source address
源端选路透明 source routing transparent {SRT}
源服务访问点 source service access point {SSAP}
源级 source level
源节点[源点] originating node, source node
源控制块 resource control block {RCB}
源路桥 source route bridge
源路由 source route
源路由算法 source route algorithm
源目录 source directory
源(码)区 source area/region/zone
源软盘片 source diskette
源输入格式 source input format {SIF}
源数据 source data
源数据项 source data item
源(程序)文本 source text
源系统 origin/source system
源语句库 source statement library {SSL}
源语言 original/source language

源(发)站 originator
源字段 source field

【yuǎn】

远 far, distant, remote
远程 long-range, remote, long-distance, distant, far-ranging 远大 long-range, ambitious 远见 foresight, forethought 远景 perspective, prospect, outlook 远期 at a specified future date, forward 远洋(大洋) ocean 远征 expedition

远程标识 remote identifier
远程操作员 teleoperator
远程测试 remote test
远程成批处理 remote batch
远程处理请求块 teleprocessing request block {TPRB}
远程传输 teletransmission, remote transmission
远程传真机 telefax
远程存取[访问] remote access
远程登录 telnet, remote login
远程方式 remote mode
远程服务 remote service, teleservice
远程复位 remote reset
远程复制 telecopier, telecopy
远程购物 teleshopping
远程管理 telemanagement
远程过程调用 remote procedure call {RPC}
远程计算机通信 telematics
远程监视器 remote monitor {RMON}
远程办公 telecommuting
远程教学 distance learning, telelecture
远程控制 handle change, remote control, telecontrol
远程目标 remote object
远程软件 telesoftware

远程事务 remote transaction
远程输入服务(功能) remote entry service {RES}
远程数据处理 remote data processing
远程数据存取 remote data access {RDA}
远程数据库 remote database
远程数据终端 remote data terminal
远程数据装置 teledata
远程探询[轮询] remote polling
远程通信 remote communication, telecommunication
远程通信存取(方)法 telecommunication access method {TCAM}
远程通信网(络) telenet, telecommunications network
远程网 long-haul network
远程文件系统 remote file system {RFS}, telefile
远程协同操作 cosession remote
远程信道 telepack
远程信号 distance signal
远程学习(系统) telelearning
远程询问 remote inquiry
远程银行 telebanking
远程(数据)站 distant/remote station
远程诊断 remote diagnosis
远程终端 remote terminal {RT}
远程终端访问方法 remote terminal access method {RTAM}
远程终端设备 remote terminal unit {RTU}
远程主机(宿主) remote host, very distant host {VDH}
远程注册 remote login
远程装入 teleload
远程咨询 telereference
远程作业输出 remote job output

远程作业输入 remote job entry {RJE}
远处 distance
远地 remote site
远端串音[串扰] far-end crosstalk {FECT}
远端故障 far end remote failure {FERF}
远景计划 advanced project, far-reaching design
远景图 perspective view
远距离学习 distance learning

【yuàn】

怨 怨恨 resentment, enmity, hate 怨言 complaint, grumble

院 (院子) courtyard, yard, compound ◇科学院 the academy of sciences 院士 academician

愿 愿望 desire, wish, aspiration 愿意 be willing, be ready

【yuē】

约 (大约) about, around, approximately 约定 convention, protocol, session 约会 appointment, engagement, date 约见 make an appointment, arrange 约略 rough, approximate 约期 fix a date, appoint a time 约束 bound, constraint, restriction
约数 ①(大约数) approximate number ②(能整除某个数的整数) divisor
约会连接 session connection
约会数据块 session data unit
约束变量 bound variable
约束程序 conformance
约束传播 constraint propagation
约束窗口部件 constraint widget
约束规范[鉴定,判定,限定] constraint qualification
约束和 restricted sum
约束集(合) constraint set
约束控制模块 bound control module {BCM}
约束类 constraint class
约束任务集 bound task set {BTS}
约束项 constraint term
约束域 constraint range

【yuè】

月 (每月的) monthly 月报 ①(月刊) monthly (magazine) ②(按月汇报) monthly report 月初 the beginning of a moon 月底 the end of a moon 月份 month 月刊 monthly magazine, monthly 月球 the moon 月息 monthly interest 月薪 manthly pay

乐 另见【lè】
music
乐器数字接口 musical instrument digital interface {MIDI}

阅 1)(检阅) review, inspect 2)(经历) experience, pass through 阅览室 reading room
阅读 read(ing), sense
阅读程序 read routine, reader
阅读方式 review mode
阅读机 reader
阅读头 read head

跃 leap, jump, spring 跃进 make a leap, leap forward
跃变 jump

yuè 越悦 yún 云匀 yǔn 允 yùn 运

跃变函数 jump function

越 1)(跨过)get over, pass, cross 2)(超出)exceed, overstep 越发 all the more, even more 越过 cross, surmount, negotiate 越来越…more and more 越权 exceed one's power or authority 越…越…the more ... the more
越权控制 override control
越权用户 unauthorized user

悦 1)(高兴)happy, pleased, delighted 2)(使愉快)please, delight

【yún】

云 cloud 云集 come together, gather, converge

匀 1)(均匀的)even, smooth 2)(使均匀)even up, divide evenly 匀称 well-proportioned, well-balanced, symmetrical

【yǔn】

允 允诺 promise, consent, undertake 允许 enabled, enable(mend), permit, allow, consent
允许保护 guard enable
允许程序 authorized program
允许复位 reset enable
允许进入 admittance
允许输出 output enable
允许输入 enable input
允许文件 authorization file
允许写入 write enable/permit
允许信元速率 allowed cell rate {ACR}
允许语句 enable statement
允许中断 enable interrupt, enabled interruption, interrupt enable
允许状态 enabled state
允许自陷 trap enable

【yùn】

运 运动 ①〈物理〉motion, movement ②(体育活动)sports, physical activities, exercise 运动会 sports meet, games 运动员 sportman, athlete, player 运费 transportation expenses, freight, carriage 运河 canal 运输 transport, convey, carry 运送 transport, ship, deliver 运算 operate, operation 运行 move, be in motion 运用 utilize, apply, put to use 运转 ①(沿一定轨道运转)revolve, turn round ②(指机器转动)work, operate, run
运筹分析 operation analysis
运筹学 operational research {OR}, operations analysis, operations research {OR, opsearch}
运动视频捕捉适配器 motion video capture adapter
运动图像 motion video
运算表达式 operation expression
运算部件 arithmetic/computation unit
运算程序 operating/production program
运算的 operative, operated
运算对象 operand
运算方法 operational method
运算方式 operate/operation/operational mode
运算放大器 computing/operation/operational amplifier
运算符 operator

yùn 蕴晕酝

运算符(号) operational symbol
运算符优先级 operator precedence
运算控制器 operation control, operation control unit
运算器 arithmetic element/organ/section/unit
运算时间 operating/operation/production time
运算速度 operating rate, operational speed
运算状态 compute mode
运行[运转] run, running
运行表 run chart, run list
运行程序 active program, run program
运行调度(表) run schedule
运行[操作]方式 operating mode
运行故障 operating trouble
运行环境 operational environment
运行记录控制(表) log control table {LCT}
运行记录前写出 log write ahead
运行记录系统 utilization logger system
运行阶段 run phase
运行结束 end of run {EOR}
运行开关 run switch
运行区 job region
运行日志[日记] log
运行时间 operable/operating time, run duration, runtime
运行数据 operating/run data
运行图 run diagram
运行系统 operation/runtime system
运行状态 running state
运用管理 operation management

蕴
蕴藏 hold in store, contain 蕴藏量 reserves, deposits 蕴涵 imply, implication
蕴涵符 implicator
蕴涵运算 subsume

晕
晕圈 halo
晕映图像 vignetting

酝
酝酿 ①(图谋) brew, ferment ②(非正式讨论) make preparations, deliberate on

Z z

【zá】

杂 1)〈形〉miscellaneous, sundry, mixed 2)〈动〉mix, mingle 杂费 ①(零碎费用)incidental expenses, incidentals ②(额外费用)sundry fees, extras 杂感 random thoughts 杂记 ①(笔记)jottings, notes ②(一种文体)miscellanies 杂乱 disorderly mixed, in a jumble, in a mess 杂项 sundry 杂项费用 miscellaneous expenses 杂文 essay 杂志 magazine, journal, periodical 杂质 impurity

杂凑函数 hash function
杂凑算法 hash algorithm
杂类函数 miscellaneous function
杂乱次序 scramble order
杂乱图像 scrambled image
杂乱信号 hash

砸 1)(撞击)pound, tamp, crush 2)(打破)break, smash 砸碎 break into pieces, smash, shatter

【zāi】

灾 calamity, disaster, catastrophe, suffering
灾难备份 disaster backup
灾难恢复 disaster recovery
灾难性错误 catastrophic error
灾难性故障 catastrophic failure

栽 (插上)stick in, insert 栽种 plant, grow

【zǎi】

载 另见〖zài〗
(记载)put down in writing, record

【zài】

在 1)(存在,生存)exist, be living 2)(表示时间、地点、情形、范围等)in, at 在场 be on the scene, be on the spot, be present 在望 ①(可以望见)be visible, be in sight, be in view ②(即将到来)will soon become true 在意 take notice of, mind, take to heart 在于 ①(事物本原所在)lie in, rest with ②(决定于)be determined by, depend on 在职 be on the job, be at one's post 在座 present, participating

在线 on-line (=on line, online)
在线操作 on-line operation
在线测试 in-circuit test
在线仿真器 in-circuit emulator {ICE}
在线服务 online service
在线求助 on-line help
在线适配器 on-line adapter

再 zài

再 1)(又一次) another time, again 2)(更加) still, more, further **再版** second edition, reprint **再次, 再度** once more, a second time, once again **再会, 再见** good-bye, see you again **再三** over and over again, time and again, repeatedly **再生产** reproduction

再初始化 reinitialize
再存入 restore
再代换 overmap
再定位 relocate, relocation, relocation bit, reposition
再定位原点 reorigin
再定位字典 relocation dictionary {RLD}
再定义 redefine
再分区 rezoning
再划分 redivide
再汇聚扇出 reconvergent fanout
再进 reentry
再聚合 reintegration
再启动 restart {RST}
再启动点 restart point
再启动条件[状态] restart condition
再启动指令 restart instruction
再入 reentry (= re-entry)
再入程序 reentrant program
再生 cloning, refresh, regen, regenerate, regeneration, restore, rewrite
再生成 regen, subgeneration
再生程序 reproducer
再生磁道 regenerative track
再生磁头 magnetic reproduce head, reproduce head
再生工程 reengineering
再生器 regenerator
再生周期 regeneration period
再循环 recirculate, recirculation, recycle, redo
再引导 reboot
再应答 reanswer
再运行 rerun
再装入 reload
再组合 reconfiguration

载 zài

载 另见【zǎi】
(装载) carry, ship, load **载运** convey by vehicles, ships, etc., transport, carry **载重** load, carrying capacity

载波 carrier {CARR}, carrier wave
载波传输 carrier transmission
载波电话机 carrier telephon
载波检测 carrier detect {CD}
载波频段 carrierband
载波频率 carrier frequency
载波系统 carrier system
载波信号 carrier signal
载波噪声 carrier noise
载量 capacity
载人卫星 inhabited satellite
载人系统 manned system
载体 carrier {CARR}

暂 zàn

暂 (短暂) of short duration **暂定** arranged for the time being, tentative **暂缓** postpone, put off **暂且** for the time being, for the moment **暂时** temporary, for the time being, for the moment **暂停** pause, halt, suspend(ed) **暂行** provisional, temporary
暂存的 temporal
暂存寄存器 temporary storage register
暂存器 scratchpad memory/ storage, temporary register, transient memory, working register/ space/ storage

zàn 赞 zāng 脏 zāo 遭糟 záo 凿 zǎo 早 zào 造

{WS}, workspace
暂存区 scratchpad area {SPA}, work(ing) area
暂存数据 temporary data
暂存文件 scratch file, temporary file
暂时存储器 scratch memory, scratchpad storage/memory, workspace
暂时的 temporary, temporal, transitory, provisional
暂时[临时]工作区 transient working area
暂时性故障 temporary fault
暂时[暂态]虚拟电路 temporary virtual circuit {TVC}
暂时状态 transient state
暂态电文延时 temporary text delay {TTD}
暂停开关 halt switch
暂停线路 dead line
暂停信号 halt signal
暂停指令 halt instruction
暂停状态 suspend(ed) state
暂驻程序 transient program
暂驻存储区 transient area
暂驻存储区描述符 transient area descriptor {TAD}

赞

赞成 approve of, favor, agree with 赞美 praise 赞赏 appreciate, admire 赞同 approve of, agree with, endorse 赞许 speak favorably of, praise, commend 赞扬 speak highly of, praise, commend 赞助 support, assist, sponsor

脏

dirty, soiled, filthy

【zāo】

遭 遭到 suffer, meet with, encounter 遭遇 suffer, be subjected to, sustain, endure

糟 糟糕 too trouble, too bad 糟粕 waste matter, useless matter 糟蹋 ①(浪费)waste, ruin ②(侮辱)insult, trample on, violate

【záo】

凿 1)〈名〉(firme) chisel, chipper 2)〈动〉cut a hole, chisel, dig

【zǎo】

早 (很久以前)long ago, as early as 早班 morning shift 早餐 breakfast 早晨 (early) morning 早期 early stage, early phase 早日 at an early date, early, soon 早退 leave earlier than one should, leave early 早些 early, in advance, beforehand 早晚 ①(早晨和晚上) morning and evening ②(迟早) sooner or later ③(将来某个时候) some time in the future, some day 早先 previously, in the past
早期失效 early/initial failure, failure initial

【zào】

造 1)(制作)make, build, create 2)(假造)fabricate, concoct 3)(编造)draw up 造成 create, cause, give rise to, bring about 造福 bring benefit to, benefit 造价 cost (of building or manufacture) 造就 ①〈动〉bring up, train, cultivate ②〈名〉

achievements　造型 ①〈动〉modelling, mold-making ②〈名〉model, mold ③〈机械〉molding　造诣(academic or artistic) attainments
造型变换 modeling transformation

噪

噪声,噪音 (acoustic) noise
噪声测量 noise measurement
噪声系数 noise factor
噪声源 noise source

【zé】

则　1)〈规范〉standard, norm, criterion 2)〈规则〉rule, regulation

责

责 duty, responsibility　责备 reproach, blame, reprove　责成 instruct (sb to fulfil a task)　责令 order, instruct, charge　责任 ①〈应做的事〉duty, responsibility ②〈应承担的过失〉responsibility for a fault or wrong
责任级别 duty class

【zěn】

怎　怎么 what, why, how
怎样 how, what

【zēng】

增 increase, gain, add　增补 augment, supplement　增产 increase production　增订 revise and expand (a book)　增多 grow in number or quantity, increase　增加 add(-in), augment, boost, increase, raise　增强 enhance, promote, improve　增刊 supplement, supplementary issue

增强 strengthen, heighten, intensify, reinforcement, enhance(ment)　增长 rise, increase, grow　增添 add, increase　增值〈经贸〉rise in value, appreciation, increment
增广矩阵 augmented matrix
增广型转换网络 augmented transition network {ATN}
增加权 add authority
增量 augmenter, increment, incremental quantity
增量表 increment list
增量参数 incremental/incrementation parameter
增量地址 increment address
增量调制 delta modulation
增量方式 incremental dimension system
增量计数器 increment counter
增量器 incrementer
增量指示器 increment pointer
增量指针 increment pointer
增亮字段 intensifier field
增强的图形适配器 enhanced graphics adapter {EGA}
增强服务 enhanced services
增强逻辑链接控制 enhanced logical link control {ELLC}
增强[提升]脉冲 enhance pulse
增强的并行端口 enhanced parallel port {EPP}
增强器 booster, enhancer
增强型 enhancement mode
增强型不归零制 enhanced non-return-to-zero {ENRZ}
增强型小型设备接口 enhanced small device interface {ESDI}
增益 gain
增益压缩 gain compression
增益因子 gain factor
增音器 repeater {RP}
增值进程 value-added process

{VAP}
增值网络 value-added network
{VAN}

憎 憎恨 hate, detest

【zèng】

赠 赠品(complimentary) gift, giveaway 赠送 give as a present, present as a gift 赠与 favor, gift, grant 赠阅 (of a book, periodical, etc.) given free by the publisher

【zhā】

扎 (刺)prick, run or stick (a needle, etc.) 扎实 ①(结实) sturdy, strong ②(实在)solid, sound, down-to-earth

【zhá】

札 (信件)letter 札记 reading notes

轧 另见【yà】
roll (steel)

闸 1)(水闸)floodgate, sluice gate 2)(把水截住)dam up water 3)(制动器) brake 闸门 ①(水闸)(sluice) gate, water gate ②(船闸)lock gate

【zhà】

乍 1)(刚开始)first, for the first time 2)(忽然)suddenly, abruptly

炸 1)(爆炸) explode, burst 2)(爆破轰炸) blow up, blast, bomb

榨 榨汁 press, extract, squeeze

栅 railings, palings, bars, 〈电子〉cascade
栅缝 slit
栅格 grill
栅格阵列 pin grid array {PGA}
栅极 grid
栅极电路 grid circuit
栅栏 barrier, fence

【zhāi】

摘 1)(取) pick, pluck 2)(选取) select, make extracts 摘记 take notes 摘录 make extracts ②〈名〉extracts, excerpts 摘要 ①〈动〉make a summary ②〈名〉summary, abstract, excerpts, brief,〈法语〉précis
摘要日志 summary journal

【zhǎi】

窄 1)(不宽)narrow 2)(气量小)narrow-minded
窄播 narrowcast
窄带调频制 narrow band frequency modulation {NBM, NBFM}
窄带信道 narrow band channel
窄频(带) narrow band

【zhài】

债 debt ◇还债 pay one's debt ∥ 借债 borrow money 债户 debtor 债款 loan 债权 creditor's rights, obligatory right 债券(government) bond, debenture 债主 creditor

【zhān】

沾 1)(浸湿)moisten, wet, soak 2)(被附着)be stained with 沾染 be infected with,

zhān 粘 zhǎn 展崭 zhàn 占战站

be contaminated by

粘 粘贴 glue, stick, paste

【zhǎn】

展 1)(张开)open up, spread out, unfold 2)(施展)put to good use, give free play to 展出 put on display, be on show, exhibit 展开①(张开)spread out, unfold, open up ②(大规模地进行)launch, unfold, carry out 展览 put on display, exhibit(ion), show 展览会 exhibition 展品 exhibit, item on display 展期①(往后推迟)extend a time limit, postpone ②(展览时期)duration of an exhibition, exhibition period 展示 open up before one's eyes, reveal, show, lay bare 展望 predict, forecast, look into the distance/future 展现 unfold before one's eyes, emerge 展销 display and sell
展开的文件 flat file
展开节点 expanding node
展开式 expansion

崭 崭新 brand-new, completely new

【zhàn】

占 占据 occupy, seize, take 占上风 gain the upper hand, have the advantage (over) 占先 take precedence, take the lead 占用 take (up), occupy and use, occupation 占有①(拥有)own, possess, have ②(占据)occupy, hold
占空率 duty ratio
占线 engage
占线信号 busy/ engaged signal
占线中断线 busy trunk
占用内存 committed memory
占用时间 busy/holding time
占用线 busy line
占有率 occupancy rate

战 战败①(打败仗)be defeated, lose (a battle or war) ②(打胜)defeat, beat, conquer 战斗①〈名〉fight, battle, combat, action ②〈形〉militant, fighting 战略 strategy, strategic(al) 战胜 defeat, triumph over, vanquish, overcome, beat 战士 soldier man, fighter 战术 (military) tactics 战线 battle line, battlefront 战役 campaign, battle 战争 war(fare), battle, fight
战略计划 strategic planning
战略决策 strategic decision-making
战略情报[信息]系统 strategic information system {SIS}
战略信息 strategic information
战略学 strategics
战争博弈 wargame

站 1)(停留)stop, halt 2)(车站)station, stop 3)(业务机构)station, center 站立 stand, be on one's feet 站住①(停止行动)stop, halt ②(站稳)stand firmly on one's feet, keep one's feet ③(理由成立)hold water, be tenable 站住脚①(停止行走)stop, halt ②(待在某地)stand one's ground, consolidate one's position ③(理

zhàn 栈 zhāng 张章 zhǎng 长涨掌 zhàng 丈

由成立) hold water, be reasonable
站布局 station arrangement
站长 board manager
站代码 station code
站接口 station interface
站空间 stage space
站控制块 station control block {SCB}
站群集器 station cluster
站识别符 station identifier

栈 1)(仓库)warehouse 2)(旅店)inn
栈 stack
栈变换 stack transformation
栈变量 stack variable
栈表 stack list
栈操作 stack manipulation, stack operation
栈处理机 stack handler
栈串 stack string
栈存储方式 stack mode
栈存储器 stack memory
栈地址 stack address
栈顶 stack top
栈顶操作数 top operand, top stack operand
栈顶算子 top operator
栈顶元素 top element, top stack element
栈顶指针 top-of-stack pointer
栈访问 stack access
栈符号表 stack symbol table
栈归约 stack reduction
栈号 stack number
栈机器 stack machine
栈深度 stack level
栈溢出 stack overflow
栈元素 stack element
栈指令 stack instruction, stack order
栈指示器 stack indicator/pointer
栈指针 stack pointer
栈指针定位 stack pointer alignment {SPA}
栈自动机 stack automata/automaton {SA}
栈作业 stack job

【zhāng】
张 1)(夸张)exaggerate, overstate 2)(开张)open a business 张开(开张)open, spread, stretch 张贴 put up 张望 peep, look around 张扬 make widely known, make public, publicize

章 (图章)seal, stamp ◇公章 official seal 章节 chapter, section 章程 constitution, rules, regulations

【zhǎng】
长 另见【cháng】
1)(年纪较大)older, elder, senior 2)(排行最大)eldest, oldest 3)(领导人)chief, head 4)(生长)grow, develop 5)(增加)acquire, enhance, increase 长进 progress

涨 rise, go up 涨价 rise in price

掌 (手掌)palm 掌管 be in charge, manage 掌权 assume power, exercise control 掌握① (支配)grasp, master, know well ② (主持,控制)control, preside over
掌上型计算机 palmtop

【zhàng】
丈 (长度单位)zhang (=3.33 meters) 丈夫① (妻子的配

偶) husband ② (男子汉) man 丈量 measure (land)

帐 帐簿 account book 帐单 bill, check 帐户 account 帐目 accounts, items of an account
帐号 account number
帐户管理 accounting management
帐户名 account name
帐务处理程序 accounting procedure

障 障碍 hinder, obstruct 障碍物 barrier, block, obstacle
障碍 balking, barrier, obstacle, occlusion

【zhāo】

招 招标 invite tenders, call for tenders 招待 attend to (guests), entertain, serve (customers) 招待会 reception 招呼 ① (呼唤) call, hail ② (问候) hail, greet, say hello to ③ (照料) take care of, look after 招领 announce the finding of lost property 招认 confess, admit 招牌 (shop) sign, signboard 招聘 give public notice of a job vacancy, put up a want ad 招生 enroll new students, recuit students 招收 recruit, enlist, enroll 招手 wave, beckon, gesture

朝 另见【cháo】
1) (早晨) (early) morning 2) (日, 天) day 朝气 youthful spirit, vigor, vitality 朝气蓬勃 full of youthful spirit, full of vigor and vitality

【zháo】

着 另见【zhuó】
着急 become worried, feel anxious 着迷 be fascinated, be captivated

【zhǎo】

找 look for, try to find, seek

【zhào】

召 召唤 call, summon 召回 recall 召集 gather together, convene, assemble 召开 convene, convoke

兆 1) (预兆) sign, omen, portent 2) (预示) portend, foretell
兆 million, (单位前缀) mega-. (= 10^6) {M}
兆比特 megabit
兆赫 megahertz {MHz}
兆流 mega stream
兆位 megabit
兆总线 megabus
兆字节 megabyte {MB, Mbyte}

照 1) (依照) according to, in accordance with 2) (比照) contrast 照办 act accordingly, act in accordance with, follow 照常 as usual 照发 ① (照例发给) issue as before ② (文件批语) approved for distribution 照顾 ① (考虑到) take into account/ consideration, make allowance(s) for ② (照料) look after, take care of, attend to 照会 ① 〈动〉present a note to (a government) ② 〈名〉note 照镜 reflect, mir-

zhào 罩 zhē 遮 zhé 折哲 zhě 锗 zhè 这 zhēn 针珍

ror 照旧,照例 as before, as usual, in the same old way 照看 look after, attend to, keep an eye on 照明 illumination, lighting 照片 photograph, picture 照射 shine, illuminate, radiate 照相 take pictures/photographs 照相机 camera 照样 ①（依照样式）after a pattern or model ②（依然）in the same old way, all the same, as before
照排机 phototypesetter
照相通真 photorealism
照相存储器 photographic storage
照相复制 photocopy, photographic copy
照相排版 film setting, photo(type)setting
照相显影 photographic process
照相制版机 imagesetter

罩 （遮盖）cover, wrap 罩子 cover, shade, shield, casing

【zhē】
遮 遮蔽 ①（挡住）hide from view, cover, screen ②（拦住）obstruct, block 遮挡 shelter from, keep out 遮盖 ①（遮住）cover, overspread ②（隐瞒）hide, conceal, cover up
遮光器 chopper
遮罩 hood

【zhé】
折 1)（弯曲）bend, twist 2)（转向）turn back, change direction 折叠 fold 折断 break, snap 折扣 discount, rebate 折合 convert into, amount to 折旧〈经贸〉depre-

ciation 折旧费 depreciation charge 折中 compromise
折半查找 dichotomizing search
折半搜索 binary search
折线 broken line, polyline
折线图 broken line graph, line chart

哲 哲理 philosophic theory, philosophy 哲学 philosophy 哲学家 philosopher

【zhě】
锗 germanium (Ge)

【zhè】
这 this 这边,这里,这儿 this side, here 这次 this time, present, current 这个 this one, this 这回 this time 这么 so, such, this way, like this 这时 now 这些 these 这样,这般 so, such, like this, this way

【zhēn】
针 1)（缝衣针）needle ◇大头针 pin 2)（缝的一针）stitch 针对 ①（对准）be directed against, be aimed at ②（依照）in the light of, in accordance with
针点矩阵 pin dot matrix
针孔馈送 pinfeed
针式打印机 needle/stylus/matrix/wire printer
针网阵列 pin grid array {PGA}

珍 珍贵 valuable, precious 珍品 treasure 珍惜 treasure, value, cherish 珍重 ①（爱惜）highly value, treasure ②（保重）take good care of yourself

真 1)(的确) really, truly, indeed 2)(清楚确实) clearly, unmistakably, distinctly 真诚 sincere, genuine, true 真谛 true essence, true meaning 真理 truth 真情 ①(真实情况) the real situation, the facts, the truth ②(真诚感情) true feeling, real sentiments 真实 true, real, authentic, genuine 真相 fact, (naked) truth, the actual state of affair 真心 wholehearted, heartfelt, sincere

真 true
真彩色 true color
真出口 true exit
真空带盘 vacuum tape reel
真空台 vacuum bed
真命题 true proposition, true statement
真感 realism
真实感图像 reality picture
真实感图形 realistic graphics
真实性 realism, reality
真实智能 real intelligence
真语句 true statement
真值(值) truth value
真值保持系统 truth maintenance system {TMS}
真值表 Boolean operation table, truth table
真值集 truth set

甄 甄别 ①(审查辨别) examine and distinguish, screen, discriminate ②(考核鉴定) reexamine a case

【zhěn】
诊 examine (a patient)
诊断 diagnosis, diagnostic, diagnose
诊断部件 diagnostic package
诊断测试程序 diagnostic test program
诊断程序 diagnosis/ diagnostic program, diagnostor
诊断跟踪程序 diagnostic trace program/routine
诊断工具 diagnostic tool
诊断功能测试(程序) diagnostic function test {DFT}
诊断控制管理程序 diagnostic control manager {DCM}
诊断码 diagnostic code
诊断软件 diagnostic software
诊断软盘 diagnostic diskette
诊断树 diagnostic tree
诊断图 diagnostic graph
诊断指令 diagnostic instruction
诊断专家系统 diagnostic expert system

缜 缜密 careful, meticulous, deliberate

【zhèn】
阵
阵列乘法器 array multiplier
阵列打印机 array printer
阵列计算机 array computer
阵列逻辑 array logic
阵列模块 array module
阵列运算 array operation

振 振兴 develop vigorously, promote, vitalize
振荡 oscillation
振荡器 oscillator
振动 oscillation, vibrate, vibration, shake
振动试验 vibration test
振幅 amplitude
振铃(字)符 bell character {BEL}

镇 1)(城镇) town 2)(抑制)

press down, ease 镇定 calm, cool, at ease

震 1)(情绪激动)greatly excited, deeply astonished, shocked 2)(地震)earthquake 震动 shake, shock, vibrate, quake 震惊 shock, stun, astound

【zhēng】
争 争辩 argue, debate, dispute 争端 controversial issue, dispute, conflict 争夺 fight for, contend for 争光 win honor for 争论 argument, controversy, dispute, debate 争取 strive for, fight for 争先 try to be the first to do sth 争议 dispute, controversy, dispute 争执 disagree, dispute, argue
争用 contention
争用时间间隔 contention interval
争执模型 conflict model

征 征集 ①(收集)collect, gather ②(征募)draft, call up, recruit 征聘 advertise for a job vacancy 征求 solicit, seek, ask for 征税 levy taxes, taxation 征文 solicit articles or essays 征询 consult, seek advice of 征兆 sign, omen, portent
征求评议文件 request for comments {RFC}
征求性 solicit request
征求性信息 solicited message

蒸 蒸发 evaporate, vapo(u)rize 蒸汽 steam 蒸煮 steam

【zhěng】
拯 拯救 save, rescue, deliver
拯救点 rescue point

整 (完整)whole, complete, full, entire 整顿 rectify, consolidate, reorganize 整个 whole, entire 整洁 clean and tidy, neat 整理 put in order, straighten out, arrange, collate, sort out 整齐 orderly, in good order, neat, tidy 整数 ①(无小数)integer, whole number ②(无零头)round number, round figures 整体 inblock, integer, unity 整体化 integration, integrate 整天 the whole day, all day, all day long
整边界 integral boundary
整变量 integer variable
整常数 integer constant
整块 inblock, monoblock
整理操作 decluttering
整理程序 collator
整理装置 collating unit
整流 rectification
整流变压器 rectifying transformer
整流电路 rectifying circuit
整流二极管 rectifier diode
整批上传 batch upload
整批下载 batch download
整数部分 integer(al) part
整数规划 integer programming
整数线性规划 integral linear programming
整数项 integer item
整数值 integer value, integral quantity
整套 full set
整体部件 global facility

整体大楼综合布线系统　total building integration cabling
整体结构　overall structure
整型表达式　integer expression
整型解　integer solution
整直器　aligner
整字换行　word wrap

【zhèng】

正 1)〈物理〉positive, plus 2)(大于零的) positive 3)(端正) regular 4)(色、味纯正) pure, right 5)(恰好) just, right, precisely, exactly 6)(时间正好是) punctually, sharp ◇ 十点正 at ten o'clock sharp　正北　due north　正常　normal, regular　正常化　normalize; normalization　正当 ①(正处在) just when, just the time for ②(合理合法的) proper, rightful　正道,正路 the right way, the correct path　正点　on schedule, on time, punctually　正对 (straight, upright) due　正方 square　正方形 square　正规 standard, normal, regular　正好,正巧 ①(恰好) just in time, just right, just enough ②(碰巧) happen to, chance to, as it happens　正门 main entrance　正面 ①(非ުǎ的) front, face, facade ②(主要使用的一面) the obverse side, the right side　正品 certified products, quality products　正确 correct, right, proper　正如 exactly as, just as　正式 formal, official, regular　正视 face squarely, face up to　正文 text, body matter, main body　正午 high noon　正误 correct (typographical) errors　正误表 errata, corrigenda　正在 in process of, in course of　正直 honest, upright, honorable　正职的, chief, principal　正中 main, situated in the middle
正半定矩阵　positive semi-definite matrix
正本　master, original
正比例　direct proportion
正步　positive step
正常回答　normal response
正常检查　normal inspection
正常流向　normal direction flow, normal flow
正常模式　normal pattern
正常入口　normal entry
正常输出　normal output
正常响应方式　normal response mode {NRM}
正常形式　normal form
正常运行　failure-free operation, regular service
正的　plus, positive
正定函数　positive definite function
正定矩阵　positive definite matrix
正反馈　positive feedback
正方的　dimetric
正负号　sign
正规表达式　regular expression
正规定义　formal definition
正规[态]方程　normal equation
正规集　regular set
正规模式　normalized mode
正规属性　normal attribute
正规网络　regular network
正规文法　normal/regular grammar
正规文件　normal file
正规语言　normal/regular

language
正规子群 normal subgroup
正号 positive sign
正号穿孔 plus punch
正交 quadrature
正交变换 orthogonal transformation
正交表 orthogonal list
正交补 orthocomplement, orthogonal complement
正交调制 quadrature modulation
正交幅度调制 quadrature amplitude modulation {QAM}
正交(性)关系 orthogonality relation
正交集 orthogonal set
正交矩阵 orthogonal matrix
正交链表 orthogonal linked list
正交链接 orthogonal linkage
正交群 orthogonal group
正交向量 orthogonal vector
正交坐标 orthogonal coordinate
正零 plus zero
正逻辑 positive (true) logic
正面馈送 face-up feed
正片 positive
正切 tangent
正区 plus zone
正确的 exact, valid
正确构造的 well formed
正确性 accuracy, correctness
正确性证明 correctness proof, proving correctness
正式的 formal
正视图 front elevation, orthograph
正态 normal
正态变量 normal variable
正态分布 normal distribution
正态随机过程 normal random/stochastic process
正文字体 body type
正弦 sine {SIN}
正弦波 sine wave, sinusoid, sinusoidal wave
正弦函数 sine function
正相关 positive correlation
正向错误校正 forward-error correction {FEC}
正向电流 forward current
正向恢复 forward recovery
正向兼容 compatibility forward
正向链 chaining forward
正向搜索 forward search
正向引用 forward reference
正像 positive image
正则表达式 regular expression
正则矩阵 regular matrix
正则搜索 regex search
正则图 regular graph
正则语言 regular language
正值性 positivity

证 证件 credentials, papers, certificate 证据 evidence, proof, testimony 证明 ① 〈动〉proof, prove, testify, bear out ② 〈名〉certificate, identification, testmonial (letter) 证券 bond, security, negotiable securities 证券交易所 stock exchange, securities exchange 证人 evidence, witness 证实 affirm, confirm, verify 证书 certificate, credentials, license
证据语句 evidence sentence
证明程序正确性 proving program correctness
证明规则 proof rule
证券问题 portfolio problem
证实 acknowledge {ACK}
证书管理 certificate authority

政 (事务) affairs of a family or an organization 政策 poli-

zhèng 症郑挣帧 zhi 之支

cy 政府 government 政权 state/political power, regime 政治 politics, political affairs

症 症状 symptom
症状模式 syndrome pattern

郑 郑重 serious, solemn

挣 (挣钱等) earn, make 挣脱 struggle to get free, try to throw off the bondage

帧 frame
帧编号 frame number
帧标识器 frame marker
帧表 frame table
帧表入口 frame table entry {FTE}
帧捕获 frame grab
帧差异 frame difference
帧长 frame length
帧窗口 frame window
帧存储 frame store
帧大小 frame size
帧的继承 frame inheritance
帧的缺省值 frame default
帧地址 frame address
帧封装 frame encapsulation
帧格式 frame format
帧级 frame level
帧级接口 frame level interface
帧间距 frame pitch
帧检验序列 frame check sequence {FCS}
帧结构 frame structure
帧控制 framing control
帧控制程序 frame handler {FH}
帧理论 frame theory
帧频 frame frequency, frames per second
帧速率 frame rate
帧同步 frame lock, frame synchronization
帧校验序列 frame check sequence {FCS}
帧栈 frame stack
帧指针 frame point
帧中继 frame relay {FR}
帧中继交换设备 frame-relay switch equipment {FRSE}
帧中继终端设备 frame-relay terminal equipment {FRTE}
帧状态字段 frame status field

【zhi】

之 ① of ② for ③ it, them
之后 later, after, afterwards 之间 between, among 之类 and so on, and so forth, and the like 之内 in, within 之前 before, prior to, ago 之上 over, above 之外 besides, except, beyond 之下 under 之中 in, in the midst of, among

支 支撑 ①(抵抗压力)prop up, sustain, support ②(勉强维持)struggle to maintain 支持 ①(勉强维持)sustain, struggle to provide for ②(鼓励)support, back, stand by 支出 ①〈动〉pay, extend ②〈名〉expenses, expenditure 支付 pay (money) 支配 ①(安排)arrange, allocate, dispose ②(控制)control, dominate, govern 支票 check, cheque 支票簿 checkbook 支取 draw (money) 支援 support, assist, help
支撑函数 support function
支持系统 support system
支持硬件 support hardware
支点 fulcrum, pivot, pivot point

支付利息 interest expense
支付日期 due date
支付手段 tender
支付装置 payment mechanism
支架 boom, cartridge, crossarm, pedestal, tray
支配关系 dominance relation
支配数 dominance number
支票核准记录 check authorization record {CAR}
支线 branch line, feeder line
支援工具 support tool
支援芯片 support chip

知 1)(知道)know, realize, be aware of 2)(使知道)inform, notify, tell 知觉 perception, consciousness 知名 well-known, noted, famous 知识 knowledge, intellect 知识分子 intellectual, the intelligentsia
知名端口 well-known port
知识编码 knowledge encoding
知识编译 knowledge compilation, knowledge compiling
知识表示系统 knowledge representation system {KRS}
知识产生 knowledge production
知识处理语言 knowledge processing language {KPL}
知识创建 knowledge creating
知识存取 knowledge access
知识的模糊性 ambiguity/fuzzy of knowledge
知识的属性 knowledge attribute
知识获取工具 knowledge acquisition tool {KAT}
知识获取系统 knowledge acquisition system {KAS}
知识件 knowledgeware
知识结构 knowledge structure
知识经济 acknowledge economics
知识科学 knowledge science
知识空间 knowledge space
知识库 knowledge base
知识库管理系统 knowledge base management system {KBMS}
知识库机 knowledge base machine {KBM}
知识库系统 knowledge base system {KBS}
知识模型 knowledge model
知识提取 knowledge elicitation
知识推理 knowledge inference/reasoning
知识系统 knowledge system
知识信息处理系统 knowledge information processing system {KIPS}
知识性工作 knowledge work
知识源 knowledge source

织 1)(纺织)weave 2)(编结)knit

指 另见【zhǐ】finger 指甲 nail

肢 limb ◇四肢 the four limbs

【zhí】

执 1)(拿着)hold, grasp 2)(坚持)stick to, persist 3)(回执)receipt 执笔 write, do the actual writing 执法 administer the law 执行 administer, execute, execution, implement, implementation, perform(ance) 执意 insist on, be determined to, be resolute 执照 license, permit
执行保护 execute protection

执行标志 execute flag
执行部件 execution unit
执行程序 executive, executive program/ routine, executor, supervisory program/routine
执行存储器 executive memory
执行单元 execution element {EE}
执行方式 executive mode
执行级 execution level
执行(总)开销 executive overhead
执行轮廓文件 execution profile
执行模型 execution model
执行请求 executive request
执行请求块 execution request block {ERB}
执行时间 execute/ execution time {E-time}
执行输入输出 execute input or output {EXIO}
执行位 execute bit
执行[行政]信息系统 executive information system {EIS}
执行循环语句 DO loop, do-loop statement
执行优先级 execution level, execution priority
执行语句 exec(ution) statement {EXEC statement}, perform statement
执行元件 execution element {EE}
执行指令 execute/execution/executive instruction
执行状态 executing state, executive mode/state

直 1)(成直线的)straight 2)(垂直)vertical, perpendicular 3)(挺直)straighten 4)(公正)just, upright 直到 until, till, up to 直观 directly perceived through the senses, audio-visual 直接 directly, straight 直径 diameter 直属 directly under, directly subordinate to 直线 straight line 直爽 frank, straightforward 直译 literal translation, word-for-word translation

直播卫星 direct broadcast satellite {DBS}
直拨网络 in-dialing network
直插封装 in-line package
直观代码 visual code
直观推断法 heuristic method
直观[可视]显示终端 visual display terminal {VDT}
直观[可视]信息处理器 visual information processor {VIP}
直观[可视]终端 visual terminal
直积 direct product
直角坐标 rectangular coordinate
直接编址[寻址,定址] direct addressing
直接拨号 direct dialing
直接插入函数 in-line function
直接产生式 direct production
直接存储存取 direct memory access {DMA}
直接存取 direct access
直接存取存储器 direct access memory, direct access storage {DAS}, direct access unit
直接调用 direct call
直接读出 direct reading, direct read-out
直接广播地址 direct broadcast address
直接广播卫星 direct broadcast satellite {DBS}
直接控制 direct control
直接连接 direct attach/connect/link, straight linkage
直接连网存储 network attached storage {NAS}

直接路由 direct route
直接耦合的 direct coupled {DC}
直接派生[导出] direct derivation
直接输出 direct output, on-line output
直接输入 direct/ substantive input
直接数(字)控(制) direct digital control {DDC}, direct numerical control {DNC}
直接图形接口规范 direct graphics interface specification {DGIS}
直接系统输出 direct system output {DSO}
直接线路附属装置 direct line attachment {DLA}
直接向内拨号 direct inward dialing {DID}
直接向外拨号 direct outward dialing {DOD}
直接寻址 immediate addressing
直觉(知识) intuition
直流 continuous current, direct current {DC}
直流传输网络 DC transmission network
直流断电(状态) DC dump
直流耦合 DC coupling
直通 end to end
直纹面 ruled
直线拟合 line-fitting
直线扫描 linear sweep
直叙语言 scripting language
直译 literal translation, transliteration

值 value 值班 be on duty
值得 be worth, merit, deserve
值钱 costly, valuable
值参数 value parameter
值单元 value cell
值调用 value call
值集 value set
值属性 value attribute
值特征 value tag
值域 range

职
职别 official rank 职称 the title of a technical or professional post 职工(staff and) workers 职能 function 职权 power 职守 post, duty 职位 position, post, office 职务 post, duties, job, assignment 职业 vocation, profession, occupation 职员 office worker, staff member 职责 duty, obligation, responsibility, charge

植
plant, grow 植物 plant, flora, vegetation

【zhǐ】

止
1) (停止) stop, cease, discontinue 2) (到…为止) to, till

只
only, merely, just 只得, 只好 be obliged to, have to, be forced to 只顾 ① (专一) be absorbed in ② (只顾到) only cared for 只管 ① (尽管)by all means, not hesitate to ② (只顾) merely, simply, just 只是 ① (仅仅是) merely, only just ② (但是) however, but then, only 只要 so long as, provided
只读 read-only {RO}
只读标志 read-only flag
只读窗口 read-only view
只读存储器 read-only memory {ROM}, read-only storage {ROS}
只读方式 read-only mode

只读光盘(存储器) read only optical disk, compact disc read only memory {**CD-ROM**}
只接收 receive-only {**RO**}
只写 write-only {**WO**}

旨 (目的)purport, purpose
旨趣 purport, objective 旨意 decree, intention

纸 paper
纸币 paper money/bill/currency, note 纸烟 cigarette 纸张 paper
纸抽取 paper extraction
纸带 paper tape
纸带机 paper tape equipment/unit/driver/handler
纸带馈送 tape feed
纸带设备 tape unit
纸架 paper holder
纸馈送符 form feed character {**FF**}
纸芯 paper core
纸用完 paper out

指 另见【zhi】
指标 target, quota, norm, index 指出 point out 指导 guide, direct 指点 give directions/ tips/ advice 指定 appoint, designate 指尖 finger tip 指令 ① instruct, order, direct ② 〈计算机〉instruction 指明 show clearly, demonstrate, point out 指南 directory, guide book, manual 指派 appoint, designate, assignment 指使 induce, instigate, agitate 指示 ① (指给人看)indicate, point out, designate ② (指示下级)instruct ③ (指示内容)directive, instructions 指头 finger 指向 point at, point to 指引 point (the way), guide, show 指针 indicator, pointer, needle 指正 point out the mistakes for correction, make a comment or criticism
指标 denotation
指触终端 touch terminal
指错信息 error message
指导程序 instructor
指导委员会 steering committee
指导[情报]系统 informing system
指定表 assign table
指定的 named
指定任务异步出口 specify task asynchronous exit {**STAE**}
指挥 instructor
指挥和控制 command and control {**2C**}
指挥仪 director
指令 instruction, order, dictation, directive
指令表 instruction list/ catalog/ repertoire/table
指令步进 instruction step
指令部件 instruction unit
指令操作代码 instruction operation code
指令长度 instruction length
指令重复执行 instruction retry
指令代码 instruction code
指令地址 instruction address
指令调度 instruction scheduling
指令断点 instruction breakpoint
指令方式 instruction mode
指令格式 instruction/ order format, order structure
指令集 instruction set
指令寄存器 instruction register
指令计数器 instruction counter
指令结构 order structure
指令控制器 instruction control

指令类型 instruction type
指令流 instruction flow, instruction stream
指令流水线 instruction pipeline
指令区 instruction area/storage
指令取出 instruction fetch
指令停机 instruction stop
指令系统 instruction system/set/repertoire, order set
指令相关性 instruction dependency, interdependency of instruction
指令译码器 instruction decoder
指令预取 instruction prefetch
指令周期 instruction cycle
指令字 coding line, instruction word
指示笔 stylus
指示灯 indicator, indicator light
指示符 designator, indicator, pointer
指示孔 designation/function punch
指示器 indicator, cursor, pointer, pointing device
指示位 qualifying bit {Q-bit}
指示语句 directive statement, indicator term
指数 characteristic, coefficient, exponent, index mark, power of number
指数记数[表示]法 exponential notation
指数平滑法 exponential smoothing method
指数衰减模型 exponential decay model
指纹 fingerprint
指纹分析 fingerprint analysis
指纹模式 fingerprint pattern
指引线 leaders
指针[指示字]变量 pointer variable
指针地址 pointer address
指针数据 pointer data
指针数组 pointer array
指针值 pointer value

趾 〔脚指〕toe

酯 〈化学〉ester ◇聚酯 polyester

【zhì】

至 1)(到)to, until, till 2)(极,最)extremely, most 至迟 at the latest, no later than 至多 at most, no more than 至关紧要 of utmost importance 至今 up to now, to this day, so far 至上 supreme, the highest 至少 at least 至于 ①(以至于)go so far as to ②(关于)as far as, as to

治 治安 public order/security, the peace 治理 ①(管理)administer, govern ②(整修)harness, bring under control, put in order

制 制裁 sanction, punish 制成品 finished products, manufactured goods, manufactures 制订 work out, formulate 制定 lay down, draw up, formulate, draft 制度 system, rules, regulations 制品 products, goods 制胜 get the upper hand of, subdue 制约 restrict, condition, confine 制造 ①(加工原材料)make, manufacture ②(制造气氛)create, fabri-

cate, make up 制止 check, curb, prevent, stop 制作 make, manufacture
制表 reporting, tabbing, tabulate, tabulation, tabulator
制表符 tab(ulation) character
制表机 tabulator
制表机构 tabulator mechanism
制表间隔 tab interval, tabulating space
制表键 tab(ulator) key
制表组 tab group
制导 guidance, guiding
制导码 guidance code
制导面板 guidance panel
制导武器 guided weapon
制动按钮 stop button
制式 system
制图 graph plotting
制图机 draft(ing) machine, graphic plotter, graphical tool, graphics unit
制图学 graphics
制图仪 graphic plotter
制图作业处理程序 graphic job processor {GJP}
制造厂 manufactory
制造厂家提供的软件 manufacturer software
制造业 manufacture
制造[生产]自动化协议 manufacturing automation protocol {MAP}

质 1)(性质) nature, character 2)(物质) matter, substance 质变 qualitative change 质地 quality 质量 ①〈物理〉mass ②(产品质量) quality 质问 question, interrogate 质询 address inquiries to, ask for an explanation 质疑 call in question, query
质量 quality
质量保证技术 quality assurance technique {QAT}
质量服务 quality of service {QOS}
质量控制 quality control
质量控制系统 quality control system {QCS}
质量诊断 quality diagnostic
质量指数 quality index {QI}
质数 prime, prime number
质蕴涵(项) prime implicant

致 1)(给与) send, extend, deliver 2)(集中于) devote 3)(招致) incur, result in, cause 致辞 make a speech 致词 make/deliver a speech 致富 become rich, acquire wealth 致敬 salute, pay one's respects to, pay tribute to 致力 devote oneself to, work for 致命 causing death, fatal, mortal, deadly 致使 cause, result in 致谢 express one's thinks, extend thanks to 致意 give one's regards, present one's compliments, send one's greetings
致冷 chill, chilling
致冷器 cryostat
致密性 compactness
致命标志 fatal flag
致命错误 fatal error
致命故障 catastrophic/ critical failure
致性 mortality

秩 秩序 order, sequence

智 智慧 wisdom, intelligence 智力,智能 intelligence, intellect, aptitude 智谋 resourcefulness 智囊 brain trust

智囊团 think group/ tank, brain trustee   智商 intelligence quotient (IQ)   智育 intellectual education/ development
智慧人 knowledgeman
智件 knowledgeware
智力 mentality, mind
智能 intellect, intelligence
智能办公室自动化系统 intelligential office automation system {IOAS}
智能编辑系统 intelligent editing program
智能程序设计 intelligent programming
智能磁盘控制器 intelligent disk controller {IDC}
智能打印数据流 intelligent printer data stream {IPDS}
智能大楼 intelligent building
智能代理 intelligent agent
智能多媒体 intelligent multimedia
智能分布系统 distributed intelligence system {DIS}
智能感知 intellisense
智能工作站 intelligent workstation
智能管理 intelligent management {IM}
智能光元 smart pixels
智能(计算)机 intelligent computer
智能机器人 intelligence/ intelligent robot
智能集线器 intelligent hub
智能技术 intellectual technology
智能计算机辅助工程 intelligent computer-aided engineering {ICAE}
智能计算机辅助教学 intelligent computer-aided instruction {ICAI}, intelligential computer assisted instruction {ICAI}
智能计算机辅助设计 intelligential computer-aided design {ICAD}
智能计算机辅助制造 intelligential computer-aided manufacturing {ICAM}
智能检索 intelligent retrieval
智能接口 intelligent(ial) interfacing
智能卡 smart card
智能控制 intelligence/ intelligent control
智能库 intelligence base
智能模拟 intelligence simulation
智能能力 intelligent capability
智能数据库 intelligent database {IDB}
智能数据库机 intelligent database machine {IDM}
智能通道 intelligent cable
智能外设 intelligent peripheral {IP}
智能外围接口 intelligent peripheral interface {IPI}
智能网 intelligent network {IN}
智能网概念模型 intelligent network conceptual model {INCM}
智能网络 intelligent network
智能系统 intelligence/ intelligent system
智能学习系统 intelligent learning system {ILS}
智能仪器 intelligence/ intelligent instrument
智能用户电报 teletex
智能知识库系统 intelligent knowledge base system {IKBS}

智能终端(设备) intelligent terminal
智能自动化系列 intelligent automation system {IAS}

滞 stagnant, sluggish 滞留 be detained, be held up 滞纳金 fine for delaying payment, fine for paying late, overdue fine 滞销 unsalable, slow-selling 滞销货 unsalable goods
滞后 lag
滞后(现象) hysteresis
滞后时间 lag time
滞后网络 phase-lag network

置 1)(搁,放) place, put 2)(设立,布置) set up, establish, install 置办 buy, purchase 置疑 doubt
置"0" reset, set to zero, unset
置换 permutation, permute, replace, replacement, substitute, substitution
置换表 substitution list
置换码 permuted code
置"0"脉冲 quench/reset pulse
置"1"脉冲 set pulse
置位 set
置位复位脉冲 set reset pulse
置位逻辑 set logic
置位脉冲 set pulse
置位时钟 set clock
置信 confidence
置信带 confidence belt
置信度 degree of belief/ confidence, (level of) confidence
置"0"信号 clear signal
置信系统 belief system {BS}
置"0"置"1"触发器 reset- set flip-flop {R-S flip-flop}, R-S flip-flop

【zhōng】

中 另见【zhòng】
1)(内部) in, among, amidst 2)(在…过程中) in the process of, in the course of 中班 middle shift 中部 central section, middle part 中等 secondary, medium, intermediate 中东 the Middle East 中断, 中止 suspend, break off, discontinue 中国 China 中国人 Chinese 中间 ①(里面) among, between ②(两者之间) intermediate, interspace, middle, mean 中介 intermediary, medium 中立 neutrality 中年 middle age 中期 mid-term, medium term 中枢 center 中途 halfway, midway 中文 the Chinese language, Chinese 中午 noon, midday 中心 center, centre, heart, core, middle 中型 medium-sized, middle-sized 中学 middle/ high/ secondary school 中旬 the middle ten days of a month 中央 ①(中心) center, middle ②(最高领导机构) central authorities
中导孔 center feed, feed/ guiding/ sprocket hole, space-hold
中断 blackout, break, interrupt {INT}, interruption
中断编码 gap coding
中断标志位 interrupt flag bit
中断表 interrupt table
中断查询 interrupt inquiry
中断超时 interrupt time-out
中断触发器 interrupt flip-flop
中断处理程序 interrupt handler, interrupt handling routine, interrupt processing

routine, interruption handling program/routine

中断等待(时间) interrupt latency

中断点 breakpoint

中断堆栈 interrupt stack

中断队列 interruption queue

中断对象 interrupt object

中断返回 interrupt return, return from interrupt

中断返回地址 interrupt return address

中断返回指令 interrupt return instruction

中断方式 interrupt mode

中断分配表 interrupt dispatch table {IDT}

中断分析程序 interrupt analyzer

中断分组 interrupt packet

中断俘获 interrupt trap

中断服务 interrupt servicing

中断服务任务 interrupt service task {IST}

中断级 class interrupt, interrupt level

中断级工作区 level work area {LWA}

中断键 attention/break key

中断接口 interrupt interface

中断结构 interrupt structure

中断控制块 interrupt control block {ICB}

中断控制字 interrupt control word

中断类 interrupt class

中断码 interrupt(ion) code

中断模式 interrupt mode

中断屏蔽寄存器 interrupt(ion) mask register {IMR}

中断屏蔽位 interrupt mask bit

中断屏蔽指令 interrupt mask instruction

中断起因 interruption source

中断启用 interrupt enable

中断嵌套 interrupt nesting

中断请求[要求] interrupt request {IR}, break request {BR}

中断请求线 interrupt request line

中断驱动 interrupt-driven

中断设备 interrupt facility

中断识别 interrupt identification/recognition/sensing

中断矢量表 interrupt vector table

中断输入线 interrupt input line

中断条件 interrupt condition

中断位表 interrupt bit table {IBT}

中断系统 interrupt system

中断现场 interrupt spot

中断陷阱 interrupt trap

中断响应 interrupt response

中断向量 interrupt vector

中断向量地址 interrupt vector address

中断信号 interrupt signal

中断信息字节 interrupt information byte {IIB}

中断应答 acknowledge interrupt, interrupt acknowledge

中断优先表 interrupt priority table

中断优先权 interrupt priority

中断源 interrupt(ion) source, source of interrupt

中断指令 interrupt instruction

中断周期 intermediate cycle

中断驻留程序 terminate and stay resident program {TSR program}

中断装置 interrupt device

中断状态 interruption status

中断状态字 interrupt status word

中断自陷 interrupt trap

中规模集成 medium-scale integration {MSI}
中继连接器 trunk connector
中继连接线 trunk junction
中继器 repeater {RP}
中继线 junction line, trunk
中继站 relay station, repeater {RP}, repeater station
中继状态 relay state
中继字 relay word
中间程序 interlude
中间代码[编码] intermediate code
中间定位 interfix
中间段 interlude
中间会晤路由 intermediate session routing {ISR}
中间计算 subtotaling, tweaking
中间件 middleware
中间结果 intermediate result
中间结果存储单元 scratchpad
中间配线架 intermediate distributing frame {IDF}
中间数据集 intermediate data set
中间体 middleware
中间位 sandwich digit
中间文本块(符) intermediate text block {ITB}
中间文件 intermediate, intermediate file
中间系统 intermediate system
中间循环轨道(系统) intermediate circular orbit {ICO}
中间语言 interlanguage, intermediary/ intermediate language {IL}
中近景 medium close-up {MCU}
中景 medium shot, mid-shot
中括号 bracket
中枢开关 backbone switch
中枢网 backbone network
中枢线路 backbone line
中数 mean
中速(的) medium speed
中文信息处理系统 Chinese information processing system {CHIPS}
中线 centerline, mean line
中项 mean
中心点 centered dot
中心服务 central service
中心节点 center node
中心局 central office {CO}
中心控制系统 center control system
中心站 hub site/station
中型计算机 medium-size/scale computer, midicomputer
中性线 neutral
中性总线 neutral bus
中序 inorder
中序遍历 inorder traversal, inorder traverse
中央操纵 central control
中央处理器[机,单元] central processing unit {CPU}, central processor
中央存储器 central memory
中央交换(机) centerx
中央局 central office {CO}
中央控制器 central control unit {CCU}, central controller
中央目录服务器 central directory server {CDS}
中央文件[档案]系统 central file system {CFS}
中央预订系统 central reservation system {CRS}
中央站 central site/station
中央终端设备[装置] central terminal unit {CTU}
中值 median
中值定理 mean value theorem
中止 disable, fall into abeyance, hang-up, kill, outage,

pause, suspend
中止权标 stop token
中止陷阱 abort trap
中止循环 stop loop
中止语句 abort statement
中缀 infix
中缀次序 inorder
中缀形式 infix form

忠
忠诚 loyal, faithful, devoted 忠告 ①〈动〉sincerely advise/ counsel ②〈名〉(sincere) advice 忠实 true, faithful, reliable 忠心 loyalty, devotion, dedication 忠于 true to, loyal to, faithful to, devoted to

衷
衷心 wholehearted, heartfelt, cordial 衷心欢迎 give a cordial welcome

钟
1)(响器)bell 2)(计时器) clock 钟点 ①(指某一时间) a time for sth to be done or to happen ②(小时)hour
钟控的 clocked

终
1)(最终)end, finish 2)(人死)death 终点(point), destination, finish, end (point), dead end 终归, 终究 eventually, in the end, after all 终极 ultimate 终端 end, final stage 终局 end, outcome 终年(全年) all the year round, throughout the year 终身, 终生 lifelong, all one's life 终于 at last, in the end, finally 终止 ①(结束) stop, cease, terminate, end ②(停止) termination
终点集合 destination set
终点[终端]控制 end point control
终点[末端]设备 end device
终端 terminal (station), termination, end, tag end
终端办公室 end office {EO}
终端表 terminal list/table
终端表目 terminal table entry {TTE}
终端操作员 terminal operator
终端处理机 terminal (handling) processor {TP}
终端打印机 terminal printer
终端地址 end/terminal address
终端对话(期) terminal session
终端仿真[模拟] terminal emulation
终端访问机制[设施] terminal access facility {TAF}
终端访问控制器 terminal access controller {TAC}
终端符(号) termination symbol, terminal symbol
终端会话设备 terminal transaction facility {TTF}
终端机模式 terminal mode
终端监督程序 terminal monitor program {TMP}
终端接口处理机 terminal interface processor {TIP}
终端轮询 terminal polling
终端名 terminal name
终端屏幕 terminal screen
终端设备 terminal device/ equipment/installation/unit
终端事务处理程序 terminal transaction facility {TTF}
终端适配器 terminal adapter {TA}
终端系统 end system
终端显示语言 terminal display language {TDL}
终端线路 terminal line
终端用户 terminal user
终端支持 terminal support

终端中继线 terminal trunk
终端装置 end equipment, terminal device/installation
终端作业 terminal job
终结符 terminal (symbol), terminator
终结状态 terminal state
终态 final state
终行 end line
终值 end/final/terminal value
终止单元 stopper
终止符号 terminating symbol
终止码 stop code
终止位 stop bit
终止语句 terminate statement, termination statement
终止状态 finite state

【zhǒng】
种 另见【zhòng】
（物种）species 种类 kind, sort, type 种种 all sorts of, a variety of 种子 seed 种族 race

【zhòng】
中 另见【zhōng】
1)（命中）fit exactly, hit 2)（遭受）be hit by, fall into, be affected by, suffer 中毒 poisoning, be poisoned 中肯 pertinent, to the point 中选 be chosen, be selected
中毒计算机 poisoning computer

仲 仲裁 arbitration
仲裁器 tiebreaker
仲裁签名 arbitrated signature

众 1)〈形〉many, numerous 2)〈名〉crowd, multitude 众多 multitudinous, numerous 众所周知 it is common knowledge that, as everyone knows, as is known to all

种 另见【zhǒng】
（种植）grow, plant, cultivate

重 另见【chóng】
1)（分量）weight ◇净重 net weight ∥ 毛重 gross weight 3)（程度深）deep, serious
重大 great, major, significant 重担 heavy burden, difficult task 重点 focal point, emphasis, key, priority 重量 weight 重视 attach importance to, lay stress on 重心(事情的主要部分) heart, core, focus 重型 heavy-duty, heavy 重要 important, significant, major 重要性 importance, significance 重音 stress, accent
重要产品数据 vital product data {VPD}
重要语汇索引 concordance

【zhōu】
洲 1)（大陆）continent 2)（沙洲）islet in a river, sand bar 洲际 intercontinental

周 1)（圈子）circumference, periphery, circuit 2)（绕一圈）make a circuit, move in a circular course 3)（普遍,全）all, whole, all over, all around 4)（星期）week 周报 weekly (publication) 周到 thoughtful, considerate 周刊 weekly (magazine/publication) 周密 careful, thorough 周末 weekend 周年 anniversary 周期 ①〈名〉peri-

od, cycle (time) ② 〈形〉cyclic(al), periodic(al) 周围 around, round, about 周转〈经贸〉turnover
周期挪用 cycle steal(ing)
周期图表 cyclogram
周期中断 cycled interrupt, periodic interrupt
周围[外围]的 environmental, peripheral
周游窗口 navigation window

【zhóu】

轴 axis, axes, axle, shaft, spindle
轴对称的 axisymmetric

【zhòu】

昼 daytime, daylight, day
昼夜 day and night, round the clock

皱 1) (皱纹) wrinkles, lines 2) (起皱纹) wrinkle, crease, crumple

【zhū】

珠 (小的球形东西) bead 珠宝 pearls and jewels, jewelry 珠子 pearl

诸 all, various 诸多 a good deal, a lot of 诸如 such as 诸如此类 and so on and so forth

猪 pig, hog, swine 猪肉 pork

【zhú】

竹 竹子 bamboo

逐 1) (追赶) pursue, chase 2) (驱逐) expel, drive out 3) (接着次序) one by one 逐步 step by step, progressively 逐个 one by one 逐渐 gradually 逐年 year by year, year after year 逐日 day by day, every day
逐步记录 step record
逐步求精程序设计 refinement programming
逐步执行 step execution
逐次 serially
逐次代法 successive substitution method
逐位法 digit by digit method
逐位进位 cascade(d) carry, step-by-step carry
逐项 term by term
逐行倒相正交平衡调幅制(PAL制彩色电视广播标准) phase alternative line {**PAL**}
逐行汇编程序 line by line assembler {**LBLA**}
逐字 word by word
逐字翻译 word for word translation

【zhǔ】

主 1) (所有者) owner, master 2) (当事人) person/ party concerned 主办 direct, sponsor, organize 主编 ① 〈名〉chief editor ② 〈动〉edit, supervise the publication 主持 ① (负责处理) take charge of, manage, direct ② (负责掌握) preside over, chair 主次 primary and secondary 主从 (关系) principal and subordinate, master-slave 主导 leading, predominant, guiding 主动 initiative, active 主观 subjective 主管 ① 〈动〉be responsible for, be in charge of ②〈名〉person in charge, director, supervisor **主讲** be the speaker, give a lecture **主课** main subject, major course **主力** main force, main strength of an army **主流** ①(主要水流) main stream, main current ②(主要方面) main aspect, main trend **主权** sovereign rights, sovereignty **主权国** sovereign state **主人** ①(财物所有人) owner ②(权力所有人) master ③(与"客人"相对的) host ◇女主人 hostess **主任** director, head, chairman **主使** instigate, be the principal plotter **主题** subject, theme **主体** subject, superior, main body/ part, principal part **主席** chairman **主修** specialize, major **主要** main, chief, primary, principal, major **主意** ①(办法) idea, plan ②(主见) decision, view **主语** subject **主张** ①〈动〉advocate, maintain, hold ②〈名〉view, position, stand, proposition **主旨** gist

主板 mainboard
主部件 master unit, mother unit
主菜单 main/ master/ primary menu
主操作员 chief operator
主程序 host/ main/ primary program, main/ master routine, master program {**MP**}
主程序体 main body
主处理机[器] host processor, main processor
主窗口 main window
主磁道 primary track
主从调度 master/ slave scheduling
主从关系 master-slave relation
主从结构 host- slave architecture
主从控制装置 puppet
主从系统 host- slave system, master-slave system
主存(储) main memory, primary store
主存储器 primary memory/store/storage, main memory/store/storage
主存储器划分 main storage partition
主存[内存]分配程序 core allocator
主存分区 main storage partition
主存库 main storage pool
主单元 mother/primary unit
主动打开 active open
主动的 active
主动目录 active directory
主动数据库 active database
主动位寻址 active position addressing {**APA**}
主动系统 active system
主方式 master mode
主干 backbone
主干网络 backbone netork, backbone
主干线 main trunk
主干线路 trunk line
主(要)功能 primary function
主构件 major structure
主关键字 major key, primary key, prime key
主规划 master program {**MP**}
主过程 main procedure
主函数 main, main function
主环路径 main ring path
主机 host, mainframe computer {**MC**}
主机(架) main(-)frame

主机地址 host address
主机监督协议 host monitoring protocol {HMP}
主机交互的 mainframe interactive {MFI}
主机系统 mainframe system
主机信息系统 mainframe information system {MIS}
主机总线 host bus
主机组 master unit, host group
主计算机 main(frame) computer, prime/ principal/ service computer
主记录 master/owner/primary record, set owner
主键 mainkey, primary key
主叫 dialing
主叫用户 dial line
主节点 major/master node
主结构 major structure
主进程 host/master process
主卷 master/primary volume
主卡片 master card
主控程序 master control (program) {MCP}
主控代码 master control code {MCC}
主控开关 master switch
主控台 primary console
主控站 master/primary station
主控振荡器 exciter
主控制器 main control unit
主控制台 master console
主控状态 major state
主口令(字) master password
主库 master/primary library
主路径 main/primary path
主脉冲 master clock
主门控制块 master gate control block {MGCB}
主密码术键 master cryptography key
主密钥 master key

主命令 main command
主模块 commander/ main/ major/primary module
主目标 main objective
主目录 master catalog, home directory
主配线架 main distributing frame {MDF}
主请求 primary request
主任务 main/ major/ primary task
主扫描 main sweep
主色 chroma key, key color
主设备 master, primary device
主设备号 major device number
主设施 master environment
主时间片 major time slice
主时钟 master clock/timer
主时钟控制块 master timer control block {MTCB}
主事件(代)码 major event code
主属性 prime attribute
主数据 main/master data
主速率接口 primary rate interface {PRI}
主索引 master/ primary/ prime index
主态 master mode/state
主题词 subject word, top term
主题分类 subject classification
主题目录 subject/ thematic/ topical bibliography
主题索引 subject index
主体信号处理器 native signal processor {NSP}
主通道 major path, primary channel
主网 primenet
主网点 master node
主文件 master/ primary/ prime/main file, master
主文件夹 main folder
主文件清单 master file inventory
主文件索引 master file index

of ②〈名〉person in charge, director, supervisor 主讲 be the speaker, give a lecture 主课 main subject, major course 主力 main force, main strength of an army 主流 ①(主要水流)main stream, main current ②(主要方面)main aspect, main trend 主权 sovereign rights, sovereignty 主权国 sovereign state 主人 ①(财物所有人)owner ②(权力所有人)master ③(与"客人"相对的)host ◇女主人 hostess 主任 director, head, chairman 主使 instigate, be the principal plotter 主题 main subject, theme 主体 subject, superior, main body/part, principal part 主席 chairman 主修 specialize, major 主要 main, chief, primary, principal, major 主意 ①(办法)idea, plan ②(主见)decision, view 主语 subject 主张 ①〈动〉advocate, maintain, hold ②〈名〉view, position, stand, proposition 主旨 gist
主板 mainboard
主部件 master unit, mother unit
主菜单 main/master/primary menu
主操作员 chief operator
主程序 host/main/primary program, main/master routine, master program {MP}
主程序体 main body
主处理机[器] host processor, main processor
主窗口 main window
主磁道 primary track
主从调度 master/slave scheduling
主从关系 master-slave relation
主从结构 host-slave architecture
主从控制装置 puppet
主从系统 host-slave system, master-slave system
主存(储) main memory, primary store
主存储器 primary memory/store/storage, main memory/store/storage
主存储器划分 main storage partition
主存[内存]分配程序 core allocator
主存分区 main storage partition
主存库 main storage pool
主单元 mother/primary unit
主动打开 active open
主动的 active
主动目录 active directory
主动数据库 active database
主动位寻址 active position addressing {APA}
主动系统 active system
主方式 master mode
主干 backbone
主干网络 backbone netork, backbone
主干线 main trunk
主干线路 trunk line
主(要)功能 primary function
主构件 major structure
主关键字 major key, primary key, prime key
主规划 master program {MP}
主过程 main procedure
主函数 main, main function
主环路径 main ring path
主机 host, mainframe computer {MC}
主机(架) main(-)frame

主机地址 host address
主机监督协议 host monitoring protocol {HMP}
主机交互的 mainframe interactive {MFI}
主机系统 mainframe system
主机信息系统 mainframe information system {MIS}
主机总线 host bus
主机组 master unit, host group
主计算机 main(frame) computer, prime/ principal/ service computer
主记录 master/owner/primary record, set owner
主键 mainkey, primary key
主叫 dialing
主叫用户 dial line
主节点 major/master node
主结构 major structure
主进程 host/master process
主卷 master/primary volume
主卡片 master card
主控程序 master control (program) {MCP}
主控代码 master control code {MCC}
主控开关 master switch
主控台 primary console
主控站 master/primary station
主控振荡器 exciter
主控制器 main control unit
主控制台 master console
主控状态 major state
主口令(字) master password
主库 master/primary library
主路径 main/primary path
主脉冲 master clock
主门控制块 master gate control block {MGCB}
主密码术键 master cryptography key
主密钥 master key

主命令 main command
主模块 commander/ main/ major/primary module
主目标 main objective
主目录 master catalog, home directory
主配线架 main distributing frame {MDF}
主请求 primary request
主任务 main/ major/ primary task
主扫描 main sweep
主色 chroma key, key color
主设备 master, primary device
主设备号 major device number
主设施 master environment
主时间片 major time slice
主时钟 master clock/timer
主时钟控制块 master timer control block {MTCB}
主事件(代)码 major event code
主属性 prime attribute
主数据 main/master data
主速率接口 primary rate interface {PRI}
主索引 master/ primary/ prime index
主态 master mode/state
主题词 subject word, top term
主题分类 subject classification
主题目录 subject/ thematic/ topical bibliography
主题索引 subject index
主体信号处理器 native signal processor {NSP}
主通道 major path, primary channel
主网 primenet
主网点 master node
主文件 master/ primary/ prime/main file, master
主文件夹 main folder
主文件清单 master file inventory
主文件索引 master file index

主问题 master problem {MP}
主析取范式 major/ principal disjunctive normal form
主系统 main/master system
主项 basic term, subject
主选菜单 primary option menu
主循环 main loop, major cycle/loop
主要部件 main unit
主要配置 host configuration
主要器件 key device
主要设备 capital equipment
主要输入 primary input
主页 home page
主页库[池] main page pool
主用户 master user
主元素 pivot element/entry
主站 main/ master/ primary station
主帧 keyframe
主(要)指令 primary instruction
主指针 owner pointer
主终端 master terminal
主轴 primary/ principal axis, spindle
主字 major word
主字体 primitive font
主总线 primary bus

煮 boil, cook

【zhù】

助 help, assist, aid 助教 assistant 助理 assistant 助手 assistant, helper, aide 助长 encourage, foster
助记操作码 mnemonic operation code
助记 mnemonic
助记符号 mnemonic mark, mnemonics
助记名 mnemonic name

贮 store, save 贮备 store up, have in reserve, lay aside 贮藏 store up, put aside 贮存 store, keep in storage

住 1)(居住) live, reside, stay, dwell 2)(停止) stop, cease 住户 household, resident, family 住口 shut up, stop talking 住手 stop, quit, leave off 住宿 stay, put up, get accommodation 住宅 residence, (dwelling) house 住址 address

注 1)(灌入) pour 2)(集中) concentrate, fix, focus 3)(登记) record, register 注册 register, enroll, log-in, entry procedure 注定 be doomed, be destined 注脚 subscript, footnote 注解 ① 〈动〉annotate, explain with notes ②〈名〉note, remark, annotation 注目 gaze at, fix one's eyes on 注视 look attentively at, gaze at 注释 explanatory note, annotation, comment 注销 cancel, write off, cross out, cancel 注意 pay attention to, take note of; notice, remark 注重 lay stress on, pay attention to, attach importance to
注册方式 log-on mode
注册器 logger
注解行 comment line
注明日期的 dated
注入 implant, implantation, impregnating, inject
注入逻辑 injection logic
注入式激光二极管 injection laser diode {ILD}
注射 injection

zhù 柱驻祝著铸 zhuā 抓 zhuān 专

注释栏 comment field
注释项目 comment item
注销 cancel {CANCL}, cancellation, cross out, deletion, logout, log-down, log-off, sign-off, weed out
注意符号 attention symbol
注意事项 attention {ATTN}

柱 (柱子) post, upright, pillar, column 柱子 post, pillar
柱面 cylindrical surface, cylinder
柱面磁头 cylinder head
柱面故障 cylinder fault
柱面扫描 cylinder scanning
柱面索引 cylinder index

驻 (停留) halt, stay 驻扎 be stationed
驻留(的) resident
驻留段 resident segment
驻留装入模块 resident load module {RLM}

祝 express good wishes, wish 祝词 congratulatory speech, congratulations 祝福 blessing, best wishes 祝贺 congratulate 祝酒 drink a toast, toast 祝愿 wish

著 (显著) marked, outstanding 著名 famous, celebrated, well-known 著作 ① (作品) works, book, writings ② (写作) write 著作权 copyright
著者引文索引 science citation index {SCI}

铸 铸造 casting, founding

【zhuā】
抓 1) (拿在手中) grab, seize, grasp 2) (捕拿) arrest, catch, capture 抓紧 firmly grasp, pay close attention to

【zhuān】
专 专长 ① 〈形〉expert ② 〈名〉specialty 专攻 specialize in 专家 expert(ise), specialist 专刊 special issue 专科学校 training school 专栏 special column 专利 patent 专利权 patent right, patent 专卖 monopoly 专门 special, specialized 专题 special subject, special topic 专题讨论会 symposium 专心 be absorbed, concentrate one's attention on 专修 specialize in 专一 concentrate 专业 ① (学科) special field of study, specialized subject, specialty, discipline ② (业务) specialized trade or profession 专用 for a special purpose 专用的 dedicated, specific, special (purpose), private 专职 full-time job, specific duty 专注 concentrate one's attention on, be absorbed in, devote one's mind to 专著 monograph, academic works
专家决策支持系统 expert decision support system {XDSS}
专家系统 expert system {ES}
专家知识 expert knowledge
专利(品) patent
专利权所有人 patentee
专门人员 specialist
专线 dedicated circuit, dedicated/leased/private line
专业知识 professional feeling
专业组 special interest group

专用变量 special variable {SIG}
专用程序 proprietary program, specific (application) program
专用磁带 special tape
专用电路 dedicated circuit
专用[特定]方式 specific mode
专用符号 special symbol
专用符号表 special characters table {SCT}
专用服务工具 dedicated service tools {DST}
专用[特殊服务信号 specific service signal {SSS}
专用机 special machine
专用计算机 dedicated computer, limited-purpose computer, single purpose computer, special-purpose computer
专用键 private key, special-purpose key
专用键台 keypad
专用节点 dedicated node
专用卷 specific volume
专用库 private library, special base
专用码 private code
专用名词 technic
专用名词表 onomasticon
专用[私有]权 private right
专用软件 proprietary software
专用设备 dedicated device, private facilities, special hardware
专用[私有]数据 private data
专用网 private network
专用系统 dedicated system
专用线(路) dedicated/ private circut, dedicated/ individual/ private/tie line, telepack
专用小(型)交换机 private branch exchange {PBX}
专用语言 special language, special purpose language
专用终端 special terminal, special-purpose terminal
专用字段 specific field
专用字符表 special characters table {SCT}
专用总线 dedicated/ private bus
专有的 owned

砖 brick

【zhuǎn】
转 另见【zhuàn】
(改变)turn, shift, change 转变 change, transform 转播 relay 转达 pass on, convey, communicate 转动 turn, move, turn round 转告 pass on, communicate, transmit 转化 change, transform 转换 change, transform, switch 转机 a favorable turn, a turn for the better 转交 pass on, transmit 转让 transfer the possession of, make over 转送 ①(转交)pass on, transmit ②(转赠)make a present of sth given to one 转弯 turn a corner, make a turn 转向 change direction, turn, steer 转移 ①(改换位置)shift, jump, move, transfer, divert ②(改变)change, transform 转义 transferred meaning, figurative sense 转运 transport, transfer, tranship 转载 down load, reprint, reproduce 转帐 transfer accounts
转插板 plugboard
转出 dump, dump out, roll-off
转储 deposit, dump, memory

转储 transfer, unload, unloading
转储表 dump list
转储程序 dump program/ routine
转储打印 dump printout
转储方式 dump mode
转储控制 dump control
转储文件 dump file
转储校验 dump check
转存区 transient area
转发 forwarding, hop
转发器 converter, interpolator, repeater {RP}, transponder, network extension unit {NEU}
转换表 conversion/ translation table
转换程序 converse routine, conversion program, converter, switcher
转换符号 conversion symbol
转换函数 transition function
转换件 bridgeware
转换卡 transition card
转换开关 alternation switch, change-over switch, commutation switch, interconnection switch, switch(er)
转换码 switch code
转换器 converser, converter, interpreter, transducer, transposer
转换设备[装置] conversion device/equipment
转换生成语法 transformational-generative grammar {TG}
转换图 transition diagram/ graph
转换系统 switching/ transition/ change-over system
转换箱 switch box
转换页 turn page
转换主干 inverted backbone
转换字符 switch character {SW}
转接 change-over, switch, switchover, transfer
转接插头 multitap
转接点 relay node
转接器 adapter, interconnecting device, sink
转接线 patch cord
转接装置 switching device
转录 duplicate, inscribe, transcribe, transcription
转入 roll-in, roll-on
转移(指令) derail
转移 branch/ jump/ transfer table
转移菜单 jump menu
转移操作 branch(ing)/ jump/ transfer operation
转移程序 branching/ jump program
转移存储 transfer memory
转移地址 branch/ jump/ transfer address
转移点 branch point
转移方式 branch mode
转移封锁 jump lock
转移格式 branch format
转移呼叫 redirected call
转移键 transfer key
转移矩阵 transition matrix
转移例程 jump routine
转移连接 branch and link, branch linkage {BAL}
转移请求 shape request
转移条件 jump condition
转移图 transition graph
转移网络 transition network
转移语句 branch statement, transfer statement
转移指令 branch/ jump order, transfer instruction
转义符 escape character {ESC}
转义字符串 escape sequence
转置 transpose, transposition

转置文件 transposed file
转子指令 jump-to-subroutine instruction

【zhuàn】

传 另见【chuán】
biography（自传）autobiography 传记 biography

转 另见【zhuǎn】
1)（旋转）turn, revolve, rotate 2)〈量词〉(绕一圈)revolution

撰 撰写 writing, compose

赚 1)（获得利润）make a profit, gain 2)（挣钱）earn (money)

【zhuāng】

庄 （村庄）village 庄严 solemn, dignified, stately 庄重 serious, grave, solemn

桩 桩子 stake, pile, pole

装 1)（服装）outfit, clothing 2)（假装）pretend, feign, fake 3)（装入）load, pack, put in 4)（安装）install, fit, assemble 装备 ①〈动〉equip, fit out ②〈名〉equipment, outfit, installation, set-up, facilities 装订 binding, bookbinding 装配 assemble, packing, fit(ting) 装潢 ①〈动〉mount, decorate, adorn ②〈名〉decoration, mounting, packaging 装货 loading, shipment, freight 装货单 shipping order 装饰 decorate, adorn, ornament, deck 装卸 ①（运上卸下）load and unload ②（装拆）assemble and disassemble 装修（房屋）fit up 装运 shipment, loading, transport 装置 ①〈动〉install, fit, fix ②〈名〉device, equipment, instrument, installation, apparatus, set, unit, plant

装板的 on-board
装板台 loader table
装配器 assembly unit
装配图 assembly drawing, load map
装配线 assembly line
装入[载] load, loading
装入并执行 load-and-go
装入程序 load routine, loader program, loader routine, loading routine
装入程序块 load program block {LPB}
装入初始表 load initial table {LIT}
装入地址 load(ing) address
装入段 load segment
装入方式 load mode
装入键 load key
装入例行程序 load routine
装入命令 load command
装入[装配]模块 load module
装入模式 loading pattern
装入器 loader
装入设备 load facility
装入映像 load image, load map
装入指令 load instruction
装入状态 loading state
装填 padding
装填数据 padding data
装载方式 load mode

【zhuàng】

壮 1)（强壮）strong, robust 2)

(宏大) magnificent, grand **壮大** ①(使强大) strengthen ②(变得强大) grow (in strength) **壮观** grand sight/view **壮丽** majestic, magnificent, glorious

状 1)(形状) form, shape, appearance 2)(褒奖、委任等文件) certificate ◇奖状 certificate of commendation 状况 state, condition, circumstances
状态 status {STAT}, situation, state, position, condition, mode, phase {PH}, appearance
状态保留区 status save area {SSA}
状态变量 state/status variable
状态标志 status flag
状态表 state table
状态查询 status poll
状态窗口 status window
状态方程 state equation
状态复原 state restoration
状态矩阵 state matrix
状态开关 status switch(ing)
状态空间 state/phase space
状态(控制)块 status block
状态逻辑 phase logic
状态码 condition/state/status code
状态描述 state description
状态模型 state model
状态区 status area
状态数 condition number
状态特征位 status flag
状态条 status bar
状态图 state diagram/graph, status map
状态位 status bit
状态显示区 status display area
状态向量 state vector
状态信息 state/status information
状态行 status line
状态值 status value
状态转换 state conversion, status switching
状态转换图 state transition diagram
状态字 status word
状态字段 status field

撞 1)(相撞) bump against, strike, collide 2)(碰见) meet by chance, bump into, run into 撞车 collision, car crash

【zhuī】

追 追查 investigate, find out, inquire into 追赶 chase after, pursue, run after 追究 look into, find out, investigate, trace 追求 seek, pursue 追溯 trace back to, date from 追随 follow 追问 question closely, inquire about, cross-examine 追寻 pursue, search, track down 追忆 recall, recollect
追加 add-on, append
追溯检索(法) retrospective search {RS}
追踪 trace, tracing, tracking
追踪功能 trace function
追踪检测器 tracer

【zhuì】

坠 坠落 fall, drop

赘 赘述 give unnecessary details, say more than is needed

【zhǔn】

准 1)(依据) in accordance with, follow 2)(一定)

zhuō 拙捉卓桌 zhuó 灼浊酌着琢

definitely, certainly **准备** ①(预先安排)prepare, get ready ②(打算)intend, plan **准确** accurate, exact, precise **准绳** criterion, yardstick **准时** punctual on time, on schedule **准许,准予** allow, grant, permit, approve, invitation **准则** standard, norm, canon, criterion, guide rule
准备发送 ready for sending
准备接收 receive ready {RR}
准备时间 make-up time, set-up time
准备信号 ready signal
准确度 accuracy
准确性 precision
准入拒绝 admission reject {ARJ}
准入控制 admissions control
准入请求 admission request {ARQ}
准入确认 admission confirm {ARC}
准时制 just-in-time {JIT}
准同步的 quasi-synchronous
准同步信号 anisochronous signal
准写 write enable
准许 invitation
准许发送 invitation to send {ITS}

【zhuō】

拙 拙劣 clumsy, inferior, poor

捉 捉拿 catch, capture 捉住 clutch, hold, grasp

卓 卓识 judicious judgment, sagacity 卓越 outstanding, brilliant, remarkable

桌 table, desk
桌面辅助程序 desktop accessory
桌面出版软件 desktop publishing software
桌面电视会议 desktop video conferencing
桌面附件 desktop accessory
桌面管理接口 desktop management interface {DMI}
桌面会议系统 desktop conference
桌面视频 desktop video {DTV}
桌上计算机 desk-top computer

【zhuó】

灼 1)(火烧)burn, scorch 2)(明亮)bright, luminous 灼见 profound view, penetrating view 灼热 scorching hot

浊 1)(浑浊)turbid, muddy 2)(声音低沉粗重)deep and thick 3)(混乱)chaotic, confused, corrupted
浊音 voiced sound

酌 酌量 consider, deliberate, think over before one acts

着 另见【zhāo】
1)(穿)wear 2)(接触)touch, come into contact with **着力** put forth effort, exert oneself **着落** ①whereabouts ②(可指望的来源)dependable source **着手** put one's hand to, set about **着眼** have sth in mind, see from the angle of **着重** stress, emphasize
着色 colorization, coloration, color coat, render

琢 琢刻 carve

【zī】

咨 consult 咨询 seek advice from, consult with
咨询 consult, consultant
咨询机构 consulting firm
咨询系统 consultation system, consulting system

姿 (容貌) looks, appearance
姿势 gesture, carriage, posture
姿态 (态度) attitude, pose, manner

资 资本 capital 资本家 capitalist 资本主义 capitalism 资产 ①(财产) property ②(资金) capital (fund) ③〈经贸〉assets 资方 capital 资格 qualification, seniority 资金 money, expenses, fund 资历 qualifications and record of service 资料 ①(生产或生活必需品) means ◇生产资料 means of production ②(依据的材料) data, material, information 资质 natural ability, endowment, intelligence
资源 resource, wealth 资助 subsidize, support
资金预算 capital budgeting
资料采集系统 data acquisition system
资料档案库 repository
资料汇编 document assembly
资料夹 data holder
资料架 hold-down bar
资料(程序)库 material library
资料[数据]手册 data handbook
资料[数据]通信 data communication {DC}
资料[数据]文件 document file, material file
资源安全性 resource security
资源保护 resource protection
资源保留协议 resource reservation protocol {RSVP}
资源标识表 resource identification table {RSID}
资源池 resource pool
资源存取[访问] resource access
资源存取保密 resource access security
资源调度 scheduling of resources
资源定义表 resource definition table {RDT}
资源分辨表 resource resolution table {RRT}
资源分配 resource allocation
资源分配范畴[目录] resource allocation category
资源共享 resource sharing
资源管理 resource management {RM}
资源号 resource number
资源级 resource level
资源交换文件格式 resource interchange file form(at) {RIFF}
资源控制块 resource control block {RCB}
资源库 repository, resource pool
资源类型 resource type
资源名 resource name
资源识别表 resource identification table {RSID}
资源识别符 rid
资源向量表 resource vector table {RVT}
资源序号 resource sequence number {RSN}
资源重复 resource-replication

【zǐ】

子 1)(儿子) son, child 2)(种子) seed 子弹 bullet 子孙 children and grandchildren,

descendants 子夜 midnight
子半群 subsemigroup
子表 sublist, subtabulation
子菜单 submenu
子层 sublayer
子超图 subhypergraph
子[例行]程序 subroutine {SUB}
子[例行]程序段 subsegment
子[例行]程序接口 subroutine interface
子[例行]程序库 library of subroutine, sublibrary, subroutine library
子池 subpool
子串 substring
子窗口 child window, secondary window, subwindow
子存储区 subpool
子单位 subunit
子单元 subelement
子地址 subaddress
子端口 subport
子段 child, child segment, subsection, subsegment
子对象 subobject
子服务器 subserver
子过程 subprocess
子画面 graphic symbol, sprite
子画面大小 sprite size
子划分 subplot
子集 subset
子集依赖 subset dependency {SD}
子记录控制字节 subrecord control byte {SRCB}
子节点 child/ minor node, subnode
子结构 minor structure, substructure
子界 subrange
子进程 child(ren) process, subprocess
子句 clause, sub-sentence

子卷 subvolume
子空间 subspace
子控制台 subconsole
子库 sublibrary
子块 blockette, subblock
子类 child class, subcategory, subclass
子类型 subtype
子例程 subroutine {SUB}
子名称 subname
子模式 subschema
子模型 submodel
子目标 sub objective, subgoal
子目录 subcatalogue, subdirectory
子女关系 children relation
子区 subarea, subsegment
子区域 subdomain, subrange, subregion
子群 subgroup
子任务 subtask, subtasking, subordinate task, attached task
子任务控制块 subtask control block {STCB}
子入口 subentry
子设备 child device
子树 subtree
子锁 sublock
子体(图像) subvolume
子体素的 subvoxel
子通道 subchannel
子图 subgraph, submap, subpicture
子外壳 subshell
子网 subnet, subnetwork
子网编址 subnet addressing
子网访问协议 subnetwork access protocol {SNAP}
子网号 subnet number
子网屏蔽 subnet mask
子网寻址 subnet addressing
子网掩码 subnet mask
子文件 subfile

子问题 subproblem
子系列 subfamily
子系统 subsystem
子系统库 subsystem library {SLIB}
子项 subentry, subterm
子序列 subsequence
子循环 subloop
子域 son field, subfield
子元素 subelement
子值 subvalue
子中断控制块 subinterrupt control block {SICB}
子字 subword
子字体 subfont
子作业 subjob

仔 仔细 ①(细心)careful, attentive ②(小心)be careful, look out

紫 purple, violet
紫外光可擦(除) PROM ultraviolet erasable PROM {UV erasable PROM}
紫外线可擦除的 ultraviolet erasable

【zì】

自 (从)from, since 自称 ①(自己称自己)call oneself ②(自己声称)declare oneself to be, claim to be 自从 since 自动 ①(自己主动)voluntarily ②(不用人力)automatic 自发 spontaneous 自负盈亏 assume sole responsibility for its profits or losses 自己 self, oneself, one's own 自给 self-sufficient, self-supporting 自觉 conscious, aware 自来水 running water, tap water, service water 自理 take care of or provide for oneself 自立 stand on one's own feet, support oneself, earn one's own living 自流 ①(自动地流)flow automatically, flow by itself ②(自由发展)take its natural course, let it develop naturally 自满 complacent, self-satisfied 自然 ①(自然界)natural world, nature ②(自由发展)naturally, in the ordinary course of events ③(理所当然)of course, naturally ④(不勉强)at ease, natural, free from affectation 自身,自我 self, oneself 自始至终 from start to finish, from beginning to end 自习 study by oneself, self-study 自相矛盾 contradict oneself, be self-contradictory 自信 self-confident 自学 study on one's own, study independently, teach oneself 自由 ①〈名〉freedom, liberty ②〈形〉free, unrestrained 自愿 voluntary, of one's free well 自重 ①(注重自己言行)conduct oneself with dignity, be self-possessed ②(自身重量)dead weight, sole weight, dead load 自主 act on one's own, decide for oneself 自传 autobiography

自保护 self-protection
自备式 self contained type
自闭圈 self-loop
自编辑程序 self editor
自变化[适应] self-adapting
自变量 argument arg, independent variable
自补码 self-complementing code
自补图 self-complementary

graph
自测试 autonomous testing, self-test(ing)
自底向上 bottom-up
自底向上程序设计 bottom-up programming
自底向上法 bottom-up approach/method
自底向上设计 bottom-up design
自底向上推理 bottom-up reasoning
自电光效应器件 self-electro-optic effect devices {SEED}
自调度 self-scheduling
自顶向下 top-down
自顶向下程序设计 top-down programming
自顶向下法 top-down approach
自顶向下推理 top-down reasoning
自顶向下语法分析 top-down syntax analysis
自定义 self-defining
自动安装 automount
自动备份 automatic backup
自动编程工具 automatically programmed tools {APT}
自动编码 autocode, autocoding, automatic code/coding
自动编排 autopath
自动编索引 autoindex
自动编译 automatic compilation
自动变量 automatic variable
自动变址 autoindex(ing)
自动拨号 autodial
自动布局 automatic placement, autoplacement
自动布线 autorouting
自动步进 automatic stepping
自动操作程序 automated operator {AO}

自动测试模式生成 automatic test pattern generation
自动测试设备 automatic checkout equipment, automatic test equipment {ATE}
自动产生 autogeneration
自动程控工具语言 automatically programmed tools {APT}
自动程序设计 automated/automatic programming {AP}
自动程序设计工具 automatic programming tool, automatically programmed tools {APT}
自动程序设计语言 automatic programming language {APL}
自动出纳机 automated tellers, automatic teller machine {ATM}
自动窗孔 autowindow
自动窗口调节 automatic window adjust
自动存储 autosave
自动答录器 voice response unit {VRU}
自动打字机 automatic typewriter
自动代码发生器[生成程序] automatic code generator {ACG}
自动登录 autologin
自动电话交换机 dial exchange
自动调节器 automatic controller
自动调整 automatic adjustment
自动定位 automatic positioning, automatic static keeping
自动对齐 automatic justification
自动发送接收机[装置] automatic send/receive set {ASR}

自动返回 automatic return

自动分页 automatic pagination/paging

自动复制 auto-dup

自动跟踪 automatic following {AF}, autotrace

自动管理终端系统 administrative terminal system {ATS}

自动柜员机 automatic teller machine {ATM}

自动号码识别 automatic number identification {ANI}

自动呼叫分配[发送] automatic call distribution {ACD}

自动呼叫装置 automatic calling unit {ACU}

自动划线 autoscore

自动化 automate, automatics, automation

自动化办公室 automated office {AO}

自动化设备 automation equipment

自动化数据处理 datamation

自动化银行存款 automatic bank deposits

自动话音网 automatic voice network {AUTOVON}

自动换行 automatic line feed

自动回车 automatic carriage return

自动回答 automatic answer, autoanswer

自动回退 automatic rollback

自动回询重发 automatic repeat request {ARQ}

自动绘图机 automatic drafting machine, autoplotter

自动绘图仪 autoplotter, variplotter

自动机 automaton, automata, robot

自动机理论 automata theory

自动机逻辑 automata logic

自动计算 automatic calculation/computation

自动记录 automatic logging

自动记忆 automatic memory

自动监督程序 automonitor (routine)

自动检测 automatic testing

自动检索 autoindex, automated retrieval, automatic indexing

自动检验[验证]系统 automatic checkout system

自动减(量) autodecrement

自动减量方式 autodecrement mode

自动键 auto key, typematic

自动交换 automatic exchange

自动交换方式 autoswap mode

自动截取中心 automatic intercept center {AIC}

自动纠错码 automatic error correction code

自动卷(体)识别 automatic volume recognition {AVR}

自动控制 automatic control, auto-control

自动控制器 automatic controller

自动零位器 nullifier

自动流程图 autoflow

自动路由选择 automatic route selection

自动逻辑图 automated logic diagram {ALD}

自动模式识别 automated pattern recognition

自动旁路 auto bypass

自动配写脚注 automatic footnote tie-in

自动配置 automatic configuration

自动匹配(程序) automatch

自动拼写检查 automated spelling check

自动频率控制 automatic fre-

quency control {AFC}
自动启动 automatic activation, autostart
自动请求 automatic request, autorequest
自动取款机 case device
自动任务 autotask
自动设计 autodesign
自动审计 automated audit
自动收发(机) automatic send/receive {ASR}
自动售货机 vender
自动数据记录 automatic data logging
自动数字报文交换中心 automatic digital message switching center {ADMSC}
自动数字网络 automated digital network {AUTODIN}
自动缩放 autoscaling
自动缩进 auto-indent
自动索引 autoindex
自动提示 autoprompting
自动停机 automatic stop
自动同步机 selsyn
自动推理 automated reasoning, automatic deduction
自动限界 autoranging
自动校验 automatic check, build-in check, built-in check
自动校正 autocorrection, automatic correction
自动写程序 autowriter
自动选择 automatic selection
自动验证工具 automated verification tools
自动页边调整 automatic margin adjust
自动仪 robot
自动应答 autoanswer {AA}, automatic answer
自动优先权组 automatic priority group {APG}
自动右对齐 automatic ragged-right justification
自动语音识别 automatic speech recognition
自动再启动 automatic restart, autorestart
自动造型 autoshape
自动增量 autoincrement, autoincrementing, automatic incrementing
自动增益控制 automatic gain control {AGC}
自动制টা加工计划 automated manufacturing planning {AMP}
自动制图 autodraft
自动重发请求 automatic repeat-request {ARQ}
自动重复键 automatic repeat key
自动重启动 autorestart
自动注册 automatic log-on
自动装配 automated assembly
自动装置 auto-plant
自动准备 auto provisioning
自动走线 automatic routing
自读的 self-reading
自对偶图 self-dual graph
自反 reflexive
自反闭包 reflexive closure
自反关系 reflexive relation
自反性 reflexivity
自复位循环 self-resetting loop
自供电的 self-powered
自规划 self-planning
自含式系统 self-comtained system
自恢复的 serially reusable
自回归 autoregression
自汇编程序 self-assembler
自激的 self-excitation
自激振荡 self-excited oscillation
自检测 self-test
自检查 self-check
自举 bootstrap

自举电路 bootstrap circuit
自举放大器 bootstrap amplifier
自举协议 bootstrap protocol {BOOTP}
自控 self-control
自嵌入 self-embedding
自清洗 self-erasure
自然单位 natural unit
自然对数 natural logarithm
自然范数 natural norm
自然数 natural number
自然推理 natural inference
自然语言 human/ natural language, spontaneous speech
自然语言接口 natural language interface
自上而下 top-down
自适应(的) self-adapting
自适应差分脉冲编码调制 adaptive differential pulse code modulation {ADPCM}
自适应处理 adaptive process
自适应共振理论 adaptive resonance theory {ART}
自适应过程 adaptive process
自适应结构 adaptive organization
自适应均衡[量化] adaptive equalization
自适应控制 adaptive control, self-adapting, self-adaptive control
自适应滤波器 adaptive filter
自适应模糊联想记忆 adaptive fussy associative memories {AFAM}
自适应能力 adaptive ability
自适应数据库系统 adaptable database system {ADABAS}
自适应系统 adaptive system
自适应选路 adaptive routing
自适应预测编码 adaptive predictive coding
自索引文件 self-indexed file
自同步 self-clocking, self-synchronizing
自同构 automorphism
自同态 endomorphism
自下而上 bottom-up
自陷 trap, trapping
自陷操作 trap operation
自陷方式 trapping mode
自陷号 trap number
自陷位 trap bit
自陷悬挂 trap pending
自陷状态 trap state
自陷字 trap word
自相关 autocorrelation
自相关图 autocorrelogram
自相容性 self-consistent
自校验系统 self-checking system
自协方差 autocovariance
自行试验 self-testing
自修理 self-repair
自学习 self-learning
自学习网桥 learning bridge
自学习系统 self-learning system
自引用 self-reference
自由变量 free/ unrestricted variable
自由表 free list
自由池 free pool
自由存储区 free storage
自由格式 free format, free-form
自由件 freeware
自由空间 free space
自由令牌 free token
自由路径[路由]选择 free routing
自由区 free area
自由网 freenet
自由域 free field
自由状态 free state
自愿中断 voluntary interrupt
自诊断 self-diagnostic

自治模型 autonomous model
自主[自治]系统 autonomous system {AS}
自主性保护 discretionary protection
自主制导 self-contained guidance
自组织 self-organization
自组织机 self-organizing machine {SOM}
自组织模型 self-organizing model
自组织文件 self-organizing file
自组织系统 self-organizing system

字 (文字)word, character
字典 dictionary 字据 receipt, written pledge 字母 letters, alphabet 字体 ①(书写形式)script, typeface ②(书法派别)style of calligraphy
字 word
字边界 word boundary
字标 word mark
字表 word table
字长 length, machine length, word capacity, word length, word size
字处理 word processing {WP}
字处理机 word processing machine, word processor, wopro
字传送 word transfer
字词间隔 word spacing
字单元 location
字地址 word address
字典次序 dictionary order
字典排序 lexicographic sort
字典式的 lexicographic
字段 field {FLD}, parcel
字段保护 field protect
字段标记 field mark/tag
字段标识 field identification

字段长 field length
字段存取 field access
字段定界符[分隔符] field delimiter
字段分隔符 field separator
字段检索变元 field search argument {FSA}
字段类型 field type
字段描述 field description
字段名 field name
字段属性 field attribute
字段数据 field data
字段选择 field selection
字段制表 field tab {FTAB}
字对齐 word alignment
字/分 words per minute {WPM, wpm}
字分隔 word separation
字分界符 word delimiter
字符 character {CHAR}
字符编码 character code/encoding
字符变量 character variable
字符标识符 character identifier
字符表 character table/repertoire
字符参考表 table reference character {TRC}
字符操作 character manipulation
字符处理 character handling/manipulation
字符传输率 character (transfer) rate
字符串 catena, (character) string, text string
字符串操作 string operation
字符串处理系统 string process system {SPS}
字符串匹配 string matching
字符串数据 character string data
字符串语言 string language
字符大小 character dimension/

字符代码 character code, code character
字符单元 character cell
字符地址 character address
字符定界符 character delimiter
字符发生器 character generator
字符方式 character mode
字符高度 character height
字符格式 character format
字符光标 character cursor
字符集 character set
字符计数 character count {CC}
字符记号 character token
字符间距 (character) pitch
字符键 character key
字符结构 character structure
字符界 character boundary
字符矩阵 character matrix
字符控制块 character control block {CCB}
字符块 character block
字符宽度 character duration/space
字符扩展 character expand, character expansion
字符类型 character type, type char(acter)
字符流 character stream
字符轮廓 character outline
字符码 character code
字符模式 character mode
字符频率 character frequency
字符闪烁 character blink
字符设备 character device
字符设计 character design
字符识别 optical character recognition {OCR}
字符视图 character view
字符数据 character data
字符数组 character array
字符体 character font
字符图像 character image

字符图形 character graphic(s)
字符歪斜 character skew
字符外形 character outline
字符文件 character file
字符显示器 character display
字形形式[风格] character style
字符行 character row, Hollerith string
字符/英寸 character per inch {CPI}, characters per inch
字符终端 character tty/ terminal
字符组 burst, character set
字号 word number/size
字盒 type box
字计数 word count
字间间隔 interword gap/space
字节 byte, syllable
字节操作数 byte operand, byte-oriented operand
字节地址 byte address
字节多路转接器 byte multiplexer
字节格式 byte format
字节交叉 byte interleave
字节连字符 syllable hyphen, syllable hyphen character {SHY}
字节/秒 bytes per second, bytes/s {bps}
字节/英寸 bytes per inch {BPI}
字节运算 byte operation
字节组 gulp
字界 character boundary
字距 pitch, word gap
字开关 word switch
字空间 word space
字宽度 word width
字模 matrix, matrices, type
字模板 grid, type plate
字模库 magazine
字模[字型]盘 font disk
字模条 type bar/slug

字母编码字符集 alphabetic coded character set
字母表 alphabet, alphabetic list
字母表序 alphabet order
字母代码 alphabet(ic) code, letter code
字母符号 alphabetic character/ symbol, letter character/symbol
字母格式 alphameric style
字母换档 alphabetic shift, letters shift {LTRS}
字母换档键 alphabetic shift
字母间隔 escapement
字母键 letter key
字母紧排 kern
字母数字(的) alphameric {A/N}, alphabetic-numeric, numeric-alphabetic
字母数字分类[排序] alphanumeric sort
字母数字符号 alphameric symbol
字母数字键 alphameric key(s)
字母数字显示设备[装置] alphameric display device
字母显示器 alphascope
字母行 letter row
字频率 word frequency
字驱动 word drive
字识别 word recognition/ spotting
字数 word number
字顺索引 alphabetical index
字体 character/type font
字体尺寸 font size
字体结构 font architecture
字体卡 font card, font cartridge
字体宽度 set width
字体设计 font design
字体[字模,字形]文件 font file
字下划线符 word underscore

character {WUS}
字型 font, font style, type face
字型号 font number
字型模板[母板] font master
字形 character form, character pattern, font (pattern), picture, type font
字形编码法 calligraphical encode method
字形变换键 shift key {PSK}
字形规格 face size
字形区 font area
字形生成器 font generator
字选择 word select
字选择线 word select line
字寻址计算机 word addressable computer
字样 type face, type style
字元 element
字运算 word operation
字转行 word wrap
字状态 word state
字组 block, block of words
字组交换 block switching
字组结束 end of block {EOB}

【zōng】

宗 1) (祖宗) ancestor 2) (家族) clan 宗教 religion 宗旨 principal aim, purpose

综 put together, sum up 综观 make a comprehensive survey 综合 ①〈动〉synthesize ②〈形〉synthetical, comprehensive ③〈名〉synthesis 综括 sum up 综览 view generally 综述 summarize, sum up 综上所述 to sum up, to mention above
综合测试系统 integrated test system
综合程序 packaged program

综合程序设计系统环境 integrated programming system environment {IPSE}

综合电子办公软件 comprehensive electronic office {CEO}

综合计算机辅助制造 integrated computer-aided manufacture {ICAM}

综合生产系统 integrated manufacturing system {IMS}

综合数据处理 integrated data processing {IDP}

综合数据存储 integrated data storage {IDS}

综合数据库管理系统 integrated database management system {IDMS}

综合网络管理系统 integrated network management system {INMS}

综合问题 master problem {MP}

综合业务 complex service

综合业务局部网 integrated services local network {ISLN}

综合业务数字网 integrated services digital network {ISDN}

综合因素 skinware

综合制造系统 integrated manufacturing system {IMS}

棕 棕色 brown

踪 踪迹 trace, track, trail

踪迹分析程序 trace analysis program {TAP}

【zǒng】

总 (总的) general, overall, total, gross, entire 总代理 general agency 总代理人 general agent 总的来说 generally speaking, by and large 总额 total, the total amount 总(而言)之 in short, in a word, in brief 总方针 general policy, general principle 总纲 general program, general principles 总括 assemble, put together, sum up 总工程师 chief engineer, engineer-in-chief 总共 in all, altogether 总管 manager 总和 sum, total, amount 总机 switchboard, telephone exchange 总计 accumulating/ grand/ major total, totalizing, summarizing 总监 inspector general, chief inspector 总结 ①〈动〉sum up, summarize ②〈名〉summary, summing up 总理 premier, prime minister 总领事 consul general 总领事馆 consulate general 总目 comprehensive table of contents 总评 general comment, overall appraisal 总是 anyway, after all, sooner or later 总算 (终于) at long last, finally 总统 president 总务 ①(指工作) general affairs, general service ②(指人员) person in charge of general affairs 总预算 general budget 总则 general rules, general principles 总值 total value

总包件 skinware

总处理能力 throughput (capacity)

总代理 general agent

总额 aggregate, extended price, footing

总费用 total cost

总结构 total architecture

总开关 main switch

总开销 overhead

总控钥匙 turnkey

总控制台 total console
总量 all-up weight, gross
总设计 overall design
总数 gross, sum, total
总体 aggregation, ensemble, integer, population
总体结构 architectural/ global structure
总体模式 metaschema
总体设计 system design
总体组成 main assembly
总线 bus, trunk
总线标准 bus standard
总线裁决器 bus resolver
总线簇 bus family
总线方式 bus mode
总线分配器 bus allocator
总线监控器 bus monitor
总线接插件 bus connector
总线接口部件 bus interface unit {BIU}
总线结构 bus structure
总线结构[布局] bus topology
总线空闲状态 bus idle state
总线控制器 bus control unit, bus controller
总线扩展槽 bus extender
总线扩展卡 bus extension card {BEC}
总线类别 bus category
总线类驱动程序 bus class driver
总线耦合器 bus coupler
总线判优器 bus arbiter
总线请求 bus request
总线[长线]驱动器 line driver
总线式结构 bus-organization, bus-organized structure
总线适配器 bus adapter
总线受控 bus slave
总线输出奇偶校验 bus out parity {BOP}
总线鼠标 bus mouse
总线占用期 bus tenuer
总线占用争用 bus contention

总线中枢 bus hub
总线仲裁 bus arbitraction
总线周期 bus cycle/tenuer
总线主控 bus master
总线装置 bus unit
总线资源 bus resource
总需求 total demand
总装配 general assembly

【zòng】

纵 1)(放任)indulge in, let loose 2)(释放)release, set free 纵然 even if, even though 纵向 lengthwise, longitudinal, vertical 纵深 depth
纵横开关 crossbar, crossbar switch
纵向磁化 longitudinal magnetization
纵向奇偶性 longitudinal parity
纵向冗余检验 vertical redundancy check {VRC}
纵向冗余校验 longitudinal redundancy check {LRC}
纵向扫描 longitudinal scan
纵向校验 longitudinal check
纵坐标 ordinate, Y-axis

【zǒu】

走 1)(走动)walk, go 2)(跑)run, move 3)(离开)leave, go away 走访 ①(访问)interview, have an interview with ②(拜访)pay a visit to, go and see 走私 smuggle 走运 be in luck, have good luck
走步测试 walking test
走带机构 deck, tape deck/drive, (tape) transport
走纸 form feed {FF}
走纸滚 paper feed roller
走纸托架 paper feed tray

【zòu】

奏 1)(演奏)play, perform, strike up 2)(取得)achieve, produce 奏效 prove effective, be successful, get the desired result

【zū】

租 (出租)rent out, let out, lease 租户 ①(租房人)tenant, leaseholder ②(租物人)hirer 租借 rent, hire 租金 rent, rental 租赁 rent, lease, hire 租赁合同 contract of tenancy, lease contract 租期 lease term 租用 rent, hire, charter, take on lease 租约 lease
租赁计算机 rental computer
租用线(路) leased line
租用信道 leased channel

【zú】

足 (脚)foot, leg 足够 sufficient, enough, ample 足球 football, soccer 足以 enough, sufficient 足足 full, as much as

族 1)(家族)clan 2)(种族,民族)race, nationality 3)(大类)family, group, set, population, series 4)〈数学〉assemblage 5)〈化学〉cluster
族集合 family set
族系统 family system

【zǔ】

阻 阻碍 hinder, block, impede 阻挡 stop, resist, obstruct, countercheck 阻隔 separate, cut off 阻拦 stop, obstruct, bar the way 阻力 obstuction, resistance 阻挠 obstruct, stand in the way 阻止 inhibit, prevent(ion), interrupt, arrest
阻挡层 barrier
阻抗 impedance
阻抗函数 impedance function
阻抗矩阵 impedance matrix
阻抗匹配 impedance matching
阻纳 immittance
阻尼 antihunt, damping
阻尼控制 damping control
阻塞 blocking, bottleneck, choke
阻塞网络 blocking network
阻塞信号 jam signal
阻止者 checker

组 group, cluster, unit, set 组成 form, make up, compose, constitute, build-up 组合 ①〈动〉make up, compose, constitute ②〈名〉combination, grouping, associaton, building up 组织 ①〈动〉organize, form ②〈名〉organization, entity, web
组地址 group addressing
组标志 group indicate, group mark(er) {GM}
组表目 group entry
组长度 group length
组成体 constituent object {CO}
组窗口 group window
组地址 group address {GADDR}
组分隔符 group separator (character) {GS}
组函数 group function
组号 group number
组合磁头 composition disk head
组合电路 combinational circuit

组合键 composite key
组合理论 combinatorial theory
组合逻辑 combinational/ combinatory/random logic
组合门 combinational gate
组合配线(框)架 combined distributing frame {CDF}
组合器 combiner
组合软件 integrated software
组合数学 combinatorial mathematics, combinatorics
组合算法 combinational/ combinatorial algorithm
组合条件 combined/ compound condition
组合网络 combinational/ combining network
组间间隔 interblock gap {IBG}, interblock space
组件 bank, chip, component, element, groupware, pack(age)
组件对象模式 companet object model {COM}
组件选通 chip enable {CE}, chip select {CS}
组交换 group switching
组块 blocking
组码 group code
组名 group name, set name
组权 group authority
组入口 group entry
组数 cardinality
组说明 group profile
组态位 configuration bit
组特许权 group authority
组项 group item
组延迟 envelope/group delay
组元 component
组帧位 framing bit
组装结构 package assembly
组装密度 packing density

祖

祖父 grandfather 祖国 homeland, native land, motherland, fatherland 祖母 grandmother 祖宗 ancestor
祖先节点 ancestor node

【zuān】

钻 另见【zuàn】
钻研 study intensively, dig into

【zuǎn】

纂 (编纂)compile, edit

【zuàn】

钻 另见【zuān】
钻孔工具 drill, auger, bit, borer 钻石 diamond, jewel

【zuǐ】

嘴 mouth 嘴唇 lip

【zuì】

最 most 最初 initial, first; prime 最大 maximum, maximal 最低 lowest, mimimum, bottom 最多 at most, maximum 最高 highest, top, maximum, on-peak, supreme, tallest 最好 ①(顶好的)best, first-rate ②(最好还是)had better, it would be best 最后 final, last, ultimate 最惠国 most-favoured nation 最近 ①(近来)recently, lately ②(距离最近的)nearest ③(最近的将来)in the near future, soon 最小 minimum, minimal 最先 the first, the earliest 最优 optimum; optimal 最终 final, ultimate
最初成本 initial cost
最大包生存期 maximum packet lifetime {MPL}

最大传输单位 maximum transfer unit {MTU}
最大等待时间 maximum latency
最大分段长度 maximum segment size {MSS}
最大分段存活时间 maximum segment lifetime {MSL}
最大公约数 greatest common divisor {GCD}, greatest common measure
最大化 maximize, maximizer
最大流 maximal/ maximum flow
最大容量 peak capacity
最大突发长度 maximum burst size {MBS}
最大下界 greatest lower bound {GLB}
最大项 maxterm
最大元 greatest element/ member
最大值 crest/ maximal value, maxima, maximum
最大最小 maxmini
最低点 lowest point
最低位 low order bit, lowest order
最低位有效(数字) least significant digit {LSD, lsd}
最低信元速率 minimum cell rate {MCR}
最低有效位 least significant bit {LSB}
最低有效位片 least significant slice {LSS}
最短路径树 shortest path tree
最短路线问题 shortest route problem
最短通路算法 minimum path-length algorithm
最短通路选路 shortest path routing
最短字 shortest word

最短作业 shortest job first {SJF}
最多有效片 most significant slice {MSS}
最高点 tiptop
最高级 top class
最高位 highest order, highest significant position, most significant bit {MSB}, most significant digit {MSD}
最高位字符 most signification character {MSC}
最高优先权 highest priority
最高有效片 most significant slice {MSS}
最后单元 last location
最后结果 conclusion
最后项 last term
最坏情况 worst-case
最佳 optimum
最佳编码 forced coding, optimum code/coding
最佳策略 best policy/strategy
最佳程序设计 forced/optimum programming
最佳订货量 economic order quantity {EOQ}
最佳[优]控制 optimum control
最佳路径[路径] optimal path
最佳配合 best fit
最佳[优]算法 optimal algorithm
最近最少使用的 least recently used {LRU}
最少使用的 least frequently used {LFU}
最先适配策略 first-fit strategy
最小覆盖 minimal cover
最小割 minimal cut
最小加权路径 minimum weight path
最小距离编码 minimum distance code

zuì 罪 zūn 尊遵 zuó 昨 zuǒ 左

最小冒险原则 least commitment principle
最小权路由 least-weight route
最小上界 least upper bound {LUB}
最小网络 minimal network
最小项 lowest term, minterm
最小有效数字 least significant digit {LSD, lsd}
最小元 least member
最优并行算法 optimal parallel algorithm
最优策略 optimal policy/strategy, optimum strategy
最优调度 optimal scheduling
最优方案 optimal plan
最优方针 optimal policy
最优化 optimization
最优化方法 optimization method
最优化技术 optimization technique
最优化控制(法) optimalizing control
最优化理论 optimization theory
最优化模型 optimizing model
最优化算法 optimization algorithm
最优解 optimal solution
最优决策规则 optimal decision rule
最优先位 override bit
最优向量 optimal/ optimum vector
最优值 optimal/ optimum value
最右边的 rightmost
最右节点 rightmost node
最终产品 end product
最终副本 final copy
最终信号单元 final signal unit {FSU}
最终用户 end-user
最终值 end value

最左树 leftmost tree
最左位 leftmost bit
最左子串 leftmost substring
最左字符 leftmost character

罪 1)(犯法的行为) crime, guilt 2)(过失) fault, blame
罪恶 crime, evil 罪名 charge, accusation 罪证 evidence of a crime

【zūn】

尊 (敬重) respect, venerate, honor 尊贵 honorable, respectable, respected 尊敬 ① respect, honor, esteem ② honorable, respectable, respected 尊严 dignity, honor
尊重 respect, value, esteem

遵 遵从 defer to, comply with, follow 遵守 observe, abide by, comply with 遵循 follow, abide by, adhere to
遵照 obey, conform to, comply with, act in accordance with

【zuó】

昨 昨天 yesterday

【zuǒ】

左 (左边) the left (side) 左面 the left side, the left-hand side 左右 ①(左和右两方面) the left and right sides ②(大约) about, or so ③(操纵) control, influence
左部 left part
左侧入口 left entry
左乘 premultiplication, premultiply
左递归 left recursion
左递归规则 left recursive rule

左调节 left-adjust
左调整 left justify
左端对齐 left justify
左对齐 flush left, left-align
左方 left hand side {LHS}
左截断 left truncation
左括号 begin/left bracket, left parenthesis
左零元 left-zero element
左逆元 left inverse, left-inverse element
左陪集 left coset
左斜字 backslant
左幺元 left identity, left-identity element
左页 verso
左页面对齐 ranged left
左移 left shift, shift left
左移操作 shift left operation
左值 l value

【zuò】

作 1)(做)do, make 2)(写作)write, compose 4)(当作)regard as, take sb or sth for 5)(成为)act as, be, become **作弊** practice fraud, cheat **作法**(做法)way of doing things **作废** become invalid **作风** style (of work) **作家** writer **作价** set a price for sth, evaluate **作品** works, writing **作为** ①(行为)conduct, deed, action ②(作出成绩)accomplish ③(当作)regard as, take for ④(从某个角度来说)as **作息** work and rest **作息时间表** daily schedule, timetable, work schedule **作业** ①(功课)school assignment ②(生产活动)work, job, activity, operation, production **作用** ①〈动〉act on, affect ②〈名〉action, effect, function **作者** author, writer **作证** testify, give evidence, bear witness

作标记 marking
作废 cancel {CANCL}, mortality, nullify, revoke, undo
作废标志 cancel indicator
作废键 cancel key
作废码 cancel code, reject code
作判决 decision making
作图语言 graphics language
作业包装区 job pack area {JPA}
作业表 job table {JT}
作业步 job step
作业步再启动 step restart
作业成批 job batch
作业处理 job processing
作业传送与操纵 job transfer and manipulation {JTM}
作业单 worksheet
作业调度 job schedule, job scheduling
作业调度程序 job scheduler
作业定义 job definition
作业队列 job queue
作业管理 job/operation management
作业号 job number
作业级 operational level
作业接口 job interface
作业结束指示(符) end-of-job indicator {EJ}
作业控制表 job control table
作业控制程序 job control (program), job controller
作业控制记录 job control record
作业控制权 job control rights
作业控制设备 job control facility

作业控制语言 job control language {JCL}
作业库 job library
作业类别 job class
作业流 job flow, job stream
作业流程图 job flowchart, operations process chart
作业名 job name
作业任务 job task
作业日志 job journal
作业输入控制语言 job entry control language {JECL}
作业输入文件 job input file
作业输入系统 job entry system
作业输入子系统 job entry subsystem {JES}
作业统计 job accounting
作业系统 on-link system {OLS}
作业优先(级) job priority
作业运行记录 job log
作业注销 job logout
作业装配区 job pack area {JPA}
作业状态 job status
作用点 action spot
作用期 action period
作用区 active region
作用域单位 scope unit

作用域规则 scoping rule

坐 (搭乘) travel by **坐落** be situated, be located **坐下** sit, take a seat
坐标 coordinate
坐标变换 coordinate transformation
坐标数字化仪 coordinate digitizer
坐标系 system of coordinates
坐标仪 coordinate machine

座 basis **座谈** have an informal discussion **座位** seat, place **座右铭** motto, maxim

做 1)(制造) make, produce, manufacture 2)(写作) write, compose 3)(从事) do, act, engage in 4)(用) be used as 5)(担任) be, become **做法** way of doing or making a thing, method of work, practice **做人**(待人接物) conduct onself, behave **做事** handle affair, do a deed

作业控制语言 job control language {JCL}
作业库 job library
作业类别 job class
作业流 job flow, job stream
作业流程图 job flowchart, operations process chart
作业名 job name
作业任务 job task
作业日志 job journal
作业输入控制语言 job entry control language {JECL}
作业输入文件 job input file
作业输入系统 job entry system
作业输入子系统 job entry subsystem {JES}
作业统计 job accounting
作业系统 on-link system {OLS}
作业优先(级) job priority
作业运行记录 job log
作业注销 job logout
作业装配区 job pack area {JPA}
作业状态 job status
作用点 action spot
作用期 action period
作用区 active region
作用域单位 scope unit
作用域规则 scoping rule

坐 (搭乘) travel by **坐落** be situated, be located **坐下** sit, take a seat
坐标 coordinate
坐标变换 coordinate transformation
坐标数字化仪 coordinate digitizer
坐标系 system of coordinates
坐标仪 coordinate machine

座 basis **座谈** have an informal discussion **座位** seat, place **座右铭** motto, maxim

做 1)(制造)make, produce, manufacture 2)(写作)write, compose 3)(从事)do, act, engage in 4)(用作)be used as 5)(担任)be, become **做法** way of doing or making a thing, method of work, practice **做人**(待人接物) conduct oneself, behave **做事** handle affair, do a deed

ISBN 7-5439-1927-3